THE BEST PLAYS OF 1955–1956

THE BURNS MANTLE YEARBOOK

Drawings by HIRSCHFELD

from "My Fair Lad

THE BEST PLAYS OF 1955–1956

EDITED BY LOUIS KRONENBERGER

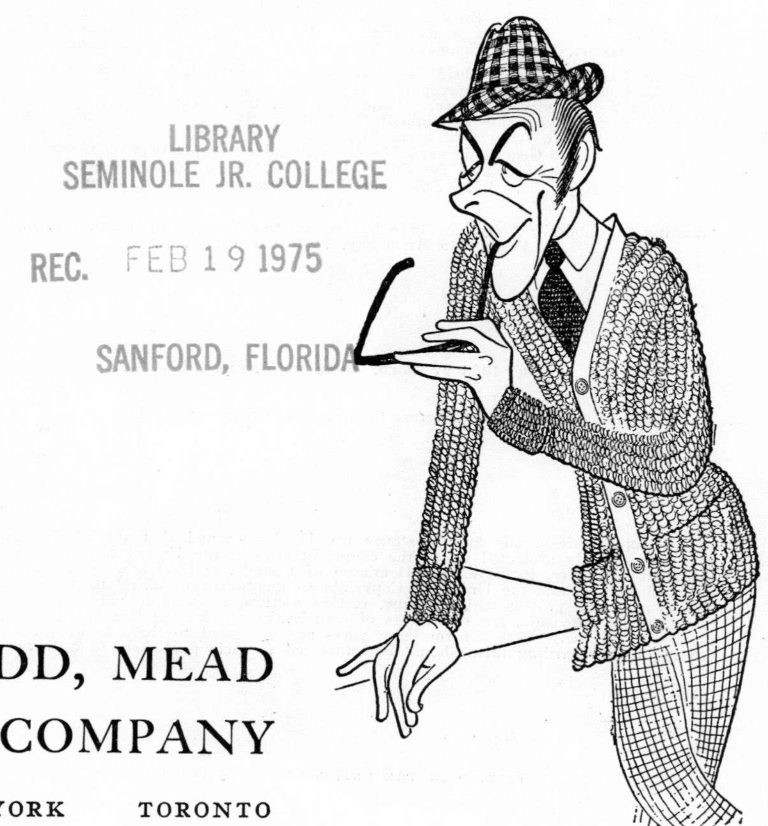

DODD, MEAD
& COMPANY

NEW YORK TORONTO

Library of Congress Catalog Card Number: 20-21432

PRINTED IN THE UNITED STATES OF AMERICA

EDITOR'S NOTE

IN editing this thirty-ninth volume in the *Best Plays* series, I find myself once again under very pleasant obligations. My wife, Emmy Plaut, has again provided help that is more fairly called collaboration. For editorial assistance, I am greatly indebted to Barbara Kamb and Phyllis Terry. For the use of photographs, I must thank the Editors of *Life* Magazine and Doris O'Neill, and for the use of its tabulation of Hits and Flops, *Variety* and Mr. Abel Green. Particular thanks are due, for their several reports, to Miss Cassidy, Mr. Tynan, M. Josset, Mr. McLaughlin, Mr. Nichols and Mr. Sherwood, and for very kindly granting the use of their sketches to Cecil Beaton, Alvin Colt, Ben Edwards, Eldon Elder, Leslie Hurry, Peter Larkin, Jo Mielziner and Oliver Smith.

And I must say once more how great a pleasure it is to be associated in this project with Mr. Hirschfeld.

LOUIS KRONENBERGER

CONTENTS

EDITOR'S NOTE . . . v

SUMMARIES OF THE SEASONS
- The Season on Broadway . . . 3
- The Season in Chicago . . . 25
- The Season in London . . . 29
- The Season in Paris . . . 40
- The Season in California . . . 47
- Off Broadway . . . 55
- The Season in Television . . . 60

THE TEN BEST PLAYS
- A View from the Bridge . . . 69
- Tiger at the Gates . . . 89
- The Diary of Anne Frank . . . 111
- No Time for Sergeants . . . 140
- The Chalk Garden . . . 163
- The Lark . . . 189
- The Matchmaker . . . 214
- The Ponder Heart . . . 238
- My Fair Lady . . . 266
- Waiting for Godot . . . 295

A GRAPHIC GLANCE BY HIRSCHFELD . . . 319

PLAYS PRODUCED IN NEW YORK . . . 333

FACTS AND FIGURES
- *Variety's* Tabulation of Financial Hits and Flops . . . 397
- Statistical Summary . . . 399
- Long Runs on Broadway . . . 400
- New York Drama Critics Circle Awards . . . 402
- Pulitzer Prize Winners . . . 403
- Books on the Theatre . . . 405
- Previous Volumes of Best Plays . . . 409
- Where and When They Were Born . . . 423

Necrology 431
The Decades' Toll 448

INDICES
Index of Authors and Playwrights 451
Index of Plays and Casts 456
Index of Producers, Directors, Designers, Stage Managers, Composers, and Choreographers 466

SUMMARIES OF THE SEASONS

THE SEASON ON BROADWAY

IT was a very good season. If part of its distinction, if something of its aura, lay in its notable superiority to the run of seasons past, 1955-56 might yet make absolute claims to merit. It might yet—in a world, and a theatre world, bursting with pain and error—make a happy mark to shoot at. At least, during such a season, the play reviewer could derive real enjoyment from his playgoing; could take a certain actual pride in his job. And there were those occasions—which is alone how stage triumphs can be reckoned—when the playgoer emerged from the play in a mild swoon of excitement. In fact, even for emotional conservatives there were a fair number of such nights. And there were a number of other nights that called forth less heady adjectives, but nonetheless proved stimulating or managed to be fun. Even so late as April, when playwriting usually sports its lightest-weight and illest-fitting clothes, here a play still looked tidy, there a play still showed substance.

Just why 1955-56 constituted by so plump a margin the most rewarding season in years, is pleasant to reflect on but not too easy to explain. It is certainly not because Broadway of a sudden eschewed the fleshpots or acquired a soul; during 1955-56, a host of producers were still peddling tinny or flashy or downright incompetent wares; while sometimes rewardingly, though oftener not, Formula was still the most frequent hostess. But it did seem that, besides those producers offering popular work at a respectable level and those concerned with box-office at all costs, there were others who cared about the quality of what they produced; and that there were those who—at least with other people's money—were really willing to take a chance. (And when in one season people bring a *Tiger at the Gates* to Broadway, and a *Chalk Garden*, and a *Waiting for Godot,* they can't help creating an atmosphere that must infect other producers.) It is also true that '55-'56 was part of a general period of prosperity, and an increasingly prospering Broadway; while a revitalized Off-Broadway had an influence also. Finally, many of the season's more creditable successes owed much to production, or at any rate specific acting; had there been no Joseph Schildkraut and Garson Kanin, no Ruth Gordon and Tyrone Guthrie, no Tyrone Guthrie and Anthony Quayle, no Rex Harrison and Julie Andrews and Moss Hart, something in the way of strength or sheen would have been missing from the works they graced.

Most of the season's plays that boasted any real distinction possessed foreign blood. From England came the one play boasting an assured high style, with an elegant savagery to boot; as from France, the one play written in a high humanistic tradition, with compassionate irony. From France, by way of Ireland, there came in *Waiting for Godot* the latest of those works to be steeped, controversially, in allegory and symbolism; but one which no less merited than inspired controversy. And beyond the foreign blood in *The Lark* and *Tamburlaine* and the prize-winning *Anne Frank,* there was the miming of Marcel Marceau and the performing of the Comédie Française.

As for choosing the ten best plays, happily for once there was some question of what to leave out as well as what to put in. At least, for any of several plays included, certain omitted ones may seem to have as good or better claims. There will certainly be those to speak up for O'Casey's *Red Roses for Me;* and certainly in its best moments it speaks eloquently for itself. But for me the play, as a whole, quite definitely fails, and not least on the score of its writing. There will be those to press the claims of *A Hatful of Rain* and *Time Limit,* and to set them above the claims of, say, a *No Time for Sergeants.* But for me *A Hatful of Rain* and *Time Limit* have merit at the level of theatre alone; and are worse, rather than better, for merely flirting with seriousness. Neither play, moreover, can boast any real merits as writing. A *No Time for Sergeants,* on the other hand, makes plain what it's up to at the outset and very generally succeeds at it.

In contrast to the previous season, 1955-56 saw comedy outstrip drama. Much as its predecessor had offered something respectable or better at almost every dramatic level, 1955-56 did so at almost every comic one. The comedy achievement is the more marked if, reaching over into drama, one requisitions the comic elements in *Waiting for Godot;* or again if one claims for the Muse of Comedy that charmer of musical comedy, *My Fair Lady.* But there is no need to reach over: in the undisputed realms of comedy itself, Broadway could boast sound work reaching from the high philosophic to straight low farce. If there was a weak area, it was that midway one of domestic or bourgeois comedy which Broadway ordinarily has rather a gift for—so that, for the nonce, it could not too regretfully be done without.

Certainly in *Tiger at the Gates* there was what Broadway does without all too often; there was high comedy at the philosophic level.

This is something more (if also in some ways less) than Shaw commonly provided in his comedies of ideas; for this, like all successful work in the genre, is shot through with a ruefully ironic view of mankind, is touched with the tragic sense of life. If one would call *Tiger* a propaganda play against war, then one must go on to say that its author is not only a kind of poet in his propagandizing, but also a pessimist enough to surmise that his propaganda must fail. Giraudoux's French title is *The Trojan War Will Not Take Place,* and Trojan Hector's fierce, fruitless efforts to substantiate this claim constitutes, of course, Giraudoux's action. In Hector's determination to send Helen back to Menelaus, and so avoid war, it's not the shallow, minxlike Helen who proves the stumbling block: it is Troy's idealists, idealizing war; Troy's aging poets, so eager to commemorate young men's deaths; its common people, gleefully spoiling for a fight; its international lawyers reckoning a legalistic victory well worth an international holocaust. His own Troy unavailing, Hector finds an ally in the skeptical but for once aidful Ulysses—only for a single warmonger to unleash the dogs of war, and for Giraudoux's story to pass over into Homer's.

Just how good a *play* is Giraudoux's sunburst of wit and dialectics is no doubt open to question; what is beyond question is the elegance, the aerated reflectiveness, the ironic lyricism of the modern theatre's most civilized playwright. Very much of this, moreover, is retained in Christopher Fry's translation, which may well be Fry's solidest writing for the stage. Before the end is reached, the play surely achieves—though on its own ironic rather than the customary dramatic terms—a kind of wry grandeur. It has its own charming loquacity en route, and very much its own dawdling relentlessness. And if a protest against war, it is much more a lament for war's inevitability. Like all masters of humane irony, Giraudoux pierces to a tragic fundament, to a world that is never governed, for long, by sense and logic; or spurred on by a love of truth; or saved by a love of virtue. As between such differing masters of dialectics and irony, there is something poignant in Giraudoux's writing—because more pessimistic—not found in Shaw's. Yet here the two men rather touch, for Shaw wrote a kind of *Tiger at the Gates* in *Caesar and Cleopatra.* Each man, at any rate, saw worlds about to be overturned through a queen's lure; in the Caesar of Shaw as in the Hector of Giraudoux the great warrior is the passionate hater of war; in Shaw's Caesar as in Giraudoux's Ulysses, the wise man apprehends how impotent is wisdom. And both plays seem as autumnal in their ruefulness as they remain vernal for their wit.

The Chalk Garden offered high comedy, too—at the drawing-room

Robert Weede, Jo Sullivan and Art Lund

in "The Most Happy Fella"

level. And while preserving a desirable drawing-room atmosphere, *The Chalk Garden* is one of those rare plays that are genuinely and fascinatingly individual. The play may descend in places from comedy of manners to outright comedy of mannerisms, and Miss Bagnold sometimes have with her eccentrics an expected and usual sort of fun. But it is soon enough evident that a special mind and temperament are at work, creating a grande-dame method of playwriting, at once wayward and relentless; but achieving a wit that enchants and an authority that mesmerizes.

Exhilarating as are Miss Bagnold's manor-house characters in themselves—self-indulgent dowager exerting a Lady-Macbeth manner on trifles; adolescent granddaughter who stirs up mischief and thinks up melodrama; on-stage Shavian manservant, off-stage moribund butler—they would after a time become mere drawing-room-comedy furniture. What transforms the play, as she transforms everything in it, is the granddaughter's companion; and she also, amid so much merely decorative oddity, effects something mutedly real. Not without cost has she achieved her green thumb for people as well as plants, or without reason known how to make things flourish in a garden built on chalk.

Despite all the chalk, there is no lecture at the blackboard. There are rather too many (and too vaporous) whiffs of facile symbolism; but Miss Bagnold is not mystical or didactic. Her play remains high comedy; and after the fashion of high comedy, small moments become the more touching for having first seemed brittle, the more penetrating for having seemed like pure façade. There are also, among all the blank-cartridged witticisms, a few real bullets; and the long paper-chase of upper-class didoes and insolences does lead in the end to the human heart. *The Chalk Garden* may be no more than superior entertainment for civilized theatre-goers; but it is entertainment that on Broadway such theatre-goers sometimes wait ten years to see.

There was beguiling entertainment in much of *The Ponder Heart,* too—where Joseph Fields and Jerome Chodorov retained from a delicate tale a good deal of Eudora Welty's delicate tailoring. The small-Southern-town story of a lovable eccentric, put on trial for the murder of his birdbrained bride who died of fright during a thunderstorm, had a nice light pastel daffiness about it, a way of making things look delightfully woozy through wrong-prescription rose-colored glasses. If occasionally cute, it was surprisingly oftener charming. If as chatty and dawdling at times as a rural postman, it also—as against the flails and wind machines that keep so many Broadway comedies in motion—seemed to catch a fresh creative breeze. And it proceeded—in neither the pretty-pretty ballet slippers of fantasy nor the hobnailed boots of farce—to a generally hilarious third-act trial scene. The defendant, there, was a modern-day Uncle Toby; the antics of the trial called to mind those in *Pickwick Papers* or *Alice in Wonderland.*

If the rest of the season's comedy fell to noticeably lower levels, at least twice more—once in the form of a classically old-fashioned, once in the form of obstreperously contemporary, farce—it still came off well. Much in the success of both *The Matchmaker* and *No Time for Sergeants* must be set down to staging; not in years, in fact, has there been better farce staging than *The Matchmaker*'s. But both plays are written and set about in a proper right style; both give their performers words to say and things to do that production can only enhance; and contrary to so much else in the theatre, neither play, while succeeding at its own level, pretends to be functioning at a higher one.

A reworking of Thornton Wilder's *Merchant of Yonkers* of 1938, *The Matchmaker* now worked amazingly well—careened where it once only clattered, and where it once sputtered, here exploded sky-high. Wilder's yarn (itself born of an old Viennese farce) of a tight-fisted Yonkers merchant of the '80s in search of a wife, and of a scheming lady matchmaker who blows out every match she gets lighted till she herself is made the conquering flame, is all quenchless, incorrigible farcicality, which does nothing so genteel as unfold. It catapults and ricochets; it has people bouncing out of trapdoors, squeezing into closets, hiding under tables, snooping behind screens; it has identities mistaken and purses mislaid, boys dressing up as girls and cabdrivers looping with drink. Thornton Wilder so wrote it that Tyrone Guthrie could open triumphantly the sluice-gates of farce; and if Wilder was sometimes, in the writing, a little cute, he was also sometimes bashfully philosophical. Everyone connives with too much good nature for any real claw to lurk beneath such a catcher's mitt of a play. But there are at least intimations that mankind is most wonderfully foolish and that money can loom immoderately large; there are moments that prove genuinely touching; and there is the sense that however madly it capers, *The Matchmaker* does not too wildly misrepresent mankind.

Nothing even bashfully philosophical obtrudes upon *No Time for Sergeants;* here, in simon-purest form, is simple-minded fun. Instead of philosophy's pale aura, we get formula's familiar profile; we are offered, once again, the theme of rube-conquers-all. And a formula that in the past has yielded satiric rewards this time provides only farcical ones. Will Stockdale, rookie and hillbilly, puts his foot in his mouth as blithely as though it were his pipe; and triumphs over every crisis by failing to realize he is involved in one. So backwoods as not to know that a sergeant is a recruit's natural enemy, Will practically kills his own sergeant with kindness; all but gives the Air Force psychiatrists ulcers through his own unshatterable normality. Whatever he does is done at an endearingly comic-strip level, and hence emerges as a bright exercise in sustained improbability and morning-fresh outrageousness. The Air Force seems like something personally invented rather than anything ever previously known or observed; and sex—on the rare occasions when it is acknowledged—sounds rather like a wholesome breakfast food. On its own terms, the play has only one real fault—it runs on too long. Somehow in the course of its demented airplane flight it ought to vanish, dissolve, disappear; instead, it is permitted to get earthbound.

The season's comedy was pleasant enough for even its also-rans to bring something in the way of pleasure. If William Marchant's *The Desk Set,* after a fairly bright beginning, became far less a play than a mere feedbox for Shirley Booth, and if Lindsay and Crouse's *The Great Sebastians* was little more than a series of well-planned opportunities for the Lunts, two other comedies might boast something in their own right. George Axelrod's *Will Success Spoil Rock Hunter?* was a satiric free-for-all about Hollywood and sex, centering in a young fan-magazine writer who sells his soul in 10% slices to a Hollywood agent with satanic powers. At 10% a throw, the Faustling becomes a Don Juan, a Croesus and a Lionel Strongfort, and cops an Oscar; and is at length saved from Hell by a script-writer who simultaneously saves himself from Hollywood. Concerning his script-writer, Mr. Axelrod gets much too solemn; but so long as he is kidding a movie siren's curves, or mixing a 20th-century Faust with 20th-Century Fox, he is fun. Not much of a play, and more of a family joke than a satire, *Will Success Spoil Rock Hunter?* offered, at its best, funnier and fresher lines than anything in Mr. Axelrod's *The Seven Year Itch.*

Carolyn Green's *Janus,* too, had its—actually more unified—rewards. An agreeably light sex farce that brought an American pinch of wackiness to a French-style exercise in sin, it told how each summer a shipping tycoon's wife and a lady librarian's husband put slipcovers over their morals and spent two secret months in New York. In time the tycoon walked in on them; and by making everybody behave in pleasantly unbourgeois fashion, *Janus* whipped up a nice comic froth. A little later an Internal Revenue man stirred up some nice fiscal commotion; and though the play eventually went downhill, it did even that with a certain grace. With truly witty dialogue,

Janus might have been quite superior of its kind; quite lacking such wit, it needed a good cast to make of it just a very agreeable evening.

By actual count, more of the season's dramas than of its comedies were worth noting; yet very few of its dramas were notable. Time and again a dramatic play aroused interest, or proved good theatre, or displayed good acting, or possessed something provocative by way of character or striking by way of theme. Yet there was about all this a kind of ragged plenty, of unpruned profusion: in one play sensationalism would be masquerading as truth, in another television palmed itself off as theatre. Somewhere else again, what seemed fine silk while the play lasted had turned by midnight into Cinderella's rags.

Fortunately, there were dramatic plays of actual merit; and plays whose very mistakes were honest ones. Certainly the play so highly esteemed by critics and public alike—*The Diary of Anne Frank*—did credit to the sensibility of its dramatizers, Frances Goodrich and Albert Hackett. They brought off, by a right approach, what might easily have been ruined through a lachrymose or stagy one. They took an adolescent girl's real-life chronicle of Jews hiding out in an Amsterdam garret and contrived vivid stage pictures of their huddled, muffled, strangely commingled existence. They portrayed it as a weird blend of the brightly ordinary and the hideously abnormal, of all-too-human squabbles and all-but-superhuman control, of comic fault-finding and heroic adjustment. The play, for me, was at its best in portraying the group life; in revealing the always thorny problem, here a hundred times thornier, of two families living under one roof. Neither in the sudden jabs of midnight terror nor in the explosions of boarding-house farce was anything prettified; there was no more of an attempt at heartbreaking gaiety than at lurid gloom; there was chiefly a demonstration of people learning to walk—and on tiptoe—among eggs. With the brattish, as with the girlish, side of Anne herself the play also generally succeeded. But in the theatre, Anne's more intimate scenes, where her secret self had to be made vocal and visual, seemed far less happy; nothing is so private as a diary nor so public as a stage, and the two refused, on occasion, to coalesce. The play, which owed much to production, was very often extolled, I think, at the wrong level. The appeal of *Anne Frank* is in the final sense documentary and "human"; it nowhere suggests—indeed, how could it?—the deeply creative, the world of art.

In a different way, there was no sense of high creation about *The Lark*. In Lillian Hellman's trenchant adaptation, it proved a generally engrossing theatre piece, but never a really fused and illuminating play. One reason why will perhaps be found in M. Anouilh's own confession that his play does not attempt to "explain the mystery of Joan"—which is hardly justified by his insistence that "you can't explain" her. In any case, there is not in *The Lark* the sense of *trying* to pierce to an ultimate explanation: so that, however vibrant its episodes, one comes away feeling that something was left out, that one must have failed to note a key scene, or let one's mind wander during a crucial passage. The parts of the play are almost all lively or vivid or challenging; the drawback is that the play adds up to less than the sum of its parts.

But taken for what it is, it works well. In adapting it, Miss Hellman has endowed it with some of her own blunt, which is to say sharp, vigor; and if the Joan of *The Lark* never seems explained, on the surface at least she is graphically characterized. No other Joan has seemed so hardheaded and practical; and if she is never history's Joan revealed, she is not just someone else's Joan revamped. The adaptation has plainly done all it could to differentiate *The Lark* from the thing it could not rival—*Saint Joan.* By drastically cutting the script, Miss Hellman certainly did not add to what there was of meaning; but she vastly enhanced its movement.

Arthur Miller's *A View from the Bridge* came closest to real achievement among the season's dramas, yet in the final sense fell a little short. Mr. Miller's is a story of a decent man undone by blind passion and ignorance; of a kindly longshoreman who does not realize his strong sexual feeling for his orphan niece (whom he brought up in his own house and regards as his daughter). When she falls in love with a Sicilian cousin of his wife's who entered the country illegally, he first taunts the girl that the youth only wants to marry her so he can become a citizen; then insinuates to the neighborhood that the youth is a homosexual; and finally, still thwarted, blabs to the immigration officers of the illegal entry. It is a powerful theme and Mr. Miller, in his writing, has often the power to match it. Except near the end, there is real stress and tension, and a feeling of something more than good theatre—of genuine drama. But just as Mr. Miller's hero never grasps the true nature of his feelings, so Mr. Miller has himself not grasped the true character of his story. Mr. Miller has linked it to Greek tragedy; and has not only introduced a Brooklyn lawyer as a kind of Greek chorus: he has let the lawyer speak poetically of Sicily's ties with Greece and of their historic pasts. *A View from the Bridge* thus explicitly seeks to evoke the drama's first great home of incestuous passion and fatal ignorance. But the play itself seems not to derive from it, or to comport with it; the play itself reveals how little its peasantlike psychology and hot Sicilian natures have in common with highborn Greek tragedy. Only now and then does there jut up the fated blundering of life; far oftener it seems not the Furies' shears that slit, but the vendetta's dagger. The play is almost glaringly primitivist, and in feeling, operatic: the right analogy seems not with the Greeks but with Mérimée, the Mérimée not only of *Carmen* but of *Mateo Falcone*. Analogies wouldn't matter much but for Mr. Miller's Greek-chorus apparatus, which often intrudes an inharmonious note. But the note of power, too, if not everywhere sustained, constantly asserts itself.

There was no lack of analogies—or of seeking them—in the case of *Waiting for Godot,* with its ability to be puzzling, or to arouse invective and rhapsody. And certainly Samuel Beckett's play is the latest of those works that pose philosophic question marks with all the emphasis of exclamation points; like Henry James' *Turn of the Screw,* Kafka's *The Castle,* Pirandello's *Right You Are,* Wilder's *The Skin of Our Teeth,* it makes of who's who at times—and at other times, of what's what—a kind of philosophic quiz show. Not in some years has Broadway been given anything that, in terms of meaning and merit, was more inevitably "controversial."

Godot offers, in a sense, storytelling without story: gaunt indeed is Beckett's account of two penniless, hapless, evil-smelling tramps waiting, in a barren countryside, for a neighborhood personage named Godot—who, despite periodic announcements that he is coming, never comes. With its disconsolate, straw-clutching outcasts; with the bullying (and later blinded) magnate they encounter, driving a harnessed slave before him; with its endless rain of symbolic and allegorical smallshot, and its scarred and almost sceneryless universe, *Waiting for Godot* can be most variously interpreted; and has been. Whether Godot is God or man's unconquerable hope; or the slave is the bought or housebroken artist; whether the two tramps, the one so often asking, the other answering, are the divided self, or each is to the other that friend or mate or makeshift companion that saves man from an intolerable loneliness—all these are sufficiently evocative symbols to mean something to almost everybody. And clearly, the play's is not a casual but a thematic plotlessness, and not a blundering but a planned garrulity.

In other words, regardless of how far Mr. Beckett's little parable throws its beams, he is plainly a man who knows what he is about, who is in firm control of his material. Perhaps one can help rescue his play from outraged splutters and arty rhapsodizings alike by suggesting that—in contrast to the major truths he confronts—Beckett exhibits a genuine but essentially minor talent. He is neat, accomplished, literary, with also a kind of inverted theatre sense: *Godot* rather proves, among other things, that storytelling that lacks a story can constitute a *kind* of play. Beckett has a gift for the theatricality of nothing happening, for small sudden changes of key, for the humor of despair. For all its vernacular and even outhouse touches, his is a sophisticated style, a succinct loquacity. *Godot,* at bottom, is both a neatly fingered exercise in wit and a pointillist rendering of humanity's dark moods.

To be sure, its very neatness gives it rather a symbolic mere rat-tat-tat than something whose reverberations leave behind great gashes and rents. Beckett dispenses with the usual stage clothing, but hardly to get closer to nakedness—for nakedness implies flesh, and *Godot* often seems ghostly. The best symbolic writing, from *Moby Dick* and *Don Quixote* down, never wears its symbolism on its sleeve; the symbolism brings added depth and resonance to an always three-dimensional creation. *Godot* lacks any real fictional creativeness; it is perhaps more justly, and more appositely, to be treated as a mood piece or a poem. But, whatever one calls it, it has its own persistent fascination; and for once in a way, in a theatre rampant with pointless hurry-scurry, they very distinctly serve who only stand and wait.

Among the season's other dramas, a baker's half-dozen that were also very much of a mixed bag had, certainly, their good points. One was an Irish play, another an English; one was adapted from short-stories, one from a novel, while one got its start on TV. The earliest of them to reach Broadway, N. C. Hunter's *A Day by the Sea* might as easily, in its Chekhovian way, be called comedy as drama. A hit in London, where the cast included Sir John Gielgud, Sir Ralph Richardson, Dame Sybil Thorndike and Irene Worth, it fell pretty flat in a production whose cast was merely good. Often nicely written, sometimes neatly observed, Mr. Hunter's Dorsetshire study of has-beens and never-weres yet seemed very watery custard; showed no really personal talent or original insight. The characters were so many musical instruments for a sophisticated enough but tediously scored tone poem; devoid of pasts or futures or both, they were all drowning with the utmost politeness, making it hard, at times, to distinguish their sense of desperation from mere lethargy. Had there never been a Chekhov, *A Day by the Sea* might have provided a welcome breath of fresh-airlessness. As it was, the effect seemed both too faint and too familiar.

Weaving together a clutch of Scott Fitzgerald short-stories, Sally Benson portrayed, in *The Young and Beautiful,* an affectedly blasé young thing out of the early Jazz Age. Immature, self-centered, perhaps incapable of emotional response, she could only—in her romantic quest of the perfect love—cast her suitors aside the moment she conquered them. Even what she thought the perfect love left her untouched; revealed her a seeker after a grand passion, incapable of any passion; a charmer whose swains were burned, one and all, by lack of fire. Beginning like one more romp about a junior miss up to junior mischief, the play as it proceeded grew more serious in character, more sinister in tone. It had a certain sobering shock value, a certain vivid relentlessness, along with nice entertainment value in its lighter moments; and a pinch of real substance at the end. Yet there was something not quite focused, not quite flexed about its storytelling; and something a little undefined about its heroine. It remains, all in all, more interesting than successful.

Michael V. Gazzo's *A Hatful of Rain* was the first of two highly theatrical problem plays. Concerned with Johnny Piper, a drug addict who picked up the habit while a hospitalized war veteran, then shook it off, and is now again addicted, it showed him tormented both by his cravings and the brutal drug-peddlers who could satisfy them. It showed Johnny's well-meaning brother giving him money for drugs; it showed Johnny's unhappy wife blaming his neglect of her on another woman. With the help of good acting, the play had scenes of frightening power. If it yet proved an unsatisfying whole, it was partly from possessing more facets than a shaky craftsman could handle, partly from letting theatricalism have the edge on truth. The play sought to dramatize Johnny's relations to himself, his wife, his father, his brother; the morality of his brother's giving him money for drugs and being in love with his wife; the problem of getting hold of drugs as well as being addicted to them. A better artist might, through using all these facets, have deepened his story; Mr. Gazzo merely diffused it, and made it seem not more real, but less. In the same way, by stressing the junkie's behavior rather than his psychology, by highlighting the vicious brutalities of "pushers," the play comes off more a scare piece than a serious study: its naturalistic manner simply gives a New Look to melodrama. The big fault of *A Hatful of Rain* is not so much its being more sensational than serious as its somehow pretending to be the reverse.

Something of the same uneasy blend of truth and theatre reduced the value and blurred the integrity of *Time Limit*. A flash-backed tale of an American army officer who had gone Communist in a Korean prison camp, it begins with a judge advocate studying the evidence for court-martialing the man and getting worried by the letter-perfectness of the case against him. Further prodding reveals that Cargill had committed treason—after being on the horns of a lacerating dilemma—from decent motives. And Cargill's having finally committed treason inspires, in turn, a debate on how it should be judged; on whether the law, however tyrannic, must be placed above lawbreaking, however understandable. The debate asks at what point cracking up might be forgivable, and how far a moment of capitulation must cancel out a lifetime of loyalty. It asks finally whether Communist brainwashing tactics may not call for revised standards of judgment—and justice.

In asking such questions, *Time Limit* offered, beyond scenes that proved vibrant and tense, a nice new twist for a thriller. What cost it distinction was its commonplace writing; what reduced its importance was its letting a serious theme too often defer to a lurid plot; what blurred its point was having Cargill, even when he turned traitor, act from such worthy motives. This last maneuver meant salvaging the play's hero at the cost of jettisoning its problem.

Sean O'Casey's *Red Roses for Me*—his first "new" play to reach Broadway since *Within the Gates* in 1934—was perhaps the weakest of those standing so long without the gates, craving admittance. Despite some fine moments of vernacular comedy, *Red Roses* is chiefly a reminder of how distinguished O'Casey could be: it has no measurable distinction of its own. The play was written in 1942; and its story, very loosely treating the 1913 Dublin transport workers' strike, bears all the marks of O'Casey's later, less realistic writing. The themes are the expected ones, but the orchestration is more mystical and ornate, the form more vagrant and diffuse. Though pivoting on a strike and an O'Casey-like young idealist who is killed in it, the events—far from displaying any clear dramatic line—are never really dramatized at all. Garrulous minor characters outrank those involved in action; and in line with the play's lyrical atmosphere, speech passes into song, movement into ballet. If all this is occasionally rewarding, things far oftener seem windy than Aeolian. The best moments have the comic smack and grizzle of *Juno and the Paycock*—reinforcing the fact, indeed, that O'Casey's true genius has always been comic; but these moments are set round with much that quite lacks their vibrancy. Regrettably often Mr. O'Casey's later style is mere brummagem, the sort of fine writing that fails of magic by striving after it. And the play fails of power as well. If it bears O'Casey's signature, it is with altogether too many loops and flourishes—and in the gaudiest purple ink.

Middle of the Night, the first Broadway play by TV's star playwright, Paddy Chayefsky, was—even with Edward G. Robinson's fine performance to aid it—decidedly disappointing. Concerned with a well-to-do fifty-three-year-old widower who falls in love with a girl

Edward G. Robinson in "Middle of the Night"

of twenty-four, the play chiefly scored with minor characters—with the author's ability to envelop commonplace people in a steam bath of their own commonplaces or of intense but clotted family feelings. But the strong point of the playwright became the weak point of the play: its small talk and small talkers seemed mere padding; seemed finally not just to interrupt but actually to replace a vibrant Man-Meets-Girl story. And vibrant it needed to be, since the play is less about December and May than December and March. The stormy, immature, unhappily married heroine is a full-fledged neurotic, and Chayefsky's concern was with a problem personality as well as a problem marriage. For this he lacked both capacity and concentration; and very likely too, the stern realism that would disdain a sudden happy ending. His play trades, besides, in banalities more pretentious than any it chronicles; and he himself remains rather a phonograph than a voice.

Earle Hyman's fine performance in the title role of *Mister Johnson* was also not enough to save the play; though here the problem, and the cause of failure, proved different. In adapting Joyce Cary's novel about a childlike young West African Negro who yearns to be a full-fledged, "civilized" Briton, Norman Rosten ran head-on into difficulties of stagecraft. It is to his credit that, with Mr. Hyman's help, he communicated a genuine sense of his hero—of a bumbling, guileful, sunny-natured orphan of two cultures; of a culturally displaced person whose miscomprehensions are comic until, in a flash, there is tragedy. But in treating its very central figure, the play resorts to peculiarly centrifugal stagecraft; contains far too many hurried, discontinuous episodes that seem flashes of ethnic scenery rather than stretches of dramatic mileage. Concerned with a man who cannot keep to the road, *Mister Johnson* unfolds a story with almost no road to keep to, and is itself a displaced narrative, no longer a novel, not yet a play, nor good sustained theatre, either.

Even during such a season of plenty, Broadway—or at any rate Broadway producers—continued to behave disgracefully in the matter of revivals. Off-Broadway, or the City Center, or the Phoenix Theatre might be fairly prodigal reviving the classics; from England might come Tyrone Guthrie's production of *Tamburlaine,* from France Mr. Sol Hurok might import the Comédie Française; ANTA might bring back from France *The Skin of Our Teeth:* Broadway money saluted the past with *Fallen Angels* and *Goodbye Again.* That, thanks to Nancy Walker's terribly funny performance, *Fallen Angels* was worth reviving as it had never been worth producing when new, hardly exculpates Broadway from never once aspiring higher. But, as I think I suggested last year, it is perhaps just as well that the line keeps growing sharper between Off-Broadway, with its con-amore attitude toward the classics, and Broadway, with its box-office logic that only name actors permit of giving Shakespeare house room. We can meanwhile be grateful for the chance of seeing Marlowe's *Tamburlaine* with no name actor by Broadway standards, but merely a fine actor, Anthony Quayle. Admittedly two plays that never convey the feeling of any real play at all, *Tamburlaine,* in Guthrie's brilliant production, yet emerged a brilliant "failure"—an evening full of stunning theatre, of slashing rhetoric, of gorgeous spectacle, with scene after scene suggesting a kind of richly lighted Delacroix canvas.

Reaching Broadway for the first time some 275 years after it was founded, the Comédie Française provided a succession of very happy evenings. One might regret that during its first conquest of America, the Comédie had not chosen Racine to be one of the conquerors; or that it had ventured with Molière no farther than *Le Bourgeois Gentilhomme*. But in seeking, in its first campaign, perhaps not so much to play safe at the moment as to provide for the future, it offered, besides expert Molière, such things as a Musset *Caprice,* Marivaux's *Jeu de l'Amour et du Hasard* and Beaumarchais' *Figaro*. To see the Marivaux or the Musset done with not only every last nuance of phrasing and diction, but with a ballet lightness and wit, was to grasp that sense of tradition that not just enriches the most celebrated of all theatres, but lights up a whole very eminent culture. Broadway, also, thanks to the Phoenix Theatre, offered France's incomparable mime—who in his finest effects is one of the world's great living artists—Marcel Marceau. By comparison, France's more habitual ambassador, Maurice Chevalier, seemed a little too clever a showman: even without comparisons, his charm had begun to wear thin. From England came Joyce Grenfell, with a real gift for well-bred nonsense and lightly barbed social satire, but who would perhaps come off better starring in an intimate revue than dividing a whole long evening with a dance trio.

The Phoenix, in its third season, was uncomfortably upsy-downsy; but beyond putting New York very much in its debt for importing Marcel Marceau, it could boast a sensitive and successful revival of Turgenev's oddly neglected *A Month in the Country*—one of those small classics that, no matter how long they are kept in mothballs, never lose their charming bouquet.

In terms of acting, it was an unusually newsworthy season—and beyond such news as Susan Strasberg's being made a star in *Anne Frank* at seventeen, or Orson Welles' enacting *Lear* in a wheelchair. Not only did a large number of established stars—Joseph Schildkraut, Ruth Gordon, David Wayne, Edward G. Robinson, Bert Lahr —gain added luster; there were such comparative newcomers to celebrity, or to our shores, as Julie Andrews, Siobhan McKenna, Earle Hyman and Andy Griffith.

Though it produced in *My Fair Lady* one of the very finest of all musical comedies, the musical field was creatively the season's weakest one. Except for *The Most Happy Fella*—too much redeemed by its music to be voted a failure, but otherwise too faulty

Carol Channing in "The Vamp

to be dubbed a success—there was nothing not wholly ringed with mediocrity. To what extent things went wrong may be inferred from the fact that a number of large-scale musicals perished out of town.

Though musical comedy is theatrically America's outstanding invention, it constitutes in America, as anywhere else, one of the most

hazardous of stage forms; one in which the sense of the whole must outshine the sum of the parts; one in which a dozen virtues often go for nothing if, say, the pacing proves a vice. The musical-comedy stage is a kind of chessboard where you have to anticipate a dozen danger points at once. And the very qualities that have helped give American musicals their primacy and their cachet—the glossiness, the gorgeousness, the profusion—are in a fair way to contributing to their decline. The tired businessman at whom all this opulence is aimed should by now, you would think, be a little bit tired of it. In any case, almost everyone else is. But musicals seem built to bear out Veblen's theory of conspicuous waste; you get the feeling that they would rather cost $462,000 and fold out of town than cost half that much and flourish on Broadway.

Lavishness was not, however, the villain in *Almost Crazy,* the intimate revue that opened the fall season; the best thing about it, indeed, was its clean, fresh, summery look. But not for a long while had so passably professional a revue so largely consisted of just going through the motions; of just exhibiting the manner of the torch song or the satirical or nonsensical skit. Number after number had an all-too-familiar look while simultaneously lacking a face; while, by way of contrast, an occasional dance creation ventured way out beyond symbolism into pure irrelevancy.

The heavy artillery (in a field where light cavalry might always bring better results) was wheeled into place with *The Vamp.* This extravaganza went for its fun to the early silent-film days, and came back empty-handed. That proved something of an accomplishment, for Carol Channing alone should lend an aura to defeat. But *The Vamp* often seemed to be Carol Channing alone, who was herself, perhaps, somewhat defeated. As for the show, it for the most part just lay on its side and stubbornly refused to move. For all its up-from-corsets movie magnates and snake-hearted ingenues, its Oriental shenanigans and Biblical films, the story never put forth one green leaf of satire: it merely seemed drenched in lavish dullness.

Where *The Vamp* outdid what it sought to spoof, *Pipe Dream* whitewashed what it set out to paint red. For their newest musical, Rodgers and Hammerstein had gone to John Steinbeck's *Cannery Row* and imported the flophouse and bordello set. Unhappily, for their own moral sensibilities, they reached too low: their bims and bums represented something they could only bear to look at through rose-colored glasses. They portrayed them on a basis of "Who touches pitch shall be drycleaned"; and when their lowlifes weren't heaving and pushing at a constantly stalled romance, they were making bawdy-house doings seem as sinful as a YMCA supper. Not just the madam had a heart of gold; where people's hearts were concerned, *Pipe Dream* showed a positive Midas touch. There was nice music and some nice lyrics, but little more—not just a want of the raffish but an excess of the dull.

With *Mr. Wonderful,* which thanks to Sammy Davis Jr.'s personal following became good box-office, Broadway once again failed to provide a good show. Very possibly, in this instance, it could not;

for Davis's is still the kind of talent that belongs in a nightclub. His amiably urgent personality blends with drinks on tables; and his unusual versatility would come off best if very compactly displayed—if it could quick-change, nightclub style, from tap-dancing (Sammy's one real talent) to vocalizing to clever imitations to blowing a trumpet to banging the traps. As it was, Sammy spent most of the evening fighting his way out of a musical-comedy frame as though it were a cage, and only at the end emerged his true right nightclub self. As for the show itself, it bedded down this young master of loud sounds in pointless noise, surrounded this demon of driving energy with feckless hullabaloo.

In the final sense, *The Most Happy Fella* did not properly come off, either. For his first Broadway show since *Guys and Dolls,* Frank Loesser wrote the book, the lyrics and the music to produce what is in style more like opera than straight musical; and, as is proper with opera, the music stands notably foremost. The varied and exuberant score ranged from perky show tunes to the fullest-throated romantic duets. Almost all that was light, or rather lightly lyrical, had gaiety and charm; only where things got old-fashionedly lush or gaudily melodramatic did nice vintage music smack of the show's own California vineyards—or even of Hollywood, California's Vine.

But the music stands too glaringly foremost. The small human story with the wise human moral that was once, in *They Knew What They Wanted,* packed into a single room, here has been wildly scattered and frequently submerged all over the Napa Valley countryside. Folkish but never touchingly simple; sentimental, but with no real emotional charge, *Fella* has been choked up, and even hoked up, with rustic razzle-dazzle and vineyard party-going. Nor, in the absence of any distinctive dancing, are the parties ever really festive. Nor, in the flatness of some of Loesser's lyrics, are his ditties always sufficiently bright. In seeking something more spacious than the standard Broadway musical, *Fella* was at worst a misstep forward, and the score remains among Broadway's most opulent in years. But about even such opulence, there is something overdone and oppressive.

Thus just one of all the season's musicals could be hailed as a success; but, everything considered, just one like *My Fair Lady* might make any season bright. To have gilded *Pygmalion,* to have retained all of Shaw's lustre, as a variety of craftsmen have done while adding a brightness, an ebullience, a festive mockery of their own, is a truly notable achievement. If the show's one small fault could be a slight disregard for length, most audiences wish the show were longer. And in addition to ebullience, it has breeding. To adapt a critical remark of G.B.S.'s own, those concerned have set Shaw to music and not merely set music to Shaw.

To be sure, *Pygmalion* the play—and certainly in combination with *Pygmalion* the movie—handsomely lends itself to musical comedy; while *Pygmalion*'s playwright possesses as often an operatic exuberance as a Gilbert-and-Sullivanish absurdity. Shaw freely milks those staples of opera—the heroic, the romantic, the melodramatic—in the very process of mocking them; introduces dazzling speeches that are pure arias, interjects satiric roulades and verbal coloratura. A number of other Shaw plays might lend themselves to music with no greater concessions than occur in *My Fair Lady*—where, at the end, it is Galatea who brings Pygmalion to life.

In the theatre, those concerned with *My Fair Lady* triumphed, like dancers, in pairs. On the acting side, Rex Harrison and Julie Andrews play Higgins and Eliza to perfection; and Harrison, in the one place where he is handicapped, suitably makes his singing a triumph of phonetics over voice. Miss Andrews, with her enchanting voice and looks, takes the grime-to-glamour phase of Eliza in her stride; but she plays after that with such charm and force as to make the much trickier second act hardly inferior to the effulgent first. Similarly high tribute must go to Moss Hart for his staging and Hanya Holm for her dances; to Cecil Beaton for his costumes and Oliver Smith for his sets. And on the creative side Mr. Lerner and Mr. Loewe provide, between them, something that—short of pure Rossini-like opera—could not better consort with Shaw. If Loewe's score is a pastiche of melodic and lyrical styles, it is a very pleasant one; while Mr. Lerner, besides making the most liberal and discerning use of Shaw's dialogue, has contrived wittily mocking lyrics and delightfully abusive patter songs. In a season where, thanks to *Tiger at the Gates* and *The Chalk Garden,* a civilized tone has penetrated the legitimate theatre, *My Fair Lady* does more than echo it. Other American musicals may contest its right to be called greatest; none could claim for a moment to be more authentically civilized.

THE SEASON IN CHICAGO

By Claudia Cassidy

Drama Critic, Chicago *Tribune*

RICH in music, ballet and the restoration, however embattled, of its resident opera, Chicago had in the season of 1955-56 less than twenty shows. Only a handful stood out. Many were mediocre, or made so, or more so, by tarnish on the gleam that sparked their original glint. There was nothing genuinely ghastly, unless you want to count *Anniversary Waltz,* which on second thought I think I do. Worth remembering were some cherishable performances, a gesture or two in our bereft direction, and that handful of shining shows.

The Skin of Our Teeth came calling because Helen Hayes and Mary Martin wanted to bring it. Burgess Meredith's rueful, gleeful Sakini ripened *The Teahouse of the August Moon* into thirty-six Erlanger weeks, the season's longest run. Herman Shumlin invested $100,000 in a Melvyn Douglas production of *Inherit the Wind* as pungently fresh as if he had aimed it at Broadway. We had a tryout look at Leslie Stevens' *The Lovers,* which fascinated some of us as much as it bored others. In the "do it yourself" line a group of Chicagoans leased the Studebaker Theatre for five years and announced forty weeks of subscription plays with a resident troupe and guest stars for 1956-57.

In hopeful interpretation, the Studebaker Theatre Company could turn out to be, not stock, which always sounds stodgy, but resident theatre, which as absurdly sounds alluring. Other producers could emulate Mr. Shumlin in shooting the works in Chicago duplication before the shine wears off. More interesting plays might choose to come our way in tryout. More stars might put their heads together and decide that something as special as the Thornton Wilder revival really should play Chicago—not that those special stars may want to risk it again.

For not all the sins are of visitors' commission. When *The Skin of Our Teeth* opened on a scalding August night the scalpers had all the tickets, an augmented crew fought to get the curtain up a half-hour late, and wilting wags maintained that the air conditioning consisted of J. J. Shubert blowing on two ice cubes. Furthermore, the

Mary Martin, Helen Hayes, George Abbott and Florence Reed i

sins of the summer were visited on the spring. *Inherit the Wind,* which played the same theatre, the Blackstone, flatly refused to risk going broke while its audience melted. Having arrived in February, it preferred a seventeen-week run to taking a chance on the weather past June 2nd.

In any case, *Inherit the Wind* was first rate, as *The Skin of Our Teeth* was adventurous. *Bus Stop* lassoed that wild mustang, Albert Salmi, with Peggy Ann Garner a wan little girl under the warpaint.

"The Skin of Our Teeth"

Nancy Kelly came in *Bad Seed,* with Kimetha Laurie as the child. *Teahouse*'s inexplicable delay was caused, so John Patrick said, by his feud with the original producer, Maurice Evans. Howard Lindsay and Russel Crouse, who took over, gave us a brilliant production which Chicago spent more than a million dollars to see. Meredith promised to stay with it until he got that glaze in his eye, and after thirty weeks the glaze was that Texas *Hamlet*. No one could have replaced him, but Eddie Bracken turned out to be an agreeable Sakini in his own surprisingly gentle fashion.

Marcel Marceau had the whole town talking. So did *Anastasia,* but out of the wry side of its mouth. The disastrous miscasting of Dolly Haas in the title-role had Eugenie Leontovich playing in a vacuum, and dismayed a city which had been enchanted by Miss Haas in *Lute Song.*

The D'Oyly Cartes looked in, with Peter Pratt diminutive, squinty, droll and dry. *Can-Can* without Gwen Verdon and *Pajama Game* without Eddie Foy Jr. left little to brag about. *Kismet* had its opulence and sometimes its drolleries, but little public. *Plain and Fancy* was a patchwork show.

This was slim picking in a season sparked by the Lyric Theatre's flaring precocity, the quality of Fritz Reiner's concerts with the Chicago Symphony orchestra, the peak of concert visitors and a wide range of dance attractions culminating in three weeks of George Balanchine's *The Nutcracker* in the 3,750-seat Civic Opera house. Theatre-wise, it could be we are waiting for Godot.

To count it out, 1955-56 brought nineteen shows in six theatres for a total of 150 weeks, by comparison with twenty shows in six theatres for 159 weeks the previous season.

The record:

Shubert Theatre: 38 weeks—*Can-Can,* 14; *Pajama Game,* 22; *Sing, Man, Sing,* 2.

Erlanger Theatre: 36 weeks—*The Teahouse of the August Moon.*

Blackstone Theatre: 33 weeks—*The Skin of Our Teeth,* 2; D'Oyly Carte Opera company, presenting *The Mikado, Yeomen of the Guard, Pinafore* and *Trial by Jury, Iolanthe* and *The Pirates of Penzance,* 2; *The Solid Gold Cadillac,* 7; *Anastasia,* 5; *Inherit the Wind,* 17.

Harris Theatre: 27 weeks—*The Tender Trap,* 5 this season, 12 in all; *Anniversary Waltz,* 13; Kabuki Theatre, 1; Marcel Marceau, 3; *Bad Seed,* 5, so far.

Great Northern Theatre: 11 weeks—Katherine Dunham Dance Revue, 1; *Kismet,* 4; *Plain and Fancy,* 3; *The Lovers,* 3.

Selwyn Theatre: 5 weeks—*Bus Stop.*

THE SEASON IN LONDON

By Kenneth Tynan

Dramatic Critic, London *Observer*

The New Plays

AT what should have been the height of the London theatre season, four months elapsed—between October and February—in which no new English play appeared in the West End. Everything that arrived was imported, and the critics, seeing the writing on the wall (or the lack of it), began to make plans for the surely imminent day of their dismissal. Then, late in April, the laggard season bloomed; and when it did, it bloomed spectacularly, giving us astonished onlookers the healthiest crop for a decade. I will begin at the bad beginning.

If acting is an imitative art, the cast of *Lucky Strike,* a sorry farce about industrial relations, was essentially unemployed; the characters, workers and managers alike, were parodies of parodies. On the same level of triviality, we had *Ring for Catty,* a tragicomedy of life in a sanatorium ward run by a briskly maternal young nurse: the program was memorably adorned with a sparkling cartoon of the heroine sprinting with a bed-pan. Gerald Savory's *A Likely Tale* was a forbidding hybrid, a half-hearted Chekhovian comedy crossed with a half-hearted Robert Morley farce: Mr. Morley played two parts, in both of which he was playfully miscast, with his accustomed panache. That exiled guardian of empire, Noel Coward, contributed a rather elderly comedy called *South Sea Bubble;* set in an imaginary British colony, it promoted the guileless fiction that all native peoples are Tories at heart. The dialogue, full of entreaties to "rise above it" and nicknames like "good old Boffin," was an anthology of Coward cliché lacking only "too, too" to make it complete. Out of the past the author's imperial aphorisms came winging, to fall wetly (the phrase is Coward's own) like pennies into mud. Vivien Leigh, as the governor's wife, hit the right note of cool, immaculate condescension.

The best two homegrown comedies came late. One was Peter Ustinov's *Romanoff and Juliet,* the neatest trick this Protean polyglot has yet pulled. Comedy, for Ustinov, derives from the clash of national attitudes; he is our greatest expert on the ways in which nations differ. Here we saw the American and Russian Embassies facing each other across the central square of the smallest country in Europe. Soviet son falls for Yankee daughter in a sudden outbreak of peace that appalls their respective families: the Americans conventionally bluster, while the Russians are caricatured as poker-faced killjoys. Romance, in the upshot, prevails. If you feel that this outline shows no very great expertness in national distinctions, let me remind you that a third country is involved, the tiny domain where the action happens, a dwarf dreamland radically different from any other on earth. It has a religious sect called the Mauve Friars, who neither sit nor stand but walk about on their knees; and its policy is to maintain "the balance of feebleness," since it has been overrun and liberated so often that every day is Independence Day. Ustinov (who plays its President himself) authenticates his midget Utopia in loving detail, contrasting its happy vagueness with the great grim dogmas of West and East, and thus providing us with a satiric touchstone against which to test the pretensions of both.

Enid Bagnold's *The Chalk Garden* may well be the finest artificial comedy to have come from an English (as opposed to an Irish) pen since the death of Congreve. Its style recalled that of Ronald Firbank's *The Princess Zoubaroff:* it had the same exotic insolence, evoking a world full of hard, gem-like flamethrowers. We eavesdrop on a group of thoroughbred minds, expressing themselves in speech of an exquisite candor, tiptoeing across frail causeways of simile and vaulting over gorges impassable to the rational soul. London gave Miss Bagnold the actors she needed. Superbly caparisoned, the old West End cavalry went into action, perhaps for the last time. Edith Evans, enraged by what she calls "this *mule* of a garden," resembled a crested wave of eccentricity dashing itself against the rocks of contemporary life; and Peggy Ashcroft beautifully played her granddaughter's dumpy governess-with-a-past. In this production (by Sir John Gielgud) one saw English actors doing consummately what few actors can do at all: reproduce in the theatre the spirited elegance of a Mozart quintet.

The serious plays were dimmer. Graham Greene's *The Power and the Glory* was adapted for the stage: this tale of a fugitive priest in Communist Mexico pointed Greene's familiar moral that, soak and seducer though you may be, you are still saved if you go to the right church. You may be 20,000 leagues below the Holy See, but you are still the elect, ever to be preferred to the merely elected, thuggish egalitarians who are assuredly damned. Through six vivid scenes we accompany the priestly sot on his search for communion wine;

British comedienne, "Joyce Grenfell Requests the Pleasure . . ."

we see his vocation leading him irrevocably to his death; and yet the tears will not come. The message, I suppose, is to blame; only certain Catholics can fully savor it. Peter Brook's production planted us firmly south of the border, and Paul Scofield brought off a prodigious hit as the trudging, wizened hero. Puffing on a cheroot, with lines of resignation etched as if by acid on his cheeks, he presented the authentic face of Mexico, flyblown and God-bitten.

Much more impressive was Brendan Behan's *The Quare Fellow,* produced by the East End company called Theatre Workshop. This took place in an Irish prison on the eve of an execution, with the author lodging his protest against capital punishment in a spirit of laconic detachment; so far from trying to gain sympathy for the condemned man, Behan keeps him off-stage throughout the play and shows us merely the effect on the prison population of the knowledge that one of them is soon to drop rope-necklaced through the untender trap. They behave with hair-raising jocularity. The tension is intolerable, but it is we, not they, who feel it; we are moved precisely in the degree that they are not. Behan's supreme dramatic achievement comes at the moment of the hanging. The stage is empty; the hour strikes; and an unseen wag, bawling from some lofty window, launches into an imaginary commentary on the hundred-yard dash from cell to scaffold—they're coming into the straight now, the chaplain's leading by a head. . . . Joan Littlewood's production of this unforgettable play was a model of restraint and disciplined naturalism.

The spring saw an organized attempt to break London of the long-run habit. At the Royal Court Theatre, the English Stage Company opened its "First Season of Modern Repertory," directed by George Devine. It struck off with *The Mulberry Bush,* a first play by the waspish novelist Angus Wilson: its theme—that pre-war progressives have lost touch with reality—was handled in dialogue that showed uncommon faith in the audience's intelligence: but the production was feeble. It was followed by Arthur Miller's *The Crucible,* a half-success. The third play, *Look Back in Anger,* was the real proof that the new enterprise meant business. Written by a 27-year-old actor named John Osborne, it caused a grand upheaval by telling the truth about post-war youth for the first time on the London stage. Its hero, a provincial university graduate who runs a candy-stall, was dismissed by many elder critics as a young pup. And indeed, what with his introspection, his gift for parody, his scorching frankness and his love of soliloquy, Jimmy Porter is the completest young pup in British drama since Hamlet. He has a wife who is talked into leaving him by an actress friend: Jimmy's instant riposte is to go to bed with the actress. *Look Back in Anger* does for the theatre what

Kingsley Amis's *Lucky Jim* did for the novel. All the qualities of the lower-middle intelligentsia are there—the instinctive leftishness, the love of jazz, the automatic rejection of "official" dogmas, the surreal sense of humor, the conviction that all the crusades worth fighting in have been either won or discredited, and—beneath all these—the determination that nobody who dies shall go unmourned. I take this piece to be the best young play of its decade.

Continental imports did well. The season began with hints of a vogue for the late Ugo Betti. His *The Queen and the Rebels,* one of those plays about a frontier incident in an unnamed country torn by revolution, made a short-lived impact. It dealt with a prostitute who takes pity on a hunted queen and offers herself to the rebels as a substitute martyr; what became abrasive was the author's refusal to let a moment pass without giving some evidence of high seriousness. "It's the smell of history," someone had to remark when someone else observed that corpses stank. "Serious" is actually the wrong word for this kind of stuff. As Hemingway said: "A serious writer may be a hawk or a buzzard or even a popinjay, but a solemn writer is always a bloody owl." Betti's tragedies are flawless, except that they are not tragic; and his comedies are everything comedy should be, except funny. This latter point was dismally proved by *Summertime,* a flimsy-dimsy-whimsy account of an Alpine flirtation.

France had its usual enlivening quota of London successes. Jean-Paul Sartre's *Nekrassov,* heavily and sensibly cut since its Parisian *débâcle,* was staged by the amateur Unity Theatre, who revealed it to be the best political satire since Shaw's perihelion. Sartre's story of a confidence man who passes himself off as an escaped Soviet diplomat was politically fairly pink, but it was pink without bitters: the dialogue bristled with buoyant ironies, ideas turned upside down and inside out with dizzying intellectual agility. Then we had Marcel Aymé's *The Count of Clérambard,* a serious farce about a sadistic count who becomes even more objectionable when he turns religious. London did not like it: this kind of ribald rat-tat on the gates of Heaven was something we had not heard since the medieval morality plays. And the production managed to turn Aymé's dangerous firework into a sputtering squib.

Fritz Hochwalder's *The Strong Are Lonely,* a passionate debate about the spiritual rights and wrongs of a Jesuit settlement in Paraguay, was similarly marred by British casting. As the Father Provincial, Donald Wolfit slogged for God like a true worker-priest; but it is of the English theatre, not of a Jesuit college, that this hard-touring actor is the true provincial father. He had one peerless scene of old-time *rodomontade* with Ernest Milton as a Spanish spy: I shall long recall the picture of these two experts, stealthily upstaging each other for the greater glory of God.

The brightest Parisian entrants were Feydeau's *Hotel Paradiso* and Anouilh's *Waltz of the Toreadors.* The former, adapted by Peter Glenville, was a sixty-year-old farce of clockwork cunning and impregnable plausibility: a henpecked husband takes his best friend's wife to a shady hotel intermittently occupied, in the course of one night, by almost everyone he knows. The dazzling economy of the construction and the lurid speed of the direction more than made up for the paucity of verbal wit. Martita Hunt, swooping about like a wounded pterodactyl, was formidably funny; and Alec Guinness, as her husband, gave a classic display of stealth—a chubby, crafty little chap, obsessed by the urge to break his bonds and live dangerously. Anouilh, of course, cut deeper. In *The Waltz of the Toreadors* he takes a stock sentimental situation—robust husband tethered to crippled wife—and treats it with lacerating candor. The hero, a lecherous old general, understands his ghastly wife well enough to loathe her but too well to leave her. Moral: never seek to understand anyone, or you will die of it. Hugh Griffiths gave us all of the general, mind, groin and gullet; one saw, beneath the savage humor, a heart splitting with misguided romanticism.

Broadway, for once in a while, sent us practically nothing. There was *Anniversary Waltz,* a queasy farce about premarital relations that bore the same relationship to drama that gossip does to biography. Then came Sigmund Miller's *One Bright Day,* a prettily written variant on *An Enemy of the People,* about the problem that faces a millionaire druggist whose best-selling product, a sedative pill, is proved to have toxic properties. Should he tell or keep mum? Clive Brook's creased and scowling dignity almost reconciled me to a very flabby *dénouement.* But the happiest American visitor was Geraldine Page in Richard Nash's *The Rainmaker,* in which a braggart dream-peddler awakens love in the heart of a farmer's bluestocking daughter. The fable is an old one: but Miss Page can make a soiled cliché shine like a coin new-minted. The play charts Lizzie Curry's painful trek from self-loathing to self-respect, and Miss Page took us with her every blushing, stumbling, lyrically faltering step of the way.

The Revivals

Fewer and better than usual: a doubly healthy sign. Frankie Howerd, one of the two or three best clowns in British show business, played an historic *Charley's Aunt;* rather than dwindle into a wife, like Millamant, he tumesced into an aunt, or rather into a sort of nightmare landlady, frantic, villainous and disgruntled. Two theatres, the Saville and the Phoenix, offered classics for limited runs. John Clements, at the Saville, presented *The Wild Duck* in Christmas week: a stroke of sharpest irony, to stage in the season of good will the greatest attack on good will ever penned! Emlyn Williams exposed the paltriness of Hjalmar Ekdal with the cold disdain of an accountant listing forged entries in the company's books; but he did not feel for the man; nor, in consequence, could we. Nothing else blemished Ibsen's impact: the play came over not only as a supreme tragedy but as a supreme comedy to boot. This production was succeeded by a frisky and ornamental revival of *The Rivals,* Sheridan's sportive tilt at the romantic spirit.

The Peter Brook-Paul Scofield season at the Phoenix was wholly devoted to sin and damnation. In addition to *The Power and the Glory,* it included *Hamlet* and T. S. Eliot's *The Family Reunion;* a bleaker gallery could hardly be imagined. Scofield, on the surface, is a born Hamlet; he has the right sadness and the right spleen, and he can freeze a word with an irony at once deadly and mournful. But in Brook's oddly tentative production, he gave us just one long, loud sulk. The evening's best thing was Alec Clunes, who made Claudius convincing for the first time by playing him from Claudius's own point of view, as a man who has committed a *crime passionnel* after an internal struggle that has left scars on his conscience. One saw a man of action growing weary and defeated as his new world of crime falls stone by stone about his ears. Under Clunes's influence *Hamlet* was the tragedy not only of a prince but of a whole doomed house. It brought the House of Atreus much closer than *The Family Reunion* did. Scofield's sleepless mien and haggard voice almost succeeded in making us care about Eliot's hero, a posh young neurotic pursued by the Furies because his father once wanted to knock off his mother. But the poetry vanquished him. Eliot is very good at lowering the temperature, at imposing a sudden chill on events; but he cannot melt or warm us, which is why the theatre, which strives on strong emotions, must ultimately reject him. Sybil Thorndike and Gwen Ffrancgon-Davies performed magisterially in Brook's production of this would-be, has-been masterpiece.

The Old Vic finished its third year of plowing through the Shakespearean First Folio: Paul Rogers, a stout supporting actor, and John Neville, a lithe blonde *jeune premier,* led an unremarkable company. They were, respectively, Brutus and Antony in *Julius Caesar;*

Lynn Fontanne and Alfred Lunt in "The Great Sebastians"

next, Rogers scored as a waddling, effeminate Falstaff in *The Merry Wives of Windsor;* and Neville replied with a smart Autolycus in *The Winter's Tale.* Richard Burton joined the troupe for *Henry V,* which he played fearlessly, as a ruthless warrior unafraid of harshness or of curling the royal lip. There ensued the season's grand stunt: Neville and Burton alternating the leading roles of *Othello,* two born Cassios (as one thought) attempting to play Othello and Iago. Both lacked the age and weight for the Moor, and Neville's Iago was no more than a capering spiv. But when Burton played Iago, the whole production rose with him. He had the secret of the part, which is that Iago must respect Othello. Earthy and transparently sincere, Burton never gave the vile game away; not by the smallest wink or leer did his outward action demonstrate the native act and figure of his heart. The imposture was total and terrifying; it would have deceived any jury on earth.

This performance apart, the Vic's peak was Tyrone Guthrie's re-creation of *Troilus and Cressida*. He mounted this great anti-war play in Edwardian costumes, the trappings of the last era that thought war glamorous. The Trojans were played as glass-smashing cavalry officers: the Greeks, scarred and monocled, were all graduates of Heidelberg. Pandarus became the Baron de Charlus, and Cressida was a militant flirt, an interpretation that quite deliberately threw romance out of the window. Of the play's many styles Guthrie chose one—broad satire—and let the rest go hang. After ten minutes of protest, one surrendered to a masterly and meaningful joke. This production reestablished Guthrie as the most inventive of British directors, ahead of the three Peters—Glenville, Brook and Hall.

The Musicals

Broadway shipped us *Plain and Fancy,* a warm and witty contrast of city slickness and rural simplicity that I thought as gay as a harvest festival: but the score issued no irresistible command to whistle, and London did not take to it. A more emphatic hit was *The Pajama Game,* which fantastically succeeded in making music out of a disputed wage increase at a factory in Dubuque, Iowa. The new eternal triangle was Capital, Labor and Personnel Management, sparked into song by the late Jerry Ross's melodic gusto and Richard Adler's fish-eyed lyrics. As the strike-leader heroine, Joy Nichols had the right limpid brassiness.

The Threepenny Opera, transferred from Broadway in Marc Blitzstein's adaptation, set another kind of reality to music: the cynical reality of Berlin in the twenties. The anger of Bert Brecht's lyrics is as salty as ever, and Kurt Weill's plaintive saxes are the ideal ironic setting: the words bang, and the music whimpers. The cast, in Sam Wanamaker's seductive production, played and sang with enormous bite, and the show pulled in enthusiastic audiences.

British musicals continued their slow awakening. According to the program, *The Water Gipsies* (by A. P. Herbert and Vivian Ellis) took place in a Thames-side suburb called Hammersmith; but it was a Hammersmith unrecognizably pastoral, peopled with quaint bargees whose joys were homely and whose destiny, they were regretfully reminded, was obscure. Snobbish is really too mild a word for this astounding exercise in mass condescension. The starring role (played by Dora Bryan with undeserved wit) was that of a hoyden who takes an "aperient" before her meals and a bottle of "Bummery" with them; and in the big emotional scene the low-born heroine did a strip-tease and then knelt in prayer, pledging her faith in "the state of life to which it pleases God to call me."

Having looked back on the twenties in *The Boy Friend,* Sandy Wilson looked back on the kindergarten in *The Buccaneer,* which is the title of an outmoded boys' magazine that is saved from extinction by a highly articulate bunch of rescuing tots. The lyrics were mettlesome and gay: where one faulted Wilson was in his dialogue, which was flat and torpid. But the book is all that one could throw at him: the tunes stayed in one's ear. His limitations are now becoming clear. He is an obstinate innocent, permanently enthralled by the pipes of Peter Pan. And his future will last as long as his nostalgia.

The year's musical novelty was *Cranks,* written, devised and directed by the young choreographer John Cranko. Using swing on a spinet and a company of four (three men and a cool girl), it mingled mime, dance and song in surrealist fashion, including a song about a niece who turns her bowler-hatted uncles into bats and a number about the liberated future in which, according to the lyric, Blackpool Tower may burst into flower. Every item brought into play the full equipment of theatre—limbs, lights and larynxes. With hands and fingers, interlaced and spot-lit, Cranko works especial wonders: his mime sketch about a live pair of white gloves would entrance Chaplin. The whole show was very Left Bank. In fact, a better title would have been: *Anything Gauche.*

To conclude, Robert Dhéry, who is a genius. M. Dhéry, who has been staging crazy revues in Paris for over eight years, brought his company to London in an extravaganza called *La Plume de ma Tante.* With amiable distress, he compères the show; and there is reason for his disquiet, for this is a revue in which everything goes quietly—not loudly—wrong. The cast, inured to calamity, faces it stoically. When Christian Duvaleix (announced by M. Dhéry, for some reason, as "my brother-in-law, Amsterdam") slinks leering into sight with an electric guitar, the instrument explodes with a blinding blue flash. At this he betrays absolutely no surprise. He does not even shrug. He simply exits. So with Jacques Legras, another clown to whom terrible things are always happening. To console himself, he eats dog-biscuits: nothing more. M. Dhéry's sense of humor is neither topical nor satirical; it is tethered neither to time nor place. Its only parallel is in the films of Jacques Tati and in parts of *Waiting for Godot.* This is the comedy of quiet desperation. It teaches us, when confronted with disaster, to react with none but the faintest of blinks. Some such impassive response, I suppose, is ideally appropriate to the crashing and alarming events of our time. M. Dhéry is not only hysterically funny: he is also a global philosopher. It is a pity that his greatest clown, Louis de Funès, refused to join him in England. All the same, he brought about what I pray will be a lasting revolution in British comedy technique.

THE SEASON IN PARIS

By André Josset

Playwright; and Secretary-General of the International Theatre Institute, UNESCO

THE opening of the theatre season, this year, coincided with the opening of the hunting season. With hounds and halloos the victims were pursued through thickets, plains, and hills. This is why the first game that was scented, called *Le Bal des Adieux* (Farewell Ball) was massacred by the critics who were still full of the energy they had stored up during their vacations.

Le Bal des Adieux was written by the author of this chronicle, and directed by one of France's first-rank stage directors (who three years ago received the Grand Prize for his work in this field), Jean Mercure. The hunting party under discussion took place at the Théâtre Gaston Baty, one of the great theatres of Paris.

Actually, the author of the play could not have been more ill-treated had he written a vaudeville to be performed in tights. *Le Bal des Adieux* paints a quite different pair of portraits from the usual ones of Louis XVI and Marie Antoinette. In any case, the external side of their histories was respected: only the hidden life, along with the character of Louis XVI, had been completely changed. Thus, after chronicling a strange series of facts in the life of the unfortunate king, the author saw Louis XVI not at all as weak or mediocre, but as a man who was insufficiently loved, a humiliated majesty who could find no way out except in death—a death that was premeditated. The character thus conceived became, I think, extremely fascinating and as disquieting as anyone must be who ruins his own life and those of others without admitting or even knowing what he does.

But for whatever reason, the play was assassinated. The author could find some consolation, however, in the fact that the Laurence Olivier Productions acquired the English-language rights to *Le Bal des Adieux* and that Vivien Leigh will play Marie Antoinette.

Next came a prewar play by Armand Salacrou called *Histoire de Rire* (Funny Story), which, if memory serves, had been put on during the "phony war" early in 1940. This play out of the past was a lively success. A comic and bitter work, its action concerns two couples who are friends. Although some critics thought it fell off in the last act, I personally believe its success was fully deserved.

The next evening, at the Théâtre des Ambassadeurs, the late Henri Bernstein's *Espoir* (Hope) was revived with only moderate success. It is quite true that this extremely well-constructed play, written in grayish tones and with muted conflicts, seemed a bit faded. It is a species of the theatre "that dare not speak its name"; that hides behind a thousand precautions, ruses, and clever tricks which, however agreeable, remove all strength from the subject treated. The audience saw in *Espoir* the rather fragile shadow of what really goes on—amid smothered sounds and words—in a bourgeois salon, and left the theatre with a faint feeling of disappointment. This type of playwrighting seems passé.

On September 28 appeared André Roussin's new play (*L'Amour Fou* (Mad Passion), an obviously very clever work. But although I adore such Roussin plays as *Les Oeufs de l'Autruche* (The Eggs of the Ostrich), *Nina* and *La Petite Hutte* (The Little Hut), I must admit that this play was not completely satisfying. The upside-down situations and some of the characters showed a rather too systematic search for originality at all costs, which yet did not entirely hide the author's talent and verve. You will get the idea of what I mean when I tell you that a 45-year-old lover comes to ask a married woman's daughter for her mother's hand in marriage. The play managed to survive its rather lukewarm reviews.

At the Palais de Chaillot on October 3, the U.S.S.R. presented the "Moisseiev Ballets" which had great success, thanks to their color and precision, to the poetry in certain of their themes, and to the liveliness of the ensemble.

The next night *Le Proces de Famille* (Family Trial), a translation from the Italian of Diego Fabbri, was well received though the play fell down very badly in its last act. A marvelous cast enacted this drama centering in a fight to gain possession of a child, which was quite good till it turned moralistic.

Next Jean-Louis Barrault offered an extraordinary production of Aeschylus' *Oresteia:* shadowy, violent, poetic, strange. The work was performed by Barrault, Marie Bell, and Marguerite Jamois (the manager of the Gaston Baty theatre) and conveyed a tragic intensity, an odor of blood, of pagan madness, of divine vengeance, that aroused my highest admiration. Among other exciting moments, I shall always remember the sight of the Erinnys lying like snoring, funereal dogs, whistling in their sleep, growling indistinctly in the ghostly light; and then greeting Clytemnestra with frenzied cackles, as she wanders through Hell in inconsolable rage and grief.

The next day Marcel Pagnol, the author of *Marius, Fanny* and *Topaze,* met defeat with a play about Judas. This is to my knowledge the fourth French play about Judas to have appeared lately. What a shower of bad disciples and traitors! What a storm of pleas, of ingenuity, of tender comprehension! Despite the vigor of Pagnol's text, and the competence of the performers, the critics were very hard on the play, which soon closed.

Then on November 4 came Jean Anouilh's *Ornifle ou le Courant d'Air* (Ornifle, or, The Draft), with Pierre Brasseur in the title role. The play was murdered, though it was actually very interesting, and very daring for its stage treatment of a cynical character. It is natural for an audacious playwright who offers theatre with all the stops pulled out to arouse indignation; but after all, we are no longer children. Furthermore, the end of the cynical character proves edifying, since he dies in the very act of committing a new nastiness. Despite the drawn knives of the critics, the play survived, and is still being performed as I write this.

At a theatre of which I am very fond, the Théâtre National Populaire, Victor Hugo's *Marie Tudor* was marvelously presented in the style of a melodrama for the tender-hearted. With inimitable seriousness, the actors uttered tirades which, had they been written by a modern author, would have provoked storms of laughter, but the play is so well constructed, the beat of its verse is so vigorous, the action so strong and rapid, that the audience could not but be swept along. Once more the most essential quality of the theatre shone forth.

Then at the Théâtre Antoine, came a play by Marcelle Maurette, one already famous in England and America. It is therefore unnecessary for me to discuss *Anastasia* at length. In Paris it was not much of a success, despite a remarkable performance by Lucienne Bogaert and the stage debut of the popular singer Juliette Greco.

Next came an 18th-century play at the Comédie Française—Diderot's *Est-il Bon, Est-il Mechant* (Is He Good, Is He Bad). It appears that this play is a self-portrait—both charming and amusing —of the famous writer; profound in that it tries to go as deeply as possible into the not always clear or lovely motives of supposedly benevolent people. The play understandably provoked esteem rather than enthusiasm.

A few days later the Japanese came to Paris to present a series of richly colorful little scenes in the Kabuki tradition. One of the attractions not foreseen was the absolutely ravishing timidity of the young and pretty Japanese society girl who presented the program

French mime, Marcel Marceau, as BIP

in French; her long eyelashes lowered, her voice lightly trembling, she provided a glimpse of the respectful politeness of old Japan.

On November 30 Peguy's *Jeanne d'Arc* was presented at the Comédie Française without success. This work, full of admirable lyricism and beauty of style, is simply not for the theatre. Then Jean-Louis Barrault gave us *Le Chien du Jardinier* (The Gardener's Dog), a charming comedy by Lope de Vega with a very luminous atmosphere; and, on December 10, Marcel Achard's *Le Mal d'Amour* (Pangs of Love) was neatly assassinated. A week later, a comedy entitled *José* was a triumph. Although its plot was very thin, the play, which aimed at amusement, completely achieved its goal.

On December 18 *Les Oiseaux de Lune* (The Moon Birds) rose in the air before our amazed and ravished eyes. The author, Marcel Aymé, always combines a great store of bizarre wit with a sense of solid human truth; introduces unexpected and hilarious developments, worked out with faultless logic. *Les Oiseaux de Lune,* treating satirically of a young provincial teacher who finds he can change people into birds, has been, in my opinion, the greatest success of the present season.

There exists also in Paris a "Théâtre en Rond," quite small and very well managed. So far, fortune has only given it half a smile, but certain plays shown there have proved the singular effectiveness of this type of production. Certainly the adaptation of an Italian play called *Entre Chien et Loup* (Between the Dog and the Wolf) was enhanced by theatre-in-the-round, though the subject itself was not adequately treated. Nevertheless, the Arena Theatre is a fascinating experiment in that it frees us from the eternal question of sets and allows free play to the imagination and audacity of playwrights. It also facilitates the production of plays by so greatly reducing their cost.

The Comédie Française had to wait until January 15, 1956, to get even for *Jeanne d'Arc* with Molière's *Les Femmes Savantes* (The Bluestockings), in a new production by Jean Meyer, with a brilliant cast and a perfect set. But plainly Molière's immense genius was the principal cause of this triumph. The play, the producer, and the actors were acclaimed.

Next there sounded the brasses of success and laughter: thanks to Jean Vilar there was a successful revival of Marivaux's *Le Triomphe de l'Amour* (The Triumph of Love). The complex plot, in which the sentiments of love are dissected with witty minuteness, does not at all harm the construction of the whole. Much was said about how very French the presentation was, though I really wonder why, for I constantly had the impression of being at Potsdam—in the grounds of Frederick the Great's San Souci—among the philosophers and rather analytical lovers of the day. For a change, the stage of the Théâtre National Populaire was not bare. Formal potted trees represented the garden in which the action took place, but the background, with its distant draperies, was austere.

It is good to note that despite the frequent error of putting ideology ahead of action, characters, and conflicts, the classic conception of well-constructed and well-developed theatre has not yet been killed. I say this à propos of *Cyrano de Bergerac,* which the Théâtre Sarah Bernhardt presented this winter in a production by Pierre Dux. The play's enormous success with the public was due, it is only fair to say, not only to its fame and innate appeal, but to Pierre Dux's clever staging and to his own direct and moving performance.

Another Italian play translated into French, *Le Seducteur* (The Charmer), was put on by François Perier in January, with considerable personal success. This great actor is capable, all by himself, of filling the stage. *Il Pleut, Bergère* (It's Raining, Shepherdess) followed at the Théâtre de la Renaissance and lasted about as long as a summer shower. Then Jean-Louis Barrault, at the Petit Théâtre Marigny, put on a play by a new author, *Le Personnage Combatant* (The Struggling Character). The Petit Théâtre Marigny is more like a gymnasium than a theatre; trapezes hang from the ceiling; enormous benches with hard wood backs fill the auditorium. Hirsute youths and pony-tailed girls from the Latin Quarter sometimes squeeze themselves onto them. This time Jean-Louis Barrault offered a two-character play of some interest, which had a pretty success with the young people.

On February 3 the famous Théâtre de l'Oeuvre, which once brought to France the works of the Scandinavian playwrights, notably Ibsen, offered that drama of the disintegration of the Slav soul, *Les Bas Fonds* (The Lower Depths) of Gorki. I will not be so foolish as to discuss a play you are so certain to know: the new element was the son of Georges and Ludmilla Pitoeff, Sacha, who, with his frightening thinness and tormented, anguished face, would seem to be the ideal interpreter of plays of despair and resignation. The play had a fine success.

And suddenly, on March 5, the growling tom-toms of the Fodeiba African Ballets began to sound, seeming to have fallen from another planet and to have come out of another age. This was a picturesque and savage excursion into prehistoric times. Fires burned in the brush, and around them were black and furiously contorted silhouettes, armed with lances, and decked out in clinking bracelets and exotic feather headdresses.

Almost immediately afterward, the Théâtre Hébertot had the audacity to present a play called *La Dame sans Merci* (The Merciless Lady), which contained a poisonous and ferocious diatribe against the critics. The actor who delivered this diatribe directly addressed the audience and pointed at the critics it inveighed against. Certain critics reacted adversely, for they did not at all like getting their own sharp arrows back: they preferred soliloquy to dialogue. The amusing thing is that the author of the play in question was himself once a critic.

After this intermezzo, Jean Cocteau's *La Machine à Ecrire* (The Typewriter) was put on at the Comédie Française. The danger of these mechanical titles is that they evoke only the vaguest memories when those who see the plays are asked to recollect them. Telephone calls to the box office often ran: "Could you please reserve a pair of seats for *La Machine à Laver* (The Washing Machine)." I found the first act excellent, the second and third a bit less so. Nevertheless the play had an honorable career, thanks partly to Jean Meyer's production and to some remarkable acting.

On May 14 the Festival of Paris opened. From year to year this great international theatre exhibition develops and grows. The Lyric Theatre is now participating in the Festival on the same basis as the Dramatic Theatre. Lyric Theatre's great triumph at the time I write is the Opera of Belgrade's production of Moussorgsky's *Kavantchina* and Borodin's *Prince Igor*. In terms of drama we have seen, up to now, performances by the National Theatre of Belgrade and the Kungliga Dramatic Theatre of Stockholm; both presentations were most interesting, and the same phenomenon occurred that I noted last year: that is, the partial removal of the barrier of language. The public is given a résumé of the plot and thereafter, thanks to the actors' performances, can guess at a great many details. This year eighteen nations will participate in the Drama Festival, five in the Lyric Festival, and four in the concerts and recitals.

THE SEASON IN CALIFORNIA

By Luther Nichols

San Francisco Drama and Book Critic

TO give a general impression of theatre in California last year (May 1955-May 1956) it is not necessary to change the record much. One merely rewinds the phonograph. Pretty much the same grooves were played, and some of them were becoming ruts. Established operations flourished; semiprofessional groups advanced somewhat, and a few novel enterprises sprang up. In all, it was a reassuring year financially, an undistinguished one esthetically and one in which the public voted for frivolity over significance in a landslide.

The booming Civic Light Opera Association (hereinafter referred to as the CLO) neared its twentieth anniversary with another profitable season under the West Coast Ziegfeld, Edwin Lester. A new board of directors and a guarantor setup paralleling that of the parent Los Angeles organization was installed in San Francisco. Some criticized the CLO's tendency to be a mere booking agent for New York shows instead of creating new ones of its own, as it did with *Song of Norway, Magdelena* and *Kismet.* But the sponsors did not carp—not after a season's gross of $2,500,000 for both cities was announced.

Kismet, incidentally, returned from its New York success two years after its world premiere here, and this time most critics were forced to admit they had underestimated its potential as a tired businessman's treat. Expertly doctored, better set, faster and smoother, it starred William Johnson, Elaine Malbin and Julie Wilson, and showed the potency of a Broadway reputation by doing turnaway business. *Kiss Me, Kate* was seen in a new production with blonde Jean Fenn and Robert Wright, but like most kisses was not as thrilling as the first; *The Pajama Game* (laundered for its Southern California appearance at the Philharmonic, a church property) might have been rather flat without a gingery lass named Pat Stanley as the cutup of Hernando's Hideaway, but with her it broke all CLO records with a ten-week run in San Francisco, and *Plain and Fancy,* in a West Coast production starring Alexis Smith and her husband, Craig Stevens, was something of a disappointment.

As with *Pajama Game, Silk Stockings,* which opened the 1956

Helen Traubel, Judy Tyler and

William Johnson in "Pipe Dream"

CLO season, was kept buoyant by its comedienne. In this case she was leggy Gretchen Wyler, who overshadowed stars Don Ameche and Jan Sherwood and almost made you forget a finale that backfired in its intention to make the brassiest kind of American jazz seem more enticing than Soviet regimentation. It was the first show to be brought intact from Broadway by the CLO.

Like a fair but not overly gifted actress, the major California theatres had steady engagements, transitory loves and a certain amount of scandal during the past year.

The greatest financial success, an unlikely looking bit of crust that proved to be buttered on all sides, was the Jerome Chodorov-Joseph Fields comedy, *Anniversary Waltz.* Unaccountably, it broke the all-time record for consecutive runs in San Francisco when it entered its twenty-fourth week at the Alcazar. Marjorie Lord was the feminine star, and it says much for her abilities that she adjusted to the changing values of several leading men in the course of the play's marathonic run, including Russell Nype, Andrew Duggan, Richard Eastham and Hugh Marlowe. The last-named was charged with kissing too ardently and embroidering the script too unpredictably for the rest of the company, and left in a flurry of temperament and publicity that did attendance no harm.

Other shows at the Alcazar last year were *The Desperate Hours,* with William Gargan and Nancy Coleman, in which there was more evidence of skilled carpentry in the two-storeyed set than in the play; *Lunatics and Lovers,* Sidney Kingsley's lecherous comedy, memorable for Pamela Britton's generosity in sharing a bubble bath with Melville Cooper; *The Tender Trap,* with Lloyd Bridges, K. T. Stevens and Russell Nype in a bit of fluff about a playboy whose domesticated friend envies his profusion of women, and *The Fifth Season,* with Joseph Buloff and Gene Raymond as two clothiers staving off bankruptcy. Hardly the sort of season you recommend to friends whom you wish to impress with your intellectual fodder, but lots of fun.

All the shows in the foregoing two paragraphs also played the Carthay Circle Theatre in Los Angeles. The Carthay's hyperactive program, managed by Jack Present and Harry Zevin under the banner of the Artists Embassy Producing Company, also offered *The Shrike,* with Dane Clark, and Jean Kerr's comedy, *King of Hearts,* with Jerome Cowan, Arthur Franz and Phyllis Avery.

In the forefront of the many artists who came to the West Coast in 1955-56 was Marcel Marceau. The great French mime restored, for a few weeks anyway, a classic sense of the theatre as the quintessential place to see "the soul in action." His art, a gallery of exquisite scenes at once primitive and enduring, refined and ephemeral, drew enthusiastic crowds here as it did in New York.

Bus Stop was a reasonably touching, if minor, comedy, starring Albert Salmi and Peggy Ann Garner, who played with a feeling that presaged their later marriage. *A Day by the Sea* brought a veteran and polished crew together as Hume Cronyn, Jessica Tandy, Dennis King and Aline MacMahon were directed by Sir Cedric Hardwicke in N. C. Hunter's urbane London comedy hit about the inability of two people to synchronize their love, but the public was unresponsive. *Don Juan in Hell* made the rounds again, this time with Agnes Moorehead directing Kurt Kasznar, Ricardo Montalban, Mary Astor and Reginald Denny in a microphoned reading of Shaw's infernal comedy. Rudy Vallee was agreeable in Jean Kerr's light comedy, *Jenny Kissed Me.* Cole Porter's high-kicking musical about Paris in 1893, *Can-Can,* came and kicked. *Bad Seed* somehow failed to shock as much as expected with its pigtailed child murderess, a notable delinquent even in California, and its star, Nancy Kelly, was not in good form. And then there was a truly forgettable comedy-mystery, *Reclining Figure,* under which Gene Lockhart was pinned. It performed under raps—critical ones.

A relatively bright spot of the season was the acting of Viveca Lindfors in *Anastasia,* which sounded unusual depths in the second act as she poignantly sought love, rather than confirmation as the rightful heir to the Russian throne, from the old empress dowager. Eugenie Leontovich played the latter with odd but effective phrasing, and it was too bad the rather expository play let them down badly in Act III.

Maurice Zolotow, in an article in *Theatre Arts,* summed up the opinion of many about Los Angeles as a theatre town when he wrote that it was "spiritually apathetic, intellectually enervated and emotionally dehydrated." However, this failed to ruffle Demetrios Vilan, manager of the Huntington Hartford Theatre, which confounded the wiseacres by its resurgent activity after a shaky first year. "The theatre is now in full swing," reports Mr. Vilan. "Up to now the Biltmore had a monopoly on Theatre Guild subscription plays, but now we are getting our share. It's a terrific theatre town if you give them what they want." And the Huntington Hartford gave them *The Caine Mutiny Court Martial,* a great success with Lloyd Nolan back from his New York triumph; *A Day by the Sea* in its West Coast premiere; Mel Dinelli's *The Man,* with Dorothy Gish; *The Rainmaker,* with Don DeFore and Jan Sterling, and a musical revue, *Joyride,* which caused no one to throw his cap over the windmill when it opened, but was gradually given enough transfusions to strengthen it for bookings in Chicago, with Broadway in mind.

Highly successful was the Greek Theatre's ten-week season in Los Angeles, during which General Director James Doolittle offered a mixture of *Three for Tonight,* with Harry Belafonte; *Wonderful Town,* with Carol Channing; New York City Ballet, and Katherine Dunham and Jose Greco's dance troupes.

At the Pasadena Playhouse the more popular shows of a busy year were *Jenny Kissed Me,* with Rudy Vallee; *The White Sheep of the Family,* with Edward Everett Horton, and *The Solid Gold Cadillac,* with Zazu Pitts. The latter was a smash.

There was a great deal of miscellaneous activity. Touring international imports, all of surpassing interest, were the D'Oyly Carte Opera Company of England in its Gilbert and Sullivan repertory, the Kabuki Dancers of Japan and the Dublin Players of guess where. The Turnabout Theatre of Los Angeles at long last invaded San Francisco with its swivel seats that permit audiences to turn to either end of the house to watch puppets or people alternately perform in happy collusion. Novelty reached its zenith when Hugh Evans (brother of Maurice) and Frank Bray introduced from England their Lilliput Theatre, a "theatre in miniature" in a forty-nine-seat house in San Francisco. They presented everything from Shakespeare to whodunits of 1830 with tiny, two-dimensional cutout figures on a stage whose proscenium arch is an old fireplace.

The bashed-in television sets of *Anniversary Waltz,* the bubble bathing of *Lunatics and Lovers,* the drunk scene of *Pajama Game*—these were honored highlights of the season in major houses. This insistence on the frivolous, to say nothing of the high cost of tickets, cut the professional theatre off from great numbers of people who found satisfaction among the warmer, more intimate and more dedicated of the state's "little theatres." There they sought relief for that nagging conscience that demands "the better things" of the drama.

Best of these resident groups, in the opinion of just about all who have seen them, is the Actor's Workshop of San Francisco. It drew some 20,000 people to its long-run performances of Arthur Miller's powerful *The Crucible;* met the challenge of Tennessee Williams' *Camino Real* with a fluid staging and antic dash that made the play's dusty message about the downtrodden of the world and their oppressors seem much fresher than it was; gave Bertold Brecht's didactic, Expressionistic, anti-war drama, *Mother Courage,* a bristling production that excited much controversy among press and public (and hence good patronage), and was somewhat less fortunate with Alfred

Hayes' *The Girl on the Via Flaminia.* The group, under Jules Irving and Herbert Blau, is obviously not afraid to venture on lofty, uncertain pathways, being graced with fine actors who are sure of their footing and work with the unison of a centipede's legs.

Other noteworthy groups in San Francisco were the new Abbott-Abrams Production Company, which was never dark in a first eight months during which it presented *Picnic, The Rose Tattoo, Twelfth Night, The Rainmaker,* Luba Sharoff in her fine literary renderings, and an original musical revue by Anne Soulé. The Interplayers did *The Madwoman of Chaillot* and William Saroyan's *My Heart's in the Highlands;* the Playhouse did T. S. Eliot's *The Confidential Clerk,* and the Company of the Golden Hind widened horizons with a colorful *Theatre Carnival* under Rachmael ben Avram, mingling opera, high comedy, poetry and wonderful scene- and costume-design as a stylized pocket of resistance to the American "dirty T-shirt trend."

The Straw Hat Theatre revived with a musical revue that blended well with dinner and drinks at the Claremont Hotel in Berkeley. And the Wharf Theatre put on its usual fine season at Monterey.

Down Los Angeles way, Little-Theatre activity waxed encouragingly. The Player's Ring, an outstanding central staging group, opened a new theatre with a triangular playing area and scored a hit with Calder Willingham's *End as a Man* and other productions. A combination of central and proscenium staging was tried at the new Horseshoe Stage by Robert W. Beecher, and one of its better shows had Negro actor James Edwards in *The Member of the Wedding.* Stage Society offered a fine revival of *The Plough and the Stars;* a new play, *Storm in the Sun,* voted by one critic the best original script of the year; and an evening of Pirandello. The Ebony Theatre outgrew its old house and moved into a 400-seat ex-storehouse, changing at the time from central to proscenium staging. It did a well received *Lost in the Stars,* followed by *Tanorama,* a Negro musical revue, and *The Seven Year Itch,* in which owner-producer Nick Stewart starred.

You didn't have to be William Hazlitt to see that there was a sad dearth of good original dramatic writing last season. But the Circle Theatre did its best to ease the situation by producing only untried scripts. These reportedly included a melodrama, *The Woman with Red Hair;* a modern comedy by Hindi Brooks called *The Illustrious Uncle,* and *Once Upon a Tailor,* which had an extended run in Los Angeles.

Thus ends a rather cursory report of California's dramatic bustle during the past year. An appropriate toast to it would be drunk with much foam and little beer, and perhaps an ironic word about the fact that the poorer a theatre becomes, the more lighthearted it apparently must be to recoup its fortunes, as witness the Alcazar and *Anniversary Waltz* or the Huntington Hartford and its feathery season. Comedy was undisputably king in the theatre, and tragedy was left to the world outside—however one might wish that this arrangement could be in some measure reversed.

OFF BROADWAY

By Garrison P. Sherwood

IT is one measure of Off Broadway's greatly renewed vitality that it offered, during 1955-56, something more than ninety productions. And it is evidence of the main direction this renascence has taken that over half of these productions were revivals, and that well over half of the revivals were classics or semi-classics. Off Broadway has become, in an almost literal sense, the place to see Shakespeare or Chekhov these days—or, even more, Molière or Pinero. It thus forcibly reminds the public that the theatre has a past, and an often distinguished one. What it suggested less this season, by way of new or avant-garde productions, is that the theatre has a future.

As for the productions themselves, last season's were better than usual and on occasion even surpassed the same show's Broadway presentation. Eugene O'Neill's *The Iceman Cometh,* as revived at the Circle-in-the-Square, is a case in point. With Jason Robards, Jr., giving an outstanding performance as Hickey, it seemed a far better play than it did when first done uptown. And *Uncle Vanya,* at the 4th Street Theatre, could at least be mentioned in the same breath with the famous Jed Harris production of 1930. Signe Hasso and Franchot Tone performed ably in the roles played in the earlier production by Lillian Gish and Osgood Perkins. The 4th Street productions of Chekhov, under the direction and management of David Ross, have been so well received by both critics and public that Mr. Ross is thinking of taking over a Broadway theatre as a kind of annex. This is indeed the height of something-or-other in reverse.

The Shakespearwrights at the Jan Hus Auditorium continued to please with their remarkably vibrant productions. They offered *Macbeth, A Midsummer Night's Dream* and an especially exciting *Romeo and Juliet.* The Shakespearean Theatre Workshop was successful to a somewhat lesser degree with *Much Ado About Nothing, Romeo and Juliet* and an imaginative *As You Like It.*

Ibsen fared very well with a production of *A Doll's House*—that proved quite interesting—at the Greenwich Mews, and of *Hedda Gabbler* at the Royal.

George Bernard Shaw seemed to pop up everywhere—for one

Anthony Quayle i

"Tamburlaine the Great"

Jo Sullivan, Scott Merrill and Lotte Lenya in "The Threepenny Opera"

reason, no doubt, because 1956 constitutes the 100th anniversary of his birth. There was *The Admirable Bashville* in a good production at the Cherry Lane. There was an interesting *Candida* and a crackling *Man of Destiny* at the Downtown Theatre. Though *Heartbreak House* was given a feeble production at the Lenox Hill, the Greenwich Mews offered various scenes from Shaw very effectively, as well as a good production of *The Philanderer*.

There was a revival which did not come off, by Proscenium Productions, of Pinero's *Dandy Dick,* though earlier this group did remarkably well with Paul Osborn's *Morning's At Seven.* And I saw no better acting all winter than that done by Ruth Matteson, Nancy Sheridan, Theodore Marcuse and Lauren Gilbert in the Priestleys' *Dragon's Mouth.*

Theatre East did Saroyan's *Beautiful People,* and the Amato Theatre offered three of his one-act plays, notable among them *Hello, Out There.*

There was a rousing, youthful and altogether delightful revival of Cole Porter's musical *Out of This World* at the Actor's Playhouse, which also won praise for its revival of *He Who Gets Slapped* and *Eastward of Eden.*

A fair *Antigone* at Carnegie Hall, a tender, lovely *Cradle Song* at the Circle-in-the-Square, and Molière's *Don Juan* at the Downtown Theatre just about completes mention of the more important revivals. There may not be a true repertory company in New York, but by attentively shopping around it is possible to see any number of good established plays effectively produced. This was simply not possible until recently; revivals could not really flourish until Off Broadway itself was revived.

The Phoenix Theatre productions are taken up in another section of this volume. The long-established Equity Library Theatre and The Blackfriars continued to produce, as did the Broadway Chapel Players. There were any number of new groups doing single productions, but no really outstanding new plays were uncovered. And all the time at the Theatre de Lys—as an instance of how really valuable and successful an Off-Broadway production can be—*The Threepenny Opera,* during its third season, continued to bring pleasure.

THE SEASON IN TELEVISION

By Robert McLaughlin
Radio and TV Editor, *Time* Magazine

THE admen and network executives who have the final word on what appears on the nation's TV screens decreed this season that television drama should concentrate on "happy stories about happy people with happy problems." Most writers obediently labored to achieve the Pollyanna touch, but there was great difficulty in finding enough happy problems to go around. So they settled for happy endings. Play after play started out with a dramatic challenge, maintained it for an act or two and then, in the denouement, weakly backed down—for all the world like a man who has talked his way into a fight and then crawls out of it.

There was a play about a test explosion of the A-bomb and a misanthropic soldier who decides to let himself be immolated in the blast. At the last moment, he changed his mind. There was a play about racial discrimination which stated flatly that it was un-Christian—but it developed that the playwright was talking about Indians, not Negroes. There was a play about an Army court-martial which painted the brass as stupid, vindictive and essentially dishonest, but in the final act explained everything away as a simple bureaucratic mistake that could have happened anywhere.

Fortunately, there were a few dramas that escaped the happiness blight. Perhaps the season's best original play was James Costigan's *A Wind from the South,* shown on the U.S. Steel Hour. It was a pleasure to watch Julie Harris's brilliant playing of an unmarried woman of thirty, growing old with her thin-mouthed bachelor brother in present-day Ireland. Julie was graced with both imagination and character and the plot turned upon her one imperfect chance to escape when Donald Woods, an American tourist whose perceptions have been dulled by alcohol and an unsatisfactory marriage, falls tumultuously in love with her. Costigan's drama, infused throughout with an unusual acceptance of the hard choices life presents, made both natural and moving Julie's refusal to take the easy way out of the pit of her days. At the play's end, she had even struck an answering fire from the flinty heart of her brother (beautifully played by Michael Higgins) and viewers had the rare TV opportunity to share in a triumphant affirmation of the indomitable human spirit.

On the level of technique, the most astonishing show was Kraft TV Theatre's production of *A Night to Remember,* a live adaptation of Walter Lord's story of the first and last voyage of the "Titanic." Producer-Director George Roy Hill's task was to create for the twenty-one-inch screen the illusion of a giant liner foundering in the North Atlantic, and to give the appearance of panic-stricken thousands with scarcely a hundred actors. To do this, he jammed forty sets into NBC's big Brooklyn studio, made masterful use of his six cameras to combine action and symbolism—thus the sight of a rope spinning wildly over a bitt was enough to suggest the hurried lowering of a crowded lifeboat. Some of the sets were built in duplicate: one being shown "dry" for the early scenes, the second built to hold water to portray the sinking. The cunning fakery of the staging was matched by the inspired playing of the large cast—had one of them missed a single of the innumerable cues the play might well have been reduced to a shambles.

The business world took its usual drubbing from TV. David Levy's *Man on a Tiger* (Alcoa Hour) was a plunge deep into the Madison Avenue jungle where admen rip each other's jugulars in the fight for accounts and TV comics learn to be as fast with a knife as a wisecrack. Keenan Wynn played a funnyman whose audience rating was beginning to slide and Melvyn Douglas an adman who had risen to a vice-presidency on the comic's back and now wanted to get off. Though neither character was virtuous enough to be morally sympathetic nor villainous enough to be theatrically so, the play was filled with accurately observed scenes. A sample: two big-shots spend a day futilely trying to get together on the phone only to be thwarted because each of their secretaries is too fiercely proud to put her boss on the wire first. David Karp's *Good Old Charley Faye* (Kraft TV Theatre) took another jaundiced look at the off-camera antics of a TV comedian, while *The Drop of a Hat* by Dick Berg (Studio One) depicted the in-fighting among career girls on a fashion magazine. Jayne Meadows and Elisabeth Montgomery easily proved the excessive deadliness of the female, and Nina Foch worked herself into a convincing neurosis as their out-maneuvered victim.

Playwrights '56 made a gallant try at reducing the prolix complexity of William Faulkner's *The Sound and the Fury* to the rigid demands of the theatre. A notable cast—Franchot Tone, Lillian Gish, Ethel Waters, Janice Rule—was able to suggest the last-gasp despairs of a dying social order, but the violence that flashes only fitfully in the novel seemed too concentrated to be convincing in the ninety-minute TV play. Playwrights '56 was also responsible for the season's oddest dramas with J. P. Miller's *The Undiscovered Country* and Alvin Sapinsley's *Even the Weariest River.* The first was a curiously compelling study of an ego-maniac, played by Cyril Ritchard, who had nothing to give the world but embarrassing truths. Forced to deliver a graveside address in memory of the town ne'er-do-well, Ritchard baldly stated the man's misdeeds ("He never did anything good in his life") and concluded that the man was better off dead. This callousness drove even his daughter from him and the play ended with Ritchard still complacently capable of a world-scorning sneer that seemed to include viewers as well as his fellow-actors. *Even the Weariest River* discovered a fresh way of treating the classic Western—in blank verse. Even more surprising: it worked. Franchot Tone, Lee Grant and Christopher Plummer played the three tragic figures who ended as corpses on a dusty street, while Boris Karloff leaned confidentially into the camera as a one-man Greek chorus to give poetic expression to the eternal verities of life, death and man's irreparable foolishness.

In its revivals of past hits, television went twice to visit *The Barretts of Wimpole Street.* The first time, on Front Row Center, found Geraldine Fitzgerald as the languishing heroine but the play suffered from the TV bends, forced by its compression into sixty minutes, less commercials. The second time (on Producers' Showcase), Rudolf Beiser's 1931 study of Victorian vapors and villainy got an extra half-hour of playing time and struck fire from the opening scene, as Katharine Cornell (in her first TV appearance) lay wanly on a chaise longue, surrounded by her feckless brothers and sisters. Henry Daniell created a father tyrannical enough to cow a platoon of rebellious siblings; Anthony Quayle made a stylish Browning, while Katharine Cornell—despite her 58 years—captured a youthful intensity that was an optical as well as an acting triumph.

Noel Coward swept on camera with three of his own productions. *Together with Music* was an entertaining musical duet with Mary Martin. *Blithe Spirit,* in addition to Coward, starred Mildred Natwick, Claudette Colbert and Lauren Bacall and startled the TV audience with perhaps the raciest and most profane language yet heard on the air. Noel's sponsor, the Ford Motor Co., was so shaken that it wanted to back out of the remaining Coward production and was only reassured when Noel substituted the flag-waving *This Happy Breed* for the more titillating *Present Laughter.* On Hallmark Hall of Fame, Maurice Evans had his best TV year with handsomely mounted and performed productions of Shaw's *The Devil's Disciple,*

Maurice Evans, Ralph Bellamy, Dennis King and Teresa Wright in "The Devil's Disciple" on TV

which co-starred Evans and Dennis King; Emlyn Williams' *The Corn Is Green,* with Eva LeGallienne as the do-gooding spinster and John Kerr smoldering like a live coal as the boy rocketed from a Welsh mine to the quadrangles of Oxford, and Shakespeare's *Taming of the Shrew,* which neatly teamed Evans and Lili Palmer.

Ford Star Jubilee presented *The Caine Mutiny Court Martial* with most of the same cast that carried the show to big-money grosses across the U.S. Lloyd Nolan re-created his manic Captain Queeg with an admirable mixture of man-to-man bluster and whining paranoia, while Barry Sullivan, Frank Lovejoy and Robert Gist gave substance to their assignments in Herman Wouk's morality play. Producers' Showcase got one of the season's most bravura performances from Jose Ferrer in *Cyrano de Bergerac* and lovely Claire Bloom made all of Ferrer's romantic travail seem well worth while. Another play, *Edward, My Son* (U.S. Steel Hour), came to TV with its Broadway cast nearly intact. Britain's Robert Morley reveled as the oleaginous trickster who believes that nothing is too good for his son—or himself, either—and is ready to burn down a factory or buy up a school to prove it.

The season's musicals were headed by a pair of TV favorites: Mary Martin's *Peter Pan* and *Babes in Toyland,* starring Comedian

Jack E. Leonard. Mary Martin came soaring out of a canvas sky to enchant some 55 million viewers—only one million fewer than had watched her last year and far and away the largest audience for any TV play of the current season. This second look at Barrie's fable confirmed the remembered excellence of Jerome Robbins' production. It also enabled viewers to note that perfection did not stop with the stars: Sondra Lee was totally right as Tiger Lily, leader of the amusingly choreographed Indians, and Kathy Nolan's Wendy was witty as well as winsome.

On "Festival of Music," NBC contributed a longhair hodgepodge starring such performers as Pianist Artur Rubinstein, Violinist Isaac Stern, Cellist Gregor Piatagorsky and vocalists like Marian Anderson, Renata Tebaldi, Zinka Milanov, Risë Stevens, Jan Peerce, Jussi Bjoerling and Leonard Warren. They aimed for a mass audience with arias from such standbys as *Pagliacci, Tosca* and *Carmen,* and music by Chopin and Mendelssohn. According to the TV rating services, they got what they were after: some 23 million viewers. Equally ambitious and equally successful was the Sadler's Wells presentation of *The Sleeping Beauty* ballet which—like the "Festival"—was brought to TV by Producers' Showcase.

THE TEN BEST PLAYS

A VIEW FROM THE BRIDGE *

By Arthur Miller

[ARTHUR MILLER *was born in New York in 1915 and brought up in Brooklyn. He is a "much prized" playwright. He won the Avery Hopwood Award while an undergraduate at the University of Michigan and a second Hopwood Award a year later. After graduating he captured a Theatre Guild prize of $1250. In 1947 he won the Drama Critics Circle Award for "All My Sons"—the play which brought him his first solid fame. In the 1948-49 season he went on with "Death of a Salesman" to win both the Drama Critics Award and the Pulitzer Prize. Though it won no prize, Mr. Miller's "The Crucible" was one of the most talked of plays of the 1952-53 season.*]

A VIEW FROM THE BRIDGE plays out its tragedy in:

> ". . . Redhook, the slum that faces the bay,
> Seaward from Brooklyn Bridge—"

in one of its tenements, and in the street before it.

The district lawyer's office is suggested at one side of the stage, but the main action occurs in the sparsely furnished tenement living-dining room of longshoreman Eddie Carbone. The lofty columnar shapes that flank the tenement doorway suggest an immediate connection of the present with an ancient and classical past.

A foghorn blows. In the street, lawyer Alfieri passes two longshoremen pitching pennies against the building. Serving as Greek chorus, he addresses the audience and sets the scene. This graying, portly lawyer, regarded in this poor section as a priest might be during disaster, confesses his love for the law and the neighborhood's fascination for him. "My wife has warned me," Alfieri says, "so have my friends: they tell me the people in this neighborhood lack elegance, glamour. After all, who have I dealt with in my life? Longshoremen and their wives and fathers and grandfathers—compensation cases, evictions, family squabbles—the petty trouble of the poor—and yet . . .

"When the tide is right,
And the wind blows the sea air against these houses,
I sit here in my office,
Thinking it is all so timeless here.
I think of Sicily, from where these people came,
The Roman rocks of Calabria,
Siracusa on the cliff, where Carthaginian and Greek
Fought such bloody fights. I think of Hannibal,
Who slew the fathers of these people; Caesar,
Whipping them on in Latin.

"Which is all, of course, ridiculous.
Al Capone learned his trade on these pavements,
And Frankie Yale was cut in half
On the corner of Union Street and President,
Where so many were so justly shot,
By unjust men. . . ."

And still, thoughts of antiquity stay with Alfieri, and when as it happens once every few years there is a case—

"And as the parties tell me what the trouble is
I see cobwebs tearing, Adriatic ruins rebuilding themselves; Calabria;
The eyes of the plaintiff seem suddenly carved,
His voice booming toward me over many fallen stones.

"This one's name was Eddie Carbone,
A longshoreman working the docks
From Brooklyn Bridge to the breakwater. . . ."

Eddie Carbone is one of the penny pitchers; then as Alfieri stops, Eddie picks up the pennies he's won and, with a "Well, I'll see ya, fellas," goes in the tenement, up the steps to his own apartment. There his seventeen-year-old niece, Catherine, is waiting excitedly.

Even as Eddie takes off his jacket, he notices her high-heeled shoes and asks, as a favor to him:

"Take them off, will you please?
You're beautiful enough without shoes."

Though Catherine answers that she's only trying them out, Eddie answers:

"When I'm home I'm not in the movies,
I don't wanna see young girls
Walking around in spike-heel shoes."

Joined by his wife Beatrice, who wants to know what he has found out, Eddie says that the ship is in, that with their regular seamen papers Beatrice's relatives will walk off with the crew. "I just hope they know where they're going to sleep, heh?" Eddie says. Beatrice insists: "I told them in a letter we got no room."

Eddie doesn't care for Catherine's excitement over the men's coming. They're here for work, not parties, Eddie reminds her. He orders her off to change her shoes and badgers Beatrice for letting her dress that way.

Eddie, on the whole, is fairly good-natured in laying down the law to his wife and niece.

BEATRICE (*half-amused, half-serious*)—All right, stop it already. You want a beer? The sauce is gotta cook a little more.

EDDIE (*to* BEATRICE)—No, it's too cold. (To CATHERINE.) You do your lessons today, Garbo?

CATHERINE—Yeah; I'm way ahead anyway. I just gotta practice from now on.

BEATRICE—She could take it down almost as fast as you could talk already. She's terrific. Read something to her later, you'll be surprised.

EDDIE—That's the way, Katie. You're gonna be all right, kid, you'll see.

CATHERINE (*proudly*)—I could get a job right now, Eddie. I'm not even afraid.

EDDIE—You got time. Wait'll you're eighteen. We'll look up the ads—find a nice company; or maybe a lawyer's office or somethin' like that.

CATHERINE—Oh, boy! I could go to work now, my teacher said.

EDDIE—Be eighteen first. I want you to have a little more head on your shoulders. You're still dizzy yet. (*To* BEATRICE.) Where's the kids? They still outside?

BEATRICE—I put them with my mother for tonight. They'd never go to sleep otherwise. So what kinda cargo you have today?

EDDIE—Coffee. It was nice.

BEATRICE—I thought all day I smelled coffee here!

EDDIE—Yeah, Brazil. That's one time, boy, to be a longshoreman is a pleasure. The whole ship smelled from coffee. It was like flowers. We'll bust a bag tomorrow; I'll bring you some. . . .

All this dressing up and excitement on Catherine's part is due to the fact that one of their expected visitors is twenty-five years old and unmarried. Eddie scolds Catherine for thinking about the young man, but when she gives him a pert answer, Eddie is amused: "I shoulda been struck by lightning when I promised your mother I would take care of you," he says; and when she sasses him, Eddie is delighted—"Boy, God bless you, you got a tongue in your mouth like the Devil's wife." But somehow the way she looks and acts in front of men is very much on his mind. "If I seen you with high heels and lipstick I wouldn't a look at you," he tells Beatrice. "So you don't look at me with low heels, so I'm even," Beatrice answers, as she goes back to the kitchen.

EDDIE—I hada open my mouth. (CATHERINE *laughs.*) I ain't kiddin', baby, I'm responsible for you, I promised your mother on her death bed, so don't joke with me, I mean it. I don't like the looks they're givin' you on the sidewalk.

CATHERINE—But those guys look at all the girls, you know that.

EDDIE—I don't like you walkin' so wavy like that.

CATHERINE—Who's walkin' wavy!

EDDIE—Now don't aggravate me, Katie, you are walkin' wavy!

CATHERINE—Oh, Jesus! (*She goes out.*)

During supper, Beatrice and Eddie discuss the conditions in Sicily that drove her relatives to enter America illegally; so desperate was their search for work that they permitted a syndicate to smuggle them through in exchange for their first six months' pay. "Boy," exclaims Beatrice, "they must've been starvin' there. To go through all this just to make a couple a dollars. I'm tellin' ya, it could make you cry." And then there's the danger from the Immigration Bureau's stool pigeons once the men have arrived. This last has Eddie worried. But Catherine's offer to help the men pretend they're from Philadelphia bothers Eddie, too.

EDDIE—Do me a favor, baby, will ya? Don't teach them, and don't mix in with them. Because with that blabbermouth the less you know the better off we're all gonna be. They're gonna work, and they're gonna come home here and go to sleep, and I don't want you payin' no attention to them. This is a serious business; this is the United States Government. So you don't know they're alive. I mean don't get dizzy with your friends about it. It's nobody's business. (*Slight pause.*) Where's the salt?

CATHERINE—It's gettin' dark.

EDDIE—Yeah, gonna snow tomorrow, I think. (*Pause.*)

Beatrice (*frightened*)—Geez, remember that Vinny Bolzano years ago? Remember him?

Eddie—That funny? I was just thinkin' about him before.

Catherine—Who's he?

Beatrice—You were a baby then. But there was a kid, Vinny, about sixteen. Lived over there on Sackett Street. And he snitched on somebody to the Immigration. He had five brothers, and the old man. And they grabbed him in the kitchen, and they pulled him down three flights, his head was bouncin' like a coconut—we lived in the next house. And they spit on him in the street, his own father and his brothers. It was so terrible.

According to Eddie, a guy who could do a thing like that could never show his face again.

Eddie's nervousness has been increasing. But when Beatrice says that since these were her cousins what else could she do, he is not only understanding—he admires her spirit.

Alfieri takes up the next skein of Eddie's story: the arrival after supper of Beatrice's two cousins. Beatrice introduces Marco—a thirty-five-year-old peasant—and Rodolpho, boyish and startlingly blond, to her husband and niece. From the first, Marco behaves with enormous dignity. But Catherine's attention is focused on Rodolpho. "How come he's so dark and you're so light, Rodolpho?" she can't resist asking. "I don't know," Rodolpho answers with a laugh. "A thousand years ago, they say, the Danes invaded Sicily."

Eddie makes polite inquiries about their trip, but Rodolpho would like to know about Tony, the man who brought them here: "He says we start work tomorrow. Is he honest?" "No," says Eddie, "but as long as you owe them money they'll get you plenty of work."

Marco and Rodolpho tell of the lack of work in their little town. They did everything they could, from fishing to masonry; or when there were tourists, they would even do horses' work and push the local taxi up the hill. The town's automobile-taxi has to be pushed as well. "Everything in our town," Rodolpho says, "you gotta push." "How do you like that!" says Beatrice sorrowfully.

Marco, with a wife and three children, is forced to work in America. "What can I do?" he says.

"The older one is sick in his chest;
My wife—she feeds them from her own mouth.
I tell you the truth,

If I stay there they will never grow up.
They eat the sunshine."

Learning that in over a year he and Rodolpho may average between thirty and forty dollars a week, and that to save money they can stay as long as they want with Beatrice, Marco's eyes show tears. "My wife—my wife . . . I want to send right away maybe twenty dollars," he says. Told that by next week he will have something to send, Marco's gratitude knows no bounds. "Don't thank me," Eddie tells him. "Listen, what the hell, it's no skin off me."

Rodolpho, however, dreams of becoming a rich American. He admits that he is also something of a singer, who was a magnificent success before the local hotel guests. Marco is more guarded about his talents, but Catherine can't wait to hear him. Rodolpho obliges with "Paper Doll" in a high tenor. Over Catherine's gushing admiration, Eddie in agitated tones insists that Rodolpho be quiet unless he wants to be picked up. Marco tells his brother to be quiet. But stopping the singing is not enough for Eddie. "You got the shoes again, Garbo?" he says. "I figured for tonight—" Catherine explains. "Do me a favor, will you?" Eddie indicates the bedroom and Catherine, now angry and embarrassed in front of the men, goes toward it. But on her return she directly seeks out Rodolpho and pays attention to him alone. Eddie is increasingly troubled, as the lights dim.

Eddie has taken to hanging around the street, waiting for Catherine to come back from dates with Rodolpho. Telling him it's not a nice thing to do, Beatrice tries to calm Eddie: as far as she is concerned, Rodolpho is a pleasant, hard-working, good-looking kid, whom she wouldn't mind seeing Catherine marry. But Eddie dredges up one criticism after the other. Finally, he blurts out to Beatrice: "He sings on the ships, didja know that?" "What do you mean, he sings?" asks Beatrice.

Eddie—Just what I said, he sings. Right on the deck, all of a sudden—a whole song comes out of his mouth—with motions. You know what they're callin' him now?—Paper Doll, they're callin' him—Canary. He's like a weird. He comes out on the pier, one-two-three, it's a regular free show.

Beatrice—Well, he's a kid; he don't know how to behave himself yet.

Eddie—And with that wacky hair; he's like a chorus girl or sump'm.

BEATRICE—So he's blond, so—

EDDIE—I just hope that's his regular hair, that's all I hope.

BEATRICE—You crazy or sump'n? (*She tries to turn him to her.*)

EDDIE (*keeping his head turned away*)—What's so crazy? I don't like his whole way.

BEATRICE—Listen, you never seen a blond guy in your life? What about Whitey Balso?

EDDIE (*turning to her victoriously*)—Sure, but Whitey don't sing; he don't do like that on the ships—

BEATRICE—Well, maybe that's the way they do in Italy.

EDDIE—Then why don't his brother sing? Marco goes around like a man; nobody kids Marco. (*He moves from her—she realizes there is a campaign solidified in him.*) I tell you the truth, I'm surprised I have to tell you all this. I mean I'm surprised, B.

BEATRICE (*she goes to him with purpose now*)—Listen, you ain't gonna start nothin' here.

EDDIE—I ain't startin' nothin', but I ain't gonna stand around lookin' at that. For that character I didn't bring her up. I swear, B., I'm surprised at you; I sit there waitin' for you to wake up but everything is great with you.

Everything is not great with Beatrice. She is badly worried, and when against Eddie's will she asks point-blank: "When am I gonna be a wife again, Eddie?" he starts to retreat. "I ain't been feelin' good," he mutters. "They bother me since they come." Beatrice refuses to accept this: "It's almost three months you don't feel good —they're only here a couple of weeks. It's three months, Eddie." Eddie won't talk about it; he can't talk about it. He pleads for Beatrice to lay off him. He's worried, he says, about Catherine.

Beatrice maintains that Catherine is eighteen years old, and if, as Eddie says, she's being taken for a ride, it's her ride. "What're you gonna stand over her till she's forty?" Beatrice demands. "Eddie," she orders, "I want you to cut it out now, you hear me? I don't like it. . . ." In subdued tones, Beatrice tells him to come into the house—that it's not nice standing around in the street this way. This has no effect on him; he stays. Beatrice goes inside.

His friends, Mike and Louis, come by and want Eddie to bowl. He says he's too tired. They talk about his two "submarines," with Louis observing: "I see they're gettin' work allatime." Mike cracks: "That's what we oughta do. We oughta leave the country and come in under the water. Then we get work." "You ain't kiddin'," Eddie manages.

Giving all credit to Eddie for taking care of the men, Louis and Mike gossip about Rodolpho. He amuses them no end. "He ain't ezactly funny," Mike figures, "but he's always like makin' remarks, like, y'know? He comes around, everybody's laughin'." When the men go off, Eddie, more uncomfortable than ever, isn't laughing.

Catherine and Rodolpho, returning from a happy time at the Brooklyn Paramount, now have Eddie to face. As fast as he can, Eddie gets rid of Rodolpho so that he can speak to Catherine alone.

CATHERINE—Why don't you talk to him, Eddie? He blesses you, and you don't talk to him hardly.

EDDIE (*enveloping her with his eyes*)—I bless you, and you don't talk to me. (*He tries to smile.*)

CATHERINE—*I* don't talk to you? (*She hits his arm.*) What do you mean!

EDDIE—I don't see you no more. I come home you're runnin' around someplace— (CATHERINE *takes his arm, and they walk a little.*)

CATHERINE—Well, he wants to see everything, that's all, so we go. You mad at me?

EDDIE—No. (*He is smiling sadly, almost moony.*) It's just I used to come home, you was always there. Now, I turn around, you're a big girl. I don't know how to talk to you.

CATHERINE—Why!

EDDIE—I don't know, you're runnin', you're runnin', Katie. I don't think you listening any more to me.

CATHERINE—Ah, Eddie, sure I am. What's the matter? You don't like him? (*Slight pause.*)

EDDIE—*You* like him, Katie?

CATHERINE (*with a blush, but holding her ground*)—Yeah. I like him.

Eddie, disconsolate, and fearful that Catherine may marry Rodolpho, tries a different tack. Insisting that Rodolpho doesn't respect her, Eddie says: "Katie, he's only bowin' to his passport." Despite Catherine's bewilderment, Eddie pounds away: "That's right. He marries you he's got the right to be an American citizen. That's what's goin' on here. You understand what I'm tellin' you? The guy is lookin' for his break, that's all he's lookin' for." Catherine is hurt, but Eddie continues to rub it in: since Rodolpho's not sending money to Marco's children or saving any himself, but spending every cent on pleasure, he's only out for himself. Catherine is sure that Rodolpho doesn't even think of his papers. "What's better for him to think about?" Eddie retorts. "He could be picked up any day here and he's back pushin' taxis up the hill!"

CATHERINE—No, I don't believe it.

EDDIE (*grabbing her hand*)—Katie, don't break my heart, listen to me—

CATHERINE—I don't want to hear it. Lemme go.

EDDIE (*holding her*)—Katie, listen—

CATHERINE—He loves me!

EDDIE (*with deep alarm*)—Don't say that, for God's sake! This is the oldest racket in the country.

CATHERINE (*desperately, as though he had made his imprint*)—I don't believe it!

EDDIE—They been pullin' this since the immigration law was put in! They grab a green kid that don't know nothin' and they—

CATHERINE—I don't believe it and I wish to hell you'd stop it!

Eddie pursues the sobbing girl into the house, but comes up against a furious Beatrice, who's had just about enough: "You going to leave her alone?" Beatrice cries, "or you gonna drive me crazy?" Trying to regain his dignity, Eddie turns tail and leaves the house.

Beatrice tries to straighten things out. She explains to Catherine that if she is grown-up enough to get married, she must act like a grown-up. "It means you gotta be your own self more," Beatrice tells her. "You still think you're a little girl, honey. But nobody else can make up your mind for you any more, you understand? You gotta give him to understand that he can't give you orders no more." Pointing out to Catherine that she still thinks of herself as a child, that she parades in front of Eddie in her slip and throws herself at him like a twelve-year-old, Beatrice warns her: "But if you act like a baby and he be treatin' you like a baby—"

Catherine can't bear to make Eddie miserable. "Well, look, Katie," retorts Beatrice, "if it's gonna hurt you so much you're gonna end up an old maid here." And she's not joking. Beatrice knows that they are too close to each other. "I mean it. I tried to tell you a couple of times in the last year or so. That's why I was so happy you were going to go out and get work, you wouldn't be here so much, you'd be a little more independent. I mean it. It's wonderful for a whole family to love each other, but you're a grown woman and you're in the same house with a grown man. So you'll act different now, heh?" Beatrice explains further that it isn't only up to Eddie who doesn't understand, it's up to Catherine. Now that

J. Carrol Naish and Van Heflin in Arthur Miller's "A View From the Bridge"

she has a nice boy, she should say goodbye. Feeling the wrench acutely, Catherine agrees: "All right . . . if I can."

Eddie, having nowhere else to go for help, has sought out lawyer Alfieri. When Eddie first entered his office, says Alfieri, recalling the visit—

"His eyes were like tunnels;
My first thought was that he had committed a crime."

But then Alfieri understood why Eddie was so intense. He had come to have the law prevent Rodolpho's marriage to Catherine: there must be some law that would keep an illegal immigrant from marrying a girl for his citizenship papers. When Alfieri explains the difficulty of such an action, even were it provable, Eddie introduces his new argument. It must be for his citizenship papers that Rodolpho is doing this, Eddie confides, "Because the guy ain't right, Mr. Alfieri." Alfieri says he doesn't understand. Eddie describes Rodolpho as a platinum blond who sings high. Alfieri answers: "Well, that's a tenor."

EDDIE—I'm tellin' you sump'n, wait a minute; please, Mr. Alfieri. I'm tryin' to bring out my thoughts here. Couple a nights ago my niece brings out a dress, which it's too small for her, because she shot up like a light this last year. He takes the dress, lays it on the table, he cuts it up; one-two-three, he makes a new dress. I mean he looked so sweet there, like an angel—you could kiss him he was so sweet.

ALFIERI—Now look, Eddie—

EDDIE—Mr. Alfieri, they're laughin' at him on the piers. I'm ashamed. Paper Doll, they call him. Blondie now. His brother thinks it's because he's got a sense of humor, see—which he's got—but that ain't what they're laughin'. Which they're not goin' to come out with it because they know he's my relative, which they have to see me if they make a crack, y'know? But I know what they're laughin' at, and when I think of that guy layin' his hands on her I could—I mean it's eatin' me out, Mr. Alfieri, because I struggled for that girl. And now he comes in my house—

ALFIERI—Eddie, look. I have my own children, I understand you. But the law is very specific. The law does not—

EDDIE (*with a fuller flow of indignation*)—You mean to tell me that there's no law that a guy which he ain't right can go to work and marry a girl and—

ALFIERI—You have no recourse in the law, Eddie.

EDDIE—Yeah, but if he ain't right, Mr. Alfieri, you mean to tell me—

ALFIERI—There is nothing you can do, Eddie, believe me.

EDDIE—Nothin'?

ALFIERI—Nothing at all. There's only one legal question here.

EDDIE—What?

ALFIERI—The manner in which they entered the country. But I don't think you want to do anything about that, do you?

EDDIE—You mean—?

ALFIERI—Well, they entered illegally.

EDDIE—Oh, Jesus, no, I wouldn't do nothin' about that. I mean—

ALFIERI—All right, then, let me talk now, eh?

EDDIE—Mr. Alfieri, I can't believe what you tell me. I mean there must be some kinda law which—

ALFIERI—

Eddie, I want you to listen to me. (*Pause.*)
You know, sometimes God mixes up the people.
We all love somebody, the wife, the kids—
Every man's got somebody that he loves, heh?
But sometimes—there's too much. You know?
There's too much, and it goes where it mustn't.
A man works hard, he brings up a child,
Sometimes it's a niece, sometimes even a daughter,
And he never realizes it, but through the years—
There is too much love for the daughter,
There is too much love for the niece.
Do you understand what I'm saying to you?

EDDIE (*sardonically*)—What do you mean, I shouldn't look out for her good?

ALFIERI—

Yes, but these things have to end, Eddie, that's all.
The child has to grow up and go away,
And the man has to learn how to forget.
Because after all, Eddie—
What other way can it end?

Eddie's passion begins to break through, climaxing in: "He's stealin' from me!" "She wants to get married, Eddie," says Alfieri. "She can't marry you, can she?"

Helpless, muttering that his heart is breaking, Eddie only half-listens to Alfieri's advice to put it out of his mind. Feeling on the verge of tears, he leaves. And Alfieri, understanding the whole thing only too clearly, would like to spread the alarm; but as nothing *has* happened, he can only sit impotently and wait.

Life in the Carbone flat continues with a surface calm marred every so often by one of Eddie's outbursts. Each person goes about his business, but more watchfully. When Eddie brings the conversation around to criticizing Rodolpho for keeping Catherine out too late, Marco orders his brother to be sure to bring her home early. But Eddie goes further—as far as he dares—and tells Marco: "If he's here to work, then he should work; if he's here for a good time then he could fool around! But I understood, Marco—" Eddie says right out in the open—"that you was both comin' to make a livin' for your family. You understand me, don't you, Marco?" Marco understands him very well.

Eddie's pent-up violence is increasing. On the surface, he seems to be offering Marco and Rodolpho a treat when he says he'll take them to the prize-fights Saturday. Actually, in a "demonstration" of what they may expect to see at the fights, Eddie contrives to have the inexperienced Rodolpho spar with him. At first, the boxing looks like good-humored fun. Then comes the moment Eddie has planned for.

EDDIE—Sure, he's terrific! Look at him go! (RODOLPHO *lands a blow.*) 'At's it. Now watch out, here I come, Danish! (*He feints with his left hand and lands with his right; it mildly staggers* RODOLPHO.)

CATHERINE (*rushing to* RODOLPHO)—Eddie!

EDDIE—Why? I didn't hurt him. (*Going to help the dizzy* RODOLPHO.) Did I hurt you, kid?

RODOLPHO—No, no, he didn't hurt me. (*To* EDDIE *with a certain gleam and a smile.*) I was only surprised.

BEATRICE—That's enough, Eddie; he did pretty good, though.

EDDIE—Yeah. (*He rubs his fists together.*) He could be very good, Marco. I'll teach him again—

Marco, having watched this performance carefully, comes up with one of his own. He asks Eddie if he can lift a chair with one hand from a kneeling position; Eddie tries and fails, whereupon Marco gets to his feet and slowly, strainingly, raises the chair higher and higher until he holds it over Eddie's head. It looks like a weapon, and Marco's smile of triumph is more like a glare of warning. Eddie's own smile vanishes, as the lights dim.

A dejected Alfieri chronicles what came next:

"On the twenty-third of that December
A case of Scotch whisky slipped from a net
While being unloaded—as a case of Scotch whisky
Is inclined to do on the twenty-third of December
On Pier Forty-one. There was no snow, but it was cold.
His wife was out shopping.
Marco was still at work.
The boy had not been hired that day;
Catherine told me later that this was the first time
They had been alone together in the house. . . ."

Rodolpho is relaxing happily as he watches Catherine do some ironing. But finding this quiet moment the right one, Catherine asks Rodolpho the question Eddie has raised in her mind. If she should want to live in Italy, would Rodolpho marry her and take her there—if she thought that's where she'd be happier. "Happier!" answers Rodolpho. "What would you eat? You can't cook the view!" Catherine suggests that maybe he could be a singer in Rome. "Rome! Rome is full of singers!" "Well, I could work then," Catherine persists. "Where?" Rodolpho asks. "God, there must be jobs somewhere!" says Catherine. But Rodolpho insists there aren't—anywhere at all. He asks her how he could bring her from a rich country to suffer in a poor country:

"I would be a criminal stealing your face;
In two years you would have an old, hungry face.
When my brothers' babies cry they give them water,
Water that boiled a bone.
Don't you believe that?"

CATHERINE (*quietly*)—I'm afraid of Eddie here. (*A slight pause.*)

RODOLPHO—
We wouldn't live here.
Once I am a citizen I could work anywhere,
And I would find better jobs,
And we would have a house, Catherine.
If I were not afraid to be arrested
I would start to be something wonderful here!

CATHERINE (*steeling herself*)—Tell me something. I mean just tell me, Rodolpho. Would you still want to do it if it turned out we had to go live in Italy? I mean just if it turned out that way?

RODOLPHO—This is your question or his question?

CATHERINE—I would like to know, Rodolpho. I mean it.
RODOLPHO—To go there with nothing?
CATHERINE—Yeah.
RODOLPHO—No. (*She looks at him wide-eyed.*) No.
CATHERINE—You wouldn't?
RODOLPHO—

No; I will not marry you to live in Italy.
I want you to be my wife
And I want to be a citizen.
Tell him that, or I will. Yes.

(*He moves about angrily.*)

And tell him also, and tell yourself, please,
That I am not a beggar,
And you are not a horse, a gift,
A favor for a poor immigrant.

CATHERINE—Well, don't get mad!
RODOLPHO—

I am furious!
Do you think I am so desperate?
My brother is desperate, not me.
You think I would carry on my back
The rest of my life a woman I didn't love
Just to be an American? It's so wonderful?
You think we have no tall buildings in Italy?
Electric lights? No wide streets? No flags?
I want to be an American so I can work,
That is the only wonder here—work!
How can you insult me, Catherine?

Catherine loves Rodolpho. She tells him that she does. But Eddie is in all her thoughts. Through her tears, and the fear she admits to of Eddie's angry moods, Catherine tries to explain that she is more womanly and more understanding of Eddie than even Beatrice is; that she doesn't know why she suddenly has to make a stranger of this man. Rodolpho says tenderly: "Catherine. If I take in my hands a little bird. And she grows and wishes to fly. But I will not let her out of my hands because I love her so much, is that right for me to do? I don't say you must hate him; but anyway you must go, mustn't you, Catherine?"

Catherine wants Rodolpho to hold her; wants to be loved; wants not to wait any longer. They are alone in the flat. Rodolpho leads her lovingly into the bedroom.

Eddie, wobbly from drinking, comes home to discover them. Ordering Rodolpho to pack and get out, he grabs a trembling Catherine, who tries to follow. For all her fright, Catherine tries to be grown-up. And in spite of his tears, and her own, she manages to tell Eddie that she can't stay there any longer. "You ain't goin' nowheres," Eddie answers. "Eddie, I'm not gonna be a baby anymore! You—" He reaches out suddenly and, as she struggles, kisses her on the mouth.

RODOLPHO—Don't. (*He pulls on* EDDIE'S *arm.*) Stop that!

EDDIE (*spun around by* RODOLPHO)—You want something?

RODOLPHO—She'll be my wife.

EDDIE—But what're you gonna be!

CATHERINE—Wait outside; don't argue with him . . . !

EDDIE—That's what I wanna know. What're you gonna be!

Through tears of rage, Rodolpho cries: "Don't say that to me!" and attacks him. Eddie, laughing, pins down his arms and suddenly kisses him. Catherine screams: "Eddie! Let go, ya hear me! I'll kill you! Leggo of him!" With tears rolling down his face, Eddie laughs mockingly at Rodolpho and lets him go. Despite Eddie's ordering Rodolpho to get out and get out alone, Catherine says: "I'm goin' with him, Eddie." Both watch helplessly as Eddie —trying to catch his breath—closes his eyes. "Don't make me do nuttin', Catherine," he warns.

When Eddie next walks into Alfieri's office, the lawyer, after one look at him, wants to call the police. But still nothing has happened. Again Eddie appeals to Alfieri, more urgently this time, because Catherine and Rodolpho have announced that they are to be married. Again Alfieri says there is nothing he can do. Morally and legally, Eddie has no rights. Alfieri repeats that Catherine is a free agent, but he adds:

"I'm not only telling you now, I'm warning you—
The law is nature.
The law is only a word for what has a right to happen.
When the law is wrong it's because it's unnatural,
But in this case it is natural,
And a river will drown you
If you buck it now.
Let her go. And bless her—"

With new anxiety, Alfieri sees Eddie rise wordlessly and quickly move away. Alfieri calls after him to put what he is thinking about

out of his mind—that it won't leave him with a friend in the world. But after leaving the building, Eddie goes to a phone booth and makes the call: "I want to report something. Illegal immigrants. Two of them. That's right. Four-forty-one Saxon Street, Brooklyn, yeah. Ground floor. Heh? (*With greater difficulty.*) I'm just around the neighborhood, that's all."

Returning home, Eddie seems strangely indifferent when he hears that Marco and Rodolpho have moved upstairs to board with a Mrs. Dondero. But a minute later he starts in again on Beatrice. She's sick and tired of the subject, but Eddie says over and over again for her to remember it was he who brought her cousins over and she shouldn't forget it. "What do you want from me?" Beatrice asks. "They've moved out; what do you want now?" "I want my respect!" he shouts. "So I moved them out," she answers. "What more do you want? You got your house now, you got your respect." Eddie wants to have it out with her about Rodolpho, but for Beatrice it's all settled. Eddie wants her to believe in him and his opinions, including his about Rodolpho's not being right.

But Beatrice's answer is that Catherine loves Rodolpho, and that if she's a baby, it's because Eddie kept her one. She had no chance to go out and see the world. Eddie now decides that Catherine should be allowed to go out and meet other people. Beatrice tells him it's too late.

Beatrice begs Eddie to give Catherine a break, and let her send-off and her wedding be happy ones. Before Eddie can break away, Catherine enters and, at Beatrice's urging, invites him to her wedding. He says: "Okay. I only wanted the best for you, Katie. I hope you know that." The next moment, he's off on his new theme—that Catherine should be allowed to get out and meet people. Catherine will have none of this—she has made up her mind; and asking for some more pillow cases for some other guys upstairs, goes into the bedroom. Eddie, discovering that there are two other illegal immigrants stowed away upstairs, calls to Catherine: "What're you, got no brains? You put them up there with two other submarines?" He orders her to get Rodolpho and Marco out before the others are tracked down, and Rodolpho and Marco are caught with them. He's full of arguments and ideas, but before Catherine can be made to act, there is a knock at the door. When the order is shouted to open for Immigration officers, Catherine, with a sob of fury, realizes what Eddie has been up to. Beatrice, turning her back on her husband, refuses to talk to him.

It's over quickly. When the men aren't found in Eddie's apartment, the Immigration authorities search the house and find, not only

Marco and Rodolpho, but the other two submarines. Beatrice, confronting Eddie and seeing his terror, cries out: "My God, what did you do!"

Despite Catherine's pleas, the men are hurried down the stairs toward the street. Marco, breaking away from the others, dashes into the apartment and before the officer can catch him, spits in Eddie's face. Disregarding Beatrice's restraining hand, Eddie rushes after Marco to the street, demanding an apology.

Instead of an apology, Marco, pointing at Eddie, shouts to the gathering crowd: "That one! I accuse that one!" And again, as he is pulled away, Marco cries: "That one! He killed my children! That one stole the food from my children!" Eddie, left behind with the neighbors, shouts: "He's crazy. I give them the blankets off my bed. Six months I kept them like my own brothers!" He calls to the butcher whose nephews also were caught, but the butcher and his wife walk away in anger and disgust. Louis and Mike turn their backs. Eddie says to Catherine as she returns from the police car: "He's gonna take that back or I'll kill him!" And to the vanishing crowd he shouts: "You hear me? I'll kill him!"

Alfieri, in court, is trying to get Marco out on bail for Rodolpho's wedding. He will only do so if Marco will promise not to harm Eddie. Marco refuses to answer, until he is reminded that Alfieri can postpone the hearing for five or six weeks during which time Marco can be working for his children. Understanding this, and that Rodolpho by his marriage will become an American, Marco says: "What will I tell him? He knows such a promise is dishonorable."

ALFIERI—To promise not to kill is not dishonorable.

MARCO—No?

ALFIERI—No.

MARCO (*gesturing with his head—this is a new idea*)—Then what is done with such a man?

ALFIERI—Nothing. If he obeys the law, he lives. That's all.

Marco, ashamed and with lowered eyes, gives his promise, and says: "Maybe he wants to apologize to me."

Eddie, with maniacal stubbornness, is forbidding Beatrice to go to Catherine's wedding unless Marco apologizes. Catherine suddenly yells: "Who the hell do you think you are?" Beatrice can't quiet her. Eddie has no right, Catherine says, to tell anyone anything for the rest of his life. But now Beatrice won't leave Eddie, and Catherine demands: "How can you listen to him? This rat!"

Eddie is ready to strike Catherine, but Rodolpho's arrival sets a new current going. Rodolpho announces that Marco is on his way here. Both women beg Eddie to leave before he comes; but Eddie, all bluster one moment and self-pity the next, refuses to leave. Catherine, full of pity, embraces Eddie and apologizes: "I never meant to do nothin' bad to you in my life, Eddie," she cries. Tears in his eyes, he asks: "Then who meant somethin' bad? How'd it get bad?" Gaining confidence from her embrace, Eddie points at Rodolpho: "They made it bad! This one and his brother made it bad which they came like thieves to rob, to rob!" And now he orders Rodolpho to get away from Catherine. Beatrice tries to intervene, but as the young couple break for the door, Eddie lunges for Catherine, and holds and kisses her like a lover. Catherine, freed, pulls Rodolpho to the door; Eddie rushes after them, with Beatrice begging him to come back. As Rodolpho and Catherine race down the steps, with Eddie behind them, Marco approaches in the street. A crowd begins to gather. Eddie delivers a set speech to them, about how Catherine and Marco and Rodolpho have repaid his kindness and what they have done to his good name.

Seeing Marco, Eddie moves toward him, yelling: "I want my good name, Marco! You took my name!" Beatrice tries to push him away. Marco says: "Animal! You go on your knees to me!" and strikes Eddie powerfully on the side of the head. Eddie, falling back, draws a knife. When the struggle, which ranges as far as the columns of the tenement, is over, Eddie is on his knees, a bleeding knife in his hand. He crawls to Catherine and dies at her feet. The light dims on the weeping women.

Says Alfieri, completing the story:

"Most of the time now we settle for half,
And I like it better.
And yet, when the tide is right
And the green smell of the sea
Floats in through my window,
The waves of this bay
Are the waves against Siracusa,
And I see a face that suddenly seems carved;
The eyes look like tunnels
Leading back toward some ancestral beach
Where all of us once lived.

"And I wonder at those times
How much of all of us
Really lives there yet,
And when we will truly have moved on,
On and away from that dark place,
That world that has fallen to stones?"

TIGER AT THE GATES *

BY JEAN GIRAUDOUX

Translated by Christopher Fry

[CHRISTOPHER FRY *was born in Bristol, England, in 1908, the son of an architect, Charles Harris, who wanted him to become a clergyman. At his father's death he took his mother's maiden name. As a young man he acted and taught. Success came after World War II with "The Lady's Not for Burning," a verse-play taken from an old German short story. Since then he has done "Venus Observed," "A Sleep of Prisoners," "The Dark Is Light Enough," as well as several adaptations.*

JEAN GIRADOUX *was born in 1882 and died in 1944, before the production of "The Madwoman of Chaillot,"* which he refused to *have put on while his country was in the hands of the enemy. One of the most admired of French novelists and dramatists, he has enjoyed success in America as well. Among the plays done on Broadway are "Amphitryon 38," "Siegfried," "The Enchanted," "Ondine" and, most memorably, "The Madwoman of Chaillot."*]

ON the walls of Troy, beautiful Andromache cries: "There's not going to be a Trojan War, Cassandra!"

CASSANDRA—I shall take that bet, Andromache.

ANDROMACHE—The Greeks are quite right to protest. We are going to receive their ambassador very civilly. We shall wrap up his little Helen and give her back to him.

CASSANDRA—We shall receive him atrociously. We shall refuse to give Helen back. And there *will* be a Trojan War.

ANDROMACHE—Yes, if Hector were not here. But he is here, Cassandra, he is home again. You can hear the trumpets. At this moment he is marching into the city, victorious. And Hector is certainly going to have something to say. When he left, three months ago, he promised me this war would be the last.

To Cassandra, it doesn't matter that Paris and Helen no longer care for each other: destiny is not interested. Andromache is puzzled by her abstractions, so Cassandra describes destiny as a "sleeping tiger." Andromache would have him sleep. So would Cassandra. "But," she adds, "certain cocksure statements have been prodding him out of his sleep. For some considerable time Troy has been full of them." "Full of what?" asks a puzzled Andromache. "Of cocksure statements," continues Cassandra. "A confident belief that the world, and the supervision of the world, is the province of mankind in general, and Trojan men and women in particular." Cassandra says further: "Hector at this very moment is marching into Troy. And," she adds, "Hector's wife is going to have a child?" Andromache says: "Yes; I am going to have a child." Cassandra concludes: "Don't you call these statements a little overconfident?"

But on such a splendid day Andromache refuses to be frightened by Cassandra, feeling as she does that—"Happiness is falling on us out of the sky. . . . If ever there were a chance to see men finding a way to live in peace, it is today. To live in peace, in humility. And to be immortal." Cassandra tells Andromache how wrong she is: ". . . Hector has come home in triumph to the wife he adores. The tiger begins to rouse, and opens one eye. The incurables lie out on their benches in the sun and feel immortal. The tiger stretches himself. Today is the chance for peace to enthrone herself over all the world. The tiger licks his lips. And Andromache is going to have a son! And the horsemen have started leaning from their saddles to stroke tom-cats on the battlements! The tiger starts to prowl." "Be quiet!" cries Andromache. "He climbs noiselessly up the palace steps," Cassandra persists. "He pushes open the doors with his snout. And here he is, here he is!" "You are lying!" cries Andromache. "It is Hector!" "Whoever said it was not?" shrugs Cassandra, as Hector rushes into Andromache's arms.

As they embrace, Cassandra lingers so that Andromache urges Hector to pay no attention to her next unpleasantness. What Cassandra says, before she turns on her heel and departs, is that Andromache is going to have a child.

Andromache and Hector sit together, thinking of their child. Begging Andromache to forget wars, Hector asks her even to forget this past one in which she lost her father and brother. Hector promises to close the Gates of War and keep them closed.

ANDROMACHE—Close them, then. But they will open again.

HECTOR—You can even tell me the day, perhaps?

ANDROMACHE—I can even tell you the day: the day when the

cornfields are heavy and golden, when the vines are stooping, ready for harvest, and every house is sheltering a contented couple.

HECTOR—And peace, no doubt, at its very height?

ANDROMACHE—Yes. And my son is strong and glowing with life.

HECTOR—Perhaps your son will be a coward. That's one possible safeguard.

ANDROMACHE—He won't be a coward. But perhaps I shall have cut off the index finger of his right hand.

HECTOR—If every mother cut off her son's right-hand index finger, the armies of the world would fight without index fingers. And if they cut off their sons' right legs, the armies would be one-legged. And if they put out their eyes, the armies would be blind, but there would still be armies: blind armies groping to find the fatal place in the enemy's groin, or to get at his throat.

Andromache would rather kill her son than have that, and knowing that if Hector loves war his son will love war, she asks: "Do you love war?"

ANDROMACHE—Admit, sometimes you love it.

HECTOR—If a man can love what takes away hope, and happiness, and all those nearest to his heart.

ANDROMACHE—And you know it can be so. Men do love it.

HECTOR—If they let themselves be fooled by that little burst of divinity the gods give them at the moment of attack.

And there are certain mornings, concedes Hector, savoring the thought of them. "And then," interrupts Andromache, "the enemy comes?"

HECTOR—Then the enemy comes, frothing at the mouth. You pity him; you can see him there, behind the swollen veins and the whites of his eyes, the helpless, willing little man of business, the well-meaning husband and son-in-law who likes to grow his own vegetables. You feel a sort of love for him. Then you kill him. Such is war.

ANDROMACHE—All of them: you kill them all?

HECTOR—This time we killed them all. Quite deliberately. They belonged to an incorrigibly warlike race, the reason why wars go on and multiply in Asia. Only one of them escaped.

ANDROMACHE—In a thousand years' time, there the warlike race will be again, descended from that one man. His escape made all that slaughter futile after all. My son is going to love war, just as you do.

Hector, however, thinks that now he hates it. It is difficult for him to understand how the sounds of war, that once seemed so noble, now sound false. "This time war had no music for you?" asks Andromache. Hector tries to explain why it hadn't: "Because I am older? Or was it just the kind of weariness with your job which, for instance, a carpenter will be suddenly seized by, with a table half finished, as I was seized one morning, standing over an adversary of my own age, about to put an end to him? Up to that time, a man I was going to kill had always seemed my direct opposite. This time I was kneeling on a mirror, the death I was going to give was a kind of suicide. But after that nothing remained of the perfect trumpet-note of war. The spear as it slid against my shield rang suddenly false; so did the shock of the killed against the ground. The cries of the dying sounded false. I had come to that." "But it all still sounded right for the rest of them," insists Andromache. "The rest of them heard it as I did," Hector assures her. "The army I brought back hates war." But the sounds of Troy sounded true for them: "There wasn't a regiment which didn't halt, racked to the heart by this sense of returning music . . ."

He hasn't understood, Andromache explains. It is war right here in Troy that welcomes the soldiers at the gates. Paris, having carried off Helen, refuses to give in to the Greeks who are demanding her return. The Greek ambassador is arriving this very day. "If we don't give her up," says Andromache, "it means war." Hector, confident that he can handle Paris, and knowing that his army wants peace as badly as he does, reassures Andromache and bids her fetch Priam. Meanwhile, he intends to settle matters with Paris.

Left alone with Paris and Cassandra, Hector casually congratulates his brother for keeping so well occupied in his absence, and asks to be brought up to date. Preening, Paris wants Cassandra to tell Hector how charming Helen is. Cassandra doesn't seem too enthusiastic. "But," protests Paris, "you were the one who first said she was like a gazelle." "I made a mistake," says Cassandra. "Since then I have seen a gazelle."

Hector—To hell with gazelles! Doesn't she look any more like a woman than that?

Paris—She isn't the type of woman we know here, obviously.

Cassandra—What is the type of woman we know here?

PARIS—Your type, my dear sister. The fearfully unremote sort of woman.

CASSANDRA—When your Greek makes love she is a long way off, I suppose?

PARIS—You know perfectly well what I'm trying to say. I have had enough of Asiatic women. They hold you in their arms as though they were glued there, their kisses are like battering-rams, their words chew right into you. The more they undress the more elaborate they seem, until when they're naked they are more over-dressed than ever. And they paint their faces to look as though they mean to imprint themselves on you. And they do imprint themselves on you. In short, you are definitely *with* them. But Helen is far away from me, even held in my arms.

HECTOR—Very interesting! But, one wonders, is it really worth a war, to allow Paris to make love at a distance?

Hector cynically asks Paris if he had employed his usual seducer's tricks, but hearing that Helen was abducted while in for a swim with no witness but Menelaus, he is decidedly relieved. Paris apparently has done nothing irrevocable: "In other words: she was undressed, so neither her clothes nor her belongings have been insulted. Nothing except her body, which is negligible. I've enough acquaintance with the Greeks to know they will concoct a divine adventure out of it, to their own glory, the story of this little Greek queen who goes down into the sea, and quietly comes up again a few months later, with a look on her face of perfect innocence." What's more, Paris needn't take Helen back to Menelaus; the Greek ambassador will do it. "I don't know whether you are allowing yourself to notice how monstrous you are being, to suppose that a man who has the prospect of a night with Helen will agree to giving it up," Paris answers. "You still have an afternoon with Helen," Cassandra tells him, adding: "Surely that's more Greek?"

Paris blusters to no avail, for this is old stuff to Hector. But Paris so elaborately insists on his special love for Helen that Hector is quickly convinced that Helen doesn't return it. "If you like," concedes Paris. "But if I had to choose one out of all the possible ways of passion, I would choose the way Helen doesn't love me."

Hector's orders fall on Paris' disobedient ears; but Hector himself falls into a trap when he eagerly agrees to accept Priam's disposition of Helen. "Mind what you're doing, Hector!" warns Cassandra. "Priam is mad for Helen. He would rather give up his daughters." "For once she is telling the truth about the present instead of the future," Paris adds. And what is more, Cassandra tells Hector,

"Helen has a guard-of-honor which includes every old man in the city. Look there. It is time for her walk. Do you see, there's a fringe of white beards draped all along the battlements?" Instead of welcoming home the victorious soldiers, they are busy waiting for Helen. Cassandra points her out as Helen bends over to adjust her sandal. Hector is astounded by the size of her ancient audience, and can't make out what all the old men are shouting. Cassandra explains: "They are shouting only words without R's in them because of their lack of teeth. Long live Beauty, long live Venus, long live Helen. At least they imagine they're shouting, though, as you can hear, all they are doing is simply increasing a mumble to its highest power."

Two exponents of the "R-less" school climb with some effort up to this point of the wall.

OLD MAN—Down there we see her better.

2ND OLD MAN—We had a very good view.

1ST OLD MAN—But she can hear us better from up here. Come on. One, two, three!

BOTH—Long live Helen!

2ND OLD MAN—It's a little tiring, at our age, to have to climb up and down these impossible steps all the time, according to whether we want to look at her or to cheer her.

1ST OLD MAN—Would you like us to alternate? One day we will cheer her? Another day we will look at her?

2ND OLD MAN—You are mad! One day without looking at Helen, indeed! Goodness me, think what we've seen of her today! One, two, three!

BOTH—Long live Helen!

1ST OLD MAN—And now down we go again!

Having viewed this extraordinary scene, Hector is now confronted by Priam, who confirms the worst Cassandra has said. Surrounded by more old men, by the women of his family, by the poet Demokos and a mathematician, Priam at once wants to know: "Do you see her?" "Indeed he sees her," snaps Priam's wife Hecuba. "Who, I ask myself, doesn't see her, or hasn't seen her? She takes the road which goes the whole way round the city." Hector says he sees a young woman adjusting her sandal. Hecuba assures him that's what they all see, although Priam is put out that Hector sees no more and is impervious to such beauty. "And, consequently," spouts Demokos, "ignorant of love. And, consequently, unrealistic. To us who are poets reality is love or nothing."

HECTOR—But the old men, you think, can appreciate love and beauty?

HECUBA—But of course. If you make love, or if you are beautiful, you don't need to understand these things.

HECTOR—You come across beauty, father, at every street corner. I'm not alluding to Helen, though at the moment she condescends to walk our streets.

PRIAM—You are being unfair, Hector. Surely there have been occasions in your life when a woman has seemed to be more than merely herself, as though a radiance of thoughts and feelings glowed from her flesh, taking a special brilliance from it.

DEMOKOS—As a ruby represents blood.

HECTOR—Not to those who have seen blood. I have just come back from a close acquaintance with it.

DEMOKOS—A symbol, you understand. Soldier though you are, you have surely heard of symbolism! Surely you have come across women who as soon as you saw them seemed to you to personify intelligence, harmony, gentleness, whatever it might be?

HECTOR—It has happened.

DEMOKOS—And what did you do?

HECTOR—I went closer, and that was the end of it. And what does this we see here personify?

DEMOKOS—We have told you before: Beauty.

Hecuba finishes: "Then send her quickly back to the Greeks if you want her to personify that for long. She's a blonde. They don't last forever."

Exhausted from war, Hector makes an earnest plea for peace and happiness for all families, but Demokos dismisses it. The poet now lets the Mathematician explain to Hector why Helen is worth a quarrel with the Greeks. To the Mathematician, Helen's presence is such that even the Trojan countryside has improved: ". . . And, what is particularly evident to true mathematicians, space and volume have now found in Helen a common denominator. We can abolish all the instruments we have invented to reduce the universe to a manageable equation. There are no more feet and inches, ounces, pounds, milligrams or leagues. There is only the weight of Helen's footfall, the length of Helen's arm, the range of Helen's look or voice; and the movement of the air as she goes past is the measure of the winds. . . ."

Hector is amazed at the man's sobbing, but remains indifferent to Priam's explanation of what Helen means to the old men of Troy. Demokos tries a different tack: "Hector, as a poet I approach things by the way of poetry. Imagine if beauty, never, at any time, touched our language. Imagine there being no such word as "delight."

HECTOR—We should get on well enough without it. I get on without it already. "Delight" is a word I use only when I'm absolutely driven to it.

DEMOKOS—Well, then the word "desirable": you could get on without that as well, I suppose?

HECTOR—If it could be bought only at the cost of war, yes, I I could get on without the word "desirable."

DEMOKOS—One of the most beautiful words there are was found only at the cost of war: the word "courage."

HECTOR—It has been well paid for.

HECUBA—And the word "cowardice" was inevitably found at the same time.

The women are staunchly backing Hector. Hecuba applauds him: "You have done well to unmask them, Hector. They want you to make war for the sake of a woman; it's the kind of lovemaking men believe in who are past making love in any other way." Going even farther, Hecuba, Andromache and Cassandra join battle to show how unworthy woman is of sacrifice—how worthless she really is. But Priam, listening to this female tirade against womanhood, twists what they say into supporting what he would believe: "I can't conceive of any greater generosity than the way you now fight for peace, when peace will give you idle, feeble, chicken-hearted husbands, and war would turn them into men." "Into heroes," adds Demokos. Hecuba shows wearily that she understands that jargon too: "In war-time a man is called a hero. It doesn't make him any braver, and he runs for his life. But at least it's a hero who is running away." Andromache now adds her pleas to Hector's, but Priam deliberately distorts what she is saying: "Daughter, the first sign of cowardice in a people is their first moment of decay." "But which is the worse cowardice," argues Andromache; "to appear cowardly to others, and make sure of peace? Or to be cowardly in your own eyes, and let loose a war?" "Cowardice," intones Demokos, "is not to prefer death on every hand rather than the death of one's native land." "I was expecting poetry at this point," Hecuba sighs. "It never lets us down." Andromache, in reply, makes her last point: "Everyone always dies for his country. If you have lived in it, well and wisely and actively, you die for it too."

Hector calls attention to Paris' silence, but that young man, feeling every inch an "international problem," has nothing to say. Paris agrees, however—knowing that Priam won't—to Hector's shipping Helen back home. Priam refuses even to discuss such an impossible notion. Demokos says Helen is not Paris' to dispose of: Helen belongs to the city, to the whole country. The Mathematician chimes in: "She belongs to the landscape," and is hushed by Hecuba who has heard all she can hear.

As Helen approaches, Hector urgently begs Priam's permission to handle her alone. Priam receives Paris' cocky consent, and gives his to Hector, withdrawing with the others to make ready the Gates of War. "Those poor gates," says Cassandra. "They need more oil to shut them than to open them."

But Demokos loiters, and as Helen approaches, mouths rhymes to her. When Hector orders him to leave, Demokos asks: "What are you glaring at? You look as though you have as little liking for poetry as you have for war." "They make a pretty couple," replies Hector.

Ever so prettily, Paris escorts Helen to waiting Hector.

PARIS—Here he is, Helen darling; this is Hector. He has a proposition to make to you, a perfectly simple proposition. He wants to hand you over to the Greeks, and prove to you that you don't love me. Tell me you do love me, before I leave you with him. Tell me in your own words.

HELEN—I adore you, my sweet.

PARIS—Tell me how beautiful the wave was which swept you away from Greece.

HELEN—Magnificent! A magnificent wave! Where did you see a wave? The sea was so calm.

PARIS—Tell me you hate Menelaus.

HELEN—Menelaus? I hate him.

PARIS—You haven't finished yet. I shall never again return to Greece.

HELEN—You will never again return to Greece.

PARIS—No, no, this is about you, my darling.

HELEN—Oh, of course! How silly I am! I shall never again return to Greece.

PARIS—I didn't make her say it.—Now it's up to you.

Paris leaves, and Hector starts off carefully with Helen, asking in a casual tone about Greece. "Well," says Helen, "there are quite a great many kings, and a great many goats, dotted about on marble." "If the kings are gold, and the goats angora, that would look pretty well when the sun was rising," comments Hector. Helen wouldn't know: "I don't get up very early." And what about all those gods, Hector continues: "Paris tells me the sky is crawling with them. . . ." Helen hasn't Paris' gift for seeing them, but promises to look when she goes back.

HECTOR—You were telling Paris you would never be going back there.

HELEN—He asked me to tell him so. I adore doing what Paris wants me to do.

HECTOR—I see. Is that also true of what you said about Menelaus? Do you not, after all, hate him?

HELEN—Why should I hate him?

HECTOR—For the one reason which might certainly make for hate. You have seen too much of him.

HELEN—Menelaus? Oh, no! I have never seen Menelaus.

HECTOR—You have never seen your husband?

HELEN—There are some things, and certain people, that stand out in bright colors for me. They are the ones I can see. I believe in them. I have never been able to see Menelaus.

HECTOR—Though I suppose he must have come very close to you sometimes.

HELEN—I have been able to touch him. But I can't honestly tell you I saw him.

HECTOR—They say he never left your side.

HELEN—Apparently. I must have walked across him a great many times without knowing it.

HECTOR—Whereas you have seen Paris.

HELEN—Vividly; in the clearest outline against the sky and the sun.

Ordered to gaze down on Paris standing against the rampart below, Helen finds him not so clear as usual. And yet, Hector points out, the wall is freshly whitewashed. "It's odd," confesses Helen, "how people waiting for you stand out far less clearly than people you are waiting for." What's more, Helen isn't clear about whether Paris loves her, and even less about her feelings for him.

Having his hunch confirmed, Hector cries for Cassandra and bids her announce that this evening Helen will be returning to Greece with the Greek ambassador. Helen, however, pulls him up sharp: "You don't understand me at all, Hector. Of course I'm not hesitating. It would be very easy to say, 'I will do this or that, so that this can happen, or that can happen.' But you mustn't think, because you have convinced me, you've convinced the future, too.

Merely by making children behave as you want them to, you don't alter the course of destiny." Helen refuses to be "bullied"; she chooses what is *not* indefinite and vague, what she sees, and she finds it difficult to see herself returning to Menelaus.

HECTOR—Here you have a rival, Cassandra. Helen can read the future, too.

HELEN—No, I can't read the future. But when I imagine the future some of the pictures I see are colored, and some are dull and drab. And up to now it has always been the colored scenes which have happened in the end.

HECTOR—We are going to give you back to the Greeks at high noon, on the blinding sand, between the violet sea and the ocher-colored wall. We shall all be in golden armor with red skirts; and my sisters, dressed in green and standing between my white stallion and Priam's black mare, will return you to the Greek ambassador, over whose silver helmet I can imagine tall purple plumes. You see that, I think?

HELEN—No, none of it. It is all quite somber.

Crying that her colored picture book holds the world up to ridicule, Hector sees Helen staring ahead, looking out over the walls with blind eyes. In a voice as dead as the look in those eyes, Hector asks if she now sees the battle below . . . and the city in ruins . . . and Paris' body dragged behind a chariot.

HELEN—Oh, do you think that is Paris? I see what looks like a flash of sunlight rolling in the dust. A diamond sparkling on his hand. Yes, it is! Often I don't recognize faces, but I always recognize the jewelry. It's his ring, I'm quite certain.

HECTOR—Exactly. Do I dare to ask you about Andromache, and myself? You are looking at us. Don't deny it. How do you see us? Happy, grown old, bathed in light?

HELEN—I am not trying to see it.

HECTOR—The scene of Andromache weeping over the body of Hector, does that shine clearer?

HELEN—You seem to know. But sometimes I see things shining, brilliantly shining, and they never happen. No one is infallible.

Hector tells her she needn't go on, but looking into her tearless eyes he wonders whether she would cry if she were going to be killed. Helen can't say, but if Hector doesn't leave her alone now she is sure she will scream. As for leaving tonight for Greece, Helen says:

"But I want to leave! I'm prepared to leave! All that I'm trying to tell is that I simply can't manage to distinguish the ship that is going to carry me there." Nor can she see anything shining. Hector breaks in: "You will go back on a gray sea under a gray sun. But we must have peace."

Helen cannot see peace. Apparently others can't see it either. A messenger arrives with news that the priests of Troy are opposed to shutting the Gates of War, and are unanimously opposed to Helen's returning to Greece. Before Hector goes off to dispose of this new obstacle, he gets Helen's promise to do as he commands with no last-minute changes. And still he senses defeat. Paris has given in to him, Priam has given in to him, Helen has said "yes" to him; yet he is tempted to kill her. "If you break the mirror by killing me, will what is reflected in it cease to exist?" she asks.

After Hector goes off, Helen tells Cassandra that, had she chosen, she could have helped him understand her. But Cassandra knows that Hector understands Helen only too clearly. "And besides," says Cassandra, "I see nothing; I never have seen anything, colored or not. But I can feel the weight of every person who comes towards me. I know what is in store for them by the sensation of suffering which flows into my veins." "In fact you feel what I can see," says Helen. "What I feel in Hector," Cassandra answers, "is a suffering too deep to be suffered. He may break the reflection in your mirror, Helen. He may have hands great enough to strangle the tiger as it springs . . ."

ACT II

In front of the still open Gates of War, Helen prettily whiles away the time teasing the youth Troilus into kissing her. In an equally lighthearted fashion, Paris enters and usurps the demonstration kiss meant for the bashful youth, while Demokos approaches Helen to further his inspiration. Helen then trips off, leaving the closing of the Gates of War to others who might care.

Not one of the elderly men assembling—Demokos, the Mathematician, or a third—seem to have come for the ceremony, either. All are dead set against peace. At the moment, their only thought is how best to put poetry and music to warlike uses. Their immediate aim is to perfect a propaganda machine that will rouse the army to fighting pitch. The Mathematician concerns himself with a problem that takes precedence over poetry: the lamentable lack of insulting epithets. . . . "Before they hurl their spears, the Greek fighting men hurl insults. You third cousin of a toad, they yell!

You son of a sow!—They insult each other, like that! And they have good reason for it. They know that the body is more vulnerable when self-respect has fled. We Trojans suffer from a grave shortage of insults."

Demokos, who agrees, is determined to organize a cursing parade that evening. Paris thinks the whole thing laughable, sure that "they're big enough to find their own curses." "What a mistake!" cries Demokos. "Could you, adroit as you are, find your own effective curses?" And he accepts Paris' challenge to a contest of epithet throwing, each to let fly at ten paces.

PARIS—You old parasite! You filthy-footed iambic pentameter!

DEMOKOS—Just one second. You had better say who it is you are addressing.

PARIS—You're quite right! Demokos! Bloodshot bullock's eye. You fungus-ridden plum-tree!

DEMOKOS—Grammatically reasonable, but very naive. What is there in a fungus-ridden plum-tree to make me rise up foaming at the lips?

HECUBA—He also called you a bloodshot bullock's eye.

DEMOKOS—Bloodshot bullock's eye is better. But you see how you flounder, Paris? Search for something that can strike home to me. What are my faults, in your opinion?

PARIS—You are cowardly: your breath smells, and you have no talent.

DEMOKOS—You're asking for trouble!

PARIS—I was trying to please you.

POLYXENE—Why are we scolding Uncle Demokos, mama?

HECUBA—Because he is a cuckoo, dearest!

DEMOKOS—What did you say, Hecuba?

HECUBA—I was saying that you're a cuckoo, Demokos. If cuckoos had the absurdity, the affectation, the ugliness and the stench of vultures, you would be a cuckoo.

DEMOKOS—Wait a bit, Paris! Your mother is better at this than you are. Model yourselves on her. One hour's exercise each day for each soldier, and Hecuba has given us the superiority in insults which we badly need. As for the war-song, I'm not sure it wouldn't be wiser to entrust that to her as well.

HECUBA—If you like. But if so, I shouldn't say that war looks like Helen.

DEMOKOS—What would you say it looks like, in your opinion?

HECUBA—I will tell you when the Gates have been shut.

All now gather for the ceremony, though Hector still has trouble persuading Priam that the Gates should actually be closed. They're well-oiled and ready, but Priam insists that war, too, is ready. "The war will never take place!" cries Hector.

DEMOKOS—No? Listen! (*The sound of clamor near the Gates.*)

HECTOR—Shut the Gates. This is where we shall meet the Greeks. Conversation will be bitter enough as it is. We must receive them in peace.

PRIAM—My son, are we even sure we should let the Greeks disembark?

HECTOR—Disembark they shall. This meeting with Ulysses is our last chance of peace.

DEMOKOS—Disembark they shall not. Our honor is at stake. We shall be the laughingstock of the whole world.

HECTOR—And you're taking it upon yourself to recommend to the Senate an action which would certainly mean war?

Oh, not at all, says Demokos. He has his international lawyer to do such things. Introducing Busiris, who just happened to be passing through Troy at the moment, Demokos says that as an expert on the rights of nations, Busiris will give his unbiased opinion to the Senate.

Hector asks to hear Busiris' thoughts. In legal circumlocution, Busiris cites the impossibly offensive things the Greeks have done to the Trojans. He cites precedents for the Trojan position. He gives examples of the cities who refused to take such insulting behavior lying down. In each case, Busiris is happy to say that legal history was made, that each city's moral superiority was preserved—though the cities themselves, he admits, were wiped off the face of the earth. Triumphantly, Demokos announces: "The situation can only be resolved in two ways: to swallow an outrage, or return it. Choose." Hector chooses a third path. He summarily instructs Busiris: "You are going to provide me, here and now, with an argument which will allow our Senate to say that there has been no fault whatever on the part of our visitors, and that with our pride untouched we welcome them here as our guests." Demokos protests, and Busiris says it simply isn't in keeping with the facts.

HECTOR—My dear Busiris, all of us here know there's no better way of exercising the imagination than the study of law. No poet ever interpreted nature as freely as a lawyer interprets truth.

BUSIRIS—The Senate asked me for an opinion: I gave it.

HECTOR—And I ask you for an interpretation. An even subtler point of law.

BUSIRIS—It goes against my conscience.

HECTOR—Your conscience has seen Orphea destroyed, Magnesia destroyed: is it now contemplating, just as lightheartedly, the destruction of Troy?

HECUBA—Yes. He comes from Syracuse.

Refusing Hector's pleas, Busiris is brought up sharp by Hector's threat: "We shall hold you here for as long as the war goes on." Hecuba, over Demokos' startled protests, purrs: "During war we imprison the rights of man. There seems no reason why we shouldn't imprison a lawyer." Busiris now, with startling facility, marshals counter-arguments that wholly satisfy Hector. "So," cries Hector, "there we have our honor safe and sound, Demokos. The next step is to make this consultation with Busiris public. Meanwhile tell the port authorities to let Ulysses disembark without any loss of time."

Hector now balks at reciting the oration for the dead, and once more displeases Priam and Demokos. He insists that he said what he had to say during their last living moments on the field; he did what he could to comfort them. But eventually Hector delivers an oration concerned with the privileged living as well as the unprivileged dead. "You insult the dead!" cries Demokos. "Do you think so?" says Hector. "Either the dead or the living," Demokos insists. Ordered to speak his peroration, Hector obliges: "Breathe in this incense, touch these offerings, you who can neither smell nor touch. And understand, since I speak to you sincerely, I haven't an equal tenderness and respect for all of you. Though all of you are the dead, with you as with us who survive there are men of courage and men of fear, and you can't make me confuse, for the sake of a ceremony, the dead I admire with those I can't admire. But what I have to say to you today is that war seems to me the most sordid, hypocritical way of making all men equal: and I accept death neither as a punishment or expiation for the coward, nor as a reward to the living. So, whatever you may be, absent, forgotten, purposeless, unresting, without existence, one thing is certain when we close these Gates: we must ask you to forgive us, we, the deserters who survive you, who feel we have stolen two great privileges. I hope the sound of their names will never reach you: the warmth of the living body, and the sky."

The noise of the landing Greeks' music prompts Hector to order a royal reception and safe conduct for them, and to send a messenger to bring Ulysses back with him. In the meantime, while Hector and Priam work out what to say to Ulysses, Paris is to be kept out of the way.

While the men confer, the women wait. Andromache accosts Helen. Now that the problem of whether she goes or stays is immaterial, Andromache begs Helen to love Paris. Helen pooh-poohs her seriousness, she feels that her relationship with Paris is thoroughly happy.

ANDROMACHE—Agreement is never reached in love. The life of a wife and husband who love each other is never at rest. Whether the marriage is true or false, the marriage portion is the same: elemental discord. There is no tranquillity for lovers.

HELEN—And if I went pale whenever I saw Paris: and my eyes filled wtih tears, and the palms of my hands were moist, you think Menelaus would be delighted, and the Greeks pleased and quite satisfied?

ANDROMACHE—It wouldn't much matter then what the Greeks thought.

HELEN—And the war would never happen?

ANDROMACHE—Perhaps, indeed, it would never happen. Perhaps if you loved him, love would call to the rescue one of its own equals: generosity or intelligence. No one, not even destiny itself, attacks devotion lightheartedly. And even if the war did happen, why I think even then—

HELEN—Then it wouldn't be the same war, I suppose.

ANDROMACHE—Oh, no, Helen! You know what this struggle is going to be. Fate would never take so many precautions for an ordinary quarrel. It means to build the future on this war, the future of our countries and our peoples, and our ways of thinking. It won't be so bad if our thoughts and our future are built on the story of a man and a woman who truly love each other. But fate hasn't noticed yet that you are lovers only on paper, officially. To think that we're going to suffer and die only for a pair of theoretical lovers: and the splendor and calamity of the age to come will be founded on a trivial adventure between two people who don't love each other—that's what is so horrible.

Andromache begs Helen love Paris. ". . . Then the war will only be a scourge, not an injustice"; and she could believe in such a war.

Lightly dismissing Andromache as difficult, Helen considers her own casual, emotionless state an excellent thing. . . . "The world is nervous enough already; look at yourself!" she tells Andromache. "Fill it with pity, Helen," Andromache begs. "That's the only help the world needs." Helen, having known that the word would sooner or later be brandished, refuses to be taken in by it, sure that people pity others to the same extent as they pity themselves. Since Helen remains indifferent, Andromache cries: "I am lost." "Why?" coolly replies Helen. "If you're content with one perfect couple to make the war acceptable, there is always you and Hector, Andromache."

The first Greek to arrive is drunken Ajax, spoiling for a fight. Accosting Hector, hurling insult after insult, Ajax shows his intention of precipitating the war very quickly. But he has reckoned without Hector. No insult is too smarting for Hector to accept peacefully. Ajax changes his attack, becoming personally abusive. He calls Hector a coward; Hector lets it go unchallenged. "I've never known such unmilitary reactions!" cries Ajax in exasperation. "Suppose I tell you what the whole of Greece thinks of Troy, that Troy is a cess-pit of vice and stupidity?" "Troy is obstinate," answers Hector. "You won't get your war." Finally Ajax aims a blow at Hector; Hector lets this pass too, with Andromache a peaceable witness.

Demokos bursts in wanting to know what is wrong. Hector, backed by both Andromache and Helen, says that nothing is. Helen seems to enjoy taking the Trojan part of peace, but Demokos cries vengeance on him who raises a hand against Hector. "Who are you, you brute? I am Demokos, second son of Achichaos!"

AJAX—The second son of Achichaos? How do you do? Tell me: is it as serious to slap a second son of Achichaos as to strike Hector?

DEMOKOS—Quite as serious, you drunk. I am the head of the Senate. If you want war, war to the death, you have only to try.

Ajax tries his best: he slaps Demokos. Hector stops Demokos' cry of war with a resounding slap of his own, thus making Ajax his delighted ally.

To Priam all this noise is confusing. He can't make any sense of the commotion. "Who struck you?" he asks Demokos. "Hector! Ajax! Ajax! Hector!" Demokos bellows. "What is he talking about? He's mad!" concludes Priam. "You will pay for this, Hector," promises Demokos. But Ajax says to Hector: "My deepest respect! My dear Hector, forgive me. I withdraw my threats, I take back my slap. We have enemies in common, in the sons of Achichaos. I won't fight with anybody who shares with me an enmity for the sons of Achichaos. Not another mention of war. I don't know what Ulysses has got in mind, but count on me to arrange the whole thing."

Andromache lovingly tells Hector that he has won another round, but Hector says: "I win every round. But still with each victory the prize escapes me."

With Ulysses' arrival the contest begins in earnest. The preliminary match smacks of the "fix": Hector promises that Helen will be on board ship within the hour, and Ajax in return promises that all will be forgiven and forgotten.

ULYSSES—You don't mean to say that Helen is being given back to us?

HECTOR—Exactly that. She is ready.

AJAX—What about her baggage? She is sure to have more to take back than when she came.

HECTOR—We return her to you, bag and baggage, and you guarantee peace. No reprisals, no vengeance!

AJAX—A woman is lost, a woman is found, and we're back where we were. Perfect! Isn't it, Ulysses?

ULYSSES—Just wait a moment. I guarantee nothing. Before we say there are going to be no reprisals we have to be sure there has been no cause for reprisals. We have to make sure that Menelaus will find Helen exactly as she was when she was taken from him.

HECTOR—How is he going to discover any difference?

ULYSSES—A husband is very perceptive when a world-wide scandal has put him on his guard. Paris will have had to have respected Helen. And if that isn't so . . .

Hector blandly—with the reluctant acquiescence of Paris and the amused assistance of Helen—states Paris never even touched the virtuous lady. Ulysses hoots at the absurdity of this line. But despite his barbs, and to vain Paris' increasing discomfort, Hector finishes off the story of the unsullied queen. Helen adds her bit: "If you don't know what love is, Ulysses, I shouldn't venture on the subject." "You must admit, Helen," Ulysses answers foxily, "you would never have followed him if you had known the Trojans were impotent." But if Paris can restrain himself from telling his story, not so his sailors in the gathering crowd. Two from Paris' ship proudly fill in the details of Helen's abduction and of how she and Paris spent their nights and days aboard ship. They leave out nothing. After their triumphant tale of passion dies down, Hector says: "This is a pack of lies, isn't it, Helen?" Ulysses notices that Helen, enraptured, hasn't missed a detail. "I forgot," explains Helen, "they were talking about me. They sound so wonderfully convincing." "Do you dare to say they are lying, Paris?" demands Ulysses. "In some of the particulars, yes, I think they are," hedges Paris.

Hector tells the sailors to be quiet, but is answered defiantly: "Well, keep this quiet, if you can!" Everyone withdraws, however, as Hector and Ulysses inform each other that they are at each other's service. "Now we come to the real tussle," says Hector. "Yes," Ulysses answers, "out of which either war or peace is going to come."

If it is to be a battle of words, Hector knows his chances are small. But Ulysses thinks it will be more a battle of weight, of how they balance each other that will count. Even here, however, Hector's youth, courage, wife, unborn child, and the civilization of Troy sound less imposing than the maturity of Ulysses, his family, his wisdom, and the very "unpitying, incorruptible" air of Greece. Hector decides that the scales have already tipped to Ulysses' side. Does he want war? "I don't want it," answers Ulysses, "but I'm less sure whether war may not want us." "Our peoples have brought us together to prevent it," argues Hector. "Our meeting itself shows that there is still some hope."

"You are young, Hector," Ulysses says. "It's usual on the eve of every war, for the two leaders of the people concerned to meet privately at some innocent village on a terrace in a garden overlooking a lake. And they decide together that war is the world's worst scourge, and as they watch the rippling reflections in the water, with magnolia petals dropping onto their shoulders, they are both of them peace-loving, modest and friendly. They study one another. They look into each other's eyes. And, warmed by the sun and mellowed by the claret, they can't find anything in the other man's face to justify hatred, nothing, indeed, which doesn't inspire human affection, nothing incompatible in their languages any more, or in their particular way of scratching the nose or drinking wine. They really are exuding peace, and the world's desire for peace. And when their meeting is over, they shake hands in a most sincere brotherly fashion, and turn to smile and wave as they drive away. And the next day war breaks out. And so it is with us both at this moment. Our peoples, who have drawn aside, saying nothing while we have this interview, are not expecting us to win a victory over the inevitable. They have merely given us full powers, isolated here together, to stand above the catastrophe and taste the essential brotherhood of enemies. Taste it. It's a rare dish. Savor it. But that is all. One of the privileges of the great is to witness catastrophes from a terrace."

In the fullness of his youth and directness, Hector hopes that the universe is mistaken: "One way to recognize error is the fact that it's universal." "But," Ulysses points out, "when destiny has brought up two nations, as for years it has brought up yours and mine, to a future of similar invention and authority, and given to each a different scale of values, the universe knows that destiny wasn't preparing alternative ways for civilization to flower. It was contriving the dance of death, letting loose the brutality and human folly which is all that the gods are really contented by. It's a mean way to contrive things, I agree. But we are Heads of State, you and I; we can say this between ourselves: it is destiny's way of contriving things, inevitably."

Until that morning, Ulysses still had some doubts, but the moment he arrived on Trojan soil he knew for certain what fate had prepared: all signs pointed to it. "All our weapons and habits," explains Ulysses, "correspond with each other and balance each other like the beams of a gable . . ." The color of doom was on all the buildings, on all the figures, even the animals. The future had never appeared to Ulysses in such startling clarity, convincing him that there was nothing to be done; they were already living in the light of the Greek war. As for the other Greeks who landed with him, they were overwhelmed with the wealth of Troy and the richness of her land.

Hector cries that this last is the truth: "Greece has chosen Troy for its prey. Then why a declaration of war? It would have been simpler to have taken Troy by surprise when I was away with the army. You would have had her without striking a blow." "There's a kind of permission for war," Ulysses answers smoothly, "which can be given only by the world's mood and atmosphere, the feel of its pulse. It would have been madness to undertake a war without that permission. We didn't have it." But now, Ulysses is afraid they have. Hector batters his "Why's" against the cold logic of Ulysses' mind. It's not its crimes that are to prove Troy's downfall, but its faults: Helen was abducted badly. Ulysses agrees that the rape of one woman is wildly disproportionate to the destruction of a whole people; but—"(Helen) is one of the rare creatures destiny puts on the earth for its own personal uses. They're apparently quite unimportant. It might be not even a person, but a small town, or a village: a little queen, or a child; but if you lay hands on them, watch out!"

HECTOR—We are giving Helen back to you.

ULYSSES—The insult to destiny can't be taken back.

HECTOR—What are we discussing, then? I'm beginning to see

what is really behind your words. Admit it. You want our wealth! You had Helen carried off to give you an honorable pretext for war. I blush for Greece. She will be responsible and ashamed for the rest of time.

ULYSSES—Responsible and ashamed? Do you think so? The two words hardly agree. Even if we believed we were responsible for the war, all our generation would have to do would be deny it, and lie, to appease the conscience of future generations. And we shall lie. We'll make that sacrifice.

HECTOR—Ah, well, the die is cast, Ulysses. On with the war! The more I hate it, the more I find growing in me an irresistible need to kill. If you won't help me, it were better you should leave here.

ULYSSES—Understand me, Hector; you have my help. Don't ask me to interpret fate. All I have tried to do is to read the world's hand, in the great lines of desert caravans, the wake of ships, and the tracks of migrant birds and wandering peoples. Give me your hand. There are lines there, too. We won't search to see if their lesson tells the same story. We'll suppose that these three little lines at the base of Hector's hand contradict the waves, the wings, and the furrows. I am inquisitive by nature, and not easily frightened. I'm quite willing to join issue with fate. I accept your offer of Helen. I will take her back to Menelaus. I've more than enough eloquence to convince a husband of his wife's virtue. I will even persuade Helen to believe it herself. And I'll leave at once, to avoid any chance of disturbance. Once back on my ship perhaps we can take the risk of running war onto the rocks.

HECTOR—Is this part of Ulysses' cunning, or his greatness?

ULYSSES—In this particular instance, I'm using my cunning against destiny, not against you. It's my first attempt, so I deserve some credit for it. I am sincere, Hector. If I wanted war, I should have asked for a ransom more precious to you than Helen. I am going now. But I can't shake off the feeling that the road from here to my ship is a long way.

With the protection of Trojan guards, Ulysses starts back for his ship. Behind him, a limp and terrified Andromache goes to Hector for support and comfort. Only a minute or two more, and Ulysses will be on board his ship.

Ajax now returns drunken, and right in front of Hector starts pawing and kissing Andromache. Cassandra sharply warns Ajax away, as Hector raises his javelin. Ajax amiably gives in and says his farewells. But now Demokos bursts upon the scene.

DEMOKOS—What's this cowardice? You're giving Helen back? Trojans, to arms! They've betrayed us. Fall in! And your war-song is ready. Listen to your war-song!

HECTOR (*striking him*)—Have that for your war-song!

DEMOKOS (*falling*)—He has killed me!

HECTOR—The war isn't going to happen, Andromache! (*He tries to take* ANDROMACHE'S *hands from her ears: she resists, her eyes fixed on* DEMOKOS. *The curtain which had begun to fall is lifted little by little.*)

ABNEOS—They have killed Demokos! Who killed Demokos?

DEMOKOS—Who killed me? Ajax! Ajax! Kill him!

ABNEOS—Kill Ajax!

HECTOR—He's lying. I am the man who struck him.

DEMOKOS—No. It was Ajax.

ABNEOS—Ajax has killed Demokos. Catch him! Punish him!

HECTOR—I struck you, Demokos, admit it! Admit it, or I'll put an end to you!

DEMOKOS—No, my dear Hector, my good dear Hector. It was Ajax. Kill Ajax!

CASSANDRA—He is dying just as he lived, croaking like a frog.

ABNEOS—There. They have taken Ajax. There. They have killed him!

HECTOR (*drawing* ANDROMACHE'S *hands away from her ears*)—The war will happen. (THE GATES OF WAR *slowly open, to show* HELEN *kissing* TROILUS.)

CASSANDRA—The Trojan poet is dead. And now the Grecian poet will have his word.

THE DIARY OF ANNE FRANK *

DRAMATIZED BY FRANCES GOODRICH AND ALBERT HACKETT

[FRANCES GOODRICH *and* ALBERT HACKETT *collaborated on their first hit in 1930, were married a year later, and have been a writing team ever since. They both had first been on the stage. They have written "Western Union," the hit comedy "Up Pops the Devil," "Bridal Wise" and "The Great Big Doorstep." They have also written such motion-picture scenarios as "The Secret of Madame Blanche," "The Thin Man," "Lady in the Dark" and "Seven Brides for Seven Brothers." Miss Goodrich was born in Belleville, New York, and became interested in dramatics at Vassar College. Mr. Hackett was born in New York in 1900 and began his acting career at the age of six.*]

ON a late November afternoon in 1945 we see the "Secret Annex," the top floors of an Amsterdam warehouse and office building where eight people stayed in hiding during the German occupation.

Mr. Otto Frank, threadbare, hatless, carrying a rucksack, climbs the small stairs leading to these dark, empty, dusty rooms. With a supreme effort at self-control, he looks about him, at the upturned table and chair, at the window curtain in shreds. Opening the door to the bedroom to the right, he abruptly shuts it and turns away. Listening to a carillon strike six, he catches sight of a many-colored knit scarf hanging from a nail. After a second, he wraps this around his neck. Going back to the couch for his rucksack, he sees a woman's white glove on the floor and he picks it up. His self-control now deserts him. He buries his head in his hands.

Miep Gies, Otto Frank's Dutch stenographer of former days, climbs heavily up the stairs. She, who is going to have a child, cries compassionately: "Don't stay up here, Mr. Frank. What's the use of torturing yourself like this?" Not knowing where he will go, Mr. Frank plans to leave: he hopes to break all past ties.

Mr. Frank—I can't stay in Amsterdam, Miep. It has too many memories for me. Everywhere there's something . . . the house we lived in . . . the school . . . the street organ playing out there . . . I'm not the person you used to know, Miep. I'm a bitter old man. (*Breaking off.*) Forgive me, I shouldn't speak to you like this—after all that you did for us . . . the suffering.

Miep—No, no. It wasn't suffering. You can't say we suffered. (*As she speaks, she straightens a chair which is overturned.*)

Mr. Frank—I know what you went through, you and Mr. Kraler. I'll remember it as long as I live.

He takes one last look around the room, and starts to leave. Miep hurries to a cupboard. Bringing forth a bundle of papers, she hopes to have Mr. Frank look at them. Over her protests, he repeats: "Burn them. All of them." "Burn *this?*" she asks as she hands him a paper notebook.

Mr. Frank—Anne's diary. (*He opens the diary and begins to read.*) "Monday, the sixth of July, nineteen hundred and forty-two." (*To* Miep.) Nineteen hundred and forty-two. Is it possible, Miep? . . . Only three years ago. (*As he continues his reading, he sits down on the couch.*) "Dear Diary, since you and I are going to be great friends, I will start by telling you about myself. My name is Anne Frank. I am thirteen years old. I was born in Germany the twelfth of June, nineteen-twenty-nine. As my family is Jewish, we emigrated to Holland when Hitler came into power."

As Mr. Frank reads on, another voice joins his, as if from the air. Anne and her father tell in unison of his starting an importing business and how things went well until the Dutch capitulation in 1940, followed by the arrival of the Germans. "Then things got very bad for the Jews," Anne's voice now continues alone.

Anne's Voice—You could not do this and you could not do that. They forced Father out of his business. We had to wear yellow stars. I had to turn in my bike. I couldn't go to a Dutch school any more. I couldn't go to the movies, or ride in an automobile or even a streetcar, and a million other things. But somehow we children still managed to have fun. Yesterday Father told me we were going into hiding. Where, he wouldn't say. At five o'clock this morning Mother woke me and told me to hurry and get dressed. I was to put on as many clothes as I could. It would look suspicious if we walked along carrying suitcases. It wasn't until we were on our way that I learned where we were going. Our hiding place was to be upstairs in the building where Father used to have his business. Three other people were coming in with us—the Van Daans and their son Peter. Father knew the Van Daans but we had never met them. . . .

Scene II

It is early morning. In the bare hiding place the Van Daans wait impatiently, and somewhat nervously, for the Franks. Surrounded by her clutter of possessions, a fur-coated Mrs. Van Daan frets. Big, portly Mr. Van Daan paces and puffs away at a cigarette while their quiet sixteen-year-old son, Peter, his cat in a box at his feet, keeps watch at the bedroom window. Before Mrs. Van Daan grows too excitable over what could have happened to them, the Franks arrive.

First, a much younger Otto Frank comes briskly and confidently up the stairs, greets the Van Daans, all the while explaining that the presence of the Green Police had forced them to take the long way around. He is followed by his wife and daughter Margot, along with Miep and Mr. Kraler. Everyone carries parcels and bags. Mrs. Frank is young, reserved, gently bred; her beautiful eighteen-year-old daughter Margot looks like her; Anne, who finally appears up the steps, is quick, mercurial, interested and interesting. The minute introductions have been made, Anne is off on a tour of inspection, climbing the little stairs in the rear of the room to the attic above.

Miep and Mr. Kraler put away parcels, and Miep shows Mrs. Frank where the stores of food, drugs, soap and towels have been placed. Then hurrying off for the group's ration cards, Miep says lightly: "Don't worry. Your names won't be on them." Mrs. Frank shows immediate concern.

Mrs. Frank (*to* Kraler)—It's illegal, then, the ration cards? We've never done anything illegal.

Mr. Frank—We won't be living exactly to regulations here. (*As* Mr. Kraler *reassures Mrs. Frank, he takes various small things such as matches and soap from his pockets, handing them to her.*)

Mr. Kraler—This isn't the black market, Mrs. Frank. This is what we call the white market . . . helping all of the thousands and thousands who are hiding out in Amsterdam.

(*The carillon is heard playing quarter before eight. Anne stops at the window as she comes down the stairs, pulling back the curtains and looking out.*)

Anne—It's the Westertoren!

Mr. Kraler—I must go. I must be out of here and downstairs

in the office before the workmen get here. (*He starts for the stairs.*) Miep or I, or both of us, will be up each day to bring you food and news and find out what your needs are. Tomorrow I'll get you a better bolt for the door at the foot of the stairs. It needs a bolt that you can throw yourself and open only at our signal. (*To* Mr. Frank.) Oh—you'll tell them about the noise?

Mr. Frank—I'll tell them.

Mr. Kraler—Goodbye, then, for the moment. I'll come up again after the workmen leave.

Mr. Frank—Goodbye, Mr. Kraler.

Mrs. Frank (*shaking his hand*) How can we thank you? (*The* Others *murmur their goodbyes.*)

Mr. Kraler—I never thought I'd live to see the day when a man like Mr. Frank would have to go into hiding. When you think—

Mr. Frank follows Mr. Kraler down the stairs, bolts the door after him, returns and advises them all to get rid of some of their clothing: after that, he will instruct them about noise. Everyone peels off layer after layer of Star-of-David-marked clothing. Mrs. Frank cries out in a shocked voice: "Anne!" The girl is standing in the middle of the room, removing panties. "It's all right," Anne answers breezily. "I've got on three more." The two families, down to the normal amount of clothes, are ready to listen to Mr. Frank.

Mr. Frank—Now. About the noise. While the men are in the building below, we must have complete quiet. Every sound can be heard down there, not only in the workroom, but in the offices too. The men come about eight-thirty and leave at about five-thirty. So, to be perfectly safe, from eight in the morning until six in the evening we move only when it is necessary and then in stocking feet. We must not speak above a whisper. We must not run any water. We cannot use the sink, or even, forgive me, the W. C. The pipes go down through the workrooms. It would be heard. No trash . . . (*The sound of marching feet stops* Mr. Frank. *He goes into the bedroom on the right, followed by* Anne, *and peers out of the window. Satisfied that the marching feet are going away, he returns and continues.*) No trash must ever be thrown out which might reveal that someone is living here . . . not even a potato paring. We must burn everything in the stove at night. This is the way we must live until it is over, if we are to survive.

There is a silence. Mr. Frank adds cheerfully that after six they can laugh, have their supper and play games just as if they were in their old home. But now they must all go to their rooms and get settled before eight o'clock.

Mr. Frank assigns Mr. and Mrs. Van Daan to the attic room, already explored by Anne. Their son Peter is to have the little room over the stairwell. The room in which they are gathered will serve not only as a common living room but as Mr. and Mrs. Frank's bedroom at night. There are courteous protests from the Van Daans that the Franks must have their room. "Please," says Mr. Frank, "I've thought this out for weeks. It's the best arrangement. The only arrangement." Sure that they can never repay the Franks, Mrs. Van Daan says: "I don't know what would have happened to us if it hadn't been for Mr. Frank." "You don't know how your husband helped me when I came to this country," Mr. Frank answers; "knowing no one—not able to speak the language. I can never repay him for that."

The Van Daans climb to their room; Mr. Frank advises his wife to get some much-needed sleep. He will help the girls hang up clothes and see that Anne gets her milk. He settles his wife in the small bedroom the girls will use; he and Margot quietly hang up clothes on hooks.

Following Mr. Frank's advice, Anne and Peter take off their shoes. Anne starts making friends with Peter, but his shyness slows her down. She starts fussing over his cat Mouschi, but Peter puts the cat back in its carrier, saying, "He's a tom. He doesn't like strangers." Unabashed, Anne simply answers: "Then I'll have to stop being a stranger, won't I?" Next she brings up schools, and is surprised to find that Peter, like herself and Margot, went to the Jewish Secondary School. Peter had been aware of her, however. He used to watch her in the schoolyard surrounded by crowds of children. "Why didn't you come over?" Anne asks. "I'm sort of a lone wolf," mutters Peter, intent on ripping off his Star of David. Watching him cut away, Anne warns him: "They'll arrest you if you go out without your star." "Who's going out?" Peter answers. Realizing the good sense of his remark, Anne starts removing her own star, wondering all the while what her friends will think when she fails to show up. Peter has no such thought: he has no date. Anne, however, had made one with her best friend, Jopie. "I wonder," says Anne, "what she'll think when she telephones and there's no answer? Probably she'll go over to the house. I wonder what she'll think. We left everything as if we'd suddenly been called away . . . breakfast dishes in the sink . . . beds not made . . .

ANNE (*as she pulls off her star, the cloth underneath shows clearly the color and form of the star*)—Look! It's still there! (PETER *starts over to the stove with his star.*) What're you going to do with yours?

PETER—Burn it.

ANNE (*she starts to throw hers in, but cannot*)—It's funny, I can't throw it away. I don't know why.

PETER—You can't throw . . . ? Something they branded you with . . . ? That they made you wear so they could spit on you?

ANNE—I know, I know. But after all, it *is* the Star of David, isn't it?

Mr. Frank now joins the children and says with charming gravity: "Forgive me, Peter. Now let me see—we must find a bed for your cat." He welcomes the cat in Anne's name and gives it a washtub for a home. Having made the cat comfortable, Mr. Frank shows Peter to his room over the stairwell. "You can't grow any more," Mr. Frank warns Peter. "Not an inch, or you'll have to sleep with your feet out of the skylight." Making sure that Peter doesn't want anything to eat, Mr. Frank closes the door to Peter's room.

Alone with Anne, Mr. Frank comments on how nice Peter is, and is sure that in spite of his shyness Anne will like him. Anne very definitely hopes so—"Since he's the only boy I'm likely to see for months and months."

Mr. Frank, sitting down to take off his shoes, directs Anne to open a box he has for her. As she opens it, she tells him: "You know the way I'm going to think of it here? I'm going to think of it as a boarding house. A very peculiar summer boarding house, like the one that we—" She cries in rapture that her father has remembered to bring her picture collection of movie stars. As he goes for Anne's milk, Mr. Frank tells her to look further: thrilled, she discovers a diary. After throwing her arms around her father's neck, she excitedly demands a pencil and starts dashing to the office below to find one. Mr. Frank catches her in the nick of time and pulls her back. She is thoroughly startled. "But there's no one in the building now!" Anne cries.

MR. FRANK—It doesn't matter. I don't want you ever to go beyond that door.

ANNE (*sobered*)—Never . . . ? Not even at nighttime, when everyone is gone? Or on Sundays? Can't I go down to listen to the radio?

MR. FRANK—Never. I am sorry, Anneke. It isn't safe. No, you must never go beyond that door.

ANNE—I see.

MR. FRANK—It'll be hard, I know. But always remember this,

Anneke. There are no walls, there are no bolts, no locks that anyone can put on your mind. Miep will bring us books. We will read history, poetry, mythology. (*He gives her the glass of milk.*) Here's your milk. (*With his arm about her, they go over to the couch, sitting down side by side.*) As a matter of fact, between us, Anne, being here has certain advantages for you. For instance, you remember the battle you had with your mother the other day on the subject of overshoes? You said you'd rather die than wear overshoes. But in the end you had to wear them? Well now, you see, for as long as we are here you will never have to wear overshoes! Isn't that good? And the coat that you inherited from Margot, you won't have to wear that. And the piano! You won't have to practice on the piano. I tell you, this is going to be a fine life for you!

Anne's panic is gone. As Peter comes out of his room to get water for Mouschi, the carillon strikes the hour. Mr. Frank pantomimes that it is now too late to run water, so Peter starts back to his room. He steps on a creaking board; the three people freeze with fear. But after a minute, Anne shares her milk with the cat and silently watches it lap it up. Mr. Frank hands his fountain pen to Anne, who comes to the table in the center of the room and settles down with her diary.

Upstairs, Mr. Van Daan fans Mrs. Van Daan as they sit together on their iron bed. In the girls' bedroom, Mr. Frank puts a comforting arm about his wife's shoulders. Everyone is silent, motionless except for Mr. Van Daan's fanning. Anne starts to write in her diary.

The curtain falls. . . . Out of the darkness Anne's voice comes faintly at first, then with growing strength, trying to explain what it is like to go into hiding: never being in the fresh air, never being able to shout and jump about, the terror at night. . . . "The days," Anne writes, "aren't so bad. At least we know that Miep and Mr. Kraler are down there below us in the office. Our protectors, we call them. I asked Father what would happen to them if the Nazis found out they were hiding us. Pim said that they would suffer the same fate that we would . . . Imagine! They know this, and yet when they come up here they're always cheerful and gay as if there were nothing in the world to bother them. . . . Friday, the twenty-first of August, nineteen-forty-two. Today I'm going to tell you our general news. Mother is unbearable. She insists on treating me like a baby, which I loathe. Otherwise things are going better. The weather is . . ."

Scene III

Two months later, the nightly routine is about to start. Mr. Frank, at the window watching the last workman leave the building, gives the all-clear signal: the signal for Anne to explode—"Whee!" she cries; the signal for Mrs. Van Daan to be first at the W. C. and for Mrs. Frank to start dinner; and for Margot to end her school day in her bedroom.

Anne is on her nightly rampage. She teases Peter and hides his shoes; then he chases her and they rough-house. They wrestle on the floor till Peter gets his shoes back. Still needing activity, Anne asks Peter to dance with her. Suddenly self-conscious, Peter, on the pretext of having to feed Mouschi, goes to his room. Anne, left behind, slams the door on him and is rebuked by her mother for being undignified. Anne, flouncing away, says: "Who cares if it's dignified? I don't want to be dignified!" "You complain that I don't treat you like a grown-up," Mrs. Frank reminds her; "but when I do, you resent it." Anne only wants some fun: "Someone to laugh and clown with. After you've sat still all day and hardly moved, you've got to have some fun. I don't know what's the matter with that boy." Mr. Frank suggests that Peter just needs time to get used to girls. "Time?" says Anne. "Isn't two months time? I could cry."

Anne begs Margot to dance, but Margot is intent on helping with the supper. "You know," Anne cries, "we're going to forget how to dance. When we get out, we won't remember a thing . . ." To prevent such a state of affairs, Anne sings and dances by herself, till Mr. Frank scoops her into his arms for an elegant waltz.

Emerging from the W. C., with a cry of "Next!" Mrs. Van Daan misses Peter. Sending Anne to fetch him, Mrs. Van Daan says: "His father will kill him if he catches him in there with that cat and his work not done." Anne uses this errand as an excuse to go into Peter's room to feed the cat. Peter hates letting her into his room. Even more, he hates listening to his mother's coy remarks about his "little girl friend." Writhing with embarrassment, Peter begs her to let him alone.

Mrs. Van Daan—He acts like it was something to be ashamed of. It's nothing to be ashamed of, to have a little girl friend.

Peter—You're crazy. She's only thirteen.

Mrs. Van Daan—So what? And you're sixteen. Just perfect. Your father's ten years older than I am. (*To* Mr. Frank.) I warn you, Mr. Frank, if this war lasts much longer, we're going to be related and then . . .

MR. FRANK—Mazeltov!

MRS. FRANK (*deliberately*)—I wonder where Miep is. She's usually so prompt.

The noise of a car's sudden stop catches everyone with a sick terror; then, when the car moves on, a wave of relief sweeps over the room. And Anne, dressed absurdly in Peter's clothes, sweeps out of his room.

ANNE—Good evening, everyone. Forgive me if I don't stay. (*She jumps on a chair.*) I have a friend waiting for me in there. My friend Tom, Tom Cat. Some people say that we look alike. But Tom has the most beautiful whiskers, and I have only a little fuzz. I am hoping . . . in time . . . (PETER, *furious, calls out:* "All right, Mrs. Quack Quack." *Now* ANNE *is outraged.*)

PETER—I heard about you . . . How you talked so much in class they called you Mrs. Quack Quack. How Mr. Smitter made you write a composition . . . "Quack, quack, said Mrs. Quack Quack."

ANNE—Well, go on. Tell them the rest. How it was so good he read it out loud to the class and then read it to all his other classes!

Peter quacks at her. Anne, enraged, takes off the coat and trousers, all the while screaming: "You are the most intolerable, insufferable boy I've ever met!" And to show she means it, she hurls the clothes down the stairwell. Mrs. Van Daan eggs her on. Anne, needing no encouragement, finishes Peter off: "With all the boys in the world . . . Why I had to get locked up with one like you—" "Quack, quack, quack . . . and from now on stay out of my room!" Peter answers back. Quick as lightning, Anne's foot trips him up as he reaches his door.

Wondering at this behavior, Mrs. Frank feels her daughter's forehead. Anne pulls away irritably. "Anneke dear," Mrs. Frank says, "don't do that. You know we can't call a doctor here ever. There's only one thing to do—watch carefully. Prevent illness before it comes. Let me see your tongue." Anne refuses. Mr. Frank tells Anne to listen to her mother, whereupon Anne swiftly sticks her tongue out "at" her mother. To smooth things over, Mr. Frank says: "I think there's nothing the matter with our Anne that a ride on her bike, or a visit with Jopie, wouldn't cure. Isn't that so, Anne?"

When Mr. Van Daan comes down the attic stairs a moment later to find out what's for dinner, Anne is up to tricks. Hearing it's to be beans again, Mr. Van Daan starts his unhappy pacing. Anne paces impishly, step for step, right behind Mr. Van Daan. Mimicking him, she says: "We are now in what is known as the 'bean cycle.' Beans boiled, beans en casserole, beans with strings, beans without strings . . ." Mr. Van Daan speaks sharply to Peter about his cat; Mrs. Van Daan is ready to take Peter's part. Mr. Frank quietly changes the subject. "Anne," he says, "you got an excellent in your history paper today . . . and very good in Latin." Anne, sitting by her father, asks about algebra. "I'll have to make a confession," says Mr. Frank. "Up until now I've managed to stay ahead of you in algebra. Today you caught up with me. We'll leave it to Margot to correct." "Isn't algebra *vile,* Pim?" says Anne. "Vile!" her father agrees.

While Margot and Mr. Frank check Margot's work, Anne concentrates on Mrs. Van Daan. Asking to borrow the fur coat, Anne receives permission so long as she is careful with it. "My father gave me that the year before he died," Mrs. Van Daan recites. "He always bought the best that money could buy." Anne struts about in the coat.

ANNE—Mrs. Van Daan, did you have a lot of boy friends before you were married?

MRS. FRANK—Anne, that's a personal question. It's not courteous to ask personal questions.

MRS. VAN DAAN—Oh, I don't mind. (*To* ANNE.) Our house was always swarming with boys. When I was a girl we had . . .

MR. VAN DAAN—Oh, God. Not again!

MRS. VAN DAAN (*good-humored*)—Shut up! (*Without a pause, to* ANN. MR. VAN DAAN *mimics* MRS. VAN DAAN, *speaking the first few words in unison with her.*) One summer we had a big house in Hilversum. The boys came buzzing round like bees around a jam pot. And when I was sixteen! . . . We were wearing our skirts very short those days and I had good-looking legs. (*She pulls up her skirt, going to* MR. FRANK.) I still have 'em. I may not be as pretty as I used to be, but I still have my legs. How about it, Mr. Frank?

MR. VAN DAAN—All right. All right. We see them.

MRS. VAN DAAN—I'm not asking you. I'm asking Mr. Frank.

PETER—Mother, for heaven's sake.

MRS. VAN DAAN—Oh, I embarrass you, do I? Well, I just hope

the girl you marry has as good. (*Then to* ANNE.) My father used to worry about me, with so many boys hanging round. He told me, if any of them gets fresh you say to him: "Remember, Mr. So-and-So, remember I'm a lady."

ANNE—Remember, Mr. So-and-So, remember I'm a lady. (*She gives* MRS. VAN DAAN *her coat.*)

MR. VAN DAAN—Look at you, talking that way in front of her! Don't you know she puts it all down in that diary?

Having momentarily exhausted the resources of "The Annex," Anne puts her ear to the floor, in an effort to hear what's going on below. Around her the Van Daans argue over Peter's work. Mrs. Van Daan blames Mr. Van Daan for not helping Peter. She says to Mr. Frank: "Maybe you could help him, Mr. Frank?" With his usual tact, Mr. Frank defers to Mr. Van Daan. Admitting defeat with his son, Mr. Van Daan says: "You go ahead . . . if you want." Mr. Frank's offer to make his school coeducational wins him a kiss from Mrs. Van Daan. Mr. Frank suggests to Peter that they do their studying in the privacy of his room. The boy leads the way there eagerly, but Mrs. Frank stops her husband at the door to wipe off the offending lipstick.

Anne, hearing something through the floor, shushes the Van Daans. Mr. Van Daan objects to such rudeness, but before he can say more his own bad temper stirs up a quarrel with Mrs. Van Daan. "If you didn't smoke so much," Mrs. Van Daan says, "you wouldn't be so bad-tempered." And it's not only his bad temper, Mrs. Van Daan continues, but the bad habit of smoking itself and the smoking up of all their money. Mr. Van Daan tells her to shut up. Then finding Anne's eyes following all that he says with interest, Mr. Van Daan shouts: "What are you staring at?" "I never heard grown-ups quarrel before," answers Anne. "I thought only children quarreled." "This isn't a quarrel!" roars Mr. Van Daan. "It's a discussion. And I never heard children so rude before." Anne rises indignantly: "*I* rude!"

Before Anne can enter the "discussion," Mrs. Frank asks for the knitting, and mentions their lists for Miep. "It's a wonder," says Anne, "that Miep has a life of her own." Then sitting beside Mrs. Van Daan, Anne proceeds to discuss Miep's private life and the young Dutchman who shares it. This chattering prompts Mr. Van Daan to say: "Don't you ever get tired of talking? Suppose you try keeping still for five minutes. Just five minutes." Mr. Van Daan starts his pacing, and when Anne starts mimicking him, her mother takes her aside for a glass of milk.

Anne's constant talking, though a major source of irritation to

Mr. Van Daan, is not the only one. Now he can't find his pipe. Even if it's empty he wants to console himself with it. Anne quickly finds it and hides it. Mr. Van Daan, telling Anne what he thinks of her, is about to blow up. Now mimicking Mrs. Van Daan, Anne says: "Remember, Mr. So-and-So, remember I'm a lady." Thrusting the missing pipe in his mouth, Anne picks up her glass of milk. Mr. Van Daan restrains himself with difficulty: "Why aren't you nice and quiet like your sister Margot? Why do you have to show off all the time? Let me give you a little advice, young lady. Men don't like that kind of thing in a girl. You know that? A man likes a girl who'll listen to him once in a while . . . a domestic girl, who'll keep her house shining for her husband . . . who loves to cook and sew and . . ."

ANNE—I'd cut my throat first! I'd open my veins! I'm going to be remarkable! I'm going to Paris to study music and art. I'm going to be a famous dancer or singer . . . or something wonderful. (*She makes a wide gesture, spilling the glass of milk on the fur coat in* MRS. VAN DAAN'S *lap.* MARGOT *quickly rushes over with a towel.* ANNE *tries to brush the milk off with her skirt.*)

MRS. VAN DAAN—Now look what you've done—you clumsy little fool! My beautiful fur coat my father gave me . . .

Mrs. Van Daan, Anne's previous supporter, is now ready to kill her. Clutching her coat, she dashes up the stairs—her husband behind her—to her room.

Anne is truly upset. Mrs. Frank reprimands her; she mustn't behave that way. "You must not answer back," Mrs. Frank says. "They are our guests. We must always show the greatest courtesy to them. We're all living under terrible tension. That's why we must control ourselves. . . . You don't hear Margot getting into arguments with them, do you? Watch Margot. She's always courteous with them. Never familiar. She keeps her distance. And they respect her for it. Try to be like Margot." Not Anne; she won't have anyone walk over her. Mrs. Frank is more worried for the people that Anne will walk over. She feels it herself, in the way Anne talks to her. "If I had ever talked to my mother as you talk to me—" Anne won't accept this kind of talk of the way things used to be. In her world she has to fight things out for herself, and she doesn't want Margot thrown up at her constantly. Violently rebellious, Anne cries: "Margot! Margot! Margot! That's all I hear from everyone . . . how wonderful Margot is . . ." And paying no attention to Margot's protests, Anne keeps right on: "Everything she does is right, and everything I do is wrong! I'm the goat around here! . . . You're all against me! . . . And you the worst of all!" And she rushes off to her room: stifling her sobs, she throws herself on her settee.

Mrs. Frank keeps on getting supper, though she is sure that no one will want any. She frankly doesn't know how they can go on living this way. "I can't say a word to Anne . . . she flies at me . . ." "You know Anne," Margot says. "In half an hour she'll be out here, laughing and joking." But that isn't all Mrs. Frank is referring to. Motioning upwards to the Van Daans' room, trying to control herself, she says: "I told your father it wouldn't work. But no . . . no . . . he had to ask them, he said. He owed it to them, he said. Well, he knows now I was right! These quarrels . . . this bickering . . ."

The disagreeable pressures increase. When the buzzer rings, it is not Miep. It is Mr. Kraler, and not with his usual scraps of cheerful news, but with another Jew to hide.

Unhesitatingly, Mr. Frank agrees to take the man in. As Mr. Kraler goes to fetch the Jewish dentist from the office below, Mr. Frank apologizes to the others: "I spoke without consulting you. But I knew you'd feel as I do." He assumed too much. Mr. Van Daan brings up the question of food that is already inadequate. Mrs. Frank, making more of an effort to respond properly, can't help wondering where they can bed the man. The young are more generous. Peter, embarrassed for his father, offers his rat-ridden room, but Mr. Frank turns him down. And Anne is perfectly willing to share her room with Mr. Dussel, while eighteen-year-old Margot, for propriety's sake, can move into the common room with her parents.

This settled, Mr. Frank gets out the emergency brandy to greet Mr. Dussel with a toast. Curious over all the sudden bustle, Mrs. Van Daan comes down her stairs. "Someone's moving in with us," Mr. Van Daan tells her. "In here? You're joking," she says. "It's only for a night or two—" Margot murmurs, "until Mr. Kraler finds him another place." "Yeah, yeah!" Mr. Van Daan answers.

Mr. Kraler brings in the middle-aged, finicky, now considerably bewildered dentist, Mr. Dussel. Mr. Frank courteously takes his brief case from him; but Mr. Dussel, even as he shakes hands with everyone, clings to his medicine kit. Seeing that Dussel is in good hands, Mr. Kraler takes the borrowed raincoat from his shoulders and prepares to leave.

DUSSEL—What can I say to thank you . . . ?

MRS. FRANK—Mr. Kraler and Miep—they're our lifeline. Without them we couldn't live.

MR. KRALER—Please. Please. You make us seem very heroic.

It isn't that at all. We simply don't like the Nazis. (MR. FRANK *offers him a drink.*) No, thanks. We don't like their methods. We don't like . . .

MR. FRANK (*smiling*)—I know. I know. "No one's going to tell us Dutchmen what to do with our damn Jews!"

Mr. Frank follows Mr. Kraler to bolt the door behind him. When he returns, Anne excitedly tells her father: "It worked, Pim . . . the address you left! Mr. Dussel says that people believe we escaped to Switzerland." "I'm glad," Mr. Frank answers. "Let's have a little drink to welcome Mr. Dussel." Hardly have they toasted him than Mr. Van Daan breaks out: "Did Mr. Kraler warn you that you won't get much to eat here? You can imagine . . . three ration books among the seven of us . . . and now you make eight."

DUSSEL—Mr. Van Daan, you don't realize what is happening outside that you should warn me of a thing like that. You don't realize what's going on. (*As* MR. VAN DAAN *starts his pacing.*) Right here in Amsterdam every day hundreds of Jews disappear. . . . They surround a block and search house by house. Children come back from school and find their parents gone. Hundreds are being deported . . . people that you and I know . . . the Hallensteins . . . the Wessels . . .

MRS. FRANK (*in tears*)—Oh, no. No!

DUSSEL—They get their call-up notices: come to the Jewish theatre on such-and-such a day and hour . . . bring only what you can carry in a rucksack. And if you refuse the call-up notice, then they come and drag you from your home and ship you off to Mauthausen. The death camp!

MRS. FRANK—We didn't know that things had got so much worse.

DUSSEL—Forgive me for speaking so.

ANNE (*coming to* DUSSEL)—Do you know the deWaals? Do you know what has become of them? Their daughter Jopie and I were in the same class. Jopie's my best friend.

DUSSEL—They are gone.

ANNE—Gone?

DUSSEL—With all the others.

Margot puts her arm around the tearful girl, as Mr. Frank suggests postponing questions till later, to allow Mr. Dussel to get settled before supper.

Anne, controlling her tears, shows Mr. Dussel to their room and commiserates with him over his previous lonely bachelor state. Mr.

Dussel, spreading his medicine bottles all over the dresser, finds that it will take considerable adjustment to share this tiny room with Anne. Before, he had no desire to share his life with even so much as a pet. Fur-bearing animals give him asthma. Anne cheerfully tells him that he will be living with Peter's cat, too. "Here?" cries Dussel. "He has it here?" "Yes," says Anne, "but we hardly ever see it. He keeps it in his room all the time. I'm sure it will be all right." Mr. Dussel, fortifying himself with some pills, fervently hopes so. He ignores the little view from the window that Anne proudly calls to his attention; he is shocked at her mention of the W. C. And admitting that he is not at his best in the morning, he gets Anne to promise that during the morning hours he can have the room to himself. "Tell me," Dussel inquires, "when you're in here, what happens to me? Where am I spending my time? In there, with all the people?" "Yes," Anne says. "I see. I see," says Dussel, afraid that he does. Since supper is to be at six-thirty, Dussel decides: "Then, if you don't mind . . . I like to lie down quietly for ten minutes before eating. I find it helps the digestion." Anne, with a real effort to be polite, hopes that she won't prove too great a bother to Mr. Dussel. She seems to bother everybody else. "I always get along very well with children," says Dussel loftily. "My patients all bring their children to me, because they know I get on well with them. So don't you worry about that." Anne, pumping his hand, thanks him gratefully. As the lights dim, the curtain closes.

. . . Anne's voice tells of her appreciation of the last book that she read and now, in September, of her unhappily strained relations with Mr. Dussel. Things have reached fighting pitch. She is ready to smack him. . . . "I keep wishing that Peter was a girl," Anne's voice says. "Then I would have someone to talk to. Margot's a darling, but she takes everything too seriously. To pause for a moment on the subject of Mrs. Van Daan. I must tell you that her attempts to flirt with Father are getting her nowhere. Pim, thank goodness, won't play."

Scene IV

Several more months have passed. It is the middle of the night. What with the noise of planes droning overhead and the singing of drunken soldiers in the street below, people sleep as best they can. In Mr. Van Daan's room, just now, a match flares; a shadowy figure comes down the stairs and goes to the food cupboard, where a match flares again. Then the figure sneaks back upstairs. There is a silence, broken suddenly by Anne's nightmare screams.

Dussel, furious to be awakened, afraid that the screams might be heard, tries gruffly to silence her. Mrs. Frank, rushing to comfort her, tells Dussel to go back to bed.

DUSSEL (*picking up a book and a pillow*)—Thank you, but I'm going to the W. C. The one place where there's peace! (*He stalks out, meeting* MR. VAN DAAN.)

MR. VAN DAAN—What is it? What happened?

DUSSEL—A nightmare. She was having a nightmare!

MR. VAN DAAN—I thought someone was murdering her.

DUSSEL—Unfortunately, no.

Anne rebuffs her mother badly. She won't talk of her dream; she won't have Mrs. Frank sit with her. She turns her face away from Mrs. Frank's kiss. Dreadfully hurt, Mrs. Frank leaves the room. Crying in German to Mr. Frank that Anne will have none of her, she tells him to go to his daughter. Sensing his wife's hurt, Mr. Frank hesitates, until Mrs. Frank says that she is glad that Anne will at least turn to him.

Armed with a sleeping pill, Mr. Frank goes to Anne. Margot consolingly puts her arms around her sobbing mother. "She wants nothing of me," Mrs. Frank repeats. "She pulled away when I leaned down to kiss her." "It's a phase . . ." Margot tells her softly. "You heard Father. . . . Most girls go through it. They turn to their fathers at this age." Mrs. Frank cries: "You weren't like this . . . you didn't shut me out."

Anne, flinging her arms around Mr. Frank, pours out her fearful dream: the Green Police grabbed her as they had Jopie. Mr. Frank gives her the pill to quiet her, and asks that she try to sleep.

ANNE—I'm a terrible coward. I'm so disappointed in myself. I think I've conquered my fear . . . I think I'm really grown up . . . and then something happens . . . and I run to you like a baby . . . I love you, Father. I don't love anyone but you.

MR. FRANK (*reproachfully*)—Anneline!

ANNE—It's true. I've been thinking about it for a long time. You're the only one I love.

MR. FRANK—It's fine to hear you tell me that you love me. But I'd be happier if you said you loved your mother as well. . . . She needs your help so much . . . your love . . .

ANNE—We have nothing in common. She doesn't understand me. Whenever I try to explain my views on life to her she asks me if I'm constipated.

MR. FRANK—You hurt her very much just now. She's crying. She's in there crying.

ANNE—I can't help it. I only told the truth. I didn't want her here . . . (*Then with a sudden change.*) Oh, Pim, I was horrible, wasn't I? And the worst of it is, I can stand off and look at myself doing it and know it's cruel and yet I can't stop doing it. What's the matter with me? Tell me. Don't say it's just a phase! Help me.

MR. FRANK—There is so little that we parents can do to help our children. We can only try to set a good example—point the way. The rest you must do yourself. You must build your own character.

Anne tells of her efforts at character-building, how each night she makes an inventory of the bad things she has done that day and vows never to do them again. She grows sleepier and sleepier as she talks to her father. When she is finally asleep, Mr. Frank watches her for a moment, then turns off the light and starts out. The curtain falls.

. . . Anne's Diary Voice tells of the increasing air raids, which according to her father herald an earlier end to the war; of Mrs. Van Daan's quickly deflated fatalism when the planes are overhead; and the joyous news of the Allies' landing in North Africa.

SCENE V

It is the first night of the Chanukah celebration in December, 1942. All the "family," dressed in their best, with the men wearing hats, are seated around the table. Mr. Frank, standing with the lighted Shamos candle in his hand, reads the blessing.

MR. FRANK—"Praised be Thou, O Lord our God, Ruler of the Universe, who hast sanctified us with Thy commandments and bidden us kindle the Chanukah lights. Praised be Thou, O Lord our God, Ruler of the Universe, who hast wrought wondrous deliverances for our fathers in days of old. Praised be Thou, O Lord our God, Ruler of the Universe, that Thou hast given us life and sustenance and brought us to this happy season." (*He lights one candle of the Menorah.*) We kindle this Chanukah light to celebrate the great and wonderful deeds wrought through the zeal with which God filled the hearts of the heroic Maccabees, two thousand years ago. They fought against indifference, against tyranny and oppression, and they restored our Temple to us. May these lights remind us that we should ever look to God, whence cometh our help. Amen.

Passing the book to Mrs. Frank, she reads the 121st Psalm. All say Amen. Mr. Dussel, rising, says: "That was very moving." Told that there is much more to Chanukah than that, that there are songs and presents too, Dussel is reminded of his St. Nicholas Day. "No! Not like St. Nicholas!" cries Mrs. Van Daan. "What kind of a Jew are you that you don't know Chanukah?" Each person now recalls what Chanukah means to him, what he remembers most happily. Margot recalls the presents of her childhood. Mrs. Frank, having served the supper, now sits down and says: "We are all here alive; that is present enough."

Not for Anne, who swiftly and excitedly whips out a satchel full of presents for everyone. Out of odds and ends, imagination and plain hard work, she has rigged up a batch of appropriate Chanukah gifts. But the best present of all is a slip of paper she hands to her mother, while pulling Mrs. Frank to her feet.

MRS. FRANK (*reads*)—"Here's an I.O.U. that I promise to pay.
Ten hours of doing whatever you say.
Signed, Anne Frank."

(MRS. FRANK *takes* ANNE *in her arms, holding her close.*)

DUSSEL (*to* ANNE)—Ten hours of doing what you're told? *Anything* you're told?

ANNE—That's right.

DUSSEL—You wouldn't want to sell that, Mrs. Frank?

MRS. FRANK—Never! This is the most precious gift I've ever had! (*She sits, showing her present to the others.* ANNE *hurries back to the satchel and pulls out a scarf, the same scarf we saw in the first scene.*)

ANNE (*offering it to her father*)—For Pim. (*He takes it, unfolding it and showing it the others.*) It's a muffler—to put around your neck. Like an Ascot, you know. I made it myself out of odds and ends. . . . I knitted it in the dark each night, after I'd gone to bed. I'm afraid it looks better in the dark!

MR. FRANK (*putting it on*)—It's fine. It fits me perfectly. Thank you, Anneke.

Anne hands Peter a ball of paper, with a string attached, for Mouschi. And for Peter, she has a real second-hand razor that she commissioned Miep to find for her. Anne has recognized Peter's need: "Look on his upper lip. . . . You can see the beginning of a mustache." Dussel sniggers: "He wants to get rid of that? Put a little milk on it and let the cat lick it off." Peter storms to his room, crying: "You think you're funny, don't you?" and slams the door behind him.

Anne hasn't forgotten even Mr. Dussel. She has concocted some ear plugs for him, the test for which will be if Mr. Dussel can then hear her. Dussel can't try them out: they disappear inside his ears. His main concern, as everyone laughs, is to get them out as quickly as possible.

They all gratefully agree that because of Anne it has been a real Chanukah. But to Anne, the Chanukah song is the whole thing, and she starts to sing. Mr. Frank, quieting her, says: "I'm afraid, Anne, we shouldn't sing that song tonight. It's a song of jubilation, of rejoicing. One is apt to become too enthusiastic." Promising not to shout, Anne starts to sing.

The good humor continues as Peter now gives Mr. Dussel his deserts. Persuading him that he has Mouschi under his coat, though actually he has nothing, he soon has Mr. Dussel wheezing and snorting. The others all appreciate the joke, but at the mention of the cat, Mr. Van Daan introduces a less pleasant note: saying that the cat looks fatter every day, Mr. Van Daan threatens to get rid of him. Peter threatens to leave if the cat does. "You're not going and the cat's not going," interrupts Mrs. Van Daan, and tells Anne to go on with the song. Mr. Frank, wishing to save the candle for the following night—a shortage he is sure God will understand—starts to blow it out. "Praised be Thou, O Lord our God, who hast sustained us and permitted us to celebrate this joyous festival." There is a crash of something from below. They all freeze in horror, straining to listen. Then Mr. Frank, turning off the light near him, motions to Peter to turn off the center lamp. Trying to reach the lamp by standing on a chair, Peter crashes; the chair goes over; the iron lampshade falls to the floor. From below there is a sound of feet running downstairs; upstairs there is complete terror.

A hysterical Mrs. Van Daan is sure that it was the Green Police; Mr. Van Daan thinks it might be the Gestapo. Adds Mr. Frank: "Or a thief looking for money." He again motions for silence. Anne suddenly faints. As Margot goes for water, Mr. Van Daan grabs her, saying: "No, no. No one's going to run water!" "If they've found us, they've found us. Get the water," Mr. Frank orders. He also decides to go down to investigate. Over Margot's terrified cries, he says: "This is Saturday. There is no way for us to know what has happened until Miep or Mr. Kraler come on Monday morning. We can't live with this uncertainty."

Once Mr. Frank has gone, there is a nasty scene between the Van Daans, with Mr. Van Daan and Peter almost coming to blows. Mrs. Frank does her best to comfort Anne, who cries for her father. Pulling her close, she prays softly: "I lift up mine eyes unto the mountains, from whence cometh my help. My help cometh from the Lord Who made heaven and earth. He will not suffer thy foot to be moved . . . He that keepeth thee will not slumber—"

Mr. Frank comes back, bringing the news that after all it *was* a thief, who had run off with the cashbox and the radio. "The danger has passed," he says quietly. "Don't be so terrified, Anne. We're safe." But Dussel knows better, and has to blurt it out, pointing at Peter: "Thanks to this clumsy fool, there's someone now who knows we're up here! Someone now knows we're up here hiding!" They are terrified once more as Dussel continues: "I think some day he'll be caught and then he'll make a bargain with the Green Police. . . . If they'll let him off, he'll tell them where some Jews are hiding!"

MR. VAN DAAN—He's right.

ANNE—Father, let's get out of here! We can't stay here now. . . . Let's go.

MR. VAN DAAN—Go! Where?

MRS. FRANK (*sinking to her chair at the table*)—Yes. Where?

MR. FRANK (*to them all*)—Have we lost all faith? All courage? A moment ago we thought that they'd come for us. We were sure it was the end. But it wasn't the end. We're alive, safe. . . . We thank Thee, O Lord our God, that in Thy infinite mercy Thou hast again seen fit to spare us. (*He turns to* ANNE.) Come on, Anne. The song! The song! (*He starts to sing.*)

Hardly audible at first, Anne starts to sing. The others gradually join in, and with growing courage they sing the song of jubilation and rejoicing. They are still singing when the curtain falls.

ACT II

In the darkness, Anne's voice reads from her diary: "Saturday, the first of January, 1944. Another new year has begun and we find ourselves still in our hiding place. We have been here now for one year, five months, and twenty-five days. It seems that our life is at a standstill."

As the lights come up, life is going on as usual: seated at the table, Anne continues to write in her diary. "We are all a little thinner.

The Van Daans' 'discussions' are as violent as ever. Mother still does not understand me. But then I don't understand her either. There is one great change, however. A change in myself. I read somewhere that girls of my age don't feel quite certain of themselves. That they become quiet within and begin to think of the miracle that is taking place in their bodies. I think that what is happening to me is so wonderful . . . not only what can be seen . . .

Miep's V-for-Victory on the buzzer signals a surprise New Year's visit. Miep and Mr. Kraler have not only brought flowers for Mrs. Frank and Mrs. Van Daan, but Miep has brought a tiny cake that she made for all of them. Mrs. Frank, after thanking her, adds: "You must have used all of your sugar ration for weeks." Unfortunately, the cake brings trouble rather than cheer: slighting Mrs. Van Daan, Mr. Dussel decides that Mrs. Frank should be the one to cut it. Both Van Daans immediately take offense.

DUSSEL—Mrs. Frank divides things better.

MRS. VAN DAAN—What are you trying to say?

MR. VAN DAAN—Oh, come on, stop wasting time.

MRS. VAN DAAN—Don't I always give everybody exactly the same? Don't I?

MR. VAN DAAN—Forget it, Kerli.

MRS. VAN DAAN—No. I want an answer. Don't I?

DUSSEL—Yes. Yes. Everybody gets exactly the same . . . except Mr. Van Daan always gets a little bit more. (MR. VAN DAAN, *the knife still in his hand, advances on* DUSSEL.)

MR. VAN DAAN—That's a lie!

MR. FRANK—Please, please! You see what a little sugar cake does to us? It goes right to our heads.

Overhearing Peter ask Miep to search for his lost cat Mouschi, Dussel, with ever-increasing insensibility, tells him he can be sure that "someone has had a nice big dinner from that cat!" Peter is left inarticulate with rage.

Mr. Van Daan now blights the celebration completely. While his wife shrieks, he hands her fur coat to Miep, to be sold. "It should fetch a good price," he says, adding: "And, by the way, will you get me cigarettes? I don't care what kind they are . . . get all you can." As she goes away carrying the coat, Miep says with noticeable restraint: "It's terribly difficult to get them, Mr. Van Daan. But I'll try. Goodbye."

Mr. Kraler stays behind, ostensibly to talk to Mr. Frank about some business matters. Margot senses that something is wrong.

MR. FRANK—If it's something that concerns us here, it's better that we all hear it.

MR. KRALER (*turning to him quietly*)—But . . . the children?

MR. FRANK—What they'd imagine would be worse than any reality. (*All listen with intense apprehension.*)

MR. KRALER—It's a man in the storeroom . . . I don't know whether or not you remember him . . . ?

Out of the blue this man, Carl, had asked about Mr. Frank; then shortly afterwards, his eyes on the office bookshelves, he was reminded of the door to the loft that had once been there, whereupon he asked Mr. Kraler for more money—twenty guilders a week more. Mr. Van Daan cries out: "Blackmail!" Mr. Frank says reasonably: "Twenty guilders? Very modest blackmail." Dussel theorizes that it was Carl they heard during the Chanukah celebration. Mr. Kraler doesn't know what to do. Mr. Frank finally decides that they'd better offer him half: "Then we'll soon find out if it's blackmail or not." "And if it is?" cries Dussel, "we've got to pay it, haven't we? Anything he asks we've got to pay." "Let's decide that when the time comes," says Mr. Frank, and Mr. Kraler, ready to follow his advice, leaves.

Margot, who has not been at all well, suddenly says she sometimes wishes the end would come—whatever it might be. Mrs. Frank says she should be ashamed of herself: "Talking that way! Think how lucky we are! Think of the thousands dying in the war every day. Think of the people in concentration camps." Anne, with her arms around Margot, answers for her.

ANNE—What's the good of that? What's the good of thinking of misery when you're already miserable? That's stupid!

MRS. FRANK—Anne!

ANNE—We're young, Margot and Peter and I! You grown-ups have had your chance! But look at us. . . . If we begin thinking of all the horror in the world, we're lost! We're trying to hold on to some kind of ideals . . . when everything—ideals, hopes . . . everything, are being destroyed! It isn't our fault that the world is in such a mess! We weren't around when all this started! So don't try to take it out on us!

Anne rushes off to her room, slamming the door behind her. Peter goes after her, carrying her piece of cake. Shyly, he confesses his admiration not only for the way Anne spoke up, but for what she said. Anne contradicts him: "I do it all wrong. I say too much.

I go too far. I hurt people's feelings. . . ." Peter thinks she's just fine; he wouldn't know what to do around here if it weren't for Anne. Her gratitude knows no bounds. She offers him some of her pictures for the room he spends so much time in. He tries to explain that he uses his room to avoid listening to fights and arguments.

ANNE—You're lucky, having a room to go to. His lordship is always here. I hardly ever get a minute alone. When they start in on me, I can't duck away. I have to stand there and take it.

PETER—You gave some of it back just now.

ANNE—I get so mad. They've formed their opinions—about everything; but we . . . we're still trying to find out. . . . We have problems here that no other people our age have ever had. And just as you think you've solved them, something comes along—and bang! You have to start all over again.

PETER—At least you've got someone you can talk to.

ANNE—Not really. Mother . . . I never discuss anything serious with her. She doesn't understand. Father's all right. We can talk about everything . . . everything but one thing: Mother. He simply won't talk about her. I don't think you can be really intimate with anyone if he holds something back, do you?

PETER—I think your father's fine.

ANNE—Oh, he is, Peter! He is! He's the only one who's ever given me the feeling that I have any sense. But anyway, nothing can take the place of school and play and friends of your own age—or near your own age—can it?

PETER—I suppose you miss your friends and all.

ANNE—It isn't just . . . (*She breaks off, staring up at him a second.*) Isn't it funny, you and I? Here we've been seeing each other every minute for almost a year and a half, and this is the first time we've ever really talked. It helps a lot to have someone to talk to, don't you think? It helps you to let off steam.

PETER (*going to the door*)—Well, any time you want to let off steam, you can come into my room.

. . . The curtain has fallen. Anne's Diary Voice now tells of the bad news they've had: the people from whom Miep got their ration cards have been arrested. There has been a further cut in their meager food supply. March 6th records yet another blow: Mr. Kraler is in the hospital with ulcers. Mr. Frank says that "they" are his ulcers. Miep now has to run the business and "them."

The Americans have landed on the southern tip of Italy. . . .

Anne's emotions are too much for news items in her diary: "Have I been skipping too much from one subject to another? I can't help it. I feel that Spring is coming. I feel it in my whole body and soul. I feel utterly confused. I am longing, so longing, for everything . . . for friends . . . for someone to talk to . . . someone who understands . . . someone young, who feels as I do . . ."

Scene II

In the evening, after supper, most of them are gathered in the main room. Mr. Dussel, impatiently waiting for Anne to get out of their bedroom, can stand it no longer. He raps sharply on the door. "No, no, Mr. Dussel," Anne trills. "I am not dressed yet." Defeated and furious, Dussel sits down in a chair and buries his head in his hands.

Anne, with Margot's help, continues to dress, all the while primping and fishing for compliments. Mrs. Frank comes to Dussel's assistance. Asking politely if she may come in. Mrs. Frank says gently: "Anne dear, you're not going in again tonight to see Peter?" "That," says Anne, "is my intention." Mrs. Frank doesn't want Anne to give Mrs. Van Daan the chance to be unpleasant. "I'm sorry, Mother," Anne answers. "I'm going to Peter's room. I'm not going to let Petronella Van Daan spoil our friendship." Mrs. Frank gives up. Anne's one worry is that she may be hurting Margot. "You don't feel badly? Really?" Anne asks Margot. "Truly? You're not jealous?" "Of course I'm jealous," Margot answers; "jealous that you've got something to get up in the morning for. But jealous of you and Peter? No." With a last look in the mirror, Anne says: "Maybe there's nothing to be jealous of. Maybe he doesn't really like me. Maybe I'm just taking the place of his cat . . ." But she picks up a pair of white gloves, puts them on, adjusts her mother's pink stole elegantly about her shoulders, and is ready to run the gauntlet. With a nod in Dussel's direction, Anne teeters out of the room on Margot's high-heeled shoes and starts toward Peter's room. "My God, look at her!" screams Mrs. Van Daan. Anne, ignoring this, knocks on Peter's door. Mrs. Van Daan begins to fuss with Peter; Mrs. Frank says quietly: "Anne won't stay late. She's going to bed promptly at nine. Aren't you, Anne?" After the two young people shut the door, Mrs. Van Daan announces: "In my day it was the boys who called on the girls. Not the girls on the boys."

Peter receives Anne as a true host should. He has prepared a place for her to sit, and provided a bottle of pop and glasses. Their conversation is somewhat formal. Anne, fishing again, leads it into more personal channels, and finally asks shyly: "Peter, did you ever kiss a girl?" "Yes. Once," Peter answers.

ANNE (*to cover her feelings*)—That picture's crooked. (PETER *goes over and straightens the photograph.*) Was she pretty?

PETER—Huh?

ANNE—The girl that you kissed.

PETER—I don't know. I was blindfolded. (*He sits opposite her.*) It was at a party. One of those kissing games.

ANNE. Oh. (*Relieved.*) I don't suppose that really counts, does it?

PETER—It didn't with me.

ANNE—I've been kissed twice. Once a man I'd never seen before kissed me on the cheek when he picked me up off the ice and I was crying. And the other was Mr. Koophuis, a friend of Father's, who kissed my hand. You wouldn't say those counted, would you?

PETER—I wouldn't say so.

ANNE—I know almost for certain that Margot would never kiss anyone unless she was engaged to him. And I'm sure too that Mother never touched a man before Pim. But I don't know . . . things are so different now. . . . What do you think? Do you think a girl shouldn't kiss anyone except if she's engaged or something? It's so hard to try to think what to do, when here we are with the whole world falling around our ears and you think . . . well . . . you don't know what's going to happen tomorrow and . . . What do you think?

PETER—I suppose it'd depend on the girl. Some girls, anything they do's wrong. But others . . . well . . . it wouldn't necessarily be wrong with them.

The carillon strikes nine. Anne, without budging, says she must go. At last starting for the door, she suggests that she might bring her diary along the next time. "Although," she adds, "I wouldn't want you to see some of it. I thought you were a nothing, just the way you thought about me." Peter hopes she has changed her mind. Anne still hesitates, longing for him to kiss her. Nothing happens, so she turns to go. With an awkward grab, Peter manages to plant a kiss on Anne's cheek. In a blissful daze, she leaves the room, sleepwalks to her parents, whom she kisses; kisses Margot, and catching sight of Mrs. Van Daan at the sink, goes to her quickly. Taking Mrs. Van Daan's face in her hands, Anne kisses one cheek and then the other. She then wafts herself to her room. Mrs. Van

Daan stares after her, glances toward Peter's room and gives a knowing "Ah hah!"

The lights dim; the curtain falls.

. . . Anne's voice gives an account of the further difficulties that befell all of them in April, 1944: rats. Rats have carried off some more of their precious food.

Outside, according to Miep, invasion fever grips everyone; while inside, Anne's own world has become much more pleasant. Her after-supper visits to Peter's room have made life more bearable. In a P. S. Anne's voice confesses that she actually lives for each new meeting: "Is there anything lovelier than to sit under the skylight and feel the sun on your cheeks and have a darling boy in your arms? I admit now that I'm glad the Van Daans have a son and not a daughter. I've outgrown another dress. That's the third. I'm having to wear Margot's clothes after all. I'm working hard on my French and am now reading 'La Belle Nivernaise.'"

Scene III

In the middle of the night a few weeks later, Mrs. Frank catches Mr. Van Daan stealing their food. Her screams awaken everyone. Dussel is ready to strangle Mr. Van Daan, and it is only with Peter's help that Mr. Frank is able to separate the men. Never having lifted her voice, never before having been able to fight, Mrs. Frank now turns into an avenging fury. The unforgivable sin is that Mr. Van Daan has stolen food from the almost starving children. Mrs. Frank orders the Van Daans out of the Annex forever. She's ready to give them money, her own money, to have them leave. Mr. Frank can't cope with her; he has never seen his wife like this. Mrs. Van Daan recalls what her husband did for Mr. Frank. Mrs. Frank, adamant, continues to count out her money, snapping: "If my husband had any obligation to you, he's paid it, over and over." "You can't be nice to some people," says Dussel. "There would have been plenty for all of us, if *you* hadn't come in here!" Mrs. Van Daan screams. His head in his hands, Mr. Frank says: "We don't need the Nazis to destroy us. We're destroying ourselves."

Anne, terribly upset, rushes to the defense of Peter's family and of Peter. "He'll stay, of course," Mrs. Frank says. "When I say I must protect the children, I mean Peter, too." But Peter, with newfound dignity, says that if his father goes he will go, too. Anne cries: "I don't care about the food. They can have mine! I don't want it! Only don't send them away. It'll be daylight soon. They'll be caught . . ." Margot too pleads with her mother. Mrs.

Frank compromises by banishing Mr. Van Daan to his room; he must stay out of her sight. They'll send him his share of the food, but he must never again come down to the living room. Dussel at once starts dividing up a sack of potatoes. "Oh, no," Margot cries. "No. We haven't sunk so far that we're going to fight over a handful of rotten potatoes." But Mrs. Van Daan does just that.

Into this atmosphere, Miep brings the news of the invasion. Pandemonium rules. Now everyone hugs everyone else in a wild demonstration. Miep heard the news through the BBC: "They said they landed on the coast of Normandy. . . . British, Americans, French, Dutch, Poles, Norwegians . . . all of them! More than four thousand ships. Churchill spoke, and General Eisenhower. D-Day they call it." Miep then rushes off to tell Mr. Kraler the good news.

Reaction sets in. Mr. Van Daan is engulfed with shame; Mrs. Frank is filled with remorse. Anne hates to think how she has treated her mother. To brighten matters, Mr. Frank pours Mr. Van Daan some brandy: "Here," he says, "here! Schnapps! Locheim!" Mrs. Frank's sobs break in. "When I think of the terrible things I said . . ." Taking her his untouched glass of cognac, Mr. Van Daan assures her: "No. No. You were right." But Mrs. Frank continues: "That I should speak that way to you . . . our friends . . . our guests . . ." "Stop it," orders Dussel, "you're spoiling the whole invasion!"

The lights dim; the curtain falls.

. . . July has come, Anne's voice says, and the invasion seems to have bogged down. Mr. Kraler has to have an operation. The Gestapo found the radio that was stolen, and so, according to Mr. Dussel, it's now just a matter of time till they get to them. Everyone is depressed. . . . "Even poor Pim can't raise their spirits. I have been downcast myself . . . but never in despair, I can shake off everything if I write. But . . . and that is the great question . . . will I ever be able to write well? I want to so much. I want to go on living even after my death. Another birthday has gone by, so now I am fifteen. Already I know what I want. I have a goal, an opinion—"

Scene IV

The curtain rises. It is Friday, the fourth of August. Everyone is keyed to an unbearable tension. Miep hasn't been near them in three days. Today, not a man came to work. Downstairs, the telephone has been constantly ringing. All Mr. Frank can say is: "If we wait patiently, quietly, I believe that help will come."

Under this pressure, the Van Daans once again are hurling accusations at one another. Mrs. Van Daan is hysterical.

Anne has gone to Peter's room to try to console him. She calls his attention to the lovely day she can glimpse through the skylight, but he lies unconsolable on his bed. Anne so wishes that he had some sort of religion . . . "Just to believe in something. When I think of all that's out there . . . the trees, and flowers, and seagulls . . . when I think of the dearness of you, Peter . . . and the goodness of the people we know—Mr. Kraler, Miep, Dirk, the vegetable man, all risking their lives for us every day . . . When I think of these good things, I'm not afraid any more. I find myself, and God, and I—" Peter bursts out: "That's fine! But when I begin to think, I get mad! Look at us, hiding out for two years. Not able to move! Caught in here like . . . waiting for them to come and get us . . . and all for what?" Anne's philosophy does not comfort Peter. She goes to him.

ANNE—I know it's terrible, trying to have any faith . . . when people are doing such horrible— But you know what I sometimes think? I think the world may be going through a phase, the way I was with Mother. It'll pass, maybe not for hundreds of years, but someday . . . I still believe, in spite of everything, that people are really good at heart.

PETER—I want to see something now . . . Not a thousand years from now.

ANNE—But Peter, if you'd only look at it as part of a great pattern . . . that we're just a little minute in the life— (*She breaks off.*) Listen to us, going at each other like a couple of stupid grown-ups! Look at the sky now. Isn't it lovely? (*She holds out her hand to him.* PETER *stands at the window, looking out, his arms around her.*) Someday, when we're outside again, I'm going to . . .

She breaks off. Everyone suddenly hears the screech of stopping cars. Then the doorbell starts ringing. Mr. Frank goes down the steps quietly, Dussel and Peter follow. The others stand rigid with terror. When Mr. Frank and Dussel return, all realize that what they feared has happened. Mr. Frank goes to a cupboard to get their bags while from below the sound of pounding begins. "For the past two years we have lived in fear," says Mr. Frank. "Now we can live in hope."

Gun-butts start breaking in the Annex door. Peter gives Anne a farewell kiss. Bags in hand, the elder Franks stand together: Anne smiles across at them. The lights dim as a mighty crash is heard.

Scene V

It is again November, 1945. Miep and Mr. Frank have been joined by Mr. Kraler. Mr. Frank turns a few blank pages of the diary. "No more," he says and closes it.

It had been the thief who informed the police, Mr. Kraler says. After a pause, Mr. Frank tells them that Anne had actually been happy in the Dutch concentration camp, happy that she was once again in the sunshine. And the news of the invasion was so good, they all felt that the Allies would reach them in time. But in September they were shipped to Poland: the men to Auschwitz and the women to Belsen. . . . "In January we were freed, the few of us who were left. The war wasn't yet over, so it took us a long time to get home. We'd be sent here and there behind the lines where we'd be safe. Each time the train would stop—at a siding, or a crossing—we'd all get out and go from group to group. . . . 'Where were you?' 'Were you at Belsen?' 'At Buchenwald?' 'At Mauthausen?' 'Is it possible that you knew my wife?' 'Did you ever see my husband?' 'My son?' 'My daughter?' That's how I found out about my wife's death . . . about Margot, the Van Daans . . . Dussel. But Anne . . . I still hoped. . . . Yesterday I went to Rotterdam. I'd heard of a woman there—she'd been in Belsen with Anne . . . I know now. (*He picks up the diary again and turns the pages back to find a certain passage. As he finds it we hear—*

ANNE'S VOICE—In spite of everything, I still believe that people are really good at heart. (MR. FRANK *slowly closes the diary.*)

MR. FRANK—She puts me to shame. (*They are silent. The curtain falls.*)

NO TIME FOR SERGEANTS *

By Ira Levin

Adapted from the novel by Mac Hyman

[Ira M. Levin *was born in New York 27 years ago. He went to Horace Mann, Drake University in Des Moines, and New York University. His first book, "A Kiss before Dawn," was a Mystery Guild selection which the Mystery Writers of America picked as the best first novel of the year. He has written several TV scripts; in fact, "No Time for Sergeants" was first done as a TV play.*

Mac Hyman *was born in Cordele, Georgia, in 1923 and was educated at North Georgia College, Duke University, and Auburn. "No Time for Sergeants" was his first book and he is at present working on another.*]

ON the stage of the Callville Township Meeting Hall, against a backdrop showing their Confederate-Army forbears, the Preacher introduces Callville's favorite son in uniform: Will Stockdale.

After a gangling, shy entrance, and a first false start, Will Stockdale says his piece: How I Won My Medal. "Well," he says, "I didn't *win* it exactly; more like this fellow just *slipped* it to me . . ." It all began, Will tells the audience, when he went into the draft.

He went into the draft very much against his Pa's wishes. His Pa turned his rifle on the Draft Man who came to get him from their mountain shack. Apparently, it wasn't the first time Pa had turned his rifle on the Draft Man.

Draft Man—Are you threatening me with a firearm? I'm a government representative on government business.

Pa—Bustin' up here without sayin' Howdy or nothin' . . . What government?

Draft Man—U. S. Government! The draft board! This boy's been called for the April draft and never reported. He's a draft-dodger! (*He points at* Will.)

PA—Fold in that finger, sir! I'm warnin' you, fold in that finger!

DRAFT MAN (*lowering his hand*)—He can be put in jail for that. He's in tomorrow's group. (*Turning to* WILL.) This is your last chance, and by God, if you don't leave with that group at 7:00 A.M., you're gonna be in more trouble than you ever seen! You already got one offense against you for not answering my letters! . . .

Will wants to go with the man. He doesn't think this draft a bad idea at all, and over his father's protests that city folk will jeer and laugh at him, Will says: "But they *want* me. They even sent a man to come an' fetch me, didn't they? And that ain't all. Last spring I seen this sign out on the sidewalk down there in town. This big picture of Uncle Sam. And '*Uncle Sam* wants you,' he's sayin'—just like this fellow here, Pa, pintin' straight in my face. And don't you think this soldier fellow come up to me right then and there, invitin' me to come along with all the other fellows? I told him how you was ailin' then and would he kindly wait a while. (*Pause.*) You been tearin' up them letters, haven't you, Pa? And you ain't ailin' no more. . . ."

Will says goodbye to his Pa, asks him to say goodbye to his hound-dog when he wakes, and goes off with the Draft Man.

In the town square the inductees are gathering. Standing in front of his bus, the driver who is to run the men to camp hands out forms and takes their draft cards. "Fill it out," the driver calls, "last name first, first name, middle name last. . . . Fill it out. Last name first, first name, middle name last."

Irvin Blanchard, a superior draftee in sunglasses and leather jacket, accepts a form from the driver, but refuses all directions. He knows. As he is filling out the form, Will arrives, handcuffed to the Draft Man. After ordering everyone to stand back and away from Will, the Draft Man transfers the cuffs from his wrist to a gas pump at the side of the square. Will is handed his card and a pencil, and directed to fill it in: "Last name first, first name, middle name last."

The Draft Man asks whether any of the inductees has had ROTC. Irvin had close to a year of it, so he is chosen to head the group and to turn them (and their forms) over to the sergeant at the Classification Center. Warned to keep an eye on Will, whom it has taken two months to flush out of those hills, Irvin swaggers across the square: "You hear what he said, plowboy?" Irvin asked. "I don't want any trouble, you understand?" Will couldn't be more amiable, and offered Irvin his unshackled hand. "Are you gettin' smart with me, plowboy? I don't want to hear one peep out of you. Not a peep!" Irvin snaps. Will resumes his writing.

The Draft Man turns the men over to Irvin: "Do like he tells you an' don't give him any trouble. Callville is proud of her sons in uniform. Show them what kind of men we raise down here. Be good, and if you can't be good, be careful." Intoxicated with his own humor, the Draft Man goes away.

Irvin takes over. "O.K., O.K.," he yells. "Into the bus when I call your name. De Roy, Richard S." "Here," answers De Roy, and goes into the bus. When Irvin reaches the S's, Will answers: "Here," but can't move. After Irvin repeatedly bellows "Whitledge, Benjamin B!" a small, spindly, frenetic fellow runs on.

Waving a pink envelope for the Draft Man, Ben shouts, "I got to find him! I got a letter for him!" Plucking the letter from Ben's hand, Irvin announces he's in charge, and shoves a card at him to fill out. Ben is full of fight. "Don't get sore at Irvin, fellow," counsels Will. "He's had ROTC." Ben, boiling with wrath, refuses to be shoved around by anyone. Trying to be helpful, Will offers to explain to Ben how to fill out his card, giving him his own card as a sample. Ben reads. "Stockdale, Will, Will, Stockdale, Stockdale, Stockdale . . ." Ben, in turn, offers to help Will.

As Ben checks through the list of children's communicable diseases that Will has never had, Irvin is collecting a small crowd to share the reading of Ben's letter.

BEN—Ever break any bones?

WILL—Leg bone once.

BEN—Which leg?

WILL—The right. No, it was the left. Yeh, the left.

BEN (*writing*)—Any member of your family belong to groups planning to overthrow the government by unconstitutional means?

WILL (*thinks*)—No, we're pretty satisfied. (BEN *writes.* WILL *thinks.*) He still limps a mite.

BEN—Who does?

WILL—That fellow whose leg bone I broke. (BEN *looks annoyedly at* WILL, *begins erasing.*) He hit me first. . . .

Ben continues with the questions: "Did you ever have ROTC?" "No," says Will, adding: "Irvin had it—close to a year. I figure he's still got a touch of it in him." Ben explains: "Look, Will, ROTC ain't a disease. It's training. Reserve, Officer, Training—uh—Corporation." Will is full of wonder, Ben, of facts. Says Ben: "There's Cavalry ROTC, Artillery ROTC, Infantry ROTC. . . . Infantry's the best . . ." Will nods wisely, but wants to be sure that Irvin's not sick. He's not sick, says Ben, and what's more, since Irvin didn't finish the course, Irvin doesn't rank them.

IRVIN (*removing glasses and holding up sheet of pink paper*)—"So I beg of you, Mr. McKinney, please get my enclosed letter to the commanding officer in the Air Force."

BEN—Hey, you . . . (BEN *flies at* IRVIN *but the inductees grab him.*)

IRVIN—". . . so that my son Ben will be put into the Infantry the same as his six brothers . . ."

BEN—Give me that! You big—let go of me!

IRVIN—"All his life little Ben has been dreaming of being a real Infantry soldier like all the men in our family." (INDUCTEES *roar.*) Little Ben wanna be a big soldier!

WILL (*loud. Silencing them*)—Irvin! That there letter belongs to Ben. You give it to him.

IRVIN—I told you to keep your mouth shut, plowboy! (*Resumes reading.*) "It will break his poor heart if he's put in the Air Force instead of . . ." (WILL *wrenches his shackled arm free, along with a piece of gas pump.*)

WILL—Give Ben his letter, Irvin.

IRVIN (*a bit pale*)—I'm in charge here. . . . I'm warning you. . . .

WILL—Ben, are you absolutely sure about that ROTC? (BEN, *still held captive, nods;* WILL *hits* IRVIN *a blockbuster. As* IRVIN *collapses,* WILL *plucks the letter out of his hand and gives it to* BEN. . . .)

Will enjoyed the bus trip to camp with Ben: all those big places like Pinehurst and Macon, that it took them half an hour to get through. He enjoyed hanging out the windows and whistling at girls, and those funny cracks from the inductees like "Oh, you kid" and "I want you in my stockin' for Christmas." . . .

At the Classification Center, Sergeant King, a very tired man who is somewhat pained by it all, gives the routine orientation speech, winding up in his sleepy monotone with: "My name is King, K-I-N-G, *Sergeant* King and I'm in charge of this barracks in which you will be billeted for approximately two weeks. During this period the barracks *will* be kept spotlessly clean; maybe it's just a stopping place to you, but to me—*it's home.* Before turning in tonight every one of you will write a letter to your nearest of kin informing them that you have arrived safely and *are in the best of health.* If at any time a problem should arise, feel free to consult me about its solution. (*Opens door of his room.*) I am here to help you during these first difficult days of military service. *Knock before entering.*"

Before Sergeant King can settle down in his homey quarters, with its hot plate, its percolator, and its sampler inscribed MOTHER on the wall, Irvin knocks, and enters, and intrudes.

Irvin has come to hand over the inductees' forms, and to complain about draft-dodger Will Stockdale. King, bored, says he'll make a note of it. Irvin urges disciplinary action for Stockdale because of the swing he took at ". . . one of the men." "In the barracks here?" inquires King. "Back at the bus," concedes Irvin. "I'll make a note of it," King repeats. Irvin can't rest: he feels duty-bound to report this to the squadron commander. Sergeant King freezes: "Any reporting is done around here, I do it." Irvin persists.

KING (*sitting on bed*)—Sonny, look; how long have you been in the service?

IRVIN—About six hours, I guess. I had ROTC, though.

KING—Uh-huh. . . . And they told you it was all efficiency and getting things done and standing at attention and running around? (*Taking off shoes.*) I been in for eighteen years, and it ain't like you think at all. It's a quiet, peaceful life . . . if everybody minds their own business. It's like there's a big lake, nice and calm; I'm in one canoe, you're in another, the captain's in a canoe, the colonel . . . You know what you do when you complain to somebody, or report somebody, or request something? (IRVIN *shakes his head.*) You make waves. (*Puts his feet into big woolly slippers, rises, goes to table, takes cup and saucer from shelf, pours coffee.* IRVIN, *meanwhile, puts handcuffs over forms and goes to door.*)

IRVIN—Well, I thought the captain would want to know if he's got a troublemaker in the outfit.

KING—Look, Sonny. I hate to pull rank, but for your information, you got the smallest canoe in the whole damn lake! Good afternoon, private. (IRVIN *exits, closing door.* KING *stretches out on his bunk.*)

RADIO ANNOUNCER—Our next request comes from Master Sergeant Orville C. King at the Air Force Classification Center. Here you are, sergeant. (KING *beams. The radio plays* "Flow Gently, Sweet Afton" *as* KING *sips his coffee. . . .*)

In the bunk house, Ben and Will are sashaying as to who should have the top bunk and who the lower one. Ben, from the top bunk, rules that because Will was the first to sit on the lower one, it's his:

"First come, first served. That's the military way." As Will politely pulls at Ben's bag, Irvin comes along. "Stockdale!" he yells, "get your hands off that man's things." Wide-eyed, Will pulls back. Not Ben. When Irvin says "If you want to start some more fighting, go after somebody your own size, not some skinny, little—" Ben is hopping mad. "You watch your mouth!" shouts Ben, swinging his feet from the top bunk. Irvin is flustered. "I was only trying to do you a favor, junior!" he says. "Who you calling junior? Who asked you anything anyhow?" Ben snaps. Irvin says: "All right. If that's the way you feel about it, all right. You want to be buddies with the draft-dodger, *be* buddies with the draft-dodger. Go ahead. . . ." "That's the way I feel about it," finishes Ben.

Irvin's followers take cracks at Will on their way to the latrine. Ben is doubly enraged—at their *plowboy* remarks, and at Will's continued amiability. "Taking their insults all day," he berates Will, "and hee-hawing like a danged donkey!" "Ah, they don't mean nothin', Ben," says Will, "and besides, that one about sleepin' with the hogs was kind of funny." Ben disgustedly yanks up his blankets and says, "You think laughin' is gonna stop these guys? A good licking is all they understand." Will thinks this over as Ben turns his back on him.

Taps sounds as Will, in his underwear, is still thinking this over. He sits on the edge of his bunk and is the butt of another inductee crack. This time he laughs half-heartedly. "I reckon," he tells the audience, "Ben knew what he was talkin' about when he said laughin' warn't gonna do no good. But I figgered I couldn't start bangin' away at 'em with no reason so I set around waitin' for someone to give me a reason."

FOURTH INDUCTEE (*passing* WILL)—Ain't used to sleeping indoors, are you, plowboy?

WILL (*to audience*)—I didn't feel as how that was quite enough. (IRVIN *and his two side-kicks return.*)

IRVIN—Get in bed, plowboy.

WILL (*to audience*)—That warn't enough.

IRVIN (*to* WILL)—That is, if you can lift those big clumsy feet of yours.

WILL (*to audience*)—That warn't enough either.

IRVIN (*to* BEN)—Don't wet the bed, Junior, or Mama will spank.

WILL (*to audience*)—That were. (*He slugs* IRVIN *and* IRVIN *goes down.*) No stayin' power at all. (*Other* INDUCTEES *attack.* BEN *hops onto one's shoulders and pummels his head.* WILL *dispatches the others with ease, punctuating the action with the following lines.*) No more muscle than a rabbit. . . . Livin' in town, that's what does it. . . . They stay up till close on ten o'clock every night! Eat all them fancy foods. . . . Orange juice. Won't touch green peas unless the shells is off 'em! . . . Surprises me they got what little strength they have. . . . (*By now all the assailants are floored. They get up and stagger away.* WILL *brushes off his hands.*) But there was a whole lot of 'em, so it was a pretty good fight anyhow! Warn't it, Ben?

To Will's surprise, Ben is more disgusted than ever. He is convinced that this fighting will prevent their being transferred. It's bound to leak out. Will reassures him that he'll clean up on the first one who opens his mouth. Ben lectures him: "Now there you go again, Will! You think they want folks in the Infantry that acts like that? No sir, they want folks who can take it and keep their mouths shut, the way a man ought to do. Transfer? We'll be lucky if they don't transfer us into the Navy—walking around in them li'l ole white uniforms!" Ben tries to make Will understand what they'll be missing: "It's the Infantry does the real fighting . . . the rest is just helpers. Look at the War Between the States. How about that?" Thinking how every man in his family, way back to his great grandpa were in the Infantry, Ben vows that in the morning he's going to present his ma's letter to the captain.

Will tries to make Ben realize that the Air Force isn't that bad. "Bad!" howls Ben. "You know what they call men in the Air Force? Airmen! Like something out of a danged funny book! How you gonna like it when somebody calls you airman?" Will says he just won't stand for it, and that very minute decides to take matters in his own hands. Ben has turned in for the night, so Will, Ben's letter in his hand, gets into some clothes and bangs on Sergeant King's door.

Sergeant King, hearing Will bang, thinks he has overslept. He stumbles into uniform, opens the door, sees Will. "I didn't hear no whistle. Tell the men to line up in back. If the captain comes around tell him I'm checking on who overslept. I'll be out as soon as I . . . (*Looks at* WILL, *looks around, looks at his wrist watch.*) It's ten o'clock . . . at night." "It is?" asks Will. "Ooh!" he adds, "that's the prettiest watch."

The enormity of Will's offense dazes the sergeant. Why did he wake him? Will goes into a rambling request, via Ben's relatives, for Ben's and his transfer to the Infantry. "Why?" the sergeant wonders, "do they send all the bums and idiots to my barracks?" "They do?" says Will. "Yes," says King, "yes, they do." "Sho' must be a mess," sympathizes Will.

Will, starting for the door, happens to mention that Ben said the captain was the one to see. King jumps as if shot, catches Will. "Stockdale," King says, ready to scream, "you're . . . you're . . . You can't *do* this. This captain'll rip off your stripes as soon as look at you." "I ain't got no stripes," Will says. "You'll never get transfers waking him up. He won't understand; believe me, he won't." Will isn't convinced. In utter desperation, King says that for the captain to do Will a favor, Will must first do one for the captain. Almost dragging Will along across the hall, Sergeant King illustrates: "You do one for him, he'll do one for me, and I'll do one for you. That's the way it works in the service."

King guides Will into the latrine. Will ventures it's kind of a big outhouse, but King tells Will that this is kind of the captain's hobby: when it sparkles, the captain sparkles too. Taking a long-handled brush from the wall, the sergeant presents it to Will with the understanding that Will is to be officer in charge. He's not to go away. Will, overwhelmed with pleasure, assures him he'll remain on duty. Sergeant King murmurs an incredulous good-night.

"Well," Will tells the audience, "it just goes to show you how good things happen to you when you least expect 'em. . . ." And he hums at his work, and by morning Sergeant King is amazed. "Beautiful! Beautiful . . . beautiful . . . (*at the commodes*) . . . beau-ti-ful!" the sergeant exclaims.

WILL—Shucks, it ain't hard. . . .

KING (*looks around incredulously*)—Wait till the *captain* sees this! He inspects this place like it was an operating room where they was getting ready to *cut out his heart!* Never in your life have you seen such a man for sticking his head *right down into* things!

WILL—You figger he'll like what I done?

KING—He'll be a new man. . . . (KING *stares some more, then goes to* WILL *and puts his hand solemnly on his shoulder.*) Will . . . how would you like to be . . . permanent latrine orderly?

WILL—Permanent latrine orderly . . .

KING—P.L.O.!

WILL—Golly!

KING—You'll keep this place all the time like it is now, the captain'll get off my back. . . .

WILL—Gee, I sure would like to do it, sergeant. Only I was set on helpin' Ben get those transfers. He's my buddy.

KING—Ain't I your buddy?

WILL—You are?

KING—You help me, I'll help Ben. But don't say a word about

this outside of this room, you understand? I'm going straight over to the Record Section, and fix it with some friends of mine.

WILL—Don't I have to go get them tests you talked about yesterday, to get myself classified?

KING—No, Will . . . (*A final enraptured look at latrine.*) you've been classified.

All week long Will is happy, despite Ben's protests that permanent latrine duty is against the rules. What Will hasn't been able to scrub or polish, he's painted.

On Saturday, the captain is delighted at Will's incredible work. When Will lets slip that this was not a day's work, but a week's, the captain swivels on the sergeant, demanding an explanation. Before the sergeant can wriggle out, Will has given a literal transcription of what the sergeant told him, remarks about the captain included. Sergeant King writhes in agony. Doing his sergeant an extra special favor, Will winds up with: "Sir, you really ought to get up off'n his back." King half dies.

CAPTAIN—How long have you been a sergeant? Speak up!

KING—Sixteen years, sir.

CAPTAIN—How long do you expect to remain a sergeant?

KING (*hopefully*)—Twelve years?

CAPTAIN—You will remain a sergeant for exactly one week. One week! Unless this man completes the entire classification process and is shipped out with the group he came in with. Do you understand? Unless this man is out of here by the end of next week, you will not be in charge of this barracks, you will not be a sergeant; you will in all probability be a permanent latrine orderly. P.L.O.!

He turns on his heel. Sergeant King, hearing Will say that he told the captain all this as a favor to the sergeant, controls himself. Desperate once more, he promises Will if he works hard and gets classified within the week, he'll give Will his watch. Will is mighty pleased.

Sergeant King has been on the job: he's "borrowed" all the tests and stuffed Will with the answers. At the testing center, he's slipped with Will into the Manual Dexterity room. The corporal doing the testing there hands Will two irregular steel links which can be interconnected. The corporal shows Will how, but Will is puzzled. "I put 'em together?" "That's right, you 'put them together,' " says the corporal. "I'll time you. Three minutes is passing." King hovers over Will cheering him on: "At-a boy! Put 'em together!" he yells. The corporal draws King aside, leaving Will to his own devices. Will wrenches open one link, shoves it through its mate, and compresses the whole into a close resemblance of a bowknot. "I'm done," says Will. "Stop the watch!" yells King, but the corporal, taking one look at Will's handiwork, and making one attempt to separate the links, runs screaming into the corridor. Hysterically he asks of another corporal how to mark such a mess. "You're supposed to be grading this," sneers the other corporal. "Can't you do a simple thing like that?"

Sergeant King approaches. Offering to pay for the ruined equipment if Will passes the test, he takes the corporal's arm and leads him off: "Now let's take this logically," he says, "you need some money and I need for him to pass the test. . . ."

Meeting in the Classification Corridor, Ben and Will find that if they both pass the eye test, they will go on to Gunnery School together. Ben's pleasure is marred by his longing for the Infantry. Will's interest in an Air Force indoctrination film leaves Ben cold. "Wait till my brothers find out," he rants. "Airman!"—with which he hurls his cap to the floor.

A passing Negro lieutenant tells Ben: "That's no way to treat government property." Ben snaps to attention, retrieves his cap, tucks in his tie, follows orders. The lieutenant, who is looking for Sergeant King, moves off, leaving Will to gape after him. Irritated at his behavior, Ben wants to know what's the matter: "Don't you know enough to stand at attention and salute an officer?"

WILL (*still gaping after the lieutenant*)—You know, he talked whiter than I do.

BEN—Whiter than you do? Listen, he was an officer, that's all!

WILL—And I'll bet he's a good one, too, so snappy and all. . . . (*Pause.*) I'm homesick. . . .

BEN—Will, when a man's in uniform, he ain't black or white or yellow or nothing! You ain't supposed to notice the color of a man in uniform!

WILL—You ain't?

Ben drives the point home. All Ben saw was a lieutenant. "A colored lieutenant," interrupts Will. "A lieutenant! Can't you understand nothing, Will?" says Ben. "The only thing that's important in the service is rank. If a man's an officer, he's higher than you, even if he's green with purple spots." "Oh, now, Ben . . ." says Will.

Sergeant King, what with his intimate knowledge of the service and sixteen good dollars, has smoothed things over with the corporal. "Well," says King on his return, "it looks like we're just liable to get you classified after all. It goes to show what the Air Force has come down to."

A corporal from the psychiatrist's office brings King a bulletin on Ben: "Psychiatrist says he has a secondary anxiety with inferiority and systematized delusions of persecution." Sergeant King isn't in the least surprised. Furthermore, the psychiatrist recommends that Ben be considered for an Infantry transfer.

Ben, overjoyed, immediately fills out the form. "Soon as he's finished," the corporal tells King, "buck it through to the colonel for approval." "O.K.," says King, "if that's what the crazy kid wants."

The moment has now arrived when Sergeant King finds himself helpless: Stockdale is called into the psychiatrist's office. "Oh Lord," groans King. "Now, Will, listen carefully. The psychiatrist's test is one I couldn't get the questions for because there ain't any. . . . The doctor just asks you whatever pops into his head. So keep your wits about you. . . ."

As the lights come on, the psychiatrist, a major, is at his desk signing papers, with Will seated near him. He looks at Will's form, looks at Will, looks back at the form.

Psychiatrist—Where you from, Stockdale?

Will—Georgia.

Psychiatrist—That's . . . not much of a state, is it?

Will—Well . . . I don't live all over the state. I just live in this one little place in it.

Psychiatrist—That's where "Tobacco Road" is, Georgia.

Will—Not around my section. (*Pause.*) Maybe you're from a different part than me?

Psychiatrist—I've never been there. What's more I don't think I would ever *want* to go there. What's your reaction to that?

Will—Well, I don't know.

Psychiatrist—I think I would sooner live in the rottenest pigsty in Alabama or Tennessee than in the fanciest mansion in all of Georgia. What about that?

Will—Well, sir, I think where you want to live is your business.

The psychiatrist stares at Will, wondering if he realizes what he's said. Will wonders in turn whether the psychiatrist realizes what *he* was saying. This attitude the psychiatrist brands as "resistance": Will must be feeling himself in danger. "Well," concedes Will, "kind of I do. If'n I don't get classified, Sergeant King won't give me the wrist watch. . . ."

A little subdued, the psychiatrist tries again: "You get along all right with your mother?" "No, sir," answers Will, "I can't hardly say that I do." Regaining his confidence, the psychiatrist gets ready for the kill, only to learn that Will's mother had died when he was born. After a long, sick pause, the psychiatrist manages: "You . . . could have told me that sooner. . . ." "Do you hate *your* Mama?" asks Will sympathetically. "I figgered as how you said it was so common . . ." As the psychiatrist hears all the questions boomerang, he consoles himself by saying: "This is a transference." Will, leaping at the word, begs for a transfer to the Infantry along with Ben. "Stop!" says the psychiatrist. He has a few more questions, and brightens up a bit when Will admits to his father's beating him. But it turns out that Will isn't antagonistic to his father—he's merely proud of his father's methods. There's an uncle that Will brings into the picture, whom Will isn't particularly partial to. The psychiatrist's not interested.

The question of girls or—as the psychiatrist puts it—of "sex," merely has Will regaling the psychiatrist with one of his father's traveling-salesman stories. "Stop!" yells the psychiatrist. "Stop!" he yells again. "Go!" says the psychiatrist. "Goodbye, you're through. You're normal. Goodbye. Go. Go."

While fretting in the corridor, King corrals Irvin to coach Will for the eye test. He figures that with all the carrots he's fed Will, this additional help should produce results.

Will, coming out of the psychiatrist's office, is still telling the psychiatrist about girls, but catching sight of the Negro lieutenant, salutes him vigorously, and says: "It's been real nice bein' here. We'll sure miss y'all." The lieutenant passes on.

King has just one more pointer to Will: "None of them wisecracks to the eye doctor. Just be nice and polite."

IRVIN (*crossing to* WILL)—He'll be polite, all right. (*Saluting.*) "Yes, sir. No, sir. Been real nice bein' here, sir." You're even polite to niggers, ain't you?

WILL—I don't know what you're talkin' about, Irvin.

IRVIN—That lieutenant, that's what.

WILL—Was the lieutenant . . . colored? (*Glances at* BEN.)

IRVIN—What are you, blind?

WILL—I didn't notice whether he was black or white or what. (*Glances at* BEN.)

KING (*looking at* WILL *with dawning horror*)—You . . . didn't . . . notice . . .

Will—I don't notice *no color*. He might've been black or white or yellow or even green with purple dots; it's all the same to me. All I seen was the uniform. I never notice color nohow.

Will is called to take his eye test; King is sunk. Ben tears up his infantry transfer, saying: "I changed my mind!" and goes off. King is left outside the oculist's room with Irvin, who brings no comfort. "I get all the nuts!" wails King. "Now what am I going to do with *that* one? If he's color-blind, Gunnery won't take him, and if they won't take him, nobody'll take him. I'm going to be permanent latrine orderly . . ." "Unless," says Irvin, "Stockdale gets into some real trouble."

Irvin sells King on the idea of inviting Will to the Purple Grotto, to get him to have a few drinks and see what happens. King thinks this a pretty stinking idea, but to get the captain off his back, he agrees. "Yeah, I guess we better. . . . Tell you one thing though, Irvin . . . I'm glad I didn't think of it."

At that sink of iniquity, the Purple Grotto, King and Irvin ply Will with a huge glassful of mixed liquor. Will is fine, and thinks of heading back to the barracks. "With the colonel coming," Will says, "the place has got to be fixed up special."

To prevent him, King gets unsteadily to his feet and gives Will his watch: "My mother give it to me . . ." he manages, ". . . to Will Stockdale because, because—because I'm proud of him for doing such a good job getting classified and cleaning the latrine and all. . . ." Touched, Will toasts the sergeant: "The best danged sergeant in the whole danged Air Force!" A few gigantic drinks later, Will does the unusual and invites a startled drunken infantryman to their table. It's not long before drunken service squabbling breaks out between Irvin and the Infantry. Irvin brags that the Air Force sergeants are tougher than Infantry ones. Sergeant King thereupon has to prove himself. Once started, the fighting quickly gathers momentum. In the midst of the ensuing riot, Will taps King on the shoulder. "Go on away!" yells King while strangling a stranger, "you're drunk—" "No I ain't," says Will. "My fingers is a mite tingly but—" "Go 'way!" yells King, above the noise of crashing bottles and wailing sirens.

Not wishing to be a spoilsport, Will returns to barracks to prepare something special for the colonel's inspection. Sergeant King misses the inspection and Ben takes over. Will returns to the latrine to be sure his gadget's working.

Ben tells the captain and the colonel that the barracks are ready for inspection. "All right, all right . . ." says the captain. "Sir (*to the colonel*), before we go any further, I'd like you to take a look at this latrine. There's a man in this barracks whose latrine work is quite surprising."

In goes the colonel. "Ten-shun!" cries Ben. Down bangs Will's foot on his gadget, up fly all the toilet seats, clattering, banging, quivering at attention. The officers recoil but then come back for another look. The captain, in a daze, would like to know just what this all means. Told that it's a form of welcome, the colonel takes it in the proper spirit. "It's all right, captain," says the colonel, "I've been welcomed in many ways; with ticker-tape, with waving flags, the women of a French village once threw rosebuds at me. . . . But this . . . this . . ."

When the captain and the colonel depart, King totters in. A bruised, battered, ragged wreck, he gains the latrine without being observed.

Stumbling on the treadle board, King causes a horrendous noise of clattering toilet seats just as the officers return. Will can't prevent the captain from opening the door to the latrine and discovering King in shreds.

The colonel, after one look, ordains that King be shipped out at once. The captain plucks King's sergeant stripes from his arm and drops them to the floor. Yelling "Private!" he marches off, intending to give everybody as many black marks as possible.

"You ain't a sergeant no more," says Will. "No, I ain't a sergeant no more! I'm a private—a forty-five-year-old private!" answers King. He has one bit of hope left, however: to be shipped to Gunnery School, a thousand miles from Will. But this hope also fades. Will and Ben are going there—they've been classified for Gunnery. They can all be buddies, says Will. "Buddies!" yowls King, in a voice full of hate. After all, Will answers, didn't King give him his watch; didn't he put him in charge of the latrine? "Oh my God," cries King, and appeals to Ben. "Cleaning the latrine," Ben explains, "isn't a good job, Will. It's the worst job there is. It's a punishment job."

Will slowly unfastens the watch. King is uncomfortable, but he accepts it. His parting shot is to Ben: "You glad now you tore up your transfer?"

Will is heartbroken that Ben should have done that for him: "I'll make it up to you, honest I will, Ben." But Ben goes off to pack. Will looks out at the audience: "I didn't realize . . . honest . . . I was just . . .

ACT II

Will briefs the audience on happenings at Gunnery School where he and Ben, having finished the two lowest in the class, are happily together again. But King, having passed those tests at the very top of the heap ("The instructors said they never seen nothing like it. It was just as if he had copies of the tests before they were given them. . . .") was rewarded with stripes and made General Bush's orderly.

On the airstrip, a medium-sized plane—complete with mounting ladder—awaits the worst crew on the base. The officers, too, were apparently taken from the bottom of their class. As they await their tardy officers, Ben declares furiously: "All other planes got off on time except ours. These officers are a disgrace to the Air Force."

They are indeed the sleepiest, sloppiest, blankest group of officers in the Air Force. The pilot, Lt. Bridges, comes on, weaves right past the plane, and has to be pulled back. The engineer, Lt. Kendall, hasn't quite got the hang of putting on a parachute yet. The co-pilot, Lt. Gardella, when approached by Will for permission to visit him up forward, says: "Sorry. Only crew members allowed on board." Will tells him he's been a member of the crew for the past two months. "I *knew* I'd seen you some place," says Gardella as he enters the plane. Next a scurrying, busy little fellow, loaded down with map, sextants, slide-rules, etc., bustles up the ladder, oblivious of Will's salute. "He's the serious one of the bunch," remarks Will about navigator Lt. Cover.

A very efficient Sergeant King, complete with stripes, armband, and clip board, comes on: "All right," he barks, "get this plane off on the double." "We can't," says Will. "Everyone ain't here yet. The radio operator and the front gunner." "You heard me, get moving," says King with sergeant-like toughness.

Up in the wild blue yonder, around three in the morning, the plane's running lights blink rythmically while the pilot sleeps. The co-pilot sleeps. The engineer sleeps. Only Lt. Cover works; he, at six different instruments at once. Will, back in the gunner's tail, suggests a game of mumblety-peg to Ben who turns it down to continue reading his comic.

With nothing much to do, Will decides to go up front, where he momentarily wakes everyone up. On his return he visits Cover, whose harassed activity he watches with great interest.

Cover takes to the intercom: "Navigator to pilot, navigator to pilot. Over." Lt. Bridges answers: "Pilot to navigator. Fred, I wish you wouldn't call me once we're off the ground. Over." Lt. Cover would just like him to know that they're heading for Mexico, that's all. "Now Fred," says Lt. Bridges, "everything is automatic and you know it. Every time we go off on a mission you start fussing with those maps and things, and all you do is to confuse everybody." But not wanting to be mean, Bridges extends his toes to the control panel and gives a little push and moves them up ninety degrees: "Are you happy?" he says. "Over and out."

On Will's return to his post, Ben—his nose in his comic—crabs that they're taking an awful long time getting to Denver, Colorado. Says Will, in defense of the officers: "They're about as good a crew as you can find, when they're sober like this."

The plane continues through the night with sporadic outbursts from Cover: "We're over the Gulf of Mexico, you idiot," he shouts to Bridges.

BRIDGES—Now, Fred, how can we be over the Gulf of Mexico when there's a city below us half the size of New York?

COVER—You want to come back here and check the maps? I figured our position by dead reckoning and we're smack-dab in the middle of the Gulf of Mexico!

BRIDGES—Well, by God, I can see, can't I? I can look right out the window and *see*, can't I?

KENDALL (*taking earphones, partially awake*)—Engineer to pilot. Are we lost again?

Now a little more awake, Kendall realizes with some surprise: "Heh, fellows, number two engine is dead."

GARDELLA AND COVER—Oh Lord!

BRIDGES—Prepare for landing!

COVER—This is *not* a seaplane!

BRIDGES—Cover, will you please look out the ever-loving window. What do you think that is down there?

GARDELLA—Wait a minute, wait a minute! That gunner fellow said he was going to watch from the blister. . . . Co-pilot to rear gunner, co-pilot to rear gunner, over. Co-pilot to rear gunner. . . . (*A red light blinks in rear of plane.* WILL *goes to it, takes earphones.*)

WILL—Howdy. Over.

GARDELLA—Hey, you seen anything below that might've been a body of water?

Will—No, sir, I ain't seen nothin'. I been sweepin' up.

Bridges—What the hell's the radio operator doing? Pilot to radio operator, pilot to radio operator, over.

Gardella—Co-pilot to radio operator. Over.

Cover—Navigator to radio operator, over.

Will—Rear gunner to everybody. Radio operator missed the plane. Over.

Bridges will settle for anyone on the damned radio. Between Ben and Will, they man it. "Watch out!" shouts Kendall, "those are mountains there!" "Pull up! Pull up! *Pull up!*" shouts Gardella. "How do you pull up with only one engine, Mr. Rickenbacker?" demands Bridges. "You're the pilot, Mr. Lindbergh," Gardella replies.

Will finally gets the radio to work by spitting on it. It lights up. Ben tells him to keep saying hello until he gets an answer, but be careful because it might be the enemy. "What enemy?" asks Will. Ben doesn't know but wants him to be careful anyway.

In a sandbagged bunker, General Pollard and party, including a visiting senator, are about ready. The senator hears an airplane. "My dear senator," says General Pollard, "a plane couldn't conceivably slip in here unless they had Lindbergh for pilot and Rickenbacker for co-pilot. Ha ha ha. When General Pollard is in charge of an operation, safety is the prime consideration. You can mention that in your report to your committee if you'd like." The senator is ushered off.

Over the radio come strange sounds, like someone spitting. Will's voice can be heard asking if anyone's there. Pollard is there and answers: "This is Command Post, Operation Prometheus. Are you in . . . an airplane?" "Sure are," answers Will.

It's too late to stop the detonator; Pollard advises: "You're right over Yucca Flats! Now listen to me, you turn that plane around and go right back where you came from! This minute!" The lieutenant points out that the plane is heading right for the tower.

Ben refuses any orders that don't come from General Bush. Pollard gets a line through to "that idiot," and at zero minus two, the call gets through. The two generals yell at each other. "Shut up and listen!" shouts Pollard, "I'm trying to re-establish radio contact. What kind of idiot radio operators did you *put* in those planes?" "What kind of idiot operators," says Bush to King, "did you *put* in those planes?"

The radio spits to life, and General Pollard holds the mike for General Bush's telephone message. Will gives his name over the radio; Sergeant King makes for the nearest exit and is stopped by General Bush. Will, at Ben's instigation, demands solid identification from General Bush. Sergeant King yells frantically: "Tell him Sergeant King will give him his watch!" That's good enough for Will, and twenty seconds before zero Will tells Bridges to reverse their course. In the radarscope, General Pollard sees them turn, then turn again, and then again turn right at the tower. As Bush and Pollard blame each other over the phone, the lieutenant counts. He reaches zero. There is a blinding flash of light and a thunderous explosion. Everything goes black.

High in the predawn sky, Will, holding Ben by the scruff of his neck, floats down in a parachute. Ben is sore as he can be that they left their posts. He feels they are deserters and would rather be a dead hero than a live deserter any day. "I ain't gonna drop you," says Will stubbornly, "no matter *what* you say."

Back at the base, General Bush is about ready to award medals to that band of battle-hardened air aces who challenged the power of the atom bomb. Two medals are to be given posthumously to Privates Stockdale and Whitledge, whose bodies Sergeant King identified from a heap of dust. General Bush, hoping that he won't choke on their names, is determined, once things quiet down, to send the whole battle-hardened crew to Iceland.

On this solemn occasion the grandstands are packed: General Bush has made sure of an audience by canceling all soldiers' leaves. The base is swarming with reporters, and there are two senators in the reviewing stand.

Then Will and Ben walk into the general's anteroom. Before they can give themselves up as deserters, the general dresses them down for failing to be dressed up on the proudest day in the base's history. "What squadron are you in?" snaps the general.

BEN—The ninth squadron, sir.

BUSH—The ninth! Stackpole and Whitehead's own outfit. . . !

WILL AND BEN (*coming to attention and saluting*)—Stockdale and Whitledge, sir!

BUSH—Well, whoever they were. By God, you're going to stay right here until I finish the ceremony and then we'll see if we can put a little decency and *esprit de corps* into you! I don't want our visitors to get even a *glimpse* of you! Dirty uniforms, today of all days! (*He goes out.*)

WILL—Well, we turned ourselves in. I *think* . . .

Andy Griffith, Howard Freeman, Myron McCormick, Royal Beal ar

oddy McDowall in "No Time for Sergeants"

Ben, sulking, goes back into the anteroom, picks up a copy of *Time* and prepares to wait. Will follows him. To Ben's shocked surprise, he finds Lt. Bridges' picture on *Time*'s cover.

Sergeant King comes into the general's office next door, and settles down at the general's desk with his shoes off and his feet up. He's prepared to spend a peaceful hour listening to the broadcast of the ceremonial tribute to Stockdale and Whitledge.

Through the door, Will and Ben hear the broadcast, too. "We are heroes, Ben," cries Will. "But," Ben points out, "we ain't dead." And Sergeant King, now confronted by Will and Ben, repeats hollowly: "You ain't dead . . . you aint' dead."

When he comes to, the sergeant goes frantically into action: yowls for the lieutenant, tells him the whole sad story, places the men under his care, and rushes out to stop the general from awarding posthumous medals! The lieutenant shoves Will and Ben back into the anteroom with orders to stay there, and not divulge their names.

Sergeant King is too late. When he returns, the gathering staff lieutenants ask what General Bush said. At that moment there is a fearful bellow of: *"I'll court-martial everybody in the whole damn Air Force."* "That's what he said, sir," croaks King.

The general himself, certain that when the story gets out he'll be a ruined man, now totters into the room. He blames Sergeant King for the whole mess.

With the reporters on his heels, the general jumps in desperation at a fresh suggestion of Sergeant King's. Transfer Will and Ben immediately to another base and then let them disappear. General Bush orders one lieutenant to get the proper forms, another lieutenant to have a car brought quietly around to the back—an old car with window shades.

Then Will and Ben are shown in. Greeting them in the style of a department store Santa Claus, General Bush asks for a little cooperation. Ben wants to be court-martialed.

BEN—We deserted when we should've stuck to our posts!

BUSH—Well, accidents will happen, and sometimes . . .

BEN—Throw the book at us, sir!

BUSH (*to* WILL)—What's the matter with *him?*

WILL—He's worryin' he ain't dead.

BUSH—Oh, for pity's sake!

The reporters are clamoring to see the general, as Ben cries grandly: "I'll make a full confession, sir!" The general stalls the reporters while he has Ben rushed to the car with the drawn window shades. He then turns his attention to Will, expecting to clear up the business quickly. There will be no punishment, merely a transfer to another air base.

The word *transfer* sticks in Will's mind; he associates the word with the Infantry; he insists, now, on being transferred to the Infantry. "Out of the question!" shrieks Bush. "Airmen can *not* transfer into the Infantry. Now if you don't get into that car before someone sees you, so help me Hannah, I'm going to have you court-martialed." Will starts to go, then stops: "Excuse me for sayin' it, sir," he says, "but if you done that a whole lot of people would see me, wouldn't they?" "What!" shouts a dazed Bush. He turns to King and says softly: "Every bit of this is your fault, sergeant. If you hadn't sent that plane up with this nincompoop at the radio." Will just reckons that he and Ben will stay right where they are unless they go into the Infantry.

Sergeant King promises Will his watch; General Bush promises Will his watch if he'll only give up that idea. Will refuses. "You're asking the impossible, Stockdale!" shouts the general. "It would take an act of Congress! Absolutely impossible!" (*Blackout except for a light on grinning* WILL.)

Will steps forward and tells his audience: "Now *you* know, when you put your mind to it there ain't *nothin'* impossible. General Bush, he got the reporters in there and told 'em about how it was such a proud day in the history of the base and all like that, and then the reporters left and him and Sergeant King let me out of the closet. . . . And then General Pollard come over and him and General Bush talked some . . . argued, you might say . . . well, what it was was cussin'. All I said to General Pollard was "Howdy" and he knowed who I was right off. He did. Then he left and the next thing you know, me and Sergeant King was all pilin' into his great big car. With window shades. And did we drive! Till after dark and then some . . ."

In a clearing in the woods, in the dead of night, General Bush has pitched camp. There are guards, sentries with passwords and orders to shoot, and a tent with a corporal typing away by the light of a lantern.

Except for the slight mishap of General Pollard's forgetting the password, and almost getting shot, things are all set: Ben is removed from the locked trunk of General Bush's car, and the generals go into the tent prepared to do their bit. "We are in trouble, Vernon," General Bush tells General Pollard, "clear up to our pensions. Now come on, sign those papers."

This last minute of his life—as he supposes—Ben takes time to forgive Will. Then on Sergeant King's orders, he marches straight and alone into the tent to sign everything in triplicate.

Sergeant King says his farewells to Will, throwing in his watch to square everything once and for all. The generals re-emerge.

BUSH—King, what's the matter with that Whitledge? He keeps saying he's sorry he has only one life to give for his country.

WILL—He figgers you brought us here to get shot, sir.

BUSH AND POLLARD (*they look at each other speculatively*)—Ridiculous. All these witnesses, Vernon. . . . All right, Stockdale, I've just got a couple of letters for you to sign and then we'll be through with this mess. This one is to your folks, saying that you're on a very important secret mission, and this one certifies that you've never heard of "Operation Prometheus" and have never been on my base in your entire life. Sign here."

Will won't sign. If he signs they get no medals, and he wants Ben to have his medal. It appears to him they're better off dead. A collapsing general agrees to everything Will asks. Bush, having no medals, only ribbons, even manages to get one of General Pollard's medals off General Pollard's unwilling chest. And under Will's happy stage-managing, all corporals, lieutenants, even generals are ordered to attention. This far General Pollard refuses to go. But Will signs now, and Ben is led from the tent.

Sergeant King reads aloud Ben's transfer to the Infantry. Ben's joy is boundless. Sergeant King opens up and wishes he could go along with Will and Ben. No sooner said, than unfortunately done. Will asks General Bush for the sergeant's transfer: it is granted. The sergeant's feeble protests are to no avail: he too is transferred to the Infantry.

General Bush shouts: "Detail, attenshun!" "Damned if I'll stand at attention," repeats General Pollard, sitting cross-armed on his shooting stick. There is a drum roll. "It gives me great pleasure," says General Bush, "to award this medal which through a regrettable error was previously awarded posthumously, to Private Benjamin B. Whitledge, U. S. Army, Infantry." The band on the radio breaks into its closing piece for the night: the national anthem. As the *Star Spangled Banner* reverberates through the woods, General Pollard leaps to attention and salutes.

And that is how Will got his ribbon and Ben his medal.

THE CHALK GARDEN *

By Enid Bagnold

[Enid Bagnold *was born in Kent, England, but spent her early childhood in Jamaica. At 12 she returned to England and went to Prior's Field School, run by the mother of Aldous Huxley. She is the author of "A Diary without Dates," "Serena Blandish," "National Velvet" and "Dear Judas" and her play, "Gertie," was produced in New York in 1952.*]

NEAR an English seaside village there is a country house with a much-worked-over chalk garden that defies its gardener's skill. In the house, things seem to flourish. The living room, with its traces of elegance and culture amid marks of country clutter, looks very much lived in.

At the moment, four chairs in this room, arranged as if for an interview or meeting of some kind, form a cold line. Three of the chairs are empty. On the fourth sits Miss Madrigal, a contained, enigmatic woman. Elsewhere sits another applicant, whose nervousness is in marked contrast to Madrigal's rigid calm. A houseman in a white coat leaves the two women to the mercies of a sixteen-year-old girl named Laurel.

Laurel, wearing rolled-up white ducks, a shirt open at the collar and an astonishing amount of jewelry, and carrying a book, wanders back and forth in front of the women. Her stare borders on insolence and so does her conversation. She refuses the offered hand of the nervous applicant, announcing: "I never shake hands. It's so animal." And as the older woman sinks to her chair in confusion Laurel says: "So one of you has come to look after me? We were expecting four applicants—the ones my grandmother selected from the letters. And now there are only two to choose from. What are your qualifications?" Having already confused the nervous applicant, Laurel adds: "I set fire to things. I am not allowed alone, except in the garden." "Such lovely weather from the garden," the woman murmurs; then determined to carry on, tries: "The advertisement said 'with handicraft.' I am clever with my fingers. I am fond of making pretty things. Now," she adds coyly, "can *you* make a lampshade?" "All the lampshades here are made already," says Laurel.

Having asked her questions, Laurel obligingly supplies information about the household: the family consists of her grandmother; herself; Maitland, the houseman; the terrible old man upstairs, Mr. Pinkbell and his hospital nurse. Mr. Pinkbell was the butler, but he had a stroke. "Who was that then?" the second applicant asks. "That was Maitland," says Laurel. "He wears a grocer's coat. Mr. Pinkbell, and his hospital nurse. Mr. Pinkbell was the butler, but The elderly applicant is appalled there is no one else, but Laurel explains: "Oh, we are rich! If we have only one servant, it is part of my grandmother's newest theory about life. She says true devotion is only to be got when a man is worked to death and has no rival."

After describing the household, Laurel is now only too willing to tell of herself and her parents; of her father whom she saw shoot himself when she was only twelve; and of her mother (who married again for *love*) for whom she has an "adolescent repugnance." Now she turns to Madrigal, all set for further inquiries. Madrigal, however, refuses the opportunity, preferring to wait for the grandmother. When Laurel persists in asking Madrigal what she can do, Madrigal retorts: "What I cannot do is wait much longer."

Maitland, swooping down, first brusquely removes the grandmother's jewelry from Laurel's neck, next removes Laurel. But as soon as the girl is sent out of the room, a decayed beauty, the third applicant, trips in and quickly fires her own set of questions. "Are you the butler?" she demands. "I am the manservant," Maitland answers.

THIRD APPLICANT—A world of difference! In my days it was thought common to wear a white coat. (*Crosses to desk. Picks up and inspects a letter.*) A relic of our occupation in India.

MAITLAND (*following her*)—Will you sit down, please?

THIRD APPLICANT—In those days, in the Hill Stations, I was thought to have extraordinary charm. (*To applicants as she comes in front of them.*) Good morning. How do you do. (*To* MAITLAND.) Is this a house where there are gentlemen?

MAITLAND—I am not to give information.

THIRD APPLICANT—But you have only to nod. (*Moves about, to a table.*) Gardening gloves . . . nicotine for wood lice . . . is your lady going up in the world or coming down? (*To* MADRIGAL, *confidentially.*) One has to be so careful.

MAITLAND (*outraged*)—Mrs. St. Maugham has a house in Belgrave Square!

The third applicant has no intention of applying for the post: she wouldn't think of staying in a house where there wasn't even a nephew, and off she drifts. As for the second applicant, while ostensibly leaving Madrigal alone for her interview, she too vanishes. Maitland anxiously tells the remaining Madrigal: "Don't *you* be flitting! If there's nobody here—after all the advertising—who do you think's going to get the brunt!" As if to herself, Madrigal says that she cannot hope to be acceptable at this first encounter. Reassurances burst from Maitland: "*You* don't need to worry! Madame's up a tree! Today's the deadline. She's got her daughter coming. A shy lady. A nice one . . . Oh, there's wheels within wheels. If you ask me . . . Madame's afraid she'll take the child." Madrigal wonders whether she'd prove suitable, only to have Maitland cry: "*She'll* take you! Madame loves the unusual! It's a middle-class failing—she says—to run away from the unusual!"

Mrs. St. Maugham can now be heard, first calling for Maitland, then for her bottom teeth. Discovering them wrapped in a handkerchief, Maitland presents them to his lady at the garden door, saying: "There's a dentist taken the empty house by the church. *He* might make you comfortable!" "I've tried all the dentists," says Mrs. St. Maugham, her back turned as she fits in her teeth. "You can't fit false teeth to a woman of character. As one gets older and older, the appearance becomes such a bore." The old, overpowering, one-time beauty sees Madrigal and promptly expresses her displeasure that there are not four waiting applicants. But immediately thereafter, with the ribbons of her garden hat untied, her old professional charm switches on and she asks the respectful Madrigal to be seated. "Now what questions do total strangers put to one another?" asks Mrs. St. Maugham.

MADRIGAL—The name is Madrigal . . . I am the daughter of the late Ronald Bentham Madrigal, Rajpootnah Hussars, Indian Army. He was the son of General Bentham Madrigal—the Honorable East India Company.

MRS. ST. MAUGHAM (*gaily; takes off scarf and gloves and drops them into a small basket at her feet*)—No, no! *That* you can't be! The Honorable East India Company was dissolved in 1860! I'm an expert! My great-grandfather was Tarr Bethune, Governor of Madras, tried for corruption in 1859, and found guilty!

MADRIGAL (*calmly*)—My grandfather had my father at the age of seventy-five.

MRS. ST. MAUGHAM—*That* might make it possible. What experience have you?

MADRIGAL—I have small private means. I have not taken such a post before.

MRS. ST. MAUGHAM—Why do you apply to me?

MADRIGAL—The advertisement attracts me. I have been somewhat alone.

MRS. ST. MAUGHAM—You will be able, I suppose, to give me references?

MADRIGAL (*coldly*)—That will be difficult.

MRS. ST. MAUGHAM—What?

MADRIGAL—In fact, impossible.

Interrupted by Mr. Pinkbell's nurse come to complain: "Our breakfast tray was late again," Mrs. St. Maugham dismisses her, saying: "One can't have everything," and picks up the threads of the interview. "Ask *me* questions, Miss Madrigal," she requests. Madrigal wishes to know if she will have a room of her own. "Life without a room to oneself is a barbarity," says Mrs. St. Maugham, but immediately draws a cry of frustration from Maitland when she adds that a tray with Madrigal's evening meal will be served in that room. "It can't be done!" shouts Maitland. "Ma'am," Mrs. St. Maugham interjects. "Ma'am," adds Maitland. Then asked why, Maitland retorts: "Because I shall be busy serving at Madame's table." "I hear the telephone," answers Mrs. St. Maugham. The telephone interruption prompts Madrigal to announce: "I don't answer the telephone." It disturbs her to join two worlds—"the outside . . . and the inside one."

Maitland relays a telephoned request that Mrs. St. Maugham open the village Summer Festival. Mrs. St. Maugham first wishes to find out what attendance they can promise; the last time she opened something there was no one there. Maitland tells her: "Madame is so unpopular." Asking for her engagement book, and ignoring the fact that it is last year's, Mrs. St. Maugham vaguely leafs through it as she describes to Madrigal what it is like to live in a village. "In a village one is down to the bones of things. When I was at my height—though I lived here—I never knew them! They were waiting for my old age like wolves, it seems! Tell them I *won't* open it." And she returns the empty book to Maitland.

Back once more to the interview, Madrigal tells of the handicraft she has done: she had ornamented a chapel by painting twining plants on the altar candles. "But," exclaims Mrs. St. Maugham, "as the candles burnt down the painting must have melted away!" "That was the beauty of it," answers Madrigal. She asks: "Is this a quiet house?" Mrs. St. Maugham answers firmly: "Absolutely," as wild screams come from the garden, and Maitland bursts through the pantry door, garden-bound.

With a quiet, fond look in the direction of the screamer, Mrs. St. Maugham asks if when Laurel talked to Madrigal she mentioned the suicide of her father, and appears quite delighted that she had. Actually, Laurel's father died of his liver. "Oh, I *knew* there would be *something,*" says Mrs. St. Maugham. "She has a need for fantasy."

MADRIGAL (*as though it were a foible*)—She does not care for the truth?

MRS. ST. MAUGHAM (*while arranging flowers*)—No. But I encourage her. She loves a small limelight! One must be tender with her. Alas, he *died* when she was three. Rich and a fine estate. Four Van Dykes and unique Sheraton furniture. (*Bitterly.*) Her mother's one success . . . But why speak of it! She married again."

Mrs. St. Maugham is loathe to think of her daughter's arrival: ". . . I have an unworldly daughter! She was always crying out after to be simple. Privilege and power make selfish people—but gay ones. It seems such a waste, with all the chances of life, to want to be simple . . ." She quickly apologizes for introducing this personal note into the interview, and Madrigal, just as quickly, changes the subject back to Laurel.

Mrs. St. Maugham can't say how Laurel feels towards her Colonel stepfather, but is delighted to tell of the girl's interesting "mother-hatred." Asked if she is able to cope with such things, Madrigal answers dreamily: "For the worse . . . or the better," drawing Mrs. St. Maugham's sharp comment: "You seem to be absent in mind!" Pulling herself together, Madrigal says: "Not in mind . . . But in manner. Your granddaughter is naturally alienated—that a sex life has broken out again in her mother."

MRS. ST. MAUGHAM—You put it well. Exactly. The child was frenzied. (*The house phone rings.*) When nothing would stop the wedding—she ran from the hotel into the dark . . .

MADRIGAL—There seems to be a bell ringing.

MRS. ST. MAUGHAM (*getting up and talking as she crosses to house telephone*)— . . . and by some extraordinary carelessness she was violated in Hyde Park at the age of twelve. It has upset her nerves. We are waiting, as it were, for calmer weather. . . . You want me, Pinkbell? One moment . . . (*Hand over phone.*) Of course we put it less strongly to her mother. Apart from certain fixations connected with fire, she is a charming, intelligent girl. (*Into phone.*) *What's that!* (*Listens.*) *I did.* I ordered it. The Extract of Humus—for the seed boxes. (*Listening.*) It should have come. I'll ring. I'll ring and ask him. (*Is about to put the receiver from her but is recalled by the voice. In despair.*) *I know!* I know! But one can't get perfection, Pinkbell! (*Replaces receiver on hook. To herself.*) Oh . . . Isn't *jealousy* terrible!

MADRIGAL (*with surprising force*)—YES.

MRS. ST. MAUGHAM (*gets small silver handbell from small table*)—You made me jump! He's my butler. Forty years my butler. Now he's had a stroke but he keeps his finger on things. (*Rings handbell.*)

MADRIGAL—He carries on at death's door.

MRS. ST. MAUGHAM—His standards rule this house.

MADRIGAL (*absently*)—You must be fond of him.

MRS. ST. MAUGHAM—Alas, no. He trains Maitland—but now Maitland won't go near him. But I shall overcome it. He's so good with the garden. (*Rings bell again.*)

MADRIGAL—Maitland?

MRS. ST. MAUGHAM—Pinkbell. He directs mine from his window. All butlers dream of gardening. We spoke of references? Who will speak for you?

MADRIGAL (*in her singsong voice, staring above* MRS. ST. MAUGHAM'S *head*)—No one will speak for me— Extract of Humus is too rich for summer biennials.

On Maitland's return from the garden, Mrs. St. Maugham finds that the bag of Humus was delivered days ago, and Maitland has ignored Pinkbell's orders to report everything that comes to the back door. "I won't take orders from the old bastard!" cries Maitland. "Am I to have trouble with you, Maitland?" says Mrs. St. Maugham. "Oh, if I could please and be sure of myself," Maitland wails. When he continues, "Oh, if things would go smoothly!" Mrs. St. Maugham deliberately orders crème de menthe and two glasses. Although ready to burst, Maitland rushes to obey. "Touch and go!" cries Mrs. St. Maugham. "How frail is authority."

Asked to explain her remark about summer biennials and Humus, Madrigal intones: "Don't pep up the soil before birth. It leads them on to expect . . . what life won't give them." Mrs. St. Maugham now asks the name of the plant Madrigal painted on the candles. With eyes fixed on some distant point, Madrigal answers: "Lapagaria. Sub-tropical. With waxy umbels." Mrs. St. Maugham wonders where she learned about such things. Madrigal says: "I was put in charge of . . . a garden."

Once again the correct servant, Maitland enters with the crème de menthe on a silver tray, but he brings his notice, too. Mrs. St. Maugham's eyes become steely as she warns him that if she accepts his notice he won't be given it back. Outbluffed, Maitland promptly collapses. He can't stand criticism. Every time a word is said against him, a month's work is undone. And as Mrs. St. Maugham says that everyone makes mistakes, Maitland passionately cries: "But nothing should be said about them! Praise is the only thing that brings to life again a man that's been destroyed!" Amid his pacing about and talk of leaving, he thinks about her need for him, and as Laurel screams again from the garden, Maitland rushes off to her, crying, ". . . and what will the child do!" Crowing that Maitland will never leave her, Mrs. St. Maugham admits to getting pleasure from his scenes. She writes them off as the result of five years in prison. Startled, Madrigal wonders whether she had no objections. "Now that there are no subject races," replies Mrs. St. Maugham, "one must be served by the sick, the mad and those who can't take their places in the outside world. . . . And served I must be."

Laurel joins the ladies, and quickly shows Madrigal what a doting grandmother she has made of Mrs. St. Maugham. "Freedom is Captain here!" says Mrs. St. Maugham. "Calm is its Lieutenant!" *Calm* seems to be the slippery word. On cue Pinkbell's nurse rushes in with the ominous news that all the lilies have blown down. *"All,"* triumphs the nurse. "And not for want of warnings!" Beside herself, Mrs. St. Maugham dashes out to view the wreckage, while Laurel happily tells Maitland that the lilies blew down because he forgot to stake them. "Oh, are they down!" Maitland rushes to the window. "The nurse told me and I forgot! How the old bastard will be crowing!" "Stake in May," Madrigal says primly. Fiercely asking if this is intended as criticism, Maitland proclaims that he isn't merely the gardener. "I'm everything! I'm the kingpin and the pivot and the manservant and the maidservant and the go-between *and the fire-extinguisher!"* In deeply tragic tones, Laurel explains to Madrigal that Maitland was five long years in prison. Madrigal responds politely, inquiring whether it was Maitland's first conviction. "Conviction!" shouts Maitland. "It was for my ideals! I was a Conscientious Objector." "And didn't you find it trying?" Madrigal asks. This sets Maitland off again on his hideous experience. Having right on his side brought him no consolation: "I went in there because I wouldn't take a life, but before I came out I would have killed a warder!" "All acts become possible," says Madrigal. "What can *you* know of life?" demands Maitland. "True," says Madrigal, "it's been sheltered."

Knowing full well she won't be held responsible, Laurel now downs the crème de menthe. As Maitland rants, Laurel purrs: "What do you expect of me! A child that's been forsaken by its mother!" Retrieving the crème de menthe tray, Maitland turns on Laurel, crying: "That's as may be! That's as those think it to be! I was found in a field but I don't make a fuss about it!" and out he rushes towards the kitchen.

Laurel finally has a chance to interview Madrigal. But it is Madrigal who asks politely what *she* is interested in. Laurel doesn't care to be questioned, and when Madrigal agrees with her, Laurel says she doesn't care to be agreed with in case she might argue. Nor does she care to be read to, unless she suggests it, and if read aloud to, she does not care to have it done with emphasis. Madrigal notes that she must have had lady-companions before, and is curious how Laurel got rid of them. Pinkbell was Laurel's agent, and since her grandmother loved to advertise for the sake of what might turn up, it was easy for Laurel to develop this system of hiring and firing.

Finding Madrigal wonderfully odd, Laurel is curious about her, too: "What life have you been used to?" she asks. Madrigal answers softly: "Regularity. Punctuality. Early rising . . ." Laurel tosses back: "It sounds like a prison!" Madrigal asks: "And what are you used to?" "Doing what I like," Laurel answers.

Hoping that Madrigal knows of her peculiarity, Laurel promises that if she comes to live with them, the two of them will talk for hours and hours about *it,* and about why she hates her mother. "I too hated my mother," says Madrigal. "I should say it was my stepmother." To Laurel, that's the usual kind of hate; hers, on the other hand, is very special.

MADRIGAL—The dangerous thing about hate is that it seems so reasonable.

LAUREL (*unnoticing*)—But you see my mother is Jezebel! She is so overloaded with sex that it sparkles! She is golden and striped—like something in the jungle!

MADRIGAL—You sound proud of her. Does she never come here?

LAUREL—To see me? Never! She's too busy with love! Just now she's in Arabia with her paramour!

MADRIGAL—With her . . . ?

LAUREL—If you pin me down he is my stepfather!

MADRIGAL—How old were you when your father shot himself?

LAUREL—How old did I say I was?

MADRIGAL—I was asking you.

LAUREL—All right. I was three. I can see in your eye that you know. Have you read *Hamlet?* It tipped my mind and turned me against my mother.

MADRIGAL—Does she know you feel discarded?

LAUREL—I don't. I left her! (*Pause.*) The night before she married—she forgot to say goodnight to me . . . Do you think that sounds a little thing?

MADRIGAL (*passionately*)—Oh, no! It lights up everything.

LAUREL—Are you talking of *you?* Or of *me?*

MADRIGAL—When one feels strongly—it is always of *me!*

Feeling at home with Madrigal, Laurel offers to let her in on a favorite pastime—collecting, with Maitland, a crime library of the Notable Crime Series. With a certain difficulty, Madrigal asks just which trials they have. When Laurel tells of her delight in the case records of Mrs. Maybrick, Lizzie Borden, and Doctor Crippen, and of Maitland's preference for murderesses, Madrigal becomes speechless. Asked "Why does the prisoner have so little to say?" Madrigal doesn't answer. Laurel notices: "What a habit you have—haven't you—of not answering." Madrigal brings back her gaze from that far-off point to Laurel, and says in a very low voice: "I made an answer." "Only to yourself, I think," Laurel decides.

Her arms full of the broken lilies, Mrs. St. Maugham sweeps in like a tragedy queen. When things die in her garden she is as upset as when she reads the daily announcements of her friends' deaths. Not bothering to look up from a book, Laurel says: "I should have thought as one got older one found death more natural."

MRS. ST. MAUGHAM (*beginning to sort out the lilies on the chaise*)—Natural! It's as though the gods went rook-shooting when one was walking confident in the park of the world! and there are pangs and shots, and one may be for me! *Natural!*

MADRIGAL (*involuntarily*)—That is why a garden is a good lesson . . .

MRS. ST. MAUGHAM—What?

MADRIGAL— . . . so much dies in it. And so often.

Mrs. St. Maugham—It's not a lesson I look for!

And pushing Madrigal towards the garden door, she instructs Laurel to take her out.

Madrigal doesn't want to go into the garden, doesn't want to stay at all, and doesn't want to waste Mrs. St. Maugham's time—but Mrs. St. Maugham has other ideas. With no intention of keeping her, she wants Madrigal to see the garden so as to get her opinion of it. Once Laurel and Madrigal are in the garden, Mrs. St. Maugham disappears to arrange her broken lilies.

As quickly as possible, Madrigal escapes from Laurel and, returning to the living room, finds a woman standing there. Intent upon leaving the house, Madrigal tells this unknown woman that the post can be hers, but warns her: "Looking at you I wouldn't come here if there is any other post open to you." "Why?" asks Olivia. "Because," Madrigal says, "the child will make hay of you!" "She *has* made hay of me!" says Olivia—Laurel's mother. Begging Madrigal to go once more into the garden with Laurel and to keep her there, Olivia has an answer to Madrigal's protest that she is a stranger: "I know but sometimes one speaks the truth to a stranger. I'm not supposed to see her. First I must see my mother. Please, go out—" Hearing Mrs. St. Maugham call her daughter, Madrigal goes back into the garden.

Mrs. St. Maugham also has plans to keep Laurel out of the way—by having Maitland light a bonfire in the garden. On greeting Olivia, she immediately reveals her prickliness by her veiled criticism of her daughter's sunburned appearance. Olivia brushes this aside, but Mrs. St. Maugham's tone, as she asks about her daughter's trip, is not encouraging. "I flew," says Olivia simply. "I got here this morning." "Like one of those crickets that leap from a distance and fall at one's feet!" adds Mrs. St. Maugham. "How did you do it?" Olivia tells quietly of flying from Baghdad to England for the Refresher Course at Aldershot. "Aldershot!" says Mrs. St. Maugham with marked distaste. "Oh—who would have thought you could have taken on that look—so quickly—of the Colonel's Lady!" Sidestepping a quarrel, Olivia gets to the point of her visit: she has come about Laurel. All Mrs. St. Maugham will answer is: "Did you wear that scarf on purpose to annoy me! What you wear is a *language* to me!" Olivia indignantly recognizes her mother's old tactics, and insists on seeing her child.

Mrs. St. Maugham— . . . and risk the mending of her? Oh—do you think only of *yourself*, Olivia!

OLIVIA—Not of myself.

MRS. ST. MAUGHAM (*rises*)—That is how it has always been. To ask is to be refused! I have asked you not to come—but you *come!* I have asked you to warn me—but you ignore it! (*Turning on her.*) *How* can you wear beige with your skin that color!

OLIVIA—Does it never become possible to talk as one grown woman to another!

MRS. ST. MAUGHAM—The gap's lessening! After fifty I haven't grown much wiser! (*Warming to the indignity.*) . . . But at least I know what the world has to have. Though one cannot pass anything on! When I count my ambitions and what you have made of them!

OLIVIA—*I did what you wanted!*

MRS. ST. MAUGHAM—But how you resisted me! I was burning for you to cut ice in the world—yet you had to be driven to gaiety! I had to beat you into beauty! You had to be lit—as one lights a lantern! Decked—like a maytree!

OLIVIA—Can't we be three minutes together . . .

MRS. ST. MAUGHAM—Even your wedding dress you wore like wrapping paper! Plain, shy, obstinate, silent. But I did what a mother should do. I married you . . .

OLIVIA—But you won't meet the man *I* married—the man I love!

MRS. ST. MAUGHAM—Love can be had any day! Success is far harder.

To her mother's surprise, Olivia talks back; but she is not above begging her mother this *one* time to be on her side, to help her find Laurel again, to help her take Laurel back. "Take her back!" shrieks Mrs. St. Maugham. "What, now? Just now! When I have such a companion for her! A woman too of the highest character! Of vast experience! I have put myself out endlessly to find her!" Arguing that the woman can then prepare Laurel for the time when she will come for her, Olivia says passionately that she cannot bear to have Laurel grow up without ever knowing her, that she must have her before the new baby arrives to claim a share of her love. Full of high-toned bluster, Mrs. St. Maugham describes turning her old age into a nursery for Laurel who came to her of her own free will. "And God," adds Olivia, "has given you a second chance to be a mother!"

As Mrs. St. Maugham glares, and her daughter waits for her next move, Madrigal bursts in from the garden, in full battle regalia. "Mrs. St. Maugham," she cries, *"there must be some mistake! This* is a chalk garden! Who has tried to grow rhododendrons in a *chalk* garden?" Mrs. St. Maugham flounders under this attack, finding refuge with her seed catalogue. Madrigal continues her list of the garden's horrors—pure lime for soil, not even a little leaf mold, and a stone-cold compost heap: *"Nothing in the world,"* she cries, *"has been done for them!"* Pulling on her gloves as she prepares to leave, she ignores a blood-curdling scream from the garden. "Not so fast!" cries Mrs. St. Maugham, frantically searching through the catalogue. "I want to ask you . . . the bergamot . . . and the gunnera . . ." "Won't thrive on chalk," answers Madrigal.

MRS. ST. MAUGHAM—There's an east slope I can grow nothing on.

MADRIGAL—The soil can't give what it has not got. (*Goes to door as* MRS. ST. MAUGHAM *pores over catalogue.*)

OLIVIA (*stops her at door*)—Don't go! The wind blows from the sea here and growing things need protection!

MADRIGAL (*low*)—. . . and the lilies have rust . . . there is black spot on the roses . . . and the child is screaming in the garden.

MRS. ST. MAUGHAM—The *roses!* What would you have done for them! Pinkbell ordered . . . and I *sprayed* them!

MADRIGAL (*turning, magnificent, contemptuous*)—With what, I wonder! You had better have prayed for them! (*They measure each other for a moment. Then very quiet and meaningful she crosses to* MRS. ST. MAUGHAM, *forcing her backwards.*) If you will accept me . . . I will take this situation, Mrs. St. Maugham. (OLIVIA *quietly exits as* MRS. ST. MAUGHAM *sinks into armchair.*) You have been very badly advised—I think—by Mr. Pinkbell.

ACT II

A month later, a much improved Laurel sits by a living room window, absorbed in painting a flower. Nearby Maitland arranges a table for a company lunch. He is happy to give "the Boss," Madrigal, full marks for Laurel's impressive showing: no longer does she try to curdle the blood with piercing screams or burn down the house. Laurel admires Madrigal just as much as Maitland, but neither one can figure out where she learnt to deal so competently with them or with life.

Laurel and Maitland differ only on Madrigal's mysterious past. But since Madrigal arrived with no mementos or revealing possessions, they can't tell whether she is a maiden lady, as Maitland believes, or a woman of passionate experience, as Laurel would like to. Not a letter has arrived, either, to assist their speculations.

Whatever Madrigal's past may have been, her present influence has so spread throughout the house that even Pinkbell has been made to feel it. Laurel is sure that there will be rows. Madrigal has coolly sent back a huge shipment of rhododendrons ordered by Pinkbell. "Whew!" says Maitland, "I'm for Miss Madrigal! I've no mercy on him!" "*Poor* Mr. Pinkbell," croons Laurel. "A man's no better when he's dying," rules Maitland.

As Laurel, ever on the track of clues, cleans Madrigal's paint box, Maitland daydreams about their lunch guest, the Judge, but is interrupted by Mrs. St. Maugham, bent on a feverish last-minute check of preparations.

MRS. ST. MAUGHAM—The green-handled ivory knives . . . !

MAITLAND (*at sideboard*)—Locked away.

MRS. ST. MAUGHAM—And the key of the safe! It's years since I've seen it! We used to have celery with the Stilton . . . and the Bristol finger bowls . . . and those glasses for the brandy.

MAITLAND—They broke.

MRS. ST. MAUGHAM—There was a gold cigar box that played a tune—that King Edward gave me . . .

LAUREL—Is it *gold?* I used to keep a mouse in it!

MRS. ST. MAUGHAM (*frantic*)—Go and get it!

Laurel can't remember where she put it and wonders at all this excitement. Isn't the man who's coming—old? "Puppy?" cries Mrs. St. Maugham. "The *Judge,*" answers Laurel, but her grandmother now is dashing frantically to the window to see what boys dare play cricket outside her house. Then mixing her order for sherry with prophecies about broken windows, Mrs. St. Maugham decrees two wine glasses at each place, though but one wine is to be served. She then countermands her previous directions on how to place the silver. Thoroughly rattled, Mrs. St. Maugham plans to ask Pinkbell for instruction on how things should be. She herself can no longer remember.

Laurel warns her that this is not the time to approach Pinkbell: he is raging against his "enemy," Madrigal, while she is nursing the agapanthus lilies with a diluted cow urine. Treacherously sly, forgetting Pinkbell, Mrs. St. Maugham dashes into the garden to watch Madrigal.

Having got rid of her grandmother, Laurel asks Maitland to look at her latest discovery. Cleaning Madrigal's paint box, she has uncovered three faint initials on the box; Maitland helps her make out a faint *C. D. W.* just as Madrigal enters.

There is an air of excitement in the room over the imminent guest.

Maitland is ecstatic that he is to feed a man with so much power. When Madrigal finds out the guest is a judge, she reacts sharply. "He's here for the Courts," says Maitland. "He's on circuit." Madrigal at once asks his name, but neither of the others knows. "It's in the newspapers," says Maitland, as he carries mustard pot and napkins to the table, "but the old bastard's got them. They are carried up to him. But I have to read them on the doorstep." Unhesitatingly, Madrigal decides that Laurel and she will sit at a separate table for lunch. Maitland's explosion dwindles as with easy flattery Madrigal persuades him to set up another table. "Oh," cries Maitland on his way to the kitchen, "if we had guests oftener! The sense of rising to something!"

Laurel comments: "How you twist him round your finger!" Then she wants to know why she and Madrigal should sit apart from the guest. "It used to be done at luncheon—in the best houses," says Madrigal. Laurel launches her attack: "Had you a life in them?" When there is no answer, she demands: "*Had* you?" Next she inquires: "Who is C. D. W.?" Madrigal is taken aback, but says after a moment: "My married sister," and puts her palette in the paint box and closes it. Unabashed, Laurel asks whom they should write to if Madrigal drops down dead. Madrigal answers firmly: "I shall not drop down dead."

An angry Pinkbell calls Madrigal on the telephone. She is unyielding. "The rhododendrons?" says Madrigal over the phone. "*I* sent them back again. I reversed the labels! And," she says, launching her own attack, "if I could I would reverse everything! And I may yet— We shall see! No, I'm afraid on that you are wrong, Mr. Pinkbell. Your facts are wrong—also your deductions! Yes, and alas it is the wrong time of year to plant them. And the wrong soil. (*Listens.*) Not at all. Don't blame yourself. Amateur gardeners very often make that mistake."

Maitland, overhearing enough of this conversation to become Madrigal's slave, starts by promising: "My God, you shall have two tables! You shall have three if you like! And the breast off both the chickens!" But all this is just the preliminary excitement; for Maitland the main event is still the arrival of the Judge, and the case he is to try. Madrigal tries in vain to keep his mind on the lunch. Loathe to talk about the man on trial, Madrigal finally bursts out: "Why do you think only of the Judge? It's the jury they work on."

MAITLAND—But it seems when you read about such trials that it must be the Judge.

MADRIGAL (*fiercely*)—*Read* more and you'll see it's neither. But fate.

MAITLAND—How can that be?

MADRIGAL—Because, when it starts, there's no free will any more.

MAITLAND (*earnestly*)—But they work, don't they, to get at the truth?

MADRIGAL—Truth doesn't ring true in a court of law.

MAITLAND—What rings true then?

MADRIGAL (*to herself, trancelike*)—The likelihood. The probability. They work to make things hang together. What the prisoner listens to there is not his life. It is the shape and shadow of it. With the accidents of truth taken out of it . . .

Madrigal refuses to satisfy Laurel's unnatural curiosity about trial lore with anything further. Instead she tries to talk to Laurel about reading or painting. But bored, and suddenly taken with an unexpected homesickness, Laurel for the first time speaks of her former home and the little games her mother played with her. Madrigal suggests a plan for the next day: "I will light that candle in the green glass candlestick and you can try to paint that." Laurel is weary of fire. "Let's have a game!" suggests Madrigal. Laurel at once comes to life, ready with a guessing game, and from the glint in her eye, she is in hot pursuit of Madrigal's past.

In spite of her allotted questions, Laurel finds out surprisingly little: Madrigal is too finished a player. The sole information Laurel comes up with is a name for Madrigal's sister—"Clarissa Dalrymple Westerham."

Madrigal, when it is her turn, launches her questions as purposefully as Laurel had: "Was your famous affair in Hyde Park on the night of your mother's marriage?" Says Laurel: "About that time."

MADRIGAL—What was the charge by the police?

LAUREL (*wary*)—The police didn't come into it.

MADRIGAL (*airily*)—Did someone follow you? And try to kiss you?

LAUREL (*off her guard*)—*Kiss* me! It was a case of criminal assault!

MADRIGAL—How do you know that—if there wasn't a charge by the police?

LAUREL (*pausing a second; on a different tone*)—That's one too many questions! *Now* for the deduction!

This, says Laurel—though she had failed to mention it before—is the real purpose of the game. She quickly starts: ". . . That you've changed so much you must have been something quite different. When you came here you were like a rusty hinge that wanted oiling. You spoke to yourself out loud without knowing it. You had been *alone*. You may have been a missionary in Central Africa. You may have escaped from a private asylum. But as a maiden lady you are an impostor. You have had a sex life of fire and brimstone. (*Changing her tone slightly—slower and more penetrating.*) About your assumed name I am not so sure . . . But you have no married sister."

Madrigal, ever so pleasantly, says her deduction will keep, and since Laurel has been good enough to give her so much warning, she intends to go to her room to be sure that she has left no clues unlocked.

Laurel can't wait to tell Maitland how outmaneuvered she had been by Madrigal: "No game would uncover her! But, Maitland—she knows about life!" "What sort of knowledge?" asks Maitland. "Something—intense," confides Laurel. "Something too dreadful. Something cut in stone over her mind—to warn you when you walk in."

In spite of Madrigal's fascinating mystery, neither Maitland nor Laurel wishes to have her horrid past overshadow their own unhappy ones. But there is a difference; there has been a change. Maitland, as if by rote, now mentions his prison term with enormous self-pity, though Laurel is sure that it couldn't have been as dreadful as Madrigal's. Laurel makes a play for Maitland's sympathy along the old lines, but it is Maitland's turn to show a new sort of toughness. He will hear no bad talk about Laurel's mother. Forbidden to talk as she chooses, Laurel decides to revive her former screaming act. "Scream away!" Maitland tells her. "Now we've got the Boss to get after you! Oh, the relief of it!" Laurel notices this sudden toughness. "It comes over me," Maitland admits; "the Right comes up in me. Like when they tried to make a soldier of me. All of a sudden I *see* how things should be!"

A change, too, has come into Mrs. St. Maugham's life. She is no longer only accountable to Pinkbell: she has to smooth things over with Madrigal, too. Coming in with flowers for the room, she encounters Madrigal and tells her that Pinkbell is crying with rage.

MADRIGAL (*calmly*)—I corrected him.

MRS. ST. MAUGHAM—But for forty years Pinkbell has never been corrected! He is the butler who was the standard of all London!

MADRIGAL—Let him take his standard from the garden! I corrected his ignorance of details, dates, fundamentals, application of manure. I spoke—not of his spoons and forks—but of his shallow knowledge of the laws of growth. You can leave the room, Maitland.

MRS. ST. MAUGHAM—That should have been said by me! But—go, Maitland. (*He exits hurriedly.* MRS. ST. MAUGHAM *is severe, majestic.*) Now— *Now,* Miss Madrigal—this is a crisis!

MADRIGAL (*equally severe, majestic*)—Yes. Now you have to make your decision.

Completely taken aback, Mrs. St. Maugham hears that she must choose between Madrigal and Pinkbell. With driving oratory, Madrigal accuses Pinkbell of laxness and worse in regard to the garden. Like a prosecutor, she lists his wrongdoings, and with a sweeping gesture towards the garden she decries: "Out there every corner is crying aloud! Must I be dumb when you and I approach together the time of year when all next summer must stand or fall by us! Have you time—before death—to throw away season after season?"

Immediately Madrigal sweeps out, and Laurel is after her grandmother to do something or she will lose her. At the moment, Mrs. St. Maugham wouldn't lose Madrigal for anything in the world; she'd sooner strangle Pinkbell. Laurel cries: "Go after her! Promise her the earth . . . *Promise her the garden!*" Glancing upwards to the ceiling, Mrs. St. Maugham hesitates. She doesn't know what to say to Pinkbell. "You are not *afraid* of him!" cries Laurel. In a low voice, as she leaves the room, Mrs. St. Maugham admits: "I have always . . . *always* been afraid of Pinkbell."

The Judge finally arrives and proves disappointing, first to Laurel and then to Mrs. St. Maugham. He looks so old and tweedy; then plagued by an allergy to the country's dusts and smells, he puts on dark sun glasses. "But now we can't see you!" Laurel cries. "You will!" the Judge answers. "Twenty minutes will cheat my old nose that we are back at the Old Bailey."

As Maitland hurries out for the food, Mrs. St. Maugham pours some sherry, which the Judge passes up. Laurel sidles over to her grandmother, to find out if she has spoken to Madrigal. "Speak louder," Mrs. St. Maugham orders. "Never whisper. My Laurel," she tells the Judge, "has a companion. A charming woman. Able—but passionate. At war just now with Pinkbell." Still anxious, Laurel leans over her grandmother for reassurance. "The door was closed, Sweet," says Mrs. St. Maugham. "One is not at one's best through mahogany. But I heard no sound of packing."

The name Pinkbell has aroused all sorts of memories for the

Judge: "*What* it brings back!" he says. "What incorruptible ritual! How I remember—after the summer glare of Piccadilly—the young man that I was, crossing your hall . . . like a pawn across a chess-board . . . and how after the first and second footmen, one arrived at last at Pinkbell. *He* stood at the foot of the stairs! The apprehension one had of his sour displeasure. *His* severity, his corklike dryness—later on, when I had to rebuke the public eye, I remembered Pinkbell! My demeanor on the bench is Pinkbell's."

Maitland explodes: "Everything—*now*—is at your service—Madame! *On the sideboard!*" His manner is less, though his volume more, than Pinkbell's. *"Simply. Simply,"* corrects Mrs. St. Maugham. "Times have changed, Maitland!" As Madrigal sweeps in, in pointed silence, Mrs. St. Maugham effusively introduces her to the Judge, but she silently passes them by and as silently looks out of the window. Refusing her sherry, Madrigal, when asked to sit down to lunch, takes her place at the other table. "But why this segregation?" cries Mrs. St. Maugham. "The Boss's orders," answers Laurel, as she sits down at Madrigal's table.

JUDGE (*seating himself; to* LAUREL)—Are you below the salt? Or are we?

LAUREL—Miss Madrigal means this to be the schoolroom.

MRS. ST. MAUGHAM (*seated*)—She is so witty!—Now you can start, Maitland. You can give us your cold chicken. (*To* JUDGE.) I don't entertain any more. The fight's over. Even the table is laid with fragments of forgotten ritual.

JUDGE—Faith is handed down that way.

MRS. ST. MAUGHAM—When Pinkbell is dead we shall not know why we used two glasses for one bottle.

Though the Judge protests at being served wine, feeling that "Alcohol in the middle of the day disperses the old brains I try to keep together," Laurel begs that it be served, and Mrs. St. Maugham tells Maitland to bring forth the bottle.

Madrigal refuses to be drawn into conversation, so Laurel says that she'll listen in on the other table's talk.

MRS. ST. MAUGHAM—You'll overhear the flavor of the past. Life was full of great rules then. And we high women were terrible. Would you have youth back, Puppy? (MAITLAND *serves* LAUREL.)

JUDGE—No. For a man youth *isn't* the triumph.

MRS. ST. MAUGHAM—I'd have it back if I could—even life's reverses! Wouldn't you, Miss Madrigal?

MADRIGAL (*high and sharp*)—You have spilled the salt, Laurel.

MRS. ST. MAUGHAM—I was asking . . . do you think grief tastes more sharply than pleasure on the palate?

MADRIGAL (*startled*)—I beg your pardon . . .

MRS. ST. MAUGHAM—You can do better than that, Miss Madrigal!

Having shown Mrs. St. Maugham the wine, Maitland goes to the sideboard to draw the cork. Hearing that sound, the Judge knows he will have to nap after luncheon. Mrs. St. Maugham is thoroughly startled. "That shocks you?" says the Judge. "In my job old age is part of the trappings!" "One gets old—all the same," answers Mrs. St. Maugham. "Judges don't age," says the Judge. "Time decorates them. You should come and hear me! Learned and crumpled like a rose leaf of knowledge I snuffle and mumble. I sham deaf. I move into court with the red glory of a dried saint carried in festival . . ." Laurel excitedly asks, for Maitland and herself, how the Judge will look as he enters court tomorrow. "In ermine," says the Judge. "In scarlet. With a full-bottomed wig. Magnificent! Seeing me now as I am—(*He takes off his sun glasses with a flourish.*)—you wouldn't know me!" A glass crashes to the floor. Madrigal cries out, then says it was her hand that knocked it. Ready to send Maitland to the pantry for another glass, Mrs. St. Maugham hearkens to Laurel's plea that Maitland hear what the Judge has to say. Mrs. St. Maugham says she forgot: "Maitland has been in prison, Puppy." "Have you indeed?" asks the Judge. "Five years, m'lord," is Maitland's cheerful reply. The Judge hopes it wasn't too unpleasant. "It's given me a fascination and a horror, m'lord, if you can understand," Maitland says, admitting to being "a little stage-struck." "Dear me," exclaims the Judge, "I hope that's not the usual effect. It's supposed to be a deterrent." Maitland is wound up, but Mrs. St. Maugham checks any further oratory by ordering him to fill Miss Madrigal's glass. Laurel demands more wine and more details from the Judge.

As Maitland picks up the broken glass he leaves the bottle on Madrigal's table, and from then on, as more and more of the judicial ritual and trappings are described, Miss Madrigal drinks more and more of the wine.

With his description of his procession to the court, the Judge arrives at the end of his histrionics: "*Then*—garbed and toffed with medieval meanings, obscured by ritual, carrying the gloves of justice and the cap of death—on a hollow knock—*I go in.*"

Mrs. St. Maugham tells Laurel to stop asking questions and to help bring Madrigal into the conversation. But Laurel persists. "Not yet!" her grandmother orders. "I am trying to weave in . . . Oh, whoever invented *two* tables! Can't one *join* them?" "Not across fifty years," says the Judge. "Not the Past and the Present!"

The Judge stiffens as Laurel insists on asking whether he will be trying a murderer tomorrow, whereupon Mrs. St. Maugham delightedly sees a resemblance, in his change of manner, to Pinkbell. But Laurel will not be put off. She and Maitland are mad for murder and the excitement that goes with murder trials: "Isn't it true that to you, Judge, everything is told for the first time?" "In principle," the Judge concedes. "But Miss Madrigal says," reports Laurel, "that the judge isn't even interested! That he sleeps." "I said he *seemed* to sleep," Madrigal corrects her. "With one eye open. Like a tiger," qualifies the Judge.

Mrs. St. Maugham wishes Madrigal to tell her whether she has been to a trial. Laurel breaks in, but Mrs. St. Maugham orders Madrigal to speak for herself.

JUDGE (*to* MADRIGAL, *politely*)—Have you heard me on the bench, Miss Madrigal?

MADRIGAL—When I spoke to Laurel of judges it was in a general sense. (*Pause.*) But I heard you give a judgment.

JUDGE—I hope it was a good one. (*No answer.*) I trust that it was one of my better days.

MADRIGAL—I think, if I remember, that I would not have come to your conclusion.

MRS. ST. MAUGHAM (*to* JUDGE)—Miss Madrigal has such answers to life! (*To* MADRIGAL, *in quite a different tone.*) But *that* was a strange one.

JUDGE—Well, a judge does not always get to the bottom of a case.

MADRIGAL—No. It takes the pity of God to get to the bottom of things.

Mrs. St. Maugham has had enough. Having provided the wine to loosen Madrigal's tongue, she now orders coffee to stop it. But Laurel can't get enough: she wants to know how the Judge feels, whether he suffers when he must determine if a man is to live or die. Madrigal says no one will suffer: "They all go into a dream together!" Laurel pries further, recalling the end of the trial procedure, before the sentencing of the prisoner. "Miss Madrigal says," Laurel continues, "that when all has gone against him—" Wildly, Madrigal shouts: "I am quoted enough!" ". . . that after the verdict," Laurel says, "when he is asked 'Have you anything to say?'—" Madrigal interrupts: "The prisoner is punch-drunk! And says nothing."

JUDGE—Not always. Some have said remarkable things. There comes to my mind a woman. . . . Have you the trial, Maitland, of Connie Dolly Wallis?

LAUREL—Of *whom?* (*Seizes flap of* MAITLAND'S *pocket.*)

MAITLAND (*stammering, disengaging himself*)—I . . . I haven't all the volumes, m'lord. I haven't that one.

JUDGE—It was not one of my successes. But you should read it for what the woman said when she stood before me. It was just before I sentenced her. (*Tilting his head back, looking at the ceiling, fingering his chin thoughtfully.*) Fine eyes, she had. I think I should remember them. A tall woman with a face like an eagle. "What I have been listening to in court," she said, "is not my life. It is the shape and shadow of my life. With the accidents of truth taken out of it."

LAUREL—What was she tried for, Judge?

JUDGE—Murder.

MADRIGAL—I remember the case. A liar! A pathological imaginer! A girl who lied! And lied! And when she told the truth it didn't save her!

JUDGE (*leans toward* MADRIGAL)—Have you been to many trials?

MADRIGAL—One trial. One. But it isn't the duplication—that makes the impression! It's the first time . . . the first time . . . (*A window breaks offstage.*)

MRS. ST. MAUGHAM—Quick, Maitland! *It's the fishmonger's boy! . . . the fishmonger's boy . . .* (MAITLAND *rushes out the hall door followed by* MRS. ST. MAUGHAM.) Catch him!

LAUREL (*to* JUDGE)—Did they hang her? (JUDGE *slowly rises and looks at* MADRIGAL.) Did they hang her?

ACT III

As much as the Judge would like to sleep after lunch, he is constantly prevented from doing so. The first intruder is Laurel, who, not having enough of crime, wishes to hear what the woman was tried for. Annoyed, the Judge disapprovingly informs her that it was for the murder of her stepsister. But, insatiable, Laurel asks whether the motive was jealousy and if she were hanged. "She was reprieved," snaps the Judge; there was a doubt, but it was not his. He wishes to put a quick end to this talk. Mercifully, Mrs. St. Maugham rids him of Laurel.

No nearer to sleep, the Judge satisfies his own curiosity about Laurel's companion: how did she come to be here? "I advertised," says Mrs. St. Maugham. "I took a chance and was justified. Miss Madrigal came to me like rain from heaven." "With references?" asks the Judge. "I never listen to what one woman says of another," answers Mrs. St. Maugham, peering around for her glasses. "References are a want of faith in one's own judgment! Finish your sleep, Puppy! Since you must have it." And out sails Mrs. St. Maugham with her retrieved pair of glasses, leaving the Judge not to sleep but to deal with his third visitor, Miss Madrigal.

Anxious to know, desperately waiting for him to say something, Madrigal cries: "Judge, I can't wait seven hours twice! You sent me to my maker on a Tuesday—but that was altered! I have done what they call 'time.' It was a lifetime!" The Judge says he wouldn't presume to judge her twice, but he doesn't care for this situation that has caused him so much embarrassment, and he points out quite angrily: "And now you have planted me with human perplexity . . . and ethical perplexity. It's most unpleasant!" She might have considered his old friend and the child. "It's the child I'm considering!" Madrigal says. "When I came here I thought I had met myself again!" But if she stays on, Madrigal wants to know, will the Judge tell who she is? Sure that crime is a flaw in character, the Judge is caught by Madrigal's impassioned idea of her kind of character: "I come of a stock—who in some insensate way—*cannot* accept defeat! My father was cashiered. And after forty years of appeals—reinstated. My grandfather died upright, on his feet. He said God wouldn't give a fallen general houseroom. For fifteen years, and alone, I have hammered out what I am! I did not know I was as dogged as any of them!"

JUDGE—You were a girl of considerable feeling, if I remember.

MADRIGAL—Not now. I am burnt out, white—like the moon, lunar!

JUDGE—Are you not—if I may gently say so—somewhat a stranger to life?

MADRIGAL—The girl I was! She was the stranger!

JUDGE—You have greatly changed.

MADRIGAL—At our last meeting I died. It alters the appearance.

Madrigal suggests that it is the Judge who should leave, but he, too, has his reason for staying—"Because," the Judge explains, "I belong to a guild of men—who feel responsibility. And a deep distaste for situations."

Olivia, Laurel's mother, now enters and adds to the Judge's burdens. Seeing her mother's old friend, Olivia immediately seeks his help with her mother. This—fond as the Judge is of Olivia—is almost too much. He looks at his watch, planning escape. Olivia pleads: "Surely you are not afraid of life?" "On the contrary," the Judge replies, "the law has made me nervous of life."

Mrs. St. Maugham, knowing full well that Olivia has arrived for Laurel, catapults into the room, prepared to fight her to the end.

Laurel, silently entering from the garden, prepares to do her own bit of fighting. She says accusingly: "You haven't been here in four years." Olivia, with a glance in her mother's direction, cries warmly that she has come for Laurel now. When Laurel loudly insists that there will be no room for her with the arrival of the new baby, Olivia sweetly tells her: "There's room! There's always been room! A heart isn't a house—with a room for each person! I can't wait any longer! Come just as you are . . ."

Madrigal comes to Olivia's assistance with an offer to pack Laurel's things. Mrs. St. Maugham is furious; Laurel wildly asks her mother if she has thought of the risk . . . "the risk that—if you take me—I might murder my stepsister!"

The Judge is horrified, but Madrigal bluntly tells Laurel that she has missed her effect. Laurel, fighting a rear-guard action, threatens Madrigal with exposure.

Olivia accosts her mother: "Each time I came you promised you would tell her." Not to be pinned down, Mrs. St. Maugham, with words and accusations, avoids an answer, insisting instead that because of her very special knowledge of Laurel she must keep her. "My mother," says Olivia, "uses words in her special fashion! For a phrase—she would make capital of anything!" "Charming for a mother to hear!" Mrs. St. Maugham lashes back, "and in front of an old friend! If—at a luncheon party—you want to have out the damage of a lifetime . . ." Madrigal takes the cue: "Let's have it!"

The Judge tries his best to calm Mrs. St. Maugham and says with a gesture: "Anything may precipitate . . ." "What?" cries Mrs. St. Maugham. "Anything," calls out Madrigal, brushing aside the Judge's wish to advise Mrs. St. Maugham. "No. Your advice is foreseen! That I must leave here—but it is the *child* who must leave! Laurel must go, Mrs. St. Maugham, go with her mother."

Over Mrs. St. Maugham's indignant cry—"This girl of special soil! Transplant her?"—Madrigal tells her: "You have not a green thumb, Mrs. St. Maugham, with a plant or a girl. This is a house where nothing good can be made of her." Mrs. St. Maugham roars: "*My* house!" "*Your* house!" returns Madrigal. "Why, even your garden is demented! By the mercy of God you do not keep an animal!"

Once again the Judge wants Madrigal to avoid complications. But, "If the past is useful," she retorts, "I shall not hesitate to use it. What I have been has long been done with—" And she goes purposefully to Laurel and says to her: "What you are is yet to come. This is the end to your fancy life." With the Judge's warnings in her ears, and Laurel's threats not to go too far, Madrigal answers: "Don't drive me to it! Who else can tell you that when your moment comes, when truth might serve you—you will not make it sound." Laurel bluffs that everyone knows about her. "They know what you have told them!" says Madrigal. "Shall we now deprive your grandmother of your famous seduction?"

Olivia is incredulous that Laurel could have told her mother such a thing and that her mother could have believed it: "Why was it done?" "Odd things are done for love," answers Madrigal. Laurel starts for the door, but is brought up sharp by Olivia's plea to—"Give it up, Laurel! It isn't worth going on." Turning to Madrigal, Laurel says: "Has it got to be the truth?" "One can lie," says Madrigal with a half-smile, "but truth is more interesting!" Laurel surrenders: "And you get better and better at spotting it! You win, Boss!" And turning to Olivia, she leaves the room with her.

The Judge's one wish is to retreat, leaving the women to fight it out alone. Accused by Mrs. St. Maugham of being a coward, he still prefers to be left out of her battle with Madrigal. In the heat of anger, Mrs. St. Maugham hurls at both of them: "*Hints*—since lunch—have been flying like gnats from side to side of the room! Nobody tells me—in plain English—anything! *Have you two met before then?*" Exchanging a look with the Judge, Madrigal, in matter-of-fact tones, answers: "I was once sentenced to death by the Judge here."

Mrs. St. Maugham sinks to her chair, but not for long. In a moment she starts seething again, ready to have Madrigal thrown bag and baggage from her house. Maitland, however, wouldn't dream of throwing out his newest idol.

The Nurse enters abruptly and announces Pinkbell's death, but Mrs. St. Maugham is so dazed by the afternoon's events that she merely says: "You can go, Nurse. I'll attend to it later." As the horrified Nurse backs to the door, Mrs. St. Maugham reminds her: "I say we have *friends*, Nurse." The Judge's exclamation and Maitland's remarks finally penetrate: "Is *that* what she said?" asks Mrs. St. Maugham. "They've downed him," says Maitland, "stiff as a rod. He hasn't tomorrow . . . He hasn't the *rest of today!*" "*Dead* . . . and my past goes with him . . ." Mrs. St. Maugham cries out.

The past comes crowding in on Mrs. St. Maugham: "When I was a young woman he educated me . . . my manner with distinguished foreigners . . . He saw to my Ascots. He bought my wine for me. Is there an afterlife, Puppy?" "I don't give judgments easily," the Judge answers. "But in *this* life you will miss him." But Mrs. St. Maugham knows that she won't.

Gathering herself together, Mrs. St. Maugham asks the Judge if he will come to see her soon. Starting for the door, the Judge confesses: "Too much happens in this house—for an old man." But he does not neglect to inquire of Madrigal: "What shall you do?" "I shall continue to explore—the astonishment of living," replies Madrigal. "Goodbye, Miss Madrigal," says the Judge. "No man's infallible."

Maitland, deciding to serve Madrigal forever, hands in his notice to Mrs. St. Maugham. Back after accompanying the Judge to the door, Mrs. St. Maugham says weakly: "Yet *now* you have it all your own way, Maitland." And as if in proof of this, she says on her way to see dead Pinkbell: "Stiff as a rod . . . the poor old bastard . . ."

Left alone with Maitland, Madrigal hastily gives him last-minute instructions for the care of the garden, all the while brushing off his interruptions. He finally manages to get in: "*But what's to become of my decision!*" "Oh—don't give notice so often!" brusquely says Madrigal. "It's a fidgety habit!" Mrs. St. Maugham, with some of her former spirit, comes back in time to see Laurel and Olivia depart. "Well, Laurel," she says sharply, "now you have a mother! It's not so rare! Every kitten has one!" Laurel's imploring looks to both her grandmother and Madrigal fail. "Don't begin badly," raps out Mrs. St. Maugham; then making sure that Laurel has her gloves, she refuses further goodbyes. But Olivia, sending Laurel ahead to the car, demands an explanation of her mother's behavior. "Why did you want her?" Olivia asks. Caught off-guard, Mrs. St. Maugham says: "Is it a crime to want to be remembered? The Pharaohs built the Pyramids for that reason." At the door, Olivia says quietly: "The thoughts of a *daughter* are a kind of memorial."

Left alone, with Madrigal about to depart, Mrs. St. Maugham wants some last gardening help. But there are other things on her mind: "You, who have an impertinent answer to everything—" Mrs. St. Maugham starts. "Is there an afterlife?" Unhesitatingly, Madrigal answers: "Certainly." She surprises Mrs. St. Maugham. "One does not sit alone for fifteen years without coming to conclusions." "Is there . . . affection in it?" pleads Mrs. St. Maugham. Calmly, Madrigal says: "But you have been living all this while without affection! Haven't you noticed it?"

Mrs. St. Maugham picks up the catalogue and aimlessly asks about one exotic plant after another. Madrigal reminds her that she lives on chalk, and has no sheltered spot to offer. Slowly, Mrs. St. Maugham says: "If you stay here—you can grow windbreaks . . ." Then with real curiosity she too wants to know: *"Did you do it?"*

MADRIGAL (*unperturbed and calm*)—What learned men at the top of their profession couldn't find out in nine days—why should *you* know?

MRS. ST. MAUGHAM (*looking down at the catalogue and putting on her glasses after a second's pause*)— . . . the Dierama . . . the Wand Flower . . .

MADRIGAL—It won't grow on chalk. But if *I* stay with you—and we work together . . . with potash—and a little granular peat . . . We can *make* it do so.

THE LARK *

By Jean Anouilh

(Adapted by Lillian Hellman)

[Lillian Hellman *was born in New Orleans and educated in New York. Before she began a notable career as a playwright, she was a book reviewer and play reader. Her first play, "The Children's Hour," ran for 691 performances. Her other plays include "Days to Come," "The Little Foxes," "Watch on the Rhine" (which won the Critics' Circle Award), "The Searching Wind," "Another Part of the Forest" and "The Autumn Garden."*

Jean Anouilh *was born in Bordeaux in 1910 and has been an increasingly prominent figure in the Paris theatre since 1932 when his first play, "L'Hermine," was a success. A year later he wrote "Mandarine," a comedy, which was also a success. This was followed by, among others, "Eurydice," "Antigone," "Cry of the Peacock," "Ring round the Moon" and "Mademoiselle Colombe."*]

THE trial of Joan—presaged by music, with voices singing the words *Qui tollis*—is entering another day.

On the gray cyclorama there projects bars of a jail. The cast assembles on a series of platforms while Joan, on a stool, awaits the seating of the Priests, her Judges.

Cauchon and the Promoter stand near Joan, while the Inquisitor sits on a stool near the Judges. In the background Joan's family forms one group; the royal family forms another. Through the crowd of village women carrying faggots and crossing past the English soldiers, the French soldier La Hire and the Squire Beaudricourt, steps the Earl of Warwick. He demands action: an end to the trial, and a start to the burning. Over Cauchon's protests that the whole story of Domremy, the Voices and Chinon be played out, Warwick asks for an end to this children's story of the warrior virgin.

WARWICK—If they have time to waste, they can make the statues that way, in days to come. Different politics may well require different symbols. We might even have to make her a monument in London. Don't be shocked at that, sire. The politics of my government way well require it one day, and what's required, Englishmen supply. That's our secret, sire, and a very good one, indeed. (*Moves downstage to address the audience.*) Well, let's worry about only this minute of time. I am Beauchamp, Earl of Warwick. I have a dirty virgin witch girl tucked away on a litter of straw in the depths of a prison here in Rouen. The girl has been an expensive nuisance. Your Duke of Burgundy sold her high. You like money in France, Monseigneur, all of you. That's the French secret, sire, and a very good one, indeed. (*He moves toward* JOAN.) And here she is. The Maid. The famous Joan the Maid. Obviously, we paid too much. So put her on trial, and burn her, and be finished.

Cauchon repeats that Joan's short life must be played out; and Warwick, claiming patience as an English virtue, agrees to be patient. Granted permission to start anywhere, Joan chooses to start at the beginning: "It's always nicer at the beginning . . ." So, a happy, dancing child, Joan is watching after her sheep. She is in her little corner of the earth, near Domremy, still untouched by the invading English. It is here that her first Voice, her Blessed Saint Michael, spoke and appeared to her—"in a beautiful clean robe that must have been ironed by somebody very careful."

Warwick's is not the sort of patience to endure this "nonsense," but Cauchon overrides him, and Joan enacts her conversations with Saint Michael. How she protests against Saint Michael's choosing her, an ignorant girl, to save France! She can't save France, she can't even ride a horse, or dare approach the Squire Beaudricourt, much less have him take her to the Dauphin. Joan is completely practical as she ticks off the things she can't do—among them, sending men to their death. She longs to go home; but held by a command, she begs Saint Michael to have pity on her. As "Alleluiah" sounds to a shepherd's music, Joan, listening, smiles. Then, coming back to the trial and the present, Joan says matter of factly that Saint Michael didn't have pity on her. . . . "And that was the day I was saddled with France. *And* my work on the farm."

And on the farm there was growing unpleasantness for Joan. Her father threatened to beat her if he caught her with whoever she was waiting for under the lady tree.

Joan confesses to the court that she was with someone—someone with great white wings who worried over the state of France and reported that God would have Joan delay no longer. She was sure that it was all a mistake, but then Saint Michael asked whether God made mistakes. "You understand," says Joan to the court, "that I couldn't very well say yes?"

THE PROMOTER—Why didn't you make the Sign of the Cross?

JOAN—That question is not written in your charge against me.

THE PROMOTER—Why didn't you say to the archangel, *"Vado retro Satanas"?*

JOAN—I don't know any Latin, Messire. And *that* question is not written in your charge against me.

THE PROMOTER—Don't act the fool. The devil understands French. You could have said, "Go away, you filthy, stinking devil."

JOAN (*angry*)—I don't talk that way to the Blessed Saint Michael, Messire.

THE PROMOTER—The Devil told you he was Saint Michael and you were fool enough to believe him.

JOAN—I believed him. He could not have been the Devil. He was so beautiful.

THE PROMOTER—The Devil *is* beautiful!

Cauchon breaks in that the Promoter shocks Joan without reason; but Joan cries bluntly that the Promoter lies. To Joan, what is beautiful is the work of God. In pushing this point, the Promoter becomes involved in his own rather special conception of the Devil's true appearance, and is ordered by Cauchon to cease. "Canon," Cauchon says sharply, "let us not get mixed up in our private devils." Joan wonders how the Promoter would have people recognize the Devil if he is beautiful. Instructed to go to her priest for such help, Joan says realistically: "But only the rich have their priests always with them—the poor can't be running back and forth."

Protected by Cauchon from the Promoter's anger, Joan can't help breaking into laughter as he asks about Saint Marguerite and Saint Catherine: "Were they naked?" "Oh, Messire!" cries Joan. "Don't you think our Lord can afford to buy clothing for his Saints?" Again Cauchon comes to her defense, but cautions her: "You forget who you are and who we are. We are your priests, your masters, and your judges. Beware of your pride, Joan."

JOAN—I know that I am proud. But I am a daughter of God. If He didn't want me to be proud, why did He send me His shining Archangel and His Saints all dressed in light? Why did He promise me that I should conquer all the men I have conquered? Why did He promise me a suit of beautiful white armor, the gift of my king? And a sword? And that I should lead brave soldiers into battle while riding a fine white horse? If He had left me alone, I would never have become proud.

CAUCHON—Take care of your words, Joan. You are accusing our Lord.

JOAN (*makes the Sign of the Cross*)—Oh. God forbid. I say only that His Will be done even if it means making me proud and then damning me for it. That, too, is His Right.

The Promoter cries heresy at such an assertion, and the Inquisitor, getting abruptly to his feet, directs the young priest, Ladvenu, to prompt Joan the fateful question: "Are you in a State of Grace?" Joan answers: "If I am not, God will help me in Grace. If I am, God will keep me in Grace." Ladvenu is pleased; the Inquisitor again seats himself; the Promoter remains angry.

Thus made aware of the Inquisitor's presence, Warwick asks why he wasn't told of his arrival. "He is one of us, sire," answers Cauchon. "We do not acknowledge your authority here." "Only," says Warwick, "when you count our money and eat our food. Never mind, the formalities do not matter to me. But time does and I hope his presence will not add to the confusion. I am almost as bewildered as the girl. All these questions must be very interesting to you gentlemen of the Church, but if we continue at this speed we'll never get to the trial and the girl will be dead of old age. Get to the burning and be done with it."

Incensed, Cauchon holds that they are here to save the girl, but Warwick thinks that—"the fine points of ecclesiastic judgments may be a little too distinguished for my soldiers and for the rest of the world. Propaganda is a soft weapon: hold it in your hands too long and it will move about like a snake, and strike the other way. Whatever the girl is or has been, she must now be stripped and degraded. That is why we bought her high, and it is what we will insist upon." Warwick smiles as he admits that he's come to like Joan, that he admires the way she stands up to the court, and the way she rides. . . . "I'd like to have known her in other circumstances, in a pleasanter world. Hard for me to remember that she took France away from us, deprived us of our heritage. We know that God is on the side of the English. He proved himself at Agincourt. 'God and my right,' you know. But when this girl came along, and we began to lose, there were those who doubted our motto. That, of course, cannot be tolerated. 'God and my right' is inscribed on all

English armor, and we certainly have no intention of changing the armor . . ." He wishes them to get on with her story.

Joan, re-enacting her difficulties with her father, endures again the beating he administered when she insisted on obeying her Voices. Young Ladvenu hates seeing Joan so hurt, but Cauchon reminds him that in the end they will hurt Joan far more. Warwick, altogether unmoved and finding this very similar to the way he was brought up, remarks that it makes for character. What's more, had the English but known about this girl from the outset, they could have reached an agreement with her father.

Joan resumes re-enacting her past: her mother tries to be more understanding than her father, but in the end she too reacts so violently to Joan's wish to follow Saint Michael's orders that Joan is ready to give up. Saint Michael will not permit this. With soft, persuasive anger, he urges Joan to take the first step, telling her that since God has placed His trust in her, she must go. And she goes, shivering from fear and the elements as she plods along. "I was on my way," she says, "to the first fool I had to deal with. And I had plenty of them to deal with."

Mishandled by Squire Beaudricourt's soldiers, Joan still manages to gain entry to the manor and to Beaudricourt's presence. Point-blank she demands a horse, man's clothing, and an armed escort. "You," she tells Beaudricourt, "will give them orders to take me to Chinon to see the Dauphin." "Of course," answers Beaudricourt. "And I will also kick you in the place where it will do you the most good." Untouched by such threats, Joan repeats her demands, though this is not easy with Beaudricourt dangling her in the air close to his face.

BEAUDRICOURT—That's a new idea—a horse. You know who I am and what I usually want? Did the village girls tell you? When they come to ask a favor it usually has to do with a father or a brother who has poached my land. If the girl is pretty, I have a good heart, and we both pitch in. If the girl is ugly, well, I usually have a good heart, too, but not so good as the other way. I am known in this land for good-heartedness. But a horse is a nasty kind of bargain.

JOAN—I have been sent by Blessed Saint Michael.

BEAUDRICOURT (*puts her down hurriedly, makes the Sign of the Cross*)—Don't mix the Saints up in this kind of thing. That talk was good enough to get you past the sentries, but it's not good enough to get you a horse. A horse costs more than a woman.

You're a country girl. You ought to know that. Are you a virgin?

JOAN—Yes, sire.

BEAUDRICOURT—Well, maybe we'll talk about a small horse. You have lovely eyes.

Joan's one-track mind in following her Voice's commands is upsetting to Beaudricourt's equally one-track mind. Her being a virgin may be attractive, and her innocence an asset, but her request for a horse—and now for an armed escort to Chinon—unnerves Beaudricourt. "Stop that crazy talk," he bawls, threatening to have her thrown out. But his curiosity has been piqued by her reference to Chinon. "As I said before, sire," Joan tells him, "I wish to find Monseigneur the Dauphin." Beaudricourt can't imagine why, since the Dauphin runs away from women and war alike. "I want an army, Messire," says Joan, "an army to march upon Orléans." This time Beaudricourt yells for his soldiers, intending to throw Joan out once and for all. Unconcernedly, Joan tells him what a kind man he is. "Sometimes yes," grumbles Beaudricourt, "sometimes no. But I don't like virgins whose heads come off at night—" "And you're very intelligent," Joan adds, "which is sometimes even better than being kind. But when a man is intelligent and kind," Joan throws in as a clincher, "then that's the very best combination on God's fine earth."

Beaudricourt, by now, not only waves away his soldiers, but offers Joan wine. He would like to go into this subject more thoroughly. Joan is not averse to adding that he is also handsome. Beaudricourt settles down to a real talk, though he tries to pass off talking to a shepherd girl as comic. Ripe for flattery, Beaudricourt asks: "I should like to know from your mouth what connection you see between beauty and intelligence? Usually people say that handsome men are stupid."

JOAN—Hunchbacks talk that way, and people with long noses, or those who will die of a bitter egg that grows in their head. God has the power to create a perfect man—(*she smiles at him*) and sometimes He uses His power.

BEAUDRICOURT—Well, you can look at it that way, of course. But you take me, for example. No, I'm not ugly, but sometimes I wonder if I'm intelligent. No, no, don't protest. I tell you there are times when I have problems that seem too much for me. They ask me to decide something, a tactical or administrative point. Then, all of a sudden, I don't know why, my head acts like it's gone some place else, and I don't even understand the words people are saying. Isn't that strange? (*After a second.*) But I never show it. I roar out an order whatever happens. That's the main thing in an army. Make a decision, good or bad, just *make* it. Things will turn out almost the same, anyway. (*Softly as if to himself.*) Still, I wish I could have done better. This is a small village to die away your life. (*Points outside.*) They think I'm a great man, but they never saw anybody else. Like every other man, I wanted to be brilliant and remarkable, but I end up hanging a few poor bastards who deserted from a broken army. I wanted to shake a nation— Ah, well. (*Looks at her.*) Why do I tell you all this? You can't help me, and you're crazy.

JOAN—They told me you would speak this way.

BEAUDRICOURT—*They* told you?

JOAN—Listen to me, nice, good Robert, and don't shout any more. It's useless. I'm about to say something very important. You will be brilliant and remarkable. You will shake a nation because I will do it for you. Your name will go far outside this village—

Joan thus lines up Beaudricourt's political support with a promise that he *will* shake the world, but asks him to forget that she is a girl: he should think of her as already wearing the boy's clothes he will provide.

Having got this far, Joan now offers a picture of the English about to overrun Brittany and Anjou, with everything falling about France's little, silly, shaking, jibbering Dauphin. She finds the French army still good and brave, but tired and sick, while their brave Captain Dunois throws himself away on wine and whores. Joan flatly intends to put a stop to this.

She puts into Beaudricourt's head that he alone can see the future. "You know your soldiers," Joan says, "you know they will leave you soon. You know that to keep them you must give them faith. You have nothing else to give them now. A little bread, a little faith—good simple things to fight with." Joan cites her own faith in her Saints' orders, and practically dares Beaudricourt to disprove her belief that God is on her side.

She says boldly that Beaudricourt is already convinced, and it is thus but a short step for her to convince the Dauphin, Dunois, and the Archbishop. Believing that God is on their side, Joan is sure that she can persuade the troops that He is. She blithely concludes: "And because you know it, you are the most remarkable man in France." "You think so?" says Beaudricourt, not without hope. "The whole world will think so," says Joan, "but you must move fast. Like all great political men you are a realist. At this minute you are saying to yourself, 'If the troops will believe this girl has come from God, what difference does it make whether she has or not? I will send her to Bourges tomorrow with the courier.' "

Laughing, Joan makes her final demands for six good soldiers and a white horse: "I want a *white* horse, please. I will do the rest. But give me a quiet horse because I don't know how to ride." Told she will break her neck, Joan is betting on her Saints to keep her in the saddle, and if she doesn't fall off, Beaudricourt must then really believe in her. Beaudricourt says: "All this thinking makes a man weary. I had other plans for this afternoon, as I told you, but any kind of exercise is good for me. Come on." Off he goes, but Joan is kept from following by the prison guards who bring her back to the present—the trial.

Warwick delights in Joan's methods because he is reminded of his own. It also occurs to him that Cauchon uses these same methods to get people to believe what he wants them to. Bluntly, Warwick inquires if Cauchon really has faith. "As a child has it," says Cauchon, "and that is why my judges and I will try to save Joan. To the bitter end we will try to save her. Our honor demands that—" Seeing Warwick turn his back, Cauchon hastily explains this unfortunate mention of the word "honor": the priests' collaboration with the English was the only reasonable solution. Surrounded by eight hundred English soldiers, the priests held out for nine months against surrendering Joan. "Nine long months," Cauchon argues, "before we agreed to hand over a girl who had been deserted by everybody but us. They can call us barbarians, but for all their noble principles I believe they would have surrendered her before we did."

WARWICK—You could have given us the girl on the first day. Nine long months of endless what?

CAUCHON—It was hard for us. God had been silent since Joan's arrest. He had not spoken to her or to us. Therefore, we had to do without His counsel. We were here to defend the House of God. During our years in the seminaries we learned how to defend it. Joan had no training in our seminaries and yet, abandoned, she defended God's House in her own way. Defended it with that strange conflict of insolence and humility, worldly sense and unworldly grandeur. (*Softly.*) The piety was so simple and sweet—to the last moment of the last flame. We did not understand her in those days. We covered our eyes like old, fighting, childish men, and turned away so that we could not hear the cries of anguish. She was all alone at the end. God had not come to her. That is a terrible time for a religious nature, sire, and brings doubt and despair unknown to others. But it is then and there that some men raise their heads, and when they do, it is a noble sight.

WARWICK—Yes, it is. But as a man of politics, I cannot afford the doctrine of man's individual magnificence. I might meet another man who felt the same way. And he might express his individual magnificence by cutting off *my* head.

Cauchon, trying to console himself with the memory of all those old priests who tried to protect Joan, can't help thinking of the future— "When our names will be known only for what we did to her; when men, forgiving their own sins, but angry with ours, will speak our names in a curse."

Cauchon and Warwick fade into the background as court music and a fleur-de-lis bright on the cyclorama herald the remnants of the French Court.

At Chinon, as France tumbles, the Court pursues its usual aimless pastimes of cards and dancing under the eyes of the aimless Dauphin. The Dauphin, with neither money for his wife and mistress nor power over his people, alternates between playing the child's game of bilboquet and cowering before his courtiers and advisers. Right now Charles has jumped back in fear from La Tremouille and the Archbishop.

LA TREMOUILLE—You grow more like your father each day.

ARCHBISHOP—But his father had the decency to take to his bed.

CHARLES—Which father?

LA TREMOUILLE—You act so strangely, sire, that even I, who knew your mother, am convinced you are legitimate. (*Angrily to* CHARLES *who is still on the floor.*) Move. Move.

THE LITTLE QUEEN—Oh, please don't speak to him that way, Monsieur de la Tremouille.

ARCHBISHOP (*who has been glaring at the dancers*)—You believe this is the proper time for dancing?

THE LITTLE QUEEN—But if the English take us prisoner, we have to know a little something. We can't disgrace our country— (LA TREMOUILLE *stares at her, exits.*)

YOLANDE—What harm do they do, sire? They are young—and there isn't much ahead for them.

ARCHBISHOP—There isn't much ahead for any of us. (*He moves off.*)

Yolande begs the Dauphin to get up, hating to see him frightened of so many men. Charles confesses to having been scared of those two always, and with good reason.

Yolande, the little Queen's mother, wishing to be helpful, urges the Dauphin to see Joan: "There is something strange about this girl, something remarkable. Or so everybody thinks, and that's what matters. She even thinks that a peasant at their council tables might do some good. Charles, however, has no illusions: he has seen men of the people become kings amidst massacres and mistakes. . . . "At least," says Charles, "I'm harmless. The day may come when Frenchmen will regret their little Charles. At least I have no large ideas about how to organize happiness and death."

La Tremouille, having received daily reports on Joan's activities, says that the townspeople are marching toward them, shouting that God commands the Dauphin to receive Joan.

CHARLES—He hasn't said a word to me.

LA TREMOUILLE—The day God speaks to you, sire, I will turn infidel.

ARCHBISHOP—Put up that toy, your majesty. You will have the rest of your life to devote to it.

LA TREMOUILLE—Get ready to leave here.

CHARLES—Where will I go? Where will you go? To the English?

ARCHBISHOP—Even from you, sire, we will not accept such words.

Yolande, moving between the men, suggests that Charles be allowed to see the girl. The Archbishop declares angrily that he is against seeing every charlatan who craves an audience. But La Tremouille, completely defeatist, thinks it doesn't matter one way or the other. But when told by Yolande, "We have nothing to lose, sire," La Tremouille corrects her: "When you deal with God you risk losing everything. If He has really sent this girl, then He has decided to concern Himself with us. In that case, we are in even worse trouble than we thought. People who govern states should not attract God's attention. They should make themselves very small and pray that they will go unnoticed."

Small and frightened, Joan enters bowing respectfully to the Archbishop. But, asked what she wants, she bows before Charles and comes to the point: "I am Joan the Maid. The King of Heaven has sent me here. I am to take you to Reims and have you anointed and crowned King of France." Neither Charles' sarcasm nor La Tremouille's disdain nor the Archbishop's desire to get rid of her can stop her. Rather surprisingly, Charles, with Joan at his side and Joan's hand in his, finds the strength to order his advisers and courtiers to leave him alone with her. Obeyed for the first time in his memory, Charles bursts into gales of giggling.

Joan's honest looks comfort him; and oddly enough, he isn't frightened of her. "I've lived so long with those pirates," Charles confesses, "that I've almost forgotten what an honest face looks like. Are there other people who have honest faces?" "Many, sire," Joan answers gravely.

CHARLES—I never see them. Brutes and whores, that's all I ever see. And the little Queen. She's nice, but she's stupid. And Agnes. She's not stupid—and she's not nice. (*He climbs on his throne, hangs his feet over one of the arms and sighs.*) All right. Start boring me. Tell me that I ought to be a great King.

JOAN (*softly*)—Yes, Charles.

CHARLES—Listen. If you want to make an impression on the Archbishop and the council, we'll have to stay in this room for at least an hour. If you talk to me of God and the Kingdom of France, I'll never live through the hour. Let's do something else. Do you know how to play at cards?

JOAN—I don't know what it is.

CHARLES—It is a nice game invented to amuse my Papa when he was ill. I'll teach you. (*He begins to hunt for the cards.*) I hope they haven't stolen them. They steal everything from me around here and cards are expensive. Only the wealthiest princes can have them. I got mine from Papa. I'll never have the price of another pack. If those pigs have stolen them— No. Here they are. (*He finds them in his pocket.*) My Papa was crazy. Went crazy young —in his thirties. Did you know that? Sometimes I am glad I am a bastard. At least I don't have to be so frightened of going crazy. Then sometimes I wish I were his son and knew that I was meant to be a king. It's confusing.

JOAN—Of the two, which would you prefer?

CHARLES—Well, on the days when I have a little courage, I'd risk going crazy. But on the days when I haven't any courage—that's from Sunday to Saturday—I would rather let everything go to hell and live in peace in some foreign land on whatever little money I have left.

JOAN—Today, Charles, is this one of the days when you have courage?

CHARLES—Today? (*He thinks a minute.*) Yes, it seems to me

I have a little bit today. Not much, but a little bit. I was sharp with the Archbishop, and—

JOAN—You will have courage every day. Beginning now.

And Joan promises him that she has a charm that will make this so. Hearing her charm is not for sale, but a gift, Charles says distrustfully: "What you get free costs too much."

His father having been mad, Charles has feigned madness so as to be left alone. But he warns Joan: "Don't think you can catch me too easily. I know a little about the world." Joan assures him that he knows too much, that he is too smart. "Yes," says Charles, "because I must defend myself against these cutthroats. They've got large bones, I've got puny sticks. But my head's harder than theirs and I've clung to my throne by using it." "I would like to defend you against them, Charles," Joan says gently. "I would give my life to do it."

Since he wishes it, Joan agrees to play cards, provided Charles will then learn the game she will teach him: of not being too smart, and of not being afraid. When Joan substitutes God for the ace in the card game, Charles becomes irritable. She maintains that God is more powerful than kings. "Oh, leave God alone for a minute," Charles snaps. "It's called the ace. Are you running this game? God this and God that. You talk as if you dined with Him last night. Didn't anybody tell you that the English also say their prayers to God? Every man thinks God is on his side. The rich and powerful know He is. But we're not rich and powerful, you and I—and France." Joan is sure that God doesn't care about any of that, only about their lack of courage. As Charles petulantly complains that God then could have given him that courage, Joan loses her patience: "Is God your nurse? Couldn't you have tried to do a little better? Even with those legs?"

Joan prevents a fresh flow of self-pity by reminding Charles that it is not only his legs that are ugly, but his head, too. Inside his head, however, things are not ugly; there is the sense that God gave him. And arguing against Charles' continuous plaint of being afraid, Joan stresses that she, too, is afraid: that during her trip to Chinon she was terrified every step of the way. Joan wants neither to suffer nor to die, but when she gets scared she proceeds as though she weren't. And, slowly and carefully, having won Charles' attention, Joan tells him where she will go: to the English at Orléans. And though frightened and outnumbered, she will march right through, because she will have had the good sense to get frightened first. Over Charles' objection that it can't be done, Joan—with a story that shows how common sense can achieve miracles—persuades him. Then she demands the army of France.

The Dauphin shies away, but Joan will have no delay. "You are ready," she coaxes him. "Come on, Charlie." Nervously he admits that perhaps he is, and the temptation to see the faces of Le Tremouille and the Archbishop when he makes the announcement is almost too much to resist. But a minute later Charles is afraid all over again. "Are you as afraid," asks Joan, "as you ever can be, ever were or will be, then, now and in the future? Are you sick?" He is. "Good. Good," says Joan. "Then the worst is over. By the time they get scared, you'll be all over yours. Now, if you're as sick as you can get, I'll call them." She runs and calls: "Monseigneur the Archbishop. Monseigneur de la Tremouille. Please come to the Dauphin." She hurries back to seat the Dauphin properly on his throne, arranging his hands and feet as effectively as possible, telling him all the while: "God is smiling. He is saying to Himself, 'Look at that little Charles. He is sicker than he's ever been in his life. But he has called in his enemies and will face them. My, such a thing is wonderful.' Hang on, Charles. We'll be in Orléans. We'll march right up."

When all the courtiers have assembled, Charles announces in a very sharp voice that he has placed Joan in command of the army, and that he will brook no arguments. There are none.

Joan, thanking God, falls to her knees. Charles, knowing there is no time to lose, asks the Archbishop's blessing. He orders La Tremouille to kneel, and the courtiers follow. As the Archbishop gives the blessing, the *Benedictus* is sung by the chorus, and a page hands a sword to the Dauphin, who presents it to Joan.

Whereupon the Englishman, Warwick, comes into the scene and walks toward the audience. "In real life," he points out, "it didn't work out exactly that way. As before, now, and forever, there were long discussions in the French fashion. The council met. Desperate, frightened, with nothing to lose, they decided to dress the girl in battle flags and let her go forth as a symbol of something or other. It worked well. A simple girl inspired simple people to get themselves killed for simple ideals."

ACT II

To the accompaniment of a song celebrating her victories, Joan flashes by in full armor. She raises her sword to salute a throng of admiring women and passes on.

Once more the court convenes: Warwick comes forward. "She

was in the field," says Warwick. "From that day, laws of strategy no longer made any difference. We began to lose. They say that Joan worked no miracles at Orléans. They say that our plan of isolated fortresses was absurd, that they could have been taken by anyone who had courage enough to attack. But that is not true. Sir John Talbot was not a fool. He's a good soldier, as he proved long before that miserable business, and after it. By all military laws his fortified positions could not have been broken. And they could not have been broken except by— Well, by what? What shall we call it even now? The unknown, the unguessed—God, if that's the way you believe. The girl was a lark in the skies of France, high over the heads of her soldiers, singing a joyous, crazy song of courage. . . ." She was the soul of France to the French, and she was that even to this Englishman, who admits with a backhand compliment that he likes France very much. He wishes, however, to get on with the business at hand.

The lark has been captured, the King and the court she saved are about to abandon her. "They are returning as fast as they can," Warwick comments, "to the old, stale political games."

Joan, back in the trial, calls out to Charles, but he turns his back on her as he half-heartedly protests to the Archbishop concerning the letter he was instructed to send. "I didn't like the letter," is all Charles has to say about his treachery. Cauchon quietly explains to Joan: "Yesterday, Charles disavowed you in a letter sent to all his cities." Again Joan calls out, "Charles!" but getting no answer, says: "Well. He is still my King and he is your King." Not Cauchon's: *he* is now a loyal subject of Henry of Lancaster, King of England and France. Put suddenly in the position of having to defend his new allegiance, Cauchon says sharply that this is not a political trial, that they are here to return a lost girl to the Mother Church. Joan won't change the subject: "That puppet man is the king God gave you," she says, pointing to Charles. "He is a poor, skinny, miserable thing, but given a little time—" Charles loudly objects to being defended in this fashion. The Archbishop, telling Charles to turn away, maliciously reminds him that it will all soon be at an end, that Joan will be burnt at the stake. And Chalres can count himself lucky, for without the English to do his dirty work, the French would have had to condemn her to death. "I will never do that, Monseigneur. After all, the girl loved me," Charles answers. "I will never do that," he repeats. "No, sire," answers the Archbishop. "We will do it for you." They move off.

Though Cauchon denies the political aspects of the trial, he says to Joan: "You are not stupid. You can understand what we think.

You swear that you heard voices and you swear to the messages they sent you. But because we believe in another king, we cannot believe that it was God Who sent you to fight against us. We are priests but we are men. And man cannot believe that God has turned against him." Joan stands as stoutly by her Voices as she stood by her king.

Cauchon, telling her that every village priest has had his share of young girls having emotional crises, finds Joan altogether understandable. Yet she had good sense: she was commander-in-chief of an army. Joan proudly adds: "I commanded brave men. *They* believed in me, and *they* followed me." Cauchon asks what if one of these men had heard voices of his own—ordering him not to follow Joan. She laughs, and is answered by a sudden burst of soldier laughter. Joan calls out to it: "The Seigneur Bishop is a priest—he has never been close to you, my soldiers." Amused, she tells Cauchon: "A good army fights, drinks, rapes—but they don't hear voices." Not caring for this explanation, Cauchon answers: "You know that a disobedient soldier in your army, in any army of this world, would be silenced. The Church Militant is also an army of this earth and we, its priests, do not believe in the Divine Origin of *your* disobedience. Nobody believes in you now, Joan."

But whatever the consequences, Joan will not call black white: she must go on thinking as she thinks. Angered again by such stubbornness, the Promoter insists on knowing the spell she cast on her king. Repeating sharply that she had no secret, Joan answers: "I gave him courage. That is the only word I know for what was between us. When a girl says one word of good sense and people listen to her, that's proof that God is present and no strange spells or miracles are needed." Leaping on her answer, the Promoter aks whether she denies the miracles of Cana and the raising of Lazarus. "No, Messire," Joan answers. "Our Seigneur changed the water into wine and retied the thread of Lazarus' life. But for Him Who is Master of life and death, that is no more miracle than if I were to make thread for my loom."

THE PROMOTER (*with great anger, to the* JUDGES)—Mark her words. Write them down. She says that Jesus made no miracles.

JOAN (*runs toward the* JUDGES, *with great force*)—I say that true miracles are not tricks performed by gypsies in a village square. True miracles are created by men when they use the courage and intelligence that God gave them.

CAUCHON—You are saying to us, to *us,* that the real miracle of

God on this earth is man. Man, who is naught but sin and error, impotent against his own wickedness—

JOAN—And man is also strength and courage and splendor in his most desperate minutes. I know man because I have seen him. He is a miracle.

Ladvenu tries to cover up Joan's blunders, but the Promoter goes to the heart of the matter: "Do you believe," he demands, "that man is the greatest miracle of God?" "Yes, Messire," Joan answers.

THE PROMOTER (*shouts*)—You blaspheme. Man is impurity and lust. The dark acts of his nights are the acts of a beast—

JOAN—Yes, Messire. And the same man who acts the beast will rise from a brothel bed and throw himself before a blade to save the soldier who walks beside him. Nobody knows why he does. He doesn't know. But he does it, and he dies, cleansed and shining. He has done both good and evil, and thus twice acted like a man. That makes God happy because God made him for just this contradiction. We are good and we are evil, and that is what was meant.

A silence falls among the indignant Judges as the Inquisitor rises. Choosing this moment to begin speaking, he says icily that he is indifferent to who rules what country, or to what alliances have been formed. He has no interest whatever in defending the temporal dignity of the Church (he will leave that to the bishops and priests) nor is he at all concerned with the Promoter's dreams of the Devil. "The Holy Inquisition," he intones, "fights in the dark world of the night, against an enemy it alone can recognize"—a great enemy with a great name.

Joan finds this all very hard to follow, but quickly understands and responds to the Inquisitor's knowledge of the smallest details of her early life, of her piety and even of her tenderness. Ladvenu can't help expressing his relief: "Messire Inquisitor, Joan has always acted with kindness and Christian charity, but this court has buried it in silence. I am happy to hear you remind them that—" He gets no further. The Inquisitor turns and rebukes him: "Silence, Brother Ladvenu. I ask you not to forget that the Holy Inquisition alone is qualified to distinguish between theological virtues and that troubled brew that man so boastfully calls the milk of human kindness." The Judges are given a chilly reminder, too: "What strange matters concern you all," says the Inquisitor. "Your business is to defend the Faith. But you see the kind eyes of a young girl and you are overwhelmed."

The Inquisitor tells Joan: "I am going to shock you—there is nothing very exceptional about the Voices you heard in those days. Our archives are full of such cases. There are many young visionaries. Girls frequently experience a crisis of mysticism. It passes. . . ." Her experience, it is true, was more prolonged; and her Voices used very strange words to an ignorant peasant girl. "Not so strange, Messire," answers Joan, "because it turned out to be the truth." What is more, Joan is convinced: "Our Lord could not want the English to kill us and conquer us. He could not want us to live by their laws and wishes. When they have gone back across the sea, to their own land," she adds magnanimously, "I will not go and pick a quarrel with them. They can rest easy in their own house. I've always said that." The Inquisitor breaks in: "And I say your presumption is not suited to my taste." He finds, too, that it would have been more fitting had Joan prayed for the defeat of the English. Saying that she did all that, Joan still sticks to the idea that God really wishes one to strike first and pray later. And knowing that this is warlike, knowing that she thinks often about the fine battles she shared with her devoted warriors, Joan confesses that God must absolve her of such a sin. "But I did not like pain or death," she pleads. "At night, on the battlefield, I would weep for the dead—"

THE PROMOTER—You would weep at night for the dead, but by morning you were shouting for a new battle.

JOAN (*moves to him, with great force*)—I say God did not wish one Englishman to remain in France. That's not so hard to understand, is it? We had to do our work, that's all. You are wise men, you think too much. Your heads are filled with too much celestial science. You don't understand even the simplest things any more—things that my dullest soldier would understand without talk. Isn't that true, La Hire?

She stumbles away from the Judges; she falls to the ground. To the whistling of the soldier's song, La Hire appears in full armor and moves toward Joan.

LA HIRE—The morning has come, Madame Joan. (*She sits up, shivers, stares at him.*)

JOAN—The night was cold, La Hire. (*He sits beside her, warms her hands in his own.* JOAN *looks toward the trial, then up, then back to* LA HIRE, *as if she were confused by the place and the time.*)

Good La Hire. Great La Hire. You've really come to help me as I knew you would.

La Hire (*takes out an onion and begins to peel it*)—Come to help you? I was sleeping fifty feet from you, Madame Joan, watching over you as I always do. (*She laughs and moves closer to him.*) Don't come too close. I stink of wine and onions.

Joan—No, no. You smell fine.

La Hire—Usually you tell me I stink too much to be a Christian. You say I am a danger to the army because if the wind is behind me the English will know where we are.

Joan—Oh, La Hire, I was so stupid in those days. You know how girls are. Nothing ever happens to them, they know nothing, but they pretend they know everything. But I am not so stupid any more. You smell good because you smell like a man.

La Hire—I can't stand a man who washes in the field because to me a man like that isn't a man. I was brought up on an onion in the morning. The rest can have their sausage. The smell is more distinguished, you tell me. I know you think a breakfast onion is a sin.

Joan (*laughs*)—A breakfast onion is not a sin. Nothing that is true is a sin, La Hire. I was a fool. I tormented you. But I didn't know anything then. I didn't. (*Softly.*) Ah, you smell so good. Sweat, onions, wine. You have all the smells a man should have. And you curse, you kill, and you think of nothing but women.

In spite of all La Hire's sins, Joan feels confident that he is like a "bright new coin in the hand of God." His blasphemy still shocks her, and yet, hearing his trepidations about the after-life, Joan reassures him with a picture of Paradise: "It's full of men like you," she cheers him. "It's the others who are kept waiting at the gates—" The gates of Orléans loom ahead now for Joan and La Hire. Holding the reins of her imaginary horse in her hands, standing tall on her stool (with La Hire girt for battle at her side), she rides off in the beauty of the early morning.

Knowing that Joan has never used a sword, La Hire goes after three Englishmen single-handedly, crying: "I'll kill them—God damned English bastards." Joan, left alone, kneels in prayer: "Dear God, he is as good as bread—I answer for him. He's my friend." Then she turns angrily and defiantly on the Judges: "The last word will not be spoken at this trial. La Hire will come to deliver me. He will bring three hundred lancers. I know them all and they will take me from my prison."

Told that La Hire and his men had come, and after seeing how many English awaited them, had gone away again, Joan is shaken. With a real effort at bravado, she says: "Yes, of course. It was *I* who taught them to do just that. I would say to them, 'Have a little sense—it doesn't cost a sou. Learn not to be brave when you are outnumbered, unless—' That's what they did. They went to get reinforcements for me—" She will not listen to Cauchon's insistence that La Hire won't return. "La Hire will return," she proudly insists, "because there is no other way to save me now." Cauchon thrusts harder: "La Hire, the mercenary, will not return because he has marched his men towards Germany in search of a new prince to pay him.

"You have been abandoned," Cauchon tells Joan. "It will sound strange to you, but the priests of this court are the only men who care for your soul and for your life. Humble yourself, Joan, and the Church will take your hand. In your heart you are a child of the Church." "Yes," Joan says softly.

CAUCHON—Trust yourself to the Church. She will weigh your deeds and take from you the agony of self-judgment.

JOAN (*after a long silence*)—For that which is of the Faith, I turn to the Church, as I have always done. But what I am, I will not denounce. What I have done, I will not deny. (*There is a shocked silence. Then there is great movement in the courtroom, as if this were the answer from which judgment will come. The* INQUISITOR *rises. The* PRIESTS *are suddenly silent. The* INQUISITOR *slowly moves before the* PRIESTS *and peers into their faces. The* PRIESTS *draw back, frightened.*)

THE INQUISITOR (*to one* PRIEST)—Not you. (*To another* PRIEST.) Not you. (*To a third* PRIEST.) Not you. (*Pauses before* CAUCHON, *stares at him.*) And not you, Bishop of Beauvais. I have spoken of the great enemy, but not even now do you know his name. You do not understand on whom you sit in judgment, nor the issues of the judgment. I have told you that the Holy Inquisition is not concerned with royal rank or merchant gold or peasant birth. To us, a scholar in his room is equal in importance to an emperor in his palace. Because *we* know the name of our enemy. His name is natural man. (*There is silence.* LADVENU *moves forward.*) Can you not see that this girl is the symbol of that which is most to be feared? She is the enemy. She is man as he stands against us. Look at her. Frightened, hungry, dirty, abandoned by all, and no longer even sure that those Voices in the air ever spoke to her at all. Does her misery make her a suppliant begging God for mercy and for light? No. She turns away from God. She dares to stand under torture, thrashing about like a proud beast in the stable of her dungeon. She raises her eyes, not to God, but to man's image of himself. I have need to remind you, Masters, that he who loves Man does not love God.

Ladvenu protests loudly, and is ordered from the court. He makes a final plea for this small, lonely enemy and goes. The Inquisitor now sees no further need for questioning; Joan's deeds no longer matter. What alone matters is why she did them, and the one fearful answer that she made. "You wish to say it again?" the Inquisitor asks Joan. "Say it." Slowly, softly, Joan repeats what she had said. Down through the ages, cries the Inquisitor, the whole insolent breed has said the same thing! "The men who dare our God. Those who say no to us—" Moving towards Joan, he whips out: "You and all like you shall be made to say yes. You put the Idea in peril, and that you will not be allowed to do . . ." He now demands of the court that she be excommunicated from the Church. He demands that she be returned to the secular authority, there to receive her punishment. "I ask," he concludes, "the secular arm to limit her sentence to this side of death and the mutilation of her members." Cauchon moves towards the Inquisitor as if to stop his judgment. Warwick, turning to Cauchon, remarks: "A passionate man and so sincere. I think he means simply to throw the dirty work to me. I am the secular authority here. Why didn't your French Charles have her burned? It was his job." Charles, very disturbed, is heard to protest that he would not want to do it.

Cauchon calls out to the Executioner, who advises that all is ready. Hearing this, Joan remembers a childhood dream and screams out as if in pain.

Desperate, Cauchon for the last time offers Joan the saving hand of the Mother Church. "We wish to save you," he repeats, "but we can delay no longer." Outside the crowd has gathered for the burning. Joan, as if in a dream, forgives the mob and Cauchon, too. The Promoter considers this another impertinence, but Joan recognizes Cauchon's gentleness. "But," she adds, "I do not know whether he means to save me or conquer me. In any case, he will be obliged to have me burned." Cauchon offers to save her if she will but confess her sins. Joan clings to his robe while pleading for the Holy Communion so long denied her. Promising it to her after she shall have confessed and begun her penance, Cauchon wonders if she is not afraid to die. "Yes. I am afraid," says Joan. "What difference does that make? I've always been so afraid of fire—" She gasps as she thinks of her old dream.

With a show of real tenderness, Cauchon now draws her to him, asking her to trust the priests of her Church and to put herself in their hands. Joan, dog-tired, has difficulty understanding what he says.

CAUCHON—I talk to you thus because my pride is less than yours.

JOAN—Pride? I have been a prisoner so long—I think my head is sick and old, and the bottom of me does not hold any more. Sometimes I don't know where I am and my dungeon seems a great beech tree. I am hungry, or I was, and I want a taste of country milk—

CAUCHON (*desperately, as if he were at the end*)—Look at me, Joan, keep your mind here. I am an old man. I have killed people in the defense of my beliefs. I am so close to death myself that I do not wish to kill a little girl. Be kind. (*Cries out.*) Help me to save you.

JOAN (*very softly; broken now*)—What do you want me to say? Please tell me in simple words.

CAUCHON—I am going to ask you three questions. Answer yes three times. That is all. (*With passion.*) Help me, Joan.

She asks to be allowed to sleep a few hours, but is refused. Told to make a complete and total act of submission, and to ask to be returned to the bosom of the Church, Joan says: "Yes, but—" The Inquisitor rises, and Cauchon becomes increasingly nervous. "I don't want to say," adds Joan, "the opposite of what my Voices told me. I don't ever want to bear false witness against Charlie. I fought so hard for the glory of his consecration. Oh, that was a day when he was crowned. The sun was out—" Charles, speaking to Joan, remembers the nice day, but would rather not have people remember that God sent Joan to him. What with her now being tried for a sorceress and heretic, he thinks it better that she just forget him.

Joan, with bowed head, is ready at last to go on her knees to the Church. She pleads with Cauchon: "Messire, deep in your heart do you believe that our Lord wishes me to submit to the judgment?" "I so believe," Cauchon answers. "Then," says Joan softly, "I submit."

She renounces forever the bearing of arms. She doesn't so quickly renounce wearing her man's uniform: it finally comes out that the reason she repeatedly asked to be taken to a Church prison where she would undress, and repeatedly refused to undress otherwise, was the presence day and night of two English soldier guards in her cell. "The nights are long," she finally tells Cauchon. "I am in chains.

I try hard not to sleep, but sometimes I am too tired. (*She stops, embarrassed.*) In this uniform it is easier for me to defend myself."

CAUCHON (*in great anger*)—Have you had so to defend yourself since the beginning of this trial? (WARWICK *moves to* JOAN.)

JOAN—Every night since I've been captured. I don't have much sleep. In the mornings, when I am brought before you, I am confused, and I don't understand your questions. I told you that. Sometimes I try to sleep here in the trial so that I will stay awake in the night—

CAUCHON—Why haven't you told us this before?

JOAN—Because the soldiers told me they would be hanged if I said anything.

WARWICK (*very angry*)—They were right. (*To* CAUCHON.) Detestable bastards. It's disgusting. They've learned such things since they came to France. It may be all right in the French Army, but not in mine. (*Bows to* JOAN.) I am sorry, Madame. It will not happen again.

Promised the protection of the Church, Joan agrees to put on woman's dress.

Over the Promoter's protests, Cauchon is permitted to recall Ladvenu, who has drawn up the Act of Renunciation.

THE PROMOTER—This trial has been conducted with an indulgence that is beyond my understanding. (*To the* INQUISITOR.) I am told that there are those here who eat from the English manger. I ask myself now if they have arranged to eat better from the French manger.

THE INQUISITOR (*rises, moves towards* JOAN)—It is not a question of mangers, Messire Promoter. I ask myself how did it happen that this girl said yes when so many lesser ones did not bow the head. I had not believed it to be possible. (*Points to* CAUCHON.) And why was tenderness born in the heart of that old man who was her judge? He is at the end of a life worn out with compromise and debasement. Why now, here, for this girl, this dangerous girl, did his heart— (*He kneels, ignoring the others. As he prays, we hear only the words* . . .) Why, O Lord . . . ? Why, O Lord . . . ? Consecrate it in peace to Your Glory. . . . Your Glory—

Ladvenu, first gently telling Joan how he had prayed for her, next reads the Act of Renunciation, and helps her to sign her name to it. Cauchon, exhausted, pronounces her saved. Condemning her to solitary imprisonment for the remainder of her days, Cauchon declares her delivered of the danger of excommunication, and, making the Sign of the Cross, he orders her to be led away.

A soldier pushes Joan away from the trial; Ladvenu helps a stumbling Cauchon, and the Judges slowly move off. Warwick remains, and as Cauchon passes commends him: "The making of a martyr is dangerous business. The pile of faggots, the invincible girl in the flames, might have been a triumph for the French spirit. But the apologies of a hero are sad and degrading. You did well, sire; you are a wise man." Bitterly, Cauchon answers: "I did not mean to earn your praise."

The spears of four soldiers form the bars behind which Joan is imprisoned. To this cell Charles now makes a weak-kneed, apologetic visit. All Joan says to him is: "Goodbye, Charlie." "You must stop calling me Charlie," he tells her. "Ever since my coronation I am careful to make everyone say sire." "Sire," says Joan.

After Charles goes, Joan tries to drink from the bucket of filthy water and retches. She tries to reach her Voices and fails. Warwick finds her in utter misery.

WARWICK—I am sorry to disturb you. I only came to say that I am glad you are saved. You behaved damned well. I, er—well, it's rather difficult to say in my language, but the plain fact is that I like you. And it amused me to watch you with the Inquisitor. Sinister man, isn't he? I detest these intellectual idealists more than anything in the world. What disgusting animals they are. He wanted only to see you humiliate yourself, no matter your state or your misery. And when you did, he was satisfied.

JOAN (*softly*)—He had reason to be satisfied.

WARWICK—Well, don't worry about him. It all worked out well. Martyrs are likely to stir the blood of simple people and set up too grand a monument to themselves. It's all very complex and dangerous. Tell me, are you a virgin?

Warwick, having satisfied his curiosity, is reminded of his virgin fiancée in England. Then, with a compliment to Joan's horsemanship and an offer to be of any further help, he is about to leave. Joan, finding him a kind man to have visited her, desperately finds herself talking things over with him: "I still believe in all that I did, and yet I swore against it. God can't want that. What can be left for me?" Warwick thinks things may eventually work out for her; her nasty little Charles may even show her some trace of loyalty. Thinking of a future which at best may find her growing fat on a small court pension and at worst will leave her to rot in all this filth and darkness, Joan cries: "What good is life either way?"

WARWICK—It is good any way you can have it. We all try to save a little honor, of course, but the main thing is to be here—

JOAN (*rises, calls out, speaking to the Voices*)—I was only born the day you first spoke to me. My life only began on the day you told me what I must do, my sword in hand. You are silent, dear my God, because you are sad to see me frightened and craven. And for what? A few years of unworthy life. (*She kneels. Softly as if she is answering a message.*) I know. Yes, I know. I took the good days from You and refused the bad. I know. Dear my God, forgive me and keep me now to be myself. Forgive me and take me back for what I am. (*She rises. She is happy and cheerful.*) Call your soldiers, Warwick. I deny my confession.

WARWICK—Joan. No nonsense, please. Things are all right as they are. I—

JOAN—Come. (*She holds out her hand to him.*)

WARWICK—I don't want anything to do with your death.

JOAN (*smiles*)—You have a funny gentleman's face. But you are kind. Come now. (*She calls out.*) Soldiers! Englishmen! Give me back my warrior clothes. And when I have put them on, call back all the priests. (*Stops, puts her hands in prayer and speaks simply.*) Please, God, help me now.

The trial judges, the courtiers, soldiers, villagers all gather. Women pass bearing faggots as two soldiers bring on a crude stake. Joan walks to it; and lashed to it, is being carried off when the Executioner moves through the crowd with a lighted torch. An English soldier, answering Joan's plea for a cross over the Promoter's angry refusal, quickly improvises one before Joan is led away.

As the flames rise on the cyclorama, Ladvenu raises a Church Cross for Joan to see. Each of her accusers cries out in his own fashion. The Inquisitor wishes her death to be quick, for—"In five minutes, the world will be crying." Warwick agrees. Ladvenu calls out to give Joan courage. Cauchon cries: "May God forgive us all," as he falls to his knees to pray for the dead. Charles and his court ladies have found it too awful to watch. The Inquisitor, too, has turned away, but asks what Joan does. Ladvenu, reporting that she neither lowers her head nor falters, says to the Inquisitor: "It is a terrible and noble sight, Messire. You should turn and see." The Inquisitor, moving away, answers: "I have seen it all before."

As the flames die out, darkness settles over Cauchon, the Promoter, Ladvenu and Warwick. Suddenly La Hire, in full flashing armor, appears: "You were fools to burn Joan of Arc." Cauchon knows it was a sin; Warwick admits it was a grave mistake: "We made a lark into a giant bird who will travel the skies of the world long after our names are forgotten, or confused, or cursed down." La Hire begs that the story of Joan not be ended in this fashion. Ladvenu agrees: "The true story of Joan is not the hideous agony of a girl tied to a burning stake. She will stand forever for the glory that can be. Praise God." La Hire says curtly: "The true story of Joan is the story of her happiest day. Anybody with any sense knows that. Go back and act it out."

In a burst of light, the Coronation of Charles is shown in the Cathedral at Reims. Lighted candles flare behind the altar, stained glass windows glow on the cyclorama, and amid the gaily dressed royal courtiers, Joan shines in a white robe stamped with a fleur-de-lis.

Warwick, moving into the scene, stands bewildered.

WARWICK—This could not have been her happiest day. To watch Holy Oil being poured on that mean, sly little head!

CHARLES (*turns to* WARWICK, *amused*)—Oh, I didn't turn out so bad. I drove you out of the country. And I got myself some money before I died. I was as good as most.

WARWICK—So you were. But certainly the girl would never have ridden into battle, never have been willing to die because you were as good as most.

JOAN (*comes forward, smiling, happy*)—Oh, Warwick, I wasn't paying any attention to Charlie. I knew what Charlie was like. I wanted him crowned because I wanted my country back. And God gave it to me on this Coronation Day. Let's end with it, please, if nobody would mind.

And so it ends with the chorus singing the *Gloria* of the Mass.

THE MATCHMAKER *

A Farce in Two Acts

BY THORNTON WILDER

[THORNTON WILDER *was born in Madison, Wis., in 1897, the son of a newspaper editor. However, he spent most of his youth in China when his father was sent to the east as an American Consul General. He was sent home to school and studied at Oberlin and Yale Universities. He wrote a first play "The Trumpet Shall Sound" which he did not like and turned to novels. His "Bridge of San Luis Rey" won him a Pulitzer Prize. He returned to the theatre with an adaptation of "Lucrece" which he did for Katharine Cornell. After the Pulitzer winning "Our Town" he wrote "The Merchant of Yonkers" for Jane Cowl and it is from this "The Matchmaker" is made. In 1942-43 he won another Pulitzer Award with "The Skin of Our Teeth."*]

IN the late 80s, Merchant Vandergelder, who lives above his Yonkers store, is being shaved by his barber.

There are none of the comforts of home in this miser's house: pots and pans hanging on the wall are its only ornament; an iron cookstove, rough chairs, a bench, a table, and a desk are its only furnishings. And in spite of Vandergelder's blustering vanity his own appearance is as slovenly as his surroundings. A soiled dressing gown covers his special lodge-parade trousers.

To his barber's annoyance, Vandergelder is telling his niece's suitor in pompous, positive tones that he hasn't a chance. Artist Ambrose Kemper protests that it's a free country and not Vandergelder's private kingdom. "There are no free countries for fools, Mr. Kemper," says Vandergelder, rising to his feet with the barber following suit. "Thank you for the honor of your visit—good morning." Vandergelder's jerk of the head has Joe, the barber, exclaiming: "Mr. Vandergelder, will you please sit still one minute. If I cut your throat it'll be practically unintentional."

Vandergelder again pontificates. Ambrose, trying to get a word in edgewise, assures him that he can make a good living. Vandergelder says that no artist can. "A living is made, Mr. Kemper," says Vandergelder, "by selling something that everybody needs at least once a year . . . and a million is made by producing something that everybody needs every day—you artists produce something that nobody needs at any time." Ambrose protests that not only can he support Ermingarde right now, but that he has very real expectations.

Vandergelder, while stamping on the floor for his clerk, tells Ambrose what *he* thinks of expectations: "We merchants don't do business with them. I don't keep accounts with people who promise somehow to pay something some day, and I don't allow my niece to marry such people. No. No, Mr. Kemper. You go back to your studio and when you've finished painting your sunset on the Hudson, why don't you try 'Hope' feeding a family or how about 'Love' melting a snowbank? There is a subject for you."

Ambrose announces that since there is no law against it, any way he and Ermingarde find to get married will be fair. Vandergelder has something to say on this subject, too: "Let me tell you something, Mr. Kemper: most of the people in the world are fools. The law is there to prevent crime; we men of sense are there to prevent foolishness. It's I, and not the law, that will prevent Ermingarde from marrying you, and I've taken some steps already. I've sent her away. . . ."

Vandergelder is pleased with himself. His old deaf servant entering at that moment is equally pleased with herself. She announces in clear deaf tones that Ermingarde's trunks are all marked care of: "Miss Van Huysen, 8 Jackson Street, New York." Vandergelder's pleasure turns to irritation. Breaking away from the barber he cries: "Hell and damnation! Didn't I tell you it was a secret?" Ambrose, picking up his hat and coat, deposits a kiss on the deaf servant's cheek and departs with Ermingarde's New York address. Vandergelder shouts: "It won't help you, Mr. Kemper!"

Clerk Cornelius pokes his head up through the trap door in answer to Vandergelder's stamped summons. He is ordered to carry Ermingarde's trunks to the station, to bring the carriage round to the front door in half an hour, and to wait.

Vandergelder seats himself at the table, giving Joe a chance to shave his neck. "This morning," says Vandergelder, "I'm leading my Lodge Parade down to Spuyten Duyvil; this afternoon I'm going to New York. Before I go, I have something important to say to you and Barnaby. Fact is—I'm going to promote you. How old are you?" Cornelius answers thirty-three, which Vandergelder considers a foolish age to be at. "I was thinking of promoting you to chief clerk," he adds. "What am I now, Mr. Vandergelder?" asks Cornelius. "You're an impertinent fool, that's what you are. Now, if you behave yourself, I'll promote you from impertinent fool to chief clerk, with a raise in your wages. And Barnaby may be promoted from idiot apprentice to incompetent clerk." With which he sends Cornelius off to get the trunks.

Having special reasons for looking his best today, Vandergelder wonders if there isn't some extra special little thing that Joe could do for him. Highly indignant, Joe has no intention of doing more than his usual fifteen cents' worth, which he says includes everything that's decent to do to a man. Vandergelder confides that he's about to be married again, and today is the day he's calling on his refined intended in New York. "Your gettin' married is none of my business, Mr. Vandergelder," snaps Joe. "I done everything to you I know, and the charge is fifteen cents like it always was and . . ." (*as* CORNELIUS *carries in the trunk with* ERMINGARDE *and the deaf servant following*), Joe makes clear: "I don't dye no hair, not even for fifty cents, I don't!" Barked at to be off, Joe fires back a final shot: "It looks to me like you're pretty rash to judge which is fools and which isn't fools, Mr. Vandergelder. People that's et onions is bad judges of who's et onions and who ain't. . . . Good morning, ladies; good morning, Mr. Vandergelder."

Vandergelder orders the deaf servant off for his parade regalia, and turns to Ermingarde. He gives her the gist of his talk with Ambrose, and asks her to leave such matters to him. Ermingarde, weeping, insists that if she doesn't marry Ambrose she'll die. "What of?" demands Vandergelder. "A broken heart," sobs Ermingarde. Vandergelder's never heard of it.

Informing Ermingarde that Mrs. Levi is to take her to her mother's New York friend, Miss Van Huysen, for several weeks, Vandergelder decrees that while there she may receive nobody's letters but his, and that he will call on her there tomorrow.

A sardonic, patently false character of about fifty comes in. Malachi Stack has heard that Vandergelder needs a new apprentice in his hay, feed, provision, and hardware business. "An apprentice at your age?" remarks Vandergelder. But before settling down to read Malachi's references Vandergelder reminds Ermingarde to let him know the minute Mrs. Levi arrives. Ermingarde obediently trots off.

Ruffling through the worn letters reporting unfavorably on Malachi as seaman, as typesetter, as hospital cook, Vandergelder encounters one from his former partner: ". . . For the most part honest and reliable . . . occasionally willing and diligent." There seems something hesitant, he notes, about these recommendations; still, seeing that Malachi has at some point been a barber and valet, Vandergelder—despite indications that Malachi drinks—hires him. He gives him a dollar to get to New York where he is to reserve Vandergelder a room. He has a minute to catch the train. "Hurry now," cries Vandergelder, "the station's across the street." Told he'll never regret this, Vandergelder, ordering Malachi off, regrets it already.

VANDERGELDER (*addressing the audience*)—Ninety-nine percent of the people in the world are fools and the rest of us are in great danger of contagion. But I wasn't always free of foolishness as I am now. I was once young, which was foolish; I fell in love, which was foolish; and I got married, which was foolish; and for a while I was poor, which was more foolish than all the other things put together. Then my wife died, which was foolish of her; I grew older which was sensible of me; then I became a rich man which is as sensible as it is rare. Since you see I'm a man of sense, I guess you were surprised to hear that I'm planning to get married again. Well, I've two reasons for it. In the first place, I like my house run with order, comfort, and economy. That's a woman's work; but even a woman can't do it well if she's merely being paid for it. In order to run a house well, a woman must have the feeling that she owns it. Marriage is a bribe to make a housekeeper think she's a householder. Did you ever watch an ant carry a burden twice its size? What excitement! What patience! What will! Well, that's what I think of when I see a woman running a house. What giant passions in those little bodies—what quarrels with the butcher for the best cut—what fury at discovering a moth in a cupboard! Believe me!—If women could harness their natures to something bigger than a house and a baby carriage—tck! tck!—they'd change the world. And the second reason, ladies and gentlemen? Well, I see by your faces you've guessed it already. There's nothing like mixing with women to bring out all the foolishness in a man of sense. And that's a risk I'm willing to take. I've just turned sixty and I've just laid side by side the last dollar of my first half-million. So if I should lose my head a little, I still have enough money to buy it back. (*He goes behind the bench and picks up the sword.*) After many years' caution and hard work I have the right to a little risk and adventure, and I'm thinking of getting married. (*Goes towards center door.*) Yes, like all you other fools, I'm willing to risk a little security for a certain amount of adventure. Think it over. (*He exits.*)

Ambrose, equally bent on adventure, comes back to elope with Ermingarde. She is utterly horrified: "Ambrose Kemper! How can you use such an awful word!" Ambrose says that she has the soul of a field mouse. Amidst tears and recriminations, Mrs. Levi saunters in.

Of seedy elegance and uncertain age, and with masses of some kind of bright hair, Mrs. Levi dangles a handbag and a paper bag. She announces her interest in the lovers' predicament and accepts Ermingarde's introduction to Ambrose: "Mrs. Levi, born Gallagher," amplifies Mrs. Levi. "This thing you were planning to do is a very great mistake," says Mrs. Levi. Shooing Ermingarde off to keep an eye on her uncle, Mrs. Levi prepares to talk to Ambrose.

Explaining that she was one of Ermingarde's mother's oldest friends, Mrs. Levi assures Ambrose that she is entirely on his and Ermingarde's side. She wants them to marry soon but there must be no elopement. Dusting off a chair with swipes of her paper bag, Mrs. Levi settles herself.

Mrs. Levi—Believe me, Mr. Vandergelder wishes to get rid of Ermingarde, and if you follow my suggestions he will even permit her to marry you. You see, Mr. Vandergelder is planning to get married himself.

Ambrose—What? That monster?

Mrs. Levi—Mr. Kemper!

Ambrose—Married! To you, Mrs. Levi?

Mrs. Levi—Oh, no, no. . . . I am merely arranging it. I am helping him find a suitable bride.

Ambrose—For Mr. Vandergelder there are no suitable brides.

Mrs. Levi—I think we can safely say that Mr. Vandergelder will be married to someone by the end of next week.

Ambrose—Well, what do you suggest, Mrs. Levi?

Mrs. Levi—I am taking Ermingarde to New York on the next train. I shall not take her to Miss Van Huysen's as is planned; I shall take her to my house. I wish you to call for her at my house at five-thirty. Here is my card.

Ambrose—"Mrs. Dolly Gallagher Levi. Varicose veins reduced."

Mrs. Levi—I beg your pardon. . . . (*Takes bunch of cards from purse, goes through them.*) I meant to give you my other card. Here. Wasn't that funny?

Ambrose—Yes. "Mrs. Dolly Gallagher Levi. Aurora Hosiery. Instruction in the guitar and mandolin." You do all these things, Mrs. Levi?

Mrs. Levi—Two and two make four, Mr. Kemper—and they

always did. So you will come to my house at five-thirty. At about six I shall take you both with me to the Harmonia Gardens Restaurant on the Battery; Mr. Vandergelder will be there and everything will be arranged.

Ambrose—How?

Mrs. Levi—Oh, I don't know. One thing will lead to another.

Ambrose—How do I know that I can trust you, Mrs. Levi? You could easily make our situation worse.

Mrs. Levi—Mr. Kemper, your situation could not possibly be worse. (*Pats his hand.*)

Ambrose—I wish I knew what you get out of this, Mrs. Levi.

Mrs. Levi—That is a very proper question. I get two things: profit and pleasure.

Ambrose—How?

Mrs. Levi—Mr. Kemper, I am a woman who arranges things. At present I am arranging Mr. Vandergelder's domestic affairs. Out of it I get—shall we call it: yes, why don't we?—little pickings? I need little pickings, Mr. Kemper, and especially just now, when I haven't got my train fare back to New York. You see: I am frank with you.

Ambrose—That's your profit, Mrs. Levi; but where do you get your pleasure?

Mrs. Levi—My pleasure? Mr. Kemper, when you artists paint a hillside or a river you change everything a little, you make a thousand little changes, don't you? Nature is never completely satisfactory and must be corrected. Well, I'm like you artists. Life as it is is never quite interesting enough for me—I'm bored, Mr. Kemper, with life as it is—and so I do things. I put my hand in here, and I put my hand in there, and I watch and I listen—and speaking of pleasure, as we were—a good deal of the time I am amused.

Ambrose (*rises, picks up hat*)—Not in my affairs, Mrs. Levi.

Mrs. Levi—Wait, I haven't finished. . . . There's another thing. I'm very interested in this household here—in Mr. Vandergelder and all that idle, frozen money of his. I don't like the thought of it lying in great piles, useless, motionless, in the bank, Mr. Kemper. Money should circulate like rain water. It should be flowing down among the people, through dressmakers and restaurants and cabmen, setting up a little business here, and furnishing a good time there. Do you see what I mean?

Ambrose—Yes, I do.

Mrs. Levi—New York should be a very happy city, Mr. Kemper, but it isn't. My late husband came from Vienna, Mr. Ephraim Levi: now there's a city that understands this. I want New York to be

Ruth Gordon in Thornton Wilder's "The Matchmaker"

more like Vienna and less a collection of nervous and tired ants. And if you and Ermingarde get a good deal of Mr. Vandergelder's money, I want you to see that it starts flowing in and around a lot of people's lives.

Ermingarde dashes in to report her approaching uncle; Ambrose disappears through the store trap door, as Vandergelder, wearing his uniform and holding a banner aloft, struts into the room.

Between gasps of admiration directed in Vandergelder's direction, Mrs. Levi pushes his niece out of the door. She then gives Vandergelder all possible attention and flattery. He gets younger every day, says Mrs. Levi. Vandergelder finds this likely enough, though he concedes that he won't see sixty—er—fifty-five again. "Fifty-five!" shrieks Mrs. Levi. "Why I can see at a glance that you're the sort that will be stamping about at a hundred—and eating five meals a day, just like what's-his-name . . . my Uncle Harry." She improvises: "At fifty-five my Uncle Harry was a mere boy—I'm a judge of hands, Mr. Vandergelder—show me your hand." His life line proves too much for Mrs. Levi: "It runs right off your hand. I don't know where it goes." She turns his hand over, looks up his sleeve, and concludes: "They'll have to hit you on the head with a mallet. They'll have to stifle you with a sofa pillow. You'll bury us all."

Having thus paved the way for business matters, Mrs. Levi guesses that Mr. Vandergelder has changed his mind again and has given up all thought of marriage. "Mrs. Levi," Vandergelder informs her, "I've practically decided to ask Mrs. Molloy to be my wife." Mrs. Levi is incredulous: "You have?" But she quickly accepts it: "Oh, you have! Well, I guess that's just about the best news I ever heard. Oh dear me! So there's nothing more for me to do but wish you every happiness under the sun and say goodbye." Over Vandergelder's protests, Mrs. Levi decides she won't make a little suggestion she had in mind.

Vandergelder would like to hear it. Mrs. Levi admits grudgingly to have found a wonderful girl, an ideal wife for him. Agog, Vandergelder asks: "Another? What's her name?" Mrs. Levi, after a pause, plays by ear: "Her name!—Ernestina—Simple. *Miss* Ernestina Simple." Even though Mrs. Levi knows that he is practically engaged to Irene Molloy, the attractive widow (four visits and a pot of geraniums constitute practically an engagement), she can't help letting Vandergelder know that this young, practical, domestic girl already has fallen in love with him. Vandergelder's tongue is hanging out: "Can she cook?" he asks. "Cook, Mr. Vandergelder?" cries Mrs. Levi. "I've had two meals from her hands, and—as I live—I don't know what I've done that God should reward me with such meals." Mrs. Levi tosses in: "And I'm the best cook in the world myself, and I *know* what's good."

What is more, this Ernestina Simple has a horror of brainless young men. According to Mrs. Levi, give her a fine head of gray hair any day. Vandergelder finds this not usual. "Usual?" cries Mrs. Levi, "I'm not wearing myself to the bone hunting up usual girls to interest you, Mr. Vandergelder. Usual, indeed. Listen to me. Do you know the sort of pictures she has on her wall? Is it any of these young Romeos and Lochinvars? No!—it's Moses on the mountain—that's what she's got. . . ." Mrs. Levi lets her imagination next play on Ernestina's appearance, so that when she suggests that Vandergelder come to New York today (knowing he was going anyway) he replies by asking her and her protégée to dine with him.

There is a slight snarl. With her handbag open before her, Mrs. Levi declares she is busy with her wretched lawsuit to own half of Staten Island and right now is at her wit's end digging up enough money to finish it. She digs into her bag while confessing that with fifty dollars Staten Island would be as good as hers. Above Vandergelder's allergic snorts and coughs, Mrs. Levi mentions how she has been working in his behalf these last two months. A compromise is reached: Vandergelder parts miserably with twenty-five dollars.

Mrs. Levi now gets back to the matter of the dinner. She hopes that for this once Mr. Vandergelder may be persuaded to order them a good dinner. Mr. Vandergelder, though reluctantly, is persuaded this once.

Mr. Vandergelder is full of plans. First he'll visit Mrs. Molloy, then see Ernestina Simple. Hoping he means business, Mrs. Levi says: "Because there's Ernestina Simple *and* Irene Molloy. Now this is a free country, Mr. Vandergelder, but it's not so free it's going to let you marry the both of them—so make up your mind!" And Mrs. Levi departs.

Cornelius and Barnaby now enter by the trap door to receive Vandergelder's last-minute instructions. Vandergelder, after announcing he's about to be married, asks his clerks if they have any questions. Cornelius has the temerity to ask one: "Does the chief clerk get one evening off every week?" Vandergelder lets him know what he thinks of such heresy: "An evening! If you keep on asking for evenings free you'll find yourself with all your days free! And evenings free!" Vandergelder, after reminding Cornelius to put the lid on the sheep dip, marches off.

Cornelius rebels. He wonders when he is going to begin to live. At thirty-three he is yet to have an evening free. Thinking back to their few holidays, Cornelius reminds Barnaby that last Christmas afternoon they spent cleaning up after all those canned tomatoes exploded.

CORNELIUS—You and I are going to New York.

BARNABY—Cornelius! We can't! Close the store?

CORNELIUS—Some more rotten tomatoes are going to explode.

BARNABY—Holy cabooses! How do you know?

CORNELIUS—I know they're rotten. All you have to do is to light a match under them. They'll make such a smell that customers can't come into the place for twenty-four hours. That'll get us an evening free. We're going to New York, too, Barnaby, we're going to live. I'm going to have enough adventures to last me until I'm a *partner*. So go and get your Sunday clothes on.

And not only that, but Cornelius promises that they're going to have a good meal, live dangerously, nearly get arrested, spend all their money and not come back to Yonkers until they've kissed a girl. This last, seventeen-year-old Barnaby doesn't feel so impatient about, but he agrees to go with Cornelius, and now follows him down the ladder.

Mrs. Levi, entering with Ermingarde, advises the timid girl to take a last look at her girlhood home. This scares the exiting Ermingarde all over again. Before she follows Ermingarde, Mrs. Levi with a quick look herself addresses the audience: "You know I think I'm going to have this room with blue wallpaper." She hurries out.

The explosions start, with Barnaby supervising them from the trap door. When they are well under way, Cornelius joins him and they dash off. A final explosion hurls a shower of cans through the trap door.

Scene II

In Irene Molloy's millinery shop Mrs. Molloy tells her assistant Minnie that, should Horace Vandergelder ask her, she will certainly marry him. Bustling about, crawling into the show window under the curtain rail, Mrs. Molloy sings at the top of her lungs. She crawls out again and goes to the counter where Minnie tries to ask: ". . . But do you . . . do you . . . ?" "Minnie," says temperamental Mrs. Molloy, "you're a fool. Say it: Do I love him? Of course I don't love him. But I have two good reasons for marrying him just the same. Minnie, put something on that hat. It's not ugly enough."

Her first reason, to Minnie's horror, is that she hates hats. With that Irene Molloy trills a snatch of song, takes two hats and crawls into the window again. When she crawls out she wonders what the two young men are doing out there on a park bench, and rocks Minnie with: "Take my word for it, Minnie, either I marry Horace Vandergelder, or I break out of this place like a fire engine. I'll go to every theatre and ball and opera in New York City." Minnie doesn't find Vandergelder attractive. "But what I think he is—" says bouncy Mrs. Molloy, "and it's very important—I think he'd make a good fighter."

MINNIE—Mrs. Molloy!

MRS. MOLLOY—Take my word for it, Minnie: the best of married life is the fights. The rest is merely so-so.

MINNIE (*her fingers in ears*)—I won't listen.

MRS. MOLLOY—Now Peter Molloy—God rest him!—was a fine arguing man. I pity the woman whose husband slams the door and walks out of the house at the beginning of an argument. Peter Molloy would stand up and fight for hours on end. He'd even throw things, Minnie, and there's no pleasure to equal that. When I felt tired I'd start a good blood-warming fight and it'd take ten years off my age; now Horace Vandergelder would put up a good fight; I know it. I've a mind to marry him.

Enjoying herself, Mrs. Molloy sings:

"So remember while you can
What became of Nelly Ann,
Who trusted in the promise
of a drinking man."

Warned by Minnie that the young men seem to be coming to the store, Mrs. Molloy says it's high time they had some men, and assigns Minnie the younger, while itching after the older one herself. "Mark my words, Minnie," she tells the shocked girl, "we'll get an adventure out of this yet. Adventure, adventure! Why does everybody have adventures except me, Minnie?" Flustered, Minnie follows her Irish boss into the workroom to wait for the men.

Having spent most of their money, Cornelius and Barnaby come into the store to hide from the approaching Vandergelder. If this is adventure, Barnaby is so tired he's not sure whether he could enjoy it. But to be sure he recognizes it when it appears, Barnaby asks Cornelius to give him the signal: *"Pudding."*

Cornelius, rehearsing what he will say to Mrs. Molloy, forgets it as soon as he sees her. From then on, as she displays and models hats for them, he is equally distracted by her charm and by the fear of Vandergelder's arrival. Barnaby remains at the door to spot trouble if it approaches.

Hearing that Cornelius is from Yonkers, where he offers to show her around, Mrs. Molloy asks if he knows Mr. Vandergelder. With that, Cornelius's mind turns to all possible hiding places and all available exits in Mrs. Molloy's store. As Mrs. Molloy pins ribbons to the back of her hat, and assumes that Mr. Vandergelder has a large circle of friends, Cornelius replies: "Yes, indeed—five or six." As she says that as a matter of fact she's expecting a call from Mr. Vandergelder, Barnaby with a whoop and a "Look out!" leaps over the window rail and flings himself under the table. Begging Mrs. Molloy's pardon, and pleading "Help us just this once, Mrs. Molloy! We'll explain later!" Cornelius jumps into the large cupboard. Over Mrs. Molloy's cries that she can't have this, Barnaby calls: "Cornelius! Cornelius! Pudding?" "Pudding!" answers Cornelius, disappearing from sight.

Vandergelder and Mrs. Levi enter the store. Mrs. Molloy, noticing that the boys have left their hats behind, trims them swiftly with flowers and chiffon. Then, pushing her guests along, she urges them to see her workroom. Cornelius and Barnaby, instead of using this breather for a getaway, discuss how much they like women and womanly surroundings.

Busy Mrs. Levi, having had enough of the workroom, discovers the boys. Cornelius, wildly smitten by now with Mrs. Molloy, confesses that he finds her the finest person in the world. Mrs. Levi asks: "And does she think you're the finest person in the world?" Cornelius doubts whether Mrs. Molloy knows he's alive. "Well," says Mrs. Levi, "I think she must notice that you're alive in that cupboard, Mr. Hackl. Well, if I were you I'd get back into it right away. Somebody could be coming in any minute."

Mr. Vandergelder and Mrs. Molloy, returning to the shop, settle themselves for a chat. Vandergelder's box of sweets is placed on the table hiding Barnaby.

Wasting no time, Mrs. Molloy asks Vandergelder if he knows that quite well-to-do Cornelius Hackl, of Yonkers. Vandergelder knows his chief clerk like his own book and inquires where Mrs. Molloy came to know him. Mrs. Molloy is nonplused. "Blah—blah—blah!" shouts Mrs. Levi, leaping into the breach, "one of those chance meetings—" she supposes. Vandergelder won't allow Cornelius the right to chance meetings. His severity gets Mrs. Molloy's back up, and her imagination working: "He's in New York often," she says, "and he's very well liked." This is business and pleasure as well as meat and drink to Mrs. Levi.

Mrs. Levi—Well, the truth might as well come out now as later. (Mrs. Molloy *rises in alarm.*) Mr. Vandergelder, Irene is quite right. Your head clerk is often in New York. Goes everywhere; has an army of friends. Everybody knows Cornelius Hackl.

Vandergelder (*laughs*)—He never comes to New York. He works all day in my store and at nine o'clock at night he goes to sleep in the bran room.

Mrs. Levi—So you think. But it's not true.

Vandergelder—Dolly Gallagher, you're crazy.

MRS. LEVI—Listen to me. You keep your nose so deep in your account books you don't know what goes on. Yes, by day, Cornelius Hackl is your faithful trusted clerk—that's true; but by night! Well, he leads a double life, that's all! He's here at the opera; at the great restaurants; in all the fashionable homes. . . . (MRS MOLLOY *sits next to* MRS. LEVI.) Why, he's at the Harmonia Gardens Restaurant three nights a week. The fact is, he's the wittiest, gayest, naughtiest, most delightful man in New York. Well he's just *the* famous Cornelius Hackl!

Mrs. Levi describes exploit after exploit of that Cornelius Hackl. Mrs. Molloy is fascinated, and urges her on. Vandergelder stubbornly insists that it must be a different Cornelius: his Cornelius doesn't have the money. Mrs. Levi, spreading it thicker by the minute, says his Cornelius is very rich; he is one of *the* Hackls; and *they* built the Raritan Canal. "Then," demands Vandergelder, "why should he work in my store?" Mrs. Levi is ready to tell him, but Vandergelder doesn't want to hear; he has a headache. He's had enough. "You can't get away from facts," he says. "I just made him my chief clerk." "If you had any sense," Mrs. Levi answers, "you'd make him partner."

Mrs. Levi next tells the sadly perplexed Mrs. Molloy not to think of marrying that heartbreaker, Cornelius. Mrs. Molloy blushes with pleasure over Dolly Levi's exaggerations, but next is barring the cupboard against Minnie. Minnie needs a coat for the errand girl and discovers, to her terror, a man instead. Mrs. Molloy pushes Minnie to the door but can't hush her.

Vandergelder is ready to use his stick. Masterful Mrs. Levi goes to the cupboard, stirs her umbrella around among the coats, closes the door and says there's no one. A sneeze interrupts her. Everyone jumps up. Mrs. Levi merely gives a broad shrug and cries: "Well, God bless you."

Disdaining explanations, Mrs. Molloy grandly confesses to hiding a man and bids her guests good afternoon. Barnaby sneezes. Vandergelder jerks off the table cloth, and with it the box of sweets. Barnaby jerks the cloth back and rolls in it.

"Lord," says Mrs. Levi, "the room's *crawling* with men! I'll never get over it!" Nor will Vandergelder, who won't trouble Mrs. Molloy further. He snatches back his box of candy from her hands and stalks off to Ernestina Simple. Mrs. Levi, telling Mrs. Molloy to make the most of all the interesting things she has in this room, raps on the cupboard and the table with her umbrella and departs.

Mrs. Molloy, needing no advice from Mrs. Levi, tells Cornelius that if he doesn't take her to a gay spot that he frequents she'll have him jailed. He's going to take Minnie and her to dinner at the Harmonia Gardens Restaurant. Mrs. Molloy orders Minnie to come with her and get ready to go. The penniless Cornelius grits his teeth and determines, jail or no jail, to take these lovely ladies to dinner.

When the ladies return, Cornelius speaks of their walking. Mrs. Molloy says that she won't go where she is not wanted; she refuses to be an unfashionable burden to him. Now it's his turn to beg. If they can't smile about it, says Mrs. Molloy, at least they can do something lively—something to prove themselves. They should sing. Cornelius can't sing. "We're wasting our time, Minnie," says Mrs. Molloy. "They don't want us." She wins.

Barnaby and Cornelius confer, then stand stiffly and deliver "Tenting Tonight." The ladies join in; the four together repeat the refrain, harmonizing softly.

The boys wait outside gaily while Mrs. Molloy locks up. To Minnie's consternation, Mrs. Molloy's eyes are full of tears: "Oh, Minnie," she says, "the world is full of wonderful things. Watch me, dear, and tell me if my petticoat's showing."

ACT II

Vandergelder, with Malachi in tow, has reached the Harmonia Gardens Restaurant on the Battery. There on the veranda Vandergelder tries to order his table for three, and the dinner and wine, only to have Malachi greet each request with: "You'll regret it." Vandergelder tells him to hold his tongue, which he does briefly. Vandergelder makes a final request to have one of the two veranda tables removed: he wants privacy for his party.

Malachi calls Vandergelder's attention to the arrival of his niece in the company of Ambrose and Mrs. Levi. Vandergelder would be at them but Malachi advises him to be like Napoleon and hide behind the adjacent screen: "Hear what they are planning. Napoleon—be Napoleon, sir. Outsmart them, Mr. Vandergelder." Vandergelder takes his place behind the screen.

Ermingarde is horrified to be in a *public restaurant*. Mrs. Levi reassures her: "That's all right, dear, there are some lovely private rooms upstairs, just meant for shy timid girls like us." And the three go off.

Vandergelder rushes into action: he sends Malachi, very much against his will, for a cabman, and composes a letter for Miss Van Huysen. That lady must hold the runaway couple in her home until Vandergelder arrives.

The cabman, as seedy as Malachi but not so full of ideas, refuses to do this alone. Vandergelder offers Malachi's help. Says Malachi to the audience: "Now I'm pushing people into houses." The cabman is so reluctant that he is offered another bill, and commanded, once the couple is in Miss Van Huysen's house, to sit in the hall to keep the man from running off with the girl.

Vandergelder scatters a few last orders around: Malachi must see that his table is set for three, that nobody else dines on the veranda, and that afterwards he joins the cabman on the box. Vandergelder leaves. The cabman asks: "Who's your friend?" "Friend!" says Malachi. "That's not a friend; that's an employer I'm trying out for a few days." After enlightening the cabman on the subject of employers, Malachi suggests that the two of them retire to the kitchen for some whisky: Malachi can't push people into houses when he is sober.

The foursome arrives. Mrs. Molloy is in particularly fine fettle; she decides that the veranda is just the place to eat, that this is just the table, that they should all address one another by their first names, and should call the waiter. Cornelius is suddenly mute. Mrs. Molloy remembers: ". . . Mrs. Levi gave us to understand that every waiter in New York knew you." "They will," sighs Cornelius.

Minnie proves an inexpensive date: she orders sardines. Mrs. Molloy, on the other hand, doesn't even require a menu. All by herself, she rolls off: soup, pheasant, chestnuts, salad, and some nice red wine. Impulsively, Cornelius decides he may as well be hanged for a sheep. He tells the waiter: "Neapolitan ice cream, hot-house peaches; champagne . . ." All cry: "Champagne!" and Barnaby spins around in his chair. Cornelius isn't through: ". . . and a German band," he says. Mrs. Molloy won't let him be that extravagant: champagne, yes, but a German band, no.

Mrs. Molloy starts to wander off with Minnie, leaving the men to look forward to a jail sentence of many years. But Mrs. Molloy, with a nose for champagne, meets a waiter carrying a cooler to the mayor of New York. This she appropriates for her own group. The waiter is miserable, so she gives him a glass. Barnaby toasts the ladies, and in exchange receives Mrs. Molloy's kiss, which on top of champagne, has him reeling. "Now I can go back to Yonkers, Cornelius. Pudding. Pudding. Pudding!" He spins around and falls flat on his back. As the waiters set their table, Mrs. Molloy cries: "Minnie, I'm enjoying myself. To think that this goes on in hundreds of places every night, while I sit at home darning my stockings."

Next a gypsy musician slides in. Mrs. Molloy wants to dance.

The men won't, but Minnie will. Mrs. Molloy and Minnie whirl about together, with Mrs. Molloy complimenting Minnie on how beautifully she dances.

The waiters start setting up a table nearby. Mrs. Molloy scents a little trouble. She orders them to take the table down and then, spoiling for a fight, orders Cornelius to throw out Malachi who is supervising the procedure. Drunken Malachi appreciates her insults. Gaining momentum, Mrs. Molloy orders Cornelius to upset the offending table. The quartet just laugh their heads off.

Then the rush is on. Everyone talks at the top of his voice. Malachi now tries to upset the table; Mrs. Molloy and Minnie rush to save it; the gypsy comes in playing and goes out on his hands and knees. As Cornelius rushes Malachi out through a door, a waiter tries to bring down the dividing screen. Cornelius and Barnaby try to close it as the waiter clutches it madly. Mrs. Molloy, with a fight on her hands, feels ten years younger.

Malachi now announces the arrival of his employer. Seeing Vandergelder, Cornelius quickly votes for the screen, which, when pulled out, divides the veranda in half.

Vandergelder rages that Malachi couldn't manage so simple a thing as having a place reserved for him. He hangs up his hat and stick and asks Malachi to help him off with his coat without killing him. In the fussing over the coat, Vandergelder's purse drops out of his pocket and falls by the screen. Wanting to read his paper undisturbed while awaiting his guests, Vandergelder won't listen to Malachi's question about his purse. Asked whether he hasn't dropped something, Vandergelder answers peevishly: "No, don't bother me no more. Do as I tell you."

Malachi starts to take the purse around the screen to Cornelius. But before he does so, and without even peeking inside it, Malachi explains to the audience, why, surprisingly enough, he is not taking the purse himself. He believes in nursing one vice alone. ". . . Give it the attention it deserves," he tells the audience, "and let your virtues spring up modestly around it. Then you'll have the miser who's no liar; and the drunkard who's the benefactor of a whole city. Well, after I'd had that weakness of stealing for a while, I found another: I took to whisky—whisky took to me. And then I discovered an important rule that I'm going to pass on to you: Never support two weaknesses at the same time. It's your combination sinners—your lecherous liars and your miserly drunkards—who dishonor the vices and bring them into bad repute. So now you see why I want to get rid of this money: I want to keep my mind free to do the credit to whisky that it deserves. And my last word to you, ladies and gentlemen, ladies and gentlemen, is this: one vice at a time."

Passing to the other side of the screen, Malachi is greeted with all sorts of apologies. Malachi brushes them off airily: "Oh, it's nothing," he says, and calls Cornelius to one side. Malachi asks him if he has lost something. "Mr. Stack," says Cornelius, "in this one day, I've lost everything I own." "There it is," says Malachi, handing him the purse, "don't mention it." To Cornelius, this is a miracle. Then finding out that Stack, too, works for Vandergelder, Cornelius repeats: "It's a miracle." He offers to give Malachi something. "Don't mention it," Malachi repeats, with his hand out. But when offered a third bill, Malachi refuses it with a "No, I might get to like them."

Feeling immeasurably better, Cornelius bounds back to Mrs. Molloy, ready to tell her the truth. "If I tell the truth," he asks, "will you let me . . . will you let me put my arm around your waist?"

(MINNIE *screams and flings her napkin over her face.*)

MRS. MOLLOY—Hold your tongue, Minnie. All right, you can put your arm around my waist just to show it can be done in a gentlemanly way; but I might as well warn you: a corset is a corset.

CORNELIUS (*his arm around her, softly*)—You're a wonderful person, Mrs. Molloy.

MRS. MOLLOY—Thank you. All right, now that's enough. (*Turns to face him.*) What is the truth?

CORNELIUS—Irene, I'm not as rich as Mrs. Levi said I was.

MRS. MOLLOY—Not rich!

CORNELIUS—I almost never came to New York. And I'm not like she said I was—bad. And I think you ought to know that at this very minute Mr. Vandergelder's sitting on the other side of that screen.

MRS. MOLLOY—Well, now! He's not going to spoil any party of mine. So that's why we've been whispering. Let's forget all about Mr. Vandergelder and have some more wine.

Mrs. Molloy starts them singing "East Side, West Side." They are at it when Mrs. Levi, sans Ernestina, saunters in.

Mrs. Levi says to Mr. Vandergelder that she'll never trust a woman as long as she lives: "She ran away and got married . . . to a young feller only fifty-one years old." She's as disappointed as Vandergelder: "I—can't—eat—a—thing—what—have—you—ordered?" Mrs. Levi doesn't think that she can face a chicken, but with the waiter at her elbow, she just about takes over the restaurant, and insists upon perfect service in the name of poor Mr. Vandergelder. Mr. Vandergelder is not cheered.

Wasting no time, Mrs. Levi pops up just to see who's on the other side of the screen. She goes through the screen door; Cornelius rises; Mrs. Levi, taking no notice, circles the table, picks up the refrain of their song, and without pausing, swishes her way back to Vandergelder. Asked who it was, Mrs. Levi answers: just some city sparks entertaining their girls.

VANDERGELDER—Always wanting to know everything; always curious about everything; always putting your nose into other people's affairs. Anybody who lived with you would get as nervous as a cat.

MRS. LEVI—What? What's that you're saying?

VANDERGELDER—I said anybody who lived with you would—

MRS. LEVI—Horace Vandergelder, get that idea right out of your head. I'm surprised that you even mentioned such a thing. Understand once and for all that I have no intention of marrying you.

VANDERGELDER—I didn't mean that. (MRS. MOLLOY *goes to the screen for a peek.*)

MRS. LEVI—You've been hinting around at such a thing for some time, but from now on put such ideas right out of your head.

VANDERGELDER—Stop talking that way. That's not what I meant at all.

MRS. LEVI—I hope not. I should hope not. Horace Vandergelder, you go your way (*Points finger.*) and I'll go mine. (*Points finger in same direction.*) I'm not some Irene Molloy, whose head can be turned by a pot of geraniums. (MRS. MOLLOY *turns and looks at* CORNELIUS.) Why the idea of you even suggesting such a thing.

VANDERGELDER—Mrs. Levi, you misunderstood me.

MRS. LEVI—I certainly hope I did. If I had any intention of marrying again it would be to a far more pleasure-loving man than you. Why I'd marry Cornelius Hackl before I'd marry you.

The waiter arrives with the food; Mrs. Levi proposes to do the serving herself. She dishes it out to Vandergelder; she supervises the pouring of the wine, without forgetting the subject at hand.

MRS. LEVI—We'll have forgotten all about it in a moment, but—sit down, sit down, we'll close the matter forever in just a moment, but there's one more thing I ought to say! (VANDERGELDER *sits down.*) It's true, I'm a woman who likes to know everything that's going on; who likes to manage things, you're perfectly right about that. But I wouldn't like to manage anything as disorderly as your household, as out-of-control, as untidy. You'll have to do that yourself, God helping you. (*Takes a mouthful of food and mumbles the last three words.*)

VANDERGELDER—It's not out of control.

MRS. LEVI—Very well, let's not say another word about it. Take some more of that squash, it's good. No, Horace, a complaining, quarrelsome, friendless soul like you is no sort of companion for me. (*Picks up pepper pot.*) You go your way (*Peppers her own plate.*) and I'll go mine. (*Peppers his plate.*)

VANDERGELDER—Stop saying that.

MRS. LEVI—I won't say another word.

VANDERGELDER—Besides . . . I'm not those things you said I am.

MRS. LEVI—What?—Well, I guess you're friendless, aren't you? Ermingarde told me this morning you'd even quarreled with your barber—a man who's held a razor to your throat for twenty years! Seems to me that's sinking pretty low. (*Eats.*)

VANDERGELDER—Well, we had a little discussion and I said . . . but . . . my clerks, they . . .

MRS. LEVI—They like you? Cornelius Hackl and that Barnaby? Behind your back they call you Wolf-Trap. (*All on the other side move close to the screen, the better to hear.*)

VANDERGELDER (*blanching*)—They don't.

MRS. LEVI—No, Horace. It looks to me as though I were the last person in the world that liked you, and even I'm just so-so. No, for the rest of my life I intend to enjoy myself. You'll be able to find some housekeeper who can prepare you three meals for a dollar a day—it can be done you know, if you like cold baked beans. You'll spend your last days listening at keyholes, for fear someone's cheating you. Take some more of that. (*Offers a dish.*)

She has made a dent. Vandergelder wishes she hadn't said such things; wishes that she wouldn't constantly harp on his age. And his house, he assures Mrs. Levi, is not in confusion. "What?" she answers, "with your niece upstairs in the restaurant right now?" Regaining some of his smugness, Vandergelder says that he's fixed that. "And your clerks," Mrs. Levi throws at him, "skipping around New York behind your back?" In proof of that, Cornelius Hackl is to be seen right on the other side of the screen, if Vandergelder will but look. Vandergelder rises, but decides against it. And he doesn't want to hear any more. He doesn't want to talk.

On the other side of the screen, Cornelius thinks they should pay and go. Mrs. Molloy proposes instead that she dress the men in the women's coats and veils, and should Vandergelder stomp about, he'll only find girls. She and Minnie take the men away to dress them.

Having had more than his fill, Vandergelder is ready to pay and leave for Miss Van Huysen's. To his horror, and to Mrs. Levi's amusement, he finds that he has no purse. Mrs. Levi thinks it funny: "Impossible! I can't imagine you without your purse." Vandergelder is greatly shaken. Mrs. Levi, advising him to calm himself, says he can always borrow from Ambrose Kemper or Cornelius Hackl. Mrs. Molloy and Cornelius—who are back again on the other side of the screen—now know whose purse it is.

As loud gypsy music starts up, things really begin to happen. Vandergelder and the waiters chase one another, now back and forth, now up and down, now in and out of doors—with the waiters dropping things. And with the reappearance of the gypsy, the be-veiled men are taught to dance by Minnie and Mrs. Molloy. Mrs. Levi interrupts Vandergelder's search to remind him what a good dancer he used to be. "Don't confess to me," she says, "that you're too old to dance." At this point everybody, Mrs. Levi and Vandergelder included, begins to dance. Mrs. Molloy and Cornelius pass the screen. Vandergelder shoots out his leg, Russian style, shouting: "Hey! Hey! Hey!" He trips Cornelius, and recognizes him, on the floor, under his veil. Cornelius gets up and collapses in a chair. Mrs. Levi just laughs and laughs. "You're discharged," bellows Vandergelder, "you're fired. Where's that idiot Barnaby Tucker?" He then chases him round a pillar, with Barnaby first on one side, then the other.

Ambrose, coming on with his luggage, now gets embroiled. Ermingarde, arriving, is confronted by Vandergelder's fist and faints into Ambrose's arms. Vandergelder goes after his hat and coat, yelling as he leaves: "You're discharged!" Mrs. Molloy, as she leaves, cries: "You're discharged!" "You're discharged!" shouts Vandergelder again.

The waiters, with the bills, await Vandergelder, now that the others have flown. Mrs. Levi runs to Vandergelder, too.

MRS. LEVI—There's your life, without niece, without clerks . . . (*The waiters are in full cry.*) . . . without bride, without purse. Will you marry me now?

VANDERGELDER (*continuing round screen*)—NO!

MRS. LEVI (*to audience*)—Well *DAMN!* (VANDERGELDER *runs out through the service door. Both waiters pursue.* MRS. LEVI *flounces round and through screen.*)

Scene II

To Miss Flora Van Huysen's bird-cage decorated, lace-curtained, upholstered, china-ornamented, aspidistra-cluttered house, drunken Malachi and the drunken cabman kidnap Cornelius and Barnaby.

Huge, sentimental, snuff-taking Miss Van Huysen receives them as the Ambrose and Ermingarde of Vandergelder's letter. (Barnaby still wears Minnie's veiled hat and coat.) Telling the cook to make coffee, ordering the drunken pair to the hall, Miss Van Huysen repeatedly tells the other pair they have nothing to fear. Then, oozing affection towards Barnaby, she offers him fresh clothes and a hot bath. Barnaby retreats.

Miss Van Huysen—Believe me, Ermingarde, your troubles are at an end. You two will be married tomorrow. (Cornelius, *overcome, crosses to window. To* Barnaby, *hand under his chin.*) My dear, you look just like I did at your age, and your sufferings have been as mine. While you're bathing, I'll come and tell you the story of my life.

Barnaby—Oh, I don't want to take a bath. I always catch cold.

Miss Van Huysen—No, dear, you won't catch cold. I'll slap you all over. I'll be back in a minute. (*She exits to kitchen.*)

Cornelius—Barnaby, do you think we could jump from this window?

The boys feel their situation is becoming increasingly desperate.

The doorbell rings. Cook and Miss Van Huysen skip for joy at all this activity. Cook lets in Ambrose and Ermingarde, as Miss Van Huysen pulls and pushes Barnaby and Cornelius to the kitchen.

Cook doesn't think Miss Van Huysen will like having someone insist she is Ermingarde when they already have an Ermingarde in the kitchen. She says: "I'll tell Miss Van Huysen who you *think* you are, she won't like it."

Left alone, except for the swigging pair in the hall, Ambrose tells Ermingarde that he'd better leave her before Vandergelder arrives. "You can't leave me in this crazy house with these drunken men in the hall," she answers. Longing for the quiet of Yonkers, she comes up with the idea that Ambrose should pretend to be her uncle's clerk, Cornelius Hackl.

Miss Van Huysen doesn't remember Ermingarde, and she knows no Cornelius Hackl. At least she says: "The other Ermingarde came with the man she's in love with, and that proves she came with Mr. Ambrose Kemper." Ermingarde bursts into tears and gains Miss Van Huysen's ever-flowing sympathy. Miss Van Huysen can see that the girl is in love with this man and assumes that Horace Vandergelder is trying to separate this pair also. It is "Mr. Hackl's" turn to consider Miss Van Huysen his friend, and she ushers him and Ermingarde into the kitchen to get warm. But the real Cornelius comes out of the kitchen and adds to the confusion. The men accuse each other of being impostors. "My dear young man," says Miss Van Huysen, "what does it matter what your names are? The important thing is that you are you—you are alive and breathing—" and she goes about pinching everybody, including herself, to drive the point home. "The important thing is that you're all in love. Everything else is illusion." Leaving the men to themselves, she whisks Ermingarde off to a bath.

The doorbell rings and adds to the commotion: Malachi and the cabman make a lunge for the cook on her way to the door, fall on the floor and remain there. Returning to the parlor, Miss Van Huysen tells the men that she'll see that Vandergelder lets his nieces marry both of them.

But it is Mrs. Levi who climbs over the drunks in the hall to escort two of her own brood into the house. Minnie is in a trance-like state and barely manages to sit down. Irene is tipsy.

Mrs. Levi announces that as soon as Vandergelder pays for the cab without money, he'll be right up. Mrs. Molloy, turning the lost purse upside down and letting bills and coins fall everywhere, offers to pay for the cab. When the scramble for the money has subsided, Mrs. Molloy says that it's Vandergelder's money which she doesn't know how to return. "I'll give it back to him," says Mrs. Levi. She hands Mrs. Molloy a banknote for Vandergelder and holds on to the purse.

Vandergelder roars in like a lion, but Miss Van Huysen bids him either shake hands with everybody or get out. "Mr. Vandergelder," says Mrs. Levi, "you've had a hard day. You don't want to go out in the rain now. Just for form's sake, shake hands with them. Start quarreling again tomorrow." He barely offers a finger to Cornelius, and refuses to shake the finger Ambrose offers him.

Minnie falls off her perch; the men prop her up. "Don't push," she contributes. Mrs. Molloy smells coffee and asks for some that's good and black. Miss Van Huysen now asks everybody into her kitchen, then says to Vandergelder: "Horace, you'll be interested to know there are two Ermingardes in there."

Mrs. Levi, left alone with the bird cages and bibelots, confides in her late husband Ephraim that she's going to marry again. It won't be like *their* marriage, but Ephraim will approve of how she'll put Vandergelder's money back in circulation again.

Mrs. Levi sits down on a pouf, holding the purse, and says: "Money, money, money, it's like the sun we walk under: it can kill and it can cure. Horace Vandergelder's never tired of saying most of the people in the world are fools, and in a way he's right, isn't he? Himself, Irene, Cornelius, myself! But there comes a moment in everybody's life when he must decide whether he'll live among human beings or not—a fool among fools or a fool alone. As for me, I've decided to live among them. . . ." It wasn't always so with Mrs. Levi, she tells the audience: after her husband's death she retired into herself. ". . . You and I have known lots of people who've decided—like Horace Vandergelder—like myself for a long time—not to live among human beings. Yes, they move out among them, they talk to them, they even get married to them; but at heart they have decided not to have anything to do with the human race. If you accept human beings and are willing to live among them you acknowledge that every man has a right to his own mistakes. . . ." All this and more Mrs. Levi offers to the audience as only the opinion of the second Mrs. Vandergelder.

Vandergelder, carrying two cups of coffee and closing the hall door with his back, reports to Mrs. Levi that a lot of foolishness is going on in the kitchen: "Everybody falling in love with everybody. I forgave 'em: Ermingarde and that artist." What's more, he made Cornelius Hackl his partner. And now there's the matter of Dolly Levi. She has her faults; Mrs. Levi agrees. She's bossy, scheming, inquisitive, but she's wonderful. "Dolly," he says, falling on his knees before her, "marry me." Mrs. Levi just doesn't dare.

Mrs. Levi—You know as well as I do that you're the first citizen of Yonkers. Naturally, you'd expect your wife to keep open house, to have scores of friends in and out all the time. Any wife of yours should be used to that kind of thing.

Vandergelder—Dolly, you can live any way you like.

Mrs. Levi—Horace, you can't deny it, your wife would have to be a *somebody*. Answer me! Am I a somebody?

Vandergelder—You are . . . you are. Wonderful woman.

She clears up the point of his loading money and jewels on her, and of her being benefactress to half the town. Vandergelder gulps hard, but gets over that hurdle. And when Mrs. Levi says she has his purse—it just walked into her hand—Vandergelder is so reformed, he tells her to keep it. "Horace . . ." says Mrs. Levi, overcome, "I never thought . . . I'd ever . . . hear you say a thing like that."

Miss Van Huysen and her kitchen have straightened out everything and everybody. Everyone including Minnie, the drunks, and the cook now returns to the room. Since there is no more gingerbread or coffee, and three couples are getting married, and the play is really over, there's only one thing left to do. Mrs. Levi calls on Barnaby, the youngest, to tell the audience the moral of the play. Orders Vandergelder: "Barnaby, do as Mrs. Wolf-Trap tells you!"

Barnaby needs a minute to shake off his shyness; Mrs. Molloy helps him. "I think," she tells the audience, "it is that your life is like a new hat—you'll never know if you have the one that really suits you if you simply keep trying it on in front of your own mirror.

MRS. LEVI—That's exactly what I think, Irene. (*Crosses to* BARNABY.) Now, Barnaby, it's you, darling.

BARNABY (*coming to her*)—Oh, I think it's about . . . (MRS. LEVI *indicates the audience.*) I think it's about adventure. The test of an adventure is that when you're in the middle of it, you say to yourself, "Oh, now I've got myself into an awful mess; I wish I were sitting quietly at home." And the sign that something's wrong with you is when you sit quietly at home wishing you were out having lots of adventure. . . . (*All form a line behind him.*) So that now we all want to thank you for coming tonight, and we all hope that in your lives you have just the right amount of sitting quietly at home, and just the right amount—of adventure! (*He joins the line.*)

THE PONDER HEART *

By Joseph Fields and Jerome Chodorov

(Adapted from Eudora Welty's story of the same name)

[Joseph Fields *and* Jerome Chodorov. *Joseph Fields is the eldest son of Lew Fields of Weber and Fields fame. Jerome Chodorov is the brother of Edward Chodorov, playwright and producer. Both men were born in New York—Fields in 1895, Chodorov in 1911—and went to school there. Chodorov became a newspaperman and Fields, who first thought he wanted to be a lawyer, turned to writing revue sketches. They "found each other" in Hollywood and together wrote a play, "The Schoolhouse on the Lot," which created no great stir. Then they adapted Ruth McKenney's stories into "My Sister Eileen," which first became a big Broadway hit and later was made into the hit musical "Wonderful Town." After "My Sister Eileen" came such successes as "Junior Miss," "The Doughgirls" and "Anniversary Waltz."*

Eudora Welty *was born in Jackson, Mississippi, in 1909 and has made it her home all her life. She attended the Mississippi College for Women, the University of Wisconsin, and Columbia University. A notable novelist and short-story writer, she has written—besides "The Ponder Heart"—such books as "Curtain of Green," "The Wide Net," "Delta Wedding," "Golden Apples" and "The Bride of Innisfallen."*]

THE scene is a small Southern town a few years back—in front of that faded relic of a Southern mansion, the Beulah Hotel. The hotel is simply a paint-peeling clapboard house with verandah; and beside it, a shabby yard with a rickety swing.

As Sarah, the colored girl, sweeps the verandah, a heavy, perspiring man lugs his sample case up the walk. He wants a room; Sarah yells into the house for Miss Edna Earle, who presently appears. The harassed proprietress of indeterminate age tells the man that he has come at the very worst possible time! "Why?" he asks. "Are you full up?" "No," Miss Edna Earle answers, "it's not that! You see court's opening today and I'll have my hands full. Besides, I'm a witness at the trial so you see how it is—" The salesman doesn't see. Refusing to elaborate, Edna Earle says: "I'm just rushed, rushed, *rushed!* There's a boarding house opposite the bus depot—" When the man picks up his case, she can't refrain from adding: "But you won't like it. Nobody has yet—" He puts his case down again. She assures him: "The Beulah's the best in town. It's a Duncan Hines." And she promises to work something out.

The salesman, Mr. Springer, waits patiently while she carries on a conversation with lawyer DeYancey, who stops on his way to the courthouse. DeYancey is worried that Daniel, who's gone off for a drive, won't be back in time for his trial. "Don't worry," says Edna Earle. "He'll be here. You couldn't keep him away. How he does love the limelight and a chance to hold forth."

Mr. Springer continues to wait as Edna Earle asks the next passer-by where he's off to. Black Big John replies: "Courthouse, ma'am. Lawyer sent for me."

DEYANCEY (*takes paper and looks at it; reads*)—"In the matter of the State versus Daniel Ponder—" By God! He is a witness all right! Now what does he know about this case?

EDNA EARLE—Well, I just can't imagine. (DEYANCEY *gives* BIG JOHN *the paper, but* BIG JOHN *stands motionless in front of him.*)

DEYANCEY—All right, Big John, you can go.

EDNA EARLE—It's no use, DeYancey. Once you stop him, he won't move unless you give him a dime. (DE YANCEY *gives him a dime and he moves off.*)

DEYANCEY—I wish Daniel was here. I gotta talk to him before the trial.

SPRINGER—Excuse me, ma'am, what's he bein' tried *for?*

DEYANCEY—Murder.

SPRINGER—Murder! You mean—murder?

DEYANCEY—That's what it mounts up to.

SPRINGER—Well, how come he's runnin' around loose?

EDNA EARLE—Oh, everybody knows where to find Uncle Daniel. They claim he murdered his wife, Bonnie Dee Peacock. Now isn't that the silliest thing you ever heard? Of course it is. Her family brought the charge against him. Shiftless trash. They're the kind of people that go out and pick railroad lilies to bring in the house and wave at trains 'til the day they die. (SPRINGER *gets his case, and starts into hotel.*)

SARAH (*coming out*)—How many for dinner, Miss Edna Earle?

EDNA EARLE—I don't know yet. You better check with me at the courthouse later. Oh, it's Miss Edna Earle this and Miss Edna Earle that every minute of my day and my time. . . . Sarah, give this gentleman the first room at the head of the stairs.

SPRINGER—Where do I get a key, Miss Edna Earle?

EDNA EARLE—You won't need a key—not at the Beulah. (SPRINGER *goes into hotel.*)

DEYANCEY—Where *is* Daniel? Doesn't he realize the serious trouble he's in?

EDNA EARLE—Of course not. You couldn't make him—I couldn't make him. He knows he couldn't do anything wrong.

DEYANCEY—Well, what does he think this case is all about?

EDNA EARLE—Near as I can tell, he figures it's some kind of a contest between you and the District Attorney to see who's the best lawyer in town.

A battered pick-up truck arrives, driven by a fat colored lady. It's Narciss with a truckload of assorted children belonging to and accompanied by Mr. and Mrs. Peacock, with a small colored girl to boot. Edna Earle asks Narciss where Mr. Ponder is. Out he pops, laughing and shouting: "*Surprise!* Surprise! Edna Earle, I'm back!" She doesn't laugh as she sees how he has messed up his spotless white suit. And she becomes somewhat grim when Uncle Daniel introduces her to his odd lot of disembarking people. "Edna Earle," he says, "you remember the Peacocks. You met them at Bonnie Dee's funeral." Sliding over that as best she can, Edna Earle asks who the little colored tyke is. "That's a little one we picked up on the road," says Uncle Daniel. "Been visiting with her granddaddy and now she's on her way back to her mama's." Seeing the little colored girl can't keep her eyes off his handkerchief, Uncle Daniel says, "You like that, Eloise?" and gives it to her. "Well, you give your mama my love and tell her I expect to see her at the trial." The child laughs and runs away.

Taking Uncle Daniel aside, Edna Earle asks in a fierce whisper what he could have been thinking of, to bring the Peacocks here today. Puzzled that she could ask this, Uncle Daniel says: "Why, I brought them into town for the *trial*—my ex-mother-in-law and my ex-father-in-law, Treva, Johnnie Ree, Purdel and Bruce." It next occurs to him that it would be nice to house the whole Peacock tribe at the Beulah as his guests. By now the children are firing cap pistols as they dash about. Observing this with pleasure, Uncle Daniel suggests that Edna Earle show them all inside. She gives up.

UNCLE DANIEL—Now there's a fine upstandin' family for you! There's five *more* but they're all scattered about.

DEYANCEY—Daniel! What are you doin' mixin' up with the other side? Why, that Peacock woman brought the charge against you. (EDNA EARLE *returns.*)

UNCLE DANIEL—No, no, Tadpole. It wasn't anything personal. She told me herself. The District Attorney *made* her do it. And he did it 'cause he's runnin' for office next fall. Why, a big case like this could help him win the election. You can't blame him. Smart politics.

EDNA EARLE—Yes, dear heart. No one's to blame for anything.

UNCLE DANIEL (*beams*)—Natural course of events. You know, Edna Earle, I've been thinkin' and *thinkin'* and you know what I decided?

EDNA EARLE (*apprehensively*)—No, dear heart. What?

UNCLE DANIEL—After the trial's over, I'm goin' to move Bonnie Dee over to my cemetery plot.

DEYANCEY—Oh, no, you can't do that, Daniel! You gave your plot away to Miss Teacake Magee when you were engaged to her.

UNCLE DANIEL—Well, the way I figure it—first come first served.

Edna Earle says it's not like him to be an Indian giver, but Uncle Daniel hates to think of Bonnie Dee tucked away in the country that she loathed, when he has a plot right in the center of town—where all the excitement is, which she'd love.

Throwing a friendly arm about DeYancey's shoulders, Uncle Daniel asks him whether he has any bright ideas for the defense. "You better put your mind to work," says Uncle Dan, "or this new District Attorney'll put the monkey on your back! I hear he's a real firebrand!" DeYancey has a bright idea that makes Uncle Daniel explode: he thinks it would be smart tactics if Uncle Daniel didn't testify; let Edna Earle do all the talking for their side.

UNCLE DANIEL (*pathetically*)—But she didn't *see* it all. She fainted in the middle of it!

DEYANCEY—Shhh! That's just what I mean. We're not goin' to mention anythin' about that!

EDNA EARLE—Anyway, that was just a twinklin'—when that fireball went through the room—five or ten seconds at the most.

DEYANCEY—We're goin' to forget Miss Edna Earle faintin'.

UNCLE DANIEL—That's not honest, Tadpole. How can you do a thing like that? If I'm gonna be in your corner, you gotta win this case fair and square.

EDNA EARLE—We all know how honest you are, dear heart, but that's why people hire lawyers.

DEYANCEY—Please, Miss Edna Earle! Daniel, you listen to me! We've got to fight fire with fire! And that Dorris R. Gladney is a shyster if I ever saw one! All he wants is convictions! Now I want you to give me your word of honor you're not gonna open your mouth in that courtroom!

UNCLE DANIEL (*pleadingly*)—An awful lot of people came to Clay especially to hear my story. They're gonna be pretty mad at you, Tadpole.

DEYANCEY—Let 'em *be* mad.

UNCLE DANIEL—But it's my trial. How can you leave me out of it?

DeYancey's subterfuge is that he plans to save Uncle Daniel's testimony for a possible appeal. A sulky Uncle Daniel prefers not to accompany DeYancey to the courthouse. Remaining behind, he tells Edna Earle: "The whole thing's spoiled. I don't even feel like goin' to the darn trial." Edna Earle reminds him of his promise to Judge Waite to appear on time. "Well," Uncle Daniel pouts, "if they're not goin' to let me talk, what fun is it? I think I'll just wait for the appeal." But, because a promise is a promise, Uncle Daniel agrees to go, though his heart's not in it.

Edna Earle is relieved. Going indoors for her hat and bag, she tells him to wait outside and not roam off. Uncle Daniel's momentary unhappiness is quickly dispelled by the sight of Gladney marching to the courthouse. He jumps up and greets the startled District Attorney. Gladney tries to move on by saying he's late. "No," says Uncle Daniel cheerfully, "you got lots of time! They can't start 'til *I* get there." Gladney booms: "Whom do I have the honor of addressing, sir?" "Why, I'm Daniel Ponder," says Uncle Daniel. With a reluctant handshake, Gladney intones: "Mr. Ponder. The accused?" "I certainly am!" says Uncle Daniel happily.

Gladney has no wish to be "socializin' with the accused," but Uncle Daniel nails him down. "If you were my lawyer in this case," asks Uncle Daniel, "would you put me in the witness box?" Gladney's wily answer delights Uncle Daniel. It is easy for him to see why Gladney's up for state senator: "You see," he confides, "my attorney, Mr. Clanahan, hasn't got your experience or your courtly manner, but he's a good boy and takes things to heart. So I'd like to ask you to do me a personal favor." Uncle Daniel would like

Gladney to go light on DeYancey and let him down nice and easy. With a smirk, Gladney says that he will let him down just as easy as he's going to let Uncle Daniel down. Uncle Daniel is extremely grateful.

When Edna Earle is introduced to Uncle Daniel's new friend, her polite smile vanishes. And when Uncle Daniel is all for putting Gladney up as his guest at the Beulah, Edna Earle is horrified. But Gladney, fully expecting to finish the trial that very day, doesn't think he will be spending the night in town. Very much interested, Uncle Daniel asks: "How do you figure *that,* sir?" "Why, I figure I got a pretty open-and-shut ironclad case," says Gladney complacently as he takes his leave. Uncle Daniel is full of admiration for the man; Edna Earle is grim. Told to round up the feasting Peacocks, once more Edna Earle dutifully leaves Uncle Daniel to his own devices.

This time Uncle Daniel corrals Mr. Springer, whom he considers lucky to have arrived just in time for the start of the trial. Promising to help him get a good seat, Uncle Daniel persuades him to sit down and talk. Uncle Daniel does all the talking; his very first question naturally is, "Do you think it's fair of my lawyer to keep me off the stand?" Mr. Springer has no answer, nor has he one concerning the Shetland pony Uncle Daniel insists on presenting to the Springer children. "But—" Mr. Springer sputters.

UNCLE DANIEL—I insist! I won't take no for an answer. He's not doin' me any good just waitin' around that stall eatin' his little fool head off. My, it's too bad you didn't ever get to meet my late wife, Miss Bonnie Dee. (*Lights begin to dim.* SINGER *hums "Row After Row" offstage.*) She was smart beyond compare. Pretty as a picture—all yellow golden hair—I wish you could have seen Bonnie Dee! I do wish you could. Used to cut my hair regular! She was a natural-born barber. (*He sighs.*) She was like a little fairy creature, she was that light and dainty. I'll never find another like her. The truth is, Mr. Springer, between you and me, I just wasn't good enough for her. Here's her picture, but it doesn't do her justice. She sort of squinted up her eyes when I snapped it. I took it with my little Brownie camera when she walked in that gate for the first time just six months ago.

LIGHTS DIM OUT

On a bright, sunny afternoon, Uncle Daniel is taking a picture of Bonnie Dee, his surprise for Edna Earle. Bonnie Dee is far more interested in her shiny new toaster than in her new Ponder surroundings. She sinks wearily into a verandah rocker while Uncle Daniel bubbles over about Edna Earle and the Beulah Hotel. "Oh, you're going to adore her, sugar," he tells the apathetic girl. "She's real friendly and good. I gave her this hotel. My daddy left it to me and I gave it to *her!*"

BONNIE DEE (*flatly*)—What for?

UNCLE DANIEL (*startled*)—Why, because I *love* her, and I want her to have a place of her own.

BONNIE DEE (*same tone*)—Why?

UNCLE DANIEL (*laughs*)—Why *not?* I got that big house on the hill my daddy left me and a man don't need *two* roofs over his head . . . besides, what would I do with a hotel? I'm rich as Croesus *now*. Well, baby doll . . . how does it feel bein' a little old married woman?

BONNIE DEE—It don't feel any different yet— (*Pays no attention to him, staring into the chrome toaster with love.*) It shines beautiful—I can see my face in it.

Uncle Daniel announces that all she need do is name whatever else she wants and it is hers. Almost stirred to life, Bonnie Dee drawls a list of the things she wants most: an electric icebox, a clothes machine, a dishwasher. Uncle Daniel delightedly promises her the lot. As a reward, Bonnie Dee confers her greatest favor on Uncle Daniel: "Then you know what, Mr. Ponder? I'll cut your hair for you." "What's that?" asks Uncle Daniel. "Well, I used to cut my daddy's hair regular," explains Bonnie Dee. "I love a scissors better than anything." Uncle Daniel is most appreciative: "That's fine, baby doll, and I'll give you the four bits I always gave Vic down at the barber shop. Oh, we're gonna have good times. We'll drive into town every Saturday night, dinner at the Beulah, movies at the Gem, then the soda parlor afterwards . . . then back to our little nest. Oh, it's not gonna be lonely any more on that hill!"

At the idea of a room of her own, Bonnie Dee smiles dreamily: "Never could get any rest at home," she says. "Treva, Johnnie Ree, Suzy and Cassadel and me all in the same room. Someone always crawlin' over you to get a glass of water or yellin' from a nightmare or howlin' from a toothache or somethin' . . ." But she'd be scared to sleep *all* alone in a big room. "Well, I'll be right down the hall," Uncle Daniel tells her. "If anything frightens you, just call out. Or better still, we'll put a cot in there for Narciss." "That's right sweet of you, Mr. Ponder." "The main thing," says Uncle Daniel, "is to get marriage off on the right foot. You got to take it slow and easy, baby doll. First you get used to the house, then you'll gradually get used to havin' me around the house. Married life is just gettin' used to one thing after another. Why, in no time at all, we'll be so accustomed to seein' each other around, there won't be nothin' to it."

An excited bunch of children on their way to the Fair stop to tell Uncle Daniel about the Ferris wheel and the Wall of Death. "Wall of Death!" cries Uncle Daniel. "Lady rides a motorcycle 'round and 'round a wall! Intrepid Elsie Fleming Defies Death! Got to see that!" And he's all for joining the children when he remembers his bride. "Oh," says he, "I forgot somethin'. Come along, sugar?" "Nope," says Bonnie Dee, kicking off her shoes. "Don't feel like it." Uncle Daniel, making a real sacrifice, remains behind.

Coming out on the porch, Edna Earle discovers, with Narciss's help, Uncle Daniel's surprise. Narciss bursts out: "Mistuh Daniel took himself a bride, Miss Edna Earle!" "Narciss," cries Uncle Daniel, "I'm gonna skin you alive. You gave it away." Narciss just laughs and departs. "Edna Earle, dear heart. I want you to meet your new aunt," says Uncle Daniel with a laugh. "You see—she's my niece—and you'll be her aunt so that makes you her niece-in-law—Bonnie Dee, sugar, get up and step out into the bright a minute." Bonnie Dee, yawning all the while, wafts into the sunlight. "Look, Edna Earle, couldn't you just eat her up?" says Uncle Daniel. "Now isn't *that* a surprise?" Containing herself, Edna Earle asks when did they get married: "I didn't even know you were—keeping company."

UNCLE DANIEL (*laughs, very pleased with himself*)—To tell the truth, 'til this morning neither did I! She works over in the Jitney Jungle—at the candy counter— You know how I love Crackerjacks?

EDNA EARLE (*faintly*)—Yes, I do.

UNCLE DANIEL—Well, it was four weeks ago I first bought a box from Miss Bonnie Dee. I kept goin' back every day . . . (BONNIE DEE *looks at him wearily, then yawns, sprawling on the swing.*) An' every day I gave her the prize in the Crackerjack box, and this mornin' you know what? (EDNA EARLE *shakes her head, looking at* BONNIE DEE *steadily.*) The prize was a gold ring—like a real weddin' ring, so I knew it was a message! And I said, "Miss Bonnie Dee Peacock—I got a great big house standing empty and me rattling around in it—and no one to look after either of us. Come on—marry me this minute."

EDNA EARLE (*faintly*)—May I ask where the nuptials took place?

UNCLE DANIEL—Justice of the Peace over in Carthage, next door to the Presbyterian Church. Right after the ceremony we all went to the soda parlor and had ice-cream cones.

BONNIE DEE (*jumps up*)—I'm *hot!* I want *another* one!

Beaming, Uncle Daniel asks Edna Earle to give him some change: he's used up his whole allowance on the toaster. Bonnie Dee, her mind set on pistachio and chocolate peppermint ice cream, comes to life and runs off. Edna Earle manages: *"Well!"*

Uncle Daniel rather sadly tells his understanding, forbearing niece how lonely he's been: "Anyhow, it's so lonely up on that hill. You're always busy, Edna Earle, and everybody else is mostly workin'. An' even the kids are at school the best part of the day. But now that I got me a wife, we can fool around together and have fun all day long."

The word has traveled. Uncle Daniel's lawyer, DeYancey, and Uncle Daniel's former fiancée, Miss Teacake Magee, hurry over to find out if it's true. To soothe DeYancey's worries as lawyer and trustee, Uncle Daniel delivers the news that they're only *trying* the marriage out. This only adds to the general consternation. DeYancey demands to know whether they did or did not get married. A little hurt, Uncle Daniel shows him the marriage certificate and proceeds to explain in "coupon" terms about his trial marriage: ". . . That's what we agreed. To take each other for better or worse for a ninety-day trial. If at the end of three months we don't suit, we'll call it off." And wanting them to meet his bride, Uncle Daniel goes off to look for her.

Edna Earle defends him: "I don't care what you say. If he's happy that's all I want." Teacake is dying to know what she's like. Edna Earle puts it succinctly: "Looks like she could sit all day and try to figure out how the tail of the C got through the L in the Coca-Cola sign."

Uncle Daniel, having retrieved Bonnie Dee with her ice-cream cone, returns. She awards limp, sticky handshakes to her well-wishers; then, turning her back, pays them no further attention. But when Uncle Daniel, in his enthusiasm, upsets her ice-cream cone, there's trouble; and to prevent more tears, he has to promise her a triple-decker pistachio cone. Her sniffles subside, and in spite of the gathering crowd of old friends she once more retires to the swing. She ignores Judge Waite's congratulations, pays no heed to Dr. Eubanks and the Bodkins; but, when Narciss drives up in the truck, Bonnie Dee trebles: "What about my ice-cream cone?"

Laughing, Uncle Daniel tells her not to worry, and lifts her into the truck. He climbs in after her. Facing his friends as if he were campaigning, Uncle Daniel says: "Well, so long, folks. I'm gonna give a great big wedding party as soon as it's permanent, so keep your fingers crossed for the next ninety days. Okay, Narciss, give her the gun!"

ACT II

Out in the country, at the Ponder house, Bonnie Dee passes the time clipping and sending off coupons. The results of all this stare out from the Victorian parlor—here a refrigerator, there a clothes washer, and for final luster, a TV set.

Whenever coupon-cutting palls, Narciss is on hand for a game of jacks. Uncle Daniel arrives during one such game, bearing a surprise: a mandarin coat and tasseled cap for Bonnie Dee to wear to this afternoon's party. *"Party? What* party?" cries Bonnie Dee. "Why it's three months, sugar!" Uncle Daniel laughs. "The ninety-day trial is over and we're havin' a celebration. From today on we're permanent man and wife. Oh, I'm as happy as a mockin' bird! If I had any kind of a voice I'd sing!" Bonnie Dee changes from dazed to frightened when she's told to expect all their best friends for an anniversary dinner. Narciss protests: *"Dinner!* We ain't got no dinner for no company!" " 'Course not!" says happy Uncle Daniel. "We're goin' to have a *real* party—the kind we didn't have on our weddin' day! Edna Earle's bringin' the fried chicken and trimmin's and I ordered the cake and ice cream!" Turning to Bonnie Dee, he says: "Here's your chance to shine, baby doll! You'll be the lady of the house!"

BONNIE DEE—What am I supposed to *do?*

UNCLE DANIEL—Why, you smile pretty and greet people and welcome them at the door. Then later on you sit at the head of the table—you put Judge Waite on your right hand and Doctor Eubanks on your left hand—

BONNIE DEE—*Then* what'll I do?

UNCLE DANIEL—Why, you just see that they get served and make conversation!

BONNIE DEE—About what?

UNCLE DANIEL—Anythin' comes to your pretty little head. Then soon as a course is finished, you ring the little silver bell for Narciss to come in!

NARCISS—Don' know if we still got that little silver bell.

UNCLE DANIEL—Must be in with the flat silver . . . (*To* BON-

NIE DEE.) Tell you what. Get out Mama's bone china an' that lace tablespread an' fix them up in the dining room.

BONNIE DEE—Fix 'em *how?*

UNCLE DANIEL—You know, lay 'em out pretty like in the magazines, an' I'll get Big John to cut some flowers for the table.

Too nervous to go on playing jacks, Bonnie Dee sits brooding while Narciss announces: "If you quit, then you lose!" Taking Bonnie Dee's part, Uncle Daniel says he'll play for her. Narciss says they're up to "threesies," and Uncle Daniel, kneeling down, asks: "What are you playin' *for?*"

NARCISS—Low man makes the beds.

UNCLE DANIEL—Oh! Here I go! (*He sees* NARCISS *put the double horns on him.*) That's no fair, Narciss.

NARCISS—She started it—she put the horns on me first!

BONNIE DEE—Just single horns.

UNCLE DANIEL—Then you can only put single horns on me. It's no fair to Double Jonah me! Did you say you were up to threesies?

Edna Earle carrying flowers, Sarah loaded down with a packed picnic basket, and DeYancey break in on their game. Daniel rises to greet Edna Earle affectionately: "Welcome, on the happiest day of my life. You too, Tadpole!"

Presented with the flowers, Bonnie Dee looks helplessly at them, then runs from the room. Narciss, following to help her arrange them, is instructed by Uncle Daniel: "Move my things into the big room and you clear out with that army cot of yours." Edna Earle and DeYancey exchange looks. Happily oblivious of all this, Uncle Daniel exclaims: "Oh, happy day! Edna Earle, the next fifty years are goin' to be nothin' but bliss, just like Mama and Daddy had!"

Edna Earle heads for the kitchen, leaving Uncle Daniel, bursting with joy, to welcome two delivery men. They are carrying Bonnie Dee's latest order: an electric dishwasher. Wanting to know where the kitchen is, they are brought up sharp by Uncle Daniel. "I'm sorry—" he says; "the lady of the house wants it right here in the parlor."

FIRST MAN—You can't hook it up here. You gotta have water for a dishwasher.

UNCLE DANIEL (*smiles*)—Well, here's where she wants it, gentlemen.

SECOND MAN—Here's where she'll get it, then. Drop it, Clyde.

In his pleasure over this timely arrival of the dishwasher, Uncle Daniel begins wishing that they had electricity. "My daddy, Mr. Samuel Ponder," he tells the startled delivery man, "never would put it in. He said we were right in the middle of the storm belt. Notice the roof? Full of lightnin' rods. He sprinkled them on like my mama used to sprinkle coconuts on a cake." The men have yet to meet Bonnie Dee. She comes in, thinks the dishwasher a beauty, tells the men sharply: "Took a long time gettin' here. I ordered it two months ago."

SECOND MAN—Dishes been pilin' up, ma'am?

FIRST MAN (*writing in receipt book*)—Got here before the electricity, anyway. Sign here.

BONNIE DEE—Can I keep this little black paper?

SECOND MAN—Sure, ma'am, we give 'em away with every purchase over two hundred dollars.

DeYancey, groaning, can take no more and disappears into the garden. Uncle Daniel, wishing to discuss money matters, follows DeYancey. Left alone, Bonnie Dee fishes for a ride to Memphis on the men's truck. Told it's against orders, Bonnie Dee brags she'll get there anyway. As he starts to leave, the delivery man confides to his companion: "*She* ain't hooked up either—if you ask me."

Edna Earle runs into trouble with Bonnie Dee when she returns to the parlor and suggests that the dishwasher be moved. Bonnie Dee insists that it remain to match up with the icebox. Grim but helpless, Edna Earle can do nothing more.

DeYancey has been having his troubles, too. Uncle Daniel has demanded an increase in allowance. DeYancey blurts out that there's nothing he can do: not only will Uncle Daniel not get more money to sprinkle around, but what there is has been tied up in a trust fund so it can't be touched at all. Uncle Daniel manifests irritation: "I'm goin' to kill you dead, Tadpole. What you go an' do a fool thing like that for?" "Just because," says DeYancey, "I knew things like *this* was gonna happen!" Edna Earle wonders that Bonnie Dee's mind goes no further than down payments. Edna Earle is wrong: Bonnie Dee doesn't even make down payments. Uncle Daniel proudly tells his startled audience: "That's right! She found a place where you buy now and pay later. Smart beyond compare!"

Bonnie Dee reminds Uncle Daniel of all the stuff, including the sun lamp, that hasn't come yet. Edna Earle bursts out: "All you have to do is step outside and you'll get more sun than you can ever use." Bonnie Dee, as she leaves the room, flings at her: "Too hot outside in the real sun!"

Uncle Daniel, all set to discuss breaking the trust fund, is distracted by Big John's arrival with the ice cream and a wedding cake topped with figures of a bride and groom. By the time Big John departs with a dime extracted from DeYancey, Uncle Daniel remembers that he has a dark suit just like the one the wedding-cake groom wears: "Got it for my weddin' with Teacake Magee and never used it. Put away in camphor. Just for fun I think maybe I'll go put it on. Oh, we're goin' to have a real celebration!" This includes using the bottle of wine his father once brought back from the Mardi Gras. "Just run some hot water over it," he tells Narciss, "and clean it up."

Edna Earle, left alone with Bonnie Dee, makes a last effort to have her change from her kimono into at least a J. C. Penney frock. Bonnie Dee's only concession is to take some red shoes out of her refrigerator and put them on her bare feet. Edna Earle retreats to the kitchen, where she is sure of better results.

Narciss, on the other hand, not bothering with any of the party preparations, gives Bonnie Dee a picture of her own married life.

NARCISS—I quit.
BONNIE DEE—Why?
NARCISS—Too one-sided.
BONNIE DEE—Did you both live in the same room together?
NARCISS—That's all there was.
BONNIE DEE—Did you ever get used to it?
NARCISS—There I was. What else could I *do* but get used to it?
BONNIE DEE—Weren't you scared?
NARCISS—Scared of *what?*
BONNIE DEE—Well, I don't know. Same room—same bed—goin' to sleep at night—wakin' up in the mornin' an' there *he* is—
NARCISS—That's it, honey. That's married life! That's the heart an' backbone of it!

Edna Earle calls to Narciss to bring the silver into the dining room. Sucked into these chores against her will, Narciss, while exiting with the silver, mimics Edna Earle: "Oh, it's Narciss this an' Narciss that every minute of my day an' my time!"

Bonnie Dee has made her decision. With a final fond glance at all the shining enameled appliances, she takes a pad and pencil and laboriously writes a note and tucks it inside the refrigerator. Grabbing a stuffed animal, she runs off just as the guests arrive.

TEACAKE—Why, look at that, Judge Waite! Looks like the basement of Sears Roebuck!

JUDGE—I'll say one thing. It's unique. Somethin' you don't see in every parlor. Right, Dr. Eubanks?

TEACAKE—Uncle Daniel's been in and out of every store in Clay this mornin', stopping everyone who'd listen to spread the good word. "Great news! The trial marriage is over! And I won! I'm movin' in to Bonnie Dee's room tonight!" Now I ask you, Dr. Eubanks, does that strike you as normal behavior for a middle-aged married man?

DR. EUBANKS—Daniel's happy—and when he's happy he wants everyone to share it with him.

While Edna Earle, in absence of the host and hostess, makes everyone welcome, DeYancey approaches the Judge and Doctor with a scheme he's cooked up. Edna Earle doesn't like the sound of it.

DEYANCEY—I simply mean that the bride—so to speak—has been in escrow. And if we work fast, before he moves in with her tonight, we can have it annulled.

EDNA EARLE—*What?*

DEYANCEY—And to make sure it sticks, we could have him declared incompetent and have him committed—temporarily, of course.

EDNA EARLE—Committed!

DR. EUBANKS—That's a helluva note! Man invites you to sit down an' share his weddin' cake and you're plannin' on puttin' him away!

DEYANCEY—We got to try an' save him from himself, Doctor. He's talkin' about breakin' up the trust fund. And if he *does,* he'll dump it all in her lap—and then bye, bye, baby!

EDNA EARLE—Well, it's his money, DeYancey—let him do what he likes with it!

The melting ice cream causes Doctor Eubanks to open the refrigerator. He finds no ice, but Bonnie Dee's startling note of farewell. Edna Earle is particularly concerned about breaking the news to Uncle Daniel, but the Doctor solves that: since the note wasn't meant for any of them, Uncle Daniel must discover it himself in his own good time.

Uncle Daniel re-enters singing. His cutaway reeks of mothballs, but his joy knows no bounds. His friends' misery goes unnoticed, though it increases when Big John arrives with a message from Bonnie Dee. Big John tells Uncle Daniel to look in the parlor icebox. In a daze, Uncle Daniel reads Bonnie Dee's note. He gives a pathetic cry: "Edna Earle! Edna Earle! She's *gone!* Where did she go, Big John? Did you see *where?*" Big John says slowly: "She flag down northbound bus wid her little handkerchief . . . H'it stopped . . . she get on . . . h'it go off." Uncle Daniel gives him his dime, weeping: "Man alive, my wife done left me here by myself . . . in this empty house. She was tiny as a fairy and pretty as a doll an' smart beyond compare . . . an' now she's left me, clean as a whistle!" Edna Earle fails to comfort him, but even in his grief Uncle Daniel remembers to be hospitable. Through his tears, he orders Narciss to cut the cake for his friends, as he goes to his room.

Scene II

Men have been electrifying things right and left in the parlor: a modern light tree, the TV set, the clothes washer. Another man has tested the newly connected phone.

The men do their level best to explain to Narciss the rudiments of electricity. They've warned her that there is only enough "juice" to work two appliances at a time; otherwise the "fuse" will blow. None of this makes any more sense to Narciss than having a machine to do the wash for her. "Mistuh Ponder—" she says with a smile—"he wants everythin' hooked up and workin' for when she gets home. I been doin' the wash all my life out back and it's sure too late to change *now*." As she leaves the room, the men look after her. "What's the fuse?" says Al. "I tell you, Clyde, putting electricity in this house is like giving a baby razor blades to play with."

Though the cost of bringing electricity to Ponder Hill was so prohibitive that it drove DeYancey to Hot Springs for a cure, Uncle Daniel delightedly knows it's worth every penny of it. It will be his surprise for Bonnie Dee on her return. And he knows that she will be returning soon because, as he tells the leery men, Edna Earle addressed an ad to her in the Memphis *Commercial Apparel* classified column. It was a beautiful lyrical bribe that Bonnie was bound to see when searching for new coupons to cut. Uncle Daniel's reading of Edna Earle's poem hastens the men's departure. They, too, hope Bonnie Dee will soon return, because they just hate to think of her wandering around alone.

Not wanting to bother the operator, Miss Celeste, Uncle Daniel can't resist seeing if the telephone still works. As he is chatting away, Bonnie Dee comes back. Miss Celeste gets the news of the homecoming the minute it happens, and receives Bonnie Dee's momentous first words on the telephone: "Hello? How do? Yes, I'm back. Thank you . . . Bye." Uncle Daniel signs off with: "Miss Celeste, that was Bonnie Dee!" And deliriously happy, Uncle

Daniel treats Bonnie Dee to a demonstration of each and every electrical object in the house. Bonnie Dee is overcome.

BONNIE DEE—Mistuh Ponder—Mistuh Ponder—sit down! I'm goin' to cut your hair for you right now! (*He takes the handkerchief out of his pocket and sticks it in his collar as he sits happily.*)

UNCLE DANIEL (*over action*)—Just like old times, baby doll! You are a natural-born barber, Bonnie Dee. (BONNIE DEE *takes a pair of shears and a comb from her purse and begins clipping his hair expertly.*)

BONNIE DEE—I love a scissors better'n *anything!*

UNCLE DANIEL (*a bit anxiously*)—Just trim it, puddin'.

BONNIE DEE—I like to cut a *lot* off.

UNCLE DANIEL—Well, if you go light, you'll be able to do it every couple days, like you used to.

BONNIE DEE—That's so.

UNCLE DANIEL—Bonnie Dee, promise me you'll never go scootin' off like that again.

BONNIE DEE—Mistuh Ponder, that sure was mean of me.

Yet, in almost the same breath, Bonnie Dee is admitting that she can't *ever* start being a proper wife, and says dazedly over Uncle Daniel's patient, encouraging words: "But now I'm here, I feel like *goin'* again. I came back to stay but I just can't. Don't know why." And off she goes for her valise, crying: "It ain't you—it's *me.* I'd like to please you, Mistuh Ponder, I really would, but it's no use. I'd better ride the bus back home."

Uncle Daniel tells her that all she needs is time to get used to being married and having a man around, so he's prepared to give it to her by moving into the Beulah while she stays here with Narciss. Bonnie Dee protests, but Uncle Daniel coaxes her: "Sure, an' every Saturday I'll come out with your allowance an' you can cut my hair. That suit you, baby doll? Will you try it that way for a while?" Bonnie Dee hesitates. "Go ahead, sugar— Try it for a while, just to please me . . ." "Well, maybe I could try one more time," she concedes.

Edna Earle, brimming over with the whole town's happy news of the reconciliation, arrives. A moment later, as Bonnie Dee disappears, and Uncle Daniel speaks of moving into the Beulah, Edna Earle speaks out.

EDNA EARLE—I can't let you go on thinking this is the right way for you to be happy!

UNCLE DANIEL—But I'll see her every Saturday. I *am* happy.

EDNA EARLE (*explodes*)—You can't be! Don't forget you're a Ponder and you've got an obligation to the name. No little backwoods nobody is goin' to ride roughshod over you. From now on I'm handling Miss Bonnie Dee and what's more I'll let you know when it's *time* for you to be happy!

SCENE III

A bad storm is coming on fast at Ponder Hill. Narciss and Bonnie Dee, all alone and increasingly nervous, are bad company for each other. By showing that she's scared, Narciss makes Bonnie Dee even more so. Between claps of thunder, Bonnie Dee tries frantically to phone the Beulah Hotel, but gets nowhere.

When Big John appears in the doorway, Bonnie Dee begs him to come in and stay.

BIG JOHN—Come with a message from Mr. Daniel—

BONNIE DEE—Where is he?

BIG JOHN—In the car, down the road. Say, tell you, I'm gonna kill you dead, Miss Bonnie Dee, if you don't take me back.

NARCISS—Miss Edna Earle put him up to that sure as you're born.

BONNIE DEE (*frantically*)—Tell him to come here *quick!* Tell him I need him! I'm scared! (*He stands there.*) Get goin'! I'll give you the dime later! (*She pushes him out during a big clap of thunder; the wind rises.*)

It gets so dark that Bonnie Dee orders Narciss to turn on all the lights. Then, as lightning flashes and thunder rolls, Bonnie Dee switches on the TV and tells Narciss to "get everythin' goin' around here!" Narciss, trying to hold Bonnie Dee back, warns her: "No, no! 'Lectric man says only two at a time! Two!" Unheeding, Bonnie Dee turns on the clothes washer, and with a horrid flash all the lights go out.

Beside herself, Bonnie Dee cries for lamps, but Narciss announces there's no kerosene. Next Bonnie Dee dashes to the phone. "Operator! Operator! Gimme the 'lectricity man! Operator! Operator! No answer! Mama, Mama!"

Narciss takes her in her arms; but with the next clap of thunder, Bonnie Dee begs Narciss to help her move the sofa away from the window.

A moment later Edna Earle's flashlight picks their legs up under the sofa. Uncle Daniel, as lightning flashes, cries to Bonnie Dee:

"Come out, sugar! Your husband's here! You don't need to be afraid!"

BONNIE DEE—I don't appreciate lightning or thunder a bit! (*Another crash of thunder. She screams in terror.*)

UNCLE DANIEL—She's scared to death of lightnin'. Always was! Come on, honey. Nothin's goin' to hurt you! (*A flash and a loud clap of thunder. Then another flash of lightning. The door bangs open and there is a loud crack.* BONNIE DEE *and* NARCISS *both scream.* EDNA EARLE *huddles close to* UNCLE DANIEL. *He pulls* BONNIE DEE *by the legs as she continues to scream. She beats his chest with her little fists as he tries to quiet her down.*) It's all right, Bonnie Dee! Quieten down! Easy—*easy!* This is your husband, Daniel Ponder! He'll take care of you! He won't let nothin' hurt you! I'm comin' back and stay here! (*The thunder grows louder.*)

BONNIE DEE—Lemme go! Lemme go! Under the couch! (*She tries to pull away. He holds her tighter.*) Lemme go! Narciss, help me! (*Lightning and thunder reach climax.*)

UNCLE DANIEL (*he can't let her go now, frozen to her*)—Please, sugar! Please! Quieten down! (*The thunder is louder and the lightning more weird.*)

BONNIE DEE—Oh, God! Turn me loose! Narciss! Help! Help! (*She struggles frantically.*)

UNCLE DANIEL—Bonnie Dee! Quiet! Hold still! Stop shakin'! (*A loud crack of thunder, then a strange sulphurous ball bounces in the front door, shoots erratically across the room and out through the beaded curtains.* EDNA EARLE *slumps to the floor in a dead faint.* BONNIE DEE *continues to fight, and screams as* UNCLE DANIEL *clings to her, trying to calm her down. As lightning flashes and thunder booms*—THE CURTAIN FALLS.)

ACT III

In the pre-Civil-War courthouse, under ceiling fans that don't work, the Ponder trial is under way. Everybody—Judge Waite, the spectators, the Peacock family, the jury, the Defense—fan themselves as Prosecutor Gladney warms up in pre-war style.

Uncle Daniel, seemingly indifferent to it all, mops his neck and waves to his friends. His loud whispers to DeYancey and to Edna Earle disrupt the court.

GLADNEY—. . . And finally, Gentlemen of the Jury, I ask you to turn your gaze upon the family of the deceased—(EVERYBODY *looks at the Peacocks, who smile self-consciously.*) A lovin' mama, a dotin' poppa and affectionate little sisters and brothers, all denied Bonnie Dee's happy smile and lovin' presence. (*Shouts suddenly.*) Vengeance is mine, sayeth the Lord! An eye for an eye, a tooth for a tooth! And this sovereign state echoes those sentiments! (*He turns away, almost bowing to the jury.* UNCLE DANIEL *rises, lost in admiration, and takes* GLADNEY'S *hand as he passes him.*)

UNCLE DANIEL—Mr. Gladney, I'd just like to say I've been comin' to this court all my life—Judge Waite'll tell you—and I regard that as one of the most movin' and beautiful pleas I ever heard to a jury! (*Turns to* DEYANCEY.) Tadpole, you better get on your toes! (*Spectators laugh as* GLADNEY *pulls his hand away as though struck by a snake.*)

JUDGE (*raps his gavel angrily*)—Order! Daniel, I'll have to ask you to refrain from makin' audible remarks.

UNCLE DANIEL—Pardon me, Judge Waite. I was just carried away.

JUDGE WAITE—Then sit down and behave yourself.

GLADNEY (*indicating* EDNA EARLE)—Your Honor, may I ask what this witness is doin' sittin' at our table?

JUDGE—Yes, you may ask. I gave her special permission. That's why she's sitting at your table. Call the first witness.

The first witness is the coroner—druggist Bodkin, who signed Bonnie Dee's death certificate. Bodkin finds it difficult to give a direct answer to the simplest question; a few histrionic bellows from Gladney throw him into utter confusion. Gladney loads his questions: "And you did examine the victim of this foul murder? DeYancey objects; Judge Waite sustains the objection and instructs Gladney to refer to the "deceased" until she may be proved otherwise. With an elaborate bow to the court, Gladney rewords his question: "You examined the deceased on the day of the murder?" Again DeYancey objects. Gladney is reprimanded. Bodkin manages to give his reason for Bonnie Dee's death: "Heart failure—natural causes." But one loud roar of *"What!"* from Gladney has him amend it in haste to: "I mean *other* than natural causes—could be . . . That's what I mean—could be other than natural causes . . ." He is allowed to retire, with no questions from DeYancey.

When Big John is called next, Uncle Daniel is deeply hurt that even *he* is getting a chance to talk. DeYancey tells him to "hush up."

Sworn in, Big John proves another irritating witness to Gladney, but Uncle Daniel, at the top of his lungs, sings out Big John's praises. The Judge has to cry for "Order!" and to plead with DeYancey: "Mr. Clanahan, you'll have to keep your client in order!" Uncle Daniel confesses he's going to need time to get used to not talking. Gladney, having his troubles too, becomes almost frantic as he tries to pry testimony out of Big John. At last he coaxes from Big John the message Uncle Daniel had sent him with to Bonnie Dee during the storm: "Tell her," Big John repeats triumphantly, "go up to my house on the hill and say, 'Miss Bonnie Dee, I'm goin' to kill you dead if you don' take me back.'" Gladney dramatically repeats this, tacking on: "And now he's done it!" Gladney is through with Big John; DeYancey says he has no wish to question him. This causes Uncle Daniel to complain that DeYancey is letting Mr. Gladney get ahead of him. Judge Waite in turn cries: "Order! Is there no way, Daniel, I can get you to keep still? I'll go straight out of my mind up here!" All sympathy, Uncle Daniel answers: "Now you're absolutely right, Judge. Folks, we got to be more considerate of Judge Waite. His health comes first."

Big John hasn't budged from the witness stand. Again, Gladney tells him he's through with him. Big John continues to sit. Uncle Daniel says pleasantly: "He won't go 'way lessen you give him a dime!" In rising anger, Gladney parts with a dime to speed Big John on his way. It's DeYancey's sour opinion that his testimony was worth every bit of it. Judge Waite raps for order, but now, seeing Sarah wave from the doorway, he halts the proceedings. "I see Miss Edna Earle's girl is standin' there," he says; "she wants to know how many for dinner at the Beulah Hotel. I'll ask for a show of hands." Uncle Daniel gets joyously into the act: "Count the Peacocks in! They're my guests!" he cries. "And better make it twelve more for the jury. They're my guests, too." "You can't do that!" yowls Gladney, but no one pays any attention. Edna Earle, with a glance about the room, sums up: "Better kill a few more hens, Sarah, and plenty of hot biscuits."

The next witness is Narciss, whose testimony sounds damaging from the outset. Uncle Daniel, sure that she doesn't know what she is talking about, would like to answer for her. Judge Waite, throwing up his hands in despair, is almost ready to give up. Gladney draws Narciss out; she even agrees with his interpretations of her answers. She says that Bonnie Dee, when Edna Earle and Uncle Daniel arrived during the storm, was "alive as you is now." Once started, Narciss works herself up into a lively account of all that happened. Gladney asks her to continue.

NARCISS—Mistuh Daniel he grab hold of her and pull her out an' she still screamin' . . . (*She stops.*)

GLADNEY—Go on! What happened next?

NARCISS—Don't *know* what happened next . . . eyes closed under the sofa—can't see anythin' . . .

GLADNEY—And when did you see Mrs. Ponder again?

NARCISS—Storm pass over. I comes out of the sofa and asked did I hear my name. There, stretched out, feets pointin' other way 'round and Doctor Eubanks snapping down her eyes . . .

GLADNEY (*a hushed voice*)—Dead! (UNCLE DANIEL *stamps his foot heavily several times.*) What are you doing?

UNCLE DANIEL—Sittin' still so long and not talkin', my foot fell asleep. It's all pins and needles. (*He pounds his foot again.*) Sorry, I can't help it, your Honor!

JUDGE—Bailiff, take Mr. Ponder outside and walk him around the building.

BAILIFF—Come, Mr. Ponder. I'll help you.

JUDGE—And Bailiff—don't hurry back!

UNCLE DANIEL (*to* BAILIFF)—Mighty kind of you, Chuck. I know I'm not gonna miss anything because Narciss don't know anything about this case anyway.

GLADNEY—Woman, you were saying when you came out from under the sofa you found Dr. Eubanks snapping down her eyelids. Now, don't that prove that the company had something to do with it? Had *everything* to do with it! Dr. Daniel Ponder, like Othello of old, the Moor of Venice, pulled her out, threw her on the sofa and suffocated to death that beautiful young innocent ninety-eight pound bride of his out of a fit of pure jealousy from the well-springs of his agin' heart.

NARCISS (sharply)—No, sir! Mr. Daniel didn't do nothin' like that. His heart ain't grow old neither, by a long shot!

GLADNEY—What do you mean by that, woman?

NARCISS—Means *you* ain't lived with Mistuh Daniel and I *has*. Find you somebody *else*.

GLADNEY (*snaps*)—That's what the other side better try to do! That's just what I mean! There *wasn't* anybody else! (*To* DEYANCEY.) Your witness.

Narciss, asked for special details of this worst storm she had ever seen, obliges DeYancey with a description: "A big ball of fire . . . I feels it clicking my teeth and twangin' my bones . . . den I couldn't no more hear an' no more see . . . just smell them smokes . . ." DeYancey, addressing the Jury, says: "Gentlemen, it is our contention that this terrifyin' manifestation of nature is what caused the death of Bonnie Dee Ponder by heart failure, which we will prove beyond the shadow of a doubt by expert medical testimony. Thank you, Narciss, that's all."

Gladney stops her from leaving the witness stand. He demands to know whether this so-called ball of fire came bouncing into the parlor before or after the company came. Narciss is bewildered and downright scared when he asks her to swear which it was on the Bible. "I ain't got nothin' to do with it which come in first," she says; "if white folks and ball of fire both tryin' to get into you all's home you just *let* them . . . an' who comes in first I ain't had nothin' to do with. *I* under the sofa!" Gladney says: "With your eyes closed! Woman, you may step down! A ball of fire! I double dog dare Mr. DeYancey Clanahan to produce that ball of fire." But as usual, his effect is ruined: the Bailiff enters announcing that he's lost Uncle Daniel.

The Judge's patience snaps. Gladney sees that Uncle Daniel has escaped, and amid general pandemonium, reprimands Judge Waite: "Your Honor, I don't want to be an old I-told-you-so, but if you'd incarcerated him in the first place, like any other murder suspect, 'stead of lettin' him roam around loose—" Pounding his gavel, Judge Waite replies: "I don't need any of your back seat drivin', Mr. Gladney—you're not state senator yet! DeYancey, I let him roam in your charge and you're responsible for his appearance." DeYancey respectfully submits that it was the Judge who sent Uncle Daniel out when his foot fell asleep. "Don't give me any fool arguments!" shouts the Judge. "He's your client! Go out and find him and bring him back or I'll slap you with a contempt of court!"

Edna Earle goes out with DeYancey, while Judge Waite recesses the court. Everyone gets up. Members of the jury object to this waste of time; Teacake voices her worries to Dr. Eubanks, who laughs them off: "You know Daniel as well as I do! If he can't be the center of attention he'll light out for somewhere where he *can* be!" The Peacock children are having a fine time taking over the witness chair. The adult Peacocks are acting important and agreeing with Gladney that Uncle Daniel has undoubtedly escaped. "That's a fine way for you to talk, Mrs. Peacock," Dr. Eubanks upbraids her, "after all he's done for you folks." *"Done* for us?" shrills Mrs. Peacock. "Where's my little Bonnie Dee? *That's* what he's done for us!" All the Peacocks gather around to comfort her. Next, the foreman of the jury offers his version: " 'Way I see it, he probably took hold of her to quieten her—and held her too hard and too long." Dr. Eubanks becomes really angry: "What kind of way is that for a juror to talk? You can't air your opinions in court." The foreman says apologetically: "I'm only goin' by the testimony—an' he ain't *here*."

Edna Earle and DeYancey come back without a single clue as to Uncle Daniel's whereabouts. Now they, too, are worried. Under pressure from Gladney, though he hates to do it, the Judge is ready to call in the State Police—just as Uncle Daniel ambles happily into the courtroom.

As Gladney glares, Uncle Daniel, amid a ripple of laughter, distributes lollipops to the Peacock children. Judge Waite explodes: "Order! Order! Daniel Ponder, where in hell have you been?" "Why, Judge," answers Uncle Daniel innocently, "what's the trouble?" He had merely taken Judge Waite at his word, and hadn't hurried back. He'd gone to the bus terminal for a shoeshine and had ended up holding some woman's baby for her. That's all there was to it, except that the child had kept Uncle Daniel's watch.

While Gladney and DeYancey confer with Judge Waite, Uncle Daniel addresses the spectators: "There's one thing I want to ask you folks. You're all my friends. Do you think it's fair of Tadpole to keep me off the stand?" No one does; they had all come, in fact, to hear him. Uncle Daniel assures them that he's the only one who knows what happened.

The trial resumes with the testimony of Johnnie Ree Peacock. DeYancey asks her to tell about her trip with her sister to Memphis, to prove that Bonnie Dee left her husband (while retaining his money) in order to revel in gay, big-city nightlife. Johnnie Ree gives a long meandering account of their trip, much of it having to do with the movie *Quo Vadis*. She could tell them the whole plot, but DeYancey hastily cuts her short. Not short enough, however. The trip was indeed taken by Johnnie Ree and her sister, but the sister wasn't Bonnie Dee. As Johnnie Ree says: "Bonnie Dee's not the only sister in the world. Stand up, Treva. That's the sister I went with." "Why, Mr. DeYancey Clanahan," says Judge Waite, "I believe you've been wasting our time." DeYancey is a broken man. Uncle Daniel, laughing with everyone else, offers DeYancey consolation, but is irritably rebuffed. "Now keep your temper, Tadpole," says Uncle Daniel, "and you're going to come out with flying colors."

The next witness is Dr. Eubanks—and the only witness that Gladney is unable to shake. As Dr. Eubanks repeats that Bonnie Dee's death was due to heart failure, Gladney gives up. Uncle Daniel offers him consolation: "Now don't you take it personal, Mr. Gladney. The Doctor's always been pretty sharp-tongued 'til you get to know him."

Miss Teacake Magee is next called to the stand. Uncle Daniel feels more put out than ever. "Miss Teacake Magee, social leader," as she describes herself, can only say the nicest things about Uncle Daniel. "And in your familiar opinion," asks DeYancey, "would you say he loved his late wife?" "Loved her?" trills Miss Teacake. "Why, if she were a little Dresden doll he couldn't have treated her with more lovin' care." Thanking her, DeYancey turns her over to Gladney.

Gladney wants to know about Miss Teacake's engagement to Uncle Daniel and why it was broken off after two months. Miss Teacake resents having to air her personal affairs in public. "You go ahead, Miss Teacake," Judge Waite says. "There's nothin' you can tell us the whole town don't know anyway."

TEACAKE—Well, the fact is when Mr. Ponder's daddy gave him the Studebaker, he took to cruisin' around the countryside and just forgot his obligations to his fiancée—not that I'd have gone, mind you; I have enough to do without scootin' around the county, givin' lifts to every vagrant who stuck his thumb out. Then when he crashed into the parking meter in Meridian and they took his license away—

UNCLE DANIEL—I couldn't find the brake, that's what happened.

TEACAKE—I decided Daniel wasn't quite ready for marriage yet.

Gladney refuses to accept this explanation, and suggests that Teacake is suppressing vital knowledge and having a convenient lapse of memory. "I object!" cries Teacake, "I—" "*You* can't object!" rules Judge Waite. "Judge Waite," states Teacake, "I didn't come here to be insulted. You may go far in politics, Mr. Dorris R. Gladney, but in Clay you're goin' to be a social non-entity." Judge Waite says that she may step down.

When Edna Earle is called as witness, it looks to Uncle Daniel that he'll never get on the stand. First DeYancey goes into the Ponder family's use of the phrase: "I'm going to kill you dead—" Edna Earle says: "He got it straight from Grandma. She said, 'I'm going to kill you,' every other breath. She raised him—gentlest woman on the face of the earth—'I'll break your neck'—'I'll skin you alive' —'I'll beat your brains out.'" "My!" exclaims Uncle Daniel. "How that does bring Grandma back!"

Edna Earle's crisp description of the storm and her teamwork with DeYancey annoys Gladney. He objects to their shoddy theatrics, but is overruled. Uncle Daniel is pleased, but when Edna Earle testifies that Bonnie Dee was dead when Uncle Daniel pulled her from under the sofa, Uncle Daniel gasps: *"Edna Earle!* Wait a minute! You—" She tells him to sit down and hush, and goes on with her well-rehearsed story.

Gladney, questioning Edna Earle, wants to straighten out the matter of the "ball of fire." Gladney plays innocent and leads her on: "Do tell—" he says softly—"and while you was miratin' away at this ball of fire that was supposed to be scarin' Mrs. Ponder to death—" She breaks in that it did scare her to death. "And how did you know *that?"* asks Gladney sharply. "No need to raise your voice to me, Mr. Gladney!" says Edna Earle angrily. "I know it 'cause it like to scare *me* to death! *I* fainted dead away—" DeYancey groans as Gladney pounces on Edna Earle. *"Now* the cat's out of the bag!" he gloats. "That's right!" Uncle Daniel agrees. "Edna Earle sure let the cat outa the bag that time." The court is in a hubbub. DeYancey does what he can: "Your Honor, I refuse to let the witness be bullied by the District Attorney. He seems to forget he's talkin' to a *lady!"*

GLADNEY (*sneers*)—This *lady,* it appears, has been lying her head pretty near off all the time she's been up on that stand.

JUDGE (*rises, pounding gavel*)—Mr. Gladney, I will not stand for that kind of language to a female in my court.

GLADNEY—Perjury knows no sex, your Honor.

JUDGE—A lady is still a lady in my court, Mr. Gladney; until she is proven otherwise.

EDNA EARLE—Thank you, Judge Waite! But Mr. Gladney's a newcomer to Clay and he doesn't know what we expect of a gentleman here.

TEACAKE—Miss Edna Earle's a respected member of our community—and her family before her for at least six generations.

GLADNEY (*scathingly*)—Yes, I heard all about them! The Ponders, I have been told, did not burn their cotton when Sherman come marchin' through. That was the founding of their fortune.

Up pops a juryman, shouting: "Take that back, Gladney. I'm a cousin of the Ponders and that's a goddamn lie!" Judge Waite, pounding for order, cries that if the man weren't on the jury, he'd throw him out of this court. Edna Earle furiously denies Gladney's accusation; but Uncle Daniel is ready to admit there may be something to it. Gladney, ordered by the court to apologize to Miss Edna Earle, does do with mock-humility, but soon after makes a telling blow. He has her helpless as he brings out that she recently discussed having Uncle Daniel committed. "Is that true, Edna Earle?" Uncle Daniel begs to know. "Were you going to have me committed?" "No, no, dear heart," Edna Earle says, "just some talk . . ." Smiling, Gladney says he'll stand on the witness' testimony as it appears in the record. She is told to step down, which she does with overdone dignity.

Seeing his chance, Uncle Daniel flies to the witness chair, and entrenches himself there. DeYancey can't pry him loose; Edna Earle can't pull him out. "I demand to testify!" shouts Uncle Daniel. Judge Waite says he has a right to, but DeYancey says he'll have to fire him first. Uncle Daniel is regretful but ready. And when he learns that someone has to put the questions to him so that he can testify, he decides to have Gladney put them. "I've had my eye on him," he says, "he's up and comin'. Been at it harder than anybody. An' I give him a little pat on the back for it. Run home, Tadpole. Give your daddy my love. Where is he, by the way? I missed his face."

Gladney, dripping oil, advises Uncle Daniel that he is acting for the *State*. "Mr. Gladney," Uncle Daniel tells him, "you're actin' for the finest state in the Union!"—he bows—"Been a citizen of it all my life and that's good enough for me!" And he's sworn in.

Uncle Daniel answers every question to the fullest. When told to listen carefully to Gladney's next question—of whether, when he came into the parlor, Bonnie Dee spoke to him—DeYancey breaks in: "I object!" Uncle Daniel sweetly tells him that he can't. "You just got fired. . . . Speak?" says Uncle Daniel, answering the question. "She hollered. She hollered—'I don't appreciate thunder and lightning a bit!'" Gladney likes Uncle Daniel's testimony, as it proceeds, detail by detail. "Mr. Ponder," says Gladney in honeyed tones, "I want to congratulate you. You set us going on the right track. You've got a reliable memory. In fact, the most *reliable* memory in court, and we're all much obliged to you."

UNCLE DANIEL (*gratefully*)—Thank you, Mr. Gladney, that's mighty nice of you. (*Grasps* GLADNEY'S *hand, looks over at* DEYANCEY.) I don't know why you say he's a shyster—seems like a gentleman to me.

GLADNEY (*looking at* DEYANCEY *grimly*)—Thank you, sir. Now you just tell us the rest of it. Remember—you picked me out.

UNCLE DANIEL—That's right, Mr. Gladney, with pleasure! Now where was I, sir?

GLADNEY (*softly rising to a high pitch*)—I'll tell you where you were, Mr. Ponder—you were holdin' your little wife in your arms. You reached out your hands and like Othello of old, you suffocated her to death. You murdered your innocent ninety-eight-pound bride!

UNCLE DANIEL (*rises*)—Judge Waite, did you hear that? (JUDGE *nods sadly;* DANIEL *gets up and starts out of the courtroom.*) Well, I've heard 'bout everything there is to hear, an' I don't believe my ears. Imagine me doin' a mean thing like that, murderin' my sweet little Bonnie Dee.

GLADNEY—What did you think this trial was all *about?*

JUDGE—*Daniel!* Where are you goin'? Come back here!

UNCLE DANIEL (*regretfully*)—Judge Waite, this is no reflection on you, but I just can't stay here an' listen to crazy talk. Judge, your Honor, I'm leavin' off.

Orders to return are of no use. Only as a personal courtesy to the Judge does Uncle Daniel agree to remain and continue testifying.

Merciless, Gladney asks him why did he think his own flesh and blood were trying to put him away, then answers for him: "They considered you irresponsible and incompetent, and that was the reason they tied your money up so's you couldn't touch it." And after tieing the money up, Gladney continues, they planned on putting Uncle Daniel away. Uncle Daniel thinks about this, while Edna Earle and Dr. Eubanks try to deny it, and decides it must be true: "I have been out of step all my life. Look at me—I don't work, I fool around all day, wastin' folks' time—folks who *do* work and worry an' who are pushin' ahead to get somewhere. To *make* somethin' out of themselves. An' there was I, laughin' and jokin' like life was one big barbecue and I was the guest of honor! My daddy made the mistake, leavin' me all that money!" Gladney would like Uncle Daniel to get back to the case, but now Uncle Daniel decides to give away his entire fortune right in the courtroom. Edna Earle gets his trust fund; the Peacocks, his big house; Miss Teacake Magee, the Studebaker; and Judge Waite (if he can use it), the pick-up truck. Judge Waite tries to halt this flow of bequests, but Uncle Daniel says happily: "Take it, Judge, and welcome to it! All possessions ever did for me was give me trouble. Now that I'm rid of them I feel like I just got over the chicken pox. Bet you're gonna feel better, too, Edna Earle, now you can stop worryin' about me. You too, Tadpole. We're *all* gonna feel better. I know I do! I'm standin' right in the middle of everythin' I own! Oh, I'm as happy as a mockin' bird! If I had any kind of voice, I'd sing." Gladney, saying it's too late for this kind of atonement, adds that confession would be better for Uncle Daniel's soul. Uncle Daniel is completely receptive to this idea also. He changes his plea from "not guilty" to "guilty."

Amid the general commotion and DeYancey's objections, Judge Waite tries to get Uncle Daniel to understand what he is saying: "Daniel, did you or did you *not* murder your wife?"

UNCLE DANIEL (*reproachfully*)—Judge Waite, I expect that from a stranger, but I didn't expect it from *you*—an' I want to say right here and now, if anybody asks me that question again, I'm goin' to go straight out of my mind—

JUDGE—Will you tell us what *did* happen?

UNCLE DANIEL (*shakes his head*)—If somebody'd asked me in the first place, we could have saved the time and patience of everybody—includin' all the witnesses, who didn't know anythin'— (*Hastily.*) Not that I *blame* them—they just weren't there— It's as simple as ABC. I pulled Miss Bonnie Dee from under the sofa—I held her in my arms and I could feel her heart beatin' like a frightened rabbit. "Quieten down, Bonnie Dee," I kept sayin' to her, "your husband's back home and he's goin' to look after you from now on." She breathed her last in my arms, an' blew off like one of those little dandelion puff-balls like we used to tell time by. An' that's exactly what happened—the whole truth and nothin' *but* the truth—just like I promised Chuck here when I took the oath. (*There is a long pause.*)

JUDGE—And that's what you call pleadin' "guilty"?

UNCLE DANIEL—Well, Judge, what else can you call it? With all due respect to Dr. Eubanks, it wasn't heart failure. When I held her in my arms and told her I was comin' back to stay, I could feel a quiver go right through her body—tears came up in her eyes and her lips moved like she wanted to say somethin' to me, but her little heart couldn't stand it. It just filled up and busted with *love*. And if it wasn't for me, she'd still be alive and that naturally makes me guilty— (*Stepping down.*) So I'm asking you, Gentlemen of the Jury, don't stand on ceremony or friendship, just put me away, 'cause I'm ready to go!

Neither a despairing Gladney nor a saddened DeYancey has anything more to say. The jury, asked to render its verdict, doesn't even bother to retire. The foreman, after a mere look around, relays the verdict: "We find the defendant—not guilty!" Amid cheers and hugs, Uncle Daniel, ready to stand treat as usual, thanks everyone for coming, and sweeps out in triumph.

MY FAIR LADY *

Adapted from Bernard Shaw's *Pygmalion*

Book and Lyrics by Alan Jay Lerner

Music by Frederick Loewe

[ALAN JAY LERNER *was born in New York in 1918, went to Choate and then to Harvard, where he did two Hasty Pudding shows. He has written advertising copy, radio scripts, and vaudeville sketches. Together with Mr. Loewe he wrote, for a musical stock company in Detroit, a revue called "What's Up?" and such Broadway productions as "The Day before Spring," "Brigadoon" and "Paint Your Wagon." In 1948 he did the book and lyrics for "Love Life," which had music by Kurt Weill.*

FREDERICK LOEWE *came to America from his native Vienna at the age of 20. He was a concert pianist there, but upon arrival in this country did some flyweight boxing before he began to compose. He wrote the popular song "Katrina," as well as the Broadway shows on which he collaborated with Mr. Lerner.*

GEORGE BERNARD SHAW *wrote the play "Pygmalion" upon which "My Fair Lady" is based. Mr. Shaw, who died in 1950 at the age of 94, was the most important, influential, and successful dramatist of his time.*]

NEAR Covent Garden, on a cold March night, the colonnade of St. Paul's provides shelter for elegant opera lovers who are waiting for taxis. A smudge-pot, outside the tenement opposite, provides warmth for the poor.

As some street entertainers try to amuse the taxi-seekers, one cartwheeling performer bangs into opera-hatted Freddy Eynsford-Hill. There is a cry of "Aaaooowww!" When the crowd parts, Eliza Doolittle is discovered lying on the pavement with flowers from her upset basket strewn all about her. "Aaaooowww!" she howls once more. Freddy is distressed; but since his mother doesn't wish to catch pneumonia, he says "Sorry" once again and rushes off in search of a taxi. Eliza turns her attention to Mrs. Eynsford-Hill: "Oh, he's your son, is he? Well, if you'd done your duty by him as a mother should, you wouldn't let him spoil a poor girl's flowers and then run away without paying." "Go on about your business, my girl," says Mrs. Eynsford-Hill.

Straightening out her crumpled flowers, Eliza next spies Colonel Pickering searching for a taxi. "I say, Captain," she whines, "buy a flower off a poor girl." Pickering has no change. "I can change half a crown. Here, take this for tuppence," persists Eliza, indicating a flower. Pickering comes up impatiently with three ha'pence. Thinking this better than nothing, Eliza subsides, till a bystander breaks in: "Here, you be careful . . . Better give him a flower for it. There's a bloke there behind the pillar taking down every blessed word you're saying." Scrambling to her feet, Eliza cries in terror: "I ain't done nothin' wrong by speakin' to the gentleman. I've a right to sell flowers if I keep off the curb. I'm a respectable girl; so help me, I never spoke to him except to ask him to buy a flower off me."

Someone in the gathering crowd is sure it's a "tec" taking down Eliza's every word. Everybody stares at the pillar. Eliza, well-nigh hysterical, begs Pickering: "Oh, sir, don't let him charge me. You dunno what it means to me. They'll take away my character and drive me on the streets for speakin' to gentlemen."

Approaching from behind the pillar, Professor Higgins tush-tushes Eliza and good-humoredly tells her to shut up. "Do I look like a policeman?" he asks. Eliza, demanding to see what he wrote down in his notebook, can't make heads or tails of it. "I can," Higgins replies, reading—and reproducing her pronunciation: "I say, Captain, buy a flower off a poor girl."

Pickering intervenes in Eliza's behalf: "Really, sir, if you are a detective, you need not begin protecting me against molestation by young women until I ask you. Anybody could see the girl meant no harm." One of the bystanders now announces that Higgins is a gentleman because of his shoes.

HIGGINS—And how are all your people down at Selsey?
SELSEY MAN—Who told you my people come from Selsey?

HIGGINS—Never mind. They did. (*To* ELIZA.) How do you come to be up so far east? You were born in Lisson Grove.

ELIZA (*appalled*)—Oooooh, what harm is there in my leaving Lisson Grove? (*In tears, she picks up her basket and sits on an orange crate in front of the pillars.*) It wasn't fit for a pig to live in; and I had to pay four-and-six a week. Oh, boo-hoo-oo—

HIGGINS—Live where you like; but stop that noise.

Of the few remaining bystanders, one asks sarcastically: "Do you know where *I* come from?" "Hoxton," answers Higgins.

HOXTON MAN—Well, who said I didn't? Blimey, you know everything, you do.

ANOTHER BYSTANDER (*indicating* PICKERING)—Tell him where he comes from, if you want to go fortune-telling.

HIGGINS (*staring at* PICKERING)—Cheltenham, Harrow, Cambridge and India.

PICKERING—Quite right.

Having had their fun, the people depart. Pickering politely inquires how Higgins does it, and Higgins is delighted to tell him: "Simple phonetics. The science of speech. That's my profession: also my hobby. Anyone can spot an Irishman or a Yorkshireman by his brogue. I can place a man within six miles; I can place him within two miles in London." Bothered by Eliza's crooning as he gives a dissertation on his favorite subject, Higgins explodes: "Woman! Cease this detestable boohooing instantly; or else seek the shelter of some other place of worship." When Eliza protests feebly, Higgins waxes even more voluble. Eliza's yowl of "Aooooooooow!" sets Higgins to singing "Why Can't the English," his lament on the "cold-blooded murder of the English tongue." He concludes:

"An Englishman's way of speaking absolutely classifies him.
The moment he talks he makes some other Englishman despise him.
One common language I'm afraid we'll never get.
Oh, why can't the English learn to
Set a good example to people whose English is painful to your ears?
The Scotch and the Irish leave you close to tears.
There even are places where English completely disappears.
In America, they haven't used it for years!
Why can't the English teach their children how to speak?
Norwegians learn Norwegian, the Greeks are taught their Greek.
In France every Frenchman knows his language from 'A' to 'Zed'—

(*Aside.*) The French never cared what they do, actually, as long as they pronounce it properly.

Arabians learn Arabian with the speed of summer lightning,
The Hebrews learn it backwards, which is absolutely frightening.
Use proper English, you're regarded as a freak.
Why can't the English . . .
Why can't the English learn to speak?"

As the song ends, Higgins makes a gesture toward Eliza. "You see this creature," he says to Pickering, "with her curb-stone English, the English that will keep her in the gutter to the end of her days? Well, sir, in six months I could pass her off as a duchess at an Embassy Ball. I could even get her a place as a lady's maid or shop assistant, which requires better English." Overhearing all this, Eliza appeals once more to Pickering: "Aooow! You don't believe that, Captain?" Confessing himself a student of Indian dialects, Pickering concedes it is possible. Higgins, hearing about the Indian dialects, asks the stranger whether he knows the author of "Spoken Sanskrit"—a Colonel Pickering. When the man says *he* is Pickering, Higgins introduces himself as the author of "Higgins' Universal Alphabet." "I came from India to meet you," says Pickering. "I was going to India to meet you!" cries Higgins, and arranges for Pickering to move in at once with him at 27-A Wimpole Street. As the men go off happily to jaw about human sounds, Eliza stops Higgins: "Buy a flower, kind sir. I'm short for my lodging." "Liar," Higgins answers amiably, "you said you could change half a crown." "You ought to be stuffed with nails, you ought," is Eliza's opinion. But still full of fight, she shoves her basket at him: "Here! Take the whole bloomin' basket for sixpence!" As the bells of St. Paul's strike two, Higgins says: "Ah." He raises his hat solemnly. "The church. A reminder." And thinking about Indian dialects, Higgins tosses some coins into Eliza's basket and goes off with Pickering.

Eliza's delighted "Aooows" fill the air as she counts her haul. The Cockneys gathering around the smudge-pot kid her good-naturedly about what she will do with her fortune. They sing "Wouldn't It Be Loverly," with Eliza replying:

"All I want is a room somewhere
Far away from the cold night air.
With one enormous chair . . .
Oh, wouldn't it be loverly?

"Lots of choc'late for me to eat
Lots of coal makin' lots of heat
Warm face, warm hands, warm feet . . .
Loverly! Loverly!
Loverly! Loverly!"

Scene II

Later that evening, in a slummy part of Tottenham Court Road, there is a minor altercation in the corner pub. Two disturbers of the peace are tossed out, while the bartender at the pub's door yells back to the third: "I ain't runnin' no charity bazaar. Drinks is to be paid for or not drunk. Come on, Doolittle. Out you go. Hop it now, Doolittle. On the double. On the double." Taking his own sweet time, Doolittle swaggers forth. With a grin and a gesture, he thanks the bartender for past hospitality, and advises him: "Send the bill to Buckingham Palace."

Doolittle joins his ejected pals, who are so discouraged they are ready to call it a night. But not Doolittle: it's his idea that his daughter Eliza shall pay for the next round of drinks. Hearing her name, his friends jeer. "What's a half-crown after all I've given her?" asks Doolittle. "When," says his friend Jamie, "did you ever give her anything?" "Anything? I give her everything. I give her the greatest gift any human being can give to another: Life! I introduced her to this here planet, I did, with all its wonders and marvels. The sun that shines, and the moon that glows; Hyde Park to walk through on a fine Spring night. The whole ruddy city of London to roam about in, sellin' her bloomin' flowers. I give her all that, and then I disappears and leaves her on her own to enjoy it. . . . Now, if that ain't worth half a crown now and again, I'll take off my belt and give her what for." One of his pals indicates that Eliza has arrived.

Before Doolittle can open his mouth, Eliza refuses him even so much as a brass farthing. Doolittle grabs her arm: "Now you look here, Eliza. You wouldn't have the heart to send me home to your stepmother without a bit of liquid protection, now would you?" Eliza snorts at the word "stepmother." Doolittle argues that it's he whom that woman has enslaved, simply because he's not her lawful husband. Relenting, because she's has a bit of luck, Eliza flips a coin towards her father, warning him not to expect anything further, and disappears into the tenement.

The men are ready for a spree. "You see, boys," Doolittle crows, "I told you not to go home! It's just Faith, Hope and a little bit of Luck!" And holding forth on this theme in song and dance, he gets the boys to help him wake up the neighborhood—"With a Little Bit of Luck":

"The Lord above gave man an arm of iron
So he could do his job and never shirk.
The Lord above gave man an arm of iron—but
With a little bit of luck,
With a little bit of luck,
Someone else'll do the blinkin' work!"

Scene III

In the balconied study at 27-A Wimpole Street, Higgins is displaying to Pickering the equipment that jams the room. With a fanatic's intensity, Higgins has played so many phonetic recordings that Pickering can take no more. Fortunately, Mrs. Pearce announces a young woman with a dreadful accent who wishes to see Mr. Higgins.

Considering this a piece of luck—he can take down her speech for Pickering's benefit—Higgins asks that the girl be sent up. When she turns out to be Eliza, Higgins yells for her to be thrown out. "She's no use," he dismisses her. "I've got all the records I want of the Lisson Grove lingo; and I'm not going to waste another cylinder on it. Be off with you; I don't want you!" "Don't you be so saucy," Eliza answers. "You ain't heard what I come for yet." She asks, did Mrs. Pearce tell Mr. Higgins she had come in a taxi? "Nonsense, girl!" says Mrs. Pearce. "What do you think a gentleman like Mr. Higgins cares what you came in?" "Oh, we are proud," says Eliza. "He ain't above givin' lessons, not him; I heard him say so. Well, I ain't come here to ask for any compliment, and if my money's not good enough I can go elsewhere."

Eliza's determination to have paid lessons intrigues Higgins. "Pickering," he calls out, "shall we ask this baggage to sit down, or shall we throw her out the window?" Pickering asks courteously what she wants. Eliza tells him: "I want to be a lady in a flower shop, instead of sellin' flowers at the corner of Tottenham Court Road. But they won't take me unless I can talk more genteel. He said he could teach me. Well, here I am ready to pay—not askin' any favor—and he treats me as if I was dirt. I know what lessons cost, and I'm ready to pay."

Learning her name, Pickering says: "Won't you sit down, Miss Doolittle?" Eliza, gaining confidence, says: "Oh, I know what's right. A lady friend of mine gets French lessons for heighteenpence

Julie Andrews and Rex Harrison

"My Fair Lady"

an hour from a real French gentleman. Well, you wouldn't have the face to ask me the same for teaching me my own language as you would for French; so I won't give more than a shilling. Take it or leave it."

Higgins is interested; Pickering persuades him: "What about your boast that you could pass her off as a duchess at the Embassy Ball? I'll say you're the greatest teacher alive if you can make that good. I'll bet you all the expenses of the experiment you can't do it. And I'll even pay for the lessons." "It's almost irresistible," says Higgins, peering at Eliza. "She's so deliciously low—so horribly dirty!" "Aoooow!" Eliza protests. "I ain't dirty: I washed my face and hands afore I come, I did." "I'll take it!" Higgins decides. "I'll make a duchess of this draggle-tailed guttersnipe!"

Telling Mrs. Pearce to take Eliza away—and sandpaper the dirt off her, burn her clothes and order some new ones—he proceeds to step all over Eliza's feelings. Mrs. Pearce reprimands him, and thinks it better that Eliza go back to her parents. "I ain't got no parents," Eliza answers. "There you are," Higgins says. "She ain't got no parents. What's all the fuss about? The girl doesn't belong to anybody, and she's no use to anybody but me. . . ." Both Mrs. Pearce and Pickering want Higgins to think about the girl and what's to become of her when he's finished his teaching. "What's to become of her if I leave her in the gutter? Answer me that, Mrs. Pearce," he retorts. "That's her own business, not yours, Mr. Higgins." "Well," concludes Higgins, "when I've done with her, we can throw her back into the gutter, and then it will be her own business again; so that's all right." Eliza's had just about enough of this and starts to leave. Higgins woos her with chocolates and Pickering comes to her assistance and demands that Higgins explain what's really in store for her. But Higgins, now wound up, can't change his tune. Resigned, Mrs. Pearce takes Eliza away.

Pickering isn't satisfied. He wants it clearly understood that no advantage be taken of Eliza's position and that Higgins is a man of good character where women are concerned. "Have you ever met a man of good character where women were concerned?" asks Higgins unconcernedly. Pickering frequently has. "Well, Higgins has not. "I find that the moment I let a woman make friends with me she becomes jealous, exacting, suspicious and a damned nuisance. I find that the moment I let myself become friends with a woman, I become selfish and tyrannical. So here I am, a confirmed old bachelor, and likely to remain so. After all, Pickering . . ." And Higgins sings "I'm an Ordinary Man"—a paean to his living exactly as *he* wishes without female interference.

"I'm an ordinary man
Who desires nothing more
Than just the ordinary chance
To live exactly as he likes
And do precisely what he wants.
An average man am I
Of no eccentric whim;
Who wants to live his life
Free of strife,
Doing whatever he thinks is best for him.
Just an ordinary man.

"But let a woman in your life
And you are up against the wall!
Make a plan and you will find
She has something else in mind;
And so rather than do either
You do something else that neither
Likes at all.
You want to talk of Keats or Milton;
She only wants to talk of love.
You go to see a play or ballet,
And spend it searching for her glove."

Scene IV

Another day, another half-crown owing the bartender at the Tottenham Court Road pub. While an appreciative audience of Cockneys looks on, Doolittle's two pals are tossed out as usual, and Doolittle, as usual, is persuaded to leave under his own steam. There is one innovation, however: when Doolittle emerges from the pub, a Cockney woman greets him with the news that henceforth he can *buy* his own drinks: "Moved in with a swell, Eliza has. Left here in a taxi all by herself, smart as paint, and ain't been home for three days. And then I gets a message from her this morning: she wants her things sent over to 27-A Wimpole Street, care of Professor Higgins. And what things does she want? Her bird-cage and her Chinese fan." These the woman hands over to Doolittle, remarking: "But," she says, "never mind about sendin' any clothes!" Doolittle joins in the general laughter, and crossing to his friends, exclaims: "I knowed she had a career in front of her! Harry boy, we're in for a booze-up. The sun is shinin' on Alfred P. Doolittle." He sings:

"A man was made to help support his children
Which is the right and proper thing to do.
A man was made to help support his children—but
With a little bit of luck,
(*Crowd cheers*)
With a little bit of luck,
They'll go out and start supporting you!"

Scene V

The same day, Mrs. Pearce has come to Higgins' study to lecture him for overworking Eliza. Getting nowhere, she asks him at least to pay attention to his mail, to this third request from an American millionaire that Mr. Higgins lecture to his Moral Reform League. Higgins promises to do something about it, as the butler announces Alfred Doolittle.

Pickering senses there may be trouble, but not Higgins. When Doolittle arrives to discuss a "serious matter," Higgins highhandedly orders him to take his daughter away at once. Doolittle is momentarily stunned, but quickly rallies. Higgins, half-overcome by Doolittle's whiskey breath, accuses the man of coming to blackmail him—otherwise, why should he have sent Eliza to Wimpole Street, and, if not, how did he know that she was here? "I'll tell ya, Governor," says Doolittle, "if you'll only let me get a word in. I'm willing to tell ya. I'm wanting to tell ya. I'm waiting to tell ya." Higgins calls to Pickering: "This chap has a certain natural gift of rhetoric. Observe the rhythm of his native woodnotes wild."

When, says Doolittle, he heard that Eliza had sent for her things but wanted no clothes, as a "parient" what was he to think? "So you came to rescue her from worse than death, eh?" Higgins fills in. When Doolittle agrees, Higgins orders Mrs. Pearce to turn Eliza immediately over to her father. Doolittle asks him to wait and discuss the matter as between men of the world. Higgins suggests that in that case Mrs. Pearce had better leave the room. Announcing that he's taken a sort of fancy to him, Doolittle airily permits Mr. Higgins to keep Eliza. At the same time, he wants to put in his own claim as a father. As, plainly, Mr. Higgins is the sort of man who will understand that her father can't let Eliza go for nothing, Doolittle adds: "What's a five-pound note to you? And what's Eliza to me?" Pickering assures him that Mr. Higgins' intentions are entirely honorable. "Of course they are, Governor," Doolittle agrees. "If I thought they wasn't, I'd ask fifty." "Have you no morals?" demands Pickering.

DOOLITTLE—No! I can't afford 'em, Governor. Neither could you if you was as poor as me. Not that I mean any harm, mind ya . . . but . . . (*Cleans off the wing chair with his dirty hat and sits.*) If Eliza is going to get a bit out of this, why not me, too? Eh? Look at it my way. What am I? I ask ya, what am I? I'm one of the undeserving poor, that's what I am. Think what that means to a man. (*He is now scratching under his shirt with great delight at the pleasure of it.*) It means he's up against middle-class morality for all the time. If there's anything going and I put in for a bit of it, it's always the same story: You're undeserving, so you can't have it. (*He has been scratching through all this, with* HIGGINS *and* PICKERING *watching in fascination. His hand now reaches his buttock.*) But my needs is as great as the most deserving widow's that ever got money out of six different charities in one week for the death of the same husband. (*He sits back and roars with laughter.*) I don't need less than a deserving man, I need more. I don't eat less hearty than he does, and I drink a lot more. I'm playing straight with you. I ain't pretending to be deserving. I'm undeserving, and I mean to go on being undeserving. I like it, and that's the truth. But will you take advantage of a man's nature to do him out of the price of his own daughter what he's brought up, fed and clothed by the sweat of his brow, till she's growed big enough to be interesting to you two gentlemen? Is five pounds reasonable? I put it to you, and I leave it to you.

Pickering thinks it unwise to give him the money: "He'll make bad use of it, I'm afraid." "Not me," answers Doolittle, "so help me, Governor, I won't. Just one good spree for myself and the missus, givin' pleasure to ourselves and employment to others, and satisfaction to you to know it ain't been throwed away. You couldn't spent it better."

Higgins, between scratching and damning a flea that has traveled from Doolittle's shirt to his own, considers giving Doolittle as much as ten pounds. "No!" says Doolittle. "The missus wouldn't have the heart to spend ten, Governor; ten pounds is a lot of money—it makes a man feel prudent-like; and then goodbye to happiness. No, you give me what I ask for, Governor: not a penny less, not a penny more."

Money in hand, Doolittle bumps into a spick-and-span Eliza at the door. He wouldn't have recognized her but for the sudden violence of her language. Advising her to mind the gentlemen, Doolittle departs. Higgins then instructs Mrs. Pearce to write to the American millionaire that Mr. Alfred P. Doolittle, a common dustman, is his man.

Eliza is in open, angry rebellion against practicing her vowels any further. Higgins ignores this, and has her repeat after him: A E I O U. "That's what I said," fumes Eliza; "Ahyee, E, Iyee, Ow, You. I've been syin' them for three days, and I won't sy them no more!" Pickering tries to explain, but Higgins interrupts that as a military man he should understand that drilling is what she needs.

Ignoring Eliza's mutterings that he ain't got no heart, Higgins marches up to his balcony stairs, saying "A" with each step. Eliza echoes, "Ahyee." When he reaches the top, Higgins looks down and says: "Eliza, I promise you you will pronounce your vowels correctly before this day is out, or there'll be no lunch, no dinner, and no chocolates!" He slams his door behind him.

In a blind rage, Eliza slams her book on the floor, stamps on it, and sings her dream of gory vengeance on 'enry 'iggins (nothing is too bad for him), in "Just You Wait."

BLACKOUT

One night, while Pickering sits by and Higgins holds a metronome, Eliza sighs through: "The rine in spine sties minely in the pline." Higgins corrects: "The rain in Spain stays mainly in the plain." "Didn't I sy that?" Eliza answers. "No, Eliza, you didn't sy that. You didn't even say that . . ." says Higgins. Then with an alcohol burner in his hand, as he's about to start her on "H's," he cries out: "Pickering, this is going to be ghastly!" But bravely carrying on, he explains to Eliza that, watching the flame, she will notice that it wavers every time she says her aitch properly, and remains stationary when she doesn't. He sets her to practicing: "In Hartford, Hereford and Hampshire, hurricanes hardly ever happen." The flame never flickers. Higgins has her start from the beginning, saying, "Ha-ha-ha-ha."

While the poor girl tries to ha-ha, Higgins talks shop to Pickering. Each of Eliza's "ha's" is more tortured than the last, but—"Go on, go on!" Higgins directs. Eliza manages one last "Ha," and blows out the flame.

BLACKOUT

A chorus of be-capped maidservants now chants of the pace poor Professor Higgins sets. Night and day he slaves away: he doesn't sleep—he doesn't eat . . .

In the study at tea time, Higgins taps out just three notes on a xylophone of "How kind of you to let me come." "*Kind* of you, *kind* of you," he says. Eliza accents the *you*. "No! Kind of you. It's like 'cup of tea.' Kind of you—cup of tea. Kind of you . . . Say 'cup of tea,' " instructs Higgins, heading for the tea tray and a piece of cake. While Eliza struggles with "cappatea," Higgins and Pickering enjoy their cup of tea, cake, and strawberry tarts. Eliza gets angrier and hungrier as they devote all their attention to the tea. "Cup, cup, cup, cup, cup," she continues, her eyes on each mouthful. "By Jove," says Pickering, "that was a glorious tea, Higgins. Finish the strawberry tart, I couldn't eat another thing." Nor can Higgins, but he sees that it won't be wasted. Eliza, watching him go to the bird-cage, lets loose with an: "Aaaaaaaaaaooooooowwww!!!!"

BLACKOUT

Poor Professor Higgins—chants the chorus—plods on and on against all odds. But when the lights come up, Higgins has Eliza doing Demosthenes' stint with the marbles. And when she unfortunately swallows one, Higgins provides her with more.

BLACKOUT

By now, even the chorus begs Professor Higgins to quit. But when the lights go on at three in the morning, Higgins is still making Eliza repeat "The rain in Spain." She may be tired, she may have a headache, but Higgins merely transfers his icebag from his head to hers. Suddenly, reasonably, in a kind tone, he tells the tired girl: "Eliza, I know you're tired. I know your head aches. I know your nerves are as raw as meat in a butcher's window. But think what you're trying to accomplish. Think what you're dealing with. The majesty and grandeur of the English language. It's the greatest possession we have. The noblest sentiments that ever flowed in the heart of men are contained in the extraordinary, imaginative and musical mixtures of sounds. That's what you've set yourself to conquer, Eliza. And conquer it you will." He gets up and asks her to try it again. Inspired by his speech, Eliza says: "The rain in Spain stays mainly in the plain." Incredulous, Higgins says: "What was that?" "The rain in Spain stays mainly in the plain," answers Eliza. "Again!" orders Higgins. Joy reigns as Eliza sings "The Rain in Spain."

ELIZA
The rain in Spain stays mainly in the plain.

HIGGINS—
I think she's got it!
I think she's got it!
ELIZA
The rain in Spain stays mainly in the plain.
HIGGINS—
By George, she's got it!
By George, she's got it!
Now once again, where does it rain?
ELIZA
On the plain! On the plain!
HIGGINS—
And where's that soggy plain?
ELIZA
In Spain! In Spain!
(PICKERING *joins them.*)
ALL (*joyously*)—
The rain in Spain stays mainly in the plain! . . .

The three dance a wildly impromptu fandango, and collapse in peals of laughter on the sofa.

Aroused by the noise, Mrs. Pearce finds the men planning to try Eliza out in public—in fact, in Mrs. Higgins' box at Ascot. "You'll consult your mother first, of course?" says Pickering. Higgins decides not: "We'll surprise her. Let's go straight to bed. First thing in the morning we'll go off and buy her a dress." And adds, "Eliza, go on with your work."

When the two men have left, Mrs. Pearce tells Eliza to stop working. But the new, elated Eliza sings that: "I Want to Dance All Night"—

"I'll never know
What made it so exciting;
Why all at once
My heart took flight . . .
I only know when he
Began to dance with me,
I could have danced, danced, danced all night!"

SCENE VI

At Ascot, Colonel Pickering breaks the news to the arriving Mrs. Higgins that any moment her son will descend on her. "What a disagreeable surprise!" she answers. "Ascot is usually the place I can come to with my friends and not run the risk of seeing my son Henry." Mrs. Higgins sighs: "Whenever my friends meet him, I never see them again."

With much greater difficulty, Colonel Pickering breaks the news to Mrs. Higgins that Henry will be accompanied by a Miss Doolittle, the flower girl he picked up off a curb-stone. Mrs. Higgins warns her chauffeur to stand by: "I may be leaving abruptly," she says.

Scene VII

Inside the Ascot enclosure, elegant ladies and gentlemen, dressed to the nines, watch the beginning of the race. Their nerveless faces and motionless bodies might belong to statues rather than to high-born bettors. ". . . What a frenzied moment that was!" they murmur in sing-song, called the "Ascot Gavotte."

"Didn't they maintain an exhausting pace?
'Twas a thrilling, absolutely chilling
Running of the Ascot op'ning race. . . ."

Higgins, dressed in mere tweeds and a squashed hat, comes up to his reproachful mother. He assures her that Eliza will be all right: "I've taught her to speak properly, and she has strict orders as to her behavior. She's to keep to two subjects—the weather and everybody's health. Sort of 'fine day' and 'how do you do'—and not just let herself go on things in general. Help her along, darling, and you'll be quite safe." "Safe?" cries Mrs. Higgins. "To talk about our health in the middle of a race?" And where's the girl now? she'd like to know. At the moment, Henry answers, Eliza is being pinned up. "Some of the clothes we bought for her didn't quite fit," Higgins explains to his superbly turned-out mother. "I told Pickering we should have taken her with us." "You're a pretty pair of babies playing with your live doll," Mrs. Higgins observes.

In the group of Mrs. Higgins' friends are Freddy Eynsford-Hill and his Mama, and a lord and his lady. At the sight of them all, Higgins irritably retreats and stays in the background, watching Colonel Pickering lead Eliza up to his mother. A delicate vision in her fluttery Ascot clothes, Eliza accepts introductions with a beautifully articulated "How kind of you to let me come," and "How do you do?"

As she seats herself, Freddy and Pickering have chairs placed for them at her side. Passing Eliza her tea, Mrs. Higgins obligingly starts the ball rolling: "Will it rain, do you think?" she asks. Eliza is primed: "The rain in Spain stays mainly in the plain." (Higgins can't resist doing a few fandango steps that cause people to look at him.) "But," adds Eliza, "in Hartford, Hereford, and Hampshire hurricanes hardly ever happen." "How awfully funny," Freddy laughs. Eliza snaps: "What is wrong with that, young man? I bet I got it right." Mrs. Eynsford-Hill hopes there will be no unseasonable cold spells to cause influenza. In precise tones, Eliza informs her: "My aunt died of influenza, so they said. But it's my belief they done the old woman in." Higgins and Pickering exchange accusing looks. "Done her in?" puzzles Mrs. Higgins. Enunciating exquisitely, Eliza explains: "Yes, Lord love you! Why should she die of influenza when she come through diphtheria right enough the year before? Fairly blue with it she was. They all thought she was dead; but my father, he kept ladling gin down her throat."—Higgins balances his tea cup on his head—"Then she come to so sudden that she bit the bowl off the spoon."

MRS. EYNSFORD-HILL—Dear me!

ELIZA—Now, what call would a woman with that strength in her have to die of influenza, and what become of her new straw hat that should have come to me? (*Sips tea.*) Somebody pinched it; and what I say is, them as pinched it, done her in.

LORD BOXINGTON—Done her in? Done her in, did you say?

HIGGINS—Oh, that's the new small talk. To do a person in means to kill them.

MRS. EYNSFORD-HILL (*horrified*)—You surely don't believe your aunt was killed?

ELIZA—Do I not! Them she lived with would have killed her for a hatpin, let alone a hat.

MRS. EYNSFORD-HILL—But it can't have been right for your father to pour spirits down her throat like that. It might have killed her.

ELIZA—Not her. Gin was mother's milk to her. . . .

Freddy is so convulsed that Eliza asks: "If I was doing it proper, what was you laughing at? Have I said anything I oughtn't?" Mrs. Higgins reassures her.

The top hats and finery now assemble. Freddy, to add to Eliza's pleasure, gives her his betting ticket on a horse named Dover. Except for singing its phlegmatic song, the Royal Enclosure crowd follows the race in snooty silence. The one exception is Eliza: crouched low, fist clenched, she roots home her horse. Her control vanishes; her "Come on, Dover!" gets louder and louder till, in a final burst, she yells: "Come on, Dover!!!! Move your bloomin' arse!!!!"

SCENE VIII

Ascot has left such a scar on Eliza that when a doting Freddy rings the bell at 27-A Wimpole Street, she refuses to see not only him, but anyone ever. Not at all unhappy, Freddy plans to "drink in the street where she lives" and camp there indefinitely. He sings "On the Street Where You Live" in hazy contentment.

SCENE IX

Six weeks have passed. In the study, on the night of the Embassy Ball, Pickering and Higgins, in white tie and tails, await Eliza. Pickering is nervous; Higgins refuses to show emotion. Pickering bets that "the damned gown doesn't fit. I warned you about those French designers. You should have gone to a good English store where you knew everybody was on our side."

The Paris designer, it turns out, was on the side of the angels: as Eliza descends the balcony stairs, the effect is breathtaking. Pickering exclaims at her beauty. Inspecting Eliza, her gown, her jewels, with obvious delight, Higgins concedes: "Not bad. Not bad at all." And Eliza leaves for the ball on his arm.

SCENE X

In the Promenade outside the Embassy ballroom, Pickering seeks out Mrs. Higgins to report on Eliza's success so far. She has captivated the wife of the Ambassador. Mrs. Higgins, who has grown very fond of the girl, reports back that everywhere people are wondering who Eliza can be. The two of them pray that Eliza can take the next hurdle as brilliantly.

On Higgins' entrance, a bearded Hungarian named Karpathy rushes up to him and, kissing him on both cheeks, cries: "Maestro! Maestro!" Purportedly a former pupil of Higgins', Karpathy is now aide to the Queen of Transylvania. He claims that he knows thirty-two languages and everybody in Europe, and can always spot an impostor. He is now ablaze with curiosity concerning the glorious, fascinating creature that Higgins has brought to the ball.

Eliza, sweeping down the staircase, causes a sensation. The Queen of Transylvania is enchanted. Higgins, his eye on Karpathy, slowly waltzes Eliza into—

SCENE XI

The ballroom.

As he and Eliza whirl about, Karpathy gradually closes in on them, until at the climax of the dance, he takes Eliza away from Higgins into his own arms. Higgins maintains perfect calm as—

THE CURTAIN FALLS.

ACT II

It is three o'clock in the morning; the three of them are home from the ball. Pickering piles admiring compliments on Higgins, who nonchalantly shrugs them off. Eliza, unnoticed and uncomplimented, tired and tragic, stands by.

Pickering tells the butler, the footman, the housemaids—anyone who will listen—about Higgins' fantastic triumph. He bursts into song: "You Did It!"

"... and when the Prince of Transylvania
Asked to meet her,
And gave his arm to lead her to the floor ... !
(*Addressing* HIGGINS.)
I said to him: You did it!
You did it! You did it!
They thought she was ecstatic,
And so damned aristocratic—"

Higgins says that if it hadn't been for Karpathy, he'd have died of boredom. "He was there, all right. And up to his old tricks ..." Finally, Higgins decided it was foolish not to let him have his chance with Eliza, and in rhythms of "You Did It" tells all about it:

"... oozing charm from ev'ry pore,
He oiled his way around the floor ...
Ev'ry trick that he could play,
He used to strip her mask away.
And when at last the dance was done
And with a voice too eager,
And a smile too broad,
He announced to the hostess
That she was a fraud!"

MRS. PEARCE—No!
HIGGINS—*Ja wohl!* (*Sings.*)

Her English is too good, he said,
That clearly indicates that she is foreign.
Whereas others are instructed in their native language,
English people aren'.
And although she may have studied with an expert
Di'lectician and grammarian,
I can tell that she was born Hungarian!

(*Spoken.*) Not only Hungarian—but—of royal blood! She is a princess!

The servants and Pickering smother Higgins with final praise before they go to bed. Still unnoticed, Eliza is left alone in the study.

Higgins, having forgotten his slippers, returns and asks for them. Eliza picks them up and hurls them straight at him. Startled, he asks if anything's wrong.

ELIZA—Nothing wrong—with you. I've won your bet for you, haven't I? That's enough for you. I don't matter, I suppose?

HIGGINS—You won my bet! *You!* Presumptuous insect. *I* won it! What did you throw those slippers at me for?

ELIZA—Because I wanted to smash your face. I'd like to kill you, you selfish brute. Why didn't you leave me where you picked me out of—in the gutter? You thank God it's all over, and that now you can throw me back again there, do you?

HIGGINS—So the creature is nervous, after all? (ELIZA *instinctively darts her nails at his face, but he clutches her hands.*) Ah! Claws in, you cat! How dare you show your temper to me? (*He throws her roughly on the sofa.*) Sit down and be quiet.

ELIZA—What's to become of me? What's to become of me?

HIGGINS (*rearranging his clothes*)—How the devil do I know what's to become of you? What does it matter what becomes of you?

ELIZA—You don't care. I know you don't care. You wouldn't care if I was dead. I'm nothing to you—not so much as them slippers.

HIGGINS—"Those" slippers.

ELIZA—Those slippers. I didn't think it made any difference now.

Higgins inquires whether anyone, himself included, has treated her badly. Eliza gives a slow "no." She wishes she were dead. Now that it's over, what is she fit for: "What have you left me fit for? Where am I to go? What am I to do? What's to become of me?" she wails.

Higgins suggests that his mother might find someone to marry her—some suitable chap or other. Eliza answers: "We were above that in Covent Garden." "What do you mean?" Higgins asks. "I sold flowers," Eliza replies, "I didn't sell myself. Now you've made a lady of me, I'm not fit to sell anything else."

Higgins suggests that Pickering, with all his money, might set her up in a flower shop. "Oh, come, you'll be all right," yawns Higgins, thinking only of getting some sleep.

Eliza detains him. Wishing to determine what belongs to her when she leaves, so she won't be accused of stealing, she rouses Higgins to surprising fury. Handing over her hired ball jewels, and tossing in a ring that he bought her at Brighton, Eliza brings Higgins to boil with righteous anger. Most of all, she makes him lose his temper. As, wrapped in his wounded dignity, he marches up the stairs, Eliza calls after him: "You'd better leave your own note for Mrs. Pearce about the coffee, for it won't be done by me!" "Damn Mrs. Pearce!" cries Higgins. "And damn the coffee! And damn you! And damn my own folly in having lavished my hard-earned knowledge and the treasure of my regard and intimacy on a heartless guttersnipe!" He marches up the last few steps, trips, and bangs into the recording machine. About to close his door, he hears the recording of "vowels" sound out. Higgins snaps it off angrily, and marches off.

Tears streaming down her face, Eliza, searching on the floor for the Brighton ring, sings: "Just You Wait."

Scene II

Immediately after, Eliza escapes from the house. Carrying a wicker suitcase, she bumps smack into Freddy, who very happily has been singing "On the Street Where You Live." She wants to know if he too thinks her a heartless guttersnipe. "Oh no, darling," says Freddy in horror. "How could you imagine such a thing? You know how I feel. I've written you two and three times a day telling you. Sheets and sheets. Eliza . . ." And in song as well as words, Freddy starts telling her all over again. Disgusted, Eliza takes the tune away from him. Shouting "Words! Words! Words! I'm so sick of words!" she sings: "Show Me."

"I get words
All day through;
First from him,
Now from you!
Is that all you blighters can do?

"Don't talk of stars,
Burning above

If you're in love,
Show me!

(*Stamps foot.*)

"Tell me no dreams
Filled with desire.
If you're on fire,
Show me!"

(*She pushes him.*)

Having demonstrated that she is in an imperative mood, she gives her concluding orders:

"Show me! Show me!
Don't wait until wrinkles and lines
Pop out all over my brow.
Show me now!"

And she crowns Freddy with her suitcase.

Scene III

In Covent Garden flower market, at five in the morning, some Cockneys sing a few bars from "Wouldn't It Be Loverly." Eliza, trying to find out where she belongs, walks unrecognized among them.

One Cockney offers: "Can I get you a taxi, Ma'am? A lady like you shouldn't be walkin' around London alone at this hour of the mornin'." "No . . . thank you," Eliza answers and sits down, deep in thought, on a bench next to a flower basket. A bunch of violets in her hand, she muses:

"Someone's head resting on my knee;
Warm and tender as he can be,
Who takes good care of me . . .
Oh, wouldn't it be loverly . . . ?
Loverly! Loverly!
Loverly! Loverly!"

This mood is shattered by a loud commotion from the neighboring pub, where a bartender bows and scrapes to a cutaway-attired Doolittle and his well-dressed friends. "Do come again," he says, "we value your patronage." Doolittle grandly dispenses largess: "Thank you, my good man. Here, take the missus a trip to Brighton."

Startled, Eliza calls to her father, who is decidedly displeased at the sight of her. In fact, he is sure that Higgins has sent her to spy on him. "He's ruined me, that's all," says Doolittle of Higgins. "Destroyed me happiness. Tied me and delivered me into the hands of middle-class morality. And don't you defend him. Was it him or was it not him that wrote to an old American blighter named Wallingford that was giving five millions to found moral reform societies, and told him the most original moralist in England was Mr. Alfred P. Doolittle, a common dustman?" It sounds to Eliza like one of Higgins' jokes. "You may call it a joke," answers Doolittle. "It put the lid on me, right enough! The bloke died and left me four thousand pounds a year in his bloomin' will." His friend Jamie interrupts this: "Come on, Alfie. In a couple of hours you have to be at the church."

ELIZA—Church?

DOOLITTLE—Yes, church. The deepest cut of all. Your stepmother wants to marry me. Now I'm respectable—she wants to be respectable.

ELIZA—If that's the way you feel, why don't you give the money back?

DOOLITTLE—That's the tragedy of it, Eliza. It's easy to say chuck it, but I haven't the nerve. We're all intimidated. Intimidated, Eliza—that's what we are. And that's what I am. Bought up. That's what your precious professor has brought me to.

ELIZA—Not my precious professor.

DOOLITTLE—Oh, sent you back, has he? First he shoves me in the midde class, then he chucks you out for me to support you. All part of his plan. But you double-cross him, Eliza. Don't you come home to me. Don't you take tuppence from me. You stand on your own two feet. You're a lady now and you can do it.

Freddy, the slave, now finds Eliza and inquires diffidently if she has finished. "Yes, Freddy," Eliza answers, "I'm finished here." And with a final backward glance, she goes away from Covent Garden.

Delighted to have disposed of her so easily, Doolittle turns his attention to corraling as many drinks and girls as possible before the church bell tolls for him. To the adoring Cockney crowd, Doolittle sings: "Get Me to the Church on Time."

"I'm getting married in the morning!
Ding dong! the bells are gonna chime!
Pull out the stopper,

Let's have a whopper—
But get me to the church on time!"

The obliging crowd pulls out the stopper and has a whopper, while the bartender pours Doolittle beer after beer. He is finally carried out over the heads of the crowd, bawling, "FOR GAWD'S SAKE, GET ME TO THE CHURCH ON TIME!!"

Scene IV

In the upstairs hall of his house, Higgins is making a loudly irate discovery that Eliza has bolted. He's ready to put the police on her trail for having so inconvenienced him. Overriding Mrs. Pearce's protests, Higgins shouts: "Why not? I want to find her The girl belongs to me! I paid five pounds for her!"

Pickering, getting Scotland Yard on the telephone, sums it all up: "Yes," he informs them, "this is her residence. . . . Between three and four this morning . . . No . . . No . . . No relation at all. Let's just say a good friend." He laughs good-humoredly. "Hmph?" he asks, as a troubled look comes over his face. "Now see here, my good man, I'm not at all pleased with the tenor of that question. What the girl does here is our affair. Your affair is to get her back so she can continue doing it . . ." Pickering hangs up abruptly.

"Pickering," says Higgins, half wrathfully, half querulously. "Why can't a woman be more like a man?" And sings "Hymn to Him."

HIGGINS—
Why can't a woman be more like a man?
Men are so honest, so thoroughly square;
Eternally noble, historically fair;
Who when you win will always give your back a pat.
Why can't a woman be like that?

Why does ev'ryone do what the others do?
Can't a woman learn to use her head?
Why do they do everything their mothers do?
Why don't they grow up like their father instead?
Why can't a woman take after a man?
Men are so pleasant, so easy to please;
Whenever you're with them, you're always at ease.
(*To* PICKERING.)
Would you be slighted if I didn't speak for hours?
PICKERING—Of course not.

HIGGINS—
Would you be livid if I had a drink or two?
PICKERING—Nonsense.
HIGGINS—
Would you be wounded if I never sent you flowers?
PICKERING—Never.
HIGGINS—
Why can't a woman be like you? . . .

Not only like him—but, Higgins concludes, "Why can't a woman be like us!!?" And more to the point, Higgins adds:

"Would I run off and never tell me where I'm going?
Why can't a woman be like me?"

SCENE V

Later that morning, Mrs. Higgins, in the garden of her house, comforts and listens to Eliza over some tea. "And you mean to say," she sympathizes, "that after you did this wonderful thing for them without making a single mistake, they just sat there and never said a word to you? Never petted you, or admired you, or told you how splendid you'd been?" "Not a word," says Eliza. "That's simply appalling," Mrs. Higgins remarks. "I should not have thrown the slippers at him . . . I should have thrown the fire irons."

As Higgins can be heard bellowing for his mother, Mrs. Higgins fortifies Eliza with a final compliment, and bids her stay put. "You!" shouts Higgins, on entering the garden.

ELIZA—How do you do, Professor Higgins? Are you quite well?

HIGGINS—Am I . . .

ELIZA—But of course you are. You are never ill. Would you care for some tea?

HIGGINS—Don't you dare try that game on me! I taught it to you! Get up and come home and don't be a fool! You've caused me enough trouble for one morning!

MRS. HIGGINS—Very nicely put, indeed, Henry. No woman could resist such an invitation.

HIGGINS—How did this baggage get here in the first place?

MRS. HIGGINS—Eliza came to see me, and I was delighted to have her. And if you don't promise to behave yourself, I shall have to ask you to leave.

HIGGINS—You mean I'm to put on my Sunday manners for this

thing I created out of the squashed cabbage leaves of Covent Garden?

MRS. HIGGINS—Yes, dear, that is precisely what I mean.

HIGGINS—I'll see her damned first! (*He crosses through the arches and paces back and forth behind the flower boxes.*)

MRS. HIGGINS—How did you ever learn manners with my son around?

ELIZA—It was very difficult. I should never have known how ladies and gentlemen behave if it hadn't been for Colonel Pickering. He always showed me that he felt and thought about me as if I were something better than a common flower girl. You see, Mrs. Higgins, apart from the things one can pick up, the difference between a lady and a flower girl is not how she behaves, but how she is treated. I shall always be a flower girl to Professor Higgins because he always treats me as a flower girl and always will. But I know that I shall always be a lady to Colonel Pickering because he always treats me as a lady, and always will.

Taking her leave of the couple, Mrs. Higgins advises her son to stick to two subjects: the weather and his health.

Once they are alone, Higgins asks Eliza whether, having had a "bit of her own back," she's had enough? And avoiding a proper invitation, Higgins grandly lays down terms for her return. She may expect no change in his nature, nor in his manners (which, he contends, are the same as Colonel Pickering's).

ELIZA—That's not true. He treats a flower girl as if she was a duchess.

HIGGINS—And I treat a duchess as if she was a flower girl.

The same to everybody, is his idea. . . . "The question," Higgins rules, "is not whether I treat you rudely, but whether you ever heard me treat anyone else better."

Eliza doesn't mind this, nor would she mind a black eye; what she does mind is being passed over. "But," she begins to realize, "I can get along without you. Don't think I can't!" With one of his sudden twists, Higgins tells Eliza that he will miss her. She asserts that she wouldn't marry him if he asked her. And with gathering courage, as Higgins corrects her English, Eliza exclaims: "I'll talk as I like! You're not my teacher now. That's not what I want and don't you think it. I've always had chaps enough wanting me that way. Freddy Hill writes to me twice and three times a day, sheets and sheets."

HIGGINS—Oh, in short, you want me to be as infatuated about you as he is: is that it?

ELIZA—No, I don't. That's not the sort of feeling I want from you. I want a little kindness. I know I'm a common, ignorant girl, and you a book-learned gentleman; but I'm not dirt under your feet. What I done—(*correcting herself*) What I did was not for the dresses and the taxis: I did it because we were pleasant together and I come—came to care for you; not to want you to make love to me, and not forgetting the difference between us, but more friendly-like.

HIGGINS—Yes, of course. That's just how I feel. And how Pickering feels. Eliza, you're a fool!

ELIZA—That's not a proper answer to give me.

HIGGINS—It's all you'll get until you stop being a plain idiot. If you're going to be a lady you'll have to stop feeling neglected if the men you know don't spend half their time sniveling over you and the other half giving you black eyes. You find me cold, unfeeling, selfish, don't you? Very well: be off with you to the sort of people you like. Marry some sentimental hog or other with lots of money, and a thick pair of lips to kiss you with and a thick pair of boots to kick you with. If you can't appreciate what you've got, you'd better get what you can appreciate.

Telling him not to be so sure he can trample her down, Eliza announces her intention of marrying and supporting Freddy. She will become a teacher; she will offer her services—and, indirectly, Higgins' teaching methods—to the Hungarian. Higgins is ready to strangle her. With magnificent defiance, Eliza counters: "Wring away! What do I care." She crows: "I knew you'd strike me one day. Aha, that's done for you, 'enry 'iggins, it 'as. Now I don't care that"—she snaps her fingers in his face—"for your bullying and your big talk." Her independence won, she sings "Without You," itemizing all the things that can get along nicely without Henry Higgins:

"Art and music will thrive without you
Somehow Keats will survive without you.
And there still will be rain
On that plain down in Spain,
Even that will remain
Without you.
I can do without you.

"You, dear friend, who talk so well,
You can go to—Hartford, Hereford and Hampshire!
(HIGGINS' *anger has changed to fascination as he watches her.*)
They can still rule the land without you.
Windsor Castle will stand without you.
And without much ado
We can all muddle through
Without you—"
("You brazen hussy!" HIGGINS *cries admiringly.*)
"Without your pulling it, the tide comes in,
Without your twirling it, the earth can spin.
Without your pushing them, the clouds roll by.
If they can do without you, ducky, so can I!"

Higgins finds her magnificent. Eliza merely says: "Goodbye, Professor Higgins. I shall not be seeing you again," and leaves.

Higgins bellows again for his mother: "She's gone." "Of course, my dear," says Mrs. Higgins, "what did you expect?" "What am I to do?" Higgins asks. "Do without," Mrs. Higgins answers.

SCENE VI

But coming home at dusk, Higgins' temper, as he approaches his door, explodes for a new reason: "Damn! Damn! Damn! Damn! I've grown accustomed to her face." He sings his reluctant love song: "Accustomed to Her Face," but in the middle reverts to his old ways—

"I'm a most forgiving man,
The sort who never could,
Ever would,
Take a position and staunchly never budge.
Just a most forgiving man.

"But I shall never take her back!
If she were crawling on her knees!
Let her promise to atone!
Let her shiver, let her moan!
I will slam the door and let the hell-cat freeze!"

As he turns the key in his lock, being "Accustomed to Her Face" sweeps over him once more.

SCENE VII

Entering his darkened, empty study, Higgins feels lonely and lost. He wanders miserably about the room. First he picks up the xylophone mallets, next he turns on the recording machine. He sits on a stool at his desk and listens to Eliza's record: "I want to be a lady in a flower shop instead of sellin' flowers at the corner of Tottenham Court Road. But they won't take me unless I talk more genteel. He said he could teach me. Well, here I am ready to pay—" Unseen by Higgins, Eliza enters and stands listening by the machine. Then she picks up the arm of the instrument, and her voice takes over from the record.

ELIZA—I washed my face and hands afore I come, I did. (HIGGINS *straightens up, face front, joy on his face. He would like to run to her, but he obviously doesn't know how. With contented comfort, he stretches back on the stool, leaning against the desk, and pulls his hat down over his eyes.*)

HIGGINS—Eliza? Where the devil are my slippers? (ELIZA *smiles. The music of "I Want to Dance All Night" reaches a crescendo . . . as the* CURTAIN FALLS.)

WAITING FOR GODOT *

A tragi-comedy in two acts

BY SAMUEL BECKETT

[SAMUEL BECKETT *was born in Dublin in 1906. He was a student at Dublin's Trinity College and for a while taught French in Dublin. He has lived mostly in Paris, where at one time he served as a kind of secretary to James Joyce, and now writes for the most part in French. He is the author of "L'Innommable" and a recent work, "Textes pour Rien." "Waiting for Godot" is his first play.*]

THE scene: A country road. A tree. Evening. Estragon, sitting on a low mound, is trying to take off his boot. He pulls at it with both hands, panting. He gives up, exhausted, rests, tries again. As before.

Enter Vladimir.

ESTRAGON (*giving up again*)—Nothing to be done.

VLADIMIR (*advancing with short, stiff strides, legs wide apart*)—I'm beginning to come round to that opinion. All my life I've tried to put it from me, saying, Vladimir, be reasonable, you haven't tried everything. And I resumed the struggle. . . . So there you are again.

ESTRAGON—Am I?

VLADIMIR—I'm glad to see you back. I thought you were gone forever.

ESTRAGON—Me too.

VLADIMIR—Together again at last! We'll have to celebrate this. But how? . . . Get up till I embrace you.

ESTRAGON (*irritably*)—Not now, not now.

VLADIMIR (*hurt, coldly*)—May one inquire where His Highness spent the night?

ESTRAGON—In a ditch.

VLADIMIR (*admiringly*)—A ditch! Where?

ESTRAGON—Over there.

VLADIMIR—And they didn't beat you?

ESTRAGON—Beat me? Certainly they beat me.

VLADIMIR—The same lot as usual?

ESTRAGON—The same? I don't know.

VLADIMIR—When I think of it . . . all these years . . . but for me . . . where would you be . . . (*Decisively.*) You'd be nothing more than a little heap of bones at the present minute, no doubt about it.

ESTRAGON—And what of it?

VLADIMIR (*gloomily*)—It's too much for one man. (*Pauses cheerfully.*) On the other hand, what's the good of losing heart now, that's what I say. We should have thought of it a million years ago, in the nineties.

ESTRAGON—Ah, stop blathering and help me off with this bloody thing.

VLADIMIR—Hand in hand from the top of the Eiffel Tower, among the first. We were respectable in those days. Now it's too late. They wouldn't even let us up. (ESTRAGON *tears at his boot.*) What are you doing?

While Estragon continues his struggle with his boot, Vladimir riles him by asking if it hurts. Howls of anger at this lack of sympathy are met by equal anger on Vladimir's part that his own suffering is never taken into account. "It hurts?" Estragon returns. "Hurts!" cries Vladimir, "He wants to know if it hurts!" With a gesture, Estragon advises: "You might button it all the same." "True," agrees Vladimir, buttoning his fly, "never neglect the little things of life."

While Estragon tugs at his boot, Vladimir, musing on the condition of his pubis, takes off his hat and contemplates its inhabitants. He pokes about in the hat, shakes the hat, returns it to his head, as Estragon, with a supreme effort, extricates his foot from the boot. Vladimir comes to the conclusion nothing is to be done. Estragon echoes: "Nothing."

The hat comes off again as Vladimir resumes his search of its interior. He is deep in thought; Estragon pulls at his bare toes. "One of the thieves was saved," says Vladimir, "it's a reasonable percentage, Gogo."

ESTRAGON—What?

VLADIMIR—Suppose we repented.

ESTRAGON—Repented what?

VLADIMIR—Oh . . . (*He reflects.*) We wouldn't have to go into details.

ESTRAGON—Our being born. (VLADIMIR *breaks into a hearty laugh which he immediately stifles, his hand pressed to his pubis, his face contorted.*)

VLADIMIR—One daren't even laugh any more.

ESTRAGON—Dreadful privation.

VLADIMIR—Merely smile. (*He smiles suddenly from ear to ear, keeps smiling, ceases as suddenly.*) It's not the same thing. Nothing to be done. (*Pause.*) Gogo.

ESTRAGON (*irritably*)—What is it?

VLADIMIR—Did you ever read the Bible?

ESTRAGON—The Bible. . . . I must have taken a look at it.

VLADIMIR—Do you remember the Gospels?

ESTRAGON—I remember the maps of the Holy Land. Colored they were. Very pretty. The Dead Sea was pale blue. The very look of it made me thirsty. That's where we'll go, I used to say, that's where we'll go for our honeymoon. We'll swim. We'll be happy.

VLADIMIR—You should have been a poet.

ESTRAGON—I was. (*Gestures towards his rags.*) Isn't that obvious?

Vladimir puzzles over the two thieves who were crucified at the same time as the Saviour; the one supposed saved and the other damned. Estragon can work up little interest: "Saved from what?" he asks. The answer of "Hell" has Estragon wanting to go. He doesn't budge.

Vladimir theorizes over the Evangelists' versions of the saved thief, but interrupts himself to ask: "Come on, Didi, return the ball, can't you, once in a way?" With exaggerated enthusiasm, Estragon returns it: "I find this really most extraordinarily interesting."

Picking up the thread, Vladimir says: "Of the other three, two don't mention any thieves at all and the third says that both of them abused him." "Who?" asks Estragon. "What?" says Vladimir. "What's all this about?" answers Estragon, "abused who?"

VLADIMIR—The Saviour.

ESTRAGON—Why?

VLADIMIR—Because he wouldn't save them.

ESTRAGON—From hell?

VLADIMIR—Imbecile! From death.

ESTRAGON—I thought you said hell.

VLADIMIR—From death, from death.

ESTRAGON—Well, what of it?

VLADIMIR—Then the two of them must have been damned.

ESTRAGON—And why not?

VLADIMIR—But one of the four says that one of the two was saved.

ESTRAGON—Well? They don't agree and that's all there is to it.

VLADIMIR—But all four were there. And only one speaks of a thief being saved. Why believe him rather than the others?

ESTRAGON—Who believes him?

VLADIMIR—Everybody. It's the only version they know.

ESTRAGON—People are bloody ignorant apes.

Having terminated that, Estragon rises painfully and, limping, goes off to peer first in one direction and then in the other. Vladimir picks up one of the offending boots, peers into it, and drops it hastily. "Pah," spits Vladimir, as Estragon, surveying the mound, says, "Charming spot," turns and advances toward the audience. "Inspiring prospects," he adds. "Let's go."

They don't. Vladimir says that they are waiting for Godot. "Ah!" despairs Estragon; then after a moment asks Vladimir if he is sure it's here they are to wait. "He said by the tree," Vladimir reminds him. "Do you see any others?" The tree that they proceed to scrutinize is leafless, barren, and unidentifiable. It could even be a shrub or a bush; and, Godot hadn't said for sure that he'd come.

ESTRAGON—And if he doesn't come?

VLADIMIR—We'll come back tomorrow.

ESTRAGON—And then the day after tomorrow.

VLADIMIR—Possibly.

ESTRAGON—And so on.

VLADIMIR—The point is . . .

ESTRAGON—Until he comes.

VLADIMIR—You're merciless.

ESTRAGON—We came here yesterday.

VLADIMIR—Ah, no, there you're mistaken.

ESTRAGON—What did we do yesterday?

VLADIMIR—What did we do yesterday?

ESTRAGON—Yes.

VLADIMIR—Why . . . (*Angrily.*) Nothing is certain when you're about . . .

Although Estragon thinks he recognizes the place, he won't go on record about it. He gets Vladimir terribly confused as to whether this is the evening they were supposed to wait, whether this is the right day at all. "If he came yesterday and we weren't here," says Estragon, "you may be sure he won't come again today." And having sown considerable doubt in Vladimir's mind, he no longer wants to talk about it, and drops off to sleep. Vladimir paces agitatedly until he can stand it no longer and abruptly wakes Estragon up. Having waked with a start Estragon would like, at least, to tell Vladimir his nightmare. But Vladimir, who just couldn't stand being lonely, refuses to hear about Estragon's dream. Whereupon Estragon wonders coldly if it wouldn't be better for the two of them to part.

Vladimir—You wouldn't go far.

Estragon—That would be too bad, really too bad. (*Pause.*) Wouldn't it, Didi, be really too bad? (*Pause.*) When you think of the beauty of the way. (*Pause.*) And the goodness of the wayfarers. (*Pause. Wheedling.*) Wouldn't it, Didi?

Vladimir—Calm yourself.

Estragon (*voluptuously*)—Calm . . . calm . . . The English say cawm. (*Pause.*) You know the story of the Englishman in the brothel?

Deliberately Estragon so overexcites Vladimir that he is forced to rush off to relieve himself. Estragon, like a spectator at the prizefights, cheers him on.

On his return, after some huffy stubbornness, the two make up. Then, thinking of what to do next, they consider hanging themselves from the tree. When Vladimir says, contemplatively: "Hmmm. It'd give us an erection!" he enlists Estragon's excited co-operation. "With all that follows," elaborates Vladimir, "where it falls, mandrakes grow. That's why they shriek when you pull them up . . ." They proceed to discuss ways and means of hanging, but in the end Estragon is in agreement with Vladimir: "Don't let's do anything. It's safer." Besides, Vladimir would like to know what Godot has to offer . . . "Then we'll take it or leave it," he concludes.

What they had asked of Godot isn't too clear for them either; it might have been a kind of prayer, a supplication. But where they come in is more definite: ". . . On our hands and knees," says Vladimir. "As bad as that?" asks Estragon. "Your Worship wishes to assert his prerogatives?" replies Vladimir. Estragon keeps asking:

"We've lost our rights?" Vladimir's distinct answer is: "We got rid of them."

Estragon, feeling hungry, asks for a carrot. Vladimir rummages among the turnips and junk in his many pockets, and at length graciously uncovers a carrot. Estragon eats it with elaborate appreciation. The pretense is futile, however. Both conclude, "There's nothing to be done." There is a sudden terrible cry and they stand together waiting and cringing.

A creature of sorts called Lucky, a rope around his neck, arrives. Overburdened with a heavy bag, a folding stool, a picnic basket, and a greatcoat, Lucky reaches and passes the mound, before Pozzo, at the other end of the rope, appears. Whip in hand, Pozzo jerks hard on the rope: "Back!" he shouts. Lucky, now unseen, can be heard to fall with a terrific clatter.

At first Vladimir and Estragon mistake Pozzo for Godot. Having introduced himself, Pozzo wants to know who this Godot is. Vladimir and Estragon are hard put to it to explain that, though it's Godot they're waiting for, they wouldn't know him if they saw him.

Fascinated, they watch Pozzo bark orders at Lucky, all the while jerking the rope for emphasis. Lucky responds like a tired old trained dog. When Pozzo, whip in hand, has Lucky where he wants him, he decides to tarry. "Yes, gentlemen, I cannot go for long without the society of my likes (*He puts on his glasses and looks at his two likes.*) even when the likeness is an imperfect one." He shouts for his stool. Lucky, divesting himself of all he is burdened with, brings Pozzo the stool. He then retreats and reloads. "Closer!" booms Pozzo. Lucky repeats the performance. Pozzo, having found it acceptable, now orders the basket. Lucky brings it.

Pozzo settles down with a bottle of wine and a chicken which he proceeds to wolf, tossing the bones away after sucking them dry. With increasing boldness, Vladimir and Estragon edge close to Lucky, on a tour of inspection, until Pozzo orders them to leave Lucky in peace. Pozzo himself then begins, whip in hand, to order Lucky unpeacefully around.

Estragon, who has had his eye on the discarded chicken bones, plucks up enough courage to ask Pozzo if he'll be needing them. Vladimir is scandalized, but Pozzo says: "He does well to ask. Do I need the bones?" (*He turns them over with his whip.*) "No, personally I do not need them any more. But," he adds, halting Estragon, "in theory the bones go to the carrier. He is therefore the one to ask."

Addressed over and over, by Estragon, as "Mister," Lucky lifts his head and looks long at his interlocutor. Pozzo yells: "Pig," and

Lucky once more bows his head, but makes no move for the bones. Estragon grabs them. Pozzo remarks: "I don't like it. I've never known him to refuse a bone before— Nice business it'd be if he fell sick on me!"

Vladimir suddenly explodes: "It's a scandal!" "Are you alluding to anything in particular?" Pozzo asks. "To treat a man . . . like that," answers Vladimir. "I think that . . . no . . . a human being . . . no . . .it's a scandal!" Not to be outdone, Estragon says, between gnaws: "A disgrace!" Vladimir is in a rage to leave. Pozzo, promising them that they'll never regret it, urges him to remain. Estragon, scenting charity, says: "We're in no hurry." Pozzo stops Vladimir with: ". . . What happens in that case to your appointment with this . . . Godet . . . Godot . . . Godin . . . anyhow you see who I mean, who has your future in his hands . . . (*Pause.*) . . . at least your immediate future?"

Estragon wants to know why Lucky doesn't put down his bags. There is no answer for a long time, so he, too, decides to go. Finally, after considerable windup and spraying his throat with a vaporizer, Pozzo declares that Lucky never puts down his burden (a) so as to impress Pozzo; (b) so as to mollify Pozzo; (c) so as to coax Pozzo into keeping him. Says Pozzo: "In reality he carries like a pig. It's not his job." "You want to get rid of him?" Vladimir ventures. "He imagines," says Pozzo, "when I see him indefatigable I'll regret my decision. Such is his miserable scheme. As though I were short of slaves! . . ." Pozzo wants to get rid of him, all right; plans to sell him—mercifully—at the fair, rather than cruelly kick him out on his arse. "The truth is," says Pozzo, "you can't drive such creatures away. The best thing would be to kill them." Lucky weeps. Pozzo hands sympathetic Estragon a handkerchief to wipe Lucky's eyes. Lucky thanks Estragon by kicking him in the shins. Estragon staggers about, howling with pain, sure that he'll never walk again. Vladimir offers tenderly to carry him, if necessary.

POZZO—He's stopped crying. (*To* ESTRAGON.) You have replaced him, as it were. (*Lyrically.*) The tears of the world are a constant quantity. For each one who begins to weep somewhere else another stops. The same is true of the laugh. (*He laughs.*) Let us not then speak ill of our generation, it is not any unhappier than it's predecessors. (*Pause.*) Let us not speak well of it either. (*Pause.*) Let us not speak of it at all. (*Pause. Judiciously.*) It is true the population has increased.

VLADIMIR—Try and walk. (ESTRAGON *takes a few limping steps, stops before* LUCKY *and spits on him, then goes and sits down on the mound.*)

POZZO—Guess who taught me all these beautiful things. (*Pause. Pointing to* LUCKY.) My Lucky!

VLADIMIR (*looking at the sky*)—Will night never come?

POZZO—But for him all my thoughts, all my feelings, would have been of common things. (*Pause.*) Professional worries! Beauty, grace, truth of the first water, I knew they were all beyond me. So I took a knook.

VLADIMIR (*startled*)—A knook?

POZZO—That was nearly sixty years ago . . . (*He consults his watch.*) . . . yes, nearly sixty. (*Drawing himself up proudly.*) You wouldn't think it to look at me, would you? Compared to him I look a young man, no? (*Pause.*) Hat! (LUCKY *puts down the basket and takes off his hat. His long white hair falls about his face. He puts his hat under his arm and picks up the basket.*) Now look. (POZZO *takes off his hat. He is completely bald. He puts on his hat again.*) Did you see?

Vladimir, full of quick pity for Lucky's present misery, abuses Pozzo. Estragon joins in: "Swine!" But Pozzo, almost in tears over his own terrible plight at Lucky's hands—Lucky has been driving him mad—wins back Vladimir and Estragon's mercurial pity. Making a lightning switch, an outraged Vladimir cries: "How dare you! It's abominable! Such a good master! Crucify him like that! After so many years! Really!"

The idea crosses Estragon's mind that Pozzo might like a substitute for Lucky, but he does nothing about it. Pozzo, denying all he had said about being made to suffer, settles down to look for his pipe. With that Vladimir says quickly: "Charming evening we're having."

ESTRAGON—Unforgettable.
VLADIMIR—And it's not over.
ESTRAGON—Apparently not.
VLADIMIR—It's only beginning.
ESTRAGON—It's awful.
VLADIMIR—Worse than the pantomime.
ESTRAGON—The circus.
VLADIMIR—The music-hall.
ESTRAGON—The circus.
POZZO—What can I have done with that briar?

ESTRAGON—He's a scream. He's lost his dudeen. (*Laughs noisily.*)

VLADIMIR—I'll be back. (*He hastens away.*)

ESTRAGON—End of the corridor, on the left.

VLADIMIR—Keep my seat. (*Exit* VLADIMIR.)

POZZO (*on the point of tears*)—I've lost my Kapp and Peterson!

ESTRAGON (*convulsed with merriment*)—He'll be the death of me!

Pozzo, concerned that Vladimir has gone away without saying goodbye, is shown the reason: "Look!" says Estragon. Pozzo, having put on his glasses, looks: "Oh, I say!" he says. On Vladimir's agitated return, Estragon says: "You missed a treat. Pity."

They wait for the night to fall. Pozzo, demanding their full attention, holds forth on the sky, on the weather, on the night to come, ending with: "That's how it is on this bitch of an earth." After a silence Estragon remarks: "So long as one knows." Vladimir adds: "One can bide one's time." They are used to waiting.

Pozzo coyly asks for praise; they, as coyly, give it. Deciding that, since Estragon and Vladimir have been civil to him, they deserve a reward, Pozzo announces that Lucky will perform as a treat. They can take their pick: Lucky can either dance, sing, recite, or *think*. Estragon favors the dancing; Vladimir, the *thinking*. In a frenzy of generosity, Pozzo orders Lucky to dance first, and *think* later. "Dance, misery!" he shouts.

Lucky dances. Lucky stops. Estragon is disgusted: "Pooh! I'd do as well myself (*He imitates* LUCKY, *and almost falls down.*) with a little practice." In former days, says Pozzo, Lucky's dance was a joy to see. "Now that's the best he can do. Do you know what he calls it?" Estragon guesses: "The Scapegoat's Agony." Vladimir suggests: "The Hard Stool." "The Net," answers Pozzo, "he thinks he's entangled in a net."

Since Lucky can't *think* without his hat, Vladimir, with more courage and cunning than Estragon, manages to get the hat on Lucky's head. But Lucky does not move. Pozzo jerks the rope, shouts: "Think, pig!" Instead, Lucky begins to dance. "Stop!" roars Pozzo. "Forward!" roars Pozzo. After a second "Stop!" Lucky stops, and when Pozzo bellows "Think!" Lucky begins a monologue.

LUCKY—Given the existence as uttered forth in the public
works of Puncher and Wattmann of a personal
God quaquaquaqua with white beard

quaquaquaqua outside time without extension
who from the heights of divine apathia divine
athambia divine aphasia loves us dearly with
some exceptions for reasons unknown but time
will tell and suffers like the divine Miranda with
those who for reasons unknown but time will tell
are plunged in torment plunged in fire whose fire
flames if that continues and who can doubt it will
fire the firmament that is to say blast hell to
heaven so blue still and calm so calm with a calm
which even though intermittent is better than
nothing but not so fast and considering what is
more that as a result of the labors left unfinished
crowned by the Acacacacademy of
Anthropopopometry of Essy-in-Possy of Testew
and Cunard it is established beyond all doubt all
other doubt than that which clings to the labors
of men that as a result of the labors unfinished of
Testew and Cunard it is established as hereinafter
but not so fast for reasons unknown that as a
result of the public works of Puncher and
Wattmann it is established beyond all doubt that
in view of the labors of Fartov and Belcher left
unfinished for reasons unknown of Testew and
Cunard left unfinished it is established what many
deny that man in Possy of Testew and Cunard
that man in Essy that man in short that man in
brief in spite of the strides of alimentation and
defecation wastes and pines wastes and pines and
concurrently simultaneously what is more for
reasons unknown. . . ."

On and on and on goes the recitation until the protesting, agitated listeners, having thrown themselves on Lucky, manage to snatch his hat from his head. Lucky is silenced. Lucky falls down.

ESTRAGON—Avenged! (VLADIMIR *examines the hat, peers inside it.*)

POZZO—Give me that! (*He snatches the hat from* VLADIMIR, *throws it on the ground, tramples on it.*) There's an end to his thinking!

VLADIMIR—But will he be able to walk?

POZZO—Walk or crawl! (*He kicks* LUCKY.) Up pig!

ESTRAGON—Perhaps he's dead.
VLADIMIR—You'll kill him.
POZZO—Up scum! (*He jerks the rope.*) Help me!
VLADIMIR—How?
POZZO—Raise him up!

Under Pozzo's shouted orders, Vladimir and Estragon struggle to get Lucky to stay on his feet, to hold on to his bags. Aided by cracks of the whip, Lucky once more gets the feel of the baggage handles. Though he teeters and reels, he holds on; a moment later he totters forward.

After a bit of delay because of a lost timepiece, Pozzo gets up steam, and says his adieus on the run. There is a long silence.

VLADIMIR—That passed the time.
ESTRAGON—It would have passed in any case.
VLADIMIR—Yes, but not so rapidly. (*Pause.*)
ESTRAGON—What do we do now?
VLADIMIR—I don't know.
ESTRAGON—Let's go.
VLADIMIR—We can't.
ESTRAGON—Why not?
VLADIMIR—We're waiting for Godot.
ESTRAGON—Ah!

Estragon's other foot starts killing him, just as the Boy, from a distance, calls out: "Mister!" "Off we go again," announces Estragon.

The timid Boy approaches with a message from Mr. Godot, but has some difficulty delivering it because of Estragon's bullying and Vladimir's reasonableness.

BOY—Mr. Godot . . .
VLADIMIR—I've seen you before, haven't I?
BOY—I don't know, Sir.
VLADIMIR—You don't know me?
BOY—No Sir.
VLADIMIR—It wasn't you came yesterday?
BOY—No Sir.
VLADIMIR—This is your first time?
BOY—Yes Sir. (*Silence.*)
VLADIMIR—Words words. (*Pause.*) Speak.

Bert Lahr, E. G. Marshall, Kurt Kasznar and Alvin Epstein

Waiting for Godot"

BOY (*in a rush*)—Mr. Godot told me to tell you he won't come this evening but surely tomorrow.

VLADIMIR—Is that all?

BOY—Yes Sir.

Vladimir inquires about the boy's life with his master Godot. It is not an unhappy life. The Boy, being told he can go home, inquires: "What am I to tell Mr. Godot, Sir?" "Tell him . . ." Vladimir hesitates, ". . . tell him you saw us." He pauses. "You did see us, didn't you?" "Yes, Sir," the Boy answers, starting to run away as fast as he can.

In a moment night has fallen. The pale moon rises, shedding its pale rays. Estragon places both his boots at the edge of the stage, intending to leave them there. Vladimir protests that he can't go barefoot.

ESTRAGON—Christ did.

VLADIMIR—Christ! What has Christ got to do with it? You're not going to compare yourself to Christ!

ESTRAGON—All my life I've compared myself to him.

VLADIMIR—But where he lived it was warm, it was dry!

ESTRAGON—Yes. And they crucified quick.

Since Godot has said that he will come tomorrow, all they need do is wait on. But Vladimir insists they must take cover.

ESTRAGON (*looking at the tree*)—Pity we haven't got a bit of rope.

VLADIMIR—Come on. It's cold. (*He draws* ESTRAGON *after him . . .*)

ESTRAGON—Remind me to bring a bit of rope tomorrow.

VLADIMIR—Yes. Come on. (*He draws him after him . . .*)

ESTRAGON—How long have we been together all the time now?

VLADIMIR—I don't know. Fifty years maybe.

ESTRAGON—Do you remember the day I threw myself into the Rhone?

VLADIMIR—We were grape harvesting.

ESTRAGON—You fished me out.

VLADIMIR—That's all dead and buried.

ESTRAGON—My clothes dried in the sun.

VLADIMIR—There's no good harking back on that. Come on. (*He draws him after . . .*)

ESTRAGON—Wait!

VLADIMIR—I'm cold!

ESTRAGON—Wait! (*He moves away from* VLADIMIR.) I sometimes wonder if we wouldn't have been better off alone, each one for himself. . . . (*He sits on the mound.*) We weren't made for the same road.

VLADIMIR (*without anger*)—It's not certain.

ESTRAGON—No, nothing is certain . . . (VLADIMIR *sits beside* ESTRAGON.)

VLADIMIR—We can still part, if you think it would be better.

ESTRAGON—It's not worth while now. (*Silence.*)

VLADIMIR—No, it's not worth while now. (*Silence.*)

ESTRAGON—Well, shall we go?

VLADIMIR—Yes, let's go. (*They do not move.*)

ACT II

Next day. Same time. Same place. Vladimir enters, as agitated as ever, but halts before the tree, which has sprouted four or five new leaves. He surveys Estragon's boots, sniffs them, replaces them where they were left the previous night, and starts singing doggerel. It is this singing that most irritates a depressed Estragon when he enters.

VLADIMIR—One is not master of one's moods. All day I've felt in great form. (*Pause.*) I didn't get up in the night, not once!

ESTRAGON (*sadly*)—You see, you piss better when I'm not there.

VLADIMIR—I missed you . . . and at the same time I was happy. Isn't that a queer thing?

ESTRAGON (*Shocked*)—Happy?

VLADIMIR—Perhaps it's not quite the right word.

ESTRAGON—And now?

VLADIMIR—Now? . . . (*Joyous*) There you are again. . . . (*Indifferent*) There we are again. . . . (*Gloomy*) There I am again. . . .

Estragon doesn't know why he keeps crawling back to Vladimir. Vladimir thinks it's because he could have stopped Estragon from doing whatever it was that caused him to be beaten. "I tell you I wasn't doing anything," protests Estragon. "Perhaps you weren't," answers Vladimir, "but it's the way of doing it that counts, the way of doing it, if you want to go on living." Deep down, too, Vladimir is sure that Estragon is happy to be back with him.

ESTRAGON—Happy about what?

VLADIMIR—To be back with me again.

ESTRAGON—Would you say so?
VLADIMIR—Say you are, even if it's not true.
ESTRAGON—What am I to say?
VLADIMIR—Say, I am happy.
ESTRAGON—I am happy.
VLADIMIR—So am I.
ESTRAGON—So am I.
VLADIMIR—We are happy.
ESTRAGON—We are happy. (*Silence.*) What do we do now, now that we are happy? (ESTRAGON *groans.*)
VLADIMIR—Wait for Godot. (*Silence.*)

Vladimir indicates to Estragon that something has changed since yesterday, and has him look at the tree. Estragon asks if it is new: he doesn't recall it. "That's the way I am," says Estragon, "either I forget immediately or I never forget."

Estragon is very hazy about yesterday; except for being kicked by a fool, and sucking a chicken bone that tasted more like a fish bone, he remembers nothing. He doesn't recognize the place at all, and goes into a fury when Vladimir questions him: "Recognize!" cries Estragon, "what is there to recognize? All my lousy life I've crawled about in the mud! And you talk to me about scenery!" Looking wildly about him, he yells, "Look at this muckheap! I've never stirred from it!" Vladimir calms him. "You and your landscapes!" cries Estragon. "Tell me about the worms!"

When he's quieter, Estragon suggests that the best thing would be to kill him like the other.

VLADIMIR—What other? (*Pause.*) What other?
ESTRAGON—Like billions of others.
VLADIMIR (*sententiously*)—To every man his little cross. Till he dies. And is forgotten.
ESTRAGON—In the meantime let us try and converse calmly, since we are incapable of keeping silent.
VLADIMIR—You're right, we're inexhaustible.
ESTRAGON—It's so we won't think. . . .

Silence after silence is interrupted by their discussions of anything at all, until they revert once more to waiting for Godot. "Ah!" murmurs Estragon, despairingly.

They start all over again; occasionally, they repeat themselves—as on the subject of *nature*. "We've tried that," says Vladimir.

ESTRAGON—True.
VLADIMIR—Oh, it's not the worst, I know.
ESTRAGON—What?
VLADIMIR—To have thought.
ESTRAGON—Obviously.
VLADIMIR—But we could have done without it.
ESTRAGON—Que voulez-vous?
VLADIMIR—I beg your pardon.
ESTRAGON—Que voulez-vous.
VLADIMIR—Ah! Que voulez-vous. Exactly. (*Silence.*)

Vladimir makes another start. He refers to the tree whose leaves weren't there yesterday. Estragon states that *they* weren't here yesterday, they were somewhere else; so how could Vladimir say the leaves sprouted in a single night? And as to what they were doing yesterday, Estragon assumes they were blathering. "Oh . . . this and that I suppose, nothing in particular. (*With assurance.*) Yes, now I remember, yesterday evening we spent blathering about nothing in particular. That's been going on now for half a century." But Estragon remembers nothing . . . nothing in particular. Vladimir tries to jog his memory by speaking of Pozzo, Lucky, the bones, the kick.

A faint glimmer occurs. Vladimir has Estragon pull up his trouser legs—he doesn't even remember on which leg the kick landed and left its mark.

Estragon cannot even remember what he did with his boots. When shown the pair at the stage's edge, he insists, after carefully inspecting them, that they aren't his. He seems so certain that Vladimir now decides the boots on the stage were left by a stranger who took Estragon's.

ESTRAGON—Why?
VLADIMIR—His were too tight for him, so he took yours.
ESTRAGON—But mine were too tight.
VLADIMIR—For you, not for him.

They're back to waiting for Godot. "Ah!" says Estragon in despair. Next they mention food. There are no carrots left; Vladimir, in the depths of one of his pockets, finds a black radish. Estragon is choosy. "I only like pink ones, you know that!" he cries. "Then give it back to me," answers Vladimir. Estragon announces that he's off for a carrot, but he doesn't move.

Vladimir thinks of trying on the boots.

ESTRAGON—I've tried everything.

VLADIMIR—No, I mean the boots.

ESTRAGON—Would that be a good thing?

VLADIMIR—It'd pass the time. . . . I assure you, it'd be an occupation.

ESTRAGON—A relaxation.

VLADIMIR—A recreation.

ESTRAGON—A relaxation.

VLADIMIR—Try.

ESTRAGON—You'll help me?

VLADIMIR—I will of course.

ESTRAGON—We don't manage too badly, eh Didi, between the two of us?

VLADIMIR—Yes, yes. Come on, we'll try the left first.

ESTRAGON—We always find something, eh Didi, to give us the impression we exist. . . .

Sure enough, the boots manage to go on. Today they're too big. "Perhaps you'll have some socks some day," says Vladimir. "True," says Estragon, settling himself on the mound to sleep, as before.

This time Vladimir sings him a lullaby, and covers him with his jacket. Vladimir, jacketless in the cold, swings his arms for warmth, then rushes to comfort Estragon when he wakes up with a start. He refuses, however, to listen to his dream.

Discovering Lucky's hat on the ground, they pass it back and forth between them, they alternate wearing it with wearing their own, they try wearing all three. Vladimir finally keeps Lucky's. "Mine," he says, "irked me. How shall I say—it itched me."

Vladimir's idea of imitating Pozzo and Lucky fizzles out. It's too one sided: Vladimir has to provide all the dialogue and action. Suddenly, Estragon wanders off.

A moment later he dashes back, collapsing in Vladimir's arms. He is being pursued. There is no place to hide. Estragon tries the tree, but gives up in disgust. Estragon stations Vladimir at one side of the stage, himself at the other.

VLADIMIR
ESTRAGON } (*Simultaneously*)—Do you . . .

VLADIMIR—Oh pardon!

ESTRAGON—Carry on.

VLADIMIR—No no, after you.

ESTRAGON—No no, you first.

VLADIMIR—I interrupted you.

ESTRAGON—On the contrary. (*They glare at each other angrily.*)
VLADIMIR—Ceremonious ape!
ESTRAGON—Punctilious pig!
VLADIMIR—Finish your phrase, I tell you!
ESTRAGON—Finish your own. (*Silence: they draw closer, and halt.*)
VLADIMIR—Moron!
ESTRAGON—That's the idea, let's abuse each other. (*They turn, move apart, turn again and face each other.*)
VLADIMIR—Moron!
ESTRAGON—Vermin!
VLADIMIR—Abortion!
ESTRAGON—Scorpion.
VLADIMIR—Sewer-rat!
ESTRAGON—Curate!
VLADIMIR—Cretin!
ESTRAGON (*with finality*)—Critic!
VLADIMIR—Oh! (*He wilts, vanquished, and turns away.*)

They then decide to make up, and fall into one another's arms. "How time flies when one has fun!" cries Vladimir.

"What do we do now?" Estragon asks. Vladimir suggests doing their exercises. Estragon tires almost before starting. Vladimir suggests a bit of deep breathing, but Estragon is tired of breathing. Vladimir suggests doing "the tree" for balance. Estragon—as a staggering tree—wonders if God sees him. He would like not only God's pity but His full attention.

Pozzo now arrives. He is totally blind and is led in by Lucky on a much shorter rope. Lucky has a new hat but the same load, and when he stops short, Pozzo crashes blindly into him and they both fall down and lie helpless among the scattered baggage. Vladimir cries: "Reinforcements at last!" "Help!" answers Pozzo. "Is it Godot?" asks Estragon. "We were beginning to weaken," says Vladimir, "now we're sure to see the evening out."

The question of whether they should go to Pozzo's aid, gives Vladimir and Estragon something to discuss at length.

VLADIMIR—Let us not waste our time in idle discourse! (*Pause. Vehemently.*) Let us do something, while we have the chance! It is not every day that we are needed. Not indeed that we personally are needed. Others would meet the case equally well, if not better. To all mankind they were addressed, those cries for help still ringing in our ears! But at this place, at this moment of time, all mankind is us, whether we like it or not. Let us make the most of it, before it is too late! Let us represent worthily for once the foul brood to which a cruel fate consigned us! What do you say? (ESTRAGON *says nothing.*) It is true that when with folded arms we weigh the pros and cons we are no less a credit to our species. The tiger bounds to the help of his congeners without the least reflexion, or else he slinks away into the depths of the thickets. But that is not the question. What are we doing here, *that* is the question. And we are blessed in this, that we happen to know the answer. Yes, in this immense confusion one thing alone is clear. We are waiting for Godot to come . . .

ESTRAGON—Ah!

POZZO—Help!

VLADIMIR—Or for night to fall. (*Pause.*) We have kept our appointment and that's an end to that. We are not saints, but we have kept our appointment. How many people can boast as much?

ESTRAGON—Billions.

As an escape from boredom, Vladimir goes to Pozzo's assistance and is promptly pulled down into the helpless heap. Estragon thinks of going off and leaving the lot of them, but reconsiders and offers Vladimir a helping hand. "Pull!" says Vladimir. Instead, Estragon topples down. There is a long silence.

They now have need to get along with each other, since they can't get along away from each other. They must pass the time in a heap. For his constant cry for help, Pozzo gets kicked in the groin. Still he can crawl to another spot and shout "Help!" there.

VLADIMIR—Pozzo!

ESTRAGON }
VLADIMIR } —He moved.

ESTRAGON—Are you sure his name is Pozzo?

VLADIMIR (*alarmed*)—Mr. Pozzo! Come back! We won't hurt you! (*Silence.*)

ESTRAGON—We might try him with other names.

VLADIMIR—I'm afraid he's dying.

ESTRAGON—It'd be amusing.

VLADIMIR—What'd be amusing?

ESTRAGON—To try him with other names, one after the other. It'd pass the time. And we'd be bound to hit on the right one sooner or later.

VLADIMIR—I tell you his name is Pozzo.

ESTRAGON—We'll soon see. (*He reflects.*) Abel! Abel!

POZZO—Help!
ESTRAGON—Got it in one!
VLADIMIR—I begin to weary of this motif.
ESTRAGON—Perhaps the other is called Cain. Cain! Cain!
POZZO—Help!
ESTRAGON—He's all humanity.

They change the subject. They decide to get up. They get up. "Child's play," says Estragon.

Since they are waiting for Godot, for something to do, they get Pozzo to his feet and support him. Pozzo asks if they are highwaymen. "Highwaymen! Do we look like highwaymen?" demands Estragon. "Damn it, can't you see the man is blind!" Vladimir snaps. "Damn it, so he is," Estragon replies, "so he says." "Don't leave me!" yells Pozzo.

Pozzo would like to know whether it is evening. There is some quibbling as to whether it is evening or not. Estragon argues that the sun may be rising, that it may be dawn. How does Vladimir know that it is the west where the sun now is? Pozzo wants his answer. Vladimir gives it: "It is evening, Sir. Night is drawing nigh. My friend here would have me doubt it and I must confess he shook me for a moment. But it is not for nothing I have lived through this long day and I can assure you it is very near the end of its repertory. . . ."

Vladimir is curious about Pozzo's blindness, and asks if it came on him all of a sudden. Pozzo says: "I woke up one fine day as blind as Fortune. (*Pause.*) Sometimes I wonder if I'm not still asleep." When Vladimir says: "But no later than yesterday—" Pozzo answers violently: "Don't question me! The blind have no notion of time. The things of time are hidden from them too." "Well just fancy that!" exclaims Vladimir, "I could have sworn it was just the opposite."

Estragon is bored. He threatens to leave. "Some diversion," he says. Pozzo asks after his "menial" and wants to know what happened. "The two of you slipped and fell," says Vladimir. Pozzo first asks them to see if the menial is hurt, then orders one or the other of them to help the menial to his feet: to get him up by pulling hard on his rope, or—if he proves recalcitrant—by kicking him in the face and privates. Estragon, told the menial never defends himself, takes on the job, but hurts his foot in the process and retires moaning to the mound, where he soon falls asleep. For the first time Pozzo inquires after Lucky by name. Vladimir wants to be sure that he heard right, and that *this* is Pozzo. "Certainly I am

Pozzo," Pozzo answers. "The same as yesterday?" Pozzo can't remember having met anyone yesterday, and tomorrow he won't remember having met anyone today. He is only interested in going on.

Before he leaves, Vladimir would like him to have Lucky perform. "He's dumb," says Pozzo, "he can't even groan." "Dumb! Since when?" asks Vladimir. With sudden fury, Pozzo roars: "Have you not done tormenting me with your accursed time! It's abominable! When! When! One day—is that not enough for you?—one day he went dumb, one day I went blind, one day we'll go deaf, one day we were born, one day we shall die, the same day, the same second, is that not enough for you? (*Calmer.*) They give birth astride of a grave, the light gleams an instant, then it's night once more. (*He jerks the rope.*) On!" Pozzo and Lucky leave.

Once again, Vladimir shakes Estragon awake. Vladimir wants to talk about Pozzo's confusion, but instead feels more and more confused himself. Estragon almost has him believing that Pozzo was Godot. He doesn't know what to think any more. "Was I sleeping, while others suffered?" asks Vladimir, "am I sleeping now. . . ?"

The Boy arrives. He does not recognize Vladimir, and says that he did not come yesterday. He has a message from Mr. Godot, who will not come this evening: he will come tomorrow.

Vladimir asks about Mr. Godot. Has he a beard? The Boy says: "Yes Sir." "Fair," Vladimir hesitates, "or black?" The Boy answers: "I think it's white, Sir." "Christ have mercy on us!" says Vladimir.

Vladimir's message for Mr. Godot is: "Tell him . . . tell him you saw me and that . . . that you saw me." As the Boy recoils, Vladimir says with sudden violence: "You're sure you saw me? You won't come and tell me tomorrow that you never saw me!"

The Boy runs away. Estragon, who has fallen asleep again, wakes up, takes off his boots, gets up and, as before, puts them down at the edge of the stage. They are now ready to go, but, according to Vladimir, they can't go far. Estragon is for dropping Godot. "He'd punish us," answers Vladimir, who remarks, after looking at the tree: "Everything's dead but the tree."

Once again they think of hanging themselves. They have no rope. They decide to try the cord that holds up Estragon's trousers. But when they pull the cord, it breaks. They are back where they were except that Estragon's trousers are down.

ESTRAGON—Didi, I can't go on like this.
VLADIMIR—That's what you think.
ESTRAGON—If we parted? That might be better for us.

VLADIMIR—We'll hang ourselves tomorrow. (*Pause.*) Unless Godot comes.

ESTRAGON—And if he comes?

VLADIMIR—We'll be saved.

Vladimir takes off his hat, peers inside it, feels about inside it, shakes it, knocks on the crown, puts it on again. "Pull *on* your trousers," he says. "True," says Estragon, realizing they are down. He pulls them up. "Well? Shall we go?" asks Vladimir. "Yes, let's go," answers Estragon. They do not move.

A GRAPHIC GLANCE

American Shakespeare Festival launched at Stratford, Conn., with Leora Dana, Polly Rowles, Christopher Plummer, Jack Palance, Hurd Hatfield, Roddy McDowall and Raymond Massey in "Julius Caesar"

Brattle Theatre's production of "Othello" with Jerome Kilty, Jan Farrand and William Marshall at City Center

American Shakespeare Festival's second production, "The Tempest" with Jack Palance, Raymond Massey, Joan Chandler and Roddy McDowall

Mermaids, wooden whales and other participan

Jones Beach spectacle "Arabian Nights"

Faye Emerson and Jean Pierre Aumont in "The Heavenly Twins"

Earle Hyman and Josephine Premice in "Mister Johnson"

Oscar Hammerstein 2d's "Carmen Jone

with Muriel Smith and Cozy Cole at City Center

Broadway sees Elaine Stritch, Hildegarde Neff, Judy Tyler, M-garet Sullavan, Shelley Winters and Gusti Huber demonstrate th culinary talents

HIRSCHFELD

Orson Welles as King Lear

Helen Hayes presents the Antoinette Perry Awards

PLAYS PRODUCED IN NEW YORK

PLAYS PRODUCED IN NEW YORK

June 1, 1955—May 31, 1956

(Plays marked "Continued" were still running on June 1, 1956)

ALMOST CRAZY

(16 performances)

Musical revue in two acts. Words and music by Portia Nelson, Raymond Taylor and James Shelton; sketches by James Shelton, Hal Hackady and Robert A. Bernstein. Produced by John S. Cobb at the Longacre Theatre, June 20, 1955.

Cast of characters—

Kay Medford
Babe Hines
Karen Anders
James Shelton
Betty Colby
Kevin Scott
Alvin Beam
Vincent Beck
Ron Cecill
Nick Dana
Lorna Del Maestro
Phyllis Dorne
Mildred Hughes
Joan Morton
William Skipper
Gloria Smith
Rita Tanno
Richard Towers
Ann York

Staged by Lew Kesler; choreography by William Skipper; sketches directed by Christopher Hewett; scenery and lighting by John Robert Lloyd; costumes by Stanley Simmons; musical director, Al Rickey; orchestral arrangements by Ted Royal; production stage manager, Walter Rinner; stage manager, Frederick Nay.

Musical numbers—

ACT I

"Everything's Gonna Be Much Worse Next Year"
(Music by Lew Kesler; lyric by James Shelton)
Ladies of the Ensemble ....Rita Tanno, Betty Colby, Karen Anders, Mildred Hughes, Joan Morton, Lorna Del Maestro, Ann York and Kay Medford
Quartette ....William Skipper, Alvin Beam, Kevin Scott, Nick Dana

"Mother's Day"
(Music by Portia Nelson; lyric by Joyce Geary)
Sung by ....Mildred Hughes, Karen Anders, Ann York

"Why Not Me?"
(Music by Ed Scott; lyric by Sam Rosen)
Sung and danced by ....Phyllis Dorne and Ron Cecill

"Fort Knox, New York"
By Lester Judson

"But It's Love"
(Music by Ray Taylor; lyric by Hal Hackady)
Sung and danced by ....Gloria Smith, Ann York, Lorna Del Maestro, Rita Tanno, Joan Morton, William Skipper, Alvin Beam, Nick Dana, Ron Cecill

"Don't Bait for Fish You Can't Fry"
(Music and lyric by Portia Nelson)
Sung by .... Babe Hines

"This Is a Living"
By Hal Hackady
Ralph Deadwood .... Kevin Scott
Mary Smiles Winter .... Kay Medford
A Model .... Mildred Hughes
The Husband .... James Shelton
Maxine Madison .... Karen Anders

"Where Is the Girl?"
(Music and lyric by James Shelton)
Sung by .... Betty Colby and Kevin Scott

"Mother's Day"
(Music by Portia Nelson; lyric by Joyce Geary)
Sung by .... Mildred Hughes, Karen Anders, Ann York

"Goin' to the Moon"
(Music by Ed Scott; lyric by Lenny Adelson)
Sung by .... Rita Tanno, James Shelton, Vincent Beck, Kay Medford, Richard Towers

"Down to Eartha"
(Music and lyric by Ray Taylor)
Sung by .... Betty Colby

"Chat Noire"
(Music by Ray Taylor; lyric by Jim Kaye)
Sung by .... Kevin Scott
Chat Noire .... Joan Morton
Bartender .... Fred Nay
Cop .... Nick Dana
Sailor .... Ron Cecill
Street Cleaner .... Fred Nay
The Mouse .... Alvin Beam

"I Can Live Without It"
(Music and lyric by Ray Taylor)
Sung by .... Karen Anders

"If I Knew You Were Coming"
By Robert A. Bernstein
Announcer .... Karen Anders
Wife .... Kay Medford
Husband .... James Shelton

"Come and Get Cozy With Me"
(Music by Lew Kesler; lyric by Carley Mills)
Lifeguard .... Kevin Scott
His Girl .... Karen Anders
Kitty's Roommate .... Kay Medford
Kitty's Beau .... James Shelton
Lovers .... Betty Colby, Vincent Beck and Company

ACT II

Entr'acte

"As We Told You"
(Music by Lew Kesler; lyric by James Shelton)
Ladies of the Ensemble .... Rita Tanno, Betty Colby, Karen Anders, Mildred Hughes, Joan Morton, Ann York, Lorna Del Maestro, Gloria Smith
Quartette .... William Skipper, Alvin Beam, Nick Dana and Ron Cecill

"Burlesque"
(Music by Bill Russell; lyric by Stan Hagler)
Queenie .... Gloria Smith
Big Queenie .... Kay Medford
Barker .... Fred Nay
The Baritone .... Kevin Scott

"Vertigo"
(Music by Ray Taylor; lyric by Helen Bragdon)
Mistress of the Villa .... Betty Colby
Tender of the Grapes .... Vincent Beck

"I Thought So Too"

By James Shelton
Doctor .... Richard Towers
1st Woman .... Lorna Del Maestro
1st Man .... Kevin Scott
2nd Man .... James Shelton
2nd Woman .... Rita Tanno
3rd Woman .... Kay Medford

"Easy"
(Music and lyric by James Shelton)
Sung by .... Babe Hines

"Always Tell the Truth"
(Dialogue by Hal Hackady; music and lyric by Portia Nelson)
Truth .... Joan Morton
Veracity .... Kay Medford

"Mother's Day"
(Music by Portia Nelson; lyric by Joyce Geary)
Sung by .... Mildred Hughes, Ann York and Karen Anders

"Here Come the Blues"
(Music by Gene DePaul; lyric by Don Raye)
Sung by .... William Skipper
Danced by .... William Skipper, Joan Morton Lorna Del Maestro, Mildred Hughes and "The Leg" Phyllis Dorne

"More Fish"
Sung by .... Karen Anders

"Love in the Barnyard"
(Music and lyric by Ray Taylor)
Sung by .... Babe Hines
Danced by .... Gloria Smith, Lorna Del Maestro, Rita Tanno, Phyllis Dorne, Ron Cecill, Alvin Beam, Nick Dana, William Skipper

"Love Me or Leave Me"
By Kay Medford and James Shelton
The Grump .... James Shelton
Ruth .... Kay Medford

Finale .... Entire Company

(Closed July 2, 1955)

THE SKIN OF OUR TEETH

(22 performances)

Drama in three acts by Thornton Wilder. Produced by Robert Whitehead; revived by the American National Theatre and Academy at the ANTA Theatre, August 17, 1955.

Cast of characters—

Announcer .... Earl George
Sabina .... Mary Martin
Mr. Fitzpatrick .... Paul Morrison
Mrs. Antrobus .... Helen Hayes
Dinosaur .... Vinie Burrows
Mammoth .... Patricia Taffe
Telegraph Boy .... Fred Kareman
Gladys .... Heller Halliday
Henry .... Don Murray
Mr. Antrobus .... George Abbott
Doctor .... Frank Hamilton
Professor .... Jonathan Anderson
Judge .... Frank Silvera
Homer .... Howard Fischer
Miss E. Muse .... Eileen Lear
Miss T. Muse .... Frances Sternhagen

Miss M. Muse .... Maud Scheerer
Drum Majorette .... Norma Veney
Drum Majorette .... Alice Fay
Lifeguard .... Charles Boaz
Bingo Caller .... Maud Scheerer
Fortune Teller .... Florence Reed
Chair Pusher .... Frank Silvera
Broadcast Official .... Earl George
Asst. Broadcast Official .... Frank Hamilton
Fred Bailey .... Howard Fischer
Hester .... Maud Scheerer
Ivy .... Vinie Burrows
Mr. Tremayne .... Frank Silvera

Conveners, Tourists, Atlantic City Sightseers: Emily Cobb, Jack Delmonte, John Dorman, David Elliott, Tom Geroghty, Lily Lodge, Richard O'Neil, Ann Stanwell.

The time is Now and Always. Act I.—The home of Mr. and Mrs. George Antrobus in Excelsior, New Jersey. Act II.—The Boardwalk at Atlantic City. Act III.—The home of Mr. and Mrs. George Antrobus in Excelsior, New Jersey.

Staged by Alan Schneider; settings by Lester Polakov; costumes by Helene Pons; lighting by Feder; stage manager, Philip Mathias.

The Skin of Our Teeth was first produced November 18, 1942, at the Plymouth Theatre for 359 performances.

(Closed September 3, 1955)

CATCH A STAR!

(23 performances)

Musical revue in two acts, with lyrics by Paul Webster and Ray Golden; music by Sammy Fain and Phil Charig; and sketches by Danny and Neil Simon. Produced by Sy Kleinman at the Plymouth Theatre, September 6, 1955.

Cast of characters—

Pat Carroll
David Burns
Elaine Dunn
Jack Wakefield
Helen Halpin
Marc Breaux
Undine Forrest
Sonny Sparks
Wayne Sherwood
Kay Malone
Denny Desmond
Calvin Holt
Trude Adams

Dances and musical numbers staged by Lee Sherman; settings devised and designed by Ralph Alswang; costumes designed by Thomas Becher; sketches directed by Danny Simon; orchestrations and musical direction by Milton Greene; revue co-ordinated by Robert Nesbitt; entire production conceived and supervised by Ray Golden; additional material by Lee Adams; ballet music composed by Herb Schutz; production stage manager, Gene Perlowin; stage managers, John Foster and Bill Smillie.

Musical numbers—

ACT I

Prologue: "Catch a Star!"
(Lyric by Paul Webster, Music by Sammy Fain)
Singer .... Wayne Sherwood
"Everybody Wants to Be in Show Business"
By Ray Golden, Bud Burtson and Phil Charig

Producer .... David Burns
Stage Doorman .... Jack Wakefield
Thief .... Denny Desmond
Policeman .... Wayne Sherwood
Magician .... Calvin Holt
Magician's Assistant .... Rhoda Kerns
Model .... Undine Forrest
Woman with Baby Carriage .... Kay Malone
Ambulance Attendants .... Carl Jeffrey, Marc Breaux
Patient .... Mickey Calin
Chorus Girls .... Lillian D'Honau, Sigyn
Waitress .... Helen Halpin
Secretaries .... Louise Golden, Elaine Dunn
Charity Collector .... Kay Kingston

"New Styles in Acting"
By Danny Simon
Producer .... David Burns
Military Pilot .... Jack Wakefield
Tennis Player .... Sonny Sparks
Stage Manager .... Denny Desmond
The Ingenue .... Pat Carroll

"A Little Traveling Music"
(Lyric by Paul Webster and Ray Golden; music by Hal Borne)
The Traveler .... Elaine Dunn
Three Improper Bostonians .. Louise Golden, Sigyn, Lillian D'Honau

"Matinee Idles"
By Danny and Neil Simon
Hawker .... Denny Desmond
Pete .... Wayne Sherwood
Man .... Jack Wakefield
Trixie .... Pat Carroll
Dorothy .... Helen Halpin
Martha .... Carol Field
Lucille .... Undine Forrest
Hazel .... Rhoda Kerns
Harriett .... Kay Malone
Florence .... Kay Kingston
Actor .... Denny Desmond
Actress .... Lillian D'Honau

"One Hour Ahead of the Posse"
(Lyric by Ray Golden and Dave Ormont; music by Phil Charig)
Killer .... Wayne Sherwood
Girl .... Lillian D'Honau
Sheriff .... Marc Breaux
Posse .... Calvin Holt, Carl Jeffrey, Mickey Calin, Denny Desmond
Folk Singers .... Carol Field, Rhoda Kerns, Kay Malone

"And Then I Wrote"
By Danny and Neil Simon
Harry .... Jack Wakefield
Kitty .... Helen Halpin
Max Dillingbert .... David Burns
Gus .... Marc Breaux
Labonza .... Sonny Sparks
Phoebe .... Undine Forrest
Customer .... Denny Desmond

"Las Vegas"
By Ray Golden and Sy Kleinman. Additional lyrics by Lee Adams
Girl .... Pat Carroll
Bellhops .... Wayne Sherwood, Carl Jeffrey, Mickey Calin, Denny Desmond

"To Be or Not To Be in Love"
(Lyric by Ray Golden, Danny Shapiro and Milton Pascal; music by Phil Charig)
Girl .... Trude Adams
Boy .... Marc Breaux

"The Story of Alice"
(Music by Jerry Bock; lyric by Larry Holofcener)
Quartet .... Helen Halpin, Wayne Sherwood, Calvin Holt, Undine Forrest

"Room for Rent"
By Danny and Neil Simon
Southern Belle .... Pat Carroll

First Man .... David Burns
First Roomer .... Jack Wakefield
Second Roomer .... Sonny Sparks
Third Roomer .... Lynne Bretonn
Fourth Roomer .... Kay Malone
Second Man .... Wayne Sherwood
Truck Driver .... Denny Desmond

"What a Song Can Do"
By Bernie Wayne and Lee Morris
Helen Halpin

"Carnival in Court"
(Lyric by Ray Golden and I. A. L. Diamond; music by Jay Navarre)
Town Crier .... David Burns
Bailiff .... Calvin Holt
Two Girls .... Sigyn, Louise Golden
Judge .... Jack Wakefield
Plaintiff .... Helen Halpin
Defendant .... Sonny Sparks
Private Eye .... Marc Breaux
Private Eye's Wife .... Elaine Dunn
Co-respondent .... Pat Carroll
Three Belles .... Lillian D'Honau, Undine Forrest, Kay Malone
Two Sailors .... Mickey Calin, Denny Desmond
Basketman .... Wayne Sherwood
Basketwoman .... Carol Field

ACT II

"Theatre Piece"
Three Male Dancers .... Marc Breaux, Carl Jeffrey, Calvin Holt
Three Female Dancers .... Sigyn, Elaine Dunn, Louise Golden
Three Characters .... Wayne Sherwood, Mickey Calin, Carol Field
Glamour Girls .... Undine Forrest, Kay Malone, Rhoda Kerns, Lillian D'Honau (Harlequin)

"Arty"
By Danny and Neil Simon
Mom .... Pat Carroll
Arty .... Jack Wakefield
First Man .... Denny Desmond
Second Man .... Sonny Sparks

"Twist My Arm"
(Lyric by Paul Webster; music by Sammy Fain)
Girl .... Elaine Dunn
Boy .... Marc Breaux

"New Hollywood Plots"
(Lyric by Paul Webster; music by Sammy Fain)
David Burns
Denny Desmond
Calvin Holt

"Foreign Cars"
(Words and music by Norman Martin)
Trude Adams

"Gruntled"
By Ray Golden, Sy Kleinman and Phil Charig
Girl .... Helen Halpin
Boy .... Denny Desmond
Three Couples .... Marc Breaux, Elaine Dunn; Calvin Holt, Lillian D'Honau; Mickey Calin, Sigyn

"Matrimonial Agency"
By Danny and Neil Simon
First Woman .... Undine Forrest
Second Woman .... Kay Malone
Adrian .... David Burns
First Shopper .... Kay Kingston
First Man .... Mickey Calin
Mrs. Ennis .... Pat Carroll
Miss B. .... Carol Field
The Frenchman .... Marc Breaux
The Reject .... Jack Wakefield
The Body .... Sonny Sparks

"Fly Little Heart"
(Music by Jerry Bock; lyric by Larry Holofcener)
Girl .... Elaine Dunn

"Bachelor Hoedown"
(Music by Jerry Bock; lyric by Larry Holofcener)
Elaine Dunn, Marc Breaux, Sigyn, Louise Golden, Carol Field, Lillian D'Honau, Rhoda Kerns, Mickey Calin, Calvin Holt, Denny Desmond, Carl Jeffrey, Wayne Sherwood
"Gift of the Magi"
By Mike Stewart
Pat Carroll
"Boffola"
(Lyric by Danny Shapiro, Milton Pascal and Ray Golden; music by Phil Charig)
Entire Cast

(Closed September 24, 1955)

OTHELLO

(15 performances)

Tragedy in three acts by William Shakespeare. Produced by the New York City Center Theatre Company (Jean Dalrymple, Director) at the New York City Center of Music and Drama, September 7, 1955.

Cast of characters—

Roderigo .... Michael Wager
Iago .... Jerome Kilty
Brabantio .... Thayer David
Othello .... William Marshall
Cassio .... Paul Sparer
Officer .... John Harkins
Duke of Venice .... Arthur Malet
Gratiano .... Larkin Ford
Lodovico .... Lester Rawlins
Desdemona .... Jan Farrand
Montano .... Pernell Roberts
Sailor .... William Landis
Officer .... Stanley Jay
Emilia .... Cavada Humphrey
Bianca .... Peggy Cass

Soldiers, servants, gentlemen: David Anthony, Laurinda Barrett, Epy Baca, Joseph Everingham, Henry Holt, Joseph Mitchell, Charles Nelson, Art Ostrin, Ken Reisdorff, Ted Roberts and George Ziboran.

The action takes place in Venice and Cyprus.

Staged by John Stix; settings by Robert O'Hearn; costumes by Robert Fletcher; performed by the Brattle Shakespeare Players; production stage manager, Herman Shapiro; stage manager, Richard Baldridge.

(Closed September 18, 1955)

MARCEL MARCEAU

(32 performances)

A program of pantomime with Marcel Marceau and his partners, Pierre Verry and Alec Sandro. Produced by the Phoenix Theatre (T. Edward Hambleton and Norris Houghton) at the Phoenix Theatre, September 20, 1955. Moved to the Ethel Barrymore Theatre October 4, 1955, where it was presented by Ronald A. Wilford Associates, Inc., and Jean de Rigault in association with the Phoenix Theatre Company.

Varied programs consisting of several of the following pantomimes:

PART I

Style Pantomimes with Marcel Marceau

Walking
Walking against the Wind
The Staircase
Youth, Maturity, Old Age, and Death
The Dandy
The Bureaucrat
Tug-of-War
The Public Garden
To go up and down a Hill with a Hand-Cart
At the Clothier's
The Dice-Players
The Thief
The Tight-rope Walker

Pantomimes with Pierre Verry and Alec Sandro

The Magician
The Chess Players
The Siamese Brothers

Pantomime with Marcel Marceau, Pierre Verry and Alec Sandro

The Street

PART II

BIP and the Bumble Bee
BIP Traffic Cop
BIP Sculptor
BIP Apache
BIP Plays David and Goliath
BIP and the Butterfly
BIP Artist
BIP in the Subway
BIP Tamer
BIP Commits Suicide
BIP and the Rendez-Vous
BIP Fireman
BIP Goes Skating
BIP Tragedian
BIP Family Man
BIP Virtuoso
BIP at the Dance Hall
BIP Photographer
BIP Professor of Botany
BIP at a Social Party
BIP Goes Traveling
BIP Tailor

Production stage manager for the Phoenix Theatre, Robert Woods; presentation of cards by Pierre Verry and Alvin Epstein in the programs presented at the Ethel Barrymore Theatre.

(Closed October 16, 1955)

HENRY IV, PART I

(15 performances)

Historical comedy in three acts by William Shakespeare. Produced by the New York City Center Theatre Company (Jean Dalrymple, Director) at the New York City Center of Music and Drama, September 21, 1955.

Cast of characters—

King Henry the Fourth (Henry Bolingbroke) ....Thayer David
The Earl of Westmoreland ....Jay Lanin
Prince John of Lancaster, son to the King ....David Bowen
Sir Richard Vernon ....Clayton Corzatte
The Archbishop of Wells ....Morris Hunt
Henry, Prince of Wales, son to the King ....Michael Wager
Sir John Falstaff ....Jerome Kilty
Edward Poins ....Stanley Jay
Thomas Percy, Earl of Worcester ....Lester Rawlins
Henry Percy, Earl of Northumberland ....Larkin Ford
Henry Percy, surnamed Hotspur, his son ....Bryant Haliday
Peto ....Arthur Malet
Bardolph ....John Peters
Gadshill ....Wood Romoff
First Traveller ....James Oberlin
Lady Percy, wife to Hotspur and sister to Mortimer ....Jan Farrand
Hotspur's Messenger ....Alan Coates
Francis ....Albert Corbin
Mistress Quickly ....Peggy Cass
Sheriff ....Pernell Roberts
Edmund Mortimer, Earl of March ....John Harkins
Owen Glendower ....Paul Sparer
Lady Mortimer ....Cavada Humphrey
The Earl of Douglas ....Pernell Roberts
Sir Walter Blunt ....Paul Sparer

Soldiers and Servants: David Anthony, Bob Burland, Alan Coates, John Copeland, Jack Eames, Cornelius Prizell, Walter Gorney, Henry Holth, Joe Mitchell, James Oberlin, Art Ostrin, Naomi Powers, Ken Reisdorff, Ted Roberts.

Act I.—Scene 1—London; The Palace. Scene 2—Windsor; The Castle. Scene 3—The highway near Gadshill. Scene 4—Warkworth Castle. Scene 5—Eastcheap; the Boar's Head Tavern. Act II.—Scene 1—Wales; Glendower's Castle. Scene 2—London; The Palace. Scene 3—Eastcheap; the Boar's Head Tavern. Act III.—The plain near Shrewsbury.

Staged by Jerome Kilty; settings by Robert O'Hearn; costumes by Robert Fletcher; performed by the Brattle Shakespeare Players; production stage manager, Herman Shapiro; stage manager, Richard Baldridge.

(Closed October 2, 1955)

A DAY BY THE SEA

(24 performances)

Play in three acts by N. C. Hunter. Produced by Huntington Hartford and Stephen Mitchell at the ANTA Theatre, September 26, 1955.

Cast of characters—

Laura Anson .... Aline MacMahon
David Anson .... Halliwell Hobbes
Julian Anson .... Hume Cronyn
Doctor Farley .... Dennis King
Frances Farrar .... Jessica Tandy
Elinor Eddison .... Veronica Cole
Toby Eddison .... Barclay Hodges
Humphrey Caldwell .... Leo Britt
Miss Mathieson .... Megs Jenkins
William Gregson .... John W. Austin

The action takes place in the garden of Laura Anson's house in Dorset, and on a beach nearby. The time is the present; it is early May. Act I.—The garden of Laura Anson's house in Dorset; a morning in early May. Act II.—Scene 1—The beach, the same afternoon. Scene 2—The same, an hour later. Act III—The same as Act I; next morning.

Staged by Cedric Hardwicke; production designed by Jay Krause; stage manager, Paul A. Foley.

See "The Season on Broadway."

(Closed October 15, 1955)

THE D'OYLY CARTE OPERA COMPANY

Repertory of eight Gilbert and Sullivan operettas. Produced by Bridget D'Oyly Carte at the Sam S. Shubert Theatre, starting September 27, 1955.

IOLANTHE

(10 performances)

Cast of characters—

The Lord Chancellor .... Peter Pratt
Earl of Mountararat .... Donald Adams
Earl Tolloller .... Leonard Osborn
Private Willis .... Fisher Morgan
Strephon .... Alan Styler
Queen of the Fairies .... Ann Drummond-Grant
Iolanthe .... Joyce Wright
Celia .... Maureen Melvin
Leila .... Beryl Dixon
Fleta .... Margaret Dobson
Phyllis .... Cynthia Morey

Staged by Robert A. Gibson; orchestra directed by Isidore Godfrey; fairy costumes by Pat Freeborn; stage manager, Jerome Stephens.

THE MIKADO

(17 performances)

Cast of characters—

The Mikado of Japan .... Donald Adams
Nanki-Poo .... Neville Griffiths
Ko-Ko .... Peter Pratt

Pooh-Bah .... Fisher Morgan
Pish-Tush .... Jeffrey Skitch
Go-To .... John Banks
Yum-Yum .... Cynthia Morey
Pitti-Sing .... Joyce Wright
Peep-Bo .... Beryl Dixon
Katisha .... Ann Drummond-Grant

Staged by Robert A. Gibson; orchestra directed by Isidore Godfrey; scenery by Peter Goffin; costumes by Charles Ricketts; stage manager, Jerome Stephens.

THE YEOMEN OF THE GUARD

(8 performances)

Cast of characters—

Sir Richard Cholmondeley .... Alan Styler
Colonel Fairfax .... Leonard Osborn
Sergeant Meryll .... Donald Adams
Leonard Meryll .... John Fryatt
Jack Point .... Peter Pratt
Wilfred Shadbolt .... Fisher Morgan
First Yeoman .... Frederick Sinden
Second Yeoman .... John Banks
First Citizen .... Lawson Johnson
Second Citizen .... John Reed
Elsie Maynard .... Muriel Harding
Phoebe Meryll .... Joyce Wright
Dame Carruthers .... Ann Drummond-Grant
Kate .... Maureen Melvin

Staged by Robert A. Gibson; orchestra directed by Isidore Godfrey; scenery and costumes by Peter Goffin; stage manager, Jerome Stephens.

THE PIRATES OF PENZANCE

(8 performances)

Cast of characters—

Major-General Stanley .... Peter Pratt
The Pirate King .... Donald Adams
Samuel .... Trevor Hills
Frederic .... Neville Griffiths
Sergeant of Police .... Fisher Morgan
Mabel .... Muriel Harding
Edith .... Joyce Wright
Kate .... Joy Mornay
Isabel .... Margaret Dobson
Ruth .... Ann Drummond-Grant

Staged by Robert A. Gibson; orchestra directed by Isidore Godfrey; costumes by George Sheringham; stage manager, Jerome Stephens.

PRINCESS IDA

(8 performances)

Cast of characters—

King Hildebrand .... Fisher Morgan
Hilarion .... John Fryatt

Cyril .... Leonard Osborn
Florian .... Jeffrey Skitch
King Gama .... Peter Pratt
Arac .... Donald Adams
Guron .... John Banks
Scynthius .... Trevor Hills
Princess Ida .... Muriel Harding
Lady Blanche .... Ann Drummond-Grant
Lady Psyche .... Cynthia Morey
Melissa .... Beryl Dixon
Sacharissa .... Maureen Melvin
Chloe .... Margaret Dobson
Ada .... Jennifer Toye

Staged by Robert A. Gibson; orchestra directed by Isidore Godfrey; scenery and costumes by James Wade; stage manager, Jerome Stephens.

TRIAL BY JURY and H.M.S. PINAFORE

(13 performances)

Cast of characters of "Trial by Jury"—

The Learned Judge .... John Reed
Counsel for the Plaintiff .... Alan Styler
Defendant .... John Fryatt
Foreman of the Jury .... John Banks
Usher .... Trevor Hills
Associate .... George Cook
The Plaintiff .... Kathleen West
First Bridesmaid .... Margaret Dobson

Cast of characters of "H.M.S.Pinafore"—

The Rt. Hon. Sir Joseph Porter, K.C.B. .... Peter Pratt
Captain Corcoran .... Jeffrey Skitch
Ralph Rackstraw .... Neville Griffiths
Dick Deadeye .... Donald Adams
Bill Bobstay .... Trevor Hills
Bob Becket .... George Cook
Josephine .... Muriel Harding
Hebe .... Joyce Wright
Little Buttercup .... Ann Drummond-Grant

Staged by Robert A. Gibson; orchestra directed by Isidore Godfrey; scenery by Joseph and Phil Harker; ladies' costumes by George Sheringham; stage manager, Jerome Stephens.

RUDDIGORE

(8 performances)

Cast of characters—

Sir Ruthven Murgatroyd .... Peter Pratt
Richard Dauntless .... Leonard Osborn
Sir Despard Murgatroyd .... Fisher Morgan
Old Adam Goodheart .... John Banks
Sir Roderic Murgatroyd .... Donald Adams
Rose Maybud .... Cynthia Morey
Mad Margaret .... Joyce Wright
Dame Hannah .... Ann Drummond-Grant
Zorah .... May Sanderson
Ruth .... Joyce Farrer

Staged by Robert A. Gibson; orchestra directed by Isidore Godfrey; costumes and new settings for Act II by Peter Goffin; stage manager, Jerome Stephens.

(Closed November 26, 1955)

MAURICE CHEVALIER IN SONGS AND IMPRESSIONS

(46 performances)

A one-man show, starring Maurice Chevalier, with Fred Freed at the piano. Produced by Gilbert Miller at the Lyceum Theatre, September 28, 1955.

Stage Manager, Windsor Lewis.

Program

Introduction—Fred Freed
"Ça Va Ça Va"
(Lyrics by Maurice Chevalier; music by Fred Freed)
"Paris Oui Oui"
(Lyrics by André Hornez; music by Henri Betti)
"I Wonder Who's Kissing Her Now"
(Lyrics by M. Hough and F. Adams; music by J. E. Howard)
"Les Pas Perdus"
(Lyrics by Robert Lamoureux and Maurice Chevalier; music by Henri Bourtsyre)
"L'Orientale"
(Lyrics by André Hornez; music by Henri Betti)
"C'est Fort La Musique"
(Lyrics by Maurice Chevalier; music by Fred Freed)

Introduction—Fred Freed
"A Boy and a Girl"
(English version by Ben Smith; music by Henri Betti)
"L'Illusioniste"
(Lyrics by Vittonet; music by Jean Constantin)
"Un Gentleman"
(Lyrics and music by Maurice Chevalier)
"She and He"
(English version by Ben Smith; music by Henri Betti)
"A Las Vegas"
(English version by Maurice Chevalier; music by Louiguy)
"Folies-Bergere"
(Lyrics by Maurice Chevalier; music by Francis Lopez)
"A Barcelone"
(Lyrics by Maurice Chevalier; music by Henri Betti)
"Accents Melodiques"
(Sketch by Maurice Chevalier)
"Louise"
(Lyrics by Leo Robin; music by Richard A. Whiting)
"Seems Like Old Times"
(Lyrics by Carmen Lombardo; music by John Jacob Loeb)

(Closed November 6, 1955)

A VIEW FROM THE BRIDGE

(149 performances)

Two plays by Arthur Miller ("A Memory of Two Mondays" and "A View from the Bridge"). Produced by Kermit Bloomgarden and Whitehead-Stevens at the Coronet Theatre, September 29, 1955.

A Memory of Two Mondays

Cast of characters—

Bert .... Leo Penn
Raymond .... David Clarke
Agnes .... Eileen Heckart
Patricia .... Gloria Marlowe
Gus .... J. Carrol Naish
Jim .... Russell Collins
Kenneth .... Biff McGuire
Larry .... Van Heflin
Frank .... Jack Warden
Jerry .... Richard Davalos
William .... Antony Vorno
Tom .... Curt Conway
Mechanic .... Tom Pedi
Mister Eagle .... Ralph Bell

The entire action takes place in the shipping room of a large auto-parts warehouse in Manhattan. It is a hot Monday morning in summer, just before nine in a bygone year, and a morning in winter.

A View from the Bridge

Cast of characters—

Louis .... David Clarke
Mike .... Tom Pedi
Alfieri .... J. Carrol Naish
Eddie .... Van Heflin
Catherine .... Gloria Marlowe
Beatrice .... Eileen Heckart
Marco .... Jack Warden
Tony .... Antony Vorno
Rodolpho .... Richard Davalos
First Immigration Officer .... Curt Conway
Second Immigration Officer .... Ralph Bell
Mr. Lipari .... Russell Collins
Mrs. Lipari .... Anne Driscoll
Two "Submarines" .... Leo Penn, Milton Carney

The action takes place in the apartment and environment of Eddie Carbone, all in Red Hook, on the Bay seaward from Brooklyn Bridge. The time is the present.

Entire production staged by Martin Ritt; designed by Boris Aronson; costumes by Helene Pons; lighting by Leland Watson; stage manager, Harry Young.

See page 69.

(Closed February 4, 1956)

THE YOUNG AND BEAUTIFUL

(65 performances)

Play in three acts by Sally Benson, based on short stories by F. Scott Fitzgerald. Produced by Robert B. Radnitz, in association with Lawrence Baker, Jr., at the Longacre Theatre, October 1, 1955.

Cast of characters—

Josephine Perry .... Lois Smith
Tillie .... Jean Jeans
Travis de Coppet .... Peter Brandon
Mr. Perry .... Jay Barney
Anthony Harker .... Douglas Watson
Mrs. Bray .... Virginia Morgan
Mrs. Perry .... Margot Stevenson
Lillian .... Jane McArthur
Sonny Dorrance .... James Hickman
Ed Bement .... Barry McGuire
Capt. Dicer .... James Olson

The entire action takes place in the Perry living room, Chicago, 1915. Act I.—Scene 1—A late afternoon in March. Scene 2—Night, two weeks later. Act II.—Scene 1—Afternoon, one week later. Scene 2—Late afternoon of the following day. Act III.—A late afternoon in early June.

Staged by Marshall Jamison; settings by Eldon Elder; lighting by Feder; costumes by Motley; production stage manager, Buford Armitage; stage manager, Ed Moroney.

See "The Season on Broadway."

(Closed November 26, 1955)

TIGER AT THE GATES

(217 performances)

Play in two acts by Jean Giraudoux, translated by Christopher Fry. The Robert L. Joseph Production, sponsored by the Playwrights' Company, in association with Henry M. Margolis, presented at the Plymouth Theatre, October 3, 1955.

Cast of characters—

Andromache, wife to Hector .... Barbara Jefford
Cassandra, sister to Hector .... Leueen MacGrath
Laundress .... Judith Braun
Hector .... Michael Redgrave
Paris, brother to Hector .... Leo Ciceri
First Old Man .... Howard Caine
Second Old Man .... Jack Bittner
Priam, King of Troy, father to Hector .... Morris Carnovsky
Demekos, a Poet, Leader of the Senate .... John Laurie
Hecuba, mother to Hector .... Catherine Lacey
Mathematician .... Milton Selzer
Lady in Waiting .... Jacqueline Brookes
Polyxene, young sister to Hector .... Ellen Christopher
Helen .... Diane Cilento
Messenger .... Ernest Graves
Troilus, young brother to Hector .... Peter Kerr
Abneos, a Senator .... Howard Caine
Busiris, a Lawyer .... Wyndham Goldie
Ajax, a Greek Captain .... Felix Munso
Ulysses .... Walter Fitzgerald
A Topman, Officer on Paris' Ship .... Nehemiah Persoff
Olpides, Sailor on Paris' ship .... Jack Bittner
Senator .... Tom McDermott
Sailor .... Louis Criss

The play takes place in and around the Palace of Troy.

Staged by Harold Clurman; settings and costumes designed by Loudon Sainthill; New York Production Supervising Designer, Paul

Morrison; incidental music by Lennox Berkeley; production stage manager, James Gelb; stage manager, Louis Criss.

See page 89.

(Closed April 7, 1956)

ISLAND OF GOATS

(7 performances)

Drama in three acts by Ugo Betti, in English version by Henry Reed. Produced by Roger L. Stevens and Hardy Smith, Ltd., at the Fulton Theatre, October 4, 1955.

Cast of characters—

Edoardo	Henry Sharp
Pia	Ruth Ford
Angelo	Laurence Harvey
Agata	Uta Hagen
Silvia	Tani Seitz

The scene is a lonely millhouse on an island in the Mediterranean; the time is the present. Act I.—Late afternoon. Act II.—Afternoon, some time later. Act III.—Just before dawn, two days later.

Staged by Peter Glenville; lighting and setting by Jo Mielziner; assistant designer to Mr. Mielziner, John Harvey; costumes by Motley; song by Norman Dello Joio; production stage manager, Seymour Milbert; stage manager, Robert B. Anderson, Jr.

Symbolic drama, laid on a Mediterranean island, about an odd young stranger who becomes unpleasantly involved with the three women of a household—a widow, her daughter, and her sister-in-law. They eventually get him down a well and leave him there to die.

(Closed October 8, 1955)

THE DIARY OF ANNE FRANK

(274 performances)
(Continued)

Play in two acts by Frances Goodrich and Albert Hackett, dramatized from the book "Anne Frank: The Diary of a Young Girl." Produced by Kermit Bloomgarden at the Cort Theatre, October 5, 1955.

Cast of characters—

Mr. Frank	Joseph Schildkraut
Miep	Gloria Jones
Mrs. Van Daan	Dennie Moore
Mr. Van Daan	Lou Jacobi
Peter Van Daan	David Levin

Mrs. Frank .... Gusti Huber
Margot Frank .... Eva Rubinstein
Anne Frank .... Susan Strasberg
Mr. Kraler .... Clinton Sundberg
Mr. Dussel .... Jack Gilford

The time: during the years of World War II and immediately thereafter. The place: Amsterdam.

Staged by Garson Kanin; production designed by Boris Aronson; costumes by Helene Pons; lighting by Leland Watson; production manager, William Hammerstein; stage manager, Walter Neal.

See page 111.

THE WOODEN DISH

(12 performances)

Play in three acts by Edmund Morris. Produced by Armand Deutsch at the Booth Theatre, October 6, 1955.

Cast of characters—

Lon (Pop) Dennison .... Louis Calhern
Clara Dennison .... Polly Rowles
Bessie Bockser .... Jane Rose
Ed Mason .... John Randolph
Susan Dennison .... Jacqueline Scott
Sam Yaeger .... Edgar Stehli
Glenn Dennison .... Gordon Tanner
Floyd Dennison .... James Westerfield
Janey Stewart .... Barbara Barrie
Mr. Forsythe .... Orville Sherman

The action takes place in the Dennison home in a city in Texas. Act I.—Afternoon. Act II.—That night. Act III.—Scene 1—The following morning. Scene 2—That evening.

Staged by Louis Calhern; scenery and lighting by Donald Oenslager; costumes designed by John Boyt; assistant to Mr. Oenslager, Klaus Holm; musician, Max Hamlisch; production stage manager, Edward McHugh; assistant stage manager, Joseph L. Graham.

An old man who for years has lived unwanted with his son and daughter-in-law is now at the half-blind stage of breaking dishes and setting things on fire. His daughter-in-law decrees that either Pop goes to a "home" or she will walk out of the house. There are some sub-developments—involving the daughter-in-law's foiled elopement with the family boarder—before the old man sets out gallantly for a rest home.

(Closed October 15, 1955)

JOYCE GRENFELL REQUESTS THE PLEASURE . . .

(65 performances)

An intimate review, with book and lyrics by Joyce Grenfell; music by Richard Addinsell. Produced by Lyn Austin and Thomas Noyes, sponsored by Producers Theatre, at the Bijou Theatre, October 10, 1955.

Principals:

Joyce Grenfell	Paddy Stone
Beryl Kaye	Irving Davies

Staged by Laurier Lister; musical director, George Bauer, who supplied additional arrangements; scenic supervision and lighting by Paul Morrison; decor by Joan and David de Bethel, Victor Stiebel, Stanley Moore, Peter Rice; choreography by Wendy Toye, John Heawood, Alfred Rodrigues, Beryl Kaye, Paddy Stone, Irving Davies; additional orchestrations by Clare Grundman; stage manager, Charles Pratt, Jr.

Sketches and musical numbers—

PART I

Welcome .... Joyce Grenfell
"Three's Company" .... Beryl Kaye, Paddy Stone, Irving Davies
"The Music's Message" .... Joyce Grenfell
"Edinburgh Rock" .... Beryl Kaye, Paddy Stone, Irving Davies
"Women at Work" .... Joyce Grenfell
1. Curiosity Shop
2. Nursery School
"Two Loves" .... Beryl Kaye, Paddy Stone, Irving Davies
"Basquette" .... Beryl Kaye, Paddy Stone, Irving Davies
"Period Piece" .... Joyce Grenfell
"Heart Ride" .... Irving Davies
"The Understanding Mother" .... Joyce Grenfell
"Nothing to Do" .... Beryl Kaye
"Thought for Today" .... Joyce Grenfell
"Favour" .... Beryl Kaye, Paddy Stone
"Three Brothers" .... Joyce Grenfell
"Palais Dancers" .... Joyce Grenfell, Beryl Kaye, Paddy Stone, Irving Davies

PART II

"Slap Happy" .... Beryl Kaye, Paddy Stone, Irving Davies
"Two Young People and a Visitor" .... Joyce Grenfell
1. Travel Talk
2. Musician
3. Visitor
"Mañana" .... Paddy Stone, Irving Davies
"Running Commentary" .... Joyce Grenfell
"Ordinary Morning" .... Beryl Kaye, Irving Davies
"Paddy's Nightmare" .... Paddy Stone
"Songs My Mother Taught Me" .... Joyce Grenfell
"Life and Literature" .... Joyce Grenfell
"Three in Time" .... Beryl Kaye, Paddy Stone, Irving Davies
"Envoi" .... Beryl Kaye, Paddy Stone, Irving Davies
Farewell .... Joyce Grenfell

(Closed December 3, 1955)

THE CAREFREE TREE

(24 performances)

Play in two acts by Aldyth Morris. Produced by the Phoenix Theatre (T. Edward Hambleton and Norris Houghton) at the Phoenix Theatre, October 11, 1955.

Cast of characters—

Feng Chu, the Charm Man	Frederic Warriner
The Storyman	Larry Gates
The Actorman	Farley Granger
The Propertyman	Jerry Stiller
Mu Yi	Farley Granger
The Princess	Janice Rule
Her Maid	Dee Victor
An Old Man	Mitchell Agruss
A Soldier	Kelton Garwood
Another Soldier	Sorrell Booke
Another Soldier	Mitchell Agruss
The Empress Dowager	Blanche Yurka
Her Chancellor	Chuan
The Red Bandit	Mitchell Agruss
The Green Bandit	David Gold
The Purple Bandit	Alvin Ailey
A Wolf	Albert Corbin
The Widow Yang	Edith Meiser
The Widows Yang	Sylvia Short, Frances Sternhagen, Olga Bielinska, Nancy Baker
The Sixth Son	Thayer David
The Fifth Son	Michael Higgins
Feng Nan	Sada Thompson

Merrymakers, Refugees, Soldiers, Helpers and Gong-Boys: Nancy Baker, Alvin Ailey, David Gold, Frances Sternhagen, Rachel Armour, Albert Corbin, Diana Barth, Sylvia Short, Olga Bielinska, Harry Lum, Allen Chin.

Staged and designed by Jack Landau; costumes designed by Alvin Colt, assisted by Stanley Simmons; incidental music by Aaron Avshalomov; percussion: Frank Weisberg; piano: Arthur Kopitz; oboe: Charles Kushkin; flute: Joseph Flavo; dance sequences supervised by Pat Burch; lighting by Klaus Holm; stage manager, Richard Blofson.

Drawn from Chinese legend and done in stylized form, the play tells—with the help of a narrator—of a highborn young couple whose families have been immemorial enemies. In time, husband and wife succeed in reconciling their two families not only to the marriage but to each other.

(Closed October 30, 1955)

WILL SUCCESS SPOIL ROCK HUNTER?

(265 performances)
(Continued)

Comedy in three acts by George Axelrod. Produced by Jule Styne, with Associate Producer Sylvia Herscher, at the Belasco Theatre, October 13, 1955.

Cast of characters—

Rita Marlowe .... Jayne Mansfield
Masseur .... Lew Gallo
George MacCauley .... Orson Bean
Michael Freeman .... Walter Matthau
Irving LaSalle .... Martin Gabel
Harry Kaye .... Harry Clark
A Secretary .... Carol Grace
Bronk Brannigan .... William Thourlby
Bellman .... David Sheiner
A Swimmer .... Tina Louise
A Chauffeur .... Michael Tolan

Act I.—Rita Marlowe's suite at the St. Regis Hotel in New York City; a day in March. Act II.—The Hollywood office of Rita Marlowe Productions; four weeks later Act III.—Scene 1—The Hollywood office; one year later. Scene 2—The terrace of Michael Freeman's bungalow at the Beverly Hills Hotel in Beverly Hills, California; the following morning.

Staged by George Axelrod; production designed by Oliver Smith; lighting by Peggy Clark; production stage manager, David Kanter; stage manager, Pat Chandler.

See "The Season on Broadway."

A ROOMFUL OF ROSES

(88 performances)

Play in two acts by Edith Sommer. Produced by Guthrie McClintic and Stanley Gilkey at the Playhouse, October 17, 1955.

Cast of characters—

Willamay .... Lulu B. King
Larry Fallon .... Darryl Richard
Nancy Fallon .... Patricia Neal
Grace Hewitt .... Alice Frost
Jane Hewitt .... Ann Whiteside
Dick Hewitt .... Warren Berlinger
Jay Fallon .... Russ Conway
Bridget MacGowan .... Betty Lou Keim
Carl MacGowan .... David White

The entire action of the play takes place in the living room of the home of Nancy and Jay Fallon in Midlothian, Illinois. Act I.—Scene 1—A warm, sunny morning in early September. Scene 2—Two weeks later; late afternoon. Act II.—Scene 1—A week later; evening, about 7:30 o'clock. Scene 2—The following day, about noon.

Staged by Guthrie McClintic; setting and lighting designed by Donald Oenslager, assisted by Klaus Holm; costumes supervised by Audre; production assistant, Gertrude H. Applebaum; stage manager, Charles Forsythe.

A fifteen-year-old girl comes, in an arrogant and resentful mood, to visit her mother, who years before ran away with another man. When the mother, the step-father and the neighborhood teen-agers can do nothing to thaw the girl out and win her over, it becomes clear that her relations with her father are equally twisted, that her whole life is askew, and that what she needs desperately is love. There is no lack of it at curtain fall.

(Closed December 31, 1955)

NO TIME FOR SERGEANTS

(258 performances)
(Continued)

Comedy in two acts by Ira Levin, adapted from the novel by Mac Hyman. Produced by Maurice Evans, in association with Emmett Rogers, at the Alvin Theatre, October 20, 1955.

Cast of characters—

Preacher . . . . Don Knotts
Will Stockdale . . . . Andy Griffith
Pa Stockdale . . . . Floyd Buckley
Draft Man . . . . O. Tolbert-Hewitt
Bus Driver . . . . Michael Thoma
Irvin Blanchard . . . . Robert Webber
Rosabelle . . . . Maree Dow
Inductees . . . . Cecil Rutherford, Robert McQuade, Carl Albertson, Arthur P. Keegan, Van Williams, Jules Racine, Wynn Pearce
Ben Whitledge . . . . Roddy McDowall
Sergeant King . . . . Myron McCormick
A Captain . . . . Ed Peck
A Nurse . . . . Maree Dow
Classification Corporal . . . . Ray Johnson
Corporal, Manual Dexterity . . . . Don Knotts
A Lieutenant . . . . Earle Hyman
A Psychiatrist . . . . James Millhollin
Cigarette Girl . . . . Maree Dow
An Infantryman . . . . Arthur P. Keegan
Air Force Policeman . . . . Jules Racine
A Colonel . . . . Rex Everhart
Lt. Bridges (Pilot) . . . . Hazen Gifford
Lt. Gardella (Co-Pilot) . . . . Carl Albertson
Lt. Kendall (Engineer) . . . . Cecil Rutherford
Lt. Cover (Navigator) . . . . Bill Hinnant
General Bush . . . . Howard Freeman
General Pollard . . . . Royal Beal
A Senator . . . . O. Tolbert-Hewitt
Aide to General Pollard . . . . Ray Johnson
Lt. Abel . . . . Rex Everhart
Lt. Baker . . . . Edmund Johnston
Capt. Charles . . . . Wynn Pearce

The action takes place in and above the United States of America. Some of it is happening now and some of it happened a while back.

Staged by Morton Da Costa; sets designed by Peter Larkin; costumes by Noel Taylor; lighting by Peggy Clark; production stage manager, Edward Padula; stage manager, Jules Racine.

See page 140.

THE DESK SET

(254 performances)
(Continued)

Comedy in three acts by William Marchant. Produced by Robert Fryer and Lawrence Carr at the Broadhurst Theatre, October 24, 1955.

Cast of characters—

Sadel Meyer .... Clarice Blackburn
Peg Costello .... Dorothy Blackburn
Ruthie Saylor .... Anne-Marie Gayer
Richard Sumner .... Byron Sanders
Bunny Watson .... Shirley Booth
Abe Cutler .... Frank Milan
The Man in Shirt-sleeves .... Harry Ellerbe
The Lady in the Blue Suit .... Mary Gildea
Kenny .... Louis Gossett
Mr. Bennett .... Frank Roberts
Elsa .... Joyce Van Patten
Miss Rumple .... Doris Roberts
Elsa's Friend .... Mike Steen
Miss Warriner .... Elizabeth Wilson
A Reporter .... Wayne Carson
Photographer .... Sterling Jensen

The action of the play proceeds in the Reference Department of a large radio and television broadcasting company in midtown Manhattan. Act I.—Early December, morning. Act II.—The day before Christmas, midday. Act III.—Four weeks later.

Staged by Joseph Fields; designed and lighted by George Jenkins, assisted by Hazel Arnett; production manager, Robert Linden; stage managers, Wayne Carson, Doris Roberts.

Though the women in a TV network's research department are walking information centers, their jobs are threatened by the electronic brain that has taken over elsewhere in the organization. There is great commotion in the research department, along with some in-and-out romance for the department's head. But in the end there is job security for all and a fine husband for the head lady.

COMÉDIE FRANÇAISE

Series of five classical comedies, presented in three programs ("Le Bourgeois Gentilhomme," October 25-November 7, 1955, 16 performances; "Le Barbier de Seville" and "Arlequin Poli par L'Amour," November 8-November 13, 1955, 8 performances; and "Le Jeu de L'Amour et du Hasard" and "Un Caprice," November 15-November 20, 1955, 8 performances). Produced by S. Hurok, by arrangement with the Government of the French Republic, at the Broadway Theatre, October 25, 1955.

Le Bourgeois Gentilhomme
(The Would-Be Gentleman)

Comedy-Ballet in Five Acts, in Prose, by Molière

Cast of characters—

Dorante, Count, lover of Dorimène .... Maurice Escande
Covielle, valet to Cléonte .... Jean Meyer
Monsieur Jourdain, bourgeois .... Louis Seigner
Dancing Instructor .... Jacques Charon

Music Instructor .... Robert Manuel
Philosophy Instructor .... Georges Chamarat
Cléonte, in love with Lucile .... Jean Piat
Apprentice Tailor .... Teddy Bilis
Master Tailor .... Jean-Louis Jemma
Fencing Master .... Michel Galabru
A Lackey .... Jacques Toja
A Lackey .... Arsène Drancourt
Nicole .... Béatrice Bretty
Mme. Jourdain .... Germaine Rouer
Lucile, daughter of M. Jourdain .... Micheline Boudet
Dorimène, Marquise .... Marie Sabouret

Singers: MM. Bisson, Gavin; Mlles. Gosselin, Lapointe.

Dancers: MM. Lapointe, Ouellet; Mlles. Zorgo, Pratt, Du Sablon, St. Jean, Kerner, Jettê.

Staged by Jean Meyer; decor and costumes by Mme. Suzanne Lalique; divertissement arranged by Mme. Léone Mail, of the Paris Opera; music by Lulli; orchestra directed by André Cadou.

Arlequin Poli par L'Amour
(Love Teaches Harlequin)

Comedy in one act by Marivaux

Cast of characters—

Harlequin, who has been abducted by The Fairy ..... Jacques Charon
Trivelin, The Fairy's Servant .... Jean Piat
The Shepherd, in love with Silvia .... Jean-Louis Jemma
Dancing Master .... Jacques Toja
Silvia, a shepherdess, Harlequin's beloved .... Micheline Boudet
The Fairy .... Marie Sabouret
The Singer .... M. Arsène Drancourt

Le Barbier de Seville

Comedy in four acts, in prose, by Beaumarchais

Cast of characters—

Bazile, music teacher of Rosine .... Jean Meyer
Bartholo, Doctor, guardian of Rosine .... Louis Seigner
La Jeuness, old servant of Bartholo .... Georges Chamarat
Figaro, Barber of Seville .... Jean Piat
L'Eveillé, second servant of Bartholo .... Teddy Bilis
A Notary .... Michel Galabru
Count Almaviva, in love with Rosine .... Jacques Toja
Rosine, young noble lady .... Micheline Boudet
An Officer of the Court .... M. Arsène Drancourt

Program staged by Gaston Baty and Jacques Charon; orchestra directed by André Cadou; for "Arlequin Poli par L'Amour": decor by Emile Bertin, incidental music by André Cadou; for "Le Barbier de Seville": decor by Mme. Suzanne Lalique, incidental music by Louis Beydts.

LE JEU DE L'AMOUR ET DU HASARD
(The Game of Love and Chance)

Comedy in three acts, in prose, by Marivaux

Cast of characters—

M. Orgon . . . . Maurice Escande
Pasquin . . . . Jacques Charon
Dorante . . . . Jean-Louis Jemma
Mario . . . . Jacques Toja
Silvia . . . . Mony Dalmes
Lisette . . . . Micheline Boudet
A Servant . . . . M. Arsène Drancourt

UN CAPRICE

Comedy in one act, in prose, by Alfred de Musset

Cast of characters—

M. de Chavigny . . . . Maurice Escande

Orchestra directed by André Cadou; costumes by Mme. Suzanne Lalique; "Le Jeu de L'Amour et du Hasard" staged by Maurice Escande; "Un Caprice" staged by M. Escande.

For entire series: guest conductor, Samuel Antek; stage manager, Charles Bellin.

(Closed November 20, 1955)

THE CHALK GARDEN

(182 performances)

Play in three acts by Enid Bagnold. Produced by Irene Mayer Selznick, assisted by Irving Schneider, at the Ethel Barrymore Theatre, October 26, 1955.

Cast of characters—

First Applicant (Miss Madrigal) . . . . Siobhan McKenna
Maitland . . . . Fritz Weaver
Second Applicant . . . . Georgia Harvey
Laurel . . . . Betsy von Furstenberg
Third Applicant . . . . Eva Leonard-Boyne
Mrs. St. Maugham . . . . Gladys Cooper
Nurse . . . . Marie Paxton
Olivia . . . . Marian Seldes
The Judge . . . . Percy Waram

The time is the present; the place, a room in a manor house, Sussex, England. Act I.—A day in June. Act II.—Two months later. Act III.—Twenty minutes later.

Staged by Albert Marre; scenery and costumes by Cecil Beaton; set supervised and lighted by Raymond Sovey; costumes supervised by Anna Hill Johnstone; production stage manager, Jose Vega; stage manager, Stuart Vaughan.

See page 163.

(Closed March 31, 1956)

DEADFALL

(20 performances)

Melodrama in two acts by Leonard Lee. Produced by Martin Goodman, in association with Julius M. Gordon, at the Holiday Theatre, October 27, 1955.

Cast of characters—

Harry Dietzler .... Clarence Derwent
Judge Romagna .... Harold Vermilyea
District Attorney McDonough .... Jay Jostyn
Clerk of the Court .... Leslie Barrett
Billie Devine .... Sheila Bond
Quentin Lockridge .... Paul Huber
Jane Lockridge .... Joanne Dru
Buck Carpenter .... John Ireland
Detective-Lieutenant Martinez .... Norman Rose
Edmund Hartley .... Mercer McLeod
Dr. Alexander Newman .... Theo Goetz
Dr. Paul Stone .... Sam Gray
Court Stenographer, Policemen, Court Spectators.

The time is the present. Act I.—Scene 1—A courtroom in the Superior Court of Los Angeles County, October 16th. Scene 2—Apartment 7, Villa Palms Apartments, West Los Angeles; afternoon of the previous June 5th. Scene 3—The same; evening, June 19th. Scene 4—The same; early evening, June 29th. Act II.—A courtroom in the Superior Court of Los Angeles County, October 17th to 20th inclusive.

Staged by Michael Gordon; production designed and lighted by Ralph Alswang; television newscaster, Kani Evans; stage manager, Howard Adelman.

A thriller in which, before the curtain rises, a woman's husband has been killed. When the man accused of the murder is acquitted, the woman—convinced of the man's guilt—vows vengeance. Assuming a new name and an on-the-town personality, she strikes up an acquaintance with the acquitted man and in due time frames him for the "murder" of her fictitious self.

(Closed November 12, 1955)

THE HEAVENLY TWINS

(35 performances)

Comedy in two acts, adapted from Albert Husson's French comedy "Les Pavés du Ciel." Produced by the Theatre Guild at the Booth Theatre, November 4, 1955.

Cast of characters—

Lucile Miremont .... Faye Emerson
Henri .... Jean Pierre Aumont
Police Inspector Mourel .... Earl Montgomery
The Old Man .... Marcel Hillaire
Marie .... Lucille Patton

Philippe Ploquin ....Drew Thompson
Nicole Belcourt ....Gaby Rodgers
Pierre Belcourt ....Jean Pierre Aumont

The action takes place in the Miremont apartment in Paris. Act I.—Scene 1—Spring; early evening. Scene 2—Afternoon; two months later. Act II.—Scene 1—Late afternoon; ten days later. Scene 2—The following morning.

Staged by Cyril Ritchard; setting and lighting by Eldon Elder, assisted by Pat Campbell; costumes designed by Helene Pons; standby for M. Aumont, George Keane.

A Parisian wife shoots her chronically unfaithful husband, only to find he has substituted blank cartridges for bullets. On a second try she shoots him dead, and after being acquitted, gets involved with his caddish charmer of an illegitimate son. The son's behavior drives her into becoming engaged to a dullard; his dullness drives her into shooting *him*. But all these theatrics turn out to be Just Suppose; and wife and husband are reconciled.

(Closed December 3, 1955)

A HATFUL OF RAIN

(234 performances)
(Continued)

Drama in three acts by Michael V. Gazzo. Produced by Jay Julien at the Lyceum Theatre, November 9, 1955.

Cast of characters—

John Pope, Sr. ....Frank Silvera
Johnny Pope ....Ben Gazzara
Celia Pope ....Shelley Winters
Mother ....Henry Silva
Apples ....Paul Richards
Chuch ....Harry Guardino
Polo Pope ....Anthony Franciosa
Putski ....Christine White
Man ....Steve Gravers

The action takes place in a remodeled apartment on New York's Lower East Side. Act I.—Scene 1—Early evening. Scene 2—Very late that night. Act II.—Scene 1—Early the next morning. Scene 2—A few hours later. Scene 3—Early the same evening. Act III.—Several hours later.

Staged by Frank Corsaro; production designed by Mordecai Gorelik; production stage manager, Len Bedsow; stage manager, Edward Julien.

See "The Season on Broadway."

THE VAMP

(60 performances)

Musical comedy in two acts, with book by John Latouche and Sam Locke; lyrics by John Latouche; music by James Mundy;

based on a story by Mr. Latouche. Produced by Oscar Lerman, Martin Cohen and Alexander Carson at the Winter Garden, November 10, 1955.

Cast of characters—

Myron H. Hubbard .... Jack Waldron
Bessie Bisco .... Bibi Osterwald
Muscle Man .... Steve Reeves
Barney Ostertag .... Paul Lipson
Oliver J. Oxheart .... David Atkinson
Ticket Girl .... Phyllis Dorne
Dick Hicks (ne Stanley Hubermyer) .... Robert Rippy
Stark Clayton .... Malcolm Lee Beggs
Elsie Chelsea .... Patricia Hammerlee
Bluestone .... Jack Harrold
Flora Weems .... Carol Channing
Uncle Garvey .... Will Geer
Aunt Hester .... Sandyl Cordell
Fire Commissioner .... Roger Franklin
Snake Charmer .... David Neuman
Samson .... Steve Reeves
Whip Man .... David Kashner
High Priest .... David Neuman
Charlie .... Matt Mattox
Second Cameraman .... Dick Eskeli
Tyrolean Couples .... Cathryn Damon, Hugh Lambert, Helen Silver, Ron Cecill

Dancers: Cathryn Damon, Mary Jane Doerr, Phyllis Dorne, Suan Hartman, Barbara Heath, Betty Koerber, Lucia Lambert, Barbara Leigh, Lila Popper, Helen Silver, Pat Wharton; Mark Aldon, Chad Block, Ron Cecill, Robert Daley, Pepe de Chazza, Burnell Dietsch, Rudy Del Campo, Hugh Lambert, Robert Norris, Dom Salinaro, Mike Stevens.

Singers: Charleen Clark, Joyce Gladmond, Bernice Massi, Donna Sanders, Kelley Stephens, Kay Turner; Dick Eskeli, Roger Franklin, Stokey Gray, William Krach, Vincent McMahon, Ralph Wayne.

Act I.—Scene 1—Hubbard's Coliseum, Fourteenth Street. Scene 2—A farm in the Bronx; the following morning. Scene 3—Hubbard's Movie House; a few weeks later. Scene 4—Grand Central Station; three months later. Scene 5—A rooftop studio in Manhattan; sometime later. Act II.—Scene 1—(1) The northeast corner of Hollywood and Vine; (2) OHO Film Company, one year later. Scene 2—Interior of OHO Studios. Scene 3—Flora's dressing room. Scene 4—Executive office, OHO Film Company; the next day. Scene 5—Hubbard's Movie Cathedral, Hollywood.

Staged by David Alexander; supervised by Robert Alton; choreography by Mr. Alton; sets and costumes designed by Raoul Pène duBois; musical direction and vocal arrangements by Milton Rosenstock; incidental music composed by Jack Pfeiffer; orchestrations by James Mundy; production manager, Neil Hartley; stage manager, Charles Millang.

Musical numbers—

ACT I

Scene 1

"The Spiel" .... Hubbard, Bessie, Patrons of the Coliseum
"The Flickers" .... Ticket Girl and Patrons

Scene 2

"Keep Your Nose to the Grindstone" .... Flora, Garvey and Hester
"That's Where a Man Fits In" .... Flora
"I've Always Loved You" .... Flora and Farm Folk

Scene 3

"You're Colossal" .... Elsie and Dick
"Fan Club Chant" .... Movie Fans

Scene 4

"Have You Met Delilah?" .... Oxheart
"Yeemy Yeemy" .... Flora, Oriental Entourage
"The Vamps" ... Matt Mattox, Barbara Heath, Cathryn Damon, Fans

Scene 5

"Delilah's Dilemma" .... Flora and Movie Fans

ACT II

Scene 1

"Four Little Misfits" .... Elsie, Bessie, Dick, Charlie

Scene 2

"Samson and Delilah" .... Flora as Delilah, Matt Mattox, Samson, Whipman, High Priest, Cathryn Damon, Movie Co.

"Why Does It Have To Be You?" .... Oxheart

"Ragtime Romeo" .... Bessie, Charlie and Boys

Scene 3

"I'm Everybody's Baby" .... Flora

Scene 4

Reprise: "I'm Everybody's Baby" .... Flora, Ostertag, Dick, Hubbard and Clayton

"The Impossible She" .... Oxheart and OHO Boys

Scene 5

Finale .... Company

(Closed December 31, 1955)

THE TERRIBLE SWIFT SWORD

(8 performances)

Play in three acts by Arthur Steuer. Roger L. Stevens' New Directors' Series, Production No. 1, produced by the Phoenix Theatre (T. Edward Hambleton and Norris Houghton) and Lyn Austin at the Phoenix Theatre, November 15, 1955.

Cast of characters—

Cantrell .... Conrad Janis
Rufus .... Bob Heller
Buckley .... John Fiedler
Scobey .... John Harkins
Wilcox .... Fred Beir
Davidson .... Richard Shepard
Hunter .... Arch Johnson

The action takes place in a student room and in the armory of Mason Military Academy, Huntington, Georgia, an R.O.T.C. prep school for boys. The time is the present.

Staged by Fred Sadoff; production supervisor, Edward Parone; stage manager, George Quick.

(Closed November 20, 1955)

THE LARK

(226 performances)
(Continued)

Play in two acts by Jean Anouilh, adapted by Lillian Hellman. Produced by Kermit Bloomgarden at the Longacre Theatre, November 17, 1955.

Cast of characters—

Warwick ....Christopher Plummer
Cauchon ....Boris Karloff
Joan ....Julie Harris
Her Father ....Ward Costello
Mother ....Lois Holmes
Brother ....John Reese
The Promoter ....Roger De Koven
The Inquisitor ....Joseph Wiseman
Brother Ladvenu ....Michael Higgins
Robert de Beaudricourt ....Theodore Bikel
Agnes Sorel ....Ann Hillary
The Young Queen ....Joan Elan
The Dauphin ....Paul Roebling
Queen Yolande ....Rita Vale
Monsieur de la Tremouille ....Bruce Gordon
Archbishop of Rheims ....Richard Nicholls
Captain La Hire ....Bruce Gordon
Executioner ....Ralph Roberts
English Soldier ....Edward Knight
Scribe ....Joe Bernard

Ladies of the court: Ruth Maynard, Elizabeth Lawrence.

Monks and soldiers: Michael Price, Joe Bernard, Michael Conrad, William Lennard, Milton Katselas, Edgar Grower.

Choral singers: Russell Oberlin (countertenor), Pauline Seim, Betty Wilson, Jean Hakes, Charles Bressler, Arthur Burrows, Brayton Lewis; by arrangement with The New York Pro Musica Antiqua.

Act I.—The Trial. Act II.—The Trial.

Staged by Joseph Anthony; scenery and lighting by Jo Mielziner, assisted by John Harvey; costumes by Alvin Colt, assisted by Frank Spencer; music composed by Leonard Bernstein; production stage manager, Bill Ross; stage manager, Perry Bruskin.

See page 189.

JANUS

(217 performances)
(Continued)

Romantic comedy in three acts by Carolyn Green. Produced by Alfred de Liagre, Jr., at the Plymouth Theatre, November 24, 1955.

Cast of characters—

Jessica ....Margaret Sullavan
Denny ....Claude Dauphin
Miss Addy ....Mary Finney
Gil ....Robert Preston
Mr. Harper ....Robert Emhardt

The action takes place in the living room of a second-floor apartment in a brownstone house off Washington Square in New York City. It is July of last summer. Act I.—Scene 1—Late afternoon. Scene 2—Later that afternoon. Act II.—The following morning. Act III.—Early the next morning.

Staged by Reginald Denham; setting and lighting by Donald Oenslager, assisted by Klaus Holm; production stage manager, William Chambers; stage manager, Arthur Marlowe.

See "The Season on Broadway."

PIPE DREAM

(211 performances)
(Continued)

Musical in two acts, with music by Richard Rodgers; book and lyrics by Oscar Hammerstein 2nd, based on John Steinbeck's novel "Sweet Thursday." Produced by Rodgers & Hammerstein at the Sam S. Shubert Theatre, November 30, 1955.

Cast of characters—

Doc .... William Johnson
Hazel .... Mike Kellin
Millicent Henderson .... Jayne Heller
Mac .... G. D. Wallace
Suzy .... Judy Tyler
Fauna .... Helen Traubel
Jim Blaikey .... Rufus Smith
Ray Busch .... John Call
George Herman .... Guy Raymond
Bill .... Steve Roland
Red .... Keith Kaldenberg
Whitey .... Hobe Streiford
Dizzy .... Nicolas Orloff
Eddie .... Warren Kemmerling
Alec .... Warren Brown
Joe (The Mexican) .... Kenneth Harvey
Pancho (A Wetback) .... Ruby Braff
Agnes .... Temple Texas
Mable .... Jackie McElroy
Emma .... Marilyn Bradley
Beulah .... Mildred Slavin
Marjorie .... Louise Troy
Cho Cho Sen .... Pat Creighton
Sumi .... Sandra Devlin
Sonny Boy .... Joseph Leon
Esteban (A Wetback) .... Jerry LaZarre
A Waiter .... Kazimir Kokich
Harriet .... Patricia Wilson
Hilda .... Ruth Kobart
Fred .... Marvin Krauter
Slick .... Gene Kevin
Slim .... Don Weissmuller
Basha .... Sigyn
Bubbles .... Marsha Reynolds
Sonya .... Annabelle Gold
Kitty .... Jenny Workman
Weirde .... Patti Karkalits
Johnny Carriagra .... Scotty Engel
Pedro .... Rudolfo Cornejo
Dr. Ormondy .... Calvin Thomas

The action takes place in Cannery Row, Monterey County, California. The time is the present. Act I.—Scene 1—The Western Biological Laboratory. Scene 2—Cannery Row, a few weeks later. Scene 3—The Palace Flophouse, immediately following. Scene 4—Cannery Row, a few days later, on a Sweet Thursday. Scene 5—The Western Biological Laboratory. Scene 6—Cannery Row. Scene 7—A room in the Bear Flag Cafe. Scene 8—Cannery Row. Scene 9—Sonny Boy's Pier Restaurant. Act II.—Scene 1—A room in the Bear Flag Cafe, the following morning. Scene 2—Cannery Row. Scene 3—The Palace Flophouse, the following night. Scene 4—Cannery Row, next day. Scene 5—The Bear Flag Cafe, a few weeks later. Scene 6—Cannery Row, next evening. Scene 7—Inside "The Pipe." Scene 8—Cannery Row, next morning. Scene 9—The Western Biological Laboratory.

Staged by Harold Clurman; scenery and lighting by Jo Mielziner; costumes by Alvin Colt; orchestrations by Robert Russell Bennett; musical director, Salvatore Dell'Isola; dances and musical numbers staged by Boris Runanin; dance arrangements by John Morris; general stage manager, Charles Atkin; stage manager, Ruth Mitchell.

Musical numbers—

ACT I

"All Kinds of People" .... Doc and Hazel
"The Tide Pool" .... Doc, Hazel and Mac, to Suzy
"Everybody's Got a Home But Me" .... Suzy
Reprise: "All Kinds of People" .... Jim
"A Lopsided Bus" .... Mac, Hazel, Kitty, Sonya and the Flophouse Gang
"Bums' Opera" .... Fauna, Joe, Pancho and the Flophouse Gang
"The Man I Used To Be" .... Doc (Danced by Don Weissmuller)
"Sweet Thursday" .... Fauna
"Suzy Is a Good Thing" .... Fauna and Suzy
"All At Once You Love Her" .... Doc, Suzy and Esteban

ACT II

"The Happiest House on the Block" .... Fauna and Girls
"The Party That We're Gonna Have Tomorrow Night" .... Mac and the People of Cannery Row
"Masquerade Brawl at the Flophouse"
(a) "The Party Gets Going"
(b) "I Am a Witch" ... Fauna, Agnes, Marjorie, Beulah and Mable
(c) "Will You Marry Me?" .... Suzy, Fauna and Doc
"Thinkin'" .... Hazel
Reprise: "All At Once You Love Her" .... Fauna
"How Long?" ..... Fauna, Doc, Flophouse Boys and Bear Flag Girls
"The Next Time It Happens" .... Suzy and Doc
Reprise: "Sweet Thursday," Finale .... Entire Company

THE MATCHMAKER

(205 performances)
(Continued)

Comedy in two acts by Thornton Wilder. Produced by the Theatre Guild and David Merrick at the Royale Theatre, December 5, 1955.

Cast of characters—

Horace Vandergelder, a Merchant of Yonkers .... Loring Smith
Ambrose Kamper, Artist .... Alexander Davion
Joe Scanlon, a Barber .... Philip Leeds
Gertrude, Vandergelder's Housekeeper .... Charity Grace
Cornelius Hackl, Clerk in Vandergelder's Store .... Arthur Hill
Ermengarde, Vandergelder's Niece .... Prunella Scales
Malachi Stack .... Patrick McAlinney
Mrs. Levi, a Friend of Vandergelder's Late Wife .... Ruth Gordon
Barnaby Tucker, Apprentice in Vandergelder's Store ... Robert Morse
Mrs. Molloy, a Milliner .... Eileen Herlie
Minnie Fay, Her Assistant .... Rosamund Greenwood
A Cabman .... Peter Bayliss
Rudolf } Waiters .... { William Lanteau
August } .... { John Milligan
A Musician .... Philip Leeds
Miss Flora Van Huysen, a Friend of Vandergelder's Late Wife .... Esme Church
Her Cook .... Christine Thomas

The action takes place in Yonkers and New York City; the time the early 'Eighties. Act I.—Scene 1—A room in Vandergelder's house, above his store in Yonkers. Scene 2—Mrs. Molloy's hat store in New York City. Act II.—Scene 1—The Harmonia Gardens Restaurant at the Battery. Scene 2—Miss Flora Van Huysen's house.

Staged by Tyrone Guthrie; settings and costumes by Tanya Moiseiwitsch; production under the supervision of David Merrick; production stage manager, Samuel Liff; stage manager, Rex Partington.

See page 214.

SIX CHARACTERS IN SEARCH OF AN AUTHOR

(65 performances)

Drama by Luigi Pirandello, in a new adaptation by Tyrone Guthrie and Michael Wager, based on Frank Tauritz' translation from the Italian. Produced by the Phoenix Theatre (T. Edward Hambleton and Norris Houghton), in association with Clinton Wilder, at the Phoenix Theatre, December 11, 1955.

Cast of characters—

The Father .... Whitfield Connor
The Mother .... Katharine Squire
The Stepdaughter .... Betty Lou Holland
The Son .... Michael Wager
The Boy .... James Lacirignola
The Girl .... Karen Sue Trent
Madame Pace .... Maud Scheerer
The Director .... Kurt Kasznar
Leading Lady .... Natalie Schafer
Leading Man .... Francis Bethencourt
Second Woman .... Shirley Grayson
Second Man .... William Cottrell
Character Actress .... Aileen Poe
Juvenile .... William Whitman
Ingenue .... Hale Gabrielson
Character Juvenile .... John Glennon
Stage Manager .... Fred Warriner
Wardrobe Mistress .... Mildred Chandler
Stagehand .... Russell Morrison
Supporting Cast ..... Dario Barri, Marilyn Stevens, Mervin Williams

The entire action takes place in this theatre in the spring of 1922.

Staged by Tyrone Guthrie, assisted by Robert Wunsch; scenery designed by Klaus Holm; costumes designed by Alvin Colt, assisted by Stanley Simmons; production stage manager, Robert Woods; assistant stage manager, Stark Hesseltine.

(Closed February 5, 1956)

THE RIGHTEOUS ARE BOLD

(68 performances)

Play in three acts by Frank Carney. Produced by Eddie Dowling at the Holiday Theatre, December 22, 1955.

Cast of characters—

Michael Martin Geraty . . . . . Len Doyle
Mary Kate Geraty . . . . . Nora O'Mahony
Willie the Post . . . . . P. J. Kelly
Anthony Costello . . . . . Liam Gannon
Patrick Geraty . . . . . James Neylin
Nora Geraty . . . . . Irene Hayes
Doctor Moran . . . . . Bryan Herbert
Father O'Malley . . . . . Denis O'Dea
Mother Benedict . . . . . Frederica Going
Sister Mary of the Rosary . . . . . Mary O'Brady

The scene is the kitchen of a poor farmhouse built into the rocks on the western ridge of Croagh Patrick, in the county of Mayo, in Ireland. The time is 1945. Act I.—Evening. Act II.—About two hours later. Act III.—Early morning, a week later.

Staged by Eddie Dowling, assisted by Elizabeth Kerr; setting by Watson Barratt; lighting by Peggy Clark; costumes supervised by Audre; stage manager, Charles Durand.

Laid in a wild part of Ireland, the play concerns the daughter of a poor family who has been living in England. She comes home to County Mayo hysterical and upset—shrieks in Latin, blasphemes in English, enragedly smashes a statue of the Virgin. The local doctor, discovering she has been a spiritualist's medium, pins his hopes on medical therapy; but the local priest declares the girl possessed of a devil which must be exorcised. It finally is; but the priest saves the girl's life at the cost of his own.

(Closed February 18, 1956)

RED ROSES FOR ME

(29 performances)

Drama in four acts by Sean O'Casey, with music by Edwin Finckel. Produced by Gordon W. Pollock at the Booth Theatre, December 28, 1955.

Cast of characters—

Mrs. Breydon . . . . . Eileen Crowe
Ayamonn Breydon . . . . . Kevin McCarthy
Eeada . . . . . Ann Dere
Dympna . . . . . Katherine Hynes
Finoola . . . . . Virginia Bosler
First Neighbor . . . . . Farrell Pelly
Second Neighbor . . . . . Page Johnson
Third Neighbor . . . . . Vincent Dowling
Sheila Moorneen . . . . . Joyce Sullivan
Brennan o' the Moor . . . . . E. G. Marshall
Sammy . . . . . David McDaniel
Roory O'Balacaun . . . . . Eamon Flynn
Mulcanny . . . . . Casey Walters
Rev. E. Clinton . . . . . Michael Clarke Laurence
First Railwayman . . . . . James C. Kelly
Second Railwayman . . . . . Lou Frizzell
Inspector Finglas . . . . . Shamus Locke
Third Railwayman . . . . . David McDaniel
Lounger . . . . . Paul Sanasardo

Another Lounger .... Jeff Duncan
Old Woman .... Beatrice Seckler
Idle Woman .... Judith Coy
Lonely Man .... David Gold
Girl .... Sandra Pine
Another Girl .... Eve Beck
Drifter .... Jack Moore
Samuel .... Whitford Kane
Foster .... Barry Macollum
Dowzard .... Jock McGraw
Lamplighter .... David Ryan

The time: A little while ago. Act I.—Two-roomed home of the Breydons. Act II.—The same. Act III.—A Dublin street, beside a bridge over the river Liffey. Act IV.—Part of the grounds round the Protestant Church of St. Burnupus. In this act the curtain is lowered for a few minutes to denote the passing of a few hours.

Staged by John O'Shaughnessy; choreography by Anna Sokolow; scenery and lighting by Howard Bay; costumes by Ballou; general stage manager, William Weaver; stage manager, Arthur Barkow.

See "The Season on Broadway."

(Closed January 21, 1956)

THE GREAT SEBASTIANS

(171 performances)
(Continued)

Melodramatic comedy in three acts by Howard Lindsay and Russel Crouse. Produced by the authors at the ANTA Theatre, January 4, 1956.

Cast of characters—

Essie Sebastian .... Lynn Fontanne
Rudi Sebastian .... Alfred Lunt
Manya .... Susan Frank
First Security Policeman .... Burns Oliver
Second Security Policeman .... Martin Brandt
Josef .... Arny Freeman
Sergeant Javorsky .... Simon Oakland
General Otokar Zandek .... Ben Astar
First Soldier .... Peter Gumeny
Second Soldier .... Michael Egan
Colonel Bradacova .... Anne Francine
Vlasta Habova .... Peg Murray
Sophie Cerny .... Eugenia Rawls
Third Soldier .... Sheppard Kerman
Karel Cerny .... Jose Ruben
Novotny .... Grant Gordon
Pavlat .... Ben Hammer
Dr. Balzar .... Edward Moor
Marie Balzar .... Doris Fesette
Bacilek .... Joseph Holland
Corporal .... Ted Gunther

The entire action is laid in Prague, Czechoslovakia. The time is winter of 1948. Act I.—Scene 1—The stage of the Theatre Variete. (The scene starts just as the Great Sebastians have concluded their mind-reading act.) Scene 2—A combination sitting room and dressing room of the Theatre Variete. (The scene starts a few minutes before the end of Scene 1.) Act II.—The living room of General Zandek's home; the same night. Act III.—The same as Act II, one hour later.

Staged by Bretaigne Windust, assisted by James Adams; settings by Raymond Sovey, assisted by Ruth Morley; lighting by Jean Rosenthal; Miss Fontanne's dresses by Main Bocher; production stage manager, David Gray, Jr.; stage manager, Peter Gumeny.

A pair of ham vaudevillians with a wobbly mind-reading act find themselves in a very wobbly position performing in Prague the day Jan Masaryk dies. Invited to a Communist party and ordered to read the guests' minds, the vaudevillians get snarled up in political intrigue but save themselves by curtain-time.

KING LEAR

(21 performances)

Tragedy by William Shakespeare. Produced by the New York City Center Theatre Company (Jean Dalrymple, Director), by arrangement with Martin Gabel and Henry M. Margolis, at the New York City Center of Music and Drama, January 12, 1956.

Cast of characters—

Lear, King of Britain	Orson Welles
King of France	Robert Blackburn
Duke of Burgundy	Walter Mathews
Duke of Albany	Sorrell Booke
Duke of Cornwall	Thayer David
Earl of Kent	Roy Dean
Earl of Gloucester	Lester Rawlins
Edgar, Son to Gloucester	Robert Fletcher
Edmund, Bastard Son to Gloucester	John Colicos
Lear's Fool	Alvin Epstein
Curan	Tom Clancy
Oswald, Steward to Goneril	Francis Carpenter
Old Man, Tenant to Gloucester	Jack Aronson
Servant to Cornwall	Robert Burr
Doctor	Walter Mathews
Captain to Edmund	Robert Burr
Gentleman to King Lear	Jack Aronson
Goneril	Geraldine Fitzgerald
Regan	Sylvia Short
Cordelia	Viveca Lindfors

Knights of Lear's Train, Officers, Attendants: Art Alisi, David Anthony, Julian Barry, Richard Edelman, Richard Hill, Thomas Newman, Kenneth Mays, Lou Perri, James T. Pritchett, Don Ratka, Robert Weaver, Michael Yuda.

Staged by Orson Welles; associate director, Emerson Crocker; costumes by Robert Fletcher (executed by Frank Thompson); stage settings by Theodore Cooper; tape recorder sound score: Otto Luening and Vladimir Ussachevsky; musical score by Marc Blitzstein; musicians: harpsichord and leader, Mr. Blitzstein; flute and clarinet, Harvey Estrin; trumpet, David Jandorf; French horn, Martin Noliboff; timpani and percussion, Frank Weisberg; production stage manager, Herman Shapiro; stage managers, John Maxtone-Graham and Spofford Beadle.

(Closed January 29, 1956)

FALLEN ANGELS

(156 performances)
(Continued)

Comedy in three acts by Noel Coward. Revived by Charles Bowden and Richard Barr, in association with H. Ridgely Bullock, Jr., at the Playhouse, January 17, 1956.

Cast of characters—

Julia Starbuck .... Nancy Walker
Frederick Starbuck .... William Windom
Jasmine Saunders .... Alice Pearce
William Danbury .... William LeMassena
Jane Danbury .... Margaret Phillips
Maurice Duclos .... Efram Zimbalist, Jr.

The action takes place in the sunroom of the Starbucks' New York apartment in the spring of 1930, a quarter of a century ago! Act I.—Saturday morning. Act II.—That evening. Act III.—The next morning.

Staged by Charles Bowden; setting and lighting by Eldon Elder; costumes designed by Patton Campbell; hats by Mr. John; stage manager, Edmund Baylies.

Fallen Angels was first produced by The Actors' Theatre, Inc., at the 49th Street Theatre, December 1, 1927, for 36 performances.

TAMBURLAINE THE GREAT

(20 performances)

Melodrama in two parts by Christopher Marlowe, adapted by Tyrone Guthrie and Donald Wolfit. Produced by the Producers Theatre (Roger L. Stevens, Robert Whitehead and Robert W. Dowling), in association with the Stratford Festival Foundation of Canada, at the Winter Garden, January 19, 1956.

Cast of characters—

Prologue .... David Gardner
Mycetes, King of Persia .... Eric House
Cosroe, His Brother .... Tony Van Bridge
Meander, a Persian Lord .... Robert Goodier
Theridamas, a Persian Lord .... Robert Christie
Menaphon, a Persian Lord .... Ted Follows
Ortygius, a Persian Lord .... Edward K. Holmes
Tamburlaine .... Anthony Quayle
Zenocrate, Daughter of the Soldan of Egypt ...... Barbara Chilcott
Agydas, a Median Lord .... Donald Davis
Techelles, a Follower of Tamburlaine .... William Hutt
Usumcasane, Another Follower .... William Shatner
Scythian Soldier .... Peter Wylde
A Persian Spy .... Peter Perehinczuk
A Persian Messenger .... Neil Vipond
A Scythian Messenger .... Julian Flett
Anippe, Maid to Zenocrate .... Deborah Cass
A Basso .... Bruce Swerdfager
Bajazeth, Emperor of the Turks .... Douglas Rain

King of Fez .... John Hayes
King of Morocco .... Harry McGirt
King of Argier .... Edward K. Holmes
Zabina, Wife of Bajazeth .... Coral Browne
Ebea, Her Maid .... Margaret Braidwood
Soldan of Egypt .... Lloyd Bochner
Capolin, an Egyptian Captain .... Eric House
First Egyptian Messenger .... Richard Howard
Second Egyptian Messenger .... David Gardner
King of Arabia .... Roland Bull
Governor of Memphis .... Eric House
First Citizen .... James Manser
Second Citizen .... William Cole
Virgins of Memphis .... Myrna Aaron, Jacqueline Cecil, Colleen Dewhurst, Margot Hartman, Barbara Kay, Fay Tracey
Philemus, a Messenger .... Alan Wilkinson
Celebinus, Son of Tamburlaine .... Ted Follows
Amyras, Another Son .... Louis Negin
Calyphas, Another Son .... Neil Vipond
Callapine, Son of Bajazeth .... Lloyd Bochner
Almeda, His Keeper .... Douglas Rain
First Physician .... Bruce Swerdfager
Second Physician .... Eric House
Orcanes, King of Natolia .... David Gardner
King of Jerusalem .... Roland Bull
King of Trebizond .... Edward K. Holmes
King of Soria .... Tony Van Bridge
A Messenger .... Peter Perehinczuk
Perdicas, Servant to Calyphas .... Bruce Swerdfager
Governor of Babylon .... Robert Goodier
Maximus .... Douglas Rain
First Citizen .... Peter Perehinczuk
Second Citizen .... John Hayes
Turkish Concubines .... Colleen Dewhurst, Jacqueline Cecil, Myrna Aaron, Fay Tracey, Margot Hartman, Barbara Kay
King of Amasia .... Donald Davis
Egyptian Captain .... William Cole

Scythians, Persians, Egyptians: Thor Arngrin, Kenneth Ayers, Guy Belanger, George Blackwell, Roland Bull, John Carter, William Cole, Julian Flett, Ted Follows, David Gardner, Jay Gerber, John Hayes, Peter Henderson, Gordon Hilstad, Richard Howard, Barney Johnston, James Manser, Arne Markussen, Harry McGirt, Alex de Naszody, William Nuss, Louis Negin, Peter Perehinczuk, Adam Petroski, Orest Ulan, Gordon Shearer, Murray Vines, Neil Vipond, Alan Wilkinson, Norman Wigutow, Beverley Wilson, Peter Wylde, Allan Zielonka.

Staged by Tyrone Guthrie; scenery and costumes by Leslie Hurry; music by John Gardner; lighting and scenic supervision by Paul Morrison; musical director, Louis Applebaum; stage manager for the Stratford Festival Foundation, Jack Merigold; production stage manager for the Tamburlaine Company, Sy Milbert.

(Closed February 4, 1956)

TIME LIMIT!

(127 performances)

Play in three acts by Henry Denker and Ralph Berkey. Produced by the Theatre Guild at the Booth Theatre, January 24, 1956.

Cast of characters—

T/Sgt. Charles Baker .... Frank Aletter
WAC Corporal Jean Evans .... Allyn McLerie

2nd Lt. George Miller ....Thomas Carlin
Lt. Col. William F. Edwards ....Arthur Kennedy
Sentry ....Ch'ao-li
1st Lt. Mike Livingston ....Arthur Storch
Capt. Gus Jablonski ....Alfred Sander
1st Lt. Steve Wardell ....Lionel Ames
1st Lt. Peter "Zip" Walden ....Mark Weston
2nd Lt. "Boxer" Mueller ....Robert Drew
2nd Lt. Phil Garland ....Jerry Morris
Col. Kim ....Kaie Deei
Major Harry Cargill ....Richard Kiley
Maj. General Joseph Connors ....Harvey Stephens
Mrs. Mary Cargill ....Patricia Benoit
Capt. Joseph Connors, Jr. ....John Connell

The action takes place in the Judge Advocate's Office of an Army Post in the United States in August, 1955, and a Korean Prisoner of War camp in December, 1951. Act I.—Tuesday, 4:15 P.M. Act II.—Wednesday, 8:00 A.M. Act III.—Immediately following.

Staged by Windsor Lewis; production designed and lighted by Ralph Alswang; costumes by Noel Taylor; stage manager, Karl Nielsen.

See "The Season on Broadway."

(Closed May 12, 1956)

THE HOT CORNER

(5 performances)

Farce-comedy in three acts by Allen Boretz and Ruby Sully. Produced by Eleanore Saidenberg at the John Golden Theatre, January 25, 1956.

Cast of characters—

Bobbie Stanley ....Daryl Grimes
George "Muldoon" Wilson ....Cliff Tatum
Mae Stanley ....Vicki Cummings
Fred Stanley ....Sam Levene
J. Rupert Wilson ....Eric Brotherson
Charley O'Connor ....Harry Holcombe
Clarence "Lefty" McShane ....Don Murray
Jane Kaiser ....Camila Ashland
Maude Wilson ....Dortha Duckworth
Frances Halliday ....Nan McFarland
August Hegel ....Horace Cooper
Gus Markheim ....Dave Starr
Eddie Genaro ....Bern Hoffman
Felix Cassidy ....Ned Glass

The action takes place during the period of two days in the living room of the Stanley home, situated in a medium-sized city in New York State. Act I.—Scene 1—September, six in the evening. Scene 2—Several hours later, night. Act II.—Noon the next day. Act III.—A few minutes later.

Staged by Sam Levene, assisted by Oliver Crawford; scenery and lighting by Ralph Alswang; costumes by Virginia Volland; stage manager, Leonard Auerbach.

A farce about a hot-tempered baseball manager trying to effect a comeback from the minors to the majors. His one chance rests on packaging himself with his star pitcher; but just as Detroit is set to sign them both, the pitcher refuses to cross a peanut-vendors' picket line. Thereafter fists fly, loudspeakers blare and bottled goods abound—in advance of a happy ending.

(Closed January 28, 1956)

MARCEL MARCEAU

(15 performances)

A program of pantomime with Marcel Marceau, assisted by Pierre Verry and Paul Sanchez. Presented by the New York City Center Theatre Company, as a return engagement, at the New York City Center of Music and Drama, February 1, 1956. (See page 342 for program.)

(Closed February 12, 1956)

THE INNKEEPERS

(4 performances)

Play in three acts by Theodore Apstein. Produced by Gordon W. Pollock, in association with Richard Cook and Peter Flournoy, at the John Golden Theatre, February 2, 1956.

Cast of characters—

Esperanza	Miriam Colon
Santiago	Ernesto Gonzales
Amy McGregor	Geraldine Page
David McGregor	Darren McGavin
Georg Mainzer	Boris Tumarin
Rose Haddock	Jean Barker
Jim Haddock	Truman Smith
The Butter and Cheese Woman	Carmen Zapata
Lupe	Sandra Zapata
Refugio	Anita de Soto
Howard	Joe Maross

The entire action takes place in the Paradise Inn in Oaxaca, Mexico. Act I.—A morning in late September. Act II.—That evening. Act III.—The following morning.

Staged by José Quintero; production associate, Theodore Mann; setting and lighting by David Hays; costumes by Guy Kent; stage manager, Elliott Martin.

A U.S. government expert has been dropped as a security risk because at college his wife was for a brief time a Communist. The couple have opened an inn in Mexico, but feel uprooted and homesick. Offered a job in the U.S. that requires anonymity, the touchy husband indignantly refuses it. But neither has he the courage to fight back; and he slowly goes to pieces from his resentments, to be left, at the end, asprawl with self-pity.

(Closed February 4, 1956)

MIDDLE OF THE NIGHT

(130 performances)
(Continued)

A "love story" in two acts by Paddy Chayefsky. Produced by Joshua Logan at the ANTA Theatre, February 8, 1956.

Cast of characters—

The Girl .... Gena Rowlands
The Mother .... June Walker
The Kid Sister .... Joan Chambers
The Manufacturer .... Edward G. Robinson
The Sister .... Nancy R. Pollock
The Widow .... Betty Walker
The Daughter .... Anne Jackson
The Neighbor .... Effie Afton
The Friend .... Janet Ward
The Husband .... Lee Philips
The Son-in-Law .... Martin Balsam

The action takes place in the West Eighties, New York City, between November and February of the present year.

Staged by Joshua Logan, assisted by Joseph Curtis; settings and lighting by Jo Mielziner, assisted by John Harvey; costumes by Motley; incidental music by Lehman Engel; production stage manager, Neil Hartley; stage manager, David Ford.

See "The Season on Broadway."

SOMEONE WAITING

(15 performances)

Play in three acts by Emlyn Williams. Produced by Eddie Rich, in association with Clifford Hayman, at the John Golden Theatre, February 14, 1956.

Cast of characters—

John Nedlow .... Howard St. John
Miss Lennie .... Ludie Claire
Martin .... Robert Hardy
Vera Nedlow .... Jessie Royce Landis
Hilda .... Brook Byron
Fenn .... Leo G. Carroll
Mrs. Danecourt .... Norah Howard
A Neighbor .... Herbert Voland
His Wife .... Louise Buckley

The action takes place in the drawing room of the Nedlows' apartment, Mill Court, London. The time is the present. Act I.—Scene 1—An early evening in May. Scene 2—Three hours later, night.

Act II.—Scene 1—Four months later; an early evening in September. Scene 2—Four hours later. Act III.—Immediately afterwards.

Staged by Allan Davis; setting and lighting by Ben Edwards; costumes designed by Gene Coffin; production stage manager, Joseph Olney; assistant stage manager, Roger Hamilton.

A young Englishman has been hanged for the murder of a Swedish girl. Convinced that someone else is guilty, the dead youth's father goes to work (under an assumed name) in the household where the murder took place. He quickly spots the head of the house as the murderer and works out a proper and elaborate revenge. One thing after another, however, ruins his revenge plan—until, as a sure way of convicting the villain, the father contrives to be murdered himself.

(Closed February 25, 1956)

A STREETCAR NAMED DESIRE

(15 performances)

Drama in two acts by Tennessee Williams. Revived by the New York City Center Theatre Company (Jean Dalrymple, Director) at the New York City Center of Music and Drama, February 15, 1956.

Cast of characters—

Negro Woman .... Vinnette Carroll
Eunice Hubbell .... Jean Ellyn
Stella Kowalski .... Frances Heflin
Stanley Kowalski .... Gerald O'Loughlin
Mitch .... Rudy Bond
Steve Hubbell .... Bruno Damon
Sailor .... David Anthony
Blanche DuBois .... Tallulah Bankhead
Pablo Gonzales .... Lou Gilbert
A Young Collector .... Sandy Campbell
Mexican Woman .... Edna Thomas
A Strange Woman .... Dorritt Kelton
A Strange Man .... Bert Bertram

The scene is the two rooms of the Kowalski apartment in the French Quarter of New Orleans. The action of the play takes place in the spring, summer and early fall. Act I.—Scene 1—Spring, early May; early evening. Scene 2—Following evening 6:00 P.M. Scene 3—Later that night. Scene 4—Early the following morning. Act II.—Scene 1—Some weeks later. Scene 2—Later, about 2:00 A.M. Scene 3—Some weeks later. Scene 4—Three-quarters of an hour later. Scene 5—A while later that evening. Scene 6—A few hours later the same night. Scene 7—Some days later.

Staged by Herbert Machiz; scenery and lighting executed by Watson Barratt, based on original designs by Jo Mielziner; production designed by Watson Barratt; production manager, Herman Shapiro; stage manager, John Maxtone-Graham.

A Streetcar Named Desire was first produced by Irene M. Selznick at the Barrymore Theatre, December 3, 1947, for 855 performances.

(Closed February 26, 1956)

THE PONDER HEART

(121 performances)
(Continued)

Comedy in two acts by Joseph Fields and Jerome Chodorov, adapted from the story by Eudora Welty. Produced by the Playwrights' Company at the Music Box, February 16, 1956.

Cast of characters—

Jacob	Theodore Browne
Sarah	Vinie Burrows
Mr. Springer	David Leland
Edna Earle Ponder	Una Merkel
De Yancey Clanahan	Don Hanmer
Big John	John Marriott
Narciss	Juanita Hall
Purdel Peacock	Edwin Buckley
Bruce Peacock	Richard Klein
Treva Peacock	Helen Quarrier
Johnnie Ree Peacock	Jeanne Shelley
Mr. Peacock	Harold Grau
Mrs. Peacock	Charlotte Klein
Eloise	Barbara Jean Gilliam
Uncle Daniel Ponder	David Wayne
Dorris R. Gladney	Will Geer
Bonnie Dee Ponder	Sarah Marshall
Sam	Noel Williams
Rodney	Johnny Klein
Willie	Junior Marshall
Teacake Magee	Ruth White
Judge Waite	John McGovern
Dr. Eubanks	Donald Foster
Truex Bodkin	Dwight Marfield
Mrs. Bodkin	Mary Farrell
Al	J. Talbot Holland
Clyde	William Dwyer
Clerk	James Karr
Bailiff	Tony Kraber
Foreman	Alan Manson
Jurors and Spectators	Daniel Bergin, Joseph Bishop, Tom Geraghty, Jim Holden, Richard Rothrock, Lieselotte Singer

The action occurs in and around a small town in the South, a few years ago. Act I.—The Beulah Hotel. Act II.—The Ponder Hill House. Act III.—The Courthouse.

Staged by Robert Douglas; settings and lighting by Ben Edwards, assisted by Richard Burns; costumes by Frank Spencer, assisted by Florence Klotz; musical advisor, Lehman Engel; lighting supervisor, Klaus Holm; production stage manager, Philip Mathias; stage manager, Tony Kraber.

See page 238.

MISS JULIE
and
THE STRONGER

(33 performances)

Program of short plays by August Strindberg, freely adapted by George Tabori. Revived by the Phoenix Theatre (T. Edward Hambleton and Norris Houghton), at the Phoenix Theatre, February 21, 1956.

Miss Julie

Cast of characters—

Miss Julie .... Viveca Lindfors
Jean, the Valet .... James Daly
Kristin, the Cook .... Ruth Ford
Fiddlers, Farmhands, Servants .... Laurinda Barrett, Jamie Smith, Beverly Bruce, Brett Viken, Walter Carlin, Alice Rolph

The action is set in the kitchen and courtyard of a country house in Sweden one Midsummer Night in the eighties.

The Stronger

Cast of characters—

Miss Y, an Actress .... Viveca Lindfors
Mrs. X, an Actress .... Ruth Ford
A Waiter .... Jamie Smith

The setting is a fashionable cafe in 1913.

Entire production staged by George Tabori, assisted by Alvin Epstein; scenery and lighting by Klaus Holm; costumes designed by Alvin Colt, assisted by Stanley Simmons; production stage manager, Robert Woods; stage manager, Stark Hesseltine.

(Closed March 18, 1956)

DEBUT

(5 performances)

Comedy in three acts by Mary Drayton, based on Isabel Dunn's novel "Maria and the Captain." Produced by Richard Horner and Justin Sturm at the Holiday Theatre, February 22, 1956.

Cast of characters—

Mattie .... Alberta Hunter
Anna .... Eulabelle Moore
Maria Beraud .... Inger Stevens
Marjorie Hansford .... Grace Raynor
Captain Richard Beraud .... G. Albert Smith
Aunt Phoebe .... Edith Gresham
Lid .... Osceola Archer
Dabney Beauchamp Featherstone III .... Charles McDaniel
Wyn Spaulding .... Tom Helmore

The action takes place in the morning room of a spacious old house in the Deep South. The time is the present. Act I.—Morning in September. Act II.—Scene 1—Evening of the same day. Scene 2—Late that same night. Act III.—Scene 1—Few hours later; early morning. Scene 2—A week later; early morning.

Staged by John Gerstad; designed by John Boyt; stage manager, Jack Woods.

Yarn about a tomboyish Southern belle pledged to marry a proper Southern youth, but who falls for a dashing, cynical Yankee newspaperman. She sins with the Yankee, telling herself it will facilitate her marriage to a virginal fiancé; but she winds up marrying her fellow-sinner.

(Closed February 25, 1956)

MY FAIR LADY

(89 performances)
(Continued)

Musical in two acts, based on Bernard Shaw's *Pygmalion,* with book and lyrics by Alan Jay Lerner and music by Frederick Loewe. Produced by Herman Levin at the Mark Hellinger Theatre, March 15, 1956.

Cast of characters—

Buskers	Imelda De Martin, Carl Jeffrey, Joe Rocco
Mrs. Eynsford-Hill	Viola Roache
Eliza Doolittle	Julie Andrews
Freddy Eynsford-Hill	John Michael King
Colonel Pickering	Robert Coote
A Bystander	Christopher Hewett
Henry Higgins	Rex Harrison
Selsey Man	Gordon Dilworth
Hoxton Man	David Thomas
Another Bystander	Rod McLennan
First Cockney	Reid Shelton
Second Cockney	Glenn Kezer
Third Cockney	James Morris
Fourth Cockney	Herb Surface
Bartender	David Thomas
Harry	Gordon Dilworth
Jamie	Rod McLennan
Alfred P. Doolittle	Stanley Holloway
Mrs. Pearce	Philippa Bevans
Mrs. Hopkins	Olive Reeves-Smith
Butler	Reid Shelton
Servants	Rosemary Gaines, Colleen O'Connor, Muriel Shaw, Gloria Van Dorpe, Glenn Kezer
Mrs. Higgins	Cathleen Nesbitt
Chauffeur	Barton Mumaw
Footmen	Gordon Ewing, William Krach
Lord Boxington	Gordon Dilworth
Lady Boxington	Olive Reeves-Smith
Constable	Barton Mumaw
Flower Girl	Cathy Conklin
Zoltan Karpathy	Christopher Hewett
Flunkey	Paul Brown
Queen of Transylvania	Maribel Hammer
Ambassador	Rod McLennan
Bartender	Paul Brown
Mrs. Higgins' Maid	Judith Williams

The place: London. The time: 1912. Act I.—Scene 1—Outside the Opera House, Covent Garden; a cold March night. Scene 2—A tenement section—Tottenham Court Road; immediately following. Scene 3—Higgins' study; the following morning. Scene 4—Tenement section—Tottenham Court Road; three days later. Scene 5—Higgins' study; later that day. Scene 6—Near the race meeting, Ascot; a July afternoon. Scene 7—Inside a club tent, Ascot; immediately following. Scene 8—Outside Higgins' house, Wimpole Street; later that afternoon. Scene 9—Higgins' study; six weeks later. Scene 10—The

Promenade of the Embassy; later that night. Scene 11—The ballroom of the Embassy; immediately following. Act II.—Scene 1—Higgins' study; 3:00 the following morning. Scene 2—Outside Higgins' house, Wimpole Street; immediately following. Scene 3—Flower market of Covent Garden; 5:00 that morning. Scene 4—Upstairs hall of Higgins' house; 11:00 that morning. Scene 5—The conservatory of Mrs. Higgins' house; later that day. Scene 6—Outside Higgins' house, Wimpole Street; immediately following. Scene 7—Higgins' study; immediately following.

Production staged by Moss Hart; choreography and musical numbers by Hanya Holm; settings by Oliver Smith; costumes by Cecil Beaton; lighting by Feder; musical arrangements by Robert Russell Bennett and Phil Lang; dance music arranged by Trude Rittman; musical director, Franz Allers; production stage manager, Samuel Liff; stage managers, Jerry Adler and Bernard Hart.

Musical numbers—

ACT I

Scene 1

Street Entertainers .... The 3 Buskers
"Why Can't the English?" .... Higgins
"Wouldn't It Be Loverly" .... Eliza and Cockneys

Scene 2

"With a Little Bit of Luck" .... Doolittle, Harry and Jamie

Scene 3

"I'm an Ordinary Man" .... Higgins

Scene 4

"With a Little Bit of Luck" (Reprise) .... Doolittle and Ensemble

Scene 5

"Just You Wait" .... Eliza
"The Rain in Spain" .... Higgins, Eliza and Pickering
"I Could Have Danced All Night" .... Eliza, Mrs. Pearce and Maids

Scene 7

"Ascot Gavotte" .... Full Ensemble

Scene 8

"On the Street Where You Live" .... Freddy

Scene 11

"The Embassy Waltz" ... Higgins, Eliza, Karpathy and Full Ensemble

ACT II

Scene 1

"You Did It" ..... Higgins, Pickering, Mrs. Pearce and the Servants
"Just You Wait" (Reprise) .... Eliza

Scene 2

"On the Street Where You Live" (Reprise) .... Freddy
"Show Me" .... Eliza and Freddy

Scene 3

"Wouldn't It Be Loverly" (Reprise) .... Eliza and Cockneys
"Get Me to the Church on Time" .... Doolittle, Harry, Jamie and Ensemble

Scene 4

"A Hymn to Him" .... Higgins

Scene 5

"Without You" .... Eliza and Higgins

Scene 6

"I've Grown Accustomed to Her Face" .... Higgins

See page 266.

MR. WONDERFUL

(81 performances)
(Continued)

Musical comedy in two acts, with book by Joseph Stein and Will Glickman; music and lyrics by Jerry Bock, Larry Holofcener and George Weiss. Produced by Jule Styne and George Gilbert, in association with Lester Osterman, Jr., at the Broadway Theatre, March 22, 1956.

Cast of characters—

Unemployed Actress .... Ann Buckles
Hal .... Hal Loman
Song Plugger .... Richard Curry
Soprano .... Rina Falcone
Rita Romano .... Chita Rivera
Two Comics .... Bob Leslie, Larry B. Leslie
Audition Annie .... Pat Wilkes
Johnnie .... John Pelletti
A Singer .... Karen Shepard
Dancers .... Tempy Fletcher, Shirley Graser, Suan Hartman, Sally Neal, Patti Ann Rita, Sylvia Shay, Patti Wharton
Sister .... Gail Kuhr, Barbara Leigh, Sherry McCutcheon
Acrobat .... Dorothy D'Honau
Hoofers .... Marvin Arnold, Bill Reilly, Jimmie Thompson
Talent Scout .... T. J. Halligan
Annie's Friend .... Charlotte Foley
Bop Musicians .... Harold Gordon, Albert Popwell, Claude Thompson
Fred Campbell .... Jack Carter
Lil Campbell .... Pat Marshall
Counterman .... Herb Fields
Mr. Foster .... Malcolm Lee Beggs
Uncle .... Will Mastin
Dad .... Sammy Davis, Sr.
Charlie Welch .... Sammy Davis, Jr.
Ethel Pearson .... Olga James
Stage Manager .... Bob Kole
Script Girl .... Ginny Perlowin
Stagehands .... Frank Marti, Tony Rossi
Cigarette Girl .... Jerri Gray
Little Girl .... Marilyn Cooper
Sophie's Boy .... Ronnie Lee

The time: the present. Act I.—Scene 1—1617 Broadway, New York City. Scene 2—The Bandbox in Union City, N. J. Scene 3—1617 Broadway; two weeks later. Scene 4—Fred and Lil's apartment; several days later. Scene 5—An audition hall. Act II.—Scene 1—The Bandbox; after hours; several months later. Scene 2—An arcade in Miami, Florida; next day. Scene 3—Backstage at the Palm Club, Miami Beach. Scene 4—Charlie's dressing room. Scene 5—The Palm Club.

Entire production staged by Jack Donohue, conceived by Jule Styne, designed by Oliver Smith; costumes designed by Robert Mackintosh; lighting by Peggy Clark; musical director, Morton Stevens; musical and vocal supervision by Oscar Kosarin; orchestrations by Ted Royal and Morton Stevens; production stage manager, John Barry Ryan; stage manager, Bernard Gersten.

Musical numbers—

ACT I

Scene 1

"1617 Broadway" .... Rita, Hal and Ensemble
"Without You, I'm Nothing" .... Fred and Lil

Scene 2

"Jacques D'Iraq" .... Charlie, Uncle, Dad and Ensemble
"Ethel, Baby" .... Ethel and Charlie
"Mr. Wonderful" .... Ethel
"Charlie Welch" .... Fred

Scene 3

"Charlie Welch" (Reprise) .... Fred and Ensemble
"Talk to Him" .... Lil and Ethel
"Too Close for Comfort" .... Charlie

Scene 4

"Without You, I'm Nothing" (Reprise) .... Fred and Charlie

Scene 5

Rita's Audition .... Rita
Dance Improvisation .... Rita, Hal and Ensemble
The Audition .... Charlie, Uncle and Dad

ACT II

Scene 1

"There" .... Charlie

Scene 2

"Miami" .... Lil and Ensemble
"I've Been Too Busy" .... Ethel, Fred, Lil and Charlie

Scene 4

"Mr. Wonderful" (Reprise) .... Ethel

Scene 5

The Act .... Charlie, Uncle, Dad
Finale: "Mr. Wonderful" .... Entire Company

LITTLE GLASS CLOCK

(8 performances)

Comedy in three acts by Hugh Mills. Produced by Richard Aldrich and Richard Myers, in association with Julius Fleischmann, at the John Golden Theatre, March 26, 1956.

Cast of characters—

Gisele .... Angela Thornton
Julien .... Donald Somers
Hyppolite .... Norman Barrs
Abbe Matignon .... Reginald Gardiner
Armand, Comte de Montfort .... Douglas Watson
Gabrielle, Comtesse de Montfort .... Eva Gabor
A Lieutenant .... Robert Carroll
A Drummer Boy .... Fred Baker
A Soldier .... Theodore George
Marechal Francois de Sevres .... Bramwell Fletcher
General de Courcelles .... John McGiver
Cardinal Pio Di Amadori .... Richard Longman
His Majesty Louis XV .... George Curzon

The action takes place in a chateau in France. The period is the middle of the eighteenth century during the reign of Louis XV. Act I.—An afternoon in early fall. Act II.—Scene 1—Later that evening. Scene 2—The next day. Act III.—Immediately following.

Staged by Alan Schneider; set by Cecil Beaton, who also supervised costumes; lighting by Charles Lisanby; stage manager, Elliot Martin.

On his wedding day to a great beauty, an eighteenth-century French count is ordered off to war—not entirely by coincidence. He sends a substitute and himself remains behind disguised as a priest. A general and other notables conspire to spend the wedding night with his bride, but they are outwitted.

(Closed March 31, 1956)

MISTER JOHNSON

(44 performances)

Drama in three acts by Norman Rosten, based on the novel of the same name by Joyce Cary. Produced by Cheryl Crawford and Robert Lewis at the Martin Beck Theatre, March 29, 1956.

Cast of characters—

Mister Johnson .... Earle Hyman
Bamu .... Josephine Premice
Aliu, Bamu's Brother .... James E. Wall
Ajali .... Broc Peters
Benjamin .... John Akar
Matumbi .... Rosetta Le Noire
Gollup .... Thayer David
Bulteel .... Lawrence Fletcher
Adamu .... Charles McRae
Audu .... Rai Saunders
Moma .... Earl Jones
Rudbeck .... William Sylvester
Brimah .... Milton J. Williams
Second Brother .... La Verne French
Uncle .... David Berahzer
Girl .... Margie James
Mother .... Ruth Attaway
Policeman .... Clayton Corbin
Saleh .... Philip Hepburn
Waziri .... Jay Riley
Isa .... Harold Nurse
Celia .... Gaby Rodgers
Chief .... Percival Borde
Petitioner .... Curtis James
Guards .... Samuel Phills, Geffrey Biddeau, Alphonse Cimber

Townspeople, petitioners, wedding guests, road workers, travelers, party guests: David Berahzer, Percival Borde, Clayton Corbin, La Verne French, Louise Gilkes, Philip Hepburn, Curtis James, Esther Liburd, Harold Nurse, Pearl Reynolds, Rai Saunders, Mary Waithe.

The entire action of the play takes place within the "landscape" of the town of Fada, in Nigeria, British West Africa.

Staged by Robert Lewis, assisted by Pearl Primus; settings, costumes and lighting by William and Jean Eckart, assisted by Betty Coe Armstrong, costumes; Ralph Holmes, William Goodhart and Klaus Holm, scenery. Production stage manager, John Effrat; assistant stage managers, James E. Wall and Alan Shayne.

See "The Season on Broadway."

(Closed May 5, 1956)

A MONTH IN THE COUNTRY

(48 performances)

Drama in two acts by Ivan Turgenev, adapted by Emlyn Williams. Produced by the Phoenix Theatre (T. Edward Hambleton and Norris Houghton) at the Phoenix Theatre, April 3, 1956.

Cast of characters—

Shaaf, Kolia's German Tutor .... Lou Gilbert
Anna Semyenovna Yslaeva, Natalia's Mother-in-Law .... Mary Morris
Lizaveta Bogdanovna, Her Companion .... Ann Hennessey
Natalia Petrovna, Wife of Yslaev .... Uta Hagen
Rakitin, a Friend of the Family .... Alexander Scourby
Kolia, Son of Natalia and Yslaev .... Tony Atkins
Beliaev, His New Tutor .... Al Hedison
Matvei, a Manservant .... Stefan Gierasch
A Footman .... Sorrell Booke
Ignaty Illyich Shpichelsky, the Doctor .... Luther Adler
Vera, Natalia's Ward .... Olga Bielinska
Yslaev, Natalia's Husband, a Rich Landowner .... Michael Strong
Katia, a Maid .... Anne Meara
Bolshintsov, a Neighbor .... Martin Wolfson

The action takes place on Yslaev's estate in the country near Moscow. The time is in the early forties of the last century. Act I.—Scene 1—A summer afternoon. Scene 2—Late afternoon, the next day. Scene 3—The next morning. Act II.—Scene 1—A few hours later. Scene 2—A few hours later, early evening. Scene 3—The next morning.

Staged by Michael Redgrave, assisted by Fred Sadoff; scenery and lighting by Klaus Holm; costumes designed by Alvin Colt, assisted by Stanley Simmons; incidental music composed by Samuel Matlowsky; production stage manager, Robert Woods; stage manager, George Quick.

(Closed May 13, 1956)

AFFAIR OF HONOR

(27 performances)

Comedy in three acts by Bill Hoffman. Produced by the Theatre Guild, in association with Theatre 200, Inc., at the Ethel Barrymore Theatre, April 6, 1956.

Cast of characters—

James Mackenzie .... James Hickman
Charlotte Mackenzie .... Daryl Grimes
Mrs. Mackenzie .... Edith King
Sally Mackenzie .... Betsy Palmer
Captain Tom Cochran .... William Prince
Judiah Floyd .... William Whitehead
Charles Henry .... Charles Mendick
Cleeve Williams .... Skedge Miller
Edward Taunton .... Albert M. Ottenheimer
Martin Erskine .... Jimmy Yoham
First Soldier of the Crown .... Bruce Brighton
Second Soldier of the Crown .... Ben Janney
A Corporal .... Ross Winston
Sergeant Gerling .... Stanley Bell
Major Rogers .... Dennis King

Mary Wilston .... Anita Dangler
Maud Erskine .... Doris Rich
Betty Williams .... Mary Loane
Polly Floyd .... Toni Darney
A Traveling Lady .... Margaret O'Neill

The action takes place within a period of 36 hours. The time: September, 1777. The place: upper New York State near the Vermont border. Act I.—Scene 1—Afternoon; Mackenzie's Ordinary, a crossroads tavern. Scene 2—The same day, nightfall; living quarters of Major Rogers, Longbridge, New York. Act II.—Scene 1—Mackenzie's Ordinary; the following morning. Scene 2—The same; afternoon. Act III.—Mackenzie's Ordinary; the next day before sunrise.

Staged by Robert Douglas; production designed and lighted by Ralph Alswang; costumes by Gene Coffin; stage manager, Charles Durand.

During the Revolutionary War, a lecherous, callous British officer agrees to save seven American rebels from the noose if a pretty, high-spirited American girl will be his for the night. There follow a good many staples of melodrama and a good many would-be Shavian epigrams; but neither lives nor virtue is lost.

(Closed April 28, 1956)

THE KING AND I

(23 performances)

Musical in two acts, with music by Richard Rodgers; book and lyrics by Oscar Hammerstein 2nd; based on the novel "Anna and the King of Siam" by Margaret Landon. Revived by the New York City Center Light Opera Company (William Hammerstein, General Director) at the New York City Center of Music and Drama, April 18, 1956.

Cast of characters—

Captain Orton .... Leon Shaw
Louis Leonowens .... Kevin Coughlin
Anna Leonowens .... Jan Clayton
The Interpreter .... John George
The Kralahome .... Leonard Graves
The King .... Zachary Scott
Phra Alack .... Hubert Bland
Lun Tha .... Philip Wentworth
Tuptim .... Christine Mathews
Lady Thiang .... Muriel Smith
Prince Chululongkorn .... Patrick Adiarte
Princess Ying Yoawalak .... Lynn Kikuchi
Sir Edward Ramsay .... Ben Lackland

Princes and Princesses: Linda Campano, Louis Hernandez, Susan Kikuchi, Barbara Norman, Antonio Obregon, Valentine Obregon, Judith Ramsay, Patricia Ramsay, Ronald Harvey, Toby Stevens.

The Royal Dancers: Olga Bergstrom, Annita Beryll, Hazel Chung, Bettina Dearborn, Dorothy Etheridge, Marion Jim, Norma Kaiser, Wonci Lui, Julie Oser, Nadine Revene, Joan Sandes, Tao Strong, Alice Uchida, Dusty Worrall, Yuriko, Rosemary Zinner, Hubert Bland, John George, James McMillan.

The Singers (Wives, Priests, Amazons, and Slaves): Doris Galiber, Jean Maggio, Rose Rosett, Jeanette Scovotti, Rita Shay, Yolanda Vasquez, John Keelin, Robert Reim, Sherman Sneed.

The action takes place in and around the King's Palace, Bangkok, Siam. The time is the early Eighteen Sixties.

Staged by John Fearnley; choreography by Jerome Robbins, remounted by June Graham; musical director, Frederick Dvonch; scenery by Jo Mielziner; costumes by Irene Sharaff; lighting by Jean Rosenthal; orchestrations by Robert Russell Bennett; assistant to William Hammerstein, Michael Shurtleff; production stage manager, John Cornell; stage manager, Milton Ste.n.

Musical numbers—

ACT I

"I Whistle a Happy Tune" .... Anna and Louis
"My Lord and Master" .... Tuptim
"Hello, Young Lovers!" .... Anna
"March of the Siamese Children" .... Anna, the King, His Wives and Children
"A Puzzlement" .... The King
"The Royal Bangkok Academy" .... Anna and Pupils
"Getting To Know You" .... Anna, Wives, Children and Yuriko
"We Kiss in a Shadow" .... Tuptim and Lun Tha
Reprise: "A Puzzlement" .... Prince Chululongkorn and Louis
"Shall I Tell You What I Think of You?" .... Anna
"Something Wonderful" .... Lady Thiang
Finale .... Entire Company

ACT II

"Western People Funny" .... Lady Thiang and Wives
"I Have Dreamed" .... Tuptim and Lun Tha
Reprise: "Hello, Young Lovers!" .... Anna
Ballet—"The Small House of Uncle Thomas"
Narrator .... Christine Mathews
Uncle Thomas .... Bettina Dearborn
Little Eva .... Wonci Lui
Topsy .... Alice Uchida
Eliza .... Yuriko
King Simon .... Marion Jim
Angel .... Dusty Worrall
Royal Dancers .... Olga Bergstrom, Annita Beryll, Hazel Chung, Dorothy Etheridge, Norma Kaiser, Julie Oser, Nadine Revene, Joan Sandes, Tao Strong, Rosemary Zinner
Property-men .... John George, John Keelin, James McMillan, Robert Reim, Sherman Sneed
Drummer .... Hubert Bland
"Shall We Dance?" .... Anna and the King
Finale .... Entire Company

The King and I was first produced by Rodgers and Hammerstein at the St. James Theatre, March 29, 1951, for 1,246 performances.

(Closed May 6, 1956)

WAITING FOR GODOT

(49 performances)
(Continued)

A tragicomedy in two acts by Samuel Beckett. Produced by Michael Myerberg, by arrangement with Independent Plays Limited, at the John Golden Theatre, April 19, 1956.

Cast of characters—

Estragon (Gogo) .... Bert Lahr
Vladimir (Didi) .... E. G. Marshall
Lucky .... Alvin Epstein
Pozzo .... Kurt Kasznar
A Boy .... Luchino Solito de Solis

Act I.—A country road; a tree; evening. Act II.—Next day; same time; same place.

Staged by Herbert Berghof; scenery by Louis Kennel; costumes by Stanley Simmons; production supervisor, John Paul; assistant stage manager, Oliver K. Berg.

See page 295.

GOODBYE AGAIN

(7 performances)

Comedy in three acts by Allan Scott and George Haight. Revived by Shepard Traube and J. H. Del Bondio at the Helen Hayes Theatre, April 24, 1956.

Cast of characters—

Anne Rogers .... Polly Rowles
Kenneth Bixby .... Donald Cook
Waiter .... Jim Stevenson
Bellman .... Fred Eisley
Maid .... Denise Dorin
Julia Wilson .... Sally Gracie
Elizabeth Clochessy .... Patricia Barry
Arthur Westlake .... Tom Poston
Harvey Wilson .... Hiram Sherman
Mr. Clayton .... Burton Mallory
Theodore .... Danny Lee

Act I.—Morning. Act II.—Late that evening. Act III.—The next morning.

Staged by Shepard Traube; setting designed by Sam Leve; stage manager, Carl Judd.

Goodbye Again was first presented by Arthur J. Beckhard at the Masque Theatre, December 28, 1932, for 216 performances; and later revived November 9, 1943.

(Closed April 28, 1956)

WAKE UP, DARLING

(5 performances)

Comedy in two acts by Alex Gottlieb. Produced by Gordon W. Pollock, in association with Lee Segall and Richard Cook, at the Ethel Barrymore Theatre, May 2, 1956.

Cast of characters—

Martha .... Kay Medford
Juliet .... Paula Trueman
Polly Emerson .... Barbara Britton
Deerfield Prescott .... Russell Nype
Don Emerson .... Barry Nelson
Gloria .... Grace Raynor
First Policeman .... Robert Downing
Second Policeman .... Richard B. Shull
Granville Prescott .... Raymond Bramley
Penelope .... Ann Whiteside
Mrs. Johnson .... Jean Arley

The action takes place in the apartment of the Don Emersons on East 75th Street in New York City. The time is the present. Act I.—Scene 1—Late afternoon. Scene 2—Very late that night. Act II.—Scene 1—A morning several weeks later. Scene 2—Fifteen minutes later. Scene 3—That evening.

Staged by Ezra Stone, assisted by Robert Downing; scenery and lighting by Ballou; costumes by Guy Kent; executive assistant to Mr. Pollock, Richard B. Shull; general stage manager, Arthur A. Barkow.

A stagestruck wife gets the lead role in a prospective musical by captivating its sexually eager but still virginal author. The author proceeds to move in on his leading lady and her husband; so does an eager Chicago divorcée; and there are lots of gags and goings-on before domestic order is restored.

(Closed May 5, 1956)

THE MOST HAPPY FELLA

(33 performances)
(Continued)

Musical in three acts by Frank Loesser, based on Sidney Howard's "They Knew What They Wanted." Produced by Kermit Bloomgarden and Lynn Loesser at the Imperial Theatre, May 3, 1956.

Cast of characters—

The Cashier .... Lee Cass
Cleo .... Susan Johnson
Rosabella .... Jo Sullivan
The Waitresses .... Marlyn Greer, Martha Mathes, Myrna Aaron, Meri Miller, Beverly Gaines
The Postman .... Lee Cass
Tony .... Robert Weede
Marie .... Mona Paulee
Max .... Louis Polacek
Herman .... Shorty Long
Clem .... Alan Gilbert
Jake .... John Henson
Al .... Roy Lazarus
Joe .... Art Lund
Giuseppe .... Arthur Rubin
Pasquale .... Rico Froehlich
Ciccio .... John Henson
Country Girl, City Boy .... Meri Miller, John Sharpe
The Doctor .... Keith Kaldenberg
The Priest .... Russell Goodwin

Tessie .... Zina Bethune
Gussie .... Christopher Snell
Neighbors .... Helon Blount, Myrna Aaron, Beverly Gaines, Henry Director, Hunter Ross, Bob Daley
Neighbor Ladies ...... Lillian Shelby, Lois Van Pelt, Marjorie Smith
Brakeman .... Norris Greer
Bus Driver .... Ralph Farnworth

All the Neighbors, and All the Neighbors' Neighbors: Helon Blount, Thelma Dare, Carolyn Maye, Genevieve Owens, Lillian Shelby, Marjorie Smith, Toba Sherwood, Lois Van Pelt, Betsy Bridge, Theodora Brandon, Art Arney, Ken Ayers, Lanier Davis, Henry Director, Ralph Farnworth, Alan Gilbert, Russell Goodwin, Norris Greer, Richard Hermany, Walter Kelvin, Roy Lazarus, Louis Polacek, Evans Thornton, Myrna Aaron, Patti Schmidt, Beverly Gaines, Marlyn Greer, Martha Mathes, Meri Miller, Bob Daley, Athan Karras, Jerry Kurland, Arthur Partington, Hunter Ross, John Sharpe.

Act I.—Scene 1—A restaurant in San Francisco; January, 1927. Scene 2—Main Street, Napa, California; in April. Scene 3—Tony's barn; a few weeks later. Scene 4—Tony's front yard. Act II.—Scene 1—The vineyards in May. Scene 2—Later in May. Scene 3—The vineyards in June. Scene 4—The barn. Scene 5—The vineyards in July. Act III.—Scene 1—The barn an hour later. Scene 2—Napa Station; a little later.

Staged by Joseph Anthony; orchestrations by Don Walker; orchestra and choral direction by Herbert Greene; choreography by Dania Krupska; scenery and lighting by Jo Mielziner; costumes by Motley; production stage manager, Henri Caubisens; stage manager, Terence Little.

KISS ME, KATE

(23 performances)

Musical in two acts, with music and lyrics by Cole Porter; book by Sam and Bella Spewack. Revived by the New York City Center Light Opera Company (William Hammerstein, General Director) at the New York City Center of Music and Drama, May 9, 1956.

Cast of characters—

Fred Graham .... David Atkinson
Harry Trevor .... Harrison Dowd
Lois Lane .... Barbara Ruick
Ralph (Stage Manager) .... Vincent McMahon
Lilli Vanessi .... Kitty Carlisle
Hattie .... Delores Martin
Stage Doorman .... Robert Reim
Paul .... Bobby Short
Bill Calhoun .... Richard France
First Man .... Al Nesor
Second Man .... Tom Pedi
Harrison Howell .... Ben Lackland
"Taming of the Shrew" Players:
Bianca (Lois Lane) .... Barbara Ruick
Baptista (Harry Trevor) .... Harrison Dowd
Gremio (First Suitor) .... Philip Wentworth
Hortensio (Second Suitor) .... Ray Weaver
Lucentio (Bill Calhoun) .... Richard France
Katharine (Lilli Vanessi) .... Kitty Carlisle
Petruchio (Fred Graham) .... David Atkinson
Haberdasher .... Arthur Mitchell

Dancers: Olga Bergstrom, Patricia Birsh, Dorothy Etheridge, Kate Friedlich, Norma Kaiser, Nadine Revene, Kathleen Stanford, Rosemary Weekly, Gene Gavin, William Inglis, Donald Mahler, Gene Myers, Arthur Mitchell, Robert Norris, Baird Searles, Jon Young.

Singers: Helen Baisley, Doris Galiber, Nina Greer, Jean Maggio, Louise Pearl, Rose Rosett, Barbara Saxby, Jack Irwin, John Keelin, Vincent McMahon, Robert Reim, Jay Stern, Ray Weaver, Philip Wentworth.

Act I.—Scene 1—Stage of Ford Theatre, Baltimore. Scene 2—The corridor backstage. Scene 3—Dressing rooms, Fred Graham and Lilli Vanessi. Scene 4—Padua. Scene 5—Street scene, Padua. Scene 6—Backstage. Scene 7—Fred and Lilli's dressing rooms. Scene 8—Exterior church. Act II.—Scene 1—Theatre alley. Scene 2—Before the curtain. Scene 3—Petruchio's house. Scene 4—The corridor backstage. Scene 5—Fred and Lilli's dressing rooms. Scene 6—The corridor backstage. Scene 7—Before the asbetsos curtain. Scene 8—Baptista's home.

Staged by Burt Shevelove; choreography by Ray Harrison, assisted by Patricia Birsh, based on the original dances by Hanya Holm; musical director, Frederick Dvonch; scenery by Watson Barratt; costumes by Alvin Colt, assisted by Stanley Simmons; lighting by Jean Rosenthal; assistant to William Hammerstein, Michael Shurtleff; production stage manager, John Cornell; stage manager, Milton Stern.

Musical numbers—

ACT I

Scene 1

"Another Op'nin', Another Show" . . . Sung by Hattie and Singing Ensemble
Danced by Dancing Ensemble

Scene 2

"Why Can't You Behave?" . . . Sung by Lois Lane

Scene 3

"Wunderbar" . . . Sung by Lilli and Fred
"So In Love" . . . Sung by Lilli

Scene 4

"We Open in Venice" . . . Sung by Petruchio, Katharine, Bianca, Lucentio

Scene 5

Dance . . . By Dancing Ensemble
"Tom, Dick or Harry" . . . Sung by Bianca, Lucentio and the Two Suitors
Specialty Dance . . . Lucentio
"I've Come To Wive It Wealthily in Padua" . . . Sung by Petruchio and Singing Ensemble
"I Hate Men" . . . Sung by Katharine
"Were Thine That Special Face" . . . Sung by Petruchio
Danced by Dancing Ensemble

Scene 8

"I Sing of Love" . . . Sung by Lucentio and Singing Ensemble
Finale: "Kiss Me, Kate" . . . Sung by Katharine, Petruchio and Singing Ensemble
Tarantella . . . Danced by Bianca, Lucentio and Dancing Ensemble

ACT II

Scene 1

"Too Darn Hot" . . . Sung by Paul
Danced by Bill Calhoun, Lois Lane and Dancing Ensemble

Scene 3

"Where Is the Life That Late I Led?" . . . Sung by Petruchio

Scene 4

"Always True to You (in My Fashion)" . . . Sung by Lois

Scene 6

"Bianca" . . . Sung by Bill Calhoun and Singing Girls
Danced by Bill Calhoun and Dancing Girls
Reprise: "So In Love" . . . Sung by Fred

Scene 7

"Brush Up Your Shakespeare" . . . Sung by First Man and Second Man

Scene 8

"I Am Ashamed That Women Are So Simple" .... Sung by Katharine
Pavanne .... By Dancing Ensemble

Scene 9

Finale .... Sung by Petruchio, Katharine and Company

Kiss Me, Kate was first produced by Saint Subber and Lemuel Ayers at the New Century Theatre, December 30, 1948, for 1,070 performances.

(Closed May 27, 1956)

THE LOVERS

(4 performances)

Play in three acts by Leslie Stevens. Produced by the Playwrights' Company and Gayle Stine at the Martin Beck Theatre, May 10, 1956.

Cast of characters—

Grigoris .... Hurd Hatfield
Clothilde .... Vivian Nathan
Sextus .... Earl Montgomery
Xegan .... Norman Rose
Mattiew .... Robert Jacquin
Simon .... Harry Bergman
Volc Sturmer .... William Bramley
Marc .... Mario Alcalde
Douane .... Joanne Woodward
Chrysagon de la Crux .... Darren McGavin
Blaise .... Gerald Hiken
Draco de la Crux .... Robert Burr
Austrict de la Crux .... Pernell Roberts
Herstal de la Crux .... Robert Lansing
Probus .... Morris Carnovsky
Tomas .... Gayne Sullivan
Saul .... George Ebeling
Lisanne .... Kathe Snyder
Mairese .... Frances Chaney
Ironsmith .... George Tyne
Millwright .... George Berkeley
Wheelwright .... Bert Conway
Escavalon .... Lester Rawlins
Clement of Metz .... Bramwell Fletcher
Stewards .... Byron Mitchell, Kurt Cerf
Friars .... Edward Setrakian, Charles Chaucer
Knights Escavalon .... Robert Dowdell, John Carter, Grant Eastham, John MacKay
People of St. Omer .... Peggy Richards, Flori Waren, Lena Romano, Edith Martin, Patricia Allaben, Emily McLaughlin, Page Johnson, Norman Wigutow

The action takes place in the district of St. Omer between Flaundres and Artoys in the middle years of the Twelfth Century. Act I.—The Sign; The Three; The Wedding. Act II.—The Feast; The Night; The Morning. Act III.—The Judgment; The Lovers; The Sinner.

Staged by Michael Gordon; lighting and setting by Charles Elson; light projections supervised by Leland Watson; costumes by John Boyt; music researched and supervised by Clois Ensor; dance staged by Flori Waren; production stage manager, Seymour Milbert; stage manager, Regis Caddic.

Following the marriage of two peasants in twelfth-century France, the lord of the neighborhood invokes the *droit du seigneur.* It is not the *droit* itself, however, that leads to tragedy, but the passion that still holds the wedding-night lovers fast long after morning breaks. In the end the bride has killed herself and the husband and the lover kill each other.

The story is told retrospectively, through flashbacks, to a wandering friar, in the hope that he will give the dead couple the Christian burial that the Church has denied them.

(Closed May 12, 1956)

THE LITTLEST REVUE

(13 performances)
(Continued)

A musical revue in two acts, conceived, cast and assembled by Ben Bagley. Lyrics and music mostly by Ogden Nash and Vernon Duke; additional music and lyrics by: John Latouche, Sheldon Harnick, Lee Adams, Charles Strouse, John Strauss, Sidney Shaw, Sammy Cahn and Michael Brown. Sketches by: Nat Hiken and Billy Friedberg; Eudora Welty, Mike Stewart, George Baxt, Bud McCreery; Allan Manings and Bob Van Scoyk. Produced by the Phoenix Theatre (T. Edward Hambleton and Norris Houghton) at the Phoenix Theatre, May 22, 1956.

Principals—

Beverley Bozeman	George Marcy
Joel Grey	Tommy Morton
Tammy Grimes	Charlotte Rae
Dorothy Jarnac	Larry Storch

Production directed by Paul Lammers; choreography by Charles Weidman; settings and lighting by Klaus Holm; costumes by Alvin Colt; musical director, Will Irwin; orchestrations by John Strauss; production stage manager, Robert Woods; stage manager, Stark Hesseltine.

The Scenes—

ACT I

Opening Number .... Entire Company
(Words by John Latouche and Kenward Elmslie; music by John Strauss)
Credit Is Due .... Joel Grey
(By Allan Manings and Bob Van Scoyk)
"Good Little Girls" .... Beverley Bozeman, Tommy Morton, George Marcy
(Music and lyrics by Vernon Duke and Sammy Cahn)
Give My Regards to Mott St. (By Mike Stewart)
Compere .... *Charlotte Rae*
Man .... Larry Storch
Woman .... Tammy Grimes
"Second Avenue and 12th Street Rag"
(Lyrics and music by Ogden Nash and Vernon Duke)

Sung and danced by . . . . George Marcy
Danced by . . . Dorothy Jarnac, Beverley Bozeman, Tommy Morton
"The Shape of Things" . . . . Charlotte Rae
(By Sheldon Harnick)
"Madly in Love" . . . . Tammy Grimes
(Lyrics and music by Ogden Nash and Vernon Duke)
Two Cents' Worth of Plain (By Mike Stewart)
Compere . . . . *Joel Grey*
Man . . . . Tommy Morton
Young Woman . . . . Beverley Bozeman
Old Woman . . . . Charlotte Rae
"I Lost the Rhythm" . . . . Joel Grey
(By Charles Strouse)
Game of Dance . . . . George Marcy, Beverley Bozeman, Tommy Morton
(Choreography by Danny Daniels; music composed and arranged by Sol Berkowitz; dialogue by Don Meyer)
Diet . . . . Charlotte Rae
(By Bud McCreery)
Vignette (By George Baxt)
Man . . . . Larry Storch
Woman . . . . Tammy Grimes
"Third Avenue El" . . . . Tommy Morton
(By Michael Brown)
The Power of Negative Thinking (By Bud McCreery)
Compere . . . . *Charlotte Rae*
Dad . . . . Larry Storch
Mom . . . . Tammy Grimes
Son . . . . Joel Grey
Sister . . . . Beverley Bozeman
Grandfather . . . . Tommy Morton
Daughter-in-law . . . . Dorothy Jarnac
Junior . . . . George Marcy
Ecstasy . . . . Charlotte Rae

ACT II

"Fly Now, Pay Later"
(Lyrics and music by Ogden Nash and Vernon Duke)
Sung and danced by . . . . Tommy Morton
Danced by . . . . . Dorothy Jarnac, George Marcy, Beverley Bozeman
Beyond Reproach (By Allan Manings and Bob Van Scoyk)
Compere . . . . *Tammy Grimes*
The Playwright . . . . Larry Storch
The Vice-President . . . . Joel Grey
The Secretary . . . . Charlotte Rae
"A Little Love, A Little Money—I" . . . . . . Tommy Morton, George Marcy, Jack Kauflin
(Lyrics and music by Ogden Nash and Vernon Duke)
"Far From Wonderful"
(Lyrics and music by Ogden Nash and Vernon Duke)
The Window Washer . . . . Joel Grey
The Gamin . . . . Dorothy Jarnac
Bye-Bye Brevoort (By Eudora Welty)
Compere . . . . *George Marcy*
Millicent Fortescue . . . . Charlotte Rae
Violet Whichaway . . . . Tammy Grimes
Evans . . . . Beverley Bozeman
Desmond Dupree . . . . Larry Storch
Wreckers . . . . Tommy Morton, George Marcy
"Born Too Late" . . . . Tommy Morton
(Lyrics and music by Ogden Nash and Vernon Duke)
"Spring Doth Let Her Colours Fly"
(Music and lyrics by Charles Strouse and Lee Adams)
Brunhilde Benzine . . . . Charlotte Rae
Show Girls . . . . Mary Harmon, Beverley Bozeman
Escorts . . . . Tommy Morton, George Marcy
The Man in the Gray Flannel Space Suit . . . . Larry Storch
(By Allan Manings and Bob Van Scoyk)
Opus 9 . . . . Dorothy Jarnac
(Composed and arranged by Edward Sauter)
"Summer Is Icumen In" . . . . Charlotte Rae
(Music and lyrics by Vernon Duke and John Latouche)

"A Little Love, A Little Money—II" ......George Marcy, Tommy Morton, Jack Kauflin
(Lyrics and music by Ogden Nash and Vernon Duke)
East Is East (By Nat Hiken and Billy Friedberg)
Compere ....*Tammy Grimes*
Judge ....George Marcy
Cop ....Tommy Morton
Slave Girls ....Dorothy Jarnac, Mary Harmon
Prime Minister ....Joel Grey
Prince ....Larry Storch
Mrs. McKenzie ....Charlotte Rae
H. Drexel Groves ....Tommy Morton
"Love Is Still in Town"
(Lyrics and music by Ogden Nash and Vernon Duke)
Sung and danced by ....George Marcy
Danced by ....Dorothy Jarnac, Beverley Bozeman
"I'm Glad I'm Not a Man" ....Tammy Grimes
(Lyrics and music by Ogden Nash and Vernon Duke)
Finale ....Entire Company

CARMEN JONES

(1 performance)
(Continued)

A musical play by Oscar Hammerstein II, based on Meilhac and Halevy's adaptation of Prosper Merimee's "Carmen"; music by Georges Bizet; orchestral arrangements by Robert Russell Bennett. Revived by the New York City Center Light Opera Company (William Hammerstein, General Director) at the New York City Center of Music and Drama, May 31, 1956.

Cast of characters—

Corporal Morrell ....Sherman Sneed
Foreman ....Stefan Lind
Cindy Lou ....Reri Grist
Sergeant Brown ....Walter P. Brown
Joe ....William DuPree
Carmen ....Muriel Smith
Sally ....Glory Van Scott
T-Bone ....Walter Nicks
Tough Kid ....Peter Burke
Drummer ....Cozy Cole
Bartender ....Herbert Stubbs
Waiter ....James Wamen
Frankie ....Delores Martin
Myrt ....Audrey Vanterpool
Rum ....Joseph James
Dink ....John Bouie
Husky Miller ....Jimmy Randolph
Mr. Higgins ....Clyde Turner
Miss Higgins ....Carol Joy
Photographer ....John Greenwood
Card Players ....Mary Louise, Carol Joy, Christine Spencer, Louise Parker
Poncho ....Herbert Stubbs
Bullet Head ....John Nielsen
Dancing Boxers ....Joseph Nash, James McMillan
Referee ....Walter Nicks

Soldiers, Factory Workers, Socialites: Adelaide Boatner, Mareda Gaither, Doris Galiber, John Greenwood, Robert Henson, Addison Hill, Bernice Jackson, Carol Joy, John Keelin, Elzar Levister, Stefan Lind,

Mary Louise, Vivian Martin, John Nielsen, Louise Parker, Annabelle Parrish, Sherman Sneed, Christine Spencer, Bill Starling, Herbert Stubbs, Fred Thomas, Rodester Timmons, Clyde Turner, Ruth Tyler, James Wamen, Leontyne Watts, Alexander Yancy.

Dancers: Georgia Collins, Frank Glass, Lavinia Hamilton, Nathaniel A. Horne, Erona Harris, Jim McMillan, Arthur Mitchell, Joseph Nash, Walter Nicks, Charles Queenan, Kathleen Stanford, Elizabeth Taylor, Ella Thompson, Glory Van Scott, Elizabeth Williamson, Billy Wilson.

Children: Dennis Butler, Peter Burke, Michael Gilford, Leonard Grinnage, Deborah Jones, Gregory Clinton, Charles Stewart, Jr.

Act I.—Scene 1—Outside a parachute factory, near a southern town. Scene 2—A nearby roadside, immediately after. Scene 3—Billy Pastor's Cafe; three weeks later. Act II.—Scene 1—Terrace of the Meadow Lawn Country Club, south-side of Chicago; two weeks later. Night. Scene 2—(a) Outside a Sport Stadium; a week later. (b) The Stadium.

Staged by William Hammerstein; choreography by Onna White; musical director, Julius Rudel; settings and lighting by Howard Bay; choral direction by Leonard Depaur; costumes for original production by Raoul Pene du Bois, supervised for the City Center by Stanley Simmons; assistant director, Michael Shurtleff; production stage manager, John Cornell; stage manager, Milton Stern.

Musical numbers—

ACT I

Scene 1

Opening Scene .... Morrell, Cindy Lou and Male Chorus
"Lift 'Em Up An' Put 'Em Down!" .... Street Boys
"Honey Gal O' Mine" .... Male Chorus
"Good Luck, Mr. Flyin' Man!" .... Female Chorus—Singers and Dancers
"Dat's Love" .... Carmen and Chorus
"You Talk Jus' Like My Maw" .... Joe and Cindy Lou
"Murder—Murder!" .... Female Chorus
Finale of Scene 1 .... Carmen, Joe, Brown, Sally and Chorus
Entr' Scene: "Carmen Jones Is Goin' To Jail" .... Children

Scene 2

"Dere's A Cafe On De Corner" .... Carmen and Joe

Scene 3

"Beat Out Dat Rhythm On A Drum" .... Frankie, Drummer and Chorus
"Stan' Up An' Fight!" .... Husky Miller and Chorus
"Whizzin' Away Along De Track" .... Rum, Dink, Myrt, Frankie and Carmen
"Dis Flower" .... Joe
"If You Would Only Come Away" .... Carmen and Joe
Finale of Act I

ACT II

Scene 1

"De Cards Don' Lie" .... Frankie, Myrt and Female Chorus
"Dat Ol' Boy" .... Carmen
"Poncho De Panther From Brazil" .... Frankie, Myrt, Husky, Rum and Chorus
Dance Roma Suite .... Ballet
"My Joe" .... Cindy Lou
Finale of Scene 1 .... Carmen, Joe, Cindy Lou, Husky, Rum, Dink, Frankie and Myrt

Scene 2

"Git Yer Program For De Big Fight" .... Chorus
"Dat's Our Man!" .... Chorus
Finale

Carmen Jones was first produced by Billy Rose at the Broadway Theatre, December 2, 1943, for 503 performances.

FACTS AND FIGURES

VARIETY'S TABULATION OF FINANCIAL HITS AND FLOPS

HITS

The Desk Set
The Diary of Anne Frank
The Great Sebastians
A Hatful of Rain
Janus
The Matchmaker
No Time for Sergeants
Tiger at the Gates

STATUS NOT YET DETERMINED

Fallen Angels
The Lark
Middle of the Night
The Most Happy Fella
Mr. Wonderful
My Fair Lady
Pipe Dream
The Ponder Heart
Waiting for Godot
Will Success Spoil Rock Hunter?

FAILURES

Affair of Honor
Almost Crazy
Catch a Star
The Chalk Garden
A Day by the Sea
Deadfall
Debut
Goodbye Again
The Heavenly Twins
The Hot Corner
The Innkeepers
Island of Goats
Joyce Grenfell Requests the Pleasure . . .
Little Glass Clock
The Lovers
Mister Johnson
Red Roses for Me
The Righteous Are Bold
A Roomful of Roses
Someone Waiting
Tamburlaine the Great
Time Limit!
The Vamp
A View from the Bridge
Wake Up, Darling
The Wooden Dish
The Young and Beautiful

SPECIAL, MISCELLANEOUS (UNRATED)

Carmen Jones
Comédie Française
D'Oyly Carte Opera
Henry IV, Part I
The King and I
King Lear

Kiss Me, Kate
Marcel Marceau
Othello
The Skin of Our Teeth
A Streetcar Named Desire

CLOSED DURING TRYOUT TOUR

Amazing Adele
Dancing in the Chequered Shade
Quiet Place
Reuben Reuben
Strip for Action
Top Man
Ziegfeld Follies

Holdovers from 1954-55 Season, Since Clarified

HITS

Damn Yankees
Inherit the Wind
Plain and Fancy
Silk Stockings

FAILURES

Ankles Aweigh
The Desperate Hours
Quadrille
Seventh Heaven

STATISTICAL SUMMARY

(Last Season Plays Which Ended Runs After June 1, 1955)

Plays	*Number Performances*	*Closing Date*
Anastasia	272	September 24, 1955
Ankles Aweigh	176	September 17, 1955
Anniversary Waltz	615	September 24, 1955
Bad Seed	332	September 24, 1955
The Boy Friend	485	November 26, 1955
Bus Stop	478	April 21, 1956
Can-Can	892	June 25, 1955
Comedy in Music	849	January 21, 1956
The Desperate Hours	212	August 13, 1955
Guys and Dolls (revival)	31	June 12, 1955
Lunatics and Lovers	336	October 1, 1955
Phoenix '55	97	July 17, 1955
Plain and Fancy	461	March 3, 1956
Seventh Heaven	44	July 2, 1955
The Seven Year Itch	1,141	August 13, 1955
Silk Stockings	478	April 14, 1956
Tea and Sympathy	712	June 18, 1955
The Teahouse of the August Moon	1,027	March 24, 1956
3 for Tonight	85	June 18, 1955

LONG RUNS ON BROADWAY

To June 1, 1956

(Plays marked with asterisk were still playing June 1, 1956)

Plays	*Number Performances*
Life with Father	3,224
Tobacco Road	3,182
Abie's Irish Rose	2,327
Oklahoma!	2,248
South Pacific	1,925
Harvey	1,775
Born Yesterday	1,642
The Voice of the Turtle	1,557
Arsenic and Old Lace	1,444
Hellzapoppin	1,404
Angel Street	1,295
Lightnin'	1,291
The King and I	1,246
Guys and Dolls	1,200
Mister Roberts	1,157
Annie Get Your Gun	1,147
The Seven Year Itch	1,141
Pins and Needles	1,108
Kiss Me, Kate	1,070
The Teahouse of the August Moon	1,027
Anna Lucasta	957
Kiss and Tell	957
The Moon Is Blue	924
Can-Can	892
Carousel	890
Hats Off to Ice	889
Follow the Girls	882
The Bat	867
My Sister Eileen	865
White Cargo	864
Song of Norway	860
* The Pajama Game	860
A Streetcar Named Desire	855
Comedy in Music	849
You Can't Take It with You	837
Three Men on a Horse	835
Where's Charlie?	792
The Ladder	789
State of the Union	765
The First Year	760
Death of a Salesman	742
Sons o' Fun	742
The Man Who Came to Dinner	739
Call Me Mister	734
High Button Shoes	727
Finian's Rainbow	725
Claudia	722
The Gold Diggers	720
I Remember Mama	714
Tea and Sympathy	712
Junior Miss	710
Seventh Heaven	704
Peg o' My Heart	692
The Children's Hour	691
Dead End	687
The Lion and the Mouse	686
Dear Ruth	683

Plays	*Number Performances*
East Is West	680
The Doughgirls	671
Irene	670
Boy Meets Girl	669
* Fanny	659
Blithe Spirit	657
The Women	657
A Trip to Chinatown	657
Bloomer Girl	654
The Fifth Season	654
Rain	648
Call Me Madam	644
Janie	642
The Green Pastures	640
The Fourposter	632
Is Zat So?	618
Anniversary Waltz	615
The Happy Time	614
Separate Rooms	613
* Witness for the Prosecution	611
Affairs of State	610
Star and Garter	609
The Student Prince	608
Broadway	603
Adonis	603
Street Scene	601
Kiki	600
Wish You Were Here	598
A Society Circus	596
Blossom Time	592
The Two Mrs. Carrolls	585
Kismet	583
Detective Story	581
Brigadoon	581
Brother Rat	577
Show Boat	572
The Show-Off	571
Sally	570
One Touch of Venus	567
Happy Birthday	564
The Glass Menagerie	561
Wonderful Town	559
Rose Marie	557
Strictly Dishonorable	557
Ziegfeld Follies	553
Floradora	553
Dial "M" for Murder	552
Good News	551
Let's Face It	547
Within the Law	541
The Music Master	540
Pal Joey	540
What a Life	538
The Red Mill	531
The Solid Gold Cadillac	526
The Boomerang	522
Rosalinda	521
Chauve Souris	520
Blackbirds	518
Sunny	517
Victoria Regina	517
The Vagabond King	511
The New Moon	509
Shuffle Along	504
Up in Central Park	504
Carmen Jones	503
The Member of the Wedding	501
Personal Appearance	501
Panama Hattie	501
Bird in Hand	500
Sailor, Beware!	500
Room Service	500
Tomorrow the World	500

NEW YORK DRAMA CRITICS CIRCLE AWARDS

At their annual meeting, the New York Drama Critics Circle chose *The Diary of Anne Frank,* adapted by Frances Goodrich and Albert Hackett, as the best new American play of the season. As the best foreign play the Circle chose Jean Giraudoux's *Tiger at the Gates* (translated by Christopher Fry), and as the best musical, Frederick Loewe and Alan Jay Lerner's *My Fair Lady.*

Circle awards have been—

1935-36—Winterset, by Maxwell Anderson
1936-37—High Tor, by Maxwell Anderson
1937-38—Of Mice and Men, by John Steinbeck
1938-39—No award.
1939-40—The Time of Your Life, by William Saroyan
1940-41—Watch on the Rhine, by Lillian Hellman
1941-42—No award.
1942-43—The Patriots, by Sidney Kingsley
1943-44—No award.
1944-45—The Glass Menagerie, by Tennessee Williams
1945-46—No award.
1946-47—All My Sons, by Arthur Miller.
1947-48—A Streetcar Named Desire, by Tennessee Williams
1948-49—Death of a Salesman, by Arthur Miller
1949-50—The Member of the Wedding, by Carson McCullers
1950-51—Darkness at Noon, by Sidney Kingsley
1951-52—I Am a Camera, by John van Druten
1952-53—Picnic, by William Inge
1953-54—The Teahouse of the August Moon, by John Patrick
1954-55—Cat on a Hot Tin Roof, by Tennessee Williams
1955-56—The Diary of Anne Frank, by Frances Goodrich and Albert Hackett

PULITZER PRIZE WINNERS

For the fourth successive year the Pulitzer Prize went to the same play as the Critics Circle Award—in this case, *The Diary of Anne Frank.*

Pulitzer awards have been—

1917-18—Why Marry?, by Jesse Lynch Williams
1918-19—No award.
1919-20—Beyond the Horizon, by Eugene O'Neill
1920-21—Miss Lulu Bett, by Zona Gale
1921-22—Anna Christie, by Eugene O'Neill
1922-23—Icebound, by Owen Davis
1923-24—Hell-bent fer Heaven, by Hatcher Hughes
1924-25—They Knew What They Wanted, by Sidney Howard
1925-26—Craig's Wife, by George Kelly
1926-27—In Abraham's Bosom, by Paul Green
1927-28—Strange Interlude, by Eugene O'Neill
1928-29—Street Scene, by Elmer Rice
1929-30—The Green Pastures, by Marc Connelly
1930-31—Alison's House, by Susan Glaspell
1931-32—Of Thee I Sing, by George S. Kaufman, Morrie Ryskind, Ira and George Gershwin
1932-33—Both Your Houses, by Maxwell Anderson
1933-34—Men in White, by Sidney Kingsley
1934-35—The Old Maid, by Zoë Akins
1935-36—Idiot's Delight, by Robert E. Sherwood
1936-37—You Can't Take It with You, by Moss Hart and George S. Kaufman
1937-38—Our Town, by Thornton Wilder
1938-39—Abe Lincoln in Illinois, by Robert E. Sherwood
1939-40—The Time of Your Life, by William Saroyan
1940-41—There Shall Be No Night, by Robert E. Sherwood
1941-42—No award.
1942-43—The Skin of Our Teeth, by Thornton Wilder
1943-44—No award.
1944-45—Harvey, by Mary Coyle Chase
1945-46—State of the Union, by Howard Lindsay and Russel Crouse

1946-47—No award.
1947-48—A Streetcar Named Desire, by Tennessee Williams
1948-49—Death of a Salesman, by Arthur Miller
1949-50—South Pacific, by Richard Rodgers, Oscar Hammerstein II and Joshua Logan
1950-51—No award.
1951-52—The Shrike, by Joseph Kramm
1952-53—Picnic, by William Inge
1953-54—The Teahouse of the August Moon, by John Patrick
1954-55—Cat on a Hot Tin Roof, by Tennessee Williams
1955-56—The Diary of Anne Frank, by Frances Goodrich and Albert Hackett

BOOKS ON THE THEATRE

1955-1956

Abbott, George, and Wallop, Douglass. *Damn Yankees.* (Music and lyrics by Richard Adler and Jerry Ross.) Random House. $2.95.

Anouilh, Jean. *The Lark.* Adapted by Lillian Hellman. Random House. $2.95.

Axelrod, George. *Will Success Spoil Rock Hunter?* Random House. $2.95.

Bagnold, Enid. *The Chalk Garden.* Random House. $2.95.

Beckett, Samuel. *Waiting for Godot.* Grove Press. $4.75; paperback, $1.00.

Bentley, Eric. *From the American Drama.* Five plays, from *Captain Jinks* to *Guys and Dolls.* Anchor Books. $1.25.

Binns, Archie. *Mrs. Fiske and the American Theatre.* Crown. $5.00.

Blum, Daniel. *Theatre World 1954-1955.* Greenberg. $5.00.

Boleslavsky, Richard. *Acting: The First Six Lessons* (new edition). Theatre Arts. $2.00.

Bowers, Faubion. *Theatre in the East:* A Survey of Asian Dance and Drama. Nelson. $7.50.

Chapman, John (Editor). *Theatre '55.* Random House. $5.00.

Chodorov, Jerome, and Fields, Joseph. *The Ponder Heart.* Random House. $2.95.

Coward, Noel. *Quadrille.* Doubleday. $3.00.

Ernst, Earle. *The Kabuki Theatre.* Oxford University Press. $7.50.

Fellheim, Marvin. *The Theatre of Augustin Daly.* Harvard University Press. $5.00.

Gaver, Jack. *Critics' Choice:* The New York Drama Critics Circle Prize Plays. Hawthorn Books. $6.00.

Gazzo, Michael Vincente. *A Hatful of Rain.* Random House. $2.95.

Giraudoux, Jean. *Tiger at the Gates.* Translated by Christopher Fry. Oxford University Press. $2.75.

Green, Carolyn. *Janus.* Random House. $2.95.

Hammerstein, Oscar, and Rodgers, Richard. *Pipe Dream.* The Viking Press. $3.50.

Hawkes, Jacquetta, and Priestley, J. B. *Dragon's Mouth.* Harper's. $2.75.

Ibsen, Henrik. *The Master Builder.* Translated by Eva LeGallienne. New York University Press. $2.50.

Jones, Robert Edmond. *The Dramatic Imagination* (new edition). Theatre Arts Books. $2.75.

Kahn, E. J., Jr. *The Merry Partners:* The Age and Stage of Harrigan & Hart. Random House. $5.00.

Kerr, Walter. *How Not to Write a Play.* Simon & Schuster. $3.50.

Kronenberger, Louis (Editor). *The Best Plays of 1954-1955.* Dodd, Mead. $5.00.

Lawrence, Jerome, and Lee, Robert E. *Inherit the Wind.* Random House. $2.95.

Levin, Ira. *No Time for Sergeants.* Random House. $2.95.

Lindsay, Howard, and Crouse, Russel. *The Great Sebastians.* Random House. $2.95.

MacGowan, Kenneth, and Melnitz, William. *The Living Stage:* A History of the World Theatre. Prentice-Hall. $8.00.

Mayorga, Margaret. *The Best Short Plays of 1954-1955.* Dodd, Mead. $3.50.

McCarthy, Mary. *Sights and Spectacles.* Theatre Chronicle 1937-1956. Farrar, Straus & Cudahy. $3.50.

McClintic, Guthrie. *Me and Kit.* Little, Brown. $5.00.

Miller, Arthur. *A View from the Bridge* (the title play and *A Memory of Two Mondays*). Viking Press. $3.00.

Molière. *Six Prose Comedies.* An English Version by George Graveley. Oxford University Press. $3.75.

Monjo, Nicolas. Introduction by Jacques Barzun. *The Edge of Perfect.* Grove Press. $3.50.

Nicoll, Allardyce (Editor). *Shakespeare Survey: 9.* Cambridge University Press. $3.75.

O'Casey, Sean. *The Green Crow.* Material reprinted from *The Flying Wasp, Windfalls* and O'Casey's journalistic work. George Braziller. $3.95.

O'Casey, Sean. *The Bishop's Bonfire.* Macmillan. $3.00.

O'Neill, Eugene. *The Long Day's Journey into Night.* Yale University Press. $3.75.

Parmelin, *Hélène. Peintres et Le Théâtre: Décors et Costumes.* (Leger, Coutaud, Gischia, Labisse, Pignon.) Editions Cercle d'Art. $15.

Purdom, C. B. *Granville Barker:* Man of the Theatre, Scholar and Dramatist. Harvard University Press. $6.00.

Robbins, Phyllis. *Maude Adams: An Intimate Portrait.* Putnam. $5.00.

Scott, A. C. *The Kabuki Theatre of Japan.* Allen & Unwin. $7.50.

Shaw, George Bernard. *Advice to a Young Critic and Other Letters.* With Notes and Introduction by E. J. West. Crown. $3.00.

Shaw, Bernard. *Saint Joan; Major Barbara; Androcles.* Modern Library. $1.45.

Shipley, Joseph T. *Guide to Great Plays.* Public Affairs Press. $10.00.

Stein, Joseph, and Glickman, Will. *Plain and Fancy.* Random House. $2.95.

Strickland, F. Cowles. *The Technique of Acting.* McGraw-Hill. $5.95.

Williams, Tennessee. *Cat on a Hot Tin Roof.* New Directions. $3.00.

Winwar, Frances. *Wingless Victory:* A Dual Biography of D'Annunzio and Duse. Harper's. $5.00.

PREVIOUS VOLUMES OF BEST PLAYS

Plays chosen to represent the theatre seasons from 1899 to 1955 are as follows:

1899-1909

Barbara Frietchie, by Clyde Fitch. Life Publishing Co.
The Climbers, by Clyde Fitch. Macmillan.
If I Were King, by Justin Huntly McCarthy. Samuel French.
The Darling of the Gods, by David Belasco. Little, Brown.
The County Chairman, by George Ade. Samuel French.
Leah Kleschna, by C. M. S. McLellan. Samuel French.
The Squaw Man, by Edwin Milton Royle.
The Great Divide, by William Vaughn Moody. Samuel French.
The Witching Hour, by Augustus Thomas. Samuel French.
The Man from Home, by Booth Tarkington and Harry Leon Wilson. Samuel French.

1909-1919

The Easiest Way, by Eugene Walter. G. W. Dillingham and Houghton Mifflin.
Mrs. Bumpstead-Leigh, by Harry James Smith. Samuel French.
Disraeli, by Louis N. Parker. Dodd, Mead.
Romance, by Edward Sheldon. Macmillan.
Seven Keys to Baldpate, by George M. Cohan. Published by Bobbs-Merrill as a novel by Earl Derr Biggers; as a play by Samuel French.
On Trial, by Elmer Reizenstein. Samuel French.
The Unchastened Woman, by Louis Kaufman Anspacher. Harcourt, Brace and Howe.
Good Gracious Annabelle, by Clare Kummer. Samuel French.
Why Marry?, by Jesse Lynch Williams. Scribner.
John Ferguson, by St. John Ervine. Macmillan.

1919-1920

Abraham Lincoln, by John Drinkwater. Houghton Mifflin.
Clarence, by Booth Tarkington. Samuel French.
Beyond the Horizon, by Eugene G. O'Neill. Boni & Liveright.

Déclassée, by Zoë Akins. Liveright, Inc.
The Famous Mrs. Fair, by James Forbes. Samuel French.
The Jest, by Sem Benelli. (American adaptation by Edward Sheldon.)
Jane Clegg, by St. John Ervine. Henry Holt.
Mamma's Affair, by Rachel Barton Butler. Samuel French.
Wedding Bells, by Salisbury Field. Samuel French.
Adam and Eva, by George Middleton and Guy Bolton. Samuel French.

1920-1921

Deburau, adapted from the French of Sacha Guitry by H. Granville Barker. Putnam.
The First Year, by Frank Craven. Samuel French.
Enter Madame, by Gilda Varesi and Dolly Byrne. Putnam.
The Green Goddess, by William Archer. Knopf.
Liliom, by Ferenc Molnar. Boni & Liveright.
Mary Rose, by James M. Barrie. Scribner.
Nice People, by Rachel Crothers. Scribner.
The Bad Man, by Porter Emerson Browne. Putnam.
The Emperor Jones, by Eugene G. O'Neill. Boni & Liveright.
The Skin Game, by John Galsworthy. Scribner.

1921-1922

Anna Christie, by Eugene G. O'Neill. Boni & Liveright.
A Bill of Divorcement, by Clemence Dane. Macmillan.
Dulcy, by George S. Kaufman and Marc Connelly. Putnam.
He Who Gets Slapped, adapted from the Russian of Leonid Andreyev by Gregory Zilboorg. Brentano's.
Six Cylinder Love, by William Anthony McGuire.
The Hero, by Gilbert Emery.
The Dover Road, by Alan Alexander Milne. Samuel French.
Ambush, by Arthur Richman.
The Circle, by William Somerset Maugham.
The Nest, by Paul Geraldy and Grace George.

1922-1923

Rain, by John Colton and Clemence Randolph. Liveright, Inc.
Loyalties, by John Galsworthy. Scribner.
Icebound, by Owen Davis. Little, Brown.
You and I, by Philip Barry. Brentano's.
The Fool, by Channing Pollock. Brentano's.

MERTON OF THE MOVIES, by George Kaufman and Marc Connelly, based on the novel of the same name by Harry Leon Wilson.
WHY NOT? by Jesse Lynch Williams. Walter H. Baker Co.
THE OLD SOAK, by Don Marquis. Doubleday, Page.
R.U.R., by Karel Capek. Translated by Paul Selver. Doubleday, Page.
MARY THE 3D, by Rachel Crothers. Brentano's.

1923-1924

THE SWAN, translated from the Hungarian of Ferenc Molnar by Melville Baker. Boni & Liveright.
OUTWARD BOUND, by Sutton Vane. Boni & Liveright.
THE SHOW-OFF, by George Kelly. Little, Brown.
THE CHANGELINGS, by Lee Wilson Dodd. Dutton.
CHICKEN FEED, by Guy Bolton. Samuel French.
SUN-UP, by Lula Vollmer. Brentano's.
BEGGAR ON HORSEBACK, by George Kaufman and Marc Connelly. Boni & Liveright.
TARNISH, by Gilbert Emery. Brentano's.
THE GOOSE HANGS HIGH, by Lewis Beach. Little, Brown.
HELL-BENT FER HEAVEN, by Hatcher Hughes. Harper.

1924-1925

WHAT PRICE GLORY? by Laurence Stallings and Maxwell Anderson. Harcourt, Brace.
THEY KNEW WHAT THEY WANTED, by Sidney Howard. Doubleday, Page.
DESIRE UNDER THE ELMS, by Eugene G. O'Neill. Boni & Liveright.
THE FIREBRAND, by Edwin Justus Mayer. Boni & Liveright.
DANCING MOTHERS, by Edgar Selwyn and Edmund Goulding.
MRS. PARTRIDGE PRESENTS, by Mary Kennedy and Ruth Hawthorne. Samuel French.
THE FALL GUY, by James Gleason and George Abbott. Samuel French.
THE YOUNGEST, by Philip Barry. Samuel French.
MINICK, by Edna Ferber and George S. Kaufman. Doubleday, Page.
WILD BIRDS, by Dan Totheroh. Doubleday, Page.

1925-1926

Craig's Wife, by George Kelly. Little, Brown.
The Great God Brown, by Eugene G. O'Neill. Boni & Liveright.
The Green Hat, by Michael Arlen.
The Dybbuk, by S. Ansky, Henry G. Alsberg-Winifred Katzin translation. Boni & Liveright.
The Enemy, by Channing Pollock. Brentano's.
The Last of Mrs. Cheyney, by Frederick Lonsdale. Samuel French.
Bride of the Lamb, by William Hurlbut. Boni & Liveright.
The Wisdom Tooth, by Marc Connelly. George H. Doran.
The Butter and Egg Man, by George Kaufman. Boni & Liveright.
Young Woodley, by John van Druten. Simon & Schuster.

1926-1927

Broadway, by Philip Dunning and George Abbott. George H. Doran.
Saturday's Children, by Maxwell Anderson. Longmans, Green.
Chicago, by Maurine Watkins. Knopf.
The Constant Wife, by William Somerset Maugham. George H. Doran.
The Play's the Thing, by Ferenc Molnar and P. G. Wodehouse. Brentano's.
The Road to Rome, by Robert Emmet Sherwood. Scribner.
The Silver Cord, by Sidney Howard. Scribner.
The Cradle Song, translated from the Spanish of G. Martinez Sierra by John Garrett Underhill. Dutton.
Daisy Mayme, by George Kelly. Little, Brown.
In Abraham's Bosom, by Paul Green. McBride.

1927-1928

Strange Interlude, by Eugene G. O'Neill. Boni & Liveright.
The Royal Family, by Edna Ferber and George Kaufman. Doubleday, Doran.
Burlesque, by George Manker Watters and Arthur Hopkins. Doubleday, Doran.
Coquette, by George Abbott and Ann Bridgers. Longmans, Green.
Behold the Bridegroom, by George Kelly. Little, Brown.
Porgy, by DuBose Heyward. Doubleday, Doran.
Paris Bound, by Philip Barry. Samuel French.
Escape, by John Galsworthy. Scribner.

THE RACKET, by Bartlett Cormack. Samuel French.
THE PLOUGH AND THE STARS, by Sean O'Casey. Macmillan.

1928-1929

STREET SCENE, by Elmer Rice. Samuel French.
JOURNEY'S END, by R. C. Sherriff. Brentano's.
WINGS OVER EUROPE, by Robert Nichols and Maurice Browne. Covici-Friede.
HOLIDAY, by Philip Barry. Samuel French.
THE FRONT PAGE, by Ben Hecht and Charles MacArthur. Covici-Friede.
LET US BE GAY, by Rachel Crothers. Samuel French.
MACHINAL, by Sophie Treadwell.
LITTLE ACCIDENT, by Floyd Dell and Thomas Mitchell.
GYPSY, by Maxwell Anderson.
THE KINGDOM OF GOD, by G. Martinez Sierra; English version by Helen and Harley Granville-Barker. Dutton.

1929-1930

THE GREEN PASTURES, by Marc Connelly (adapted from "Ol' Man Adam and His Chillun," by Roark Bradford). Farrar & Rinehart.
THE CRIMINAL CODE, by Martin Flavin. Horace Liveright.
BERKELEY SQUARE, by John Balderston.
STRICTLY DISHONORABLE, by Preston Sturges. Horace Liveright.
THE FIRST MRS. FRASER, by St. John Ervine. Macmillan.
THE LAST MILE, by John Wexley. Samuel French.
JUNE MOON, by Ring W. Lardner and George S. Kaufman. Scribner.
MICHAEL AND MARY, by A. A. Milne. Chatto & Windus.
DEATH TAKES A HOLIDAY, by Walter Ferris (adapted from the Italian of Alberto Casella). Samuel French.
REBOUND, by Donald Ogden Stewart. Samuel French.

1930-1931

ELIZABETH THE QUEEN, by Maxwell Anderson. Longmans, Green.
TOMORROW AND TOMORROW, by Philip Barry. Samuel French.
ONCE IN A LIFETIME, by George S. Kaufman and Moss Hart. Farrar & Rinehart.
GREEN GROW THE LILACS, by Lynn Riggs. Samuel French.
AS HUSBANDS GO, by Rachel Crothers. Samuel French.

ALISON'S HOUSE, by Susan Glaspell. Samuel French.
FIVE-STAR FINAL, by Louis Weitzenkorn. Samuel French.
OVERTURE, by William Bolitho. Simon & Schuster.
THE BARRETTS OF WIMPOLE STREET, by Rudolf Besier. Little, Brown.
GRAND HOTEL, adapted from the German of Vicki Baum by W. A. Drake.

1931-1932

OF THEE I SING, by George S. Kaufman and Morrie Ryskind; music and lyrics by George and Ira Gershwin. Knopf.
MOURNING BECOMES ELECTRA, by Eugene G. O'Neill. Horace Liveright.
REUNION IN VIENNA, by Robert Emmet Sherwood. Scribner.
THE HOUSE OF CONNELLY, by Paul Green. Samuel French.
THE ANIMAL KINGDOM, by Philip Barry. Samuel French.
THE LEFT BANK, by Elmer Rice. Samuel French.
ANOTHER LANGUAGE, by Rose Franken. Samuel French.
BRIEF MOMENT, by S. N. Behrman. Farrar & Rinehart.
THE DEVIL PASSES, by Benn W. Levy. Martin Secker.
CYNARA, by H. M. Harwood and R. F. Gore-Browne. Samuel French.

1932-1933

BOTH YOUR HOUSES, by Maxwell Anderson. Samuel French.
DINNER AT EIGHT, by George S. Kaufman and Edna Ferber. Doubleday, Doran.
WHEN LADIES MEET, by Rachel Crothers. Samuel French.
DESIGN FOR LIVING, by Noel Coward. Doubleday, Doran.
BIOGRAPHY, by S. N. Behrman. Farrar & Rinehart.
ALIEN CORN, by Sidney Howard. Scribner.
THE LATE CHRISTOPHER BEAN, adapted from the French of René Fauchois by Sidney Howard. Samuel French.
WE, THE PEOPLE, by Elmer Rice. Coward-McCann.
PIGEONS AND PEOPLE, by George M. Cohan.
ONE SUNDAY AFTERNOON, by James Hagan. Samuel French.

1933-1934

MARY OF SCOTLAND, by Maxwell Anderson. Doubleday, Doran.
MEN IN WHITE, by Sidney Kingsley. Covici-Friede.
DODSWORTH, by Sinclair Lewis and Sidney Howard. Harcourt, Brace.

AH, WILDERNESS, by Eugene O'Neill. Random House.
THEY SHALL NOT DIE, by John Wexley. Knopf.
HER MASTER'S VOICE, by Clare Kummer. Samuel French.
NO MORE LADIES, by A. E. Thomas.
WEDNESDAY'S CHILD, by Leopold Atlas. Samuel French.
THE SHINING HOUR, by Keith Winter. Doubleday, Doran.
THE GREEN BAY TREE, by Mordaunt Shairp. Baker International Play Bureau.

1934-1935

THE CHILDREN'S HOUR, by Lillian Hellman. Knopf.
VALLEY FORGE, by Maxwell Anderson. Anderson House.
THE PETRIFIED FOREST, by Robert Sherwood. Scribner.
THE OLD MAID, by Zoë Akins. Appleton-Century.
ACCENT ON YOUTH, by Samson Raphaelson. Samuel French.
MERRILY WE ROLL ALONG, by George S. Kaufman and Moss Hart. Random House.
AWAKE AND SING, by Clifford Odets. Random House.
THE FARMER TAKES A WIFE, by Frank B. Elser and Marc Connelly.
LOST HORIZONS, by John Hayden.
THE DISTAFF SIDE, by John van Druten. Knopf.

1935-1936

WINTERSET, by Maxwell Anderson. Anderson House.
IDIOT'S DELIGHT, by Robert Emmet Sherwood. Scribner.
END OF SUMMER, by S. N. Behrman. Random House.
FIRST LADY, by Katharine Dayton and George S. Kaufman. Random House.
VICTORIA REGINA, by Laurence Housman. Samuel French.
BOY MEETS GIRL, by Bella and Samuel Spewack. Random House.
DEAD END, by Sidney Kingsley. Random House.
CALL IT A DAY, by Dodie Smith. Samuel French.
ETHAN FROME, by Owen Davis and Donald Davis. Scribner.
PRIDE AND PREJUDICE, by Helen Jerome. Doubleday, Doran.

1936-1937

HIGH TOR, by Maxwell Anderson. Anderson House.
YOU CAN'T TAKE IT WITH YOU, by Moss Hart and George S. Kaufman. Farrar & Rinehart.
JOHNNY JOHNSON, by Paul Green. Samuel French.
DAUGHTERS OF ATREUS, by Robert Turney. Knopf.

STAGE DOOR, by Edna Ferber and George S. Kaufman. Doubleday, Doran.
THE WOMEN, by Clare Boothe. Random House.
ST. HELENA, by R. C. Sherriff and Jeanne de Casalis. Samuel French.
YES, MY DARLING DAUGHTER, by Mark Reed. Samuel French.
EXCURSION, by Victor Wolfson. Random House.
TOVARICH, by Jacques Deval and Robert E. Sherwood. Random House.

1937-1938

OF MICE AND MEN, by John Steinbeck. Covici-Friede.
OUR TOWN, by Thornton Wilder. Coward-McCann.
SHADOW AND SUBSTANCE, by Paul Vincent Carroll. Random House.
ON BORROWED TIME, by Paul Osborn. Knopf.
THE STAR-WAGON, by Maxwell Anderson. Anderson House.
SUSAN AND GOD, by Rachel Crothers. Random House.
PROLOGUE TO GLORY, by E. P. Conkle. Random House.
AMPHITRYON 38, by S. N. Behrman. Random House.
GOLDEN BOY, by Clifford Odets. Random House.
WHAT A LIFE, by Clifford Goldsmith. Dramatists' Play Service.

1938-1939

ABE LINCOLN IN ILLINOIS, by Robert E. Sherwood. Scribner.
THE LITTLE FOXES, by Lillian Hellman. Random House.
ROCKET TO THE MOON, by Clifford Odets. Random House.
THE AMERICAN WAY, by George S. Kaufman and Moss Hart. Random House.
NO TIME FOR COMEDY, by S. N. Behrman. Random House.
THE PHILADELPHIA STORY, by Philip Barry. Coward-McCann.
THE WHITE STEED, by Paul Vincent Carroll. Random House.
HERE COME THE CLOWNS, by Philip Barry. Coward-McCann.
FAMILY PORTRAIT, by Lenore Coffee and William Joyce Cowen. Random House.
KISS THE BOYS GOOD-BYE, by Clare Boothe. Random House.

1939-1940

THERE SHALL BE NO NIGHT, by Robert E. Sherwood. Scribner.
KEY LARGO, by Maxwell Anderson. Anderson House.
THE WORLD WE MAKE, by Sidney Kingsley.
LIFE WITH FATHER, by Howard Lindsay and Russel Crouse. Knopf.

THE MAN WHO CAME TO DINNER, by George S. Kaufman and Moss Hart. Random House.
THE MALE ANIMAL, by James Thurber and Elliott Nugent. Random House, New York, and MacMillan Co., Canada.
THE TIME OF YOUR LIFE, by William Saroyan. Harcourt, Brace.
SKYLARK, by Samson Raphaelson. Random House.
MARGIN FOR ERROR, by Clare Boothe. Random House.
MORNING'S AT SEVEN, by Paul Osborn. Samuel French.

1940-1941

NATIVE SON, by Paul Green and Richard Wright. Harper.
WATCH ON THE RHINE, by Lillian Hellman. Random House.
THE CORN IS GREEN, by Emlyn Williams. Random House.
LADY IN THE DARK, by Moss Hart. Random House.
ARSENIC AND OLD LACE, by Joseph Kesselring. Random House.
MY SISTER EILEEN, by Joseph Fields and Jerome Chodorov. Random House.
FLIGHT TO THE WEST, by Elmer Rice. Coward-McCann.
CLAUDIA, by Rose Franken Meloney. Farrar & Rinehart.
MR. AND MRS. NORTH, by Owen Davis. Samuel French.
GEORGE WASHINGTON SLEPT HERE, by George S. Kaufman and Moss Hart. Random House.

1941-1942

IN TIME TO COME, by Howard Koch. Dramatists' Play Service.
THE MOON IS DOWN, by John Steinbeck. Viking.
BLITHE SPIRIT, by Noel Coward. Doubleday, Doran.
JUNIOR MISS, by Jerome Chodorov and Joseph Fields. Random House.
CANDLE IN THE WIND, by Maxwell Anderson. Anderson House.
LETTERS TO LUCERNE, by Fritz Rotter and Allen Vincent. Samuel French.
JASON, by Samson Raphaelson. Random House.
ANGEL STREET, by Patrick Hamilton. Constable & Co., under the title "Gaslight."
UNCLE HARRY, by Thomas Job. Samuel French.
HOPE FOR A HARVEST, by Sophie Treadwell. Samuel French.

1942-1943

THE PATRIOTS, by Sidney Kingsley. Random House.
THE EVE OF ST. MARK, by Maxwell Anderson. Anderson House.

THE SKIN OF OUR TEETH, by Thornton Wilder. Harper.
WINTER SOLDIERS, by Dan James.
TOMORROW THE WORLD, by James Gow and Arnaud d'Usseau. Scribner.
HARRIET, by Florence Ryerson and Colin Clements. Scribner.
THE DOUGHGIRLS, by Joseph Fields. Random House.
THE DAMASK CHEEK, by John van Druten and Lloyd Morris. Random House.
KISS AND TELL, by F. Hugh Herbert. Coward-McCann.
OKLAHOMA!, by Oscar Hammerstein 2nd and Richard Rodgers. Random House.

1943-1944

WINGED VICTORY, by Moss Hart. Random House.
THE SEARCHING WIND, by Lillian Hellman. Viking.
THE VOICE OF THE TURTLE, by John van Druten. Random House.
DECISION, by Edward Chodorov.
OVER 21, by Ruth Gordon. Random House.
OUTRAGEOUS FORTUNE, by Rose Franken. Samuel French.
JACOBOWSKY AND THE COLONEL, by S. N. Behrman. Random House.
STORM OPERATION, by Maxwell Anderson. Anderson House.
PICK-UP GIRL, by Elsa Shelley.
THE INNOCENT VOYAGE, by Paul Osborn.

1944-1945

A BELL FOR ADANO, by Paul Osborn. Knopf.
I REMEMBER MAMA, by John van Druten. Harcourt, Brace.
THE HASTY HEART, by John Patrick. Random House.
THE GLASS MENAGERIE, by Tennessee Williams. Random House.
HARVEY, by Mary Chase.
THE LATE GEORGE APLEY, by John P. Marquand and George S. Kaufman.
SOLDIER'S WIFE, by Rose Franken. Samuel French.
ANNA LUCASTA, by Philip Yordan. Random House.
FOOLISH NOTION, by Philip Barry.
DEAR RUTH, by Norman Krasna. Random House.

1945-1946

STATE OF THE UNION, by Howard Lindsay and Russel Crouse. Random House.
HOME OF THE BRAVE, by Arthur Laurents. Random House.

DEEP ARE THE ROOTS, by Arnaud d'Usseau and James Gow. Scribner.
THE MAGNIFICENT YANKEE, by Emmet Lavery. Samuel French.
ANTIGONE, by Lewis Galantière (from the French of Jean Anouilh). Random House.
O MISTRESS MINE, by Terence Rattigan. Published and revised by the author.
BORN YESTERDAY, by Garson Kanin. Viking.
DREAM GIRL, by Elmer Rice. Coward-McCann.
THE RUGGED PATH, by Robert E. Sherwood. Scribner.
LUTE SONG, by Will Irwin and Sidney Howard. Published version by Will Irwin and Leopoldine Howard.

1946-1947

ALL MY SONS, by Arthur Miller. Reynal & Hitchcock.
THE ICEMAN COMETH, by Eugene G. O'Neill. Random House.
JOAN OF LORRAINE, by Maxwell Anderson. Published by Maxwell Anderson.
ANOTHER PART OF THE FOREST, by Lillian Hellman. Viking.
YEARS AGO, by Ruth Gordon. Viking.
JOHN LOVES MARY, by Norman Krasna. Copyright by Norman Krasna.
THE FATAL WEAKNESS, by George Kelly. Samuel French.
THE STORY OF MARY SURRATT, by John Patrick. Dramatists' Play Service.
CHRISTOPHER BLAKE, by Moss Hart. Random House.
BRIGADOON, by Alan Jay Lerner and Frederick Loewe. Coward-McCann.

1947-1948

A STREETCAR NAMED DESIRE, by Tennessee Williams. New Directions.
MISTER ROBERTS, by Thomas Heggen and Joshua Logan. Houghton Mifflin.
COMMAND DECISION, by William Wister Haines. Random House.
THE WINSLOW BOY, by Terence Rattigan.
THE HEIRESS, by Ruth and Augustus Goetz.
ALLEGRO, by Richard Rodgers and Oscar Hammerstein 2d. Knopf. Music published by Williamson Music, Inc.
EASTWARD IN EDEN, by Dorothy Gardner. Longmans, Green.
SKIPPER NEXT TO GOD, by Jan de Hartog.

An Inspector Calls, by J. B. Priestley.
Me and Molly, by Gertrude Berg.

1948-1949

Death of a Salesman, by Arthur Miller. Viking.
Anne of the Thousand Days, by Maxwell Anderson. Sloane.
The Madwoman of Chaillot, by Maurice Valency, adapted from the French of Jean Giraudoux. Random House.
Detective Story, by Sidney Kingsley. Random House.
Edward, My Son, by Robert Morley and Noel Langley. Random House, New York, and Samuel French, London.
Life with Mother, by Howard Lindsay and Russel Crouse. Knopf.
Light Up the Sky, by Moss Hart. Random House.
The Silver Whistle, by Robert Edward McEnroe. Dramatists' Play Service.
Two Blind Mice, by Samuel Spewack. Dramatists' Play Service.
Goodbye, My Fancy, by Fay Kanin. Samuel French.

1949-1950

The Cocktail Party, by T. S. Eliot. Harcourt, Brace.
The Member of the Wedding, by Carson McCullers. Houghton Mifflin.
The Innocents, by William Archibald. Coward-McCann.
Lost in the Stars, by Maxwell Anderson and Kurt Weill. Sloane.
Come Back, Little Sheba, by William Inge. Random House.
The Happy Time, by Samuel Taylor. Random House.
The Wisteria Trees, by Joshua Logan. Random House.
I Know My Love, by S. N. Behrman. Random House.
The Enchanted, by Maurice Valency, adapted from a play by Jean Giraudoux. Random House.
Clutterbuck, by Benn W. Levy. Dramatists' Play Service.

1950-1951

Guys and Dolls, by Jo Swerling, Abe Burrows and Frank Loesser.
Darkness at Noon, by Sidney Kingsley and Arthur Koestler. Random House.
Billy Budd, by Louis O. Coxe and Robert Chapman. Princeton University Press.
The Autumn Garden, by Lillian Hellman. Little, Brown & Co.

Bell, Book and Candle, by John van Druten. Random House.
The Country Girl, by Clifford Odets. Viking Press.
The Rose Tattoo, by Tennessee Williams. New Directions.
Season in the Sun, by Wolcott Gibbs. Random House.
Affairs of State, by Louis Verneuil.
Second Threshold, by Philip Barry. Harper & Bros.

1951-1952

Mrs. McThing, by Mary Coyle Chase.
The Shrike, by Joseph Kramm. Random House.
I Am a Camera, by John van Druten. Random House.
The Fourposter, by Jan de Hartog.
Point of No Return, by Paul Osborn. Random House.
Barefoot in Athens, by Maxwell Anderson. Sloane.
Venus Observed, by Christopher Fry. Oxford.
Jane, by S. N. Behrman and Somerset Maugham. Random House.
Gigi, by Anita Loos and Colette. Random House.
Remains to Be Seen, by Howard Lindsay and Russel Crouse. Random House.

1952-1953

The Time of the Cuckoo, by Arthur Laurents. Random House.
Bernardine, by Mary Coyle Chase.
Dial "M" for Murder, by Frederick Knott. Random House.
The Climate of Eden, by Moss Hart. Random House.
The Love of Four Colonels, by Peter Ustinov.
The Crucible, by Arthur Miller. Viking.
The Emperor's Clothes, by George Tabori. Samuel French.
Picnic, by William Inge. Random House.
Wonderful Town, by Joseph Fields, Jerome Chodorov, Betty Comden and Adolph Green. Random House.
My 3 Angels, by Sam and Bella Spewack.

1953-1954

The Caine Mutiny Court-Martial, by Herman Wouk. Doubleday & Company, Inc.
In the Summer House, by Jane Bowles. Random House.
The Confidential Clerk, by T. S. Eliot. Harcourt, Brace and Company, Inc.
Take a Giant Step, by Louis Peterson.
The Teahouse of the August Moon, by John Patrick. G. P. Putnam's Sons.

THE IMMORALIST, by Ruth and Augustus Goetz. Ruth and Augustus Goetz. Dramatists' Play Service.
TEA AND SYMPATHY, by Robert Anderson. Random House.
THE GIRL ON THE VIA FLAMINIA, by Alfred Hayes.
THE GOLDEN APPLE, by John Latouche and Jerome Moross. Random House.
THE MAGIC AND THE LOSS, by Julian Funt. Samuel French.

1954-1955

THE BOY FRIEND, by Sandy Wilson.
THE LIVING ROOM, by Graham Greene. Viking.
BAD SEED, by Maxwell Anderson. Dodd, Mead.
WITNESS FOR THE PROSECUTION, by Agatha Christie.
THE FLOWERING PEACH, by Clifford Odets.
THE DESPERATE HOURS, by Joseph Hayes. Random House.
THE DARK IS LIGHT ENOUGH, by Christopher Fry. Oxford.
BUS STOP, by William Inge. Random House.
CAT ON A HOT TIN ROOF, by Tennessee Williams. New Directions.
INHERIT THE WIND, by Jerome Lawrence and Robert E. Lee. Random House.

WHERE AND WHEN THEY WERE BORN

(Compiled from the most authentic records available)

Name	Birthplace	Year
Abbott, George	Forestville, N. Y.	1889
Abel, Walter	St. Paul, Minn.	1898
Addy, Wesley	Omaha, Neb.	1912
Adler, Luther	New York City	1903
Aherne, Brian	King's Norton, England	1902
Aldrich, Richard	Boston, Mass.	1902
Anders, Glenn	Los Angeles, Cal.	1890
Anderson, Judith	Australia	1898
Anderson, Maxwell	Atlantic City, Pa.	1888
Andrews, Julie	London, England	1935
Arthur, Jean	New York City	1905
Ashcroft, Peggy	Croydon, England	1907
Bainter, Fay	Los Angeles, Cal.	1892
Bankhead, Tallulah	Huntsville, Ala.	1902
Barrymore, Ethel	Philadelphia, Pa.	1879
Barton, James	Gloucester, N. J.	1890
Behrman, S. N.	Worcester, Mass.	1893
Bellamy, Ralph	Chicago, Ill.	1904
Bergman, Ingrid	Stockholm, Sweden	1917
Bergner, Elisabeth	Vienna, Austria	1900
Berlin, Irving	Russia	1888
Best, Edna	Hove, England	1900
Blackmer, Sidney	Salisbury, N. C.	1898
Bolger, Ray	Dorchester, Mass.	1904
Bondi, Beulah	Chicago, Ill.	1892
Booth, Shirley	New York City	1909
Bourneuf, Philip	Boston, Mass.	1912
Boyer, Charles	Figeac, France	1899
Brando, Marlon	Omaha, Neb.	1924
Brent, Romney	Saltillo, Mex.	1902
Brown, Joe E.	Holgate, Ohio	1892
Burke, Billie	Washington, D. C.	1885
Byington, Spring	Colorado Springs, Colo.	1898

Cagney, James	New York City	1904
Cagney, Jeanne	New York City	1920
Calhern, Louis	New York City	1895
Cantor, Eddie	New York City	1892
Carnovsky, Morris	St. Louis, Mo.	1898
Carradine, John	New York City	1906
Carroll, Leo G.	Weedon, England	1892
Carroll, Madeleine	West Bromwich, England	1906
Channing, Carol	Seattle, Wash.	1921
Chase, Ilka	New York City	1905
Chatterton, Ruth	New York City	1893
Claire, Ina	Washington, D. C.	1895
Clark, Bobby	Springfield, Ohio	1888
Clift, Montgomery	Omaha, Neb.	1921
Clive, Colin	St. Malo, France	1900
Clurman, Harold	New York City	1901
Cobb, Lee	New York City	1911
Coburn, Charles	Macon, Ga.	1877
Collinge, Patricia	Dublin, Ireland	1894
Collins, Russell	New Orleans, La.	1897
Colt, Ethel Barrymore	Mamaroneck, N. Y.	1911
Colt, John Drew	New York City	1914
Conroy, Frank	London, England	1885
Cook, Donald	Portland, Ore.	1902
Cook, Joe	Evansville, Ind.	1890
Cooper, Gladys	Lewisham, England	1888
Cooper, Melville	Birmingham, England	1896
Corbett, Leonora	London, England	1908
Cornell, Katharine	Berlin, Germany	1898
Coulouris, George	Manchester, England	1906
Coward, Noel	Teddington, England	1899
Crawford, Cheryl	Akron, Ohio	1902
Cromwell, John	Toledo, Ohio	1888
Cronyn, Hume	London, Ontario	1912
Crothers, Rachel	Bloomington, Ill.	1878
Crouse, Russel	Findlay, Ohio	1893
Cummings, Constance	Seattle, Wash.	1911
Dale, Margaret	Philadelphia, Pa.	1880
Dana, Leora	New York City	1923
Daniell, Henry	London, England	1894
Davis, Owen	Portland, Me.	1874
Derwent, Clarence	London, England	1884
Dixon, Jean	Waterbury, Conn.	1905

Douglas, Melvyn	Macon, Ga.	1901
Dowling, Eddie	Woonsocket, R. I.	1894
Drake, Alfred	New York City	1914
Duncan, Todd	Danville, Ky.	1900
Dunning, Philip	Meriden, Conn.	1890
Durante, Jimmy	New York City	1893
Eldridge, Florence	Brooklyn, N. Y.	1901
Elsom, Isobel	Cambridge, England	1893
Evans, Edith	London, England	1888
Evans, Maurice	Dorchester, England	1901
Evans, Wilbur	Philadelphia, Pa.	1908
Evelyn, Judith	Seneca, S. Dak.	1913
Ewell, Tom	Owensboro, Ky.	1912
Fabray, Nanette	New Orleans, La.	1921
Fay, Frank	San Francisco, Cal.	1897
Ferber, Edna	Kalamazoo, Mich.	1887
Ferrer, José	Puerto Rico	1912
Field, Betty	Boston, Mass.	1918
Field, Virginia	London, England	1917
Fields, Gracie	Rochdale, England	1898
Fitzgerald, Barry	Dublin, Ireland	1888
Fitzgerald, Geraldine	Dublin, Ireland	1914
Flemyng, Robert	Liverpool, England	1912
Fletcher, Bramwell	Bradford, Yorkshire, Eng.	1904
Fonda, Henry	Grand Island, Neb.	1905
Fontanne, Lynn	London, England	1887
Forbes, Brenda	London, England	1909
Foy, Eddie, Jr.	New Rochelle, N. Y.	1907
Francis, Arlene	Boston, Mass.	1908
Fry, Christopher	England	1907
Gahagan, Helen	Boonton, N. J.	1900
Gaxton, William	San Francisco, Cal.	1893
Geddes, Barbara Bel	New York City	1922
Geddes, Norman Bel	Adrian, Mich.	1893
George, Grace	New York City	1879
Gershwin, Ira	New York City	1896
Gielgud, Sir John	London, England	1904
Gillmore, Margalo	England	1901
Gilmore, Virginia	El Monte, Cal.	1919
Gish, Dorothy	Massillon, Ohio	1898
Gish, Lillian	Springfield, Ohio	1896

Golden, John	New York City	1874
Goodner, Carol	New York City	1904
Gordon, Ruth	Wollaston, Mass.	1896
Greaza, Walter	St. Paul, Minn.	1900
Green, Martyn	London, England	1899
Greenwood, Joan	London, England	1921
Guinness, Alec	London, England	1914
Gwenn, Edmund	Glamorgan, Wales	1875
Hagen, Uta	Göttingen, Germany	1919
Hammerstein, Oscar, II	New York City	1895
Hampden, Walter	Brooklyn, N. Y.	1879
Hardie, Russell	Griffin Mills, N. Y.	1906
Hardwicke, Sir Cedric	Lye, Stourbridge, England	1893
Harris, Julie	Grosse Point, Mich.	1925
Harrison, Rex	Huyton, Lancashire, England	1908
Hart, Moss	New York City	1904
Havoc, June	Seattle, Wash.	1916
Haydon, Julie	Oak Park, Ill.	1910
Hayes, Helen	Washington, D. C.	1900
Hayward, Leland	Nebraska City, Neb.	1902
Heflin, Frances	Oklahoma City, Okla.	1924
Heineman, Eda	Japan	1891
Hellman, Lillian	New Orleans, La.	1905
Helmore, Tom	London, England	1912
Helpmann, Robert	South Australia	1911
Henie, Sonja	Oslo, Norway	1913
Hepburn, Audrey	Brussels, Belgium	1929
Hepburn, Katharine	Hartford, Conn.	1909
Herlie, Eileen	Glasgow, Scotland	1920
Hiller, Wendy	Bramhall, England	1912
Holliday, Judy	New York City	1924
Holloway, Stanley	London, England	1890
Holm, Celeste	New York City	1919
Homolka, Oscar	Vienna, Austria	1898
Hull, Josephine	Newtonville, Mass.	1886
Hull, Henry	Louisville, Ky.	1890
Hunt, Martita	Argentine Republic	1900
Hunter, Kim	Detroit, Mich.	1922
Hussey, Ruth	Providence, R. I.	1917
Inescort, Frieda	Hitchin, Scotland	1901
Ives, Burl	Hunt Township, Ill.	1909

Johnson, Harold J. (Chic)	Chicago, Ill.	1891
Joy, Nicholas	Paris, France	1889
Kane, Whitford	Larne, Ireland	1882
Kanin, Garson	Rochester, N. Y.	1912
Karloff, Boris	Dulwich, England	1887
Kaufman, George S.	Pittsburgh, Pa.	1889
Kaye, Danny	New York City	1914
Kazan, Elia	Constantinople	1909
Keith, Robert	Fowler, Ind.	1898
Kennedy, Arthur	Worcester, Mass.	1914
Kerr, Deborah	Helensburgh, Scotland	1921
Kerr, John	New York City	1931
Killbride, Percy	San Francisco, Cal.	1880
King, Dennis	Coventry, England	1897
Kingsley, Sidney	New York City	1906
Kirkland, Patricia	New York City	1927
Knox, Alexander	Ontario	1907
Kruger, Otto	Toledo, Ohio	1885
Lahr, Bert	New York City	1895
Landis, Jessie Royce	Chicago, Ill.	1904
Laughton, Charles	Scarborough, England	1899
LeGallienne, Eva	London, England	1899
Leigh, Vivien	Darjeeling, India	1913
Leighton, Margaret	Barnt Green, England	1922
Lillie, Beatrice	Toronto, Canada	1898
Lindsay, Howard	Waterford, N. Y.	1899
Linn, Bambi	Brooklyn, N. Y.	1926
Lockhart, Gene	Ontario	1892
Loeb, Philip	Philadelphia, Pa.	1892
Logan, Joshua	Texarkana, Tex.	1908
Lonergan, Lenore	Toledo, Ohio	1928
Lukas, Paul	Budapest, Hungary	1891
Lunt, Alfred	Milwaukee, Wis.	1893
Lytell, Bert	New York City	1885
MacMahon, Aline	McKeesport, Pa.	1899
Mamoulian, Rouben	Tiflis, Russia	1898
Mann, Iris	Brooklyn, N. Y.	1939
Marceau, Marcel	Near Strasbourg, France	1923
March, Fredric	Racine, Wis.	1897
Martin, Mary	Weatherford, Texas	1913

Mason, James	Huddersfield, England	1909
Massey, Raymond	Toronto, Canada	1896
Matteson, Ruth	San Jose, Cal.	1905
Maugham, W. Somerset	England	1874
McClintic, Guthrie	Seattle, Wash.	1893
McCormick, Myron	Albany, Ind.	1907
McCracken, Joan	Philadelphia, Pa.	1923
McGrath, Paul	Chicago, Ill.	1900
McGuire, Dorothy	Omaha, Neb.	1918
McKenna, Siobhan	Belfast, Ireland	1923
Menotti, Gian-Carlo	Italy	1912
Meredith, Burgess	Cleveland, Ohio	1908
Merkel, Una	Covington, Ky.	1903
Merman, Ethel	Astoria, L. I.	1909
Middleton, Ray	Chicago, Ill.	1907
Mielziner, Jo	Paris, France	1901
Miller, Arthur	New York City	1915
Miller, Gilbert	New York City	1884
Mitchell, Thomas	Elizabeth, N. J.	1892
Moore, Victor	Hammonton, N. J.	1876
Moorehead, Agnes	Clinton, Mass.	1906
Morgan, Claudia	New York City	1912
Morley, Robert	Semley, England	1908
Moss, Arnold	Brooklyn, N. Y.	1910
Muni, Paul	Lemberg, Austria	1895
Nagel, Conrad	Keokuk, Iowa	1897
Natwick, Mildred	Baltimore, Md.	1908
Neal, Patricia	Packard, Ky.	1926
Nesbitt, Cathleen	Cheshire, England	1889
Nugent, Elliott	Dover, Ohio	1900
Odets, Clifford	Philadelphia, Pa.	1906
Oenslager, Donald	Harrisburg, Pa.	1902
Olivier, Sir Laurence	Dorking, Surrey, England	1907
Olsen, John Siguard (Ole)	Peru, Ind.	1892
O'Malley, Rex	London, England	1906
O'Neal, Frederick	Brookville, Miss.	1905
Page, Geraldine	Kirksville, Mo.	1925
Palmer, Lilli	Posen, Austria	1914
Petina, Irra	Leningrad, Russia	1900
Picon, Molly	New York City	1898

Pinza, Ezio	Rome, Italy	1895
Porter, Cole	Peru, Ind.	1892
Price, Vincent	St. Louis, Mo.	1914
Quayle, Anthony	Ainsdale, England	1913
Rains, Claude	London, England	1889
Raitt, John	Santa Ana, Cal.	1917
Rathbone, Basil	Johannesburg, Africa	1892
Redgrave, Michael	Bristol, England	1908
Redman, Joyce	Newcastle, Ireland	1918
Reed, Florence	Philadelphia, Pa.	1883
Rennie, James	Toronto, Canada	1890
Rice, Elmer	New York City	1892
Richardson, Sir Ralph	Cheltenham, England	1902
Roberts, Joan	New York City	1918
Rodgers, Richard	New York City	1902
Ross, Anthony	New York City	1906
Royle, Selena	New York City	1905
Sarnoff, Dorothy	Brooklyn, N. Y.	1919
Saroyan, William	Fresno, Cal.	1908
Schildkraut, Joseph	Vienna, Austria	1895
Scott, Martha	Jamesport, Mo.	1914
Segal, Vivienne	Philadelphia, Pa.	1897
Sherman, Hiram	Boston, Mass.	1908
Sherwood, Robert Emmet	New Rochelle, N. Y.	1896
Shumlin, Herman	Atwood, Colo.	1898
Silvers, Phil	Brooklyn, N. Y.	1911
Simms, Hilda	Minneapolis, Minn.	1920
Skinner, Cornelia Otis	Chicago, Ill.	1902
Slezak, Walter	Vienna, Austria	1902
Smith, Kent	Smithfield, Me.	1910
Stanley, Kim	Tularosa, N. M.	1921
Stapleton, Maureen	Troy, N. Y.	1926
Starr, Frances	Oneonta, N. Y.	1886
Stickney, Dorothy	Dickinson, N. D.	1903
Stoddard, Haila	Great Falls, Mont.	1914
Stone, Carol	New York City	1917
Stone, Dorothy	New York City	1905
Stone, Ezra	New Bedford, Mass.	1918
Stone, Fred	Denver, Colo.	1873
Straight, Beatrice	Old Westbury, N. Y.	1918

Sullavan, Margaret	Norfolk, Va.	1910
Sullivan, Francis L.	London, England	1903
Tandy, Jessica	London, England	1909
Tetzel, Joan	New York City	1923
Thorndike, Sybil	Gainsborough, England	1882
Tozere, Frederick	Brookline, Mass.	1901
Tracy, Lee	Atlanta, Ga.	1898
Truex, Ernest	Red Hill, Mo.	1890
van Druten, John	London, England	1902
Van Patten, Dick	New York City	1929
Varden, Evelyn	Venita, Okla.	1893
Verdon, Gwen	Culver City, Cal.	1926
Walker, June	New York City	1904
Walker, Nancy	Philadelphia, Pa.	1922
Wallach, Eli	Brooklyn, N. Y.	1915
Wanamaker, Sam	Chicago, Ill.	1919
Ward, Penelope	London, England	1914
Waring, Richard	Buckinghamshire, England	1912
Waters, Ethel	Chester, Pa.	1900
Watson, Douglas	Jackson, Ga.	1921
Watson, Lucile	Quebec, Canada	1879
Wayne, David	Travers City, Mich.	1914
Webb, Alan	York, England	1906
Webb, Clifton	Indiana	1891
Webster, Margaret	New York City	1905
Welles, Orson	Kenosha, Wis.	1915
West, Mae	Brooklyn, N. Y.	1892
Weston, Ruth	Boston, Mass.	1911
Widmark, Richard	Sunrise, Minn.	1914
Wilder, Thornton	Madison, Wis.	1897
Willard, Catherine	Dayton, Ohio	1895
Williams, Emlyn	Wales	1905
Williams, Rhys	Wales	1903
Williams, Tennessee	Columbus, Miss.	1914
Winwood, Estelle	England	1883
Wood, Peggy	Brooklyn, N. Y.	1894
Wyatt, Jane	Campgaw, N. J.	1912
Wynn, Ed	Philadelphia, Pa.	1886
Wynn, Keenan	New York City	1917
Yurka, Blanche	Bohemia	1893

NECROLOGY

June 1, 1955—May 31, 1956

Allen, Fred, 61, actor. He began his career in vaudeville as a juggler and toured the United States and Australia billed under such names as Paul Huckle, Fred St. James and Freddie James. His real name was John Florence Sullivan. Gradually he altered his act until he relied more on his monologue patter. He made his Broadway debut in "The Passing Show of 1922." He was in "The Greenwich Village Follies," "The Little Show," "Three's a Crowd" and others. But it was on radio that he became best known and his "Allen's Alley" interviews became nationally famous. He was one of the real wits of our time. Born Cambridge, Mass.; died New York, Mar. 17, 1956.

Arnold, Edward (Guenther Schneider), 66, actor. As a twelve-year-old amateur he played Lorenzo in "The Merchant of Venice." His first professional job was with a company in Trenton, N. J., in 1905. He then joined the Ben Greet Players. Following this came engagements with Maxine Elliott and Ethel Barrymore. He worked in silent films but returned to Broadway in 1925. He was in "Easy Come, Easy Go," "The Third Little Show," and later, "Whistling in the Dark." He returned to Hollywood and made many pictures, often working in two at the same time. These include "Diamond Jim Brady," "You Can't Take It With You," "Dear Ruth" and "John Loves Mary." He was also well known in radio's "Mr. President" series. Born New York; died Hollywood, Apr. 26, 1956.

Ayers, Lemuel, 40, scene designer, producer. He graduated from Princeton in 1936 and later obtained the degree of Master of Theatre Arts at the University of Iowa. He designed the sets and costumes for "St. Louis Woman," "Inside U. S. A." and "My Darlin' Aida." With Saint Subber he co-produced "Kiss Me, Kate" and "Out of This World." He also did sets for the Maurice Evans-Judith Anderson "Macbeth" and for "Angel Street" and was most famous for his sets for "Oklahoma!" Birthplace not given; died New York, Aug. 14, 1955.

Baxter, Lora, 47, actress. She had been active in show business since she was 18. She was a Metro scenarist, later going into vaudeville and pictures before attempting Broadway. She appeared in such plays as "The Animal Kingdom," "Goodbye Again" and "The Sex Fable." Birthplace not given; died New York, June 16, 1955.

Beecher, Janet, 71, actress. She made her first stage appearance as a "walk on" in a revival of "The Two Orphans" at the New Amsterdam Theatre, N. Y. Her first speaking role was in "The Education of Mr. Pipp" in Utica in 1905. Other plays in which she appeared were "The Concert," "The Great Adventure," "Believe Me Xantippe," "Call the Doctor," "A Bill of Divorcement" and "Courage." She was the sister of Olive Wyndham. Her last Broadway appearance was in "The Late George Apley" in 1944. She was also seen in numerous motion pictures. Born Jefferson City, Mo.; died Washington, Conn., Aug. 6, 1955.

Beerbohm, Sir Max, 83, drama critic, caricaturist, writer. The much younger half-brother of Sir Herbert Beerbohm-Tree, he achieved a name while still an undergraduate at Oxford, and as a very young man contributed to *The Yellow Book.* In his early twenties he published his first volume, a slim collection of essays, under the title "The Works of Max Beerbohm." Best known for many volumes of delightful familiar essays, many volumes of sprightly caricatures, and his Oxford novel, "Zuleika Dobson," he in 1898 succeeded Shaw as drama critic on *The Saturday Review,* a post he held with distinction until 1910. Much of the drama criticism was published—and recently re-published—under the title "Around Theatres." In 1910 he married an American actress, Florence Kahn, and went to live in Rapallo, Italy, where he remained—except for returning to England during World War II—until his death. He was knighted in 1939. Born London, England; died Rapallo, May 20, 1956.

Bernstein, Aline, 74, designer. One of the legitimate theatre's leading scene and costume designers, she originally set out to be a portrait painter. She became interested in costuming and worked with Irene and Alice Lewisohn. She received recognition for her work on "The Dybbuk," "The Little Clay Cart" and "The Grand Street Follies." On Broadway she designed such Theatre Guild successes as "Reunion in Vienna," "Ned McCobb's Daughter" and "The Game of Love and Death." Max Reinhardt had her create the costumes for "The Miracle." She was one of the founders of the Museum of Costume Art (1937) which was eventually incorporated into the Metropolitan Museum of Art. She wrote two novels and an autobiography of her early life. Born New York; died New York, Sept. 7, 1955.

Blackwell, Carlyle, 71, actor. One of Hollywood's earliest movie idols he made over 300 movies, starring with such actresses as Mary Pickford, Marion Davies, Betty Blythe and Blanche Sweet. At the height of his career in 1916 he created a sensation with a reception at Madison Square Garden. There were 20,000 in the Garden and 10,000 more outside. He studied at Cornell University before taking up acting in 1910. Among his many movies were "Such a Little Queen," "Beloved Vagabond," "Bulldog Drummond" and "She." Born Troy, Pa.; died Miami, Fla., June 17, 1955.

Bonner, Isabel, 47, actress. She began her stage career as a child actress in her father's stock company in Pittsburgh and made her Broadway debut as the ingenue in "Let Freedom Ring." She was also seen in "Processional," "Uncle Harry," "Liliom," "Laura," "Foolish Notion" and others. She was very popular in television. She died on stage while appearing in Los Angeles in "The Shrike," the play written by her husband, Joseph Kramm. Birthplace not given; died Los Angeles, July 1, 1955.

Braham, Horace, 62, actor. His first London appearance was in "Consequences" and in 1914 he made his Broadway debut in the same play and remained in America thereafter. Among his many plays were "Androcles and the Lion," "Gold Diggers," "The Rat," "The Squall" and "The Taming of the Shrew." For five years he conducted courses in theatre at Columbia University. When taken fatally ill, he was playing in "Witness for the Prosecution." Born London; died New York, Sept. 7, 1955.

Brown, Chamberlain, 57, theatrical agent. One of the most prominent of theatrical agents in New York during the twenties and thirties. He handled most of the big stars of the period and ran several stock theatres. Birthplace not given; died New York, Nov. 11, 1955.

Bryant, Nana, 67, actress. Her career spanned fifty years from touring stock to television. She appeared on Broadway in many musicals—among them "Connecticut Yankee"—and was also seen in such legitimate plays as "Marriage Is for Single People." She made many films including "The Devil Is Driving," "Meet Nero Wolfe," "Street of Missing Men," "Harvey" and "Bright Victory." Birthplace not given; died Hollywood, Dec. 24, 1955.

Byrd, Sam, 47, actor. After attending the University of Florida he came to New York to be an actor and appeared in such plays as "The House of Wonder" and "Of Mice and Men."

He set a record in "Tobacco Road," appearing in 1151 consecutive performances. He was also the author of several books. Born Mount Olive, N. C.; died Durham, N. C., Nov. 14, 1955.

Cahill, Lily, 69, actress. After playing with Mrs. Leslie Carter in 1909 and with Leo Ditrichstein in "The Concert," she made her first real success on Broadway in "Under Cover." She was featured in "So This Is London," with the Lunts in "Caprice," with Katharine Cornell in "Alien Corn" and with Jane Cowl in "First Lady." In London she played in "Women Kind." The latter came to New York as "And Be My Love" with Miss Cahill still in the company. Her last Broadway engagement was in "Life With Father" during 1945-1946. Born Texas; died San Antonio, Texas, July 20, 1955.

Calhern, Louis (Carl Henry Vogt), 61, actor. While attending school in St. Louis he was hired as an extra for a touring company and thereafter decided to be an actor. Without finishing high school he worked as prop boy and as bit player in touring theatre and burlesque. After serving in World War I he first made a hit opposite Judith Anderson in "Cobra" and followed this with leads opposite Ethel Barrymore and Laurette Taylor. One of the best actors of his time, he is especially remembered for his "King Lear," his Justice Holmes in "The Magnificent Yankee," and his Colonel in "Jacobowsky and the Colonel." His last Broadway appearance was in "The Wooden Dish." He was on location for his 69th film, "Teahouse of the August Moon," when he died of a heart attack. Born Brooklyn, N. Y.; died Nara, Japan, May 12, 1956.

Cameron, Donald, 66, actor. As a youth he studied at the American Academy of Dramatic Arts and made his first professional appearance in 1913 in Berkeley, Calif. His first New York appearance was as Joseph in "The Taming of the Shrew." He toured with Margaret Anglin for three years and became her leading man. In the early twenties he was in such plays as "Wake Up, Jonathan," "Dice of the Gods" and "The Bride." He was with Eva LeGallienne's Civic Repertory Theatre from 1927 to 1932 and toured with her in 1935. In 1939 he was Marcellus in Maurice Evans' production of "Hamlet." Born in Canada; died West Cornwall, Conn., July 11, 1955.

Chekhov, Michael, 64, actor, director. A nephew of Anton Chekhov, he joined the Moscow Art Theatre after three years at the Souverine Dramatic School. In 1928 he left Russia, playing in Berlin, Vienna and Paris. In 1934 he brought his Moscow Art

Players to the United States for a season of repertory. He then went to England to Darlington Hall and undertook the development of the Chekhov Theatre school. In 1939 the studio moved to Ridgefield, Conn. He appeared in many motion pictures, among them "In Our Time," "Spellbound," "Spectre of the Rose" and "Invitation." Born St. Petersburg; died Hollywood, Sept. 30, 1955.

Conlan, Frank, 81, actor. He made his first Broadway appearance in "The Dummy" in 1914. He was also seen in "The Front Page," "When We Were 21" and "Strike Me Pink" and made a hit in "June Moon" and "You Can't Take It With You." Birthplace not given; died East Islip, N. Y., Aug. 24, 1955.

Dean, James, 24, actor. Before becoming famous in movies—"East of Eden," "Rebel Without a Cause" and "Giant"—he had been seen on Broadway in "See the Jaguar" and "The Immoralist." Born Marion, Ind.; died Paso Robles, Calif., Sept. 30, 1955.

Dingle, Charles, 68. He made his debut in stock at the age of 14 and played many roles in stock and repertory before his first Broadway appearance in "The Killers" in 1928. Aside from a number of Shakespearean roles he was seen in "Bury the Dead," "All for the Living," "So Proudly We Hail," "Sweet River," "Miss Liberty" and "The Immoralist." Perhaps his most impressive role was Ben Hubbard in "The Little Foxes." He also appeared in many motion pictures. Born Wabash, Ind.; died Worcester, Mass., Jan. 19, 1956.

Donaldson, Arthur, 86, actor, singer, dramatist, director, producer. He began his career at the age of 13 months when he was carried on stage in his native Sweden. His next appearance was at 7 after which he went to the Royal Academy of Dramatic Arts in Stockholm. He later came to America and worked for Henry Savage, David Belasco and the Shuberts. He created the title role in "The Prince of Pilsen," playing it 1345 times. Besides other stage roles, he is credited with producing, directing and appearing in the very first talkie—the Swedish phonofilm "Domen." Born Sweden; died Long Island, N. Y., Sept. 28, 1955.

Elliott, Madge, 59, actress. Educated in Australia she made her first stage appearance in ballet with the Melba Grand Opera Company. She came to New York with her husband Cyril Ritchard in 1950 for the Theatre Guild production of "The Relapse." She had also played with Noel Coward and done much television work. Born London; died New York, Aug. 8, 1955.

Emerson, John, 81, playwright. He studied for the ministry but was attracted to the stage and began his long career in 1904, appearing opposite Bessie Tyree in "Tit for Tat." He was leading man and stage manager for Mrs. Fiske. He was stage manager for the Shuberts from 1908 till 1911 and for Charles Frohman from 1911 to 1915. In 1914 he became active in directing and writing. With his wife, Anita Loos, he wrote such plays as "The Whole Town's Talking," "The Fall of Eve" and "The Social Register." He was president of Actors Equity during the actors' strike and was later named perpetual honorary president. He was both a writer and producer of motion pictures. Born Sandusky, Ohio; died Los Angeles, Mar. 8, 1956.

Fabre, Emile, 86, playwright. As a young man he practiced law in Marseilles. He took up playwriting and a number of successful plays decided his future. Among his early successes was "L'Argent." His "La Rabouilleuse" was done in America by Otis Skinner as "The Honor of the Family." He was general administrator of the Comédie Française from 1915 to 1936. Born France; died Paris, Sept. 25, 1955.

Garland, Robert, 60, drama critic. Educated in private schools, he became feature writer for the Baltimore *News* and later was drama editor and critic for the Baltimore *American*. In 1927 he came to New York as a columnist for the New York *Telegram*, and later became its drama critic. In 1943 he became drama critic for the New York *Journal-American*. He wrote several plays and movie scenarios, among them "The Double Miracle" and "At Night All Cats Are Gray." Born Baltimore, Md., died New York, Dec. 27, 1955.

Golden, John, 80, producer. Best known as a producer, he was experienced in many sides of the theatre. He began as a "super" in the old Niblo's Garden and the Harrigan Theatre. He then turned to writing verses, some of which he sold to newspapers and some as songs. Besides writing songs, he composed the music for several musical comedies. He collaborated with Irving Berlin, Oscar Hammerstein and Douglas Fairbanks. His best known songs were "Poor Butterfly" and "Good-bye, Girls, I'm Through." In 1916, with Winchell Smith he produced "Turn to the Right." The next play they offered was the famous "Lightnin' " which, running for 1291 performances, set a record at the time. In the years that followed he produced more than 100 plays on Broadway, among them such outstanding hits as "Three Wise Fools," "The First Year," "Seventh Heaven," "Claudia," "Susan and God," "Skylark," "Counselor-at-Law" and "Let Us Be Gay." He was founder of The Stage Relief Fund, Inc., and The American Society of Composers, Authors and Publishers and the organizer of the Stage Door Canteen. Born New York; died New York, June 17, 1955.

Gorcey, Bernard, 67, actor. After many years on the New York stage he went to Hollywood to appear in motion pictures—among them "The Unknown Guest," "Joan of Paris" and "Here Come the Marines." He was in the original cast of "Abie's Irish Rose" in 1922. Birthplace not given; died Hollywood, Sept. 12, 1955.

Grapewin, Charles, 86, actor. He ran away with a circus when he was a small boy and later went into vaudeville. At the turn of the century he was one of Broadway's top comedians. Still later he was starred or featured in more than a hundred movies. His pictures include "Shannons of Broadway," "Don't Bet on Love," "Ah! Wilderness," "The Wizard of Oz" and "Crash Dive." Perhaps his two best known pictures were "Tobacco Road" and "Grapes of Wrath." Born Xenia, Ohio; died Los Angeles, Feb. 2, 1956.

Gropper, Milton, 68, playwright. After studying at Columbia University, he began his career as a newspaper reporter, later writing a number of one-act plays for a newspaper syndicate. In 1924 he collaborated with Oscar Hammerstein II on "Gypsy Jim." The next year David Belasco produced his "Ladies of the Evening." His other plays include "Hidden Assets," "Bulls, Bears and Asses" and "Sing and Whistle." Born New York; died New York, Oct. 27, 1955.

Hammerstein, Arthur, 82, producer. The son of Oscar Hammerstein I, he was hired by his father as "personal representative" in 1906 and began his own producing career in 1912 with "The Firefly." From then on he had a number of successes, among them "High Jinks," "Katinka," "Rose Marie" and "Naughty Marietta." Altogether he put on 31 plays. He built the Hammerstein Theatre at Broadway and 53rd Street in memory of his father. Born New York; died Palm Beach, Fla., Oct 12, 1955.

Hampden, Walter, 75, actor. He had his first success in England in touring companies. He had played Shylock at 16 at Brooklyn Polytechnic Institute. He went to Harvard and studied in Paris. In England in 1905 he played Hamlet for a week when H. B. Irving was ill. He made his Broadway debut opposite Nazimova. In 1918 he embarked on a series of matinees offering "Julius Caesar," "Macbeth" and "Hamlet." The following year he formed a repertory company and toured the country. In the season of 1923-1924 he produced and played the title role of "Cyrano de Bergerac" which was a tremendous hit. In 1925 he took over the Colonial Variety house and renamed it the Hampden Theatre; he presented many plays there during the next few years. In 1927 he was elected president of The Players. He was also seen in many motion pictures, among them "All About Eve," "The Silver Chalice" and "Sabrina." His last Broadway appearance was in "The Crucible." Born Brooklyn; died Los Angeles, June 11, 1955.

Hartman, Grace, 48, dancer. After studying dancing in San Francisco she was in ballet in Ferris Luce Hartman's Comic Opera Company. She married the producer's son, Paul, and as a team, they danced their way around the world. On Broadway they were in "Red, Hot and Blue," "You Never Know," "Angel in the Wings" and others. Birthplace not given; died Van Nuys, Calif., Aug. 8, 1955.

Harvey, Paul, 71, actor. He first acted on the west coast, later joined the Selig Film Co. of Chicago, and in all appeared in hundreds of films. He was on Broadway in several plays, among them "The Trial of Mary Dugan" and "Dinner at Eight." Born Sandwich, Ill.; died Hollywood, Dec. 14, 1955.

Hodiak, John, 41, actor. After attending high school in Detroit he entered radio. In 1942 he signed a contract with MGM. Among his twenty-odd pictures were "Lifeboat," "The Harvey Girls," "A Bell for Adano" and "Command Decision." On Broadway he was in "The Chase" in 1952 and most recently was Maryk in "The Caine Mutiny Court-Martial." Born Pittsburgh; died Tarzana, Calif., Oct. 19, 1955.

Hoffman, Gertrude, 57, dancer. She danced in several Ziegfeld Follies, made a number of motion pictures and starred on Broadway in "Broadway to Paris" in 1917. Lately she had been operating as a clairvoyant in Washington, D. C. Born Montreal; died Washington, D. C., June 3, 1955.

Hoyt, Julia, 58, actress. A noted society beauty, she turned to acting in 1921 when she supported Norma Talmadge in the motion picture "The Wonderful Thing." Later that same year she was with William Faversham on Broadway in the revival of "The Squaw Man." She appeared in Stuart Walker's stock company in the middle west and in New York in such plays as "The Virgin of Bethulia," "The Rhapsody" and "Anatomy of Love." Born New York; died New York, Oct. 31, 1955.

Isaacs, Edith J. R., 78, stage expert. A leading spirit in the development of the American theatre, she was editor of Theatre Arts Magazine from 1919 to 1946. She discovered new talent and encouraged progressive trends. She was editor of "Essays on the Art of Theatre" and "Plays of American Life and Fantasy" and the author of "The Negro in the American Theatre." Born Milwaukee, Wis.; died White Plains, N. Y., Jan. 10, 1956.

Janis, Elsie (Bierbower), 67, actress. At 3 she was experimenting with scenes from "Romeo and Juliet" and at 8 made her stage debut in James O'Neil's company. At 10 she was in vaudeville offering imitations of the popular figures of the day. Her first hit was in 1905 in "When We Were Forty-one." After "The Vanderbilt Cup" there was "The Hoyden," "The Fair Co-ed," "The Slim Princess" and "A Star for a Night." She was in "The Lady of the Slipper" in 1912 and in 1914 she scored in London one of the biggest successes ever achieved by an American. She was the first American entertainer to perform for the American Expeditionary Forces in France and as such she probably achieved her greatest success. Subsequently she put together a series of soldier revues and created a new style of entertainment. There were several editions of "Elsie Janis and Her Gang" as she called these revues. Born Columbus, Ohio; died Los Angeles, Feb. 26, 1956.

Jones, Margo, 42, producer. She entered Texas State College for Women at 14 and earned an M.A. degree with a thesis on psychology. She then studied every phase of theatre at the Southwestern School of the Theatre in Dallas. She worked with the Ojai Community Players of California and the Pasadena Playhouse. In 1939 she staged plays as head of the Community Players of Houston. Her Theatre in the Round in Dallas became famous under her management and she produced more than 100 plays there. Broadway knows her best for "The Glass Menagerie," "On Whitman Avenue," "Joan of Lorraine" and "Summer and Smoke." Her last Broadway activity was as co-producer of "Inherit the Wind." Born Livingston, Texas; died Dallas, July 24, 1955.

Joyce, Alice, actress, 65. She made her first screen appearance in the old time hit "The Lion and the Mouse." She was one of the first glamour queens of the movies; among her pictures were "Stella Dallas," "Mannequin," "Beau Geste," "Dancing Mothers" and "The Green Goddess." Born Missouri; died Hollywood, Oct. 9, 1955.

Karlweis, Oscar, 61, actor. Well known both in Europe and the United States, he appeared in musicals and movies as well as legitimate dramas. In Europe his best-known role was probably that of the Baron in the German version of "Grand Hotel." In this country one of his biggest hits was Jacobowsky in "Jacobowsky and the Colonel." He was also seen here in "Cue for Passion," "I Like It Here," "Ring Round the Moon" and "Once Upon a Tailor." Born Vienna; died New York, Jan. 24, 1956.

Kemper, Collin, 87, producer. He started his career as a church organist at the age of 9. At 14 he joined a Shakespearean company as an actor. In 1887 he formed a producing partnership with Lincoln A. Wagenhals which was singularly successful. They introduced Mme. Modjeska to American audiences and had such hits as "Seven Days," "Paid in Full," "The Bat," "Spanish Love" and "Resurrection." Born Cincinnati; died Bronxville, N. Y., Nov. 27, 1955.

Kibbee, Guy, 70, actor. His career started at 15 with a small troupe in the Southwest. He barnstormed all over the country. His first real success on Broadway was in 1930 in "Torch Song." He was also in New York in "Marseilles" and "A Joy Forever." In 1931 he entered pictures and was one of the industry's busiest and most popular actors. Among his numerous films were "Man of the World," "Gold Diggers of 1933," "Easy to Love," "Babbitt," "Power of the Press" and "Captain Blood." Born El Paso, Tex.; died East Islip, L. I., N. Y., May 24, 1956.

Korda, Sir Alexander, 62, motion picture producer. In his youth he taught school and worked on a Budapest newspaper. He made motion pictures in Vienna, Rome and Berlin before going to London where he became a giant in the British film industry. In 1926 he worked in Hollywood. In 1936 he became a British subject and was knighted in 1942. His 112 films include "The Private Life of Henry VIII," "The Ghost Goes West," "That Hamilton Woman," "The Third Man" and "Richard III." Born Hungary; died London, Jan. 23, 1956.

Langford, William, 35, actor. He began his career in Canadian stock companies and soldier shows. He then made "The True and the False," a motion picture with Signe Hasso. He was with Tallulah Bankhead in her revival of "Private Lives." Born Montreal; died New York, July 27, 1955.

La Rue, Grace, 75, actress. Made her stage debut in Julia Marlowe's company, later going into vaudeville and musical comedy. On Broadway she was in "The Blue Moon" in 1906 followed by such hits as "The Ziegfeld Follies of 1908," "Betsy," "Hitchy-Koo," "Dear Me," "The Music Box Revue" and "Stepping Out." She was a tremendous hit in London when in 1913 she introduced the song "You Made Me Love You—I Didn't Want to Do It." Born Kansas City, Mo.; died San Francisco, Calif., March 12, 1956.

Loeb, Philip, 61, actor. He made his professional debut with E. H. Sothern in a revival of "If I Were King." He was stage manager of "The Green Goddess," formed a long association with The Theatre Guild, and worked as actor and stage manager for the Lunts. He was for many months Papa in the TV version of "The Goldbergs." Born Philadelphia; died New York, Sept. 1, 1955.

MacArthur, Charles, 60, playwright. He was a Chicago reporter during the Prohibition era. His first play, written with Edward Sheldon, was "Lulu Belle." Two years later he wrote "Salvation" with Sidney Howard. That same year he turned out the first of many collaborations with Ben Hecht, the hit play "The Front Page." Together they wrote "Jumbo," "Ladies and Gentlemen" and "Swan Song." On his own he wrote "Johnny on a Spot." He collaborated with Hecht on several movie scripts, among them "The Scoundrel," "Crime Without Passion," "Gunga Din" and "Wuthering Heights." His best known solo film job was "The Sin of Madelon Claudet" in which his wife, Helen Hayes, was starred. Born Scranton, Pa.; died New York, Apr. 21, 1956.

MacColl, James A. (age not given), actor. A graduate of the American Academy of Dramatic Arts, he made his professional debut as the young son of Ethel Barrymore in "Encore." Later he was in two hit revues, "Life Begins at 8:40" with Bert Lahr and "At Home Abroad" with Beatrice Lillie. He acquired a British accent and often played English roles. Born New York; died New York, April 18, 1956.

Matthison, Edith Wynne, 83, actress. She entered musical comedy in England in 1896 and later toured with Sir Henry Irving. She starred in a revival of "Everyman" in which she was brought to this country by Daniel Frohman for a two-year tour. She was noted for Shakespearean and Greek dramatic roles as well as for performances in plays by her husband Charles Rann Kennedy. In 1918 she and her husband went to the Bennett Junior College, Millbrook, N. Y., where they headed the drama department. She appeared in one early silent film, "The Governor's

Lady." Born Birmingham, England; died Los Angeles, Sept. 23, 1955.

Milne, Alan Alexander, 74, playwright, author, poet. He was educated at Westminster School and Trinity College, Cambridge. After graduation he wanted to become a journalist and was assistant editor of *Punch* from 1906 to the end of 1914. He became famous as the author of the "Winnie the Pooh" books and his three best known plays were "Mr. Pim Passes By," "The Dover Road" and "The Truth About Blayds." Born London; died Sussex, Eng., Jan. 31, 1956.

Minevitch, Borrah, 52, musician. He came to this country when he was ten. He wanted to be a violinist, but heard the harmonica and made this his chief interest. In 1925 he formed his first troupe of 25 boys and trained them in a repertoire of jazz and classical numbers. Borrah Minevitch and His Harmonica Rascals became famous in vaudeville and night clubs both here and in Europe. Born Kiev, Russia; died Paris, June 26, 1955.

Miranda, Carmen, 41, dancer and comedienne. She began her career at seventeen as a model in Rio de Janeiro. In the United States she became famous as the South American Bombshell through her performance in "The Streets of Paris." She was celebrated for her fruit basket hats. She made many motion pictures and appeared in nightclubs and on television. Her pictures include "Down Argentine Way," "That Night in Rio" and "Four Jills in a Jeep." Born Portugal; died Beverly Hills, Calif., Aug. 5, 1955.

Mistinguett (Jeanne Bourgeois), 82, music hall star. She began to work in music halls in her early teens. One of her first big successes was at the Folies Bergère in 1911 when she did her Apache dance with Maurice Chevalier. She was known as the lady with the "million dollar legs" because she said she had them insured for from 3 to 5 millions. The darling of France, she was not successful in her one Broadway appearance, in 1921, in "Innocent Eyes." At 72 she still performed in Paris nightclubs. Born near Paris; died Paris, Jan. 5, 1956.

Morris, McKay, 62, actor. Received his dramatic training under the watchful eye of David Belasco and made his first appearance on the stage in that producer's "The Governor's Lady." He was with Stuart Walker's Portmanteau Theatre for three years. He was seen in such plays as "Aphrodite," "Main Street," "Volpone," "Ghosts" and "Man and Devil." He was Romeo to Ethel Barrymore's Juliet. His last Broadway appearance was in "Lute Song" in 1946. Born Fort Sam Houston; died Forest Hills, L. I., Oct. 3, 1955.

Morton, Harry K., 67, actor. His youth he spent as a circus boy. Later he went into vaudeville and formed a team with Zella Russell whom he married. In the Twenties he began appearing in musical comedies on Broadway, among them "Love Song," "Love Dreams," "The Red Robe" and "Lady in Ermine." Birthplace not given; died New York, May 9, 1956.

Murfin, Jane, 62, playwright. In collaboration with Jane Cowl she wrote four Broadway plays, among them such hits as "Lilac Time" and "Smilin' Through." She went to California as a producer and introduced the dog, Strongheart, to pictures. Thereafter wrote sixty-odd films including "Little Women," "Roberta" and "The Silver Cord." Born Ypsilanti, Mich.; died Hollywood, Aug. 10, 1955.

Oshins, Julie, 50, actor. After graduation from New York's Morris High School he was physical instructor at the Morningside Hotel in the Catskills, and while there directed and acted in weekly comedies. During the prohibition era he worked in Times Square night spots and later in Hollywood. On Broadway he won recognition in "This Is the Army" and replaced David Burns in "Make Mine Manhattan." Born Brooklyn; died New York, May 9, 1956.

Peters, Brandon, 63, actor. He toured in Shakespearean companies before joining Margaret Anglin's company. In 1925 he came to Broadway in "The Buccaneer." He was also in such plays as "As You Desire Me," "Love on the Dole," "Too Many Boats," "The Day Will Come" and "The Curious Savage." Born Troy, N. Y.; died New York, Feb. 27, 1956.

Pogany, Willy, 72, designer. His talent brought him many awards both here and abroad. He came to the United States from Hungary in 1914 and among the productions he designed were "Sumurun," "Queen High," "Lassie," "The Jeweled Tree," "Carnival in Venice" and "Thunder Bird." His interest in art and design was almost without limit. He designed stained glass windows, swimming pools, murals, cover designs, illustrations for books. Born Szeged, Hungary; died New York, July 30, 1955.

Powers, Tom, 65. He studied for the stage at the American Academy of Dramatic Arts and made his first appearance on tour in 1911 in "In Mizzoura." His first New York appearance was with Stuart Walker's Company in "Six Who Pass While the Lentils Boil." Thereafter he was in any number of Broadway productions and was also seen in London. Among the many Broadway plays he appeared in were "The First Fifty Years," "The Wild Duck," "White Wings," "Strange Interlude," "A House in the Country" and "The Three Sisters." He also made many films. Born Owensboro, Ky.; died Hollywood, Nov. 9, 1955.

Prouty, Jed, 77, actor. He ran away from home to join a circus and made his first stage appearance at the Boston Museum at 15. He made some 500 pictures, was prominent in radio and television, and was seen on Broadway in "Something for the Boys," "Harvey," "And Be My Love," "Heads or Tails" and others. Born Boston; died New York, May 10, 1956.

Rasumny, Mikhail, 65, actor. At 14 he went on the stage, touring Europe and South America. Later he joined the Moscow Art Theatre and came to the United States with them in 1935. In 1940 he entered pictures and was in such films as "For Whom the Bell Tolls," "Tonight We Sing," "Anything Can Happen" and "This Gun for Hire." He made his English-speaking stage debut in 1954 in "Mademoiselle Colombe." Born Odessa; died Hollywood, Feb. 17, 1956.

Robins, Edward H., 74, actor. At 19 he was city editor of the Shamokin (Pa.) *Dispatch*. He made his stage debut as Bernardo in "Hamlet" in Philadelphia in 1900. Later he formed his own company and also spent several years with other troupes. In 1908 David Belasco hired him to play in "The Easiest Way" opposite Frances Starr. He was in "Ben Hur" and with Mrs. Fiske in "Erstwhile Susan." Among his many other plays were "So This Is London," "The Night of January 16th" and "Nellie Bly." Born Shamokin, Pa.; died Paramus, N. J., July 27, 1955.

Ross, Anthony, 46, actor. Educated at Brown University, the Sorbonne and the University of Nancy, he made his Broadway debut in 1932 in "Whistling in the Dark." He was with Maurice Evans in "Richard II" and "Twelfth Night," and scored his first big hit as the Gentleman Caller in "The Glass Menagerie." Other successes include "Winged Victory" and "Season in the Sun." At the time of his death Mr. Ross was appearing in "Bus Stop." Born New York; died New York, Oct. 25, 1955.

Ross, Jerry, 29, composer and lyricist. As a boy he attracted attention singing in a synagogue; he later sang in Yiddish theatres and worked on the "borscht circuit." He then met Richard Adler and together they turned out over 250 songs, including those for "Pajama Game" and "Damn Yankees." Born Bronx, N. Y.; died New York, Nov. 11, 1955.

Rouverol, Mrs. Aurania, 69, playwright. Once a pupil at Prof. George Pierce Baker's 47 Workshop. She was the author of such plays as "Growing Pains," "Young April," and "Skidding," and was the creator of the Andy Hardy series on radio and film. She appeared on the stage in "Little Women," replacing Alice Brady as Meg. Born Palo Alto, Calif.; died Palo Alto, Calif., June 23, 1955.

Seymour, Jane, 57, actress. She began her stage career in a road company of "Within the Law" and in 1925 came to Broadway in support of Fay Bainter in "The Enemy." Among her other plays were "Paris Bound," "The House Beautiful," "Both Your Houses," "The Women," "The Moon Is Down" and "Harriet." She made several motion pictures and was a prominent radio actress. Born Hamilton, Ontario; died New York, Jan. 29, 1956.

Sherwood, Robert Emmet, 59, playwright. After attending Milton Academy he studied at Harvard from 1914 to 1917. During World War I he was rejected by the Army as too tall and enlisted in the Canadian Blackwatch. He was gassed and twice wounded in France. While at Harvard, he was editor of the *Lampoon,* a magazine founded by his father. He attracted the attention of Frank Crowninshield who made him drama critic of *Vanity Fair.* His first play was "Barnum Was Right," his first big success "The Road to Rome." Later came "Reunion in Vienna" for the Lunts and then, among others, three Pulitzer Prize winners: "Idiot's Delight," "Abe Lincoln in Illinois" and "There Shall Be No Night." In 1938 he joined with Elmer Rice, Maxwell Anderson, S. N. Behrman and Sidney Howard to form The Playwrights' Company. In World War II he was overseas director of the Office of War Information and is generally credited with helping to write Mr. Roosevelt's speeches. His book "Roosevelt and Hopkins" won a Pulitzer Award in 1949. As playwright, writer and liberal he attained a high place in this country and abroad. Born New Rochelle, N. Y.; died New York, Nov. 14, 1955.

Somnes, George (age not given), producer. Reared in Boston and educated in Europe, he first appeared on Broadway in a play produced by William A. Brady. In 1914 he went to England and became the first American to become prominent in the Old Vic. He produced plays on Broadway and was director of the famous Elitch's Garden Theatre Stock Company of Denver from 1936 to 1954. Born Boston; died Denver, Feb. 8, 1956.

Stahl, Rose, 85, actress. Began her career in Philadelphia in stock. In 1888 she was with David Bandmann in "Dr. Jekyll and Mr. Hyde." In 1897 she was seen in New York in "The Captain of the Nonesuch." Her greatest successes were "The Chorus Lady" and "Maggie Pepper." Born Montreal; died Flushing, L. I., July 16, 1955.

Standing, Herbert, 71, actor. He made his theatrical debut while still a youth at London's Gaiety Theatre. He came to the United States in 1920, appearing in many silent films as well as on Broadway. His last appearance was in 1936 in "The Black Limelight." Born London; died New York, Sept. 23, 1955.

Steele, Vernon, 72, actor. In 1899 he made his first stage appearance in "The Little Minister" in London. He later came to the United States and supported many stars, among them Ethel Barrymore in "Déclassée." He was for a time prominent in pictures. Born England; died Los Angeles, July 23, 1955.

Stephenson, Henry, 85, actor. He made his stage debut in 1896 in the English provinces and appeared in London later in the same year. He first came to New York in 1901 in "The Man From Blankley's." He later acted with Mrs. Fiske and with the Lyceum and Empire Theatre companies. In 1916 he joined Jane Cowl's company and was with her for four years. He went to Hollywood in 1932 and made numerous films. His plays include "Lilac Time," "Smilin' Through," "The Fool," "Dancing Mothers," "The Adorable Liar" and "Command Performance." His last New York appearance was with Katharine Cornell in "That Lady." Born Grenada, B. W. I.; died San Francisco, Apr. 24, 1956.

Thompson, Woodman, 66, stage designer. He was scenic designer for such theatre groups as The Theatre Guild, The Actors' Theatre and Equity Theatre. He worked on over 70 shows, among them Katharine Cornell's "Candida," "What Price Glory?", "Smilin' Through," Winthrop Ames' Gilbert and Sullivan series and "The Warrior's Husband." For several years before his death he had been lecturing at the School of Dramatic Arts at Columbia University. Birthplace not given; died New York, Aug. 26, 1955.

Thurston, Harry (Marcus Cowan), 81, actor, writer. He was the creator of 'Ole Bill in "The Better 'Ole" in London and later appeared in vaudeville in this country. He wrote and produced several plays and radio shows in London and Australia. Born London; died Rumson, N. J., Sept. 2, 1955.

Wallace, David, 66, playwright. From 1910 to 1912 he was a reporter for the Syracuse, N. Y., *Herald,* later coming to New York to write reviews for the *Dramatic Mirror* and *The Morning Telegraph.* Among his plays were "Lady Lazy" and "Faith, Hope and Alice." He was also personal representative for many stars. Born Syracuse, N. Y.; died New York, June 15, 1955.

Weston, Ruth, 49, actress. She began her career in Hollywood using her knowledge of French and German to appear in foreign-language versions of motion pictures. In 1933 she understudied Ina Claire in "Biography," playing the part when the star was on vacation. She was also in the cast of "George Washington Slept Here," "The American Way" and "Three's a Crowd." In 1944 she replaced Betty Garde as Aunt Eller in "Oklahoma!" playing the role for 39 months. Born Boston; died East Orange, N. J., Nov. 6, 1955.

Wilcox, Robert, 44, actor. He appeared in 26 films, among them "Let Them Live," "Blondie Takes a Vacation" and "Dreaming Out Loud." He was on the stage most recently playing opposite his wife, Diana Barrymore, in "Pajama Tops." Birthplace not given; died Rochester, N. Y., June 11, 1955.

Wilson, Frank H., 70, actor. As a young man he sang in vaudeville and then became a postman in Manhattan for ten years. In 1914 he began writing, presenting and acting in one-act plays in Harlem. He studied at the American Academy of Dramatic Arts and in 1924 played in "All God's Chillun Got Wings." Later he was in "The Emperor Jones" and in 1926 stepped into the leading role of "In Abraham's Bosom." He was chosen for the title role of "Porgy," which he played for 367 performances in New York and later played in London. Among his many other plays were "The Green Pastures" (Moses), "They Shall Not Die," "The Big Knife" and "Memphis Bound." He also played Moses in the picture version of "The Green Pastures." Born New York; died Jamaica, N. Y., Feb. 16, 1956.

THE DECADES' TOLL

(Prominent Theatrical Figures Who Have Died in Recent Years)

	Born	*Died*
Adams, Maude	1872	1953
Anderson, John Murray	1886	1954
Arliss, George	1869	1946
Bennett, Richard	1873	1944
Bernstein, Henri	1876	1953
Calhern, Louis	1895	1956
Carroll, Earl	1893	1948
Carte, Rupert D'Oyly	1876	1948
Christians, Mady	1900	1951
Cochran, Charles B.	1872	1951
Collier, Willie	1866	1943
Cowl, Jane	1884	1950
Craven, Frank	1890	1945
Crosman, Henrietta	1865	1944
Digges, Dudley	1879	1947
Duncan, Augustin	1872	1954
Errol, Leon	1881	1951
Fields, W. C.	1879	1946
Garfield, John	1913	1952
Gaige, Crosby	1883	1949
Hampden, Walter	1879	1955
Hart, Lorenz	1895	1943
Hart, William S.	1870	1946
Hooker, Brian	1881	1947
Howard, Willie	1883	1949
Jolson, Al.	1886	1950
Jouvet, Louis	1887	1951
Kern, Jerome D.	1885	1945
Lawrence, Gertrude	1898	1952
Lehar, Franz	1870	1948
Loftus, Cecilia	1876	1943
Lord, Pauline	1890	1950
Mantle, Burns	1873	1948

	Born	Died
Marlowe, Julia	1866	1950
Merivale, Philip	1886	1946
Molnar, Ferenc	1878	1952
Moore, Grace	1901	1947
Nazimova, Alla	1879	1945
Nethersole, Olga	1870	1951
O'Neill, Eugene	1888	1953
Patterson, Joseph Medill	1879	1946
Perry, Antoinette	1888	1946
Powers, James T.	1862	1943
Reinhardt, Max	1873	1943
Romberg, Sigmund	1887	1951
Scheff, Fritzi	1879	1954
Selwyn, Edgar	1875	1944
Shaw, G. B.	1856	1950
Sheldon, Edward	1886	1946
Sherwood, Robert E.	1896	1955
Shubert, Lee	1875	1953
Tarkington, Booth	1869	1946
Tauber, Richard	1890	1948
Tyler, George C.	1867	1946
Ward, Fannie	1872	1952
Warfield, David	1866	1951
Webster, Ben	1864	1947
Whitty, Dame May	1865	1948
Woods, Al H.	1870	1951
Woollcott, Alexander	1887	1943
Youmans, Vincent	1899	1946

INDEX OF AUTHORS AND PLAYWRIGHTS

Abbott, George, 405, 411, 412, 423
Achard, Marcel, 44
Adams, Lee, 338
Ade, George, 409
Aeschylus, 41
Akins, Zoë, 403, 410, 415
Alsberg, Henry G., 412
Anderson, Maxwell, 402, 403, 411, 412, 413, 414, 415, 416, 417, 418, 419, 420, 421, 422, 423, 445
Anderson, Robert, 422
Andreyev, Leonid, 410
Anouilh, Jean, 12, 34, 42, 189, 362, 405, 419
Ansky, S., 412
Anspacher, Louis Kaufman, 409
Apstein, Theodore, 373
Archer, William, 410
Archibald, William, 420
Arlen, Michael, 412
Atlas, Leopold, 415
Axelrod, George, 10, 353, 405
Aymé, Marcel, 33, 44

Bagley, Ben, 391
Bagnold, Enid, 8, 30, 163, 358, 405
Baker, Melville, 411
Balanchine, George, 28
Balderston, John, 413
Barrie, James M., 64
Barry, Philip, 410, 411, 412, 413, 414, 416, 418, 421
Baum, Vicki, 414
Baxt, George, 391, 392
Beach, Lewis, 411
Beaumarchais, 19, 357
Beckett, Samuel, 13, 14, 295, 385, 405
Behan, Brendan, 32
Behrman, S. N., 414, 415, 416, 418, 420, 421, 423, 445
Beiser, Rudolf, 62, 414
Belasco, David, 409
Benson, Sally, 14, 348
Berg, Dick, 61
Berg, Gertrude, 420
Berkey, Ralph, 371
Bernstein, Henri, 41
Bernstein, Robert A., 335, 336
Betti, Ugo, 33, 350
Biggers, Earl Derr, 409
Blitzstein, Marc, 37
Bolitho, William, 414
Bolton, Guy, 410, 411
Booth, Clare, 416, 417
Boretz, Allen, 372
Bowles, Jane, 421
Brecht, Bertolt, 37, 52
Bridgers, Ann, 412
Brooks, Hindi, 53
Browne, Maurice, 413
Burrows, Abe, 420
Butler, Rachel Barton, 410
Byrne, Dolly, 410

Capek, Karel, 411
Carney, Frank, 367
Carroll, Paul Vincent, 416
Cary, Joyce, 18, 382
Casalis, Jeanne de, 416
Casella, Alberto, 413
Chapman, Robert, 420
Chase, Mary Coyle, 403, 418, 421
Chayefsky, Paddy, 16, 17, 374
Chekhov, Anton, 14, 29, 55, 434
Chodorov, Edward, 238, 418
Chodorov, Jerome, 8, 50, 238, 376, 405, 417, 421
Christie, Agatha, 422
Clement, Colin, 418
Cocteau, Jean, 46
Coffee, Lenore, 416
Cohan, George M., 409, 414
Colette, 421
Collinge, Patricia, 424
Colton, John, 410
Comden, Betty, 421
Congreve, William, 30
Conkle, E. P., 416
Connelly, Marc, 403, 410, 411, 412, 413, 415
Cormack, Bartlett, 413
Costigan, James, 60

Coward, Noel, 29, 62, 370, 405, 414, 417, 424, 435
Cowen, William Joyce, 416
Cowl, Jane, 443, 448
Cranko, John, 38
Craven, Frank, 410, 448
Crothers, Rachel, 410, 411, 413, 414, 416, 424
Crouse, Russel, 10, 27, 368, 403, 406, 416, 418, 420, 421, 424

Daly, Augustin, 406
Dane, Clemence, 410
D'Annunzio, Gabriele, 408
Davis, Donald, 415
Davis, Owen, 403, 410, 415, 417
Dayton, Katharine, 415
Dell, Floyd, 413
Denker, Henry, 371
Deval, Jacques, 416
Diderot, 42
Dinelli, Mel, 51
Dodd, Lee Wilson, 411
Donaldson, Arthur, 435
Drake, W. A., 414
Drayton, Mary, 377
Drinkwater, John, 409
Dunn, Isabel, 377
Dunning, Philip, 412
d'Usseau, Arnaud, 418, 419

Eliot, T. S., 35, 53, 420, 421
Ellis, Vivian, 37
Elser, Frank B., 415
Emery, Gilbert, 410, 411
Ervine, St. John, 409, 410, 413

Fabbri, Diego, 41
Fauchois, René, 414
Faulkner, William, 61
Ferber, Edna, 411, 412, 414, 416, 425
Ferris, Walter, 413
Feydeau, Georges, 34
Field, Salisbury, 410
Fields, Joseph, 8, 50, 238, 376, 405, 417, 418, 421
Firbank, Ronald, 30
Fitch, Clyde, 409
Fitzgerald, F. Scott, 348
Flavin, Martin, 413
Forbes, James, 410
Franken, Rose, 414, 418
Friedberg, Billy, 391, 392
Fry, Christopher, 5, 89, 349, 402, 406, 421, 422, 425
Funt, Julian, 422

Galantiere, Lewis, 419
Gale, Zona, 403
Galsworthy, John, 410, 412
Gardner, Dorothy, 419
Gazzo, Michael V., 15, 360, 406
George, Grace, 410
Geraldy, Paul, 410
Gibbs, Wolcott, 421
Gilbert, William S., 52
Giraudoux, Jean, 5, 89, 349, 402, 406, 420
Glaspell, Susan, 403, 414
Gleason, James, 411
Glenville, Peter, 34, 37
Glickman, Will, 380, 407
Goetz, Augustus, 419, 422
Goetz, Ruth, 419, 422
Goldsmith, Clifford, 416
Goodrich, Frances, 11, 111, 350, 402, 404
Gordon, Ruth, 3, 418, 419
Gore-Browne, R. F., 414
Gorki, Maxim, 45
Gottlieb, Alex, 386
Goulding, Edmund, 411
Gow, James, 418, 419
Granville-Barker, Harley, 407, 410, 413
Granville-Barker, Helen, 413
Graveley, George, 407
Green, Adolph, 421
Green, Carolyn, 10, 363, 406
Green, Paul, 403, 412, 414, 415, 417
Greene, Graham, 30, 422
Grenfell, Joyce, 19, 352
Gropper, Milton, 437
Guitry, Sacha, 410
Guthrie, Tyrone, 370

Hackady, Hal, 335, 336, 337
Hackett, Albert, 11, 111, 350, 402, 404
Hagan, James, 414
Haight, George, 386
Haines, William Wister, 419
Halevy, Ludovic, 393
Hamilton, Patrick, 417
Hammerstein, Oscar, II, 22, 364, 384, 385, 393, 404, 406, 418, 419, 426, 436, 437
Harrigan, Edward, 406

Hart, Joseph, 406
Hart, Moss, 413, 415, 416, 417, 418, 419, 420, 421, 426
Hartog, Jan de, 419, 421
Harwood, H. M., 414
Hawkes, Jacquetta, 406
Hawthorne, Ruth, 411
Hayden, John, 415
Hayes, Alfred, 52-53, 422
Hayes, Joseph, 422
Hecht, Ben, 413, 441
Heggen, Thomas, 419
Hellman, Lillian, 11, 12, 189, 362, 402, 405, 415, 417, 418, 419, 420, 426
Herbert, A. P., 37
Herbert, F. Hugh, 418
Heyward, DuBose, 412
Hiken, Nat, 391, 392
Hockwalder, Fritz, 33
Hopkins, Arthur, 412
Housman, Laurence, 415
Howard, Leopoldine, 419
Howard, Sidney, 387, 403, 411, 412, 414, 419, 445
Hughes, Hatcher, 403, 411
Hugo, Victor, 42
Hunter, N. C., 14, 51, 343
Hurlbut, William, 412
Husson, Albert, 359
Hyman, Mac, 140, 354

Ibsen, Henrik, 35, 45, 55, 406
Inge, William, 402, 404, 420, 421, 422
Irwin, Will, 419

James, Dan, 418
James, Henry, 13
Jerome, Helen, 415
Job, Thomas, 417
Josset, André, 40

Kafka, Franz, 13
Kanin, Fay, 420
Kanin, Garson, 419, 427
Karp, David, 61
Katzin, Winifred, 412
Kaufman, George S., 403, 410, 411, 412, 413, 414, 415, 416, 417, 418, 427
Kelly, George, 403, 411, 412, 419
Kennedy, Charles Rann, 441
Kennedy, Mary, 411
Kerr, Jean, 50, 51
Kesselring, Joseph, 417
Kingsley, Sidney, 50, 402, 403, 414, 415, 416, 417, 420, 427
Knott, Frederick, 421
Koch, Howard, 417
Koestler, Arhur, 420
Kramm, Joseph, 404, 421
Krasna, Norman, 418, 419
Kummer, Clare, 409, 415

Landon, Margaret, 384
Langley, Noel, 420
Lardner, Ring W., 413
Latouche, John, 360, 361, 422
Laurents, Arthur, 418, 421
Lavery, Emmet, 419
Lawrence, Jerome, 406, 422
Lee, Leonard, 359
Lee, Robert E., 406, 422
LeGallienne, Eva, 406, 427
Lerner, Alan J., 266, 378, 402, 419
Levin, Ira M., 140, 355, 406
Levy, Benn W., 414, 420
Levy, David, 61
Lewis, Sinclair, 414
Lindsay, Howard, 10, 27, 368, 403, 406, 416, 418, 420, 421, 427
Locke, Sam, 360
Loesser, Frank, 23, 387, 420
Logan, Joshua, 374, 404, 419, 420, 429
Lonsdale, Frederick, 412
Loos, Anita, 421, 436
Lord, Walter, 61

MacArthur, Charles, 413, 441
Manings, Allan, 391, 392
Marchant, William, 10, 355
Marivaux, 19, 44, 357, 358
Marlowe, Christopher, 18, 370
Marquand, John P., 418
Marquis, Don, 411
Martinez Sierra, G., 412, 413
Maugham, William Somerset, 410, 412, 421, 428
Maurette, Marcelle, 42
Mayer, Edwin Justus, 411
McCarthy, Justin Huntly, 409
McCreery, Bud, 391, 392
McCullers, Carson, 402, 420
McEnroe, Robert Edward, 420
McGuire, William Anthony, 410
McLellan, C. M. S., 409
Meilhac, 393
Meloney, Rose Franken, 417
Merimee, Prosper, 393

Middleton, George, 410
Miller, Arthur, 12, 13, 32, 52, 69, 347, 402, 404, 407, 419, 420, 421, 428
Miller, J. P., 62
Miller, Sigmund, 34
Mills, Hugh, 381
Milne, Alan Alexander, 410, 413, 442
Mitchell, Thomas, 413, 428
Molière, 19, 44, 55, 59, 356, 407
Molnar, Ferenc, 410, 411, 412, 449
Moody, William Vaughn, 409
Morley, Robert, 420, 428
Moross, Jerome, 422
Morris, Edmund, 351
Morris, Lloyd, 418
Musset, Alfred de, 19, 358

Nash, Richard, 34
Nichols, Robert, 413
Nugent, Elliott, 417, 428

O'Casey, Sean, 4, 16, 367, 407, 413
Odets, Clifford, 415, 416, 421, 422, 428
O'Neill, Eugene, 55, 403, 407, 409, 410, 411, 412, 414, 415, 419, 449
Osborne, John, 32
Osborn, Paul, 58, 416, 417, 418, 421

Pagnol, Marcel, 42
Parker, Louis N., 409
Patrick, John, 27, 402, 404, 418, 419, 421
Peguy, 44
Peterson, Louis, 421
Pinero, Arthur Wing, 55, 58
Pirandello, Luigi, 13, 53, 366
Pollock, Channing, 410, 412
Priestley, J. B., 58, 406, 420

Randolph, Clemence, 410
Raphaelson, Samson, 415, 417
Rattigan, Terence, 419
Reed, Henry, 350
Reed, Mark, 416
Reizenstein, Elmer, 409

Rice, Elmer, 403, 413, 414, 417, 419, 429, 445
Richman, Arthur, 410
Riggs, Lynn, 413
Rosten, Norman, 18, 382
Rotter, Fritz, 417
Roussin, André, 41
Rouverol, Mrs. Aurania, 445
Royle, Edwin Milton, 409
Ryerson, Florence, 418
Ryskind, Morrie, 403, 414

Salacrou, Armand, 40
Sapinsley, Alvin, 62
Saroyan, William, 53, 58, 402, 403, 417, 429
Sartre, Jean-Paul, 33
Savory, Gerald, 29
Scott, Allan, 386
Selver, Paul, 411
Selwyn, Edgar, 411, 449
Shairp, Mordaunt, 415
Shakespeare, William, 18, 35, 52, 55, 63, 341, 343, 369, 407, 435
Shaw, George Bernard, 5, 23-24, 33, 51, 55, 58, 62, 266, 378, 407, 449
Sheldon, Edward, 409, 410, 441
Shelley, Elsa, 418
Shelton, James, 335
Sheridan, Richard B., 35
Sherriff, R. C., 413, 416
Sherwood, Robert E., 403, 412, 414, 415, 416, 419, 429, 445, 449
Simon, Danny, 338, 339, 340
Simon, Neil, 338, 339, 340
Smith, Dodie, 415
Smith, Harry James, 409
Sommer, Edith, 354
Soulé, Anne, 53
Spewack, Bella, 388, 415, 421
Spewack, Sam, 388, 415, 420, 421
Stallings, Laurence, 411
Stein, Joseph, 380, 407
Steinbeck, John, 364, 402, 416, 417
Steuer, Arthur, 362
Stevens, Leslie, 25, 390
Stewart, Donald Ogden, 413
Stewart, Mike, 341, 391, 392
Strindberg, August, 376
Sturges, Preston, 413
Sully, Ruby, 372
Swerling, Jo, 420

Tabori, George, 376, 421
Tarkington, Booth, 409, 449
Tauritz, Frank, 366
Taylor, Samuel, 420
Thomas, A. E., 415
Thomas, Augustus, 409
Thurber, James, 417
Thurston, Harry (Marcus Cowan), 446

Totheroh, Dan, 411
Treadwell, Sophie, 413, 417
Turgenev, Ivan, 19, 383
Turney, Robert, 415

Underhill, John Garrett, 412
Ustinov, Peter, 29-30, 421

Valency, Maurice, 420
van Druten, John, 402, 412, 415, 418, 421, 430
Van Scoyk, Bob, 391, 392
Vane, Sutton, 411
Varesi, Gilda, 410
Vega, Lope de, 44
Verneuil, Louis, 421
Vincent, Allen, 417
Vollmer, Lula, 411

Wager, Michael, 366
Wallace, David, 447
Wallop, Douglass, 405
Walter, Eugene, 409
Watkins, Maurine, 412
Watters, George Manker, 412
Weitzenkorn, Louis, 414
Welty, Eudora, 8, 238, 376, 391, 392
West, Mae, 430
Wexley, John, 413, 415
Wilder, Thornton, 4, 9, 13, 25, 214, 337, 365, 403, 416, 417, 430
Williams, Emlyn, 63, 374, 383, 417, 430
Williams, Jesse Lynch, 403, 409, 411
Williams, Tennessee, 52, 375, 402, 404, 408, 418, 419, 421, 422, 430
Willingham, Calder, 53
Wilson, Angus, 32
Wilson, Harry Leon, 409, 411
Wilson, Sandy, 38, 422
Wodehouse, P. G., 412
Wolfit, Donald, 370
Wolfson, Victor, 416
Wouk, Herman, 63, 421
Wright, Richard, 417

Yordan, Philip, 418

Zilboorg, Gregory, 410

INDEX OF PLAYS AND CASTS

Bold face page numbers refer to pages on which Cast of Characters may be found.

Abe Lincoln in Illinois, 403, 416, 445
Abie's Irish Rose, 400, 437
Abraham Lincoln, 409
Accent on Youth, 415
Adam and Eva, 410
Admirable Bashville, The, 58
Adonis, 400
Adorable Liar, The, 446
Affair of Honor, **383-384**, 397
Affairs of State, 400, 421
Ah, Wilderness, 415
Alien Corn, 414, 434
Alison's House, 403, 414
All For the Living, 435
All God's Chillun Got Wings, 447
All My Sons, 69, 402, 419
Allegro, 419
Almost Crazy, 22, **335**-337, 397
Amazing Adele, 398
Ambush, 410
American Way, The, 416, 447
Amphitryon 38, 89, 416
Anastasia, 28, 42, 51, 399
Anatomy of Love, 438
And Be My Love, 434, 444
Androcles, 407
Androcles and the Lion, 433
Angel in the Wings, 438
Angel Street, 400, 417, 431
Animal Kingdom, The, 414, 432
Ankles Aweigh, 398, 399
Anna Christie, 403, 410
Anna Lucasta, 400, 418
Anne of the Thousand Days, 420
Annie Get Your Gun, 400
Anniversary Waltz, 25, 28, 34, 50, 52, 54, 238, 399, 400
Another Language, 414
Another Part of the Forest, 189, 419
Antigone, 59, 189, 419
Aphrodite, 442
Arabian Nights, 323
Arlequin Poli par L'Amour, 356, **357**
Arsenic and Old Lace, 400, 417
As Husbands Go, 413
As You Desire Me, 443
As You Like It, 55
At Home Abroad, 441
Autumn Garden, The, 189, 420
Awake and Sing, 415

Babes in Toyland, 63
Bad Man, The, 410
Bad Seed, 27, 28, 51, 399, 422
Bal des Adieux, Le, 40
Barbara Frietchie, 409
Barbier de Seville, Le, 356, **357**
Barefoot in Athens, 421
Barnum Was Right, 445
Barretts of Wimpole Street, The, 62, 414
Bas Fonds, Les, 45
Bat, The, 400, 440
Beautiful People, 58
Beggar on Horseback, 411
Behold the Bridegroom, 412
Believe Me Xantippe, 432
Bell, Book, and Candle, 421
Bell for Adano, A, 418
Ben Hur, 444
Berkeley Square, 413
Bernardine, 421
Better 'Ole, The, 446
Beyond the Horizon, 403, 409
Big Knife, The, 447
Bill of Divorcement, A, 410, 432
Billy Budd, 420
Biography, 414, 447
Bird in Hand, 401
Black Limelight, The, 446
Blackbirds, 401
Blackfriars, The, 59

Blithe Spirit, 62, 401, 417
Bloomer Girl, 401
Blossom Time, 400
Blue Moon, The, 440
Boomerang, The, 401
Born Yesterday, 400, 419
Both Your Houses, 403, 414, 445
Bourgeois Gentilhomme, Le, 19, **356-357**
Boy Friend, The, 38, 399, 422
Boy Meets Girl, 401, 415
Bridal Wise, 111
Bride, The, 434
Bride of the Lamb, 412
Brief Moment, 414
Brigadoon, 266, 400, 419
Broadway, 400, 412
Broadway to Paris, 438
Brother Rat, 400
Browne, Porter Emerson, **410**
Buccaneer, The, 38, 443
Bulls, Bears and Asses, 437
Burlesque, 412
Bury the Dead, 435
Bus Stop, 26, 28, 51, 399, 422, 444
Butter and Egg Man, The, 412

Caesar and Cleopatra, 5
Caine Mutiny Court Martial, The, 51, 63, 421, 438
Call It a Day, 415
Call Me Madam, 400
Call Me Mister, 401
Call the Doctor, 432
Camino Real, 52
Can-Can, 28, 51, 399, 400
Candida, 58, 446
Candle in the Wind, 417
Caprice, Un, 19, 356, **358**
Captain Jinks, 405
Captain of the Nonesuch, The, 446
Carefree Tree, The, **353**
Carmen Jones, 326, **393-394,** 397, 401
Carnival in Venice, 443
Carousel, 400
Castle, The, 13
Cat on a Hot Tin Roof, 402, 404, 408, 422
Catch a Star!, **338**-341, 397
Chalk Garden, The, 3, 5, 8, 24, 30, 163-188, **358,** 397, 405
Changelings, The, 411
Charley's Aunt, 34
Chase, The, 438
Chauve Souris, 401
Chicago, 412
Chicken Feed, 411
Chien du Jardinier, Le, 44
Children's Hour, The, 189, 401, **415**
Chorus Lady, The, 446
Christopher Blake, 419
Circle, The, 410
Clarence, 409
Claudia, 401, 417, 436
Climate of Eden, 421
Climbers, The, 409
Clutterbuck, 420, 433
Cobra, 434
Cocktail Party, The, 420
Come Back, Little Sheba, 420
Comédie Française, 4, 18, 19, 42, **44,** 46, **356-358,** 397
Comedy in Music, 399, 401
Command Decision, 419
Command Performance, 446
Concert, The, 432, 434
Confidential Clerk, The, 53, **421**
Connecticut Yankee, 433
Consequences, 433
Constant Wife, The, 412
Coquette, 412
Corn Is Green, The, 63, 417
Counselor-at-Law, 436
Count of Clérambard, The, **33**
Country Girl, The, 421
County Chairman, The, 409
Courage, 432
Cradle Song, The, 59, 412
Craig's Wife, 403, 412
Cranks, 38
Criminal Code, The, 413
Crucible, The, 32, 52, 69, 421, **438**
Cry of the Peacock, 189
Curious Savage, The, 443
Cynara, 414
Cyrano de Bergerac, 45, 63, 438

Daisy Mayme, 412
Damask Cheek, The, 418
Dame sans Merci, La, 46
Damn Yankees, 398, 405, 444
Dancing in the Chequered Shade, **398**
Dancing Mothers, 411, 446
Dandy Dick, 58
Dark Is Light Enough, The, 89, **422**
Darkness at Noon, 402, 420
Darling of the Gods, The, **409**

Daughters of Atreus, 415
Day Before Spring, The, 266
Day by the Sea, A, 14, 51, 343-**344**, 397
Day Will Come, The, 443
Days to Come, 189
Dead End, 401, 415
Deadfall, **359**, 397
Dear Me, 441
Dear Ruth, 401, 418
Death of a Salesman, 69, 401, 402, 404, 420
Death Takes a Holiday, 413
Deburau, 410
Debut, **377**-378, 397
Decision, 418
Déclassée, 410, 446
Deep Are the Roots, 419
Design for Living, 414
Desire Under the Elms, 411
Desk Set, The, 10, 355-**356**, 397
Desperate Hours, The, 50, 398, 399, 422
Detective Story, 400, 420
Devil Passes, The, 414
Devil's Disciple, The, 62
Dial "M" for Murder, 401, 421
Diary of Anne Frank, The, 4, 11, 19, 111-139, **350-351**, 397, 402, 403, 404
Dice of the Gods, 434
Dinner at Eight, 414, 438
Disraeli, 409
Distaff Side, The, 415
Dr. Jekyll and Mr. Hyde, 446
Dodsworth, 414
Doll's House, A, 55
Don Juan, 59
Don Juan in Hell, 51
Doughgirls, The, 238, 401, 418
Dover Road, The, 410, 442
Dragon's Mouth, 58, 406
Dream Girl, 419
Drop of a Hat, The, 61
Dulcy, 410
Dummy, The, 435
Dybbuk, The, 412, 432

Easiest Way, The, 409, 444-445
East Is West, 401
Eastward of Eden, 59, 419
Easy Come, Easy Go, 431
Education of Mr. Pipp, The, 432
Edward, My Son, 63, 420
Elizabeth the Queen, 413
Elsie Janis and Her Gang, 439
Emperor Jones, The, 410, 447
Emperor's Clothes, The, 421, **433**
Enchanted, The, 89, 420
Encore, 441
End as a Man, 53
End of Summer, 415
Enemy, The, 412, 445
Enemy of the People, An, 34
Enter Madame, 410
Entre Chien et Loup, 44
Erstwhile Susan, 444
Escape, 412
Espoir, 41
Est-il Bon, Est-il Mechant, 42
Ethan Frome, 415
Eurydice, 189
Eve of St. Mark, The, 417
Even the Weariest River, 62
Everyman, 441
Excursion, 416

Fair Co-ed, The, 439
Faith, Hope and Alice, 447
Fall Guy, The, 411
Fall of Eve, The, 436
Fallen Angels, 18, **370**, 397
Family Portrait, 416
Family Reunion, The, 35
Famous Mrs. Fair, The, 410
Fanny, 401
Farmer Takes a Wife, The, **415**
Fatal Weakness, The, 419
Femmes Savantes, Les, 44
"Festival of Music," 64
Fifth Season, The, 50, 400
Figaro, 19
Finian's Rainbow, 401
Firebrand, The, 411
Firefly, 437
First Fifty Years, The, 444
First Lady, 415, 434
First Mrs. Fraser, The, 413
First Year, The, 401, 410, **436**
Five-Star Final, 414
Flight to the West, 417
Floradora, 401
Flowering Peach, The, 422
Follow the Girls, 400
Fool, The, 410, 446
Foolish Notion, 418, 433
Fourposter, The, 400, 421
Front Page, The, 413, 435, **441**

Game of Love and Death, The, 432
George Washington Slept Here, 417, 447
Gertie, 163
Ghosts, 442
Gigi, 421
Girl on the Via Flaminia, The, 53, 422
Glass Menagerie, The, 401, 402, 418, 439, 444
Gold Diggers, The, 401, 433
Golden Apple, The, 422
Good Gracious Annabelle, 409
Good News, 401
Good Old Charley, 61
Goodbye Again, 18, **386**, 397, 432
Goodbye, My Fancy, 420
Goose Hangs High, The, 411
Governor's Lady, The, 442
Grand Hotel, 414, 440
Grand Street Follies, The, 432
Great Adventure, The, 432
Great Big Doorstep, The, 111
Great Divide, The, 409
Great God Brown, The, 412
Great Sebastians, The, 10, 36, **368**-369, 397, 406
Green Bay Tree, The, 415
Green Goddess, The, 410, 441
Green Grow the Lilacs, 413
Green Hat, The, 412
Green Pastures, The, 400, 403, 413, 447
Greenwich Village Follies, The, 431
Growing Pains, 445
Guys and Dolls, 23, 399, 400, 420
Gypsy, 413
Gypsy Jim, 437

Hamlet, 27, 35, 434, 437, 444
Happy Birthday, 401
Happy Time, The, 400, 420
Harriet, 418, 445
Harvey, 400, 403, 418, 444
Hasty Heart, The, 418
Hatful of Rain, A, 4, 15, **360**, 397, 406
Hats Off to Ice, 400
He Who Gets Slapped, 59, 410
Heads or Tails, 444
Heartbreak House, 58
Heavenly Twins, The, 324, **359-360**, 397
Hedda Gabbler, 55
Heiress, The, 419
Hell-bent for Heaven, 403, 411
Hello, Out There, 59
Hellzapoppin, 400
Henry IV, Part I, **343**, 397
Henry V, 36
Her Master's Voice, 415
Here Come the Clowns, **416**
Hero, The, 410
Hidden Assets, 437
High Button Shoes, 401
High Jinks, 437
High Tor, 415
Histoire de Rire, 40
Hitchy-Koo, 441
Holiday, 413
Home of the Brave, 418
Honor of the Family, The, **436**
Hope for a Harvest, 417
Hot Corner, The, **372**-373, 397
Hotel Paradiso, 34
House Beautiful, The, 445
House in the Country, A, 444
House of Connelly, The, 414
House of Wonder, The, 433
Hoyden, The, 439

I Am a Camera, 402, 421
I Know My Love, 420
I Like It Here, 440
I Remember Mama, 401, 418
Icebound, 403, 410
Iceman Cometh, The, 55, 419
Idiot's Delight, 403, 415, 445
If I Were King, 409, 441
Il Pleut, Bergère, 45
Illustrious Uncle, The, 53
Immoralist, The, 422, 435
In Abraham's Bosom, 403, 412, 447
In Mizzoura, 443
In the Summer House, 421
In Time to Come, 417
Inherit the Wind, 25, 26, 28, 398, 406, 422, 439
Innkeepers, The, **373**-374, 397
Innocent Eyes, 442
Innocent Voyage, The, 418
Innocents, The, 420
Inside U.S.A., 431
Inspector Calls, An, 420
Iolanthe, 28, **344**
Irene, 401
Is Zat So?, 400
Island of Goats, **350**, 397

Jacobowsky and the Colonel, 418, 434, 440

Jane, 421
Jane Clegg, 410
Janie, 400
Janus, 10-11, **363**, 397, 406
Jason, 417
Jeanne d'Arc, 44
Jenny Kissed Me, 51, 52
Jest, The, 410
Jeu de L'Amour et du Hasard, Le, 19, 356, **358**
Jeweled Tree, The, 443
Joan of Lorraine, 419, 439
John Ferguson, 409
John Loves Mary, 419
Johnny Johnson, 415
Johnny on a Spot, 441
José, 44
Journey's End, 413
Joy Forever, A, 440
Joyce Grenfell Requests the Pleasure . . . , 31, **352**, 397
Joyride, 51
Julius Caesar, 35, 320, 437
Jumbo, 441
June and the Paycock, 16
June Moon, 413, 435
Junior Miss, 238, 401, 417

Katherine Dunham Dance Revue, 28
Katinka, 437
Kavantchina, 46
Key Largo, 416
Kiki, 400
Killers, The, 435
King and I, The, **384-385**, 397, 400
King Lear, 19, 330, **369**, 397, 434
King of Hearts, 50
Kingdom of God, The, 413
Kismet, 28, 47, 400
Kiss and Tell, 400, 418
Kiss Me, Kate, 47, **388**-390, 398, 400
Kiss the Boys Goodbye, 416

Ladder, The, 401
Ladies and Gentlemen, 441
Ladies of the Evening, 437
Lady in Ermine, 443
Lady in the Dark, 417
Lady Lazy, 447
Lady of the Slipper, The, 439
Lady's Not for Burning, The, 89
L'Amour Fou, 41
L'Argent, 436
Lark, The, 4, 11-12, 189-213, 362-**363**, 397, 405
Lassie, 443
Last Mile, The, 413
Late Christopher Bean, The, 414
Late George Apley, The, 418, 432
Laura, 433
Leah Kleschna, 409
Left Bank, The, 414
Let Freedom Ring, 433
Let Us Be Gay, 413, 437
Let's Face It, 401
Letters to Lucerne, 417
L'Hermine, 189
Life Begins at 8:40, 441
Life with Father, 400, 416, 434
Life with Mother, 420
Light Up the Sky, 420
Lightnin', 400
Likely Tale, A, 29
Lilac Time, 443, 446
Liliom, 410, 433
Lion and the Mouse, The, 401
Little Accident, 413
Little Clay Cart, The, 432
Little Foxes, The, 189, 416, 435
Little Glass Clock, **381**, 397
Little Minister, The, 446
Little Show, The, 431
Little Women, 445
Littlest Revue, The, **391**-393
Living Room, The, 422
Look Back in Anger, 32
Lost Horizons, 415
Lost in the Stars, 53, 420
Love Dreams, 443
Love Life, 266
Love of Four Colonels, The, 421, 433
Love on the Dole, 443
Love Song, 443
Lovers, The, 25, 28, **390**-391, 397
Loyalties, 410
Lucky Strike, 29
Lucrece, 214
Lulu Belle, 441
Lunatics and Lovers, 50, 52, 399
Lute Song, 28, 419, 443

Macbeth, 55, 431, 437
Machinal, 413
Machine à Ecrire, La, 46
Mademoiselle Colombe, 189, 444
Madwoman of Chaillot, The, 53, 89, 420

Magdelena, 47
Maggie Pepper, 446
Magic and the Loss, The, 422
Magnificent Yankee, The, 419, 434
Main Street, 442
Major Barbara, 407
Make Mine Manhattan, 443
Mal d'Amour, Le, 44
Male Animal, The, 417
Mamma's Affair, 410
Man, The, 51
Man and Devil, 442
Man from Blankley's, The, 446
Man from Home, The, 409
Man of Destiny, 58
Man on a Tiger, 61
Man Who Came to Dinner, The, 401, 417
Mandarine, 189
Marcel Marceau, 4, 19, 28, 43, 50, **341**-342, **373**, 398, 427
Margin for Error, 417
Marie Tudor, 42
Marriage Is for Single People, 433
Marseilles, 440
Mary of Scotland, 414
Mary Rose, 410
Mary the 3d, 411
Master Builder, The, 406
Matchmaker, The, 4, 9, 214-237, **365-366**, 397
Maurice Chevalier in Songs and Impressions, **347**
Me and Molly, 420
Member of the Wedding, The, 53, 401, 402, 420
Memory of Two Mondays, A, 347-**348**, 407
Memphis Bound, 447
Men in White, 403, 414
Merchant of Yonkers, The, 9, 214
Merrily We Roll Along, 415
Merry Wives of Windsor, The, 36
Merton of the Movies, 411
Michael and Mary, 413
Middle of the Night, 16-17, **374**, 397
Midsummer Night's Dream, A, 55
Mikado, The, 28, **344-345**
Minick, 411
Miracle, The, 432
Miss Julie, 376-**377**
Miss Liberty, 435
Miss Lulu Bett, 403
Mr. and Mrs. North, 417
Mister Johnson, 18, 325, **382**, 397
Mr. Pim Passes By, 442
Mister Roberts, 400, 419
Mr. Wonderful, 22, **380**-381, 397
"Moisseiev Ballets," 41
Month in the Country, A, 19, **383**
Moon Is Blue, The, 400
Moon Is Down, The, 417, 445
Morning's at Seven, 58, 417
Most Happy Fella, The, 7, 19, 23, **387-388**, 397
Mother Courage, 52
Mourning Becomes Electra, 414
Mrs. Bumpstead-Leigh, 409
Mrs. McThing, 421
Mrs. Partridge Presents, 411
Much Ado About Nothing, 55
Mulberry Bush, The, 32
Music Box Revue, The, 441
Music Master, The, 401
My Darlin' Aida, 431
My Fair Lady, 4, 19, 23-24, 266-294, **378-379**, 397, 402
My Heart's in the Highlands, 53
My Sister Eileen, 238, 400, 417
My 3 Angels, 421, 433

Native Son, 417
Naughty Marietta, 437
Ned McCobb's Daughter, 432
Nekrassov, 33
Nellie Bly, 444
Nest, The, 410
New Moon, The, 401
Nice People, 410
Night of January 16th, The, 444
Night to Remember, A, 61
Nina, 41
No More Ladies, 415
No Time for Comedy, 416
No Time for Sergeants, 4, 9, 140-162, **355**, 397, 406
Nutcracker, The, 28

O Mistress Mine, 419
Oeufs de l'Autruche, Les, 41
Of Mice and Men, 402, 416, 433
Of Thee I Sing, 403, 414
Oiseaux de Lune, Les, 44
Oklahoma!, 400, 418, 431, 447
Old Maid, The, 403, 415
Old Soak, The, 410
On Borrowed Time, 416
On Trial, 409

On Whitman Avenue, 439
Once in a Lifetime, 413
Once Upon a Tailor, 53, 440
Ondine, 89
One Bright Day, 34
One Sunday Afternoon, 414
One Touch of Venus, 400
Oresteia, 41
Ornifle ou le Courant d'Air, 42
Othello, 36, 320, **341**, 398
Our Town, 214, 403, 416
Out of This World, 59, 431
Outrageous Fortune, 418
Outward Bound, 411
Over 21, 418
Overture, 414

Paid in Full, 440
Paint Your Wagon, 266
Pajama Game, The, 28, 37, 47, 52, 401, 444
Pajama Tops, 447
Pal Joey, 401
Panama Hattie, 401
Paris Bound, 412, 445
Passing Show of 1922, The, 431
Patriots, The, 402, 417
Pavés du Ciel, Les, 359
Peg o' My Heart, 401
Personal Appearance, 401
Personnage Combatant, Le, 45
Peter Pan, 63
Petite Hutte, La, 41
Petrified Forest, The, 415
Philadelphia Story, The, 416
Philanderer, The, 58
Phoenix '55, 399
Pick-up Girl, 418
Picnic, 53, 402, 404, 421
Pigeons and People, 414
Pinafore, 28, **346**
Pins and Needles, 400
Pipe Dream, 22, 49, **364**-365, 397, 406
Pirates of Penzance, The, 28, **345**
Plain and Fancy, 28, 37, 47, 398, 399, 407
Play's the Thing, The, 412
Plough and the Stars, The, 53, 413
Plume de ma Tante, La, 38
Point of No Return, 421
Ponder Heart, The, 8, 238-265, **376**, 397, 405
Porgy, 412, 447
Power and the Glory, The, 30, 35
Present Laughter, 62
Pride and Prejudice, 415
Prince Igor, 46
Princess Ida, **345-346**
Princess Zoubaroff, The, 30
Private Lives, 440
Proces de Famille, Le, 41
Processional, 433
Pygmalion, 23, 24, 266, 378

Quadrille, 398, 405
Quare Fellow, The, 32
Queen and the Rebels, The, 33
Queen High, 443
Quiet Place, 398

R. U. R., 410
Racket, The, 413
Rain, 400, 410
Rainmaker, The, 34, 51, 53
Rat, The, 433
Rebound, 413
Reclining Figure, 51
Red, Hot, and Blue, 438
Red Mill, The, 401
Red Robe, The, 443
Red Roses for Me, 4, 16, **367-368**, 397
Remains to Be Seen, 421
Resurrection, 440
Reuben Reuben, 398
Reunion in Vienna, 414, 432, 445
Rhapsody, The, 438
Richard II, 444
Right You Are, 13
Righteous Are Bold, The, 366-**367**, 397
Ring for Catty, 29
Ring Round the Moon, 189, 440
Rivals, The, 35
Road to Rome, The, 412, 445
Rocket to the Moon, 416
Romance, 409
Romanoff and Juliet, 29
Romeo and Juliet, 55, 439, 442
Room Service, 401
Roomful of Roses, A, **354**, 397
Rosalinda, 401
Rose Marie, 401, 437
Rose Tattoo, The, 53, 421
Roubouilleuse, La, 436
Royal Family, The, 412
Ruddigore, **346**
Rugged Path, The, 419

Sailor, Beware!, 401
St. Helena, 416
Saint Joan, 12, 407
St. Louis Woman, 431
Sally, 400
Saturday's Children, 412
Schoolhouse on the Lot, The, 238
Searching Wind, The, 189, 418
Season in the Sun, 421, 444
Second Threshold, 421
Seducteur, Le, 45
See the Jaguar, 435
Separate Rooms, 400
Seven Days, 440
Seven Keys to Baldpate, 409
Seven Year Itch, The, 10, 53, 399, 400
Seventh Heaven, 398, 399, 401, 436
Sex Fable, The, 432
Shadow and Substance, 416
Shining Hour, The, 415
Show Boat, 400
Show-Off, The, 400, 411
Shrike, The, 50, 404, 421, 433
Shuffle Along, 401
Siegfried, 89
Silk Stockings, 47, 398, 399
Silver Cord, The, 412
Silver Whistle, The, 420
Sing and Whistle, 437
Sing, Man, Sing, 28
Six Characters in Search of an Author, **366**
Six Cylinder Love, 410
Six Who Pass While the Lentils Boil, 443
Skidding, 445
Skin Game, The, 410
Skin of Our Teeth, The, 13, 18, 25, 26, 27, 28, 214, **337-338**, 398, 403, 418
Skipper Next to God, 419
Skylark, 417, 436
Sleep of Prisoners, A, 89
Sleeping Beauty, The, 64
Slim Princess, The, 439
Smilin' Through, 443, 446
So Proudly We Hail, 435
So This Is London, 434, 444
Social Register, The, 436
Society Circus, A, 400
Soldier's Wife, 418
Solid Gold Cadillac, The, 28, 52, 401
Someone Waiting, **374-375**, 397
Something for the Boys, 444
Song of Norway, 47, 401
Sons o' Fun, 401
Sound and the Fury, The, 61
South Pacific, 400, 404
South Sea Bubble, 29
Spanish Love, 440
Squall, The, 433
Squaw Man, The, 409, 438
Stage Door, 416
Star and Garter, 400
Star for a Night, A, 439
State of the Union, 401, 403, 418
Stepping Out, 441
Storm in the Sun, 53
Storm Operation, 418
Story of Mary Surratt, The, 419
Strange Interlude, 403, 412, 444
Street Scene, 400, 403, 413
Streetcar Named Desire, A, **375**, 398, 401, 402, 404, 419
Streets of Paris, The, 442
Strictly Dishonorable, 401, 413
Strike Me Pink, 435
Strip for Action, 398
Strong Are Lonely, The, 33
Stronger, The, **376-377**
Student Prince, The, 400
Summer and Smoke, 439
Summertime, 33
Sumurun, 443
Sunny, 401
Sun-Up, 411
Susan and God, 416, 436
Swan, The, 411
Swan Song, 441
Sweet River, 435

Take a Giant Step, 421
Tamburlaine the Great, 4, 18, 57, **370-371**, 397
Taming of the Shrew, 63, 433, 434
Tanorama, 53
Tarnish, 411
Tea and Sympathy, 399, 401, 422
Teahouse of the August Moon, The, 25, 27, 28, 399, 400, 402, 404, 421
Tempest, The, 321
Tender Trap, The, 28, 50
Terrible Swift Sword, The, **362**
That Lady, 446
Theatre Carnival, 53
There Shall Be No Night, 403, 416, 445

They Knew What They Wanted, 23, 387, 403, 411
They Shall Not Die, 415, 447
Third Little Show, The, 431
This Happy Breed, 62
This Is the Army, 443
Three for Tonight, 52, 399
Three Men on a Horse, 401
Three Sisters, The, 444
Three Wise Fools, 436
Threepenny Opera, The, 37, 59
Three's a Crowd, 431, 447
Thunder Bird, 443
Tiger at the Gates, 3, 4, 5, 24, 89-110, **349,** 397, 402, 406
Time Limit!, 4, 15-16, **371-372,** 397
Time of the Cuckoo, The, 421
Time of Your Life, The, 402, 403, **417**
Tit for Tat, 436
Tobacco Road, 400, 434
Together with Music, 62
Tomorrow and Tomorrow, 413
Tomorrow the World, 401, 418
Too Many Boats, 443
Top Man, 398
Torch Song, 440
Tovarich, 416
Trial by Jury, 28, **346**
Trial of Mary Dugan, The, 438
Triomphe de l'Amour, Le, 44
Trip to Chinatown, A, 401
Troilus and Cressida, 37
Trojan War Will Not Take Place, The, 5
Trumpet Shall Sound, The, 214
Truth About Blayds, The, 442
Turn of the Screw, The, 13
Turn to the Right, 436
Twelfth Night, 53, 444
Two Blind Mice, 420
Two Mrs. Carrolls, The, 400
Two Orphans, The, 432

Unchastened Woman, The, 409
Uncle Harry, 417, 433
Uncle Vanya, 55
Under Cover, 434
Undiscovered Country, The, 62
Up in Central Park, 401
Up Pops the Devil, 111

Vagabond King, The, 401
Valley Forge, 415
Vamp, The, 20, 22, **360-362,** 397
Vanderbilt Cup, The, 439
Venus Observed, 89, 421
Victoria Regina, 401, 415
View from the Bridge, A, 12, 69-88, 347-**348,** 397, 407
Virgin of Bethulia, The, 438
Voice of the Turtle, The, 400, 418
Volpone, 442

Waiting for Godot, 3, 4, 13-14, 38, 295-317, 385-**386,** 397, 405
Wake Up, Darling, **387,** 397
Wake Up, Jonathan, 434
Waltz of the Toreadors, The, 34
Warrior's Husband, The, 446
Watch on the Rhine, 189, 402, **417**
Water Gipsies, The, 37
We, the People, 414
Wedding Bells, 410
Wednesday's Child, 415
Western Union, 111
What a Life, 401, 416
What Price Glory?, 411, 446
What's Up, 266
When Ladies Meet, 414
When We Were Forty-one, 439
When We Were 21, 435
Where's Charlie?, 401
Whistling in the Dark, 431, 444
White Cargo, 400
White Sheep of the Family, The, 52
White Steed, The, 416
White Wings, 444
Whole Town Is Talking, The, 436
Why Marry?, 403, 409
Why Not?, 410
Wild Birds, 411
Wild Duck, The, 35, 444
Will Success Spoil Rock Hunter?, **10,** 353-**354,** 397
Wind from the South, A, 60
Winged Victory, 418, 444
Wings over Europe, 413
Winslow Boy, The, 419
Winter Soldiers, 418
Winter's Tale, The, 36
Winterset, 402, 415
Wisdom Tooth, The, 412
Wish You Were Here, 400
Wisteria Trees, The, 420
Witching Hour, The, 409
Within the Gates, 16

Within the Law, 401, 445
Witness for the Prosecution, 400, 422, 433
Woman with Red Hair, The, 53
Women, The, 401, 416, 445
Women Kind, 434
Wonderful Town, 52, 238, 401, 421
Wooden Dish, The, **351**, 397, 434
World We Make, The, 416

Years Ago, 419
Yeomen of the Guard, 28, **345**
Yes, My Darling Daughter, 416
You and I, 410
You Can't Take It with You, 401, 403, 415, 435
You Never Know, 438
Young and Beautiful, The, 4, 14, **348-349**, 397
Young April, 445
Young Woodley, 412
Youngest, The, 411

Ziegfeld Follies, 398, 401, **441**

INDEX OF PRODUCERS, DIRECTORS, DESIGNERS, STAGE MANAGERS, COMPOSERS, AND CHOREOGRAPHERS

Abbott-Abrams Production Company, 53
Actor's Playhouse, 59
Actors' Theatre, The, 446
Actor's Workshop, 52
Adams, F., 347
Adams, James, 368
Adams, Lee, 391, 392
Addinsell, Richard, 352
Adelman, Howard, 359
Adelson, Lenny, 336
Adler, Jerry, 379
Adler, Richard, 37, 405, 444
Alcoa Hour, 61
Aldrich, Richard, 381, 423
Alexander, David, 361
Allers, Franz, 379
Alswang, Ralph, 338, 359, 372, 384
Alton, Robert, 361
Amato Theatre, 58-59
American National Theatre and Academy, 18, 337
Ames, Winthrop, 446
Anderson, John Murray, 448
Anderson, Robert B., Jr., 350
Anglin, Margaret, 443
Antek, Samuel, 358
Anthony, Joseph, 363, 388
Applebaum, Gertrude H., 354
Applebaum, Louis, 371
Armitage, Buford, 349
Armstrong, Betty Coe, 382
Arnett, Hazel, 356
Aronson, Boris, 348, 351
Artists Embassy Producing Company, 50
Atkin, Charles, 365
Audré, 354, 367
Auerbach, Leonard, 372
Austin, Lyn, 352, 362
Avram, Rachmael ben, 53
Avshalomov, Aaron, 353
Axelrod, George, 354
Ayers, Lemuel, 390, 431
Aymé, Marcel, 44

Baker, Lawrence, Jr., 348
Baldridge, Richard, 341, 343
Ballou, 368, 387
Barkow, Arthur, 368, 387
Barr, Richard, 370
Barratt, Watson, 367, 375, 389
Barrault, Jean-Louis, 41, 44, 45
Baty, Gaston, 357
Bauer, George, 352
Bay, Howard, 368, 394
Baylies, Edmund, 370
Beadle, Spofford, 369
Beaton, Cecil, 24, 358, 379, 381
Becher, Thomas, 338
Beckhard, Arthur J., 386
Bedsow, Len, 360
Beecher, Robert W., 53
Belasco, David, 435, 437, 442, 444
Bellin, Charles, 358
Bennett, Robert Russell, 365, 385, 393
Berg, Oliver K., 386
Berghof, Herbert, 386
Berkeley, Lennox, 350
Berkowitz, Sol, 392
Berlin, Irving, 423, 436
Bernstein, Aline, 432
Bernstein, Leonard, 363
Bertin, Emile, 357
Bethel, David de, 352
Bethel, Joan de, 352
Betti, Henri, 347
Beydts, Louis, 357
Birsh, Patricia, 389
Bizet, Georges, 393
Blau, Herbert, 53
Blitzstein, Marc, 369
Blofson, Richard, 353
Bloomgarden, Kermit, 347, 350, 362, 387
Bocher, Main, 369

Bock, Jerry, 339, 340, 341, 380
Borne, Hal, 339
Borodin, 46
Bourtsyre, Henri, 347
Bowden, Charles, 370
Boyt, John, 351, 377, 390
Brady, William A., 445
Bragdon, Helen, 336
Bray, Frank, 52
Broadway Chapel Players, 59
Brook, Peter, 32, 35, 37
Brown, Michael, 391, 392
Bruskin, Perry, 363
Bullock, H. Ridgely, Jr., 370
Burch, Pat, 353
Burns, Richard, 376
Burtson, Bud, 338

Caddie, Regis, 390
Cadou, André, 357, 358
Cahn, Sammy, 391
Calhern, Louis, 351
Campbell, Patton, 360, 370
Carr, Lawrence, 355
Carroll, Earl, 448
Carson, Alexander, 361
Carson, Wayne, 356
Carte, Bridget D'Oyly, 344
Carte, Rupert D'Oyly, 448
Caubisens, Henri, 388
Chambers, William, 363
Chandler, Pat, 354
Charig, Phil, 338, 339, 340, 341
Charon, Jacques, 357
Chekhov, Michael, 434
Chevalier, Maurice, 19, 347
Chodorov, Edward, 238
Chopin, Frederic, 64
Circle Theatre, 53
Circle-in-the-Square, 55, 59
Civic Light Opera Association, 47
Clark, Peggy, 354, 355, 367, 380
Clements, John, 35
Clurman, Harold, 349, 365, 424
Cobb, John S., 335
Coffin, Gene, 375, 384
Cohen, Martin, 361
Colt, Alvin, 353, 363, 365, 366, 377, 383, 389, 391
Comédie Française, 4, 18, 19, 42, 44, 46, 356-358, 397, 436
Company of the Golden Hind, 53
Constantin, Jean, 347
Cook, Richard, 373
Cooper, Theodore, 369
Cornell, John, 385, 389, 394
Corsaro, Frank, 360
Coward, Noel, 29, 62, 424
Coxe, Louis O., 420
Cranko, John, 38
Crawford, Cheryl, 382, 424
Crawford, Oliver, 372
Criss, Louis, 350
Crocker, Emerson, 369
Crouse, Russel, 368
Curtis, Joseph, 374

Da Costa, Morton, 355
Dalrymple, Jean, 341, 343, 369, 375
Daniels, Danny, 392
Davies, Irving, 352
Davis, Allan, 375
Del Bondio, J. H., 386
Dell'Isola, Salvatore, 365
Denham, Reginald, 363
DePaul, Gene, 337
Depaur, Leonard, 394
Deutsch, Armand, 351
Devine, George, 32
Dhéry, Robert, 38-39
Diamond, I. A. L., 340
Donahue, Jack, 380
Donaldson, Arthur, 435
Doolittle, James, 52
Douglas, Melvyn, 25, 425
Douglas, Robert, 376, 384
Dowling, Eddie, 366, 367
Dowling, Robert W., 370
Downing, Robert, 387
Downtown Theatre, 58, 59
D'Oyly Carte Opera Company, The, 28, 52, 344-346, 397
Drake, Alfred, 425
Dublin Players, 52
duBois, Raoul Pene, 361, 394
Duke, Vernon, 391, 392, 393
Dunham, Katherine, 28, 52
Durand, Charles, 367, 384
Dux, Pierre, 45
Dvonch, Frederick, 385, 389

Ebony Theatre, The, 53
Eckart, Jean, 382
Eckart, William, 382
Edwards, Ben, 375, 376
Effrat, John, 382
Elder, Eldon, 349, 359, 370
Elmslie, Kenward, 391

Elson, Charles, 390
Engel, Lehman, 374, 376
English Stage Company, 32
Ensor, Clois, 390
Epstein, Alvin, 377
Equity Library Theatre, 59
Escande, Maurice, 358
Eva LeGallienne's Civic Repertory Theatre, 434
Evans, Hugh, 52
Evans, Maurice, 27, 62, 355, 425, 434

Fabre, Emile, 436
Fain, Sammy, 338, 340
Fearnley, John, 385
Feder, 338, 349
Ferrer, José, 425
Fields, Joseph, 356
Finckel, Edwin, 367
Fleischmann, Julius, 381
Fletcher, Robert, 341, 343, 369
Flournoy, Peter, 373
Fodeiba African Ballets, 45
Foley, Paul A., 344
Ford, David, 374
Ford Motor Co., 62
Ford Star Jubilee, 63
Forsythe, Charles, 354
Foster, John, 338
Fourth Street Theatre, 55
Freeborn, Pat, 344
Freed, Fred, 347
Frohman, Charles, 436
Front Row Center, 62
Fryer, Robert, 355

Gabel, Martin, 369
Gardner, John, 371
Geary, Joyce, 335, 336, 337
Geddes, Norman Bel, 425
Gelb, James, 350
Gershwin, George, 403, 414
Gershwin, Ira, 403, 414, 425
Gerstad, John, 377
Gersten, Bernard, 380
Gibson, Robert A., 344, 345, 346
Gielgud, Sir John, 30, 425
Gilkey, Stanley, 354
Glenville, Peter, 34, 37, 350
Godfrey, Isidore, 344, 345, 346
Goffin, Peter, 345, 346
Golden, John, 426, 436
Golden, Ray, 338, 339, 340, 341
Goodhart, William, 382
Goodman, Martin, 359
Gordon, Julius M., 359
Gordon, Michael, 359, 390
Gorelik, Mordecai, 360
Graham, Joseph L., 351
Graham, June, 385
Gray, David, Jr., 369
Greco, Jose, 52
Greene, Herbert, 388
Greene, Milton, 338
Greenwich Mews, 55, 58
Grundman, Clare, 352
Gumeny, Peter, 369
Guthrie, Tyrone, 3, 9, 18, 37, 366, 371

Hagler, Stan, 336
Hall, Peter, 37
Hallmark Hall of Fame, 62
Hambleton, T. Edward, 341, 353, 362, 366, 376-377, 383, 391
Hamilton, Roger, 375
Hamlisch, Max, 351
Hammerstein, Arthur, 437
Hammerstein, William, 351, 384, 385, 388, 389, 393, 394
Hardwicke, Sir Cedric, 51, 344, 426
Hardy Smith, Ltd., 350
Harker, Joseph, 346
Harker, Phil, 346
Harnick, Sheldon, 391, 392
Harris, Jed, 55
Harrison, Ray, 389
Hart, Bernard, 379
Hart, Lorenz, 448
Hart, Moss, 3, 24, 379, 403, 413, 426
Hartford, Huntington, 343
Hartley, Neil, 361, 374
Hartman, Ferris Luce, 438
Harvey, John, 350, 363, 374
Hayman, Clifford, 374
Hays, David, 373
Hayward, Leland, 426
Heawood, John, 352
Herscher, Sylvia, 353
Hesseltine, Stark, 366, 377, 391
Hewett, Christopher, 335
Hill, George Roy, 61
Hoffman, Bill, 383
Holm, Hanya, 24, 379, 389
Holm, Klaus, 351, 353, 354, 363, 376, 377, 382, 383, 391
Holmes, Ralph, 382
Holofcener, Larry, 339, 340, 341, 380
Horner, Richard, 377

Hornez, André, 347
Horseshoe Stage, 53
Hough, M., 347
Houghton, Norris, 341, 353, 362, 366, 377, 383, 391
Howard, J. E., 347
Huntington Hartford Theatre, 51, 54
Hurok, Sol, 18, 356
Hurry, Leslie, 371

Independent Plays Limited, 385
Interplayers, The, 53
Irving, Jules, 53
Irwin, Will, 391

Jamison, Marshall, 349
Jenkins, George, 356
John, Mr., 370
Johnstone, Anna Hill, 358
Joio, Norman Dello, 350
Jones, Margo, 439
Judd, Carl, 386
Judson, Lester, 335
Julien, Edward, 360
Julien, Jay, 360

Kabuki Theatre, The, 28, 42, 52, 405, 407
Kanin, Garson, 3, 351, 427
Kanter, David, 354
Kaye, Beryl, 352
Kaye, Jim, 336
Kazan, Elia, 427
Kemper, Collin, 440
Kennel, Louis, 386
Kent, Guy, 373, 387
Kern, Jerome D., 448
Kerr, Elizabeth, 367
Kesler, Lew, 335, 336
Kilty, Jerome, 343
Kleinman, Sy, 338, 339, 340
Klotz, Florence, 376
Kosarin, Oscar, 380
Kraber, Tony, 376
Kraft TV Theatre, 61
Krause, Jay, 344
Krupska, Dania, 388
Kungliga Dramatic Theatre, 46

Lalique, Suzanne, 357, 358
Lammers, Paul, 391
Lamoureux, Robert, 347
Landau, Jack, 353
Lang, Phil, 379
Larkin, Peter, 355
Latouche, John, 391, 392
Laughton, Charles, 427
Laurence Olivier Productions, 40
Lehar, Franz, 448
Lerman, Oscar, 361
Lerner, Alan J., 24
Lester, Edwin, 47
Leve, Sam, 386
Levene, Sam, 372
Levin, Herman, 378
Lewis, Robert, 382
Lewis, Windsor, 347, 372
Lewisohn, Alice, 432
Lewisohn, Irene, 432
Liagre, Alfred de, Jr., 363
Liff, Samuel, 366, 379
Linden, Robert, 356
Lindsay, Howard, 368
Lisanby, Charles, 381
Lister, Laurier, 352
Little, Terence, 388
Littlewood, Joan, 32
Lloyd, John Robert, 335
Loeb, John Jacob, 347
Loesser, Frank, 23
Loesser, Lynn, 387
Loewe, Frederick, 24, 266, 378, 402, 419
Logan, Joshua, 374, 404, 427
Lombardo, Carmen, 347
Lopez, Francis, 347
Louiguy, 347
Luening, Otto, 369
Lulli, 357

Machiz, Herbert, 375
Mackintosh, Robert, 380
Mail, Mme. Léone, 357
Mamoulian, Rouben, 427
Mann, Theodore, 373
Margolis, Henry M., 349, 369
Marlowe, Arthur, 363
Marlowe, Julia, 440, 449
Marre, Albert, 358
Martin, Elliott, 373, 381
Martin, Norman, 340
Mathias, Philip, 338, 376
Matlowsky, Samuel, 383
Maxtone-Graham, John, 369, 375
McClintic, Guthrie, 354, 407, 428
McHugh, Edward, 351
Mendelssohn, Felix, 64
Menotti, Gian-Carlo, 428

Mercure, Jean, 40
Meredith, Burgess, 428
Merigold, Jack, 371
Merrick, David, 365
Meyer, Don, 392
Meyer, Jean, 44, 46, 357
Mielziner, Jo, 350, 363, 365, 374, 375, 385, 388, 428
Milbert, Seymour, 350, 371, 390
Millang, Charles, 361
Miller, Gilbert, 347, 428
Mills, Carley, 336
Mitchell, Ruth, 365
Mitchell, Stephen, 343
Moiseiwitsch, Tanya, 366
Moore, Stanley, 352
Moorehead, Agnes, 51, 428
Morley, Ruth, 369
Moroney, Ed, 349
Morris, Aldyth, 353
Morris, John, 365
Morris, Lee, 340
Morrison, Paul, 349-50, 352, 371
Motley, 349, 374, 388
Moussorgsky, 46
Mundy, James, 360
Murfin, Jane, 443
Myerberg, Michael, 385
Myers, Richard, 381

Nash, Odgen, 391, 392, 393
National Theatre of Belgrade, 46
Navarre, Jay, 340
Nay, Frederick, 335
Neal, Walter, 351
Nelson, Portia, 335, 336, 337
Nesbitt, Robert, 338
New York City Center Light Opera Company, 384, 388, 393
New York City Center Theatre Company, 18, 341, 343, 369, 373, 375
Nielsen, Karl, 372
Noyes, Thomas, 352
Nugent, Elliott, 428

Oenslager, Donald, 351, 354, 363, 428
O'Hearn, Robert, 341, 343
Olivier, Sir Laurence, 428
Olney, Joseph, 375
O'Neil, James, 439
Ormont, Dave, 339
O'Shaughnessy, John, 368
Osterman, Lester, Jr., 380

Padula, Edward, 355
Parone, Edward, 362
Partington, Rex, 366
Pasadena Playhouse, 52
Pascal, Milton, 339, 341
Paul, John, 386
Perier, François, 45
Perlowin, Gene, 338
Pfeiffer, Jack, 361
Phoenix Theatre, 18, 19, 59, 341, 342, 353, 362, 366, 376, 383, 391
Player's Ring, The, 53
Playhouse, 53
Playwrights' Company, 349, 376, 390, 445
Playwrights '56, 61, 62
Pogany, Willy, 443
Polakov, Lester, 338
Pollock, Gordon W., 367, 373, 386, 387
Pons, Helene, 338, 348, 351, 359
Porter, Cole, 51, 59, 388, 429
Pratt, Charles, Jr., 352
Present, Jack, 50
Primus, Pearl, 382
Producers' Showcase, 62, 63, 64
Producers Theatre, 352, 370
Proscenium Productions, 58

Quick, George, 362, 383
Quintero, José, 373

Racine, Jules, 355
Radnitz, Robert B., 348
Raye, Don, 337
Redgrave, Michael, 383
Reed, Henry, 350
Reinhardt, Max, 432
Rice, Peter, 352
Rich, Eddie, 374
Ricketts, Charles, 345
Rickey, Al, 335
Rigault, Jean de, 342
Rinner, Walter, 335
Ritchard, Cyril, 359
Ritt, Martin, 348
Rittman, Trude, 379
Robbins, Jerome, 64, 385
Robert L. Joseph Production, The, 349
Roberts, Doris, 356
Robin, Leo, 347
Rodgers, Richard, 22, 364, 384, 385, 404, 406, 418, 419, 429
Rodrigues, Alfred, 352
Rogers, Emmett, 355